A BIOGRAPHY
OF THE ENGLISH
LANGUAGE

A BIOGRAPHY OF THE ENGLISH LANGUAGE

C. M. Millward

Boston University

Harcourt Brace Jovanovich College Publishers

Fort Worth Philadelphia San Diego New York Orlando Austin San Antonio
Toronto Montreal London Sydney Tokyo

Publisher, Humanities: *Charlyce Jones Owen*
Associate Editor: *Kate Morgan*
Senior Project Editor: *Lester A. Sheinis*
Copy Editor: *Kristin Camitta Zimet*
Proofreader: *Andrew Goldwasser*
Senior Production Manager: *Nancy Myers*
Design Supervisor: *Gloria Gentile*
Text and Cover Designer: *Caliber Design Planning, Inc.*

Library of Congress Cataloging-in-Publication Data

Millward, Celia M.
    A biography of the English language / C. M. Millward.
        p.   cm.
    Bibliography: p.
    Includes index.
    1. English language—History.   I. Title.
    PE1075.M64   1989
    420′.9—dc19   88-10078
                                                                                    CIP

ISBN 0-03-059431-6

Requests for permission to make copies of any part of the work should be mailed to: Permissions, Harcourt Brace Jovanovich, Publishers, 8th Floor, Orlando, Florida 32887

Printed in the United States of America

1 2 3 038 9 8 7 6 5 4 3

Harcourt Brace Jovanovich, Inc.
The Dryden Press
Saunders College Publishing

Credits

1. Drawing adapted from Roland Siegrist, ed., *Prehistoric Petroglyphs and Pictographs in Utah* (n.p.: Utah State Historical Society, 1972). Reproduced by permission of the Utah State Historical Society.

(Credits continued on p. 385.)

P R E F A C E

This book is designed primarily for a one- or two-semester introductory course in the history of the English language at the advanced undergraduate or graduate level. It can also be the basic text for a self-taught course in the subject. It does not assume any prior training in either linguistics or the history of English.

The approach is essentially traditional, stressing substance over theory. My reasons are twofold: First, I have found it impossible to do justice to both the theory and the substance of the history of English even in a two-semester course. Second, no existing theory can satisfactorily handle even a fraction of the historical data. Of course, I borrow from contemporary theories that best explain particular phenomena. Almost all of the illustrative material comes from fresh research, which affords new insights.

Three themes are emphasized throughout the text: (1) language, languages, and language change are systematic; (2) the "inner history" of English has not occurred in a linguistic vacuum, but has been profoundly affected by "outer" political and cultural events; and (3) nearly everything in the history of English has left its traces on the English of today. The historical chapters are identically organized so that students can easily trace changes in any subsystem, such as morphology, from the beginnings to the present day. Each such chapter opens with a section on the "outer history" of the English-speaking peoples.

The book's structure also conveys the progression of the language as a whole. The first three chapters introduce language, phonology, and writing systems. Thereafter, the organization is chronological, with separate chapters on Indo-European and Germanic, Old English, Middle English, Early Modern English, and Present-Day English. Although a reverse chronological order would have the advantage of proceeding from the (supposedly) familiar to the unfamiliar, it would have the overriding disadvantage of presenting results before causes. With topical organization, students would trace the entire history of subsystems but get no feeling for the whole or for how changing subsystems affect one another.

This book abounds with special features. Among them are the sections on semantics and the detailed discussions of syntax for each period. Numerous examples from actual texts illustrate all the principles and changes discussed. Brief summaries of the major characteristics of each period of English provide overviews. Because so many students know almost nothing about the nature of surviving Old English and Middle English literature (believing, for instance, that Chaucer wrote in Old English), brief outlines of Old English and Middle English literature are included at the ends of Chapters 5 and 6. The final chapter makes students aware of the importance of English around the world as well as in the United Kingdom and the United States. The extensive glossary, which includes brief examples where appropriate, makes the text accessible for those to whom the technical terminology is new. Finally, boxed vignettes add interesting sidelights to every chapter.

The book's fullness and logical structure allow instructors to tailor it to their own courses. For example, a one-semester syllabus might bypass most of the material on Indo-European, or the sections on Old English and Middle English literature, or even the final two chapters of the book. For more sophisticated or more highly motivated students, the brief bibliographies at the end of each chapter and the extensive bibliography at the end of the book encourage pursuit of more detailed information.

Students can also benefit from the workbook that accompanies this text. The workbook provides exercises designed to test the student's knowledge of text content and to illustrate the different stages and structures in the development of English.

It is a truism—but nonetheless true—that this book would have been impossible without the work of previous scholars, from Otto Jespersen to Frederic Cassidy. I am especially indebted to the late Freeman Twaddell, from whom I took my first course in historical linguistics; to Nelson Francis, whose course in the history of the English language convinced me that this subject was to be the academic love of my life; and to Angus McIntosh, who taught me what basic research in language history should be. I would also like to thank the many students who used versions of this text and made valuable suggestions; I am particularly grateful to Rachael and Brendan Lynch and Christopher Parr, who served as native informants for dialects of English with which I am less than ideally familiar.

I should also like to express my thanks for the suggestions of the reviewers chosen by the publishers, including Walter Beale, University of North Carolina–Greensboro; Julian Boyd, University of California–Berkeley; Thomas Brooks, Wheaton College; Thomas Carnicelli, University of New Hampshire; Thomas Clark, University of Nevada–Las Vegas; Virginia Clark, The University of Vermont; Robert Grindell, Kansas State University; Judith Johnson, Eastern Michigan University; Brian Joseph, The Ohio State University; Braj Kachru, University of Illinois at Urbana–Champaign; Edward Kline, University of Notre Dame; Ruth Lehmann, The University of Texas at Austin; Samuel Monsen, Brigham Young University; Norman Stageberg, University of Northern Iowa; and

Jacqueline de Weever, Brooklyn College. All of their comments were responsible, some of them were extremely useful, and a few of them helped prevent embarrassing errors in the final text.

Finally, I owe a debt that can be neither measured nor repaid to the constant and selfless support of my late husband, Richard B. Millward. To him this book is lovingly dedicated.

C.M.M.

To the memory of Richard B. Millward

C O N T E N T S

CHAPTER 3

Writing   28

CHAPTER 4

Language Families and Indo-European   37

CHAPTER 5

Old English   65

CHAPTER 6

Middle English   120

CHAPTER 7

Early Modern English   193

CHAPTER 8

Present-Day English   258

CHAPTER 9

A BIOGRAPHY
OF THE ENGLISH
LANGUAGE

CHAPTER 1

Introduction

Language is a perpetual Orphic song,
Which rules with Daedal harmony a throng
Of thoughts and forms, which else senseless and
shapeless were.
— *Percy Bysshe Shelley*

Everyone knows intuitively what language is, but it is notoriously difficult to define. Rather than become entangled in complex philosophical arguments, we shall define language for our purposes as a systematic and conventional means of human communication by vocal sounds; it may (or may not) include written symbols corresponding in some way to these vocal sounds. A single language such as English or Hungarian, is a specific, established example of such a communication system used in common by the members of a particular community.

Features Common to All Languages

All Languages Are Systematic
All languages, including of course English, are systems, or, more precisely, series of interrelated systems governed by rules. In other words, languages are highly structured; they consist of patterns that recur in various combinations and rules that apply to produce these patterns. A simple English example would be the systematic alternation between *a* and *an* produced by the rule that *an* is used before words beginning with a vowel sound, and *a* is used otherwise. Much more complex rules account for the grammaticality of such verb phrases as *might have been picking* and *will have been picking* but the ungrammaticality of **might will been picking* or **might been have picking*.[1]

---

[1] An asterisk (*) before a word, phrase, or other linguistic form means either (1) that it is ungrammatical or (2) that it is a hypothetical form, assumed to have existed but not actually recorded.

A moment's reflection will reveal that if languages were not highly system-atic and ruled, we could never learn them and use them. Speakers learn the rules of their language(s) as children and then apply them automatically for the rest of their lives. No native speaker of English, for example, has to stop in the middle of a sentence and think about how to pronounce the plurals of *rate, race,* or *raid.* Even though the plurals of all three of these words are pronounced differently, we learned at a very young age that the different forms are predictable and how to predict them. It is precisely in those areas of language that lack system or are exceptions to the rules that mistakes in usage occur. Children who say "My foots are dirty" are demonstrating, not that they do not know the rules of English, but rather that they know the rules well, although they have not mastered the exceptions.

The interrelated systems of a language include phonology, morphology, syntax, lexicon, and semantics. Languages that have a written representation (and not all languages do) also have a system of graphics. All languages have the same *set* of systems (with the possible exception of graphics), but the components of the systems and the interrelationships among the systems differ from language to language. Both German and Turkish have phonological systems, but the sounds that make up these systems differ from each other and from English sounds.

Phonology is the sounds of a language and the study of these sounds. The study of the sounds of speech taken simply as sounds and not necessarily as members of a system is called **phonetics**. The sounds themselves are sometimes called **phones**. The study of the sounds of a given language as significantly contrastive members of a system is called **phonemics**, and the members of the system are called **phonemes**. The distinction between phonetics and phonemics is important. For example, the English pronunciation of *p* in the word *pan* is accompanied by a strong puff of air called aspiration, whereas the *p* in the word *span* has no such strong aspiration. The two kinds of *p* are different phones, but not different phonemes because the two varieties of *p* never contrast. That is, the strong aspiration occurs only when *p* is at the beginning of the syllable and not when *p* follows *s.* Therefore the two varieties of *p* are not used to distinguish two different words, and the difference between them is not phonemic. On the other hand, the initial sounds in the words *pan* and *tan* serve to distinguish these two words; the *p* and the *t* contrast significantly and are classified as separate phonemes. Phonology will be discussed in much greater detail in Chapter 2; for the moment, it is sufficient to note that phonemes are building blocks of language, but have no meaning in and of themselves.

Morphology is the arrangement and relationships of the smallest meaningful units in a language. These minimum units of meaning are called **morphemes**. Although at first thought the word may seem to be the basic unit of meaning, words like *houseboat* and *playback* clearly consist of more than one meaningful element. Somewhat less obviously, the word *joyous* consists of a base word *joy* and a suffix morpheme *-ous*, which means something like "an adjective made from a noun" and appears on many other words, such as *poisonous, grievous,* and *thunderous.* The word *unsightly* consists of three morphemes: *un-, sight,* and *-ly.* The verb *sees* consists of the base morpheme *see* and the third-person singular present indicative morpheme *-s*. Note that morphemes are not identical to syllables: the form *don't* has one syllable but two morphemes, *do* and *not.* Conversely, the word *Wisconsin* has three syllables but is a single morpheme.

It is often useful to distinguish between **free** and **bound** morphemes. Free morphemes can be used alone as independent words—for example, *take, for, each, the, panda.* Bound morphemes form words only when attached to at least one other morpheme; *re-, dis-, un-, -ing, -ful,* and *-tion* are all bound morphemes. The most familiar bound morphemes are **affixes** (that is, prefixes and suffixes), but even bases (forms to which affixes are attached) can be bound. An example of a bound base is the *-cept* of such words as *except, accept, deceptive,* and *reception.*

As just noted, affixes may be either prefixes or suffixes. (Some languages also have infixes, which appear inside a word, but these are not important for English.) Another classification of affixes distinguishes **inflectional** and **derivational** affixes. For instance, the *-s* used to form plurals and the *-ed* used to indicate past tense are inflectional affixes. Present-Day English has few inflectional affixes, but Old English had many more.

Derivational affixes may be either prefixes or suffixes. Most derivational prefixes simply change the meaning of the word to which they are attached (*uni*form, *trans*plant, *micro*wave, *un*believable, *de*sensitize). Derivational suffixes normally change the part-of-speech category and may also change the meaning of the word to which they are attached. For example, the derivative suffix *-ive* in *generative* changes the verb *generate* to an adjective; the suffix *-ness* in *coolness* changes the adjective *cool* to a noun; the suffix *-ify* in *codify* changes the noun *code* to a verb. In *joyless,* the suffix *-less* not only changes the noun to an adjective, it also changes the meaning of the resulting word to the opposite of the original meaning.

Syntax is the arrangement of words into phrases, clauses, and sentences; loosely speaking, it is word order. A simple example like the difference between *I had stolen my car* and *I had my car stolen* illustrates how crucial syntax is in English. English speakers have more options with respect to syntax than they do with respect to phonology or morphology. That is, they cannot expect to be understood if they refer to a canine mammal as a *god* instead of a *dog*; but they do have the option of saying either *I like dogs* or *Dogs I like.* This freedom is limited, however; they cannot say **Like dogs I* or **Like I dogs.*

The **lexicon** of a language is the list of all the morphemes in the language. In linguistic terminology, a lexicon differs from vocabulary or a dictionary of a language in that it includes not only independent words but also morphemes that do not appear as independent words, including affixes such as *-ed, -s, mis-,* and *poly-,* and bound forms like the *-clude* of *include, exclude,* and *preclude,* which appear only as parts of words and never as independent words. The lexicon of a language is much less obviously structured and predictable than are its phonology, morphology, and syntax.

Semantics is the study of meanings or all the meanings expressed by a language. It is the relationship between language and the real world, the relationship between the sounds we make and what we are talking about. It is frequently convenient to distinguish lexical meanings (those with referents outside language) from grammatical meanings (those with reference only within the language system itself). For example, the word *run* has the lexical meaning (among many other meanings) of moving rapidly in such a way that both feet are off the ground at the same time during each stride. But the suffix *-ic* in the word *atomic* has no such external reference and means only "making an adjective out of a noun"; its meaning is grammatical.

Graphics as a linguistic term refers to the systematic representation of language in writing. A single unit in the system is called a **grapheme**. A single grapheme may represent a sound, as with the English letters *d* and *l*, a syllable, an entire word, or meaning itself with no correspondence to individual words, syllables, or sounds. (See Chapter 3 for a much more complete discussion of graphics.)

All of these various systems of language—phonology, morphology, syntax, lexicon, semantics, and even graphics—interact in highly complex ways within a given language. Changes within one subsystem can produce a chain reaction of changes among the other systems. For example, in the history of English, a sound change that entailed the loss of final unstressed syllables of words drastically affected the morphology of English by eliminating most English inflectional endings. This change in the morphology meant that the relationships among words in a sentence could no longer be made clear by inflectional endings alone. Hence word order, or syntax, became much more crucial in distinguishing meaning and also much more rigid. At the same time, prepositions became more important in clarifying relationships among the parts of a sentence. New prepositions were borrowed or formed from other parts of speech, as was the case with *except* and *during*, thus adding to the lexicon of the language. Previously existing prepositions were extended in use and meaning, thus creating syntactic and semantic change. For instance, the word *to*, which in Old English was simply a directional preposition or an adverb, took on many additional, primarily grammatical meanings, such as indicating an infinitive (*to have*, *to worry*) or even a kind of possession (*the words to the song*). Ultimately there was even a graphic change that distinguished the preposition from the adverb; the former retained its original spelling *to*, but an extra letter was added to the adverb *too*.

Interactions can also take place in the opposite direction. For example, when the grapheme þ (representing /θ/ or /ð/, the initial sounds of *think* and *they*) was abandoned and replaced by *th*, some words which were previously spelled with *th* but pronounced /t/ came to be pronounced /θ/. This is what happened to the proper name *Arthur*, formerly pronounced as if it were spelled *Arter*. Here a graphic change—the loss of the letter þ—brought about a phonological change, minor though it was.

All Languages Are Conventional and Arbitrary

All natural languages are both conventional and arbitrary. If the conventions are violated, communication fails. To take a simple example, English conventionally categorizes eating utensils as *forks*, *knives*, and *spoons*. A single English speaker cannot whimsically decide to call a *fork* a *spoon*, a *knife*, a *kiuma*, a *volochka*, or a *krof*. On the other hand, there is no particular reason why a pronged eating implement should have been called a *fork* in the first place; the French do nicely calling it a *fourchette*, and German speakers find *Gabel* quite satisfactory. The relationship between the implement itself and the sounds used to refer to it are purely arbitrary.

All Languages Are Redundant

Natural languages are also highly redundant; that is, the same information is signaled in more than one way. Redundancy may be either external or internal to language. If I make a face and point to food in a dish as I say, "I hate tapioca pudding," my distorted face signals the same thing as the word *hate*, and the pointed finger indicates the same thing as the phrase *tapioca pudding*. The face-making and finger-pointing are examples of external redundancy. Internal redundancy can be illustrated by an utterance like *He is a man*. Here the subject is signaled twice—by its position at the beginning of the sentence before the verb and by its form (*he* instead of *him* or *his*). Singularity is signaled four times: by *he* (not *they*), by *is* (not *are*), by *a* (instead of no article at all), and by *man* (not *men*). Masculinity is signaled by both *he* and *man*. Third person is signaled by *he* and *is*. Animate noun is signaled by *he* and *man*. Finally, the fact that this utterance is a statement and not a question is indicated both by word order (compare *Is he a man?*) and by intonation (if the utterance is spoken) or punctuation (if it is written). Few utterances are as internally redundant as this somewhat unlikely example, but a certain amount of internal redundancy is essential to all language in order to counteract the effects of ever-present "noise" in the environment.

METAPHORICAL DOUBLETS

All language and all languages use metaphors extensively. They may be obvious, like *the foot of the bed*, or much less obvious, like *lighthearted*. What is perhaps surprising is that, regardless of the language they speak, people tend to invent the same metaphors over and over. English has many metaphorical "doublets," pairs of expressions of which one is a colloquial, even slangy, native formation, the other a more dignified, borrowed term from Latin, but both originating as metaphors using the same semantic associations.

   For instance, *assail* is from Latin *assilire* 'to jump on'; compare this with the breezier English *to jump all over someone*. *Delirium* comes from Latin *delirare* 'to be deranged' and ultimately from *de* 'away' + *lira* 'furrow, track.' That is, one who is delirious is *off the track, off his trolley*. The Latin loan *punctual*, from Medieval Latin *punctualis* 'to the point' is completely parallel to English *on the dot*. *Incur* (Latin *incurrere*) has the same metaphorical origin as *run into*. The notion of understanding as being a kind of seizing by the mind is reflected in both *comprehend* (from Latin *com* 'together' + *prehendere* 'seize') and native English *grasp*.

All Languages Change

Finally, all natural languages change. Because they change, they have histories. All languages change in different ways, so their histories are different. The history of a given language is the description of how it has changed over a period of time. The history of English is the record of how one dialect of West Germanic has changed over the past fifteen hundred years.

   Events in language history are harder to define than most events in political history. Theoretically, a history of the English language could consist solely of statements like the ones below:

- On October 17, A.D. 784, Ecgfrith, son of Osric, used a dative *him* instead of an accusative *hine* as a direct object while speaking to his foster-brother Healfdane.
- Margery Fitzroy began pronouncing *city* with the major stress on the first syllable in 1379 after hearing her cousin Joanna, who was from London, pronounce it that way.

- On April 1, 1681, the pretentious young clerk Bartholomew Drew, while preparing a treatise on vinegar-making, decided that the English phrase "by drops" was inelegant and so paraded his learning by coining the adjective *stillatitious* from the Latin verb *stillare*.

Even assuming that we could retrieve and document such events, we quite properly feel that isolated examples of individual behavior like these are not historically significant in and of themselves. "Events" in the history of a language consist, not of isolated deviations or innovations by single speakers, but rather of changes in overall patterns or rules, changes that are adopted by a significant portion of the speakers of that language. It is of no particular interest that Ecgfrith, on one occasion, confused the dative and accusative forms of the third-person singular masculine personal pronoun. It is of interest that thousands of little Ecgfriths regularly used only dative forms of pronouns where their grandparents would have used both dative and accusative forms.

Changes in Language

What Is Language Change?

Because all language is systematic, the history of any language is the history of change in its systems. By change, we mean a permanent alteration. That is, slips of the tongue, ad hoc coinages that are not adopted by other users of the language, "new" structures that result from one person's getting his or her syntax tangled in an overly ambitious sentence are not regarded as change. Ephemeral slang that is widely used one year but that has been abandoned five years later occupies a kind of no-man's-land here; it is indeed part of the history of the language but has no permanent effect.

   Changes in language may be systematic or sporadic. The addition of a vocabulary item to name a new product, for example, is a sporadic change that has little impact on the rest of the lexicon. Even some phonological changes are sporadic. For instance, many speakers of English pronounce the word *catch* to rhyme with *wretch* rather than with *hatch*. In their dialects an isolated sporadic change has occurred in the distribution of vowels—parallel words such as *hatch*, *batch*, *match*, or *scratch* have not undergone the change. Similarly, for some speakers, the word *yukky* (from the interjection *yukh*, meaning "I don't like it") has a sound not found elsewhere in English, a heavily aspirated glottal fricative.

   Systematic changes, as the term suggests, affect an entire system or subsystem of the language. These changes may be either conditioned or unconditioned. A conditioned systematic change is brought about by context or environment, whether linguistic or extralinguistic. For many speakers of English, the short *e* vowel (as in *bet*) has, in some words, been replaced by a short *i* vowel (as in *bit*). For these speakers, *pin* and *pen*, *him* and *hem* are homophones (words pronounced the same). This change is conditioned because it occurs only in the context of a following *m* or *n*; *pig* and *peg*, *hill* and *hell*, *middle* and *meddle* are not pronounced alike for these speakers.

   An unconditioned systematic change is one for which no specific conditioning factor can be identified. An example would be the tendency among many speakers of American English to move the stress of bisyllabic words from the second syllable to the first, as in *pólice*, *défense*, *Détroit*. We can speak vaguely of a general historical drift of English to move the stress toward the beginning of the word, but the fact remains that English today is characterized by variable stress placement; indeed, many words are distinguished in pronunciation primarily on the basis of differing stress (such as *píckup/pick úp*; *pérvert/pervért*; *áttribute/attríbute*). We cannot explain the change from *políce* to *pólice* as reflecting a simple underlying rule that all words should be stressed on the first syllable.

In simplest terms, all change consists of a loss of something, a gain of something, or both—a substitution of one thing for another. Both loss and gain occur in all the subsystems of natural languages. For example, over the centuries, English has lost the distinction between long and short vowels (phonological loss), between dative and accusative cases (morphological loss), the regular inversion of subject and verb after an adverbial (syntactic loss), the verb *weorðan* (lexical loss), the meaning "to put into" for the verb *do* (semantic loss), and the letter ð (graphic loss). English has gained the diphthong represented by the spelling *oi* (phonological gain), a means of making nouns like *dropout* out of verb + adverb combinations (morphological gain), a distinction between past perfect (*I had painted my room*) and past causative (*I had my room painted*) (syntactic gain), the word *education* (lexical gain), the meaning of "helper" for the word *hand* (semantic gain), and the distinction between the letters *u* and *v* (graphic gain).

Loss may be absolute, as exemplified by the loss of *h* before *l*, *r*, and *n* (Old English *hlude*, *hring*, *hnutu*; Present-Day English *loud*, *ring*, *nut*), where the *h* (aspiration) simply disappeared. Other loss may be the result of a merger of two formerly distinct units, as when Middle English [x], a heavily aspirated *h*-like sound, collapsed with [f] in words like *tough*, *rough*, and *enough*. Such a merger is sometimes called **fusion**.

Similarly, gain may result from the introduction of an entirely new unit; an example would be the addition in Middle English, cited above, of the diphthong *oi* through such French loan words as *joy*, *poison*, and *joint*. Or the gain may result from the split of a single unit into two distinct units. For instance, Middle English *flor* underwent both semantic and graphic split to become modern English *flour* and *flower*. Such a split is sometimes called **fission**.

Losses and gains, especially in phonology, morphology, and syntax, are normally considered irreversible, but occasionally are only temporary. For example, several dialects of American English had lost the phoneme /r/ except when it appeared before a vowel, but now once again have /r/ in this position. Conversely, the use of *do* as a marker of the simple indicative (as in Shakespeare's *The cry did knock against my very heart*) was added in Early Modern English but has since disappeared.

All changes, whether major or minor, conditioned or unconditioned, disrupt a language, sometimes rather violently. But any living language is self-healing, and the permanent damage resulting from change is usually confined to the feelings of the users of the language. Many people deplore the recent introduction of *hopefully* as a sentence modifier, but the English language as a whole is none the worse for this usage. Similarly, the distinctions in meaning lost through the abandonment of the now nearly extinct subjunctive mood are today made through adverbs, modal auxiliaries, and word-order changes.

Change occurs at different rates and times within the subsystems of a language. A new loan word may be introduced and become widely accepted within a period of a few days, as with the Russian loan *sputnik* in 1957. Changes in phonology, on the other hand, operate much more slowly than isolated changes in lexicon. For any given speaker, a change in a pattern (rule) may be instantaneous, but for the total community of speakers it sometimes takes centuries for completion. The Great Vowel Shift of English took at least several generations to complete. (Some scholars claim that it is still going on today, five centuries after it began.) The loss of aspiration in such words as *which*, *whip*, and *white* began perhaps as long as a thousand years ago and is still not complete for all dialects.

In sum, for all natural languages, change is both inevitable and constant; only dead languages (languages with no native speakers) do not change. Because change is constant and has always been so, there is no such thing as a "pure" or a "decadent" language or dialect. There are only different languages and dialects, which arose in the first place only because all languages change.

The history of the English language, then, is the record of how its patterns and rules have changed over the centuries. The history of English is not the political history of its speakers, although their political history has affected their language, sometimes dramatically, as was the case with the Norman invasion of England in 1066. Nor is the history of the English language the same as the history of English literature, even though the language is the raw material of the literature. Indeed, the nature of any language influences its literature and imposes certain limitations on it. For example, quantitative verse is impossible in English today because English does not distinguish long and short syllables. Compared to other languages, English is difficult to rhyme in because of its stress patterns and great variety of syllable endings. On the other hand, because of its stress patterns, English, unlike French, lends itself easily to alliteration. Any language with a literary tradition and extensive literacy will be affected by that literature. Grammatical structures originating in writing are transferred to the spoken language. Vocabulary items and phrases introduced in literature enter the spoken language. The written tradition tends to give rise to concepts of correctness and to act as a conservative influence on the spoken language.

Why Does Language Change?

In any science, the hardest question to answer is "why?" In many cases, the question is unanswerable. From one point of view, it is strange that human beings speak so many languages and that these languages undergo any changes at all. Other human activities are identical and unchanging everywhere—all human beings smile, cry, scream in terror, sleep, drink, and walk in essentially the same way. Why should they differ in speech, the one aspect of behavior that is uniquely human? The answer is that, whereas the capacity to learn language is innate, the particular language that anyone uses is learned. That is, the ability to learn languages is universal and unchanging, but the languages themselves are diverse and constantly changing.

Given that learned behavior can and often does change, what are the forces that trigger change? One explanation for linguistic change is the principle of least effort. According to this principle, language changes because speakers are "sloppy" and simplify their speech in various ways. Accordingly, abbreviated forms like *gym* for *gymnasium* and *plane* for *airplane* arise. *Going to* becomes *gonna* because the latter has two fewer phonemes to articulate. Intervocalic *t* becomes *d* because, first, voiced sounds require less energy to produce than voiceless sounds, and, second, the speaker does not have to switch from voiced to voiceless and then back to voiced again in a word like *little*. On the morphological level, speakers use *showed* instead of *shown* as the past participle of *show* so that they will have one less irregular verb form to remember.

The principle of least effort is an adequate explanation for many isolated changes, such as the reduction of *God be with you* to *Goodbye*, and it probably plays an important role in most systemic changes, such as the loss of inflections in English. However, as an explanation for *all* linguistic change, it has shortcomings. How exactly are "difficulty" and "ease" to be defined? Judging by its rarity among the languages of the world and by how late English-speaking children master it, the phoneme /θ/ (the first sound of *think*) must be difficult to articulate and hence highly susceptible to change. Yet it has survived intact throughout the entire history of English. Further, many changes cannot be explained either by basic communicative needs or by a principle of least effort. An example would be the development in Middle English of the extremely complex system of definite and indefinite articles in English, a system that is the despair of so many foreign learners of the language. Old English got along nicely with no indefinite article at all and with a form of *that* as both demonstrative and definite article. Many languages today—for example, Russian, Chinese, and Japanese—have no articles at all. The principle of least effort by itself simply cannot explain the rise of articles in English.

Another explanation for language change is analogy. Under analogical change, two things or rules that were once different become identical or at least more alike. The principle of analogy is closely related to the principle of least effort; analogy is one way of achieving least effort. By analogy, a speaker reasons, usually unconsciously, that if A is like B in several respects, then it must be like B in other respects. If *beans* is a plural noun naming a kind of vegetable and has the singular form *bean*, then *peas*, which also names a kind of vegetable, must also be a plural and must have the singular form *pea*. (Historically, *peas*, or *pease*, was an uncountable singular noun.) If, in noun phrases, single-word modifiers precede the noun they modify, then in the noun phrase *attorney general*, *attorney* must be the modifier and *general* the noun. Therefore the plural of the phrase must be *attorney generals*, even though *general* was originally an adjective.

Analogy can operate at all levels of a language. On the semantic level, many people use the word *livid* to mean "bright," especially bright red, as in anger. Though historically *livid* means "pale," its sound association with *vivid* has led to analogical semantic change. Even spelling may be affected by analogy. The word *delight* historically contained no *-gh-*, but acquired these letters by analogy with such rhyming words as *light*, *fright*, *sight*, and *might*.

In general, the more common a word or construction, the less susceptible it is to change by analogy. Less frequently used words or constructions are more likely to be altered to fit the patterns of more common ones. Thus the verb *to be* remains wildly irregular in English because it is learned so early and used so often. But the relatively uncommon verb *thrive*, once conjugated as *thrive : throve : thriven*, is well on its way to becoming a weak (regular) verb.

Still another explanation frequently offered for language change is that children learn their native language imperfectly from their elders. Imperfect learning is surely one factor, but it cannot explain all change. For permanent linguistic change to occur, all children of a given speech community would have to make exactly the same mistakes. This intuitively seems unlikely. Further, there is ample evidence that linguistic change occurs beyond the childhood years. Many adults, consciously or unconsciously, alter their speech in various ways, changing even their phonology. For example, twenty years after moving to New England as a young adult, I have altered my own phonology to such an extent that my New York family comments on it. For a few words, this change was deliberate; because my Rhode Island neighbors mistook my pronunciation of the street on which I live (*Forest Street*) for *Fourth Street*, I deliberately altered my pronunciation of *Forest* to make the first syllable a homophone of *far* instead of *for*. In other instances, the change was unconscious; I was not aware that my pronunciation of words like *class, past, half,* and *aunt* had changed until acquaintances pointed it out to me.

More important than such anecdotal evidence is the fact that linguistic change occurs in aspects of language not even used by children learning the language. For instance, over the centuries, English has developed complex structures of subordination that did not exist in Old English. Consider the sentence *Having no weapon with which to attack the mosquitoes whining around my head, I could only curse Joel for persuading me to come camping in an area that was noted for its ferocious predators.* Underlying this compact sentence are at least seven separate "simple" statements: (1) I had no weapon, (2) I could not attack the mosquitoes, (3) The mosquitoes whined around my head, (4) I could only curse Joel, (5) Joel persuaded me, (6) I came camping in an area, and (7) This area was noted for its ferocious predators. Young children today do not spontaneously produce such elaborate structures; even adults have to be trained in their use. Clearly these changes were introduced by adults. Another example is the change of the impersonal pronoun from earlier *man* to present-day *one*. Young children almost never use *one* as an impersonal pronoun today, so it is unlikely that they were responsible for its introduction.

Internal and External Pressures for Change

In discussing the history of a language, it is often useful to distinguish **outer history** from **inner history**. The outer history is the events that have happened to the speakers of the language leading to changes in the language. For example, the Norman invasion brought French-speaking conquerors to England and made French the official language of England for about three hundred years. As a result, the English language was profoundly affected. The inner history of a language is the changes that occur within the language itself, changes that cannot be attributed directly to external forces. For instance, many words that were pronounced as late as the ninth century with a long *a* sound similar to that of *father* are today pronounced with a long *o*: Old English *ham, gat, halig,* and *sar* correspond to modern *home, goat, holy,* and *sore*. There is no evidence of an external cause for this change, and we can only assume that it resulted from pressures within the language system itself.

Among external pressures for language change, foreign contacts are the most obvious. They may be instigated by outright military invasion, by commercial relations, by immigration, or by the social prestige of a foreign language. The Viking invasions of England during the ninth and tenth centuries added, not surprisingly, many new lexical items to English. Less obviously, they contributed to (though were not the sole cause of) the loss of inflections in English because, although Norse and English were similar in many ways, their inflectional endings were quite different. One way of facilitating communication between speakers of the two languages would have been to drop the inflectional endings entirely. (Exactly the same process can be observed today when a speaker of Icelandic talks to a speaker of Swedish.) An example of the effects of the prestige of another language would be the spread of /ž/ (the sound of *s* in *usual*) in French loan words to environments where it had not previously appeared in English; examples include *garage, beige,* and *genre.*

Foreign pressures may also take the form of contact between different dialects of the same language. The changes cited above in my own speech resulting from contact with a new dialect exemplify this kind of influence. Here again, sociological factors may play a role. The reemergence of preconsonantal and final /r/ (as in *harm* and *far*) in Eastern Seaboard and Southern American dialects certainly has been encouraged by the sociological facts that *r*-lessness is frequently ridiculed in other areas of the country, that it is often associated with Black English, and that the prestige of American English vis-à-vis British English has increased in the past thirty years.

Internal pressures for language change most often appear when changes in one system of the language impinge on another system. For example, phonological changes caused the **reflexes** (the "descendants" that have undergone change) of OE *lætan* 'to allow' and OE *lettan* 'to hinder' to fall together as *let.* The resulting homonymy was unacceptable because the two verbs, opposite in meaning, often occurred in identical contexts, leading to ambiguity and a breakdown in communication. Consequently, the *let* that meant "hinder" has been all but lost in modern English, surviving only in such set phrases as *let ball* and the legal term *without let or hindrance.* On the morphological level, the verb *wear,* a weak verb in OE, has become a strong verb in modern English, despite the fact that the trend has been overwhelmingly in the opposite direction. This change can be explained by the rhyme analogy of *wear* with strong verbs like *bear, tear,* and *swear* and also, perhaps, by the semantic bond between *wear* and *tear.*

Still other changes fall on the borderline between internal and external. British English still uses *stone* as a unit of weight for human beings and large animals, although the weight of other commodities is normally expressed in pounds. American English uses the pound as a measure for both large animals and other items. One of the reasons why *stone* has remained in British English may be that *pound* is semantically "overloaded" by being both a unit of weight and the national monetary unit. Similarly, in some parts of Great Britain, at least, a small storage room – the American English *closet* – is referred to as a *cupboard.* The avoidance of the term *closet* is probably explained by the fact that what speakers in the United States refer to as a *toilet* or *john* is called a *W.C.* (for *water closet*) in Britain. The mild taboo associated with the term *water closet,* even in its euphemistic abbreviated form, has led to its avoidance in other contexts.

Predicting Change

Even though we can frequently offer convincing post hoc explanations for language change, we can seldom predict what specific changes will occur in the future. Obviously, extralinguistic events like invasions or sweeping technological changes will result in additions and losses to the lexicon. Also, once certain changes have begun, we can with some confidence predict that other changes will follow. For example, in recent American English, a *t* that appears between vowels and after the major stress of a word becomes *d* (consider the similar pronunciations of *writer* and *rider*). Because we know that the sounds *t* and *d* are paired in a system of consonants that also pairs *k* with *g* and *p* with *b,* it is quite possible that, under the same circumstances, *k* will become *g* and *p* will become *b.* Indeed, these changes have already been heard in the speech of some individuals, and seen in occasional misspellings such as *significant.* Fifty years ago, we could have accurately predicted that *t* would *not* become *u* or *f*, but we could not have predicted that it would become *d*.

Asymmetries, "weaknesses," or irregularities in the various subsystems of a language are normally prime targets for change. For example, Old English had, as a result of earlier sound changes, two sets of diphthongs, usually spelled *ea* and *eo*, that were apparently similar in pronunciation and did not fit symmetrically into the overall Old English vowel system. It is not surprising that these diphthongs had fallen together with other vowels by Middle English. By the same argument, however, we could predict a simplification of the overcrowded and asymmetric array of front vowels in English (the vowels of *beet*, *bit*, *bait*, *bet*, and *bat*). Yet these vowels have remained remarkably stable over the centuries. In sum, linguistic training and knowledge of linguistic history may allow us to predict which sorts of changes are likely, but rarely which precise changes will actually take place.

Factors Impeding Change

As a rule, if there are extensive ongoing changes in one subsystem of a language, other subsystems tend to remain fairly stable. For example, over the centuries, English has undergone drastic changes in its morphology, but has been relatively conservative in its phonology. In fact, the last major phonological change in English, the Great Vowel Shift, began only as the vast morphological alterations were ending and the morphology of English was settling down to what is essentially its present state. German, though closely related to English, has undergone many more phonological changes, but has been much more conservative than English in its morphology. Just as redundancy in language allows changes to occur in the first place, the necessity for redundancy prevents too many changes from occurring at the same time. Uncurbed change would lead to a total breakdown in communication.

Changes in the graphic system of a language come much more slowly than changes in other systems. English has not adopted a totally new grapheme (though a few have been lost and the distribution of others has been modified) since it began to be written in the Latin alphabet. Despite vast changes in pronunciation, English spelling has not been revised in any fundamental way for the past five hundred years. The third-person singular indicative ending *-th* (as in *doth*, *hath*) was still being written as late as two hundred years after all speakers were using the current *-s* ending in speech.

There are multiple reasons for this archconservatism of writing systems, most of them external to language itself. First, though speech is ephemeral, writing provides a permanent reference; we can go back to check what was written previously. Second, ever since the advent of printing, there have been practical arguments against graphic reform. The introduction of a revised spelling would entail a great deal of relearning by millions of literate adults, would necessitate complete revision of dictionaries, and would mean that earlier classics of English literature would be rendered inaccessible to current and future generations. If new letter forms were introduced for the miserably represented vowel system of English, then all existing typewriters and type fonts would immediately become obsolete. Third, agreement on whose pronunciation the revised spelling should be based upon would probably be impossible to achieve. Still another factor against graphic reform is the fact that the written language is, to a much greater degree than the spoken language, under the control of the highly educated or well-to-do, the most conservative groups in a culture.

Not only are graphic systems themselves resistant to change, but combined with a high level of literacy, they act as a brake on change in the spoken language and, occasionally, even reverse changes that have occurred in it. The reintroduction of postvocalic /r/ in some American English dialects would have been impossible without the written language, because speakers would not have known where to put the /r/ without a written model. The commonly heard /t/ in *often*, /p/ in *clapboard*, and /h/ in *forehead* are all the results of spelling pronunciations. Hundreds of lexical items survive only because they have been preserved in the written language; examples include not only nouns naming obsolete objects such as *firkin* but even structural words like the conjunction *lest*.

Demarcating the History of English

Although linguistic change is a slow but unceasing process, like a slow-motion movie, so to speak, it is impracticable to try to describe the changes in this way. Instead, we must present them as a series of still photographs, noting what has changed in the interval between one photograph and the next. This procedure fails to capture the real dynamism of linguistic change, but it does have the advantage of allowing us to examine particular aspects in detail and at a leisurely pace before they disappear. The history of the English language is normally presented in four such still photographs—Old English, Middle English, Early Modern English, and Present-Day English. We will retain these traditional divisions, but also glance at the prehistory of English and speculate to some extent about English in the future.

The dividing lines between one period of English and the next are not sharp and dramatic: the English people did not go to bed on December 31, 1099, speaking Old English and wake up on January 1, 1100, speaking Middle English. Nevertheless, the changes that had accumulated by the year 1100 were sufficiently great to justify a different designation for the language after that date.

Old English (OE) is that stage of the language used between A.D. 450 and A.D. 1100. The period from 1100 to 1500 is Middle English (ME), the period between 1500 and 1800 is Early Modern English (EMnE), and the period since 1800 is Present-Day English (PDE). For those familiar with English history, these dates may look suspiciously close to dates of important political and social events in England. The beginning of ME is just a few years after the Norman Conquest, the beginning of EMnE parallels the English Renaissance and the introduction of printing into England, and the starting date for Present-Day English is on the heels of the American Revolution.

These parallels are neither accidental nor arbitrary. All of these political events are important in the outer history of English. The Norman Conquest had a cataclysmic effect on English because it brought thousands of Norman French speakers to England and because French subsequently became the official and prestigious language of the nation for three centuries. The introduction of printing, among other effects, led to greatly increased literacy, a standard written language, concepts of correctness, and the brake on linguistic change that always accompanies widespread literacy. The American Revolution represents the beginning of the division of English into national dialects that would develop more or less independently and that would come to have their own standards.

Linguistically, these demarcation points of 450, 1100, 1500, and 1800 are also meaningful. The date 450 is that of the separation of the "English" speakers from their Continental relatives; it marks the beginning of English as a language, although the earliest surviving examples of written English date only from the seventh century. By 1100, English had lost so many of its inflections that it could no longer properly be called an inflecting language. By 1500, English had absorbed so many French loans that its vocabulary looked more like that of a Romance language than that of a Germanic language. Further, the very rhythms of the spoken language had changed under the influence of the differing stress patterns of these French loans. By 1800, the vast numbers of Latinate loans brought in by the English Renaissance had been absorbed, along with hundreds of exotic, often non-Indo-European words introduced through English exploration and colonization. Also, the grammar of English had, in most important respects, become that of the present day.

Evaluating Sources of Information

Our primary source of information about earlier stages of English is written texts. Except for the most recent times, texts outweigh in importance all other sources put together. Fortunately for the historian of the language, English has been written down almost from the beginning of its existence as an identifiable dialect of West Germanic; the earliest English texts date from the seventh century A.D.

Texts are not, however, without their problems. First, there simply are not enough of them. Further, no matter how many manuscripts we had, we would always be missing just what we needed from a given geographical area or time period. Or the text would perversely fail to contain crucial diagnostic forms. Furthermore, we cannot, of course, question a text to find out about words or structures that it does not include.

Second, texts must be interpreted. We can rarely take whatever we find at face value. Seemingly deviant forms may well be nothing more than clerical errors, the result of carelessness or of woolgathering on the part of the scribe, or, later, typesetter or proofreader. Here, patterns are important. For example, it would normally be of no particular significance if a writer of PDE spelled the word *platter* as *pladder* on one occasion. If, on the other hand, he or she also spelled *traitor*, *deep-seated*, and *metal* as *trader*, *deep-seeded*, and *medal*, respectively; and if he or she spelled *pedal* and *tidy* as *pettle* and *tighty*, we would have good reason to suspect that this writer did not distinguish /t/ and /d/ when these two came between two vowels and after the major stress of the word.

In using texts as a source of information, we also have to try to evaluate the extent to which tradition and convention have concealed real differences and similarities or, conversely, may have indicated differences or similarities that did not actually exist. If we had only spelling as evidence, we would have to assume that speakers today pronounce *I* and *eye* very differently; on the other hand, we would not know that there are two distinct pronunciations for the sequence of letters *wound*.

In this respect, the semi-educated are better informants about how a language is actually pronounced than are well-educated writers. For example, we would never know from reading the works of Roger Williams, the founder of Rhode Island, that American colonists were regularly "dropping their *r*'s" in unstressed syllables at the ends of words and after certain vowels. Williams had a

Cambridge education and had learned conventional English spellings. However, legal records written by less well educated town clerks have scores of spellings like *therefo*, *Edwad*, *fofeiture*, and *administe* (for *therefore*, *Edward*, *forfeiture*, and *administer*), clear evidence that *r*-dropping goes back several centuries in New England speech.

In interpreting texts we must also bring to bear all the extralinguistic evidence we can garner. If a contemporary Canadian man writes *The wind bloweth where it listeth*, we know that he has some familiarity with the King James Bible, and also that he does not freely alternate the endings *-eth* and *-s* for the third-person singular present indicative of verbs. Similarly, when an educated English-woman writes *There is a nice distinction to be made here*, we do not assume that she means "pleasant distinction," nor do we assume that every native speaker of English has the meaning "subtle, sensitive, precise" for the word *nice*. Such assumptions are relatively easy to make for Present-Day English texts because we are contemporaries of the writers, sharing their culture. The further back in time we go, the more difficult it is to appraise written texts because we have irretrievably lost so much information about the cultural background that surrounded the writers.

Still a third problem with written texts as sources of information is that, at least for the first thousand years of English history, so many of the texts are translations, especially from Latin or French. This fact limits the subject matter—and hence the vocabulary—of the text. More important, the original language may have influenced the vocabulary (loan words), the syntax, and even the morphology. Anyone who has ever translated a text from a foreign language into English knows how difficult it is to produce a smooth English translation that is not influenced by the vocabulary and word order of its original. Certain Old English words or structures appear *only* in translations, evidence that Old English translators had the same difficulty; still, because most of the available texts are translations, the scholar has no alternative but to use them.

Apart from written texts, other sources of information about language change include descriptive statements, recordings, contemporary dialects, loan-words in English, and contemporary spellings. All of these sources are severely limited in their usefulness. Descriptive statements about English do not appear until late; there are none of any significance prior to the seventeenth century. In addition, it is frequently difficult to interpret these early descriptions and to translate them into modern terminology. Few such early statements were intended to be objective. Their purpose was usually prescriptive, instructing readers in appropriate pronunciation and usage; hence they were biased toward what the author considered elegant speech. Indeed, if such an author says that one must *not* pronounce a word in a certain way, we can be fairly sure that many speakers of the time *were* pronouncing it that way.

Recordings of spoken English date only from the twentieth century. Many of them are less than satisfactory, particularly if the speaker is reading rather than speaking spontaneously. Also, if speakers know they are being recorded, they usually become self-conscious and even deliberately edit certain usages or pronunciations out of their speech.

The contemporary pronunciation of loanwords from other languages is helpful primarily in dating sound changes in English or the approximate time when the loanword entered English. For example, PDE *dish* and *discus* are both from Latin, but the pronunciation of the final sound in *dish* shows that it is a very early loanword, borrowed before a sound change in which *sk* came to be pronounced like *sh*; *discus*, borrowed much later, was not affected by this change.

Dialectal differences in contemporary English also provide some information about earlier stages of the language. Remoter, more rural dialects often preserve older morphological forms and vocabulary items lost in the standard dialect. Differing pronunciations of the same words also may help the scholar reconstruct earlier stages of the language. For instance, Irish and American English pronounce *beet* in essentially the same way. However, in American English *beat* is a homophone of *beet*, whereas, to American ears, the Irish pronunciation of *beat* sounds like that of *bait*. (Compare the pronunciation of the name of the Irish poet *Yeats* and that of the English poet *Keats*.) This dialectal difference, combined with the spelling difference of *ea* and *ee*, strongly suggests that Irish dialects reflect an earlier stage of English when *beat* and *beet* were not homophones.

Because English spelling is so conservative—it has not had a thoroughgoing reform in five hundred years—it has become a museum of the history of the language, and, as such, is helpful in reconstructing earlier stages. Spellings like *sword, knee, though,* and *dumb* preserve consonants long lost in the spoken language. But museum though English spelling is, it is a museum with poorly labeled contents and even with a fair number of bogus reconstructions, the Piltdown Men of spelling. The "silent" consonants in *island, ghost,* and *whole*, for example, are frauds; the *s, h,* and *w* in these words never have been pronounced in English. Hence English spelling by itself, without corroborative evidence, is not a reliable source of information.

In the later chapters of this book, as we examine the prehistory and then the history of English, we will see many of the principles introduced here applied to the English language itself. Before we begin discussing the lineage of English, though, we must make a quick excursus into the phonology of Present-Day English and another into the nature of writing systems. These brief digressions will provide a point of reference and a vocabulary of technical terms necessary for understanding the remaining chapters.

Suggested Further Reading[2]

Aitchison, Jean. *Language Change: Progress or Decay?*
Anttila, Raimo. *An Introduction to Historical and Comparative Linguistics.*
Arlotto, Anthony. *Introduction to Historical Linguistics.*
Bynon, Theodora. *Historical Linguistics.*
Harris, Roy. *The Language Makers.*
Hoenigswald, Henry M. *Language Change and Linguistic Reconstruction.*
Jeffers, Robert J., and Ilse Lehiste. *Principles and Methods for Historical Linguistics.*
Palmer, Leonard R. *Descriptive and Comparative Linguistics: A Critical Introduction.*
Pedersen, Holger. *The Discovery of Language: Linguistic Science in the Nineteenth Century.*
Robins, R. H. *A Short History of Linguistics.*
Samuels, M. L. *Linguistic Evolution: With Special Reference to English.*
Sturtevant, E. H. *Linguistic Change: An Introduction to the Historical Study of Language.*
Yule, George. *The Study of Language.*

---

[2] Full publication data for the suggested further readings in each chapter appear in the General Bibliography, pp. 369–373.

C H A P T E R 2

Phonology

*Language is called the garment of thought: how-
ever, it should rather be, language is the flesh-
garment, the body, of thought.*

—Thomas Carlyle

Most native speakers of English, even without training in linguistics, have a fairly
good intuitive understanding of morphology, syntax, lexicon, and semantics.
However, because the Latin alphabet is so inadequate for representing English
sounds and because the match between English spelling and English pronunciation
is both complex and poor, some specific training in English phonology is necessary
as background for a study of the history of English.

Partly because we are literate and accustomed to seeing speech represented
on paper as a series of separate marks, we tend to think of speech as consisting of
discrete sounds. Real speech is continuous, not discrete. In a sound spectrogram[1] of
someone saying the word *dig*, for example, there are no clear boundaries between
the *d*, the *i*, and the *g*. Nonetheless, if we are to analyze the sounds of speech, we
must treat them as if they were discrete—and, for all its shortcomings, our writing
system does just that. Further, all the evidence we have suggests that the human
brain in some way also breaks up the continuous flow of speech and sorts it out
into separate units. Therefore, the discipline of phonology is based on the fiction
that speech consists of isolable units of sound.

Theoretically, there are at least three ways to approach the analysis of
speech sounds: (1) from a perceptual point of view, or how the mind analyzes and
interprets the sounds; (2) from an acoustic point of view, or the physical properties
of the sounds; and (3) from an articulatory point of view, or how the sounds are

---

[1] A sound spectrogram is a kind of "photograph" giving a visual representation of the intensity
and frequency of sound waves in a segment of speech over time.

produced by the speech organs. However, our understanding of how the mind interprets speech is still limited, and the acoustic approach to speech sounds requires elaborate equipment and an extensive knowledge of physics. Thus, for the purposes of studying the history of English, we will use the articulatory approach. It is relatively easy for people to see and feel what is going on in their mouths as they produce speech sounds. Furthermore, apart from pathological cases such as cleft palates or missing teeth, the vocal tracts of all human beings are basically identical and have not changed over the centuries. Finally, all the changes that occur in speech sounds can be described in articulatory terms.

The Production of Speech

Speech begins when air leaves the lungs. After that, the stream of air may be impeded or modified at any point from the larynx on up through the nose or lips; the nature of the resulting speech sound depends on how and where the stream of air is modified. The **articulators** of speech are the movable parts of the speech tract: the lips, the tongue, and the uvula. The tongue is the most important articulator. The **points of articulation** are the nonmovable portions of the speech tract with which an articulator comes in contact or near contact. Figure 2.1 shows the whole vocal apparatus, apart from the lungs.

1. **Lips**. The lips may be open, closed, partially closed, spread, or rounded during speech. Sounds involving the lips as articulator are called **labials**. If both lips are involved, the sounds are often called **bilabials**.
2. **Teeth**. The teeth may be open, closed, or partially closed during speech. Sounds in which the tongue touches the back of the teeth are called **dental**; those in which the tongue protrudes slightly between the teeth are **interdental**. **Labio-dental** sounds are produced with the upper teeth on the lower lip.
3. **Alveolar ridge**. The alveolar ridge is the bony plate into which the upper teeth are fixed. **Alveolar** sounds are produced when the tip or the front of the tongue is in contact with the alveolar ridge.
4. **Hard palate**. The hard palate is the dome-shaped bony plate at the roof of the mouth. **Palatal** sounds are produced when the tip or the front of the tongue is in contact with the hard palate.
5. The **velum**, or **soft palate**, is the soft, muscular tissue behind the hard palate. (If you have a limber tongue, you can curl it back to feel the dividing line between the hard palate and the velum. Or you can find it with your forefinger.) The velum can be contracted to come in contact with the top of the throat, closing off the nasal passage. **Velar** sounds are produced when the back of the tongue, or **dorsum**, comes in contact with the velum.
6. The **uvula** is the cylindrically shaped extension of the velum that hangs down over the back of the tongue. (You can view it in a mirror if you open your mouth very wide.) The uvula is not used in forming English sounds, but it becomes an articulator in some languages when it is made to vibrate rapidly, producing a **uvular trill**.
7. The **nasal cavity** is opened to the flow of air from the lungs when the velum is lowered. The resulting sounds are called **nasals**; the specific nature of the nasal sound depends on the position of other articulators.

Figure 2.1 The Human Vocal Apparatus

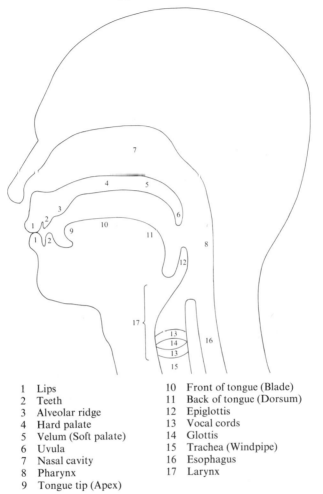

1	Lips	10	Front of tongue (Blade)
2	Teeth	11	Back of tongue (Dorsum)
3	Alveolar ridge	12	Epiglottis
4	Hard palate	13	Vocal cords
5	Velum (Soft palate)	14	Glottis
6	Uvula	15	Trachea (Windpipe)
7	Nasal cavity	16	Esophagus
8	Pharynx	17	Larynx
9	Tongue tip (Apex)		

8. The **pharynx** is the cavity at the back of the upper throat. It is not specifically involved in the production of sounds in English, though it is in some languages, for example, Arabic.
9. The **tongue tip,** or **apex** of the tongue, is one of the most important articulators. In **apical** sounds, the tongue tip is the articulator.
10. The **blade,** or front of the tongue, is that portion of the tongue just behind the tip. As an articulator, the blade may come in contact with the teeth, the alveolar ridge, or the hard palate.
11. The **dorsum,** or the back of the tongue, serves as an articulator when it comes in contact with the velum (soft palate).
12. The **epiglottis** is a piece of cartilage that folds over the trachea to channel food down the esophagus and prevent it from going down the trachea and into the lungs. It is not an articulator and is involved in speech only to the extent that, when it is sealing off the trachea, speech is impossible.

13. The **vocal cords** are a pair of elastic muscular bands rather like thick rubber bands. They are attached to the front and back of the larynx. When the vocal cords are relaxed, air from the lungs passes through them unimpeded, and the resulting sounds are called **voiceless**. When the vocal cords are tensed, the opening between them is reduced, and air passing through them makes them vibrate rapidly; the resulting sounds are called **voiced**. The faster the vocal cords vibrate, the higher the pitch of the voiced sounds.
14. The **glottis** is the opening between the vocal cords. If the glottis is momentarily closed and then released, a voiceless speech sound called a **glottal stop** results. A glottal stop appears before the vowels in the two syllables of "unh-unh," the vocal gesture meaning "no." It also separates the two syllables of "uh-oh," the sound we use to indicate trouble.
15. The **trachea** is the tube carrying air to and from the lungs.
16. The **esophagus** is the tube running parallel to the trachea, through which food passes on its way to the stomach. The esophagus is not involved in normal speech production.
17. The **larynx** is the general area between the pharynx and the trachea, including the vocal cords. It is not an articulator in English, though it is in some languages.

Phonemes and Allophones

The human vocal tract produces a wide assortment of noises. Some of them are speech sounds or suitable for use as speech sounds, and some are not. In studying phonology, we ignore snorts, sneezes, sighs, coughs, sniffs, screams, and so on. We ignore extralinguistic or supralinguistic aspects such as the pitch difference between male and female voices, whispering, and pathological conditions like harelips or malformed jaws.

Of the remaining sounds, the components of speech, no two are ever identical, even when produced by the same speaker. However, both speaker and hearer treat some sounds as if they were identical, and others as different. For example, the initial consonants of *pear* and *bear* are considered different because they distinguish two different words with two different meanings. On the other hand, the *p*-sounds in *pace* and *space* are physically different for all native speakers of English. The *p* in *pace* is accompanied by a fairly strong puff of air called **aspiration**, whereas the *p* in *space* is not. This difference in aspiration is never used to distinguish two different words in English, that is, no two words contrast on the basis of this difference alone. Thus the two sounds are treated as being the same.

A group of sounds that never contrast with one another, that speakers treat as the same sound, is called a **phoneme**. The noncontrastive variants that comprise a phoneme are called **allophones** of that phoneme. Hence *p* and *b* are separate phonemes in English, but aspirated *p* and unaspirated *p* are only allophones of the phoneme *p*. To indicate whether we are discussing phonemes or allophones, it is conventional to enclose phonemes between slashes (/ /) and allophones between square brackets ([ ]). Thus we say that [p] and [pʻ] (where the inverted apostrophe stands for aspiration) are allophones of the phoneme /p/.

Normally, all the allophones of a phoneme share many features. Both [p] and [pʻ] are voiceless, are bilabial, and involve a momentary complete stoppage of the air coming from the lungs. Their only difference lies in the force of the plosion when the stoppage is released. In a few instances, however, allophones of a single phoneme differ strikingly. For example, most allophones of the phoneme /t/ are formed by the contact of the tongue with the alveolar ridge. But one common allophone, [ʔ], does not involve the tongue at all. Instead, it is formed by the momentary contraction and then release of the vocal cords. Phonetically, it is a glottal stop, not an alveolar stop; phonemically, it is still only an allophone of /t/ in English.

Although the glottal stop [ʔ] is only an allophone of /t/ or other stops in English, it constitutes a separate phoneme in some languages. This fact illustrates an important principle of phonology: *every language has its own unique configuration of phonemes and allophones.* Even within a given language, the total set of phonemes and allophones may differ from dialect to dialect and may change over time. For example, though French and English both have /t/ phonemes, they are not the "same" /t/. Most of the allophones of the French /t/ are produced with the tongue touching the upper teeth rather than the alveolar ridge. Nor does the French /t/ have the aspirated allophone [tʻ] in initial position or the glottal allophone [ʔ]. Russian has a palatal version of its phoneme /t/ that does not occur at all in English. The concept of the phoneme and the allophone is meaningful only within the context of a specified language.

In discussing the earlier stages of a language, we normally operate at the phonemic level and not the allophonic level (though there are exceptions). Although we can identify with a fair amount of confidence the phonemes of past stages, we usually lack the precise knowledge of production required to identify the allophones.

As a means of representing actual pronunciation, English spelling is notoriously inadequate and complex. Words pronounced the same may be spelled differently (*meet, meat, mete*), and words spelled the same may be pronounced differently (*wind, arithmetic, invalid*). Some phonemes have no separate spelling of their own (for example, the two different initial consonants of *then* and *thin*). Some alphabetic symbols can stand for several different sounds—or no sound at all—as is the case of *s* in the words *sun, pays, treasure, tension,* and *aisle.* The letter *c* is totally redundant in that any phoneme that it represents also has another traditional representation: It replaces *k* in *call, s* in *cell, ch* in *cello, sh* in *social,* and stands for nothing at all in *indict.* Many words are spelled with "silent" letters (*b* in *climb, ch* in *yacht, g* in *sign, h* in *exhaust, n* in *autumn, p* in *receipt, t* in *castle,* and *w* in *answer*). In other instances, phonemes are not represented in spelling at all (the initial *w*-sound in *one* or the *y*-sound after *m* in *music*). We shall see in later chapters that there is usually a good historical explanation for these anomalies of spelling. They represent an earlier stage in the pronunciation of English—or even of Latin, French, Dutch, and so on. Knowledge of the history of English makes one more tolerant of the eccentricities of Present-Day English spelling.

In order to represent every phoneme by one and only one separate symbol, various phonemic alphabets have been devised. Most such alphabets use existing Latin symbols wherever possible, supplementing them with diacritical marks or modifications where necessary, and omitting Latin symbols that are totally redundant (such as *x* and *c*). The phonemic alphabet used in this book is one of the more common ones employed, especially by American linguists.

FOR THE BIRDS

Imitative (or echoic, or onomatopoeic) words comprise only a tiny, though entertaining, part of the total English vocabulary. Perhaps the highest proportion of such words is to be found in the names of birds and bird sounds. The word *owl*, for example, goes all the way back to an imitative Indo-European root **ul-*. Other onomatopoeic names for English birds include *chiffchaff, chough, cock, cuckoo, curlew, hoopoe, pewit,* and *quail.* The process has continued into the modern period. When English colonists encountered unfamiliar birds in North America, they frequently named them for their songs or characteristic cries; hence such names as *bobolink, bobwhite, chewink, chickadee, chuckwill's widow, killdeer, peetweet, pewee, phoebe,* and *whippoorwill.* Among the imitative words describing bird noises are *cackle, caw, cheep, chirp, cluck, cock-a-doodle-doo, coo, gobble, hoot, peep, tweet,* and *twitter.* Although bird songs are notoriously difficult to describe to someone who has not heard them, people clearly are willing to keep trying.

The Phonemes of Present-Day American English

The phonemes of all languages are conventionally subdivided into consonants and vowels. This division is convenient because of fundamental differences in the way consonants and vowels are produced and because of their different roles in the structure of syllables. In simplest terms, consonants are characterized by a stoppage or impedence of the flow of air at some point in the vocal tract, whereas vowels are characterized by an unimpeded flow of air but with modifications of the shape of the oral chamber through which the air passes. In English, every separate vowel constitutes the center of a separate syllable; the syllable may or may not include one or more consonants.

Consonants

In articulatory terms, a **consonant** can be defined by its place of articulation and its manner of articulation. The places of articulation are illustrated in Figure 2.1 and discussed on pages 18–20. Figure 2.2 shows the classes of consonants defined by manner of articulation.

STOPS

Stops, also called **plosives**, are sounds produced by blocking the stream of air completely at some point in the mouth and then fully releasing it. The type of stop is defined by the point at which the stream of air is blocked. Thus /p/ is a bilabial stop because the air is blocked at the lips, whereas /g/ is a velar stop because the air is blocked at the velum by the back of the tongue. If the vocal cords vibrate during the production of the stop, it is called a **voiced** stop; if they do not vibrate, it is a **voiceless** stop.

Figure 2.2 Consonant Phonemes of Present-Day English

Manner of Articulation		Point of Articulation					
		Bilabial	*Labio-dental*	*Inter-dental*	*Alveolar*	*Alveo-palatal*	*Velar*
Stops	Voiceless	p			t		k
	Voiced	b			d		g
Affricates	Voiceless					č	
	Voiced					ǰ	
Fricatives	Voiceless		f	θ	s	š	h*
	Voiced		v	ð	z	ž	
Nasals		m			n		ŋ†
Lateral					l		
Retroflex					r		
Semivowels		w				j	(w)‡

Key

/p/	pill	/f/	feel	/m/	hum
/b/	bill	/v/	veal	/n/	Hun
/t/	till	/θ/	thigh	/ŋ/	hung
/d/	dill	/ð/	thy	/l/	lore
/k/	kill	/s/	seal	/r/	roar
/g/	gill	/z/	zeal	/w/	wore
/č/	chill	/š/	mesher	/j/	yore
/ǰ/	Jill	/ž/	measure		
		/h/	heel		

*The fricative /h/, in modern English only a burst of aspiration preceding a vowel, is actually produced at various points in the mouth, depending on the nature of the following vowel. For the sake of convenience, it is listed here as a velar phoneme.

† The velar /ŋ/ is not phonemic for many speakers of English, but only an allophone of /n/ that occurs before /k/ and /g/. If, in your speech, the words *finger* and *singer* rhyme, [ŋ] is probably not phonemic for you.

‡ The phoneme /w/ actually has a dual articulation; it is bilabial by virtue of the rounding and near closure of the lips and velar by virtue of the raising of the back of the tongue toward the velum.

FRICATIVES

Fricatives, also called **spirants**, are produced by impeding but not totally blocking the stream of air from the lungs. This constriction of the passage produces friction, a hissing sound created by the turbulence of the stream of air. The type of fricative is defined by the point of narrowest stricture; /f/ is a labiodental fricative because the friction occurs at the point of loose contact between the upper teeth and the lower lip. Like stops, fricatives may be either voiced or voiceless in English.

AFFRICATES

Affricates are a combination of stop plus fricative. The stream of air is completely stopped very briefly and then is released relatively gradually with accompanying friction. Though some languages have several types of affricate phonemes, English has only the alveopalatal affricates /č/ and /ǰ/, the former voiceless and the latter voiced.

RESONANTS

All the remaining consonants of English can be grouped together as **resonants**; all are voiced only. The resonants include the nasals, the lateral, the retroflex, and the semivowels. The lateral and the retroflex are sometimes termed **liquids**. **Nasals** are formed by blocking the oral passage at some point but lowering the velum so that air escapes through the nose. The particular type of nasal is determined by the point at which the oral passage is blocked. The **lateral** /l/ is produced when the center of the mouth is blocked by the tongue in contact with the alveolar ridge while air is allowed to escape along the sides of the tongue (hence the term *lateral*). The most common allophone of /l/ after a vowel is [ɫ], the so-called "dark *l*," produced by raising the back of the tongue toward, but not touching, the velum. The **retroflex** /r/ is produced by curling the tip of the tongue upward and pointing it toward the alveolar ridge or hard palate. **Semivowels** are produced by narrowing the air passage greatly but still allowing air to pass without stoppage or friction at any point. Semivowels are like vowels in that the stream of air is not blocked, but they are classified as consonants because they function like consonants before regular vowels and because the air passage is more constricted than with regular vowels. Our analysis classifies only /j/ and /w/ as semivowels; some analyses also treat /r/ as a semivowel.

Vowels

Unlike consonants, vowel phonemes cannot easily be defined by manner and point of articulation because the manner of articulation is essentially the same for all vowels. Further, vowels have no real point of articulation because the articulator (the tongue) does not come into actual contact with another part of the mouth. Instead, English vowels are traditionally defined by the height of the tongue, the location of the highest part of the tongue, and the degree of tension of the tongue during articulation.

The height of the tongue is normally correlated with the degree of openness of the mouth; the lower the tongue, the more open the mouth. Vowels are accordingly classified as **high**, **mid**, or **low**. The location in the mouth of the highest part of the tongue determines whether a vowel is **front**, **central**, or **back**. Finally, if the tongue is relatively tense, the vowel is called **tense**; if the tongue is relatively relaxed, the vowel is called **lax**.

These three features are adequate for defining all the vowels of modern English. However, for other languages and for earlier periods of English, additional features are necessary. In Old English, some vowel phonemes were distinguished on the basis of rounding—a high front tense vowel, for example, could be articulated with either rounded or unrounded lips. In Present-Day English, all front vowels are unrounded and all back vowels are rounded, so the distinction is redundant and nonphonemic. In many languages, including Old and Middle English, vowel length, or the amount of time spent in producing a vowel, is distinctive. In some languages, such as modern French, nasality of vowels is phonemic; modern English vowels may have nasal coloring if the following consonant is a nasal, but no two vowels are distinguished on the basis of nasality alone.

The Latin alphabet is unsatisfactory for representing all the consonant phonemes of English, but it is hopelessly inadequate for representing the vowels. First, there simply are not enough separate vowel symbols. Second, drastic changes in the pronunciation of some vowels occurred after English spelling had become fixed, so the symbols used in standard written English today no longer correlate with their original values or with the values they have in most other European

Figure 2.3 Vowel Phonemes of Present-Day English

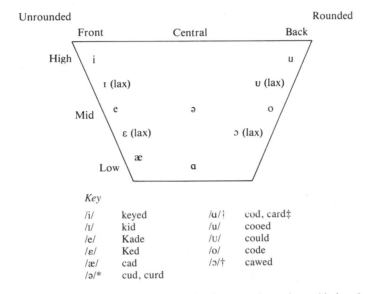

Key

/i/	keyed	/ɑ/†	cod, card‡
/ɪ/	kid	/u/	cooed
/e/	Kade	/ʊ/	could
/ɛ/	Ked	/o/	code
/æ/	cad	/ɔ/†	cawed
/ə/*	cud, curd		

* The symbol /ə/, called *schwa*, is used here for the stressed vowel sound in *but*, the unstressed final vowel in *sofa*, and the vowel preceding /r/ in words like *her, fir*, and *purr*. Many speakers will notice a definite qualitative difference in the sounds of the vowel in these three positions. However, because the three sounds are in complementary distribution (never contrast with each other), they can be treated as allophones of the phoneme /ə/. Some linguists prefer to use the symbol /ʌ/ for the stressed sound of *but* and /ɜ/ for the sound preceding /r/, leaving /ə/ only for the unstressed vowel of *sofa*. For those speakers of English who regularly omit /r/ except before a vowel, the "dropped" /r/ is often replaced by /ə/, especially after high and mid vowels. Thus, *fear* may be /fiə/ and *four* may be /foə/.

† If *cod* and *cawed* have the same vowel in your speech, you probably have /ɔ/ in both; you may have /ɑ/ in *balm* but /ɔ/ in *bomb*. If you think you have the same vowel in all of these words, /ɑ/ and /ɔ/ are probably not separate phonemes for you. You may—or may not—make the distinction by using [ɑ] in *uah* (*that's good!*) and [ɔ] in *aw* (*shucks!*).

‡ A following /r/ drastically affects the pronunciation of vowels in most dialects of English. In general, there is a tendency for the distinction between the lax and tense vowels and between /æ/ and /ɑ/ to be lost. For example, most speakers today probably do not distinguish *mourning* and *morning* by having /o/ in the former and /ɔ/ in the latter. Similarly, some speakers have /e/ in *Mary*, /ɛ/ in *merry*, and /æ/ in *marry*; others make only two distinctions here, and still others have /ɛ/ in all three words. In some dialects, both *poor* and *pore* have /ɔ/; in others, *poor* has /u/ or /ʊ/ and *pore* has /ɔ/. In some dialects, nearly all vowels are followed by a short /ə/ before an /r/; other speakers use such a glide only to distinguish pairs of words like *mare* /mer/ and *mayor* /meər/; and still other speakers do not use a schwa here at all.

languages. Therefore, in representing the vowel phonemes of English, it is necessary to use a number of symbols not in the Latin alphabet and to use the familiar Latin letters in some unfamiliar ways.

With a few exceptions, all native speakers of English have the same inventory of consonant phonemes and use these phonemes in the same places. However, there are great disparities among English speakers in both the total number of vowel phonemes and in their distribution in individual words. The configuration depicted in Figure 2.3 illustrates only the minimum number of distinctions made by most speakers of American English. Some speakers have additional distinctions, especially in the low central area, and some lack a phonemic distinction between /ɔ/ and /ɑ/.

DIPHTHONGS

In addition to so-called "pure" vowels, in which the tongue remains in one position during articulation, English also has several **diphthongs**, or **glides**. A diphthong is a vowel-like sound produced while the tongue is moving from one vowel position toward another. The two symbols used to transcribe a diphthong represent the approximate starting and ending points of that diphthong. For example, in the word *toy*, the tongue moves from the approximate position of /o/ or /ɔ/ toward the direction of /ɪ/ or /i/.

Phonetically, most English vowels, especially tense vowels, are often diphthongized in actual speech. This is particularly noticeable in final position, where the vowel in a word such as *go* may clearly move from the [o] position toward the [u] position. Nevertheless, because these diphthongized versions never contrast with nondiphthongized versions, we can treat them simply as allophones of the "pure" vowels.

Of the three diphthongs that are phonemic in English, two, /ɑɪ/ and /ɔɪ/, are fronting diphthongs, that is, they move from the lower back position toward the high front position. One, /ɑʊ/, is a backing diphthong, that is, it moves from the low central position toward the high back position. The arrows in Figure 2.4 show the directions in which the diphthongs move.

UNSTRESSED VOWELS

In most dialects of English, unstressed vowels are regularly reduced to /ɪ/ or /ə/, with the distribution of these two varying widely from dialect to dialect and even from speaker to speaker. The vowel /ɪ/ is especially common in inflectional endings (as in *patches*, *wishes*, *judges*), but it is by no means universal even here.

Figure 2.4 Diphthong Phonemes of Present-Day English

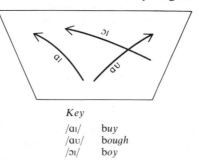

Key

/ɑɪ/	b*uy*
/ɑʊ/	b*ough*
/ɔɪ/	b*oy*

Prosody

The term **prosody** refers to the stress patterns of a language. In English, stress is distinctive both at the level of the individual word and at the level of phrases, clauses, and entire sentences. For our purposes, we need be concerned only with stress in individual words. Here English distinguishes three levels of stress—primary, secondary, and reduced (or unstressed). When it is necessary to indicate stress or stress distinctions, an acute accent (´) represents primary stress (*Ápril*, *understánd*), a grave accent (`) represents secondary stress (*álphabèt*, *bóokcàse*), and no marking at all represents reduced stress (*lánguage*). In this book, we will normally distinguish only primary and reduced stress.

Suggested Further Reading

Bronstein, Arthur. *The Pronunciation of American English.*
Jones, Daniel. *The Pronunciation of English.*
Kurath, Hans. *A Phonology and Prosody of Modern English.*
Thomas, Charles Kenneth. *An Introduction to the Phonetics of American English.*
Traugott, Elizabeth Closs, and Mary Louise Pratt. *Linguistics for Students of Literature.*

C H A P T E R 3

Writing

To be a well-favoured man is the gift of fortune; but
to write and read comes by nature.
—William Shakespeare

Speech is of course primary to language. People were speaking for hundreds of thousands—perhaps millions—of years before writing was invented. Human beings speak before they learn to read and write; even today, many people never learn to read and write, and there are still languages with no writing systems. People learn how to speak without formal training, but most have to be taught how to read and write. Further, all forms of writing are ultimately based on spoken language. In other words, writing is a derivative of speech; it is a secondary form of language. Speech is, quite properly, the focus of most linguistic study.

Nonetheless, we should not underestimate the importance of writing. Civilization as we know it depends on the written word. We study speech by means of writing and we use writing to represent the phonetics of speech. Most of our information about language, and certainly all of our information about the history of languages, is in writing.

Writing has become so important that, for the educated person, it can become almost totally independent of speech. Most of us know many words that we can read, understand, and even write but that we would hesitate to try to pronounce. For example, I think of the word *gneiss*. I know that it is a kind of rock, that it is usually metamorphic in origin, and that (to my untrained eye) it looks somewhat like granite. Yet I do not normally speak this word and I have to refer to a dictionary—another written source—to discover that *gneiss* is pronounced /nais/ and not /nis/ or /gnais/ or /nɪs/. We also use words and grammatical constructions in writing that we rarely if ever spontaneously produce in speech. Who uses the subordinating conjunction *lest* in a casual conversation? What does a paragraph sound like? Many people read and sometimes even write fluently in languages that they cannot speak. Skilled readers take in and mentally process written texts at a rate so rapid that the words cannot possibly have been silently articulated and "listened to"; clearly, for such readers, writing has become a form of language virtually independent of speech. Finally, there is even physiological evidence that writing is more than simply a secondary form of speech: Some brain-damaged people are competent in reading and writing but are unable to speak or understand speech.

The Effects of Writing on Speech

Writing has numerous effects on the spoken language, and the more literate a culture is, the greater these effects are. Because of the prestige, the conservatism, and the permanency of writing, it tends to act as a brake on changes in the spoken language. Conversely, writing tends to spread changes from one area or group of speakers to another; this is especially true of vocabulary items. Most of us can recall new words that we first encountered in a written text and only later—or perhaps never—heard spoken. Writing also preserves archaisms that have been lost in the spoken language and sometimes even revives words that have become obsolete in the spoken language. For example, Edmund Spenser probably reintroduced *rampant* in the meaning of "fierce" through his writings; the OED's last citation in this meaning prior to Spenser is nearly two hundred years earlier.

Writing and literacy give rise to spelling pronunciations, that is, the pronunciation of words as they are spelled. These may take the form of the reinsertion of lost sounds or the insertion of unhistorical sounds. Many people today pronounce the word *often* as [ɔftən], even though the [t] dropped out of the spoken language centuries ago, and even though they do not pronounce a [t] in such parallel words as *soften* or *listen*. Similarly, because English readers associate the letter sequence ⟨th⟩[1] with the sounds [θ] and [ð], words spelled with that sequence that historically were pronounced with [t] have come to be pronounced with [θ]. Examples include the given names *Katherine* and *Arthur* (compare the short forms *Art* and *Kate* that retain the [t]). The river *Thames* is pronounced [tɛmz] in Britain, but [θemz] in Connecticut because the influence of the spelling proved stronger than earlier oral tradition.

Conventional spellings for vocal gestures involving noises outside the English phonemic system may also lead to a literal pronunciation. Examples include the vocal gesture for disapproval or commiseration, an alveolar click. Because this sound is written *tsk-tsk*, it is occasionally pronounced [tɪsk tɪsk]. Even more familiar are the pronunciations [bər:] for ⟨brrr⟩, a spelling originally intended to represent a voiced bilabial trill, and [i:k] for *eek*, a spelling intended to represent a high-pitched scream.

Literacy and our alphabet so permeate our culture that even our vocabulary is affected. The widespread use of acronyms presupposes speakers who are familiar with the letters with which words begin. We even use letter shapes as analogies to describe objects: The words *T square*, *U-turn*, *ell* (as a wing of a building), *S-curve*, and *V-neck* are all derived from the names of alphabetic characters.

---

[1] When it is necessary to distinguish graphemic forms from phonological representations, angled brackets (⟨ ⟩) are used for the graphemes.

In sum, writing has been such an integral part of English for the past thirteen hundred years or so that it is impossible to imagine what the spoken language would be like today if English had never been committed to writing. Indeed, without writing, English probably would have split up into numerous mutually unintelligible dialects long ago.

Why Was Writing Invented?

Efficient as speech is, it is severely limited in both time and space. Once an utterance has been made, it is gone forever, and the preservation of its contents is dependent on human memory. Writing is as permanent as the materials used in producing it; readers can return to a written record as often as or after as long a period of time as they like. Further, speech is much more limited in space than is writing. Until the recent developments of electronic media—all of which require supplementary apparatus in the form of transmitters and receivers—speech was spatially limited to the range of the unamplified human voice. Writing can be done on portable materials and carried wherever people can go.

Although it would perhaps be esthetically comforting to think that the first writing systems were created to preserve literary works, all the evidence indicates

A POOR DEVIL

Slips of the tongue and pen have always been a part of natural language, but perhaps only medieval monks would invent a patron demon for them. Titivillus, as he was named, collected fragments of mispronounced, mumbled, or skipped words in the divine services. He put them all into a sack and carried them to his master in hell, where they were registered against the offender.

Later Titivillus' jurisdiction was extended to orthographic and printing errors. He never lacked for material to put in his sack. For instance, when Pope Sixtus V (1585–1590) authorized the printing of a new edition of the Vulgate Bible, he decided to insure against printing errors by automatically excommunicating ahead of time any printer who altered the text in any way. Furthermore, he himself proofread every page as it came off the press. Nonetheless, the final text was so full of errors that the Pope finally had to recall every copy for destruction.

Titivillus was well enough known, both in England and on the Continent, to appear as a character in medieval mystery plays and other literature. Hence his introduction in *Myroure of Oure Ladye*, an anonymous fifteenth-century devotional treatise:

> I am a poure dyuel, and my name ys Tytyuyllus ... I muste eche day ... brynge my master a thousande pokes full of faylynges, and of neglygences in syllables and wordes.

Myroure of Oure Ladye I.xx.54

that the first true writing was used for far more mundane purposes. Although "creative" literature arose long before the invention of writing, it was orally transmitted, with devices such as alliteration, repetition, and regular meter being used as aids to memory. Writing was invented for the same practical purpose to which, in terms of sheer bulk, most writing today is dedicated, commercial record-keeping—the number of lambs born in a season, the number of pots of oil shipped to a customer, the wages paid to laborers. A second important early use of writing was to preserve the exact wording of sacred texts that would otherwise be corrupted by imperfect memories and changes in the spoken language. For most of the history of writing, literacy has been restricted to a small elite of bookkeepers and priests; often, the two occupations were combined in one scribe. To the illiterate, writing would have seemed a form of magic, an impression that was not discouraged by those who understood its mysteries.

Types of Writing Systems

If we can judge by the delight a child takes in its own footprints or scribbles made with any implement on any surface, human beings have always been fascinated by drawing. The urge to create pictures is revealed by the primitive drawings—early forms of graffiti—found in caves and on rocks all over the world. But pictures as such are not writing, although it is not always easy to distinguish pictures from writing. If we define writing as human communication by means of a system of conventional visible marks,[2] then, in many cases, we do not know whether the marks are systematic because we do not have a large enough sample. Nor do we know if the marks were intended to communicate a message. For example, Figure 3.1 is an American Indian **petroglyph** (a drawing or carving on rock) from Cottonwood Canyon, Utah. Conceivably, the dotted lines, wavy lines, spiral, and semicircle had some conventional meaning that could be interpreted by a viewer

Figure 3.1 American Indian Petroglyph[3]

---

[2] The definition is adapted from I. J. Gelb, *A Study of Writing*, rev. ed. (Chicago: University of Chicago Press, 1963), p. 12.

[3] Drawing adapted from Roland Siegrist, ed., *Prehistoric Petroglyphs and Pictographs in Utah* (Salt Lake City: Utah State Historical Society, 1972), p. 62. Reproduced with permission of the Utah State Historical Society.

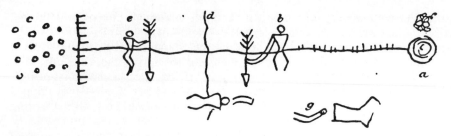

Figure 3.2 American Indian Picture Story

familiar with the conventions. If so, the petroglyph might be called prewriting, but not actual writing.

Pictograms and Ideograms

More clearly related to writing are the picture stories of American Indians. Like the modern cartoon strip without words, these **pictographs** communicate a message. Further, they often include conventional symbols. Figure 3.2 is from a birch-bark record made by Shahâsh'king (b), the leader of a group of Mille Lacs Ojibwas (a) who undertook a military expedition against Shákopi (e). Shákopi's camp of Sioux (c) was on the St. Peter's River (d). The Ojibwas under Shahâsh'king lost one man (f) at the St. Peter's River, and they got only one arm of an Indian (g).[4]

Although such pictographs do communicate a message, they are not a direct sequential representation of speech. They may include **ideographic** symbols, symbols that represent ideas or concepts but do not stand for specific sounds, syllables, or words. In Figure 3.2, the drawing at (f) means that the Ojibwas lost one man, but it does not represent a unique series of sounds or words. It could be translated as "We lost one man" or "The Sioux killed a warrior" or "Little Fox died on this expedition" or "One man fell by the river." To take a more familiar example, the picture ☛ is an **ideogram;** it does not represent a sequence of sounds, but rather a concept that can be expressed in English in various ways: "go that way" or "in this direction" or "over there" or, combined with words or other ideograms, such notions as "the stairs are to the right" or "pick up your luggage at that place." Ideograms are not necessarily pictures of objects; the arithmetic "minus sign" is an ideogram that depicts not an object, but a concept that can be translated as "minus" or "subtract the following from the preceding" or "negative."

Logograms

Ideograms are not writing, but they are the ancestors of writing. If a particular ideogram is always translated by the same spoken word, it can come to stand for that word and that word alone. At this point, **logograms**, or symbols representing a single word, have been invented, and true writing has begun. Indeed, an entire writing system may be based on the logographic principle. This is the case with Chinese, in which each character stands for a word or part of a compound word. In

---

[4] Adapted from Garrick Mallery, "Picture-Writing of the American Indians," in *Tenth Annual Report of the Bureau of Ethnology* (Washington, D.C.: Government Printing Office, 1893), pp. 559–60.

their purest forms, logographic symbols have no relationship to individual sounds, but only to entire words. For example, the Chinese character 吊 stands for a verb meaning "to hang, to suspend"; it is pronounced roughly as [diɑu] in Standard Chinese, but no particular part of the character represents [d] or [i] or [ɑ] or [u]. By itself, the top part of the character, 口, is pronounced [kou], and the bottom part, 巾, is pronounced [jin]. The character 钓 is pronounced in exactly the same way as 吊, but 钓 means "to fish with a hook and line." Like all writing systems actually used for natural languages, Chinese is less than totally pure; many characters contain both ideographic and phonetic components. Still, the Chinese system is basically logographic in that each character stands for an entire word or morpheme, and one cannot determine the pronunciation of an unfamiliar character from its components.

    The distinction between ideograms and logograms is somewhat arbitrary. If, within a given language, a symbol is always interpreted as representing one word and one word alone, it is a logogram for that language. However, if it has the same meaning but is represented by different words in other languages, it is, strictly speaking, an ideogram. An example would be the symbol &, which stands only for the word *and* in English, but for *agus* in Irish, *et* in French, *och* in Swedish, *и* in Russian, *na* in Swahili, and so forth. It is a logogram within a given language, but an ideogram across languages.

Syllabaries

Logographic systems are inefficient for most languages because, if every single word in the language is to be represented by a different symbol, an astronomical number of complex symbols is required. Therefore, while the writing is still at the ideographic-logographic stage, scribes may begin to use symbols to represent sounds instead of concepts. They probably begin by punning on existing logograms. For example, assume that English used the logogram ◉ to stand for the word *eye*. Noting that, in speech, the word *eye* sounds like the word *I*, a clever scribe might decide to use ◉ to mean *I* in writing too. If the logogram for *scream* were 😮, then *ice cream* could be written ◉😮. Symbols would now represent sound sequences or syllables instead of entire words.

    When this kind of punning becomes widely used, the writing system is turning into a **syllabary**, or a system in which each symbol stands for a syllable. Over time, the sound values of symbols become predominant and their picture values less important. As scribes simplify the symbols to save time and space, the original pictures often become unrecognizable. To use our hypothetical example from English again, the logogram for *eye* might change from ◉ to ◯ to ◁ to ◁ as a syllabic writing system evolved.

    Old Persian cuneiform provides an example of a syllabic writing system that lost its pictorial qualities completely. The symbols in Figure 3.3 are not alphabetic because one cannot separate the consonant portions from the vowel portions. That is, there is no particular part of ⊨𝕍𝕍 [ta] that represents either [t] or [a]; the sign stands only for the syllable as a whole.[5]

    The first syllabaries were developed among the Semites of the Middle East, perhaps as long ago as seven or eight thousand years, and the concept of the

---

[5] Although the signs illustrated in Figure 3.3 are purely syllabic, the Old Persian system also retained four logograms and even included alphabetic features. Real writing systems are never as tidy as theoretical ones.

Figure 3.3   Old Persian Cuneiform

ga		gu	
ka		ku	
ta		tu	
ra		ru	
ma		mu	

syllabary rapidly spread over the entire area. Although, strictly speaking, a syllabary represents vowel differences as well as consonant differences among syllables, most of the Semitic syllabaries indicated only consonants. That is, while [ba], [ma], and [ka] were represented by distinct symbols, [ba], [be], and [bi] were all written the same way.

For languages with very simple syllable structures, such as Japanese or Chinese, a syllabary provides an efficient writing system because relatively few symbols are needed to represent every possible syllable in the language. Modern Japanese has two syllabaries, the *katakana* and the *hiragana*. Each of these two syllabaries consists of only 46 basic signs, plus a few diacritical marks. Although the syllabaries are completely adequate for writing anything in Japanese, the prestige of Chinese logograms is so great that contemporary Japanese continues to use a mixture of Chinese characters and *kana* syllabic signs – illustrating how cultural factors may outweigh logic and efficiency in determining the written form of a language.

WORDS FROM MISTAKES

New words can originate in many different ways. One entertaining kind of origin is simple misreading due to confusion of similar letter forms. For example, the English word *gravy* comes from Old French *grave,* but the original French form was probably *grane;* the letters *n* and *v (u)* looked much alike in medieval handwriting. The word *sneeze* is apparently the result of misreading an *f* for an *s;* its Old English ancestor was *fneosan* (*f* and *s* were formed in much the same way in Old English times). In some instances, both the correct and the erroneous form have survived, with differentiation of meaning. Hence we have both the original Greek form *acme* and the misread form *acne.*

Alphabets

The final step in the phonemicization of writing is the **alphabet**, in which each symbol represents a separate phoneme, not an entire syllable. So far as we know, the alphabet has been invented only once. The Greeks borrowed the Semitic syllabary and, probably over a fairly long period of time, began using unneeded characters to represent vowels separately from consonants. Once there were separate characters for vowels, the originally syllabic characters could always be used for consonants alone, and the alphabet had been invented.

The precise form of the Greek letters, or **graphemes**, changed somewhat over time, and the Romans introduced still further changes when they borrowed the Greek alphabet to write Latin, partly because the sound system of Latin differed in a number of important ways from that of Greek. The Romans did not adopt the Greek letters Θ Ξ Φ Ψ or Ω at all. They modified the most common forms or orientations of Greek Γ Λ Λ Γ to C, D, L, and S, respectively, and then added a tail to C to form G. The archaic Greek letter F had represented [w], but the Romans used it for [f] instead. In Greek, H is a vowel symbol, but it became a consonant symbol in Latin. The grapheme P represents [r] in Greek, but, because the Romans used P for [p], they had to modify it to R to represent [r]. The Romans adopted the obsolete Greek character Q to represent [k] before [w], as in Latin *quo*. Because Latin used three symbols, C, Q, and K (though K was rarely used) to represent [k], the Latin alphabet almost from the beginning violated the principle of an ideal alphabet, a one-to-one correspondence between phoneme and grapheme.

Primarily through the spread of Christianity from Rome, the Latin version of the alphabet was eventually adopted in all of Western Europe. Because Russia was Christianized by the Eastern Church, whose official language was Greek, its alphabet (the Cyrillic alphabet) was borrowed independently from Greek; in many ways, it is closer to the classical Greek alphabet than the Latin alphabet is. For example, its forms Γ Д Л Н П Р Ф Х for [g d l n p r f x], respectively, are similar to their Greek originals. However, the Cyrillic alphabet uses В for [v], and Б, a modified form of B, for [b]. С represents [s], and У represents [u]. З, a modified form of Greek Z, is used for [z]. Because Russian is much richer in fricatives and affricates than Greek, new symbols were devised to represent them: Ж, Ц, Ч, Ш Щ stand for [ž, ts, č, š, šč], respectively. The Cyrillic characters И, Ы, Э, Ю, Я represent the vowels or diphthongs [i y ε ju ja], respectively. Finally, Russian also uses two graphemes as diacritics; they represent no sound of their own, but indicate that a preceding consonant is palatalized (Ь) or not palatalized (Ъ).

English has had two different alphabets. Prior to the Christianization of England, the little writing that was done in English was in an alphabet called the **futhorc** or **runic alphabet**. The futhorc was originally developed by Germanic tribes on the Continent and probably was based on Etruscan or early Italic versions of the Greek alphabet. Its association with magic is suggested by its name, the runic alphabet, and the term used to designate a character or letter, **rune**. In Old English, the word *rūn* meant not only "runic character," but also "mystery, secret." The related verb, *rūnian*, meant "to whisper, talk secrets, conspire." (See Chapter 5 for further details about the Old English alphabet.)

As a by-product of the Christianization of England in the sixth and seventh centuries, the English received the Latin alphabet. Although it has been modified somewhat over the centuries, the alphabet we use today is essentially the one adopted in the late sixth century. However, its fit to the sound system is much less accurate than at the time of its adoption because many phonological changes have not been reflected in the writing system.

An ideal alphabet contains one symbol for each phoneme, and represents each phoneme by one and only one symbol. In practice, few alphabets are perfect. Even if they are a good match to the sound system when they are first adopted (not always the case), subsequent sound changes destroy the fit. Writing is always much more conservative than speech, and, as the years go by, the fit between phoneme and grapheme becomes worse and worse unless there is regular spelling and even alphabet reform. Such reform has taken place in a number of countries; regular reform is even required by law in Finland. Major reform in the Soviet Union occurred after the 1917 revolution. In 1928, Turkey under Kemal Atatürk switched from the Arabic writing system to the Latin alphabet. However, as the history of Russian and Turkish suggests, resistance to reform is usually so strong that it takes a cataclysmic event like a revolution to achieve it. In general, reform is easier in smaller countries that do not use a language of worldwide distribution and prestige. Even under these circumstances, resistance to reform will be fierce if the country has a long tradition of literacy and literature. Icelandic, for instance, is spoken by fewer than a quarter of a million people, a large proportion of whom are bilingual or trilingual in other European languages. However, pride in their long native literary traditions has to date prevented any significant spelling reform. A person reasonably skilled in Old Norse (c. A.D. 900–c. A.D. 1350) can read modern Icelandic without much difficulty even though the spoken language has undergone vast changes since Old Norse times and even though the present match between grapheme and phoneme is poor indeed. Clearly, people become as emotionally entangled with their writing systems as with their spoken languages.

Suggested Further Reading

Diringer, David. *The Alphabet: A Key to the History of Mankind.*
Elliott, Ralph W. V. *Runes: An Introduction.*
Gelb, I. J. *A Study of Writing.*
Harris, Roy. *The Origin of Writing.*
Page, R. I. *An Introduction to English Runes.*
Ullman, Berthold Louis. *Ancient Writing and Its Influence.*

C H A P T E R 4

Language Families and Indo-European

There was no light nonsense about Miss Blimber.... She was dry and sandy with working in the graves of deceased languages. None of your live languages for Miss Blimber. They must be dead —stone dead—and then Miss Blimber dug them up like a Ghoul.

—Charles Dickens

Anyone who has even the slightest brush with a language other than English cannot fail to notice at least a few similarities between English and that language. We notice lexical similarities most easily, perhaps taking morphological or syntactic similarities for granted. For example, from a sampling of six other languages, one could list the following words as being similar in sound and meaning:

English *mom*	Welsh *mam*
English *miaow-miaow*	Chinese *mi-mi*
English *me*	Swahili *mimi*
English *pistachio*	Italian *pistacchio*
English *choose*	French *choisir*
English *glide*	Swedish *glida*

However, the reasons for the similarity differ in all six instances. English *mom* and Welsh *mam* are similar because of what might be considered a universal of all languages: The word for "mother" contains [m] and a low vowel in nearly every

37

language, probably because this sequence is among the first speech-like sounds that a human infant produces. English *miaow-miaow* and Chinese *mi-mi* are both echoic words; they are alike because the sounds they imitate are alike—all cats, English, Chinese, or Egyptian, make the same kind of noise. The resemblance between English *me* and Swahili *mimi* is pure coincidence; further examination reveals that Swahili *mimi* is an emphatic pronoun only and that the other Swahili pronouns bear no resemblance at all to English pronouns. English *pistachio* and Italian *pistacchio* are alike because English recently borrowed the word from Italian. Conversely, English *choose* and French *choisir* are similar because French borrowed the word from Gothic, a Germanic language related to English. Finally, the correspondence between English *glide* and Swedish *glida* reflects their common origin. Neither language borrowed the word from the other; both words descend from a common ancestor.

Whether all the languages of the world were once one—whether language was invented only once and then spread and diverged—is a question we cannot answer. Nonetheless, some languages share so many features not found in other languages that the conclusion that they were once the same language is inescapable. Such a clearly related group is normally called a **language family**, and the members of the group are called **cognate languages** (from Latin *cognatus* 'born together, related by birth').

The term *language family* is often criticized as a dangerous metaphor, suggesting as it does a biological analogy.[1] This criticism has some justification; languages are not discrete entities like kittens, born at one specific time and dying at another. They are not separate creatures from their "parents"; rather, they *are* their parents. Spanish is not something entirely separate from Latin; it is one of the things Latin has become over a period of two thousand years. Each member of a biological family has its own configuration of genes, and no member can influence the genes of another member after birth. But two languages, even originally unrelated languages, can influence each other's nature and structure at any time. Further, again unlike biological families, the "offspring" of a parent language do not share the same "gene pool." That is, some offspring languages of the same parent are more closely related than others.

Because of the flaws in this biological analogy, or *Stammbaum* ("family tree") theory, as it is often called, and the misconceptions it can create, scholars have suggested other models of language relatedness. In the late nineteenth century, Johannes Schmidt modified the *Stammbaum* theory with his *Wellentheorie*, or theory of "waves of innovation," that linguistic changes begin in small specific areas and spread outward to other dialects, like the concentric ripples created by dropping a pebble in a pool. One advantage of the wave theory and its later modifications is that it can account for the fact that languages in close geographical proximity to each other over long periods of time are more alike than languages separated by thousands of miles. We might think of the difference between the

---

[1]Biologists borrowed the family-tree analogy from historical linguistics, not the other way about. The family-tree analogy was being used by Indo-European philologists in the eighteenth century; nearly a century later, Charles Darwin supported his arguments for biological evolution by noting, "If two languages were found to resemble each other in a multitude of words and points of construction, they would be universally recognised as having sprung from a common source, notwithstanding that they differed greatly in some few words or points of construction." Charles Darwin, *The Descent of Man* (New York: D. Appleton and Company, 1883), p. 148.

family-tree theory and the wave theory of language change as parallel to the "nature-nurture" theories of human development. The family-tree theory stresses nature ("sister" languages are like each other by inheritance), whereas the wave theory stresses nurture (married couples come to look like each other through long association in the same environment).

Despite its flaws, the family-tree theory provides a convenient and familiar vocabulary for describing relationships among languages. We will use the term "family" in our discussions here, but it should be remembered that it is only an analogy and an imperfect analogy at that.

In deciding whether two languages are related to each other by a common origin, scholars look for patterned, consistent relationships between the two. In fact, consistent differences are more significant than absolute identity. For example, both Russian and English have the word *hydroplane*. Allowing for the differences in the phonology and alphabets of the two languages, they are pronounced and spelled similarly. The German word for the same object is *Gleitboot*, clearly from a different source. Nonetheless, this single example does not prove that English is more closely related to Russian than to German. If we take a larger number of English words and compare them with the corresponding German and Russian words, it becomes obvious that the German and English words are related, whereas the Russian words are very different.

English	German	Russian
hair	Haar	vólos
have	haben	imet'
half	halb	polovína
hand	Hand	ruká
hang	hängen	veshat'
hard	hart	tverdi

Even when English and German words begin with different letters (and sounds), the relationship between them is often regular and consistent, whereas, once again, the corresponding Russian words are totally unrelated.

English	German	Russian
pan	Pfanne	skovorodá
path	Pfad	tropá
pole	Pfahl	shest
pepper	Pfeffer	pérets
pipe	Pfeife	trubá
plant	Pflanze	rasténie

Although a much larger sample would be required to show the exact relationships among English, German, and Russian, even these short lists demonstrate that English and German are more closely related to each other than either is to Russian.

The lists above also illustrate another important principle of historical and comparative linguistics. *Hydroplane* is a technical term; its invention required a long history of literacy and intellectual activity. The words in the two lists, on the other hand, are "core" terms; with the exception of *pepper*, we would expect to find corresponding terms in any language, anywhere in the world, regardless of the level of civilization of the speakers. When comparing languages for possible relatedness, scholars concentrate on such basic, essential words because they are far less likely to be borrowed from another language.

When a word has been in a language since its beginnings as a discrete language, it is called a **native word**. A **borrowed word**, or **loanword**, is one that has been introduced at some time from another language, either from a related or an unrelated language. Both English *glide* and Swedish *glida* are native words in their respective languages. *Choose* is a native word in English, but a borrowed word in French. English *pepper* and German *Pfeffer* are both borrowed from Latin (which in turn borrowed it from Greek, which borrowed it from Sanskrit). English *head* is native, whereas *capital* is a loan from Latin; both have the same root, but developed differently in the two languages before English borrowed *capital*.

Because so many English words have been borrowed from Latin and Greek, languages that were written down before English was, it is easy to assume that Latin and Greek are "older" than English. This is not the case. No language is older than any other language. All languages are the same age—all ultimately go back to the invention of language itself. Therefore, even though English *father*, for example, is cognate with Latin *pater*, English *father* does not "come from" Latin. Both words are independent developments from the same source. English *paternal*, on the other hand, does "come from" Latin because it was borrowed from Latin into English in the early seventeenth century.

Another distinction that is sometimes confusing is the difference between a language and a dialect. Theoretically, **dialects** are mutually intelligible versions of one language. When mutual intelligibility is lost, then the two versions are separate languages. Hence the national languages of the United States, Great Britain, New Zealand, Australia, and so on, are all called English because, given a little practice and patience, speakers of any one of them can understand and communicate with speakers of any other. Unfortunately, political boundaries often influence the terminology. Danish and Swedish are mutually intelligible, but are called separate languages because Denmark and Sweden are separate nations. Conversely, the speech of a Cantonese is totally incomprehensible to a native of Shanghai; yet, because both Canton and Shanghai are within the boundaries of the People's Republic of China, both are called Chinese, or dialects of Chinese, even though they would more accurately be described as separate languages.

As mentioned earlier, we have no way of knowing whether language was invented once or many times. We do know, however, that many languages today are related and have a common origin. In other cases, there is simply not enough evidence to demonstrate relatedness. We cannot prove that two languages are *not* related; they may once have been the same but have changed so much over the millennia that all evidence of their common origin has been lost.

Major Language Families of the World

Depending on how one counts, there are anywhere from a hundred to several hundred recognized language families in the world today, and several thousand distinct languages within these families. The number of speakers of these languages varies from the hundreds of millions whose native tongue is English or Standard Chinese to the few score who speak some of the rapidly disappearing American Indian languages.

Within Europe, the dominant family is *Indo-European* (which will be discussed in much greater detail later). Finnish, Estonian, Lapp, and Hungarian all belong to the *Finno-Ugric* (or *Uralic*) family. Turkish, along with some other languages that extend across northern Asia, belongs to the *Altaic* family. (Some scholars consider Finno-Ugric and Altaic subfamilies of a larger *Uralo-Altaic* family.) Basque, spoken only in the Pyrenees, belongs to no known language family. In the Caucasus region of the Soviet Union (between the Black and Caspian seas), there are two non-Indo-European families, *Northern Caucasian* and *Southern Caucasian*; Georgian, a Southern Caucasian language, is probably the best known of the Caucasian languages. Although Etruscan is now extinct and its written language has never been decoded, it apparently belonged to still a different language family.

The dominant family in the Mideast and North Africa is the *Hamito-Semitic* (or *Afro-Asiatic*) family. Among the Semitic languages are Arabic and Hebrew, the latter extinct as a spoken language for nearly two thousand years and then revived in the twentieth century. The Hamitic branch of the family includes a number of North African languages, such as Berber, Somali, and Hausa. Ancient Egyptian was also a Hamitic language; its descendant, Coptic, is still used as a liturgical language in the Coptic (Christian) Church.

Southern Africa and scattered portions of northern Africa are dominated by two large language families, *Niger-Congo* and *Khoisan*. Among the various subfamilies of Niger-Congo is Kwa, which includes the Yoruba, Ibo, and Ewe languages; and the Bantu group, whose best-known members are Swahili and Zulu. The Khoisan family includes the distantly related Hottentot and Bushman languages.

In Asia, the dominant language family in terms of number of speakers is *Sino-Tibetan*. The Sinitic branch comprises most of the languages of China, including Mandarin and Cantonese. The most familiar representatives of the Tibetan branch are Tibetan and Burmese. As mentioned earlier, the Altaic family has members in northern Asia, including Manchu and Mongolian. Some believe that Japanese and Korean are also Altaic languages, but more conservative scholars still prefer to classify Japanese and perhaps even Korean as independent families. The *Dravidian* family probably once extended throughout most of India, but it has been replaced in the north by Indo-European languages. In southern India, Dravidian languages are spoken by as many as 150 million people; the best-known representatives are Tamil and Telugu.

In Southeast Asia, Cambodian and perhaps Vietnamese (though Vietnamese is hard to classify) belong to the *Mon-Khmer* family. Thai and Lao are members of the *Tai* family. All the native languages of Australia belong to the *Australian* family. The term *Papuan* is given to the great variety of languages spoken in New Guinea, even though these languages are so diverse and so poorly documented that their genetic relationships are uncertain.

The *Malayo-Polynesian* (or *Austronesian*) family, essentially an island family, extends all the way from Madagascar off the coast of Africa, through the islands of the Indian Ocean, and on to the islands of the Pacific Ocean. Among its member languages are Malagasy, Indonesian, Javanese, Malay, Tagalog, Maori, Samoan, and Hawaiian. Some scholars would group the Tai, Australian, and Malayo-Polynesian families into one huge *Austro-Tai* superfamily.

Although the majority of people in the Americas today speak Indo-European languages, the pre-European inhabitants spoke a wide variety of languages, apparently belonging to many different families. In the extreme north was the *Eskimo-Aleut* family. South of the Eskimo-Aleut area was the *Athabascan* family, with such members as Navaho and Apache extending down into the southwestern United States. The *Algonquian* family once extended almost from coast to coast in North America; some of its better-known members are Abnaki, Delaware, Cree, Ojibwa, Cheyenne, and Blackfoot. The *Iroquois* family was concentrated in the East; members included Mohawk, Oneida, and Seneca. More southern members of the Iroquois family are Cherokee and Tuscarora. In the southeastern parts of the United States was the *Muskogean* family, including Seminole and Choctaw. The *Siouan* family was in the Great Plains; Dakota, Crow, and Winnebago are Siouan languages. The *Uto-Aztecan* family was centered in the Southwest and extended down into Mexico. Among its members are Hopi, Shoshone, and Nahuatl. The *Mayan* family, including, for example, Mayan, Quiché, and Yucatec, extended from Mexico down into Central America.

The linguistic situation in pre-Columbian South America was extremely complex. Even today, many languages and even language families remain undescribed; some investigators believe that there were once as many as a hundred separate families in South America, although more knowledge would probably allow us to reduce this figure greatly. Among the most prominent of the recognized families are *Quechua*, of which Inca is a member. *Arawak, Carib*, and *Tupi-Guarani* are also important families.

This brief and necessarily incomplete summary of some of the world's languages has been based on "genetic" relationships among languages. However, other classificatory systems exist. One common system is based on types of morpheme or word formation. Three broad categories are recognized: inflectional languages, agglutinative languages, and isolating languages. **Inflectional languages** are those like Classical Greek and Latin in which inseparable inflections are fused with lexical stems to carry much of the grammatical information. For example, in Latin *amo* 'I love', the *-o* ending is fused with the stem, and **am* does not even occur by itself as a word. The *-o* suffix carries the information (a) first-person subject, (b) singular, (c) present tense, and (d) indicative mood. One cannot isolate the "parts" of this *-o* that refer to first person, to singular, and so forth.

Agglutinative languages such as Swahili and Turkish combine grammatical morphemes with lexical stems, but the grammatical morphemes are discrete, relatively unchanged from word to word, and strung onto the lexical stem one after the other. For example, in Swahili, the word *nitakupenda* means "I will like you." Unlike Latin, the grammatical morphemes can be isolated: *ni* means "I," *ta* means "future tense," *ku* means "second-person object," and *penda* is the main verb stem. *Nilakupenda* means "I liked you" (the *la* means "past tense"); *nitampenda* means "I will like him" (the *m* means "*him* as object"), and so on.

In **isolating languages** like Chinese and Vietnamese, every morpheme forms a separate word, and individual particles (such as prepositions, articles, and conjunctions) are used to convey grammatical information. For example, in Chinese, *ai* means "love," as either a noun or a verb. To say "I love" one uses a separate pronoun: *wo ai*. *Ni ai* means "you love," and so on. Instead of adding prefixes or suffixes to a stem, Chinese expresses the future by using particles or adverbs; hence, *mingtian wo ai* means "tomorrow I will love."

Useful as this typology is in some ways, it is not especially helpful for our purposes. First, we are concentrating on the "life history"—hence the genetic relationships—of English. Second, English does not today fit, nor has it ever fit, neatly into any one of these three categories, though it has moved from a more inflectional to a more isolating language over the centuries. English today is very much a mixed language. For example, the word *says* is characteristic of an inflectional language in that the morpheme *-s* not only changes the pronunciation of the stem *say*, but also combines indivisibly the grammatical information of (a) third person, (b) singular, (c) present, and (d) indicative. The word *unfriendliness* is more characteristic of an agglutinative language because *un-* means only "not," *-ly* means only "adjectival," and *-ness* means only "abstract noun." None of the affixes changes the stem or is affected by the stem to which it is attached. Words such as *the*, *for*, *to*, *by*, and *no* are characteristic of isolating languages, as is the relatively rigid word order of English phrases, clauses, and sentences.

Development of Historical Linguistics in Europe

Although we tend to take the existence of different languages for granted today, linguistic diversity is not necessarily an intuitive idea, and when prehistoric tribes first encountered other tribes who did not speak intelligibly (to them), they must have been astounded. After all, human beings are essentially identical in the way they perform such basic functions of life as walking, sleeping, eating, defecating, giving birth, crying. How could they differ in the one characteristic that most obviously distinguishes humans from other animals? Their first impulse upon meeting someone who did not understand their language and whose language they could not understand must have been to assume that this person was stupid, inferior, and probably dangerous. The very word *barbarian* is related to the word *babble*—a barbarian is someone whose speech is incoherent. Once people had accepted the fact of linguistic diversity, however, they began to speculate about why languages are different and to look for evidence of relatedness among diverse languages.

In medieval and Renaissance Europe, the pervasive influence of Christianity and its story of the Creation gave rise to the theory that the original language of all humanity was Hebrew and that all other languages were ultimately derived from it. At the same time, the prestige of Classical Latin and, later, Classical Greek led people to assume that contemporary European languages were decadent descendants of these "purer" tongues. People noticed similarities between various words in the different languages and devised "etymologies" for them. These etymologies were occasionally correct by chance, but most were simply fanciful. There was no concept of systematic, structured relationships, no rules of language change, no notion that proof might be necessary.

The earliest European scholar to approach the study of language and language change in a scientific way was the so-called First Grammarian of Iceland in the twelfth century, who noted, among other remarkable discoveries, the relationships between Icelandic and English. However, Iceland was soon thereafter virtually cut off from contact with Europe, and the First Grammarian's work did not become widely known until the nineteenth century. In the fourteenth century, Dante recognized the subfamilies of Greek, Latin, and Germanic languages; the common descent of Romance languages from Latin; and the origin of dialects in a single source language. By the sixteenth century, numerous scholars accepted the relatedness of the Romance languages and their common descent from Latin.

Nonetheless, progress continued to be hampered by the obsession with Hebrew as the source of all languages.

At the end of the sixteenth century, J. J. Scaliger finally refuted the notion that Hebrew was the progenitor of all languages. Scaliger also divided the languages of Europe into eleven "mother tongues"—Slavic, Germanic, Italic, Greek, Albanian, Tartar, Hungarian, Finnish, Irish, Welsh, and Basque. He did not, however, understand the exact relationships among these groups. Today we classify both Tartar (Turkish) and Basque as belonging to separate families and put Hungarian and Finnish into the larger Finno-Ugric family. All of Scaliger's remaining mother tongues are classified as Indo-European, but Welsh and Irish are grouped together as members of the Celtic branch of Indo-European. Later in the seventeenth century, Leibniz demonstrated that Hebrew was related to Arabic and that Finnish and Hungarian had a historical relationship.

The most important breakthrough in the study of Indo-European came in 1786, when Sir William Jones read a paper before the Royal Asiatic Society of Bengal. Jones' insistence that Sanskrit, Latin, Greek, Germanic, and Celtic languages were all related was not new, but his hypothesis that all of them derived from a "lost" Indo-European original was new. Friedrich von Schlegel persisted in treating Sanskrit as a parent language of Indo-European, but he did refine the classification of other Indo-European languages and insisted on the importance of regular, structured, causal relationships in historical studies (1808). Franz Bopp, although mistaken in many of his phonological analyses, furthered Indo-European studies by his highly detailed comparison of verbal systems (1816). Bopp's contemporary, Rasmus Rask, emphasized the importance of systematic phonological changes in general, and also pointed out interrelationships among various members of the Indo-European family (1818).

The work of other nineteenth-century scholars such as Grimm and Verner will be taken up in the next chapter. Here we can simply note that, by the mid-nineteenth century, historical linguistics had been firmly established as a discipline. One scholar, A. Schleicher, had so much confidence in the existing knowledge and hypotheses that he reconstructed prehistoric Indo-European forms. To Schleicher we also owe the Darwinian idea of a genealogical tree (*Stammbaumtheorie*) as a model for language relationships and change.

The Outer History of Indo-European

The earliest written records of any Indo-European language date only from about 1500 B.C. Thus all information about earlier stages of Indo-European is necessarily based on extrapolation backwards. Not surprisingly, there is less than complete agreement about the original homeland of the Indo-Europeans and the time period for which Indo-European could be considered a single language or even a single language with various mutually intelligible dialects.

In general, scholars agree that a common Indo-European language was being spoken perhaps as early as 5000 B.C. and probably as late as 3000 B.C. Because surviving Indo-European languages share common words for *cold, winter, honey, wolf, snow, beech,* and *pine,* but do not have common words for *ocean, palm, elephant,* or *camel,* we assume that the original home was inland in a relatively cool area, probably eastern Europe or western Asia. Making such assumptions on the basis of surviving vocabulary alone can be dangerous because people often apply old words to new phenomena when they move to new areas. For example, English colonists named an unfamiliar American bird "robin" because it was red-breasted like the English robin. But the American robin is a thrush (*Turdus migratorius*), not even of the same family as the much smaller English robin (*Erithacus rubecula*). Further, once common words may be lost from individual languages; the fact that surviving Indo-European languages do not all share a common word for *sky* does not imply that there was no sky in the original Indo-European homeland. Nevertheless, because we have a large sample of common roots suggesting an inland, cool area and a corresponding lack of common roots suggesting a subtropical coastal area, we can be fairly confident that the Indo-European homeland was not, say, India, North Africa, or England. Some archaeologists have identified the Kurgan culture of the region north of the Black Sea with the early Indo-Europeans. Without written records, proof is impossible, but this thesis is at least not incompatible with the linguistic evidence from surviving vocabulary.

The Indo-Europeans were Late Stone Age people, perhaps seminomadic. They had domesticated animals and probably at least primitive agriculture. They seem to have practiced a fairly well developed religion. We have no way of knowing what they looked like or even whether they were all of the same racial stock.

Sometime after about 3000 B.C., the Indo-Europeans began a series of extensive migrations that would eventually take them all over present-day Europe and into Asia. Perhaps as early as 2000 B.C., some groups of Indo-Europeans were in Greece; by about 1500 B.C., other groups had reached the Indian subcontinent. The split-up was gradual, with the Hittites breaking off first, followed by the Indo-Iranians. The Germanic, Balto-Slavic, and Celtic groups were probably the last to leave their original homeland.

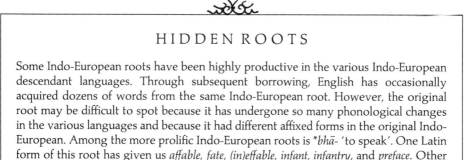

HIDDEN ROOTS

Some Indo-European roots have been highly productive in the various Indo-European descendant languages. Through subsequent borrowing, English has occasionally acquired dozens of words from the same Indo-European root. However, the original root may be difficult to spot because it has undergone so many phonological changes in the various languages and because it had different affixed forms in the original Indo-European. Among the more prolific Indo-European roots is *bhā-* 'to speak'. One Latin form of this root has given us *affable, fate, (in)effable, infant, infantry,* and *preface.* Other Latin forms are responsible for *banish, contraband, fame, infamous, confess,* and *profess.* Greek versions of IE *bhā-* give modern English *aphasia, prophet, euphemism, blasphemous, blame,* and the highly productive *phone* (as in *telephone, phonetics,* and *symphony*). From Old English itself we have *ban* and *banns,* from Old Norse *boon,* from Old French *abandon* and *banal,* and from Italian *bandit.*

In most of these derivatives, the core meaning "to speak" is still obvious. For example, *blasphemous* means speaking badly of something holy, *ineffable* means unable to be spoken or expressed in words, and a *telephone* lets us speak at a distance. In other instances, the semantic connection is harder to detect, but it can usually be ferreted out with a little effort and imagination. An *infant* is someone unable (too young) to speak. Both a *ban* and *banns* were once spoken publicly. *Bandit* comes from an Italian verb meaning to band together, that is, to have been summoned by speaking.

The Indo-European Languages

On the basis of resemblances among the member languages, scholars today recognize ten subfamilies of Indo-European, some of them now extinct. Other subfamilies have become extinct without leaving any written records. The ten groups for which we have evidence are Indo-Iranian, Tocharian, Armenian, Anatolian, Balto-Slavic, Hellenic, Albanian, Celtic, Italic, and Germanic. Figure 4.1 shows their members. These ten groups are sometimes subdivided into **satem** languages (Indo-Iranian, Albanian, Armenian, and Balto-Slavic) and **centum** languages (all the others), depending on how certain Indo-European velar sounds developed. Roughly speaking, the *satem* (from Avestan *satəm* '100') languages are to the east, and the *centum* (from Latin *centum* '100') languages are to the west. However, Tocharian, the easternmost of any Indo-European language, is a *centum* language. For purposes of the history of English, the *centum-satem* division is, however, of little importance.

Indo-Iranian

The Indic and Iranian branches of Indo-European share so many similarities that they are usually grouped together into one superbranch called Indo-Iranian. The separation into Indic and Iranian occurred when, during their migration from central Europe, perhaps beginning about 2000 B.C., one group remained in the Iranian tableland while the other continued to India. The extensive use of Persian in India during the Mogul period (A.D. 1526–1857) helped perpetuate the similarities between Indic and Iranian.

The Indic languages comprise the easternmost surviving branch of Indo-European and also have the distinction of preserving some of the oldest known written records of any Indo-European language. These religious texts, the *Vedas*, were written down after 1000 B.C. but contain portions composed several centuries earlier. To distinguish it from the later Classical Sanskrit, the language of the *Vedas* is called Vedic Sanskrit. Classical Sanskrit, which was fixed by the brilliant grammarian Panini in about 400 B.C., is the vehicle of one of the world's richest literatures, beginning about 500 B.C. and continuing almost to the present day. In addition to the monumental epic poems *Rāmāyana* and *Mahābhārata*, it includes philosophical, political, and religious treatises; drama; lyric poetry; tales and proverbs. The popular dialects corresponding to literary Sanskrit were the Prakrits, which themselves developed important written traditions.

As the sacred language of Buddhism, the Middle Indic Pāli has had enormous influence beyond the confines of India. Modern Indic has hundreds of millions of speakers in India and neighboring islands. Among the many important Indic languages today are Hindi, Urdu, Nepali, Bengali, Marathi, Gujarati, Panjabi, Assamese, and Singhalese (the major language of Sri Lanka). Romany, the language of the Gypsies, is also Indic.

The Iranian languages are divided into an Eastern and a Western branch; the oldest written records are in Avestan, an Eastern Iranian dialect. Avestan is represented in the Avesta, the sacred writings of the Zoroastrians. Although surviving texts of the Avesta are late, the language of some of its hymns is much older, perhaps as old as the Indian Vedas. Avestan has no modern descendants, but Eastern Iranian does survive in several dialects, including Afghan (or Pashtu, spoken in Afghanistan) and Ossetic (spoken in the Caucasus). The earliest written records in Western Iranian are Old Persian inscriptions of Darius from the sixth century B.C. Middle Persian, or Pahlavi, is the language of the Sassanid Empire in Persia (third through seventh centuries A.D.). Modern Iranian, dating from the tenth century A.D., is represented today by Persian, Kurdish (spoken in Iran and parts of Turkey and Iraq), and Baluchi (spoken in Soviet Baluchistan).

Tocharian

In the early part of the twentieth century, a number of texts written in an Indic alphabet but in an unknown language were discovered in Chinese Turkestan. With the aid of parallel texts in Sanskrit, the unknown language was deciphered, identified as Indo-European, and named Tocharian. Two dialects, Tocharian A and Tocharian B, are recognized. Tocharian B texts date from the seventh century A.D.; the Tocharian A texts probably extend from the fifth to the tenth centuries A.D.

Although Tocharian has been extinct for centuries, its discovery was of great interest to scholars, partly because, despite its location in Asia, its phonology resembles that of western Indo-European languages in important ways. Apparently the original speakers of Tocharian had migrated east from an original location much farther west. Tocharian also has some characteristics of its own not found in any other Indo-European language; for example, it distinguishes gender in the first-person singular nominative pronoun "I" and has at least four categories of number in the noun.

Armenian

The Armenians as a political entity are mentioned by name as early as the sixth century B.C. in Old Persian inscriptions of Darius the Great. Armenian may be the descendant of the language of the Phrygians mentioned by Greek historians, but our knowledge of Phrygian is too scanty to allow a positive identification. Because of its extensive Iranian vocabulary, Armenian was considered a member of the Iranian family until it was demonstrated that the resemblances were due to borrowing. Written records of Armenian begin with a translation of the Bible in the fifth century A.D. Among the innovations of Armenian are a fixed accent, loss of grammatical gender, and a consonant shift similar to, but independent of, that of Germanic languages.

Modern Armenian has two main branches: Eastern Armenian, spoken in the Armenian Soviet Republic in the Caucasus, and Western Armenian, with speakers in Turkey and Greece. There are also sizable pockets of Armenian speakers in Syria, the United States, Iraq, Iran, and Rumania.

Anatolian

By far the best documented Anatolian language is Hittite. Although the Hittites were familiar to history from their mention in the Bible and in Egyptian records, little was known of their language until the discovery of their archives near Boğasköy, Turkey, in 1906. The language of these cuneiform records, deciphered by Bedřich Hrozný in 1914–16, proved to be Indo-European. Dating from c. 1550–1200 B.C., these cuneiform tablets are among the oldest records of any Indo-European language, perhaps from approximately the same time as the oldest of the Vedic hymns.

Although much of the vocabulary of Hittite is non-Indo-European, the grammar and phonology are clearly Indo-European. The identification of laryngeal consonants (consonants articulated in the larynx) in Hittite was of particular interest to scholars because it supported earlier theories that Indo-European had once had laryngeal consonants even though they had been lost in all previously recognized Indo-European languages. Other Anatolian dialects of Asia Minor closely related to Hittite were Luwian, Palaic, Lydian, Lycian, and Hieroglyphic Hittite.

Balto-Slavic

On the basis of common sound changes and similarities in vocabulary and grammar, the Baltic languages and the Slavic languages are today usually grouped together as a single Balto-Slavic branch of Indo-European. West Baltic, represented only by Old Prussian (extinct since the early eighteenth century), survives in a few texts, the earliest of which date from the fifteenth century A.D. The major representatives of East Baltic are Lithuanian and Latvian (Lettish); the earliest written documents of each are from the sixteenth century. Lithuanian is of particular interest to historical linguists because of its archaic nature. It preserves the Indo-European free (unpredictable) accent and has a highly conservative vowel system and noun declensions.

The earliest written record of Slavic is from the ninth century A.D., when the bishops Cyril and Methodius translated the gospels and other religious texts into Old Bulgarian (also called Old Church Slavonic), even devising a new alphabet, the Glagolitic alphabet. At this time, all of the Slavic dialects were apparently very similar. They have since become more differentiated, and today three divisions of the Slavic languages are recognized: East Slavic, West Slavic, and South Slavic. East Slavic is spoken primarily within the Soviet Union and consists of Great Russian (or simply Russian), White Russian (or Belorussian), and Ukrainian (or Little Russian or Ruthenian). West Slavic includes Polish, Czech, Slovak, and Sorbian (or Lusatian or Wendish, spoken in a small area in East Germany). South Slavic consists of Slovenian, Serbo-Croatian, Bulgarian, and Macedonian, of which all but Bulgarian are spoken in Yugoslavia.

Hellenic

Hellenic speakers started pushing into the Greek peninsula perhaps as early as 2000 B.C., and successive waves of them continued to arrive throughout the second millennium. Probably each invading group spoke a slightly different dialect, giving rise to the subsequent division of Greek dialects into western and eastern groups. Western Greek includes Northwest Greek and Doric, whereas Eastern Greek comprises Attic-Ionic, Aeolic, and Arcado-Cyprian. With the rise in power and prestige of Athens, Attic became the dominant dialect, or *koine*, of the entire region, and the basis of Modern Greek.

Aside from an eighth century B.C. Attic inscription on a vase, the earliest known evidence of Greek had been the Homeric poems, the *Iliad* and the *Odyssey*, whose language is probably from about 800 B.C. Then in 1952 Michael Ventris deciphered the syllabic writing of Linear B, preserved in numerous Mycenaean clay tablets dating from about 1500–1200 B.C. Ventris' demonstration that this language was an archaic form of Greek allowed Greek to join Indo-Iranian and Hittite as the oldest documented Indo-European languages.

Modern Greek has two major variations: demotic or "popular" Greek, and "pure" Greek, a formal language based on the ancient *koine* and including elements from the Classical period.

Albanian

Partly because Albanian has borrowed vocabulary so heavily from Latin, Greek, Slavic, and Turkish, it was late in being recognized as an independent branch of the Indo-European family. Some scholars consider Albanian the descendant of ancient Illyrian, but this relationship is not certain. Written records of Albanian are later than those of any other Indo-European subfamily, dating only from the fifteenth century A.D. Contemporary Albanian is represented by two dialects, Gheg in the north and Tosk in the south.

Celtic

Celts are first mentioned in the fifth century B.C.; by the beginning of the Christian era, they were all over western Europe except Scandinavia. They founded the kingdom of Galatia in Asia Minor, destroyed the power of the Etruscans in Italy, and even sacked Rome in 390 B.C. They were in Britain before Caesar's conquest of that island. However, throughout their entire recorded history, speakers of Celtic have been steadily giving up their languages in favor of Germanic or Italic languages.

Celtic shares many features with Italic, and scholars once postulated an Italo-Celtic branch, though the two are usually treated separately today. One of the most striking features of all Celtic languages is initial mutation, the change in the beginning of a word due to the influence of a preceding word. For example, the Welsh word *pen* 'head' may become *mhen, ben,* or *phen,* depending on the preceding sound or word.

The earliest written records of Celtic consist of about sixty inscriptions in northern Italy. They are in Gaulish, the Continental group of Celtic, but the inscriptions are too scanty to provide much detailed information about the nature of Gaulish, which has been extinct for perhaps the past fifteen hundred years.

Insular Celtic is that group of languages centered in the British Isles. It is in turn divided into Goidelic (or *q*-Celtic) and Britannic (or *p*-Celtic). (The terms *q*- and *p*- refer to their respective developments of the Indo-European labiovelar *k^w; it became [k] in Goidelic and [p] in Britannic.) The Goidelic branch includes Irish, Scots Gaelic, and Manx. The oldest Goidelic records are fourth or fifth century A.D. Old Irish inscriptions in the unique Ogham alphabet. Irish has a rich literature in the Latin alphabet from the tenth to the sixteenth centuries. Scots Gaelic is a late offshoot of Irish brought to Scotland by Irish settlers in the sixth century A.D.; its first written records are from the fifteenth century. Manx, extinct since the mid-twentieth century, is recorded from the sixteenth century.

The Britannic (or Brythonic) branch of Celtic comprises Welsh, Cornish, and Breton. The earliest written records of Welsh date from the late eighth century A.D.; those of Cornish from the tenth century. Breton was brought to Brittany in northern France in the fifth and sixth centuries A.D. by immigrants from Cornwall and Wales fleeing the Germanic invaders.

Of all the surviving Indo-European language groups, Celtic is probably in the greatest danger of extinction today. Though there are still thousands of native speakers of Irish, Scots Gaelic, and Welsh, and perhaps a million native speakers of Breton, virtually all of these speakers are bilingual in English or French.

RELIGIOUS LOANS

Because Latin was the official language of the Roman Catholic Church, many Latin loanwords into Old and Middle English were ecclesiastical in origin, although some have since lost their religious meanings. A number of these loans are a kind of abbreviation for the names of divine services or liturgy, deriving from the first word or two of the service or prayer.

- *credo* (from Latin *credo* 'I believe') is the first word of the Apostles' and Nicene creeds.
- *dirge* (from Latin *dirige*, imperative of *dirigere* 'direct') is the first word of the antiphon of matins in the Latin office of the dead.
- *paternoster* (from Latin *pater noster* 'our father') is the first two words of the Lord's Prayer.
- *placebo* (from Latin *placebo* 'I shall please') is the first word of the first antiphon of vespers for the dead; the entire phrase is *Placebo Domino in regione vivorum* 'I shall please the Lord in the land of the living'.
- *requiem* (accusative of Latin *requies* 'rest') is the first word of the introit of the mass for the dead; the entire first phrase is *Requiem aeternam dona eis, Domine* 'Eternal rest give unto them, Lord'.

Italic

Early Italy contained within its borders a wide variety of languages and dialects, most of them Indo-European, but at least one of them (Etruscan) non-Indo-European. Although Oscan and Umbrian are today categorized as Italic, along with Latin, there is some evidence that Osco-Umbrian was a completely separate Indo-European group. Both Oscan and Umbrian were once fairly important languages in Italy; we have surviving extensive inscriptions in Oscan dating back to about 400 B.C. and in Umbrian from the second century B.C.

Latin was once confined to the minor provinces of Latium south of the Tiber River, but the power of Rome spread Latin throughout the peninsula, and Latin had replaced most of the other languages there by perhaps the beginning of the Christian era. As the Roman Empire expanded throughout Europe, the legionnaires and the administrators brought their own version of Latin with them. This was Vulgar Latin, the spoken language, which differed from Classical Latin in vocabulary and in its loss of inflections. Because the Romans moved into different areas of Europe at different times, they brought different varieties of Vulgar Latin with them; hence, modern French and modern Spanish did not have an identical direct ancestor.

The prestige of Classical Latin and learning delayed the recognition of the various offshoots of Vulgar Latin as respectable languages. Consequently, our earliest records of the Romance languages are all relatively late. French first appears in writing in the eighth century A.D., Italian in the tenth, Spanish and Portuguese in the eleventh, and Rumanian only in the sixteenth century. Aside from these major Romance languages today, there are also Rhaeto-Romansch in

Switzerland, Sardinian, Walloon (a dialect of French) in Belgium, Canadian French, and Haitian and Papiamentu creoles.

Germanic

Germanic speakers came to the attention of history when they began to move from southern Scandinavia toward the Roman Empire. Caesar first used the term *Germani* in his *Gallic Wars*; a century and a half later, Tacitus treated them in more detail in his *Germania* (A.D. 98).

Up to about the beginning of the Christian era, Germanic was probably one language with only minor dialectal differences. However, as groups migrated into various parts of Europe and became separated, dialectal differences developed rapidly. Today the Germanic languages are usually divided into East Germanic, West Germanic, and North Germanic. Although these divisions are not entirely satisfactory for encompassing the complex relationships among the various languages, they are adequate for our purposes.

All the East Germanic languages are extinct today, but we have evidence that many separate dialects—Gothic, Burgundian, Vandalic, Gepidic, Rugian, and so on—once existed. Of these, there is written evidence of only Gothic. Happily for Germanic scholars, this evidence is early and fairly extensive. About A.D. 370, Bishop Ulfilas (or Wulfila, to use the Germanic form of his name), a missionary among the Visigoths, translated most of the Bible into Gothic, even inventing a special alphabet based on Greek for his project. Large portions of his translations have been lost, but enough remains to provide detailed information about the language. Gothic was spoken and occasionally written in Italy, Spain, and France until perhaps as late as the ninth century A.D., but gradually gave way to Romance languages. The last vestiges were reported from the Crimea in the eighteenth century.

North Germanic consists of the Scandinavian languages. No extensive continuous texts appear until about the twelfth century, but briefer runic inscriptions survive from the third century A.D. on. The North Germanic languages seem to have been undifferentiated until as late as the eighth century. North Germanic today includes an eastern branch (Swedish and Danish) and a western branch (Norwegian, Icelandic, and Faroese). Although Icelandic today has only perhaps a quarter of a million native speakers, it has a long and glorious literary tradition, especially of prose sagas and of poetry, dating back to the tenth and eleventh centuries.

Like North Germanic, the West Germanic languages are traditionally divided into two groups, High German and Low German, on the basis of sound changes in the former. (The traditional terms High and Low refer to geography, not quality; a better terminology would be South German instead of High German and North German instead of Low German.) High German is attested—already with dialectal variants—from the eighth century onward. Contemporary representatives of High German are the varieties of German spoken in southern Germany, Austria, and Switzerland. Yiddish, despite heavy influence from Hebrew and Slavic, is also a High German dialect.

Written records of Low German first appear in the seventh century in England and in the ninth century on the Continent. Modern Low German languages (or dialects) include Low German (Plattdeutsch) in Germany, Dutch, Afrikaans, Luxemburgian, Flemish (in Belgium), Frisian (in the northern part of the Netherlands), and English. Frisian and English are especially closely related, and some scholars speak of an Anglo-Frisian subgroup of Low German.

Figure 4.1 Indo-European Languages

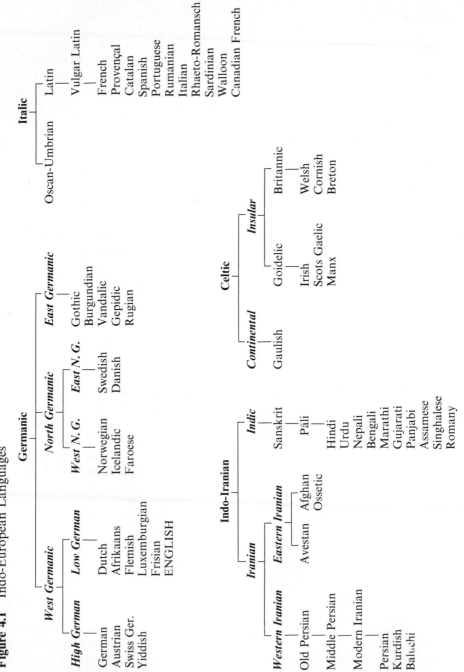

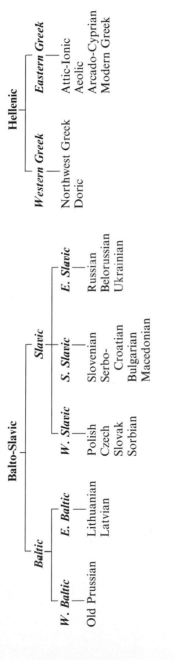

Hellenic

Western Greek	*Eastern Greek*
Northwest Greek	Attic-Ionic
Doric	Aeolic
	Arcado-Cyprian
	Modern Greek

Balto-Slavic

Baltic

W. Baltic	*E. Baltic*
Old Prussian	Lithuanian
	Latvian

Slavic

W. Slavic	*S. Slavic*	*E. Slavic*
Polish	Slovenian	Russian
Czech	Serbo-Croatian	Belorussian
Slovak	Bulgarian	Ukrainian
Sorbian	Macedonian	

Anatolian

Hittite
Luwian
Palaic
Lydian
Lycian
Hieroglyphic Hittite

Armenian

Western Armenian	Eastern Armenian

Albanian

Gheg
Tosk

Tocharian

Tocharian A
Tocharian B

From Indo-European to Germanic

As we have noted earlier, we simply do not have enough information about early Indo-European or even early stages of Germanic to speak confidently about all their details. Indeed, some of the evidence that we do have is sufficiently conflicting to suggest that neither Indo-European nor Germanic was ever a single, undifferentiated language. Hence, in the following discussion, the terms Common Indo-European (CIE) and Common Germanic (CGmc) should be interpreted only as referring to sets of common features shared by most or all of the dialects or subdivisions of CIE and CGmc. It is as if we were to describe Present-Day English by abstracting the common features of the language used by speakers from Chicago, Dublin, Manchester, and Melbourne. We would be able to give a coherent picture of the broader aspects of English, but would find conflicting evidence in the finer details. Nor can we even assign precise dates to CIE and CGmc. For the purposes of exposition, we can, somewhat arbitrarily, assume a date of 3000 B.C. for CIE and 100 B.C. for CGme.

Phonology

PROSODY
Prosody refers to the rhythmic alternations of strongly and weakly accented syllables, to the differences in stress or pitch or both between syllables. Loosely speaking, it is the pattern of accented and unaccented syllables in the flow of sound. CIE had an accent based on pitch differences. This pitch accent was "free"; that is, it could occur on any syllable (though any particular form of a given word would have the accent in the same place).

Germanic replaced the CIE pitch accent with a strong stress accent based on loudness rather than pitch. It ended up with three degrees of stress: (1) primary or major stress on the root syllable of words, (2) weak stress on following syllables, and (3) an intermediate level of secondary stress on the second element of compound words and on many prefixes. Somewhat later, Germanic fixed this stress accent on the initial syllable of the word. (A few prefixes took weak stress; then the accent was on the following syllable.) These prosodic changes were to have widespread effects on all the Germanic languages. In English they were to affect not only the phonology but also the morphology and ultimately the syntax of the language.

CONSONANTS AND THE FIRST SOUND SHIFT
CIE had three types of consonants—stops, a single fricative [s], and the resonants [m n l r j w]. Most scholars today also posit anywhere from one to four laryngeal consonants, but because they are not necessary for discussing the evolution of Germanic or English, we shall ignore them here. There is also debate over exactly how many series of stops CIE had; again, for a description of Germanic developments, we need assume only the following:

	Bilabial	*Dental*	*Velar*	*Labiovelar*
Voiceless	p	t	k	k^w
Voiced	b	d	g	g^w
Voiced Aspirated	bh	dh	gh	gh^w

(The final entries in each row ([kʷ] [gʷ] [ghʷ]) represent labiovelar stops, that is, stops with simultaneous labial and velar articulation, somewhat like the initial sounds of English *quick* and *Guatemala*.)

Figure 4.2 Grimm's Law Illustrated

Original IE Sound	*Other IE Language*	*Germanic*
p	Latin *pedis, pater*	English *foot, father*
t	Latin *tres, tonare*	English *three*, to *thunder*
k	Latin *canis, cornu*	English *hound, horn*
b*	Latin *turba* 'crowd'	Old English *thorp* 'village'
	Old Bulgarian *slabu*	English *sleep*
d	Latin *dentis, duo*	English *tooth, two*
g	Latin *granum, ager*	English *corn, acre*
bh	Latin *frater, fra(n)go*†	English *brother, break*
dh	Latin *foris, fi(n)go*†	English *door, dough*
gh	Latin *hortus, hostis*†	English *garden, guest*‡

* Examples of IE [b] are few; the sound was apparently very rare.

† IE voiced aspirates changed to fricatives in Latin.

‡ Because Gmc [g] underwent later changes in English, we here use two loanwords in English from Old Norse. Old Norse is also a Germanic language, so is acceptable to illustrate Grimm's Law.

Grimm's Law.   Beginning some time in the first millennium B.C. and perhaps continuing over several centuries, all the Indo-European stops underwent a complete transformation in Germanic. At the end of the complete cycle of changes, the following pattern had emerged:

IE	Gmc	IE	Gmc	IE	Gmc
p	> f	b	> p	bh	> b
t	> θ	d	> t	dh	> d
k	> x (h)	g	> k	gh	> g
kʷ	> xʷ	gʷ	> kʷ	ghʷ	> gʷ

In short, all the IE voiceless stops had become voiceless fricatives, the IE voiced stops had become voiceless stops, and the IE voiced aspirated stops had become voiced stops.[2] (Later changes in the individual Germanic languages have modified this pattern in certain environments, but we need not be concerned about these details at this point.)

Although certain correspondences between the consonants in Germanic languages and those in other IE languages had been observed earlier, it was Jakob Grimm (of fairy-tale fame) who codified them in 1822. Therefore the change is often termed **Grimm's Law**. Figure 4.2 illustrates resulting correspondences in cognate

---

[2] IE voiced aspirated stops first became voiced fricatives ([β] [ð] [γ] [γʷ]) before shifting to voiced stops. For the sake of simplicity, we list only the end result here.

words between Germanic and other IE languages. The IE labiovelars such as [kʷ] are omitted from the chart because their development was identical to that of the velars.

Almost as soon as Grimm's Law had been formulated, apparent exceptions began to be noticed. Many of them were soon explained as being conditioned by the phonetic environment. For example, Grimm's Law was amended to allow for the preservation of IE voiceless stops in Germanic after another voiceless stop or after [s]. Thus the following correspondences held:

After a Voiceless Stop	*After [s]*
Latin oc<u>t</u>o; OE eah<u>t</u>a 'eight'	Latin <u>sp</u>uo; PDE <u>sp</u>it
Latin ca<u>pt</u>o; PDE ha<u>ft</u>	Latin <u>st</u>ella; PDE <u>st</u>ar
	Latin <u>sc</u>alpo; PDE <u>sc</u>alp[3]

Verner's Law. A more puzzling set of exceptions involves seeming reversals of Grimm's Law. Where voiceless [f] [θ] and [x] were expected to appear as corresponding fricatives to the IE stops [p] [t] and [k], the voiced stops [b] [d] and [g] sometimes appeared instead. In addition, [r] often appeared where [s] was expected. In 1877, Karl Verner was able to explain these exceptions with what has since become known as **Verner's Law**. By examining cognate words in other languages that had preserved the original IE stress, Verner showed that when the Germanic [f] [θ] and [x] (resulting from Grimm's Law) were surrounded by voiced sounds and preceded by an unaccented vowel, they became voiced. Figure 4.3 illustrates the operation of Verner's Law by comparing forms in Germanic languages with forms in Classical languages that preserve the original Indo-European consonants; the Greek and Sanskrit forms also retain the original IE stress. In some instances Gothic forms are used to illustrate the Germanic development because subsequent changes in Old English confuse the picture.

Figure 4.3 Verner's Law Illustrated

Original IE Sound	*Classical Language*	*Germanic Language*
p	Greek heptá 'seven'	Gothic si<u>b</u>un
	Latin ca<u>p</u>ut 'head'	Gothic hau<u>b</u>iþ
t	Greek klu<u>t</u>ós 'famous'	OE hlu<u>d</u> 'loud'
	Latin cen<u>t</u>um 'hundred'	OE hun<u>d</u>red
k	Greek he<u>k</u>urá 'mother-in-law'	OE swe<u>g</u>er
	Greek de<u>k</u>ás 'group of ten'	Gothic ti<u>g</u>us*
s	Sanskrit snu<u>s</u>á 'daughter-in-law'	OE sno<u>r</u>u

*Compare Greek déka 'ten', Gothic taihun, where the original stress is on the preceding syllable. Verner's Law does not apply, and Grimm's Law operates as expected.

---

[3] We use the Old Norse loanword *scalp* to illustrate the point here because the combination [sk] underwent a further change in early Old English.

Subsequent sound changes have usually obscured the effects of Verner's Law in PDE; one exception is the varying final consonants of *was* and *were*. However, the effects can still be seen in Old English, especially in alternations among forms of strong verbs. The following examples are typical:

OE Present-Stem Forms	*OE Past Participles*
seoþan 'to seethe'	-*soden* 'sodden'
ceosan 'to choose'	-*coren* 'chosen'
slyhþ 'strikes'	-*slagen* 'struck, slain'

Verner's Law was helpful in providing a relative (though not absolute) chronology for Grimm's Law and the fixed stress of Germanic. Because it resulted from a mobile (free) stress, the change must have occurred *before* Germanic fixed stress on initial syllables. On the other hand, because it operated on the results of Grimm's Law, it must have occurred *after* the changes described by Grimm's Law had already begun—after the IE voiceless stops had become voiceless fricatives. Otherwise, the resulting voiced stops would have fallen together with the original IE voiced stops. In sum, the chronology was (1) IE voiceless stops become voiceless fricatives in Germanic (Grimm's Law); (2) under certain circumstances, Germanic voiceless fricatives became voiced stops (Verner's Law); (3) Germanic stress was fixed on the first syllable.

The term **First Consonant Shift** is often used to refer to the effects of Grimm's Law and Verner's Law taken together. It is called "First" to distinguish it from a later change, the Second Consonant Shift, that affected only High German. The Second Consonant Shift is beyond the scope of our discussion here, but we might just note that it is the cause of such English-German correspondences as *penny: Pfennig*; *copper: Kupfer*; and *dead: tot*.

The remaining IE consonants developed less dramatically in Germanic. IE [s], except when affected by Verner's Law, remained unchanged. IE also had a series of resonants ([m n l r j w]), which could serve either as consonants or vowels. In Germanic, they all remained but lost their vocalic nature. That is, they no longer could form the nucleus of a syllable, but were always supported by a regular vowel.

VOWELS AND ABLAUT

Compared to the drastic changes in the consonant system, the vowel system of Germanic remained relatively stable; the major changes are in the direction of simplification. Among the most important changes, IE *[ā] > Gmc [ō], reducing the inventory of long vowels by one. Further, IE *[o] and *[a] collapsed in Germanic, reducing the number of short vowels. The falling together of IE *[a] and *[o] also affected the diphthongs, reducing that category. IE *[ei] simplified to Gmc [ī], giving just three diphthongs in place of the six that IE had had. Subsequent sound changes in Germanic were to alter the distribution of some of its original vowels. In particular, there was a general tendency for [i] to replace [e] in unstressed syllables and before nasals.

We might note that the vowels [a] and [o] have a long history of instability in Germanic languages. To this day, the various dialects of English handle them differently, and many dialects do not phonemically distinguish the PDE reflexes of these vowels, /a/ and /ɔ/; for example, in some dialects, the words *caller* and *collar* are homophones. Even within the same dialect, different speakers often have different distribution patterns.

Indo-European vowels participated in an extensive system of **ablaut** (also called **apophony** or **vowel gradation**), whereby changes in the vowels of roots indicated such morphological categories as tense, number, or even part of speech. The basic ablaut series was $e \sim o \sim ø$, in which e represents full grade, o represents secondary grade, and ø represents lowest, or zero grade (that is, the vowel is lost completely). This basic pattern was varied by lengthening ($\bar{e} \sim \bar{o} \sim \partial$) and by forming diphthongs with elements following the original vowels ($ei \sim oi \sim i$), leading to a number of different sets of alternations, the specific details of which need not concern us here. The particular vowel that appeared in a given form originally depended upon the location of the accent in the word. (One can see the effects of shifting accent upon vowel quality in such PDE loanwords as *catastrophic* [kǽtəstrɑfɪk]/*catastrophe* [kətǽstrəfi], where the shifting of the stress from the first to the second syllable changes every vowel of the original word.)

In Germanic, the conditioning factor (a change in accent) for ablaut was eliminated when the accent was fixed on the first syllable of all words, regardless of their grammatical form or function. Nonetheless, the vowel alternations that had appeared in CIE often remained—to some extent, to the present day. They are most obvious in strong verbs like *sing, sang, sung*, but also appear in related nouns from the same root (*song*).

Graphics

Since CIE was the language of a preliterate culture, we have no graphic evidence of it. Shortly after the split of Common Germanic into East, West, and North branches, the North Germanic and West Germanic groups invented a special alphabet, the *futhorc*; it will be discussed in more detail in Chapter 5.

Morphology

In analyzing Present-Day English, many grammarians tend to lump morphology and syntax together, primarily because PDE has so few inflections that it seems more economical to treat them as special complications of syntax than as a separate level for grammatical analysis. This approach neglects two other components of morphology, derivation and composition, both of which are highly complex in PDE. In any case, no discussion can afford to dismiss IE morphology completely, for it was extremely rich in inflections.

Primarily on the basis of the inflections they took or did not take, four major word classes (parts of speech) are identified for IE: nouns/adjectives, pronouns, verbs, and prepositions. The adverb was not a separate word class. There was no article and no separate class of conjunctions. Nouns and adjectives are lumped together because in IE they took the same inflections; the rather sharp distinction we tend to make between PDE nouns and adjectives did not exist. What we say here about nouns also applies to their use as modifiers.

IE nouns, adjectives (including demonstratives), and pronouns were inflected for case, number, and gender. (**Case** refers to the use of separate inflections to express different grammatical functions such as subject or object.) IE probably had eight cases: (1) **nominative**, used for the subject of a finite verb or for predicate nouns or adjectives; (2) **genitive**, used to indicate that a noun is the modifier of another noun and to express such relationships as possession, source, and partition; (3) **dative**, used to indicate the indirect object of a verb, the object of some prepositions, and the object of some verbs; (4) **accusative**, used to indicate the direct object of a verb and also the object of some prepositions; (5) **ablative**, used to indicate separation or direction away from a source; (6) **instrumental**, used to express agency or means; (7) **locative**, used to indicate place in or at which; and (8) **vocative**, used to indicate a person or thing being directly addressed.

In Germanic, the ablative and locative fell together with the dative case, giving Germanic only six cases (nominative, genitive, dative, accusative, instrumental, and vocative). Although there was a strong tendency for the instrumental to fuse with the dative, West Germanic preserved the instrumental long enough for traces to survive in early Old English. The vocative also later became identical to the nominative, partly because many of its endings had already been the same as those of the nominative.

IE had three **numbers**—singular, plural, and dual (used to refer to only two of something). Germanic preserved all three of these numbers, although the dual was to be lost later. IE also had three **genders** (masculine, feminine, and neuter), all of which were preserved in Germanic.

In addition to this assortment of inflectional categories, IE had various classes of noun stems, and the actual form of each inflection varied according to what vowel or consonant the stem ended in. Again, Germanic tended to reduce the number of different stem types.

Although its general tendency was to simplify the IE declensional system, Germanic was unique among the IE languages in complicating the adjective declension by introducing two different sets of adjective inflections, whose use was determined by whether the adjective was preceded by a demonstrative (**definite** or **weak adjectives**) or not (**indefinite** or **strong adjectives**). See Chapter 5 for a more detailed discussion of definite and indefinite adjectives.

Indo-European pronouns had all the cases, numbers, and genders of nouns and adjectives. In addition, the personal pronouns distinguished three **persons**: first person (speaker), second person (addressee), and third person (anything else). First- and second-person pronouns did not, however, distinguish gender (nor is gender distinguished in these pronouns today).

The IE verb was even more heavily inflected than the noun. In addition to marking person and number, it also distinguished aspect, voice, and mood. **Aspect** is only roughly equivalent to what we normally mean by "tense"; it focuses more on completion, duration, or repetition of the action expressed by the verb than on time. IE verbs had six aspects: (1) **present**, referring to continuing action in progress; (2) **imperfect**, referring to continuing action in the past; (3) **aorist**, referring to momentary action in the past; (4) **perfect**, referring to completed action; (5) **pluperfect**, referring to completed action in the past; and (6) **future**, referring to actions to come. Like the Celtic and Italic languages, Germanic changed the focus of verb conjugations from aspect to tense, that is, to expressing only time relationships through inflections. Germanic also reduced the six aspect categories of IE to two tense categories, present (which included future), and past (often called **preterite**).

IE had three **voices**—active, passive, and middle (or reflexive). Except for Gothic, Germanic lost both the inflected passive and the inflected middle voices, expressing these notions by means of phrases rather than inflections. The five **moods** of IE were **indicative** (for statements or questions of fact), **subjunctive** (expressing will), **optative** (expressing wishes), **imperative** (expressing commands), and **injunctive** (expressing unreality). Germanic retained the indicative and parts of the imperative, but subsumed both the subjunctive and the injunctive under the optative (confusingly usually called the subjunctive).

There were seven major classes of verbs in IE, distinguished by their root vowels and following consonants. Without going into details at this point, we will note simply that Germanic retained these seven basic classes. Germanic also added an entirely new category of verbs, the "weak verbs" (or **dental preterite** verbs), formed from other parts of speech and characterized by past tense and past participle endings containing [t] or [d].

Figure 4.4 summarizes these changes in morphology.

Figure 4.4   Summary of IE and Germanic Inflectional Categories

	Indo-European	*Germanic*
CASE	nominative	nominative
	genitive	genitive
	dative	
	ablative	dative
	locative	
	instrumental	(instrumental)*
	accusative	accusative
	vocative	(vocative)*
GENDER	masculine	masculine
	feminine	feminine
	neuter	neuter
PERSON	first	first
	second	second
	third	third
NUMBER	singular	singular
	dual	dual
	plural	plural
MOOD	indicative	indicative
	subjunctive	
	optative	optative (= subjunctive)
	injunctive	
	imperative	imperative
VOICE	active	
	middle	active
	passive	
ASPECT (>TENSE)	present	present
	future	
	imperfect	
	perfect	
	aorist	past (= preterite)
	pluperfect	

* Survived in Germanic, but had only a marginal status in Old English.

Syntax

With no surviving speakers or texts, we have no direct information about word order in IE. However, because the plethora of inflections provided a great deal of information about the grammatical functions of the words in a sentence, word order must have been a great deal freer than in, say, Present-Day English. With the loss of distinctive inflections for the ablative, locative, and, to some extent, the instrumental cases, the various Germanic languages developed prepositions to express those grammatical relationships. However, this process was only just beginning at the time of Common Germanic. Most scholars assume that objects tended to precede verbs in IE rather than the other way about as in contemporary English.

Common Germanic apparently still retained a relatively free word order; at least, in the fourth century A.D., Ulfilas found it possible to translate the Greek Bible almost word for word into Gothic without readjusting the syntax. Although the resulting translation may have seemed somewhat unidiomatic to native speakers of Gothic, we must assume that it was at least comprehensible. Certainly, by A.D. 1000, when extensive portions of the Bible were translated into Old English, the translators changed the word order of the original Latin a great deal to fit what were by then more rigid English patterns.

Lexicon

As was mentioned earlier, enough of the vocabulary of CIE has survived in its descendant branches to give us a reasonably good outline of the original homeland and culture of its speakers. In addition to the vocabulary items listed there, we have cognates for a large number of words that any human culture must have in order for its members to communicate with each other. They include kinship terms like *father* and *mother*, basic verbs like *be*, *lie*, and *eat*, terms for natural phenomena like *sun* and *tree*, adjectives such as *long* and *red*, and nouns for bodily parts such as *foot* and *head*. The various IE languages still share cognate forms for common grammatical concepts such as interrogation and negation.

Common Germanic inherited and retained a large fund of such words from CIE. For many Germanic words, we lack evidence for a common Indo-European root, but find cognates in one or more of the other IE branches, especially for those geographically closest to Germanic, including Italic, Celtic, and Balto-Slavic. Common Germanic also borrowed words from these other IE branches. For example, the Germanic words for copper, ark, cheese, kettle, ass, and linen were borrowed from Latin. Words for doctor, king, and iron came from Celtic. (The borrowing was not all one-way; these other branches also borrowed extensively from Germanic. For example, the various words for "blue" in the Romance languages come from Germanic.)

Besides its inherited vocabulary from CIE and its loanwords from other IE languages, Germanic languages are distinguished by a large common vocabulary *not* shared by other IE languages. Present-Day English still preserves scores and scores of these words, including —and this is only a small sample—*back, bless, blood, body, bone, bride, broad, child, dear, earl, eel, game, gate, ground, oar, rat, rise, sea, soul, theft, womb.* Most scholars assume that this large, uniquely Germanic vocabulary was borrowed from non-Indo-European speakers whom the Germanic speakers encountered and probably assimilated at an early stage in their migration away from the original IE homeland. We have, however, no evidence whatsoever for what this substratum language may have been or what it was like.

No living language relies solely on borrowings for creating new vocabulary items. Common Germanic already used derivative affixes such as *-iskaz* (PDE *-ish*) to form nouns and adjectives indicating nationality. It also had inherited the process of compounding from CIE, although the kind of compounding most characteristic of Germanic languages today was a later development in the individual languages.

Semantics

Because we have no examples of either Indo-European or Germanic in context, no surviving texts, it is difficult to say much about types of semantic change between CIE and CGmc. In a few cases, all surviving words from one IE root show a meaning different in Germanic from that in other IE languages, and here we can sometimes see not only the shift in meaning but also the logic of the shift. For example, from the IE root *wespero-* 'evening, night', Latin has *vesper* 'evening' and Greek has *hesperos* 'evening'. In Germanic, the root survives in the form *west* (English *west*, German *Westen*, Swedish *väst*, etc.). Clearly, the change in reference is from the time when the sun sets to the place where the sun sets. In the case of the IE root *gembh-* 'tooth, nail', Gmc *kambaz* 'comb' reflects a change in meaning from biological bonelike structures to an object resembling such structures, a shift caused by analogy.

Texts

As we have noted, we have no texts of Common Germanic, and the earliest surviving texts in any Germanic language are in Gothic, perhaps five hundred years after the breakup of Common Germanic. For North Germanic, the earliest texts are brief futhorc inscriptions. Of the West Germanic languages, English has the first texts, but the earliest of these dates only from the early seventh century A.D. Nonetheless, the relationships among the Germanic languages are obvious even a millennium after the breakup.

Reproduced below is the text of the Lord's Prayer in the WGmc Old English (c. A.D. 1000), the NGmc Old Norse (after A.D. 1000), and the EGmc Gothic (c. A.D. 350). For comparative purposes, the Latin Vulgate and a PDE translation are also given. The Gothic is a translation from the Greek New Testament; the Old English and the Old Norse are translations from the Vulgate (itself a translation from the Greek). Cognate words among two or all three of the Germanic languages are underscored; because Latin is also an IE language, a number of the Latin words are predictably also cognate with the Germanic words, but they are not underlined.

OE	Fæder ure þu þe eart on heofonum, si þin nama gehalgod.
ON	Faðer várr sá þú ert í hifne, helgesk nafn þitt.
Gothic	Atta unsar þu in himinam, weihnai namo þein.
Vulg.	Pater noster qui es in caelis, sanctificetur nomen tuum.
PDE	Our father who is in heaven, may your name be made holy.

OE	Tobecume þin rice. Gewurþe ðin willa on eorðan swa swa on heofonum.
ON	Til kome þitt ríke. Verðe þinn vile, suá á iorþ sem á hifne.
Gothic	Qimai þiudinassus þeins. Wairþai wilja þeins, swe in himina jah ana airþai.

Vulg.	Adveniat regnum tuum. Fiat voluntas tua, sicut in caelo et in terra.
PDE	May your kingdom come. May your will be done, on earth as it is in heaven.

OE	Urne dæghwamlican hlaf syle us todæg.
ON	Gef oss í dag várt dagligt brauþ.
Gothic	Hlaif unsarana þana sinteinan gif uns himma daga.
Vulg.	Panem nostrum supersubstantialem da nobis hodie.
PDE	Give us today our daily bread.

OE	And forgyf us ure gyltas	swa swa we
ON	Ok fyrerlát oss ossar skulder	suá sem vér
Gothic	Jah aflet uns þatci skulans sijaima,	swaswe jah weis
Vulg.	Et dimitte nobis debita nostra,	sicut et nos
PDE	And forgive our debts,	just as we

OE	forgyfað urum gyltendum.
ON	fyrerlátom ossom skuldo-nautom.
Gothic	afletam þam skulam unsaraim.
Vulg.	dimittimus debitoribus nostris.
PDE	forgive our debtors.

OE	And ne gelæd þu us on costnunge,	ac alys us of yfele.
ON	Ok inn leiþ oss eige í freistne,	heldr frels þú oss af illo.
Gothic	Jah ni briggais uns in fraistubnjai	ak lausei uns af þamma ubilin.
Vulg.	Et ne nos inducas in tentationem,	sed libera nos a malo.
PDE	And do not lead us into temptation,	but deliver us from evil.

Differing spelling conventions in the three Germanic languages conceal some of the similarities or identities among them. For example, Gothic *ei* = [ī]; if it were respelled with *i*, the relationship of Gothic *þeins* with ON *þitt* would be clearer. Similarly, Gothic *q* = [kw]; respelling *Qimai* as *kwimai* would make its parallel to ON *kome* more obvious.

In some instances, cognate words were available in two or all three of the Germanic languages but simply were not used—like all languages, the earlier Germanic languages were relatively rich in synonyms. For example, in line 4, the OE text has *forgyf* 'forgive' where ON and Gothic have *fyrerlát* and *aflet*, respectively. The OE translator could just as well have used *forlǣt* here; it also meant "forgive." In line 6, where OE has *costnunge*, the translator could have used *frasung* instead, cognate with Gothic *fraistubnjai* and ON *freistne*. In the same line, where OE has *gelǣd*, OE *bring* (cognate with Gothic *briggais*) would have been possible.

The progressing rigidity of syntax of the Germanic languages is evident in the differences between the early Gothic on the one hand and the later OE on the other. Whereas the Gothic almost always follows the Greek (and the Latin) word order exactly, ON and OE alter it frequently. For example, except for the first two words in the text,[4] the possessive pronouns in ON and OE precede the words they modify, even though they normally follow them in the Latin text. (In line 2, compare Vulg. *Adveniat regnum tuum* 'come kingdom thy' with OE *Tobecume þin rice* 'come thy kingdom'.)

    The Germanic loss of the rich IE system of verbal inflections is evident in line 1, where the meaning calls for an optative present passive verb. To express this notion, Gothic uses a subjunctive present (*weihnai*). Old English has a verb phrase consisting of the present subjunctive of the verb "to be" (*si*) and a past participle (*gehalgod*). Old Norse employs a reflexive form of the verb (*helgesk*).

    Different as they may appear at first glance, these texts reveal clearly the unity of the Germanic languages as opposed to the non-Germanic Latin.

To summarize, the six most important changes that distinguish Germanic languages from other Indo-European languages are

1. Fixed stress accent on root syllable of words.
2. Grimm's and Verner's Laws (First Consonant Shift).
3. "Strong" versus "weak" adjective declensions.
4. "Weak" verbs with past tense in [t] or [d] (dental preterite).
5. Two-tense verbal system.
6. Large common vocabulary not shared by other IE languages.

Suggested Further Reading

Baldi, Philip. *An Introduction to the Indo-European Languages.*

Benveniste, Émile. *Le vocabulaire des institutions indo-européennes.*

Birnbaum, Henrik, and Jaan Puhvel, eds. *Ancient Indo-European Dialects.*

Cardona, George, Henry M. Hoenigswald, and Alfred Senn, eds. *Indo-European and Indo-Europeans.*

Chadwick, John. *The Decipherment of Linear B.*

Lockwood, W. B. *Indo-European Philology.*

Lockwood, W. B. *Languages of the British Isles, Past and Present.*

Lockwood, W. B. *A Panorama of Indo-European Languages.*

Meillet, Antoine. *General Characteristics of the Germanic Languages.*

Meillet, Antoine. *Introduction à l'étude comparative des langues indo-européennes.*

Prokosch, E. *A Comparative Germanic Grammar.*

Ruhlen, Merritt. *A Guide to the World's Languages.*

Streadbeck, Arval L. *A Short Introduction to Germanic Linguistics.*

---

[4] The inversion of noun and possessive pronoun in the opening words is due to the fact that they constitute a vocative (direct address); Old English has such inversions elsewhere with direct address. For example, in the poem *Beowulf*, Wulfgar addresses Hroðgar as *þeoden min*, literally "lord my."

C H A P T E R   5

Old English

> *One age cannot be completely understood if all the others are not understood. The song of history can only be sung as a whole.*
>
> —*José Ortega y Gasset*

OUTER HISTORY

England Before the English

The land mass now called England has been continuously inhabited since Paleolithic times, when the glaciers of the last Ice Age had so lowered the sea level that England was attached to the continent of Europe. We have no knowledge of the languages spoken by the Paleolithic and Neolithic inhabitants of Britain, apart from the fact that they were almost certainly non-Indo-European. The first Indo-European speakers to arrive were probably the Celts. The date of their arrival is a subject of much confusion and controversy; suffice it to say that Celtic speakers were in the British Isles several centuries before the birth of Christ.

Beginning in 55 B.C., Julius Caesar made several attempts to invade Britain, but met such fierce resistance from the local population that Rome left Britain alone for the next century. Then in A.D. 43, the Emperor Claudius sent a huge army to the island and, by about A.D. 50, had subjugated most of what is today England. The northern part of Britain escaped Roman domination and remained unconquered, a condition, as Edward Gibbon rather unkindly said, "for which they were not less indebted to their poverty than to their valour."

For the next four hundred years, England was Rome's westernmost outpost and was gradually but thoroughly Romanized. The Romans established cities and built a network of highways. They erected Roman-style houses and villas, complete with hypocaustic central heating, running water, and mosaic tile floors. There were Roman public baths and even theaters. Naturally, military bases and forts were set up. In the north, defensive walls were built to discourage raids by the un-Romanized Picts (natives who probably spoke a Celtic language). When the Empire adopted Christianity as its official religion, England too was Christianized. The official language was Latin, though the native Britons continued to speak their Celtic dialects.

By the beginning of the fifth century A.D., Rome itself was under such pressure from migrations and invasions from the east and north that the Roman legions were withdrawn from Britain to defend the borders closer to Rome; the traditional date of their departure from Britain is A.D. 410.

The Arrival of the English

Once the Romans had left, the political situation in Britain deteriorated rapidly. Softened by their long exposure to civilization, the Romanized Britons were ill-equipped to defend themselves from renewed attacks by the Picts in the north. Then, even as the Britons were trying to cope with their fiercer northern neighbors, a much more calamitous series of events took place: waves of Germanic-speaking people from the Continent began to invade the island. The "English" were coming to England.

Although the traditional date for the first Germanic invasions is A.D. 449, at least some Germanic immigrants had arrived earlier, and certainly many more continued to come after 449. Unfortunately for historians, the Anglo-Saxon invasions and settlements coincided with one of the lowest points in European history. The term Dark Ages is a misnomer as applied to much of the thousand-year period between A.D. 476 and 1450; nevertheless, the fifth century was indeed one of great decline and turmoil. Historical records for the period are almost nonexistent, and our knowledge of events in England at the time must depend as much on archeology and inference as on written evidence.

The most complete written description of the Germanic invasions comes from the Venerable Bede, who was writing two and a half centuries after the event. Bede says that the invaders were Angles, Saxons, and Jutes. He reports that the Angles came from eastern Schleswig and settled in what is now Suffolk, Norfolk, Cambridgeshire, Humberside, and northern Yorkshire. The Saxons came from the north German coast between the Elbe and Weser rivers and occupied Essex, Sussex and northern Hampshire. The Jutes, according to Bede, originated in southern Denmark and settled in Kent, the Isle of Wight, and the nearby coast of southern Hampshire. Bede's description, however, is suspiciously tidy, implying a level of planning and organization among the groups of invaders that surely never existed. Probably the immigrants were of mixed origins when they came and continued to intermingle long after they arrived. Further, it is highly likely that, in addition to Angles, Saxons, and Jutes, there were Frisians from the general area of Zuyder Zee.

Whatever the original tribal associations of the invaders, the Celts called them "Saxons"—and to this day *Sassenach* is an uncomplimentary term for the English among the Scots and Irish. However, they were called Angles on the Continent almost from the beginning, their common language was called English, and the Angles of course eventually gave their name to the entire country.

Germanic immigrants continued to pour into England for the rest of the fifth century, and those already there continued to push inland, further invading Celtic territory. Had the Britons been able to maintain Roman organization and discipline, they would have easily been able to repel the invaders, at least in the beginning. The Britons, however, constantly squabbled among themselves and, as a result, were steadily forced back toward the west, southwest, and north of the island. At the beginning of the sixth century, the Britons did manage to unite briefly under the leadership of King Arthur (who was probably not a king at all but rather a general of Romano-British background). They won a great victory around A.D. 500 at Mt. Badon, perhaps located near Bath. Anglo-Saxon military activity and the flood of immigrants halted for the next half century, and some of the Anglo-Saxons even returned to the Continent. The halt was only temporary, however, and, by the middle of the sixth century, Anglo-Saxon pressure on the Britons was again in full force.

Once in control of the best parts of the island, the Anglo-Saxons continued to indulge their warfaring habits by fighting among themselves. Traditionally, there were seven major kingdoms, collectively termed the Heptarchy: (1) Northumberland, extending from southeast Scotland down to the Humber River; (2) East Anglia, including present-day Norfolk and Suffolk; (3) Mercia, including the rest of central England over to Wales; (4) Essex; (5) Kent; (6) Sussex; and (7) Wessex in the southwest over into Devon. This neat division is, however, too simplistic: borders shifted with the rise or decline of petty kings, and there were several minor kingdoms about which little is known. In general, the locus of major power shifted steadily southward during the Anglo-Saxon period. Northumbria dominated in the seventh century, Mercia in the eighth, and Wessex in the ninth and tenth.

By the sixth century, Roman Britain lay in ruins. Public works like roads, bridges, and baths were neglected. Cities and towns decayed and then were abandoned. Peasants, the bulk of the population, clustered in tiny villages surrounded by their fields. At least some Anglo-Saxon kings, on the other hand, managed to amass great wealth and power, as is evidenced by the magnificent seventh-century cenotaph burial of an East Anglian king (probably Rædwald) at Sutton Hoo. The eighth-century Mercian King Offa was sufficiently prominent and confident to be offered a marriage treaty by Charlemagne—and to decline the offer. Offa even had at his disposal a large labor force, which built the 120-mile earthworks known as Offa's Dyke.

The Christianization of England

During the disorder that followed the withdrawal of the Roman legions and the coming of the Anglo-Saxons, Christianity had died out among the Britons. The only religion of the Anglo-Saxons themselves was Germanic paganism. In A.D. 597, Pope Gregory sent a mission under St. Augustine (not to be confused with the earlier St. Augustine, Bishop of Hippo and author of *City of God*) to Kent. Conversion was relatively swift, although backsliding took place occasionally during the early years, and pagan customs and beliefs survived for centuries under the veneer of Christianity. For example, the English names for four of the days of the week are still those of the Germanic divinities Tiw, Wodan, Thor, and Frig; and even the most sacred of Christian holidays, the paschal festival, is named for the Germanic goddess Eastre.

Even as Augustine's mission was proselytizing in southern England, northern England was being converted by missionaries from Ireland. At the time, the Irish church was organized somewhat differently from the Roman church, and over the years of isolation from Rome, the Irish had failed to keep up with changes emanating from Rome, primarily minor points such as the calculation of Easter, appropriate clerical tonsure, and the like. The two branches had no major doctrinal discrepancies, and, for England, their differences were resolved amicably in favor of Rome at a synod held in Yorkshire in 664.

Christianization was an important landmark in the history of the English language because it brought England and English speakers into the only living intellectual community of Europe, that of the Latin Church. England immediately adopted the Latin alphabet, and English was soon being written down extensively. New loanwords from Latin began to appear in English. During the seventh and eighth centuries, the level of Latin scholarship was so high in England that English scholars were in demand on the Continent. Alcuin of York became director of Charlemagne's Palace School.

The Anglo-Saxon church and, consequently, Anglo-Saxon learning declined sharply with the Viking invasions. The Vikings themselves were pagan and had no compunctions about robbing English monasteries, burning books, and killing or dispersing monks. After the Treaty of Wedmore (A.D. 878), King Alfred was able to achieve some revival of intellectual life, but the major rebirth of learning after the Danish invasions did not come until the reign of his grandson Edgar. In the second half of the tenth century, inspired and supported by the ongoing Benedictine Reform on the Continent, three English churchmen—Dunstan (Archbishop of Canterbury), Ethelwold (Bishop of Winchester), and Oswald (Bishop of Worcester and Archbishop of York)—reformed monastic rules, brought in better-educated clergy, had new churches built, established schools, and encouraged the copying of both English and Latin manuscripts.

The Viking Invasions and Their Aftermath

While the English—for they can be termed such by now—were still fighting among themselves, the island was subjected to a new wave of Germanic invaders. These were the Vikings, the terror of all Europe and even the Mediterranean. Their first attack on England was in 787, when a contingent of Danish Vikings landed in Dorsetshire. In 793, the Vikings (or Danes, as the English called them) sacked the wealthy Lindisfarne Priory off the Northumberland coast. England's weak defenses and rich monasteries made it a tempting target for the Danes, who continued to plague the English for another century and came close to taking the country over entirely. Early raids were primarily hit-and-run, but the Danes soon realized that England was a valuable piece of real estate and began settling in previously terrorized and conquered areas.

In 865, a huge Viking army landed in East Anglia, and within five years the Danes controlled most of northeast England and were moving toward Wessex. At last, the ruler of Wessex, King Alfred, managed to beat the Danes soundly at Ashdown in 871 and again at Edington in 878. Under the terms of the subsequent Treaty of Wedmore, Guthrum, the Danish leader, was forced to accept Christianity and to retreat to the Danelaw, a section of northeast England that the English· agreed to recognize as Danish territory in return for a cessation of the incursions into other parts of the island.

King Alfred, certainly among the greatest kings England has ever had, not only held the Danes at bay, but also fortified towns and built the first English navy.

His talents also extended beyond the military. Disturbed by the decline in learning caused by the Viking attacks on monasteries (the only real centers of intellectual activity), Alfred had important Latin texts translated into English, arranged for the compilation of other texts, founded schools, and instituted the *Anglo-Saxon Chronicle*, a log of important events that was kept continuously in some areas of England until well after the Norman Conquest. Fortunately for England, Alfred had competent heirs. His son Edward the Elder was king of Wessex and his daughter Æthelflæd ruled Mercia after her husband died; between the two of them, they kept Danish power in check and further unified the country.

In the early eleventh century, renewed Norse invasions produced more turmoil and ended with the Danish king Cnut on the English throne (1016). Cnut's sons, less able than he, so misgoverned England that power returned to Alfred's line in 1042 in the person of Edward the Confessor. Edward died without a direct heir in 1066. Of the several claimants to the throne, the most important were (a) Edward's brother-in-law Harold Godwineson, whom a group of English lords selected as king; (b) Harold Haardraade, king of Norway; and (c) William, Duke of Normandy, who insisted that Edward had promised him the throne. In 1066, Harold Haardraade landed a huge fleet in Yorkshire; he was killed at Stamford Bridge and Harold Godwineson routed his troops. Two days later, Duke William sailed from Normandy with a large army bound for Essex. Harold Godwineson force-marched his troops 190 miles south to meet William, and the two armies met near Hastings in East Sussex. William had the great advantages of fresh troops and cavalry (Harold had only infantry). After Harold was killed by an arrow through his eye, William won the battle and eventually all of England.

INNER HISTORY

In our discussions of Old English, we use a late variety of West Saxon as a model for all of Old English. This practice is misleading because, first, "classical" West Saxon represents a late stage of Old English, and second, it seems to have been a somewhat artificial literary dialect. Most important, West Saxon is not the direct ancestor of any of the standard dialects of Present-Day English. However, we really have no alternative because the overwhelming majority of surviving OE texts are written in West Saxon.

Old English Phonology

Consonants

Old English (OE) retained all the consonants of Common Germanic, although the distribution of some of them had been altered by sound changes. In addition, sound changes had given Old English three new sounds ([š č j]) that were phonemic by late Old English, if not earlier. In contrast to its vocalic system, the Old English consonant system looks surprisingly modern; Present-Day English still has all the same phonemes, though it has since acquired a few new ones. In Figure 5.1, the boxed consonants are new ones developed between Common Germanic and Old English. All the consonants of PDE except one appeared at least allophonically in OE; the one exception, PDE /ž/, developed late and is still rare in English.

Figure 5.1   Old English Consonants

		Bilabial	**Labio-dental**	**Inter-dental**	**Alveolar**	**Alveo-palatal**	**Velar**
Stops	vl.	p			t		k
	vd.	b			d		g
Affricates	vl.					č	
	vd.					ǰ	
Fricatives			f	θ	s	š	h
Nasals		m			n		
Lateral					l		
Retroflex					r		
Semivowels		w				j	

All the structurally significant changes in consonants between Common Germanic and Old English occurred with the velar consonants /k/ and /g/, both of which were affected by their environments. At first these changes would have been only allophonic, but eventually phonemic fission took place.

Gmc   OE

/k/ > [k] before a consonant or a back vowel: OE *clǣne* 'clean'; *crypel* 'cripple'; *carfulnes* 'anxiety'; *corn* 'grain'; *cū* 'cow'.

> [č] next to a front vowel (unless this front vowel resulted from umlaut; see below): OE *cēap* 'bargain'; *cild* 'child'; *dīc* 'ditch'; *þæc* 'thatch'. This change is the origin of the phoneme /č/ in OE.

/g/ > [g] before consonants, before back vowels, and before front vowels resulting from umlaut: OE *græs* 'grass'; *glǣm* 'gleam'; *gān* 'go'; *gōd* 'good'; *gyltig* 'guilty'.

> [γ] (a voiced velar fricative) between back vowels or after [l] or [r]: OE *sagu* 'saw, saying'; *beorg* 'barrow'; *fylgan* 'follow'.

> [j] before or between front vowels and finally after a front vowel: OE *ġiet* 'yet'; *ġēar* 'year'; *manig* 'many'. This [j] simply merged with the /j/ inherited from IE and Gmc. Therefore IE **jeu-* gave OE *geong* 'young'; but also IE **ghel* gave Gmc **gel-* and OE *gellan* [jɛllan] 'to yell'.

/sk/ > [š] (spelled *sc*) in all environments by late OE; indeed, all occurrences of the cluster /sk/ in PDE are from loanwords. OE examples include *fisc* 'fish'; *wascan* 'wash'; *scearp* 'sharp'.

/gg/ > [ǰ] in medial or final position; OE /ǰ/ did not appear at the beginning of a word or syllable: OE *brycg* 'bridge'; *secg* 'sedge, reed'; *mycg* 'midge'.

The only major difference between the consonant phonemes of OE and of PDE is the lack of *phonemic* voiced fricatives in OE. Voiced fricatives did, however, appear as allophones of their corresponding voiceless fricatives. When the fricative was surrounded by voiced sounds, it became voiced; otherwise, it was voiceless. Doubled fricatives were also voiceless; hence OE *rīsan* [rīzan] 'to rise', but *missan* [missan] 'to miss', *singan* [siŋgan], and *græs* [græs] 'grass'. This voiceless-voiced alternation is still reflected to some extent in the pronunciation of such PDE words as *knife* (OE *cnīf*)/*knives* (OE *cnīfas*) and *path* (OE *pæþ*)/*paths* (OE *pæþas*). Note that there was no corresponding [ž] allophone of OE [š], however.

In Old English, [ŋ] was simply an allophone of /n/ that appeared before /k/ or /g/. It was not to become phonemic until at least late ME; indeed, it is not phonemic for many speakers of English to this day. Old English /r/ was possibly an alveolar trill, but we have no way of knowing for certain.

Old English /h/ deserves some comment because its distribution was much wider in OE than in PDE and it had several allophones not present in PDE. Initially before vowels and the consonants /l r n w/, it was [h] as in PDE (OE *hand* 'hand'; *hlædel* 'ladle'; *hræfn* 'raven'; *hnappian* 'take a nap'; *hwīt* 'white'). After front vowels, it was a palatal fricative [ç]: OE *sihþ* 'sight'. Elsewhere it was the forcefully articulated velar fricative [x]: OE *þurh* 'through'; *hēah* 'high'; *eahta* 'eight'.

The OE consonant system also differed from that of PDE in having phonemically long consonants. In writing they were indicated by doubling the letter; for example, OE *bed* 'prayer'/*bedd* 'bed'; OE *fȳlan* 'to befoul'/*fyllan* 'to fill'. (To get some feeling for the difference between long and short consonants, compare the length of the [m] sound in PDE *home-made* with that of *homey*.)

Finally, Old English had some clusters of consonants that have been lost in PDE. Most noticeable are the clusters with /h/ mentioned above, of which all but /hw/ have lost the /h/ today—and even /hw/ is restricted to certain dialects, though it is still regularly spelled (as in *what, whale, whistle*). We have also lost in pronunciation the OE initial clusters /kn/ and /gn/. Again, the PDE spelling system usually retains them as "silent" letters: OE *cnēow* 'knee'; *gnæt* 'gnat'.

Despite these differences in detail, the consonant system of Old English is remarkably similar to that of PDE. Both have a basic voiced-voiceless opposition shared by three sets of stops; both have four sets of fricatives plus /h/ and two affricates. Both have a single lateral /l/, an /r/, and a series of nasals corresponding in place of articulation to the stops. Both have two phonemic semivowels. To the native speaker of English, this overall system of oppositions may be so familiar that it seems only natural for all human languages. But one does not even have to leave the IE family to find different ways of organizing consonant oppositions. Hindi, for example, has four, not three, stop positions. Chinese has the same three stop positions, but related stops are distinguished by aspiration or lack of aspiration rather than by a voiced-voiceless opposition. In short, the PDE consonant system has remained highly stable for at least the past twelve hundred years. Even the thousands and thousands of loanwords that have entered English since OE times have not affected the basic system; in general, English speakers have adapted non-English consonants in these words by substituting similar English sounds for them.

Vowels

Throughout its history—and prehistory—the vowels of English have been much less stable than its consonants. So many complex changes occurred between Common Germanic and Old English that we will not attempt to cover all of them exhaustively here. With respect to the overall system, the following qualitative changes occurred between CGmc and OE; most of these involve the Gmc diphthongs.

In addition to these general systemic changes, three types of vowel changes conditioned by the environment of the vowel took place prior to the first written records of Old English. Two of these, **breaking** and **back mutation**, had little permanent effect on English and need be dealt with only briefly here. The third, **front mutation**, is of far greater importance to the subsequent history of English.

Breaking (also called **fracture**) involved the development of a glide after certain front vowels and before velarized consonants (/l r h w/). The front vowels affected were /ǽ ĕ ĭ/, though not all these vowels were affected by all the following consonants.[1] Further, different OE dialects varied in the extent to which they showed the effects of breaking. When breaking did occur, the vowels changed as follows:

$$ĭ \quad > \quad \text{ĭo (later} > \text{ĕo)}$$
$$ĕ \quad > \quad \text{ĕo}$$
$$ǽ \quad > \quad \text{ĕa}$$

For example, pre-OE *hǽrd 'hard' became *heard*; *fehtan 'fight' became *feohtan*. Because subsequent sound changes were to eliminate all the diphthongs resulting from breaking, the process is of little significance to the later history of English.

Later, a similar diphthongization of the stressed short vowels /i e æ/ to /io eo ea/ took place when these vowels were followed by a back vowel in the next syllable. For example, earlier *hefon 'heaven' became *heofon*. The extent of this **back mutation** varied greatly from dialect to dialect; it was also influenced by following consonants. Again, because the effects of back mutation were wiped out by later sound changes, we need not concern ourselves with the complex details.

By far the most important and widespread vowel change between Germanic and Old English was **front mutation** (also known as **umlaut** or **i/j mutation**). This change predates written OE and is shared by all West and North Germanic languages. Because the fourth-century Gothic texts show no evidence of it, we assume that it occurred afterward, probably in the sixth century. Under front mutation, if a stressed syllable was followed by an unstressed syllable containing [i] or [j], the vowel of the stressed syllable was fronted or raised; that is, the preceding stressed vowel partially assimilated to the following high front [i] or [j]. Only low front and back vowels and diphthongs were affected.

Figure 5.2 summarizes the effects of front mutation. Note that the examples of words with mutated vowels show no following [i] or [j]. This is because, after

---

[1] A macron (‾) indicates a long vowel and a breve (˘) a short vowel. If no mark appears over a vowel, it is understood that either the vowel is short or that length is not phonemically significant. Both a macron and a breve over a vowel (≚) stand for (a) both the long and the short varieties of the vowel or (b) either the long or the short variety. For example, the notation ū̆ > ȳ̆ means that (long) ū becomes (long) ȳ and (short) ŭ becomes (short) y̆.

Figure 5.2 Front Mutation (Umlaut)

Original Vowel	Resulting Vowel	Nonmutated OE Example	Mutated OE Example
æ	e	-*slægen* 'slain'	-*slege* 'slaying, death'
a + nasal	e	*mann* 'man'	*menn* 'men'
ā	ǣ	*hāl* 'whole'	*hǣlan* 'to heal'
o	e*	Latin *olium* 'oil'	*ele* 'oil'
ō	ē*	*dōm* 'judgment'	*dēman* 'to judge'
u	y	*cuman* 'to come'	*cyme* 'arrival'
ū	ȳ	*mūs* 'mouse'	*mȳs* 'mice'
e	i†	*beran* 'to bear'	*bir(e)þ* 'it bears'
ea	y	*eald* 'old'	*yldra* 'older'
ēa	ȳ	*grēat* 'large'	*grȳtra* 'larger'
eo	y	*feorr* 'far'	*āfyrran* 'to remove'
ēo	ȳ	*bēodan* 'to offer'	*bȳtt* 'it offers'

* The mutation of [o] and [ō] was originally to the midrounded vowels [œ] and [œ̄]. Unrounding to [e] and [ē] soon occurred in West Saxon, and it is this unrounded result that we show here.

† The raising of [e] to [i] occurred earlier, in Common Germanic, but for simplicity's sake, we include it here under the later general front mutation.

front mutation had taken place, the [i] or [j] that had caused it in the first place either dropped out entirely or changed to [e]. If we had to rely on evidence from Old English alone, we would have an effect with no apparent cause. Gothic cognates are helpful here. For example, for OE *dōm/dēman*, the corresponding Gothic forms are *dōms* and *dōmjan*; the [j] that was to cause mutation in the OE verb is still evident.

This change in the phonology of English, regular enough in itself, had drastic effects on the morphology of English. Within a single paradigm, some suffixes might have had [i] or [j] while others did not. Those with [i] or [j] would mutate the root vowel of the words, while forms without the [i] or [j] in the suffix would remain unchanged. Four parts of the OE morphological system were especially affected:

1. One class of OE nouns had had an [i] in the endings of the dative singular and the nominative-accusative plural. The [i] mutated the root vowel, giving rise to oppositions like nom.-acc. sg. *fōt* 'foot'/nom.-acc. pl. *fēt* 'feet'. Today's irregular plurals *men, feet, teeth, geese,* and *lice* all result from mutation; OE had other such mutated plurals that have since been regularized by analogy—for example, *bōc* 'book'/*bēc* 'books', and *fēond* 'foe'/*fȳnd* 'foes'.
2. Some common adjectives had *i*-mutation in their comparative and superlative forms: compare OE *strang* 'strong' with *strengra* 'stronger' and *strengest* 'strongest'. All but one of these adjectives were regularized by PDE; the sole exception is the alternative comparative and superlative *elder* and *eldest* for *old*, which have survived beside the regularized *older* and *oldest* through a differentiation in meaning.
3. Many Germanic weak verbs were formed by adding a formative suffix beginning with [j] or [i] to another part of speech or a form of a strong verb. Again,

mutation gave the resulting new word a different root vowel from that of its etymon. Examples include *settan*, formed from the past sg. *sæt* of the verb *sittan* and giving rise to the PDE opposition *sit/set*. Similarly, the PDE oppositions *to lie/to lay*, *to fall/to fell*, *whole/heal*, and *doom/deem* all result from front mutation.

4. The second- and third-person singular present indicative forms of strong verbs had originally had [i] in their endings; after mutation, these forms had a different root vowel from the rest of the present-tense paradigm. Because any vowel subject to mutation was affected, the alternation was widespread, even though it has been totally regularized by PDE. Old English examples include *cuman* 'to come'/*cymþ* 'he comes'; *feohtan* 'to fight'/*fyht* 'he fights'; *standan* 'to stand'/*stent* 'he stands'.

Because the phonetic quality and phonemic status of several Old English vowels are uncertain, in Figure 5.3 the vowels are listed by their usual spellings, not as phonemic symbols. The diagram in Figure 5.3 represents a fairly late stage of West Saxon.

There is some controversy about the pronunciation of the diphthongs *ĕa* and *ĕo*. Because they are consistently spelled differently from each other and from simple vowels in the manuscripts, most scholars assume that they were separate phonemes and that they were diphthongs. However, because all of them were to fall together with pure vowels in Middle English, the picture is much less than clear. The most widely accepted opinion is that *ĕa* represented [æ̆ə] and *ĕo* represented [ē̆ə].

The OE short vowels *i*, *e*, *o*, and *u* were probably still tense vowels, more like the Continental vowels today than like PDE [ɪ ɛ ɔ ʊ]. We have represented them as such here, but it is possible that they were already laxer than their counterparts in, for example, French or Italian.

Prosody
Although many surviving OE texts are punctuated with marks that apparently indicated "breath-groups" and served as a guide to reading aloud, we have no

Figure 5.3 Old English Vowels

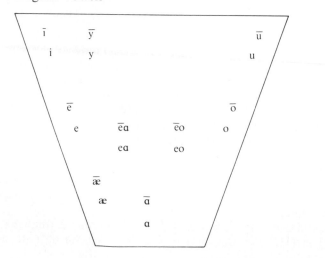

direct evidence of the prosody of OE because stress and pitch have never been indicated systematically in English writing. The differences between the intonation patterns of contemporary London English and Chicago English, for example, show that striking pitch differences are possible between dialects that are mutually intelligible, yet these differences are not revealed in any way in written English.

Stress patterns are, however, at least indirectly recoverable from Old English poetry. Old English inherited the Germanic verse traditions, which were based, not on syllable-counting and rhyme, but on alliteration and a stress-timed line. Alliteration held the line together, and the alliterating syllables took major stress. The number of syllables per line varied, but the time elapsing from one major stress to another was roughly equal. Knowing these facts, we can identify the major stresses in a line of OE verse. When we do so, we find that the stress patterns of OE correspond closely to those of native words in English today. (PDE loanwords from Latin, of course, often do not conform to the stress patterns of native words.) In other words, the root syllable took major stress and subsequent syllables much lighter stress, as in the PDE words *friéndliness*, *líkelihood*, *unwánted*, and *becóming*. Compound words took a major stress on the first element and a secondary stress on the second, again corresponding to PDE patterns like *mánslàughter*, *cándlestìck*, or *grásshòpper* (OE *mánslège*, *cándelstìcca*, *gǽrshòppa*).

Old English Graphics

The Futhorc

Some time shortly after the beginning of the Christian era, probably in the third century A.D., Germanic speakers developed a common alphabet. This alphabet, today called the **futhorc** (after its first six letters) or **runic alphabet** (from OE *rūn* 'mystery, secret'), eventually spread to all Germanic-speaking areas. As Figure 5.4 shows, it was influenced by both the Greek and the Latin alphabets, but had a number of unique signs, especially for sounds absent in Greek or Latin.

The angled forms and lack of curves in all versions of the futhorc suggest that it was designed primarily for scratching or carving on wood or stone, and, indeed, most surviving runic inscriptions are on stone. However, it is possible that it was also used extensively for writing on bark and even leather or cloth, but that these less durable materials have all perished in the damp climate of northern Europe. The fact that our word *book* derives from a Germanic word meaning "beech tree" strongly suggests that wood and/or bark was an important early writing material.

The original futhorc had 24 symbols. As Germanic split into various dialects, each dialect tended to add new signs or abandon older ones to correspond to phonological changes within the dialect. In the different versions of the futhorc used in England, the number of signs or "letters" ranged from 28 to 33.

Surviving runic inscriptions are plentiful in Scandinavia, less common in England. The two best-known English runic inscriptions are those on the Franks Casket, an eighth-century whalebone box, and the Ruthwell Cross, a large stone cross in Dumfriesshire, Scotland, which has in runic writing a portion of the Old English poem "The Dream of the Rood."

Unlike the Latin or Greek alphabets, each character of the runic alphabet was "named" by a noun. All but two of these names, *eolh* and *Ing*, begin with the sound represented by the character. (The sounds that *eolh* and *Ing* represent—[x]

Figure 5.4 The Runic Alphabet (Futhorc)

Rune	Equivalent	Probable Value	Name
ᚠ	f	[f]	*feoh* 'movable property'
ᚢ	u	[u]	*ūr* 'bison, aurochs'
ᚦ	th	[θ]	*þorn* 'thorn'
ᚩ	o	[o]	*ōs* 'god'
ᚱ	r	[r]	*rād* 'road, journey'
ᚳ	c	[k]	*cēn* 'pine (torch)'
ᚷ	g	[g]	*giefu* 'gift'
ᚹ	w	[w]	*wēn* 'hope'
ᚻ	h	[h]	*hagol* 'hail'
ᚾ	n	[n]	*nīed* 'necessity'
ᛁ	i	[i]	*īs* 'ice'
ᛄ	y	[j]	*gēar* 'year'
ᛉ	ēo	[eə]?	*ēoh* 'yew-tree'
ᛈ	p	[p]	*peorþ* 'chessman' (?)
ᛦ	h	[x]	*eolh* 'elk (sedge)' (?)
ᛋ	s	[s]	*sigel* 'sun'
ᛏ	t	[t]	*tīr* 'glory'
ᛒ	b	[b]	*beorc* 'birch'
ᛖ	e	[e]	*eoh* 'war-horse'
ᛗ	m	[m]	*mann* 'person'
ᛚ	l	[l]	*lagu* 'sea'
ᛝ	ng	[ŋ]	*Ing* (name of a god)
ᛟ	œ	[œ]	*ēþel* 'native land'
ᛞ	d	[d]	*dæg* 'day'
ᚪ	a	[ɑ]	*āc* 'oak'
ᚫ	æ	[æ]	*æsc* 'ash'
ᛣ	y	[y]	*ȳr* 'bow' (?)
ᛡ	io	[io]?[iɑ]?	*īor* 'eel' (?)
ᛠ	ea	[æə]	*ēar* 'earth'

and [ŋ]—did not occur at the beginning of a word in Germanic languages.) Figure 5.4 presents the 29-sign version of the English futhorc used in the OE "Runic Poem." This poem has a short stanza of alliterative verse describing each sign, roughly parallel to our children's alphabet books with their "A is for Apple, B is for Boy," but on a much more sophisticated level. Figure 5.4 also gives a transliteration of each symbol into the equivalent English letter or digraph, and the probable phonetic value(s) of each sign; the name of each runic sign and its meaning are also listed. Note that the order of signs in the futhorc differs from that in the Greek or Latin alphabets.

The eleventh stanza of "The Runic Poem" is that for the sign | [i]; the first three words of this stanza are *īs byþ oferceald* 'ice is very cold'. In runic characters, this phrase would be

$$\text{ᛁᛋ ᛒᛦᚦ ᚠᚠᛗᚱᚻᛏᚠᚻ}$$

Although we have written this phrase left-to-right and with spaces between the words, actual runic writing was sometimes right-to-left and either with no spaces between words or with dots separating words.

The Latin Alphabet

With the Christianization of England in the late sixth century, the Latin alphabet was adopted for writing English, and the runic alphabet, never used for longer, continuous texts, was almost—but not quite—abandoned. Despite the associations of the runic alphabet with pagan magic, the clerical scribes apparently felt that Christianity was securely established in England. At least, they themselves occasionally wrote runic signs in their manuscripts. For example, in the manuscript of the poem *Beowulf*, the rune ᛟ is twice used in place of the full word *ēþel* 'native land' (the name of the ᛟ rune is *ēþel*).

Although the well-organized official mission to Christianize England came from Rome, and England eventually followed Roman practices and rituals, Irish missionaries also worked there, especially in the north. As a result, the particular style in which the Latin alphabet was written in England was closer to Irish practice than to Roman. The letter shapes of this so-called Insular alphabet are remarkably close to those we are familiar with today, but a few letters had characteristic features no longer employed. The forms for *f, g, r*, and *s* were ꝼ, ᵹ, ꞃ, and ꞅ, respectively. Two runic characters were also incorporated into the Latin alphabet to represent sounds not occurring in Latin: *thorn* (þ), used for [θ] and [ð]; and *wen* (ƿ), used for [w]. For the sound [æ], the English used the digraph æ. In addition to thorn, a "crossed d" (ð), called *eth*, was also used to represent [θ] and [ð].

The Latin characters *q, x,* and *z* were known but were used infrequently. The character *c* was used to represent [k] in most words, although *k* was also used (*cyning* or *kyning* 'king'). In earlier OE, *y* represented the front rounded high vowel [y], but as [y] unrounded in the various dialects, *y* came to be interchangeable with *i* and *ie*. Old English [ǰ] was spelled *cg*; [š] was spelled *sc*. The character *c* represented either [k] or [č], and *g* stood for [g], [γ], or [j]. Therefore, even in its early stages, the English writing system never met the criterion for an ideal alphabetic system with one and only one unique character for each phoneme of the language.

Spelling and Punctuation

Though it is not inaccurate to say that classical Old English had a standardized spelling, the spelling of all manuscripts—or any one manuscript—was not absolutely consistent. In general, the later the manuscript, the less consistent the spelling. Most of the inconsistencies are due to changes in the language itself. For example, early OE distinguished the sounds represented by *y* and *ie*, but late OE did not. Consequently, later manuscripts interchange *y* and *ie* in the same word. Then, as [y] unrounded to [i] in some dialects, the letter *y* came to be virtually interchangeable with the letter *i*. For example, the word "shield" could be spelled *scield*, *scild*, or *scyld*, even within the same manuscript.

By late Old English, the vowels of unstressed inflectional endings had all been reduced to [ə]. The scribes themselves no longer perceived a difference in what had once been unstressed *-a*, *-e*, *-o*, and *-u*, so, if they had not learned the traditional spelling for a form, they often spelled all endings with the same vowel letter—most often *e*, but sometimes *o* or *u*. By very late Old English, unstressed final *-m* and final *-n* are also often confused, the tendency being to spell both as *-n*. Probably both *-n* and *-m* had been lost as full consonants in this position, their remaining traces being only nasalization of the preceding vowel.

Except for [h x j ɣ], most other consonants, especially those in stressed positions, had consistent spellings throughout the Old English period, and the distinction between long and short consonants was in general well preserved in the spelling. Certainly, Old English spelling is a model of consistency compared to the chaotic state of Middle English spelling. However, this consistency is somewhat misleading because most surviving manuscripts are in the West Saxon dialect, whereas the dialectal distribution of ME manuscripts is much wider.

Modern editions of Old English works designed for students usually normalize the spelling for the sake of convenience. In addition, many editions distinguish long from short vowels by placing a macron over long vowels. Old English scribes never distinguished vowel length this way. Though OE scribes often placed a kind of macron over vowels, this seems to have been intended to indicate stress in reading aloud, not vowel length.

By modern standards, punctuation in Old English manuscripts was scanty. The most important mark of punctuation was the raised point (a dot); it represented a pause, but did not correspond to PDE conventions for either the comma or the period. In later Old English, a semicolon and an inverted semicolon called a *punctus elevatus* were employed to indicate pauses.

The modern distinction between capital and lowercase letters did not exist; essentially, there was only one form for most letters. Larger versions could be used for emphasis, especially at the beginning of a new section of text or "chapter." (The words *capital* and *chapter* are cognates, both meaning "head.")

An Illustration of Old English Graphics

Reproduced below are the last five lines from a manuscript page of the Old English poem *Judith*, a late OE poem probably composed in the tenth century. It appears in the same manuscript as the much more famous poem *Beowulf*; the manuscript itself was copied about 1000. This passage includes all the regularly used characters of the classical OE alphabet. A transliteration into the modern English alphabet and a word-for-word gloss of the passage appears below each word.

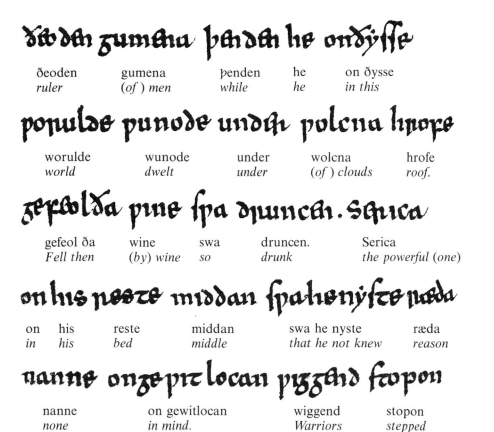

ðeoden	gumena	þenden	he	on ðysse
ruler	*(of) men*	*while*	*he*	*in this*

worulde	wunode	under	wolcna	hrofe
world	*dwelt*	*under*	*(of) clouds*	*roof.*

gefeol ða	wine	swa	druncen.	Serica
Fell then	*(by) wine*	*so*	*drunk*	*the powerful (one)*

on	his	reste	middan	swa he nyste	ræda
in	*his*	*bed*	*middle*	*that he not knew*	*reason*

nanne	on gewitlocan	wiggend	stopon
none	*in mind.*	*Warriors*	*stepped*

In general, the letters here are clearly written—English handwriting has been deteriorating ever since Old English times. A point (period) is used as punctuation in the third line, although we probably would not use a period there in PDE. In the first and last lines, the preposition *on* is written together with the following word; in the third line, the adverb *ða* is not separated from the preceding verb; and in the fourth line, the conjunction *swa*, the pronoun *he*, and the verb *nyste* are all written as one unit.

Old English Morphology

Inflections

Throughout its history—and even prehistory—English has undergone a steady decrease in its inflectional affixes. Apart from the personal pronouns, Present-Day English has only two noun inflections (possessive and plural) and four verb inflections (third-person singular present indicative, past tense, past participle, and present participle). Some linguists also consider the comparative *-er* and superlative *-est* inflections; even including them, PDE has a total of only eight inflectional endings.

Present-Day English Inflections

Noun		parrot	mouse	
Plural		parrots	mice	
Possessive	Sg.	parrot's	mouse's	
	Pl.	parrots'	mice's	
Verb		listen	sing	
3d person sg. pres. ind.		listens	sings	
Past		listened	sang	
Past participle		listened	sung	
Present participle		listening	singing	
Adjective or Adverb		fat	soon	good
Comparative		fatter	sooner	better
Superlative		fattest	soonest	best

Compared to PDE, OE looks wealthy in its inflections, but this wealth is only relative. Beside the inflectional system of classical Greek or Latin, the OE system seems meager. Further, the OE system had a number of inherent weaknesses that would contribute to its ultimate loss. First, almost no paradigm contained the maximum amount of differentiation, and some paradigms had so few distinctions as to make the entire inflectional group virtually useless in distinguishing function within the sentence. For example, the definite adjective declension theoretically could have had 30 distinct endings (3 genders × 2 numbers × 5 cases). Only 5 distinct endings appear; the ending *-an* alone fills 17 of the 30 possible slots.

A second weakness of the OE inflectional system resulted from phonology. Heavy stress on root syllables and light stress on succeeding syllables meant that all the vowels of inflections would tend to be reduced to [ə] and that most final nasals [n] and [m] would first merge as [n], then drop off while nasalizing the preceding vowel, and finally be lost without a trace. A third contributing factor to—though not necessarily a cause of—the loss of inflections is the fact that, by OE times, the language had already developed relatively fixed word orders that indicated the function of words within a clause. Thus, syntax provided a kind of backup system for assuring intelligibility when inflections were lost—but it also made the inflections less necessary. A final contributing factor to the loss of inflections in English after the Old English period is less easy to demonstrate but nonetheless important. This was the necessity of adapting hundreds and even thousands of loanwords from two other inflecting languages—Old Norse and French—into English. The simplest solution was just to leave off inflections entirely, a procedure that had already been used to some extent with Latin words in Old English.

For the basis of our discussion here, we use Late West Saxon, primarily because the bulk of surviving OE manuscripts are written in this dialect. However, OE underwent many changes between 450 and 1100. Further, West Saxon was only one of several dialects in Old English and is not even the direct ancestor of any of the contemporary major standard English dialects in England, the United States, Canada, Australia, or elsewhere. Finally, even within Late West Saxon manuscripts, often even within one manuscript copied by a single scribe, variants occur. Therefore the forms listed below are more an idealized representation than a description of the actual forms in use, even in a given place at a given time.

The discussion below is organized according to the traditional parts of speech (nouns, adjectives, pronouns, verbs, and other classes). It is a less than totally satisfactory way of describing PDE, and it is no more satisfactory for OE. Fortunately, the areas of fuzziness for OE and for PDE are much the same—the problem of distinguishing adverbs and prepositions, the highly miscellaneous nature of items called adverbs, the borderline between nonfinite verbs and adjectives, and so on. Hence, in understanding the vagaries of OE, our intuition as native speakers of PDE can usually take over when logic fails. Old English is, after all, still English.

Inflections in languages can appear in three positions: initial (prefixes), internal (infixes), and final (suffixes). Old English inflections, like PDE inflections, consisted primarily of suffixes. There was less but still significant use of infixes (vowel changes), and no use of inflectional prefixes, though there were of course derivational prefixes that changed the meaning of words.[2]

Nouns

Old English nouns were inflected for three genders (masculine, feminine, and neuter), four cases (nominative, accusative, genitive, and dative), and two numbers (singular and plural).

The gender of nouns was grammatical, not natural or biological as in PDE. That is, gender did not, except accidentally, correspond to the actual sex of the referent. Instead, the inherent gender of the word determined certain of its endings and the forms of its modifiers and pronoun substitutes. For example, the OE words for both "woman" (*wīf*) and "child" (*cild*) were neuter. OE *wīfmann*, also meaning "woman," was masculine, and *hlǣfdige* 'lady' was feminine. Proportionally, almost half of OE nouns were masculine, about one-third were feminine, and the rest were neuter.

AN UNPOPULAR PEDAGOGUE

The first university course in Old English (Anglo-Saxon) was introduced in 1825 at the then newly opened University of Virginia; it had been included in the curriculum at the urging of Thomas Jefferson. The only English course offered at the University, it was taught by a Dr. Georg Blaettermann of Leipzig, who also taught French, German, Spanish, and Italian. Dr. Blaettermann was not popular with his students, who rioted on several occasions and once even pelted him with shot during a lecture. Their petitions for his dismissal were not successful, but he was finally removed from the university in 1840 for horsewhipping his wife in public.

Information taken from Stanley R. Hauer, "Thomas Jefferson and the Anglo-Saxon Language," *PMLA*, XCVIII: 5 (Oct. 1983), p. 891.

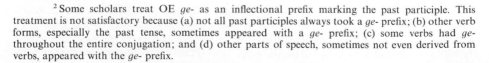

---

[2] Some scholars treat OE *ge-* as an inflectional prefix marking the past participle. This treatment is not satisfactory because (a) not all past participles always took a *ge-* prefix; (b) other verb forms, especially the past tense, sometimes appeared with a *ge-* prefix; (c) some verbs had *ge-* throughout the entire conjugation; and (d) other parts of speech, sometimes not even derived from verbs, appeared with the *ge-* prefix.

Despite the fact that grammatical gender prevailed, there were weaknesses in the system and, even as early as OE, signs of its eventual decline. First, there was heavy overlapping of endings, especially in (a) masculine and neuter nouns, (b) the genitive and dative plural of all nouns, and (c) all weak nouns. Second, only for a few words could the gender be determined by the form of the nominative singular. All agentive nouns ending in -*a* were masculine (*hunta* 'hunter'), and all abstract nouns ending in -*nes* were feminine (*glædnes* 'joy'); but for most words, the nominative singular provided no clue as to gender. Examples include masculine *gāst* 'spirit'; feminine *rest* 'rest, sleep'; and neuter *dūst* 'dust'.

Signs of deterioration of grammatical gender in OE include the use of biological gender to determine pronoun substitutes. The personal pronoun for *wīf* (neuter) was normally *hēo* 'she' and not *hit* 'it'. That native speakers of OE were not themselves always sure of the correct gender is evidenced by the fact that many OE nouns are recorded with two different genders, and a few with all three: *gyrn* 'sorrow' is both masculine and neuter; *sunbēam* 'sunbeam' is both masculine and feminine; *sūsl* 'misery' is both neuter and feminine; and *wēsten* 'wilderness' may be masculine, feminine, or neuter.

Although the instrumental case survived marginally in adjectives and pronouns in OE, it had coalesced completely with the dative in nouns. Therefore, OE nouns had only four cases. Like the gender system, the OE case system had weaknesses that would contribute to its eventual loss. The accusative was particularly feeble, always identical to the nominative in the plural, but also in the singular for many classes of nouns. All the oblique (nonnominative) cases of weak nouns except for the neuter singular accusative were identical in the singular, and the neuter accusative singular was the same as the nominative singular.

Except for the nominative-accusative of weak nouns (only about 10 percent of all OE nouns), the singular-plural distinction is well preserved in OE—and of course is still strong in PDE. Indeed, the number distinction in English has managed to accommodate and preserve, at least for educated speakers, rather a large number of irregular plurals borrowed from other languages (*crisis/crises*; *fungus/fungi*; *stratum/strata*, and so on).

In addition to being inflected for gender, case, and number, each OE noun belonged to one of several different classes. By far the most important of these classes in terms of number of members are the vocalic -*a* stem masculine and neuter nouns, the corresponding vocalic -*o* stem feminine nouns, and the consonantal -*an* declension. The -*a* and -*o* declensions are also often called "strong" nouns; the -*an* declensions are called "weak" nouns. (These labels are not especially satisfactory because they describe a pre-OE stage that was no longer apparent by OE times. Nevertheless, because they are the traditional terms, we use them here.)

Figure 5.5 gives the entire declension for -*a* and -*o* stem nouns and for -*an* nouns. The numerous minor declensions are not listed; even in OE times, they tended to overlap with and gravitate toward the larger declensional classes. The declension of nouns with mutated plurals is, however, included. Although this class was small even in OE, a number of mutated plurals have survived to the present day, partly because these nouns were so familiar and so frequently used.

Note that the OE masculine nominative-accusative -*a* stem plural (-*as*) has generalized to all regular plurals in PDE, and that the masculine-neuter genitive singular -*es* has generalized to all possessives, singular and plural. To put it another way, all the noun declensions ending in -*s* have survived and extended their domain, while almost all the other OE inflectional endings of nouns have been lost.

Figure 5.5 OE Noun Declensions

		-*a* stems			-*o* stems (fem.)	
	Case	*Masc.* 'boat'	*Neut. (long)** 'people'	*Neut. (short)** 'ship'	*short** 'grief'	*long** 'bridge'
Sg.	N	bāt	folc	scip	cearu	brycg
	A	bāt	folc	scip	ceare	brycge
	G	bātes	folces	scipes	ceare	brycge
	D	bāte	folce	scipe	ceare	brycge
Pl.	NA	bātas	folc	scipu	ceara	brycga
	G	bāta	folca	scipa	ceara	brycga
	D	bātum	folcum	scipum	cearum	brycgum

		-*an* declension			Mutated plurals	
	Case	*Masc.* 'name'	*Neut.* 'eye'	*Fem.* 'earth'	*Masc.* 'tooth'	*Fem.* 'louse'
Sg.	N	nama	eage	eorþe	tōþ	lūs
	A	naman	eage	eorþan	tōþ	lūs
	G	naman	eagan	eorþan	tōþes	lūse, lȳs
	D	naman	eagan	eorþan	tēþ	lȳs
Pl.	NA	naman	eagan	eorþan	tēþ	lȳs
	G	namena	eagena	eorþena	tōþa	lūsa
	D	namum	eagum	eorþum	tōþum	lūsum

* A long syllable has a long vowel or ends in a long consonant or consonant cluster. Thus *folc* is long because it ends in [lk], and *scip* is short because its vowel is short and it ends in a single consonant. *Brycg* is a long syllable because *cg* counts as a long consonant.

OE *cildru* 'children' belonged to a very small minor class of neuter nouns having a plural in -*ru*; the [r] has survived in PDE, but an additional weak -*n* plural has been added, giving PDE *children* a double plural. PDE *oxen* retains its weak plural but has lost its mutated vowel (OE *oxa*, pl. *exen*). Finally, OE *broþor* 'brother' had an unmarked nominative-accusative plural (*broþor*), but has since developed an alternative mutated weak plural (*brethren*) in addition to its PDE regular plural *brothers*.

The unmarked plural of OE long neuter -*a* stems has not only been preserved in some of the words in which it occurred in OE, but has actually extended its domain to some words that had other kinds of plurals in OE. *Folk* has an uninflected plural in some usages and regularly in compounds (*kinfolk, menfolk*). The unmarked plurals of *sheep* and *deer* reflect the OE plurals *scēap* and *dēor*, and the category has been extended to other kinds of nouns referring to game animals. For example, though *fish* and *elk* today have unmarked plurals, OE *fisc* 'fish' and *eolh* 'elk' were both masculine nouns with plurals in -*as*. PDE *moose* is not even a native word, but a loanword from Algonquian; it also follows the unmarked plural pattern of *sheep*.

Figure 5.6 OE Adjective Declensions

	Case	Indefinite (Strong)			Definite (Weak)		
		Masc.	*Neut.*	*Fem.*	*Masc.*	*Neut.*	*Fem.*
Sg.	N	blind	blind	blind*	blinda	blinde	blinde
	A	blindne	blind	blinde	blindan	blinde	blindan
	G	blindes	blindes	blindre	blindan	blindan	blindan
	D	blindum	blindum	blindre	blindan	blindan	blindan
	I	blinde	blinde	blindre	blindan	blindan	blindan
Pl.	NA	blinde	blind*	blinda(-e)	blindan	blindan	blindan
	G	blindra	blindra	blindra	blindra*	blindra*	blindra*
	D	blindum	blindum	blindum	blindum	blindum	blindum

* Adjectives with a short root syllable differ only in having a final *-u* in the feminine nominative singular and the neuter nominative-accusative plural. The genitive plural of the definite declension had an alternative ending in *-ena* (instead of *-ra*).

Adjectives

The adjective was the most highly inflected of any Old English part of speech. Like the noun, it was marked for gender, case, and number—all determined by the noun or pronoun that the adjective modified. Adjectives also could take comparative and superlative endings. Finally, OE preserved the Germanic innovation of two separate "weak" and "strong" declensions for each adjective.

As Figure 5.6 shows, OE adjective declensions were not identical to those of nouns. Rather, they shared characteristics of both noun and pronoun declensions.

Old English adjectives had no phrasal comparative parallel to PDE *more* and *most*. Regardless of the number of syllables in the stem, the comparative ended in *-ra* and the superlative in either *-ost(a)* or *-(e)st(a)*. A few adjectives had totally irregular comparatives and superlatives, all of which have remained irregular to the present day (the words for "good," "a little," "much," and "bad"). A number of common adjectives had *i*-mutation in the comparative and superlative forms (such as *strang* 'strong', *strengra*, *strengest*). Of them, only *elder*, the alternative comparative of *old* in PDE, has survived (OE *eald*, *yldra*, *yldest*).

The "weak" or definite declension of an adjective was used when the noun it modified was accompanied by a demonstrative ("this, that"), an ordinal numeral, or a possessive pronoun. Otherwise, the "strong" or indefinite declension was used. OE had no indefinite article at all and no definite article separate from the demonstrative for "that," but these definite and indefinite declensions served, to some extent, a similar function. The definite endings helped to particularize the noun being modified (*þæt gōde scip* 'the good ship'), whereas the indefinite endings indicated that no specific member of a class was meant (*gōd scip* 'a good ship').

In PDE, we frequently use a noun as a modifier of another noun without changing its form (*army knife*, *state court*), but only under highly restricted circumstances can we use an adjective for a noun without changing the form of the adjective. In OE, the situation was reversed. Today we can say *law book* but not **to the bloody*; OE could say *to þæm blodigan* 'to the bloody (one)' but not **lagu boc*. OE either had to make a compound noun or to decline the modifying noun in some

Figure 5.7 OE Personal Pronouns

First Person	Singular	Dual	Plural
N	ic	wit	wē
A	mē, mec	unc	ūs
G	mīn	uncer	ūre
D	mē	unc	ūs

Second Person	Singular	Dual	Plural
N	þū	git	gē
A	þē, þec	inc	ēow, ēowic
G	þīn	incer	ēower
D	þē	inc	eow

Third Person	Masc.	Fem.	Neut.	Plural
N	hē	hēo	hit	hīe
A	hine	hīe	hit	hīe
G	his	hiere	his	hiera
D	him	hiere	him	him

way, such as *laga boc* 'a book of laws', where the modifying noun is in the genitive plural.

Pronouns

PERSONAL PRONOUNS

Of all the word classes of English today, by far the most conservative are the personal pronouns. Only the personal pronouns have retained three cases (subject, object, and possessive; corresponding to OE nominative, accusative-dative, and genitive). Indeed, as an examination of Figure 5.7 will reveal, Present-Day English has lost only three of the inflectional distinctions made in OE. The first distinction, between dative and accusative, was collapsing even in OE, where it was clearly and consistently retained only in the third person. Also in PDE—but not until PDE—the distinction between singular and plural in the second person has been neutralized everywhere except in the reflexive and intensive pronoun (*yourself/ yourselves*). Finally, PDE has lost the category of dual. Here again, the category existed only in the first and second person in OE. Further, it was not an obligatory category even then.[3] In most OE texts, the regular plural (*we, us,* and so on) is used to refer to the speaker and one other person, and the dual (*wit*) is used primarily to emphasize the "twoness" of the situation.

As Figure 5.7 shows, gender distinctions in OE pronouns are preserved only in the third-person singular, as in PDE. All of the surviving OE pronouns are

---

[3] Traces of a once much more extensive dual system survive in such English words as *both, either, or, neither, nor,* and *whether.* Further, the semantic reality of "dualness" is reflected in a number of PDE nouns that refer to single objects but that have grammatically only plural forms: *trousers, shorts, eyeglasses, shears, suspenders, pliers,* and the like.

recognizable today. The PDE third-person plural pronouns in *th-* are ME borrowings from Old Norse. PDE *she* is not a regular development of OE *hēo*; the precise origin of *she* is uncertain.

In some ways, PDE actually has a more complex pronominal system than OE. We have distinct forms for possessive adjectives and possessive pronouns (*my/mine*; *their/theirs*, and so on). In OE, the genitive forms served as both adjective and pronoun. Further, OE had no separate reflexive pronouns. Instead, either the dative or the accusative forms of the regular personal pronouns were used to express reflexivity, a practice that still survives in some PDE dialects ("I got *me* a big stick"). OE did have the word *self*, but it was an intensifying pronoun, not a reflexive.

Figure 5.7 shows only one spelling for each of the OE personal pronouns. Some of them, such as *hē, his, him, wē*, and *mē*, are almost always spelled the same way in all manuscripts. Others, however, have several variant spellings; for example, *hiera* 'of them' may appear as *hira, heora, heara*, and so on.

DEMONSTRATIVE PRONOUNS
Unlike PDE, OE had no separate definite article. Instead, the pronoun/adjective corresponding to PDE *that* served not only as a demonstrative, but also as a marker of "definiteness," although it was frequently not employed where PDE would require a definite article and, conversely, was sometimes employed where PDE would not use an article or demonstrative. The OE demonstrative was fully declined for four cases (plus a separate masculine-neuter singular form for the instrumental case), two numbers, and three genders in the singular. All these forms have, of course, merged in PDE to one singular *that*, derived from the OE neuter nominative-accusative, and a somewhat irregularly derived plural *those*. None of the many OE forms is the ancestor of our definite article *the*.

As Figure 5.8 shows, OE also had a demonstrative corresponding to PDE *this*. In origin an emphatic pronoun, it often served an emphatic function in OE, but also was used in roughly the same way as it is in PDE to indicate nearness to the speaker. Again, PDE preserves only the singular *this*, based on the OE neuter singular nominative-accusative, and the plural *these*, an irregular development not based on any of the OE plural forms.

INTERROGATIVE PRONOUNS
Figure 5.9 shows that the OE interrogative pronoun had already lost any number distinction and had collapsed the three-way gender distinction into two, "human"

Figure 5.8 OE Demonstrative Pronouns

	"that, the"				"this"			
Case	Masc.	Neut.	Fem.	Plur.	Masc.	Neut.	Fem.	Plur.
N	se	þæt	sēo	þā	þes	þis	þēos	þās
A	þone	þæt	þā	þā	þisne	þis	þās	þās
G	þæs	þæs	þære	þāra	þisses	þisses	þisse	þissa
D	þǣm	þǣm	þære	þǣm	þissum	þissum	þisse	þissum
I	þȳ, þon	þȳ, þon	þære	þǣm	þȳs	þȳs	þisse	þissum

Figure 5.9 OE Interrogative Pronouns (singular only)

Case	Masculine-Feminine	Neuter
Nom.	hwā	hwæt
Acc.	hwone	hwæt
Gen.	hwæs	hwæs
Dat.	hwǣm	hwǣm
Inst.	hwǣm, hwȳ	hwȳ

versus "nonhuman." Of the six different forms in OE, all but the accusative *hwone* have survived, with some irregularities in development, in PDE *who, what, whose, whom,* and the adverbial *why* (based on the OE instrumental form).

OTHER PRONOUNS

Old English had no relative pronoun as such. Instead, it (a) used much less subordination than written PDE, (b) used an indeclinable particle *þe* as a relative, (c) occasionally used the personal pronouns alone as relatives, or (d) combined the personal pronouns with the particle *þe*.

Old English had a full range of indefinite pronoun/adjectives, which are the direct ancestors of the PDE indefinite pronouns. A few examples are OE *ǣlc* 'each', *hwilc* 'which', *ǣnig* 'any', *eall* 'all', *nān* 'none', and *swilc* 'such'. OE *sum* 'some' often served as a kind of indefinite article, corresponding roughly to the PDE unstressed use of *some* in such sentences as "Some man came by to see you today." OE *man* was a useful indefinite pronoun that has since been lost from the language. It corresponded in meaning to PDE *one* but was not restricted to formal styles. Most indefinite pronouns took the indefinite adjective declension; some were invariable in form.

Verbs

PDE verbs are normally classified into two broad groups, regular and irregular. Regular verbs form their past tense and past participle without a change in the root vowel, by adding /d/, /t/, or /əd/ in both the past tense and the past participle (*-d* or *-ed* in writing). This rough-and-ready bipartite classification is not suitable for Old English, where many of the verbs treated as irregular today were actually regular. Old English had three major types of verb conjugation: strong, weak, and other. The terms "strong" and "weak" are traditional and should not be understood as implying a value judgment.

STRONG VERBS

Old English had seven subclasses of strong verbs, varying in membership from a handful of common verbs (Class 4) to scores of verbs. All seven classes had in common the indication of past tense and past participle by a change in the stem-vowel (or ablaut; see p. 58). The first five classes had originally all had the same vowels, but different environments had altered these vowels in different ways. Class 6 verbs had had a different set of stem vowels. Class 7 verbs originally did not even belong to the ablaut series, but had been "reduplicating verbs" in IE, verbs that

Figure 5.10   OE Strong Verb Classes

Ablaut Series	Infinitive	3d sg. pres.	3d sg. pret.	Plur. pret.	Past part.
Class 1 ī-ā-i-i	scīnan 'shine'	scīnþ	scān	scinon	(ge)scinen
Class 2 ēo-ēa-u-o	smēocan 'smoke'	smycþ	smēac	smucon	(ge)smocen
Class 3 i-a-u-u	singan 'sing'	singþ	sang	sungon	(ge)sungen
Class 4 e-æ-ǣ-o	stelan 'steal'	stilþ	stæl	stǣlon	(ge)stolen
Class 5 e-æ-ǣ-e	sprecan 'speak'	spricþ	spræc	sprǣcon	(ge)sprecen
Class 6 a-ō-ō-a	scacan 'shake'	scæcþ	scōc	scōcon	(ge)scacen
Class 7 V₁-ēo-ēo-V₁ V₁-ē-ē-V₁	sāwan 'sow' slǣpan 'sleep'	sǣwþ slǣpþ	sēow slēp	sēowon slēpon	(ge)sāwen (ge)slǣpen

formed their past tense by repeating the root syllable. By OE, the reduplication had been lost, and the class had merged with the ablaut verbs.

Strong verbs in OE had four principal parts—infinitive, past singular, past plural, and past participle, each part defined by characteristic stem vowels. From these four parts, all other forms could be predicted. As Figure 5.10 illustrates for Classes 2, 4, 5, 6, and 7, the stem vowel of the second- and third-person present indicative regularly underwent mutation because of an earlier [i] in the personal endings.

Of the three hundred or so strong verbs in OE, many have been totally lost by PDE (such as *þēon* 'to prosper'; *(ge)limpan* 'to happen'; *þicgan* 'to receive'). Many more have become weak verbs (*scūfan* 'to shove'; *murnan* 'to mourn'; *wascan* 'to wash'). Still others have changed class membership or developed irregularly. For all surviving strong verbs, the number of principal parts has been reduced from four to three as the distinction between singular and plural has been lost in the preterite.

The fate of the eight verbs illustrated in Figure 5.10 mirrors the general pattern of change in strong verbs between OE and PDE. Class 1 *scīnan* has held up fairly well, although the vowel of the past participle has generalized to that of the preterite singular; if the development had been absolutely regular, we would have *shine, shone, shin* today. Class 2 *smēocan* has become a weak verb. Class 3 *singan* is well preserved; in fact, of all the OE strong verb classes, Class 3 has kept its identity the best and has the largest representation in PDE. Among surviving Class 3 verbs in PDE are *begin, bind, cling, drink, find; grind, run, sing, spring, stink, swell, swim,* and *swing.* Class 4 *stelan* also remains strong, though it has generalized the past participle vowel to the past tense. Class 5 *sprecan* has been lost entirely, giving way to an OE alternative *specan.* Class 6 *scacan* has developed completely regularly. Class 7 *sāwan* has become weak in the past tense (*sowed*) and today has an alternative weak past participle (*sowed* or *sown*). The other Class 7 verb illustrated in Figure 5.10, *slǣpan,* has become a weak verb. The differing vowels in the infinitive and past result from a Middle English sound change; the fact that /t/ is added to form the past tenses is evidence of its move to the class of weak verbs.

Despite the great attrition among OE strong verbs over the years, the category has resisted total annihilation, primarily because so many of the verbs are common ones, learned early and used frequently. Indeed, English has occasionally even added to the category. For example, OE *werian* 'to wear' and *hringan* 'to ring' were both weak in OE but have since become strong. Even a few borrowed verbs have entered English as strong verbs. For example, *dig* and *strive* came from Old French. *Fling, get,* and *take* from Scandinavian and *sling* from either Scandinavian or Low German were probably all strong verbs in their original languages, so it is less surprising that they appear as strong verbs in English.

WEAK VERBS

In terms of sheer numbers, there were far more weak verbs than strong verbs in OE. These weak verbs, descendants of the Germanic innovation of the dental preterite, were eventually to become the "regular" verbs of English. OE had several subtypes of weak verbs, depending on the length of the stem syllable and the presence or absence of -*i*- in the infinitive. As Figure 5.11 shows, the subtypes varied slightly in their personal endings, but all shared the /d/ or /t/ in the past tense and past participle. A few OE weak verbs had *i*-mutation in the infinitive but not in the past or past participle, and several of them survive as irregular verbs today (*sell, tell, buy*). Note that, despite the different vowels in the past tense, they are weak verbs because they have the dental preterite.

OTHER VERBS

Some of the most common verbs of OE did not fit neatly into either the strong or the weak classification. Most irregular of all, as it still is today, was the verb "to be." An amalgam of several roots, OE "to be" had two different present stems, one based on the infinitive *wesan* and the other on the infinitive *bēon*. Also anomalous were *dōn* 'do', *willan* 'want, wish', and *gān* 'go'.

Of particular interest are the OE **preterite-present verbs**, so called because the original present had fallen into disuse and the original strong (ablaut) preterite had taken on present meaning. A new weak (dental) preterite then developed to replace the earlier one that was now a present. Some of these preterite-present verbs were *sculan* 'have to,' *cunnan* 'know,' *magan* 'be able,' *ic dearr* 'I dare,' *āgan* 'have, own,' and *þurfan* 'need.' A number of these verbs have since been lost, but the PDE modal auxiliaries *shall, can, may, dare, must,* and *ought* are all descendants of OE preterite-presents, although most have undergone semantic change. Note that, in PDE, the OE weak past tenses *should, could, might, must,* and *ought* have all once again acquired present-tense meanings, so much so that, to express the notion of past with them, we normally have to use a perfect instead of a single past tense. That is, we cannot say "Yesterday I should go"; instead we have to say "Yesterday I should have gone."

Figure 5.11 presents the complete conjugation of an OE strong verb, three varieties of weak verbs, and the verb "to be." As Figure 5.11 shows, the inflectional endings for strong and weak verbs were similar, especially in the present tense. All OE verbs were inflected for tense, person, number, and mood, but *not* for voice; the inflected passive had been lost by the time of the first OE records, and a phrasal passive similar to that of PDE was used instead.

Figure 5.11 OE Verb Conjugations

		Strong	Wk Ia	Wk Ib	Wk II	"to be"	
Infinitive		clēofan 'cleave'	fremman 'do'	bærnan 'burn'	lōcian 'look'	wesan	bēon
Present Tense							
Indicative	Sg. 1	clēofe	fremme	bærne	lōcie	eom	bēo
	2	clȳfst	fremest	bærnst	lōcast	eart	bist
	3	clȳfþ	fremeþ	bærnþ	lōcaþ	is	biþ
	Pl.	clēofaþ	fremmaþ	bærnaþ	lōciaþ	sind(on)	bēoþ
Subjunctive	Sg.	clēofe	fremme	bærne	lōcie	sȳ	bēo
	Pl.	clēofen	fremmen	bærnen	lōcien	sȳn	bēon
Imperative	Sg. 2	clēof	freme	bærn	lōca	wes	bēo
	Pl. 2	clēofaþ	fremmaþ	bærnaþ	lōciaþ	wesaþ	bēoþ
Present Participle		clēofende	fremmende	bærnende	lōciende	wesende	bēonde
Preterite Tense							
Indicative	Sg. 1, 3	clēaf	fremede	bærnde	lōcode	wæs	
	Sg. 2	clufe	fremedest	bærndest	lōcodest	wēre	
	Pl.	clufon	fremedon	bærndon	lōcodon	wēron	
Subjunctive	Sg.	clufe	fremede	bærnde	lōcode	wēre	
	Pl.	clufen	fremeden	bærnden	lōcoden	wēren	
Past Participle		-clofen	-fremed	-bærned	-lōcod	-bēon	

OE verbs were inflected for only two tenses, present and preterite. There was no future conjugation; rather, the present was used to express future time, with adverbs added to avoid ambiguity. However, by late OE, *sculan* and *willan* often carried some sense of future time in addition to their basic meanings of obligation and desire. There was no systematically used progressive tense as we know it today. Old English did witness the beginnings of the phrasal perfect tense, using either "have" or "be" as the auxiliary with the past participle. Compound phrasal tenses like PDE future perfect passive "They will have been seen" simply did not exist.

OE infinitives were not preceded by "to"; the *-an* suffix was adequate to identify them as infinitives. Past participles normally—but not always—had a *ge-* prefix.

Uninflected Word Classes
In addition to the inflected word classes of nouns, adjectives, pronouns, and verbs, OE had other, uninflected categories of words, including prepositions, conjunctions, adverbs, and interjections.

PREPOSITIONS

Because the case endings of OE made many syntactic relations clear, the language needed fewer prepositions than are used in PDE. Nonetheless, OE had a fairly wide assortment of prepositions, most of which have survived in PDE, and many of which have retained their basic meaning to this day: *tō, for, bē* 'by', *in* (*on*), *under, ofer* 'over', *mid* 'with', *wiþ* 'against', *fram, geond* 'throughout', *þurh* 'through', *ymbe* 'around', *of* 'from'. Most of them were derived from adverbs and could also be used as adverbs.

CONJUNCTIONS

The OE supply of conjunctions was smaller than the wide array available in PDE, partly because OE used subordination less extensively than PDE does. Among the most widely used conjunctions were *and*, *ac* 'but', *gif* 'if', *þēah* 'though', and *forþæm* (*þe*) 'because'. OE had, if anything, more correlative conjunctions than PDE. Among them were

oþþe ... oþþe	'either ... or'
ge ... ge	'both ... and'
þā ... þā	'when ... then'
nā ... nā	'neither ... nor'
þonne ... þonne	'when ... then'
þȳ ... þȳ	'the ... the'
nū ... nū	'now that'
swā ... swā	'just as ... so'; 'whether ... or'

ADVERBS

In both OE and PDE, the term "adverb" is a catch-all for items that do not fit conveniently into any other word class. For OE, several broad subcategories are recognizable, all of them with parallels in PDE. As in PDE, a number of words are classified either as adverbs or as prepositions, depending on their use in the clause. Chief among them are the time and place words like *ofer* 'over', *under*, *on*, *þurh* 'through', and *æfter*. A second type of adverb includes miscellaneous indeclinable words used only adverbially: *ne* 'not', *ēac* 'also', *nǣfre* 'never', and *tō* 'too'. OE could also attach the useful suffix *-an* to other parts of speech in order to form adverbs with the general meaning "from that direction." For example, *ēastan* meant "from the east," *feorran* meant "from afar," and *siþþan* meant "from that time, afterwards."

A third source of adverbs was the inflected forms of other parts of speech, especially genitive and dative forms. For example, from *eall* 'all', OE used the genitive singular *ealles* to mean "entirely." From *gēar* 'year', there was *gēara* 'of years', meaning "formerly." From the noun *hwīl* 'time', the dative plural *hwīlum* was used adverbially to mean "at times." A number of such adverbs survive in PDE, though their genitive origins are no longer obvious: *twice*, *backwards*, *always*, *sometimes*, and so on.

By far the most numerous and productive category of adverbs was that of qualitative adverbs formed from adjectives simply by adding *-e* to the adjective stem or to the adjective stem plus *-lic*. For *riht* or *rihtlic* (both meaning "right"), the corresponding adverbs were *rihte* and *rihtlice*. Old English *-lic* (PDE *-ly*) was originally an adjective suffix, and it survives in many PDE adjectives (*friendly*, *homely*, *earthly*). But since it has become the standard way of forming an adverb, it is no longer productive for making new adjectives in PDE.

INTERJECTIONS

Like any other natural language, OE must have had a number of conventional interjections parallel to PDE *oh*, *ouch*, *dammit*, and the like. Interjections are not the sort of things that easily make their way into texts, however, so we know few of what probably was once a wide range of interjections. *Ēalā* and *wā lā wā*, both meaning "alas," appear occasionally. OE *hwæt lā* corresponded roughly to PDE *what!* In his *Grammar*, Ælfric tells us that *ha ha* and *he he* indicate laughter *on leden and on englisc* 'in Latin and in English', showing that this onomatopoeic interjection is as old as the language itself.

Old English Syntax

Word order in Old English, at least compared with that in Present-Day English, was relatively free. The speaker or writer of Old English had more options than we do today as to where to place such elements as direct objects with respect to other elements in the sentence. However, OE never had the syntactical freedom of a language like Classical Latin, and there were definite "favorite" phrase, clause, and sentence patterns that were followed quite consistently, especially in prose. Further, most of these patterns were the same as those of PDE. For example, a word-for-word translation of the following sentence from Alfred's *Orosius* (c. 895) produces a completely idiomatic PDE sentence.

> Hē sǣde ðæt Norðmanna land wǣre swȳþe lang and swȳþe smæl.
> *He said that (the) Northmen's land was very long and very narrow.*

Syntax Within Phrases

NOUN PHRASES
As in PDE, modifiers in OE tended to be close to the words they modified. Single-word adjectivals generally preceded their nouns:

> Ðā ungelǣredan prēostas   mihtig dryhten
> *Those ignorant priests*   *mighty lord*

This order could, however, be reversed, especially in poetry. Titles used with proper names normally followed the name, and adjectives modifying nouns used in direct address often did:

> bearn unweaxen   Ælfrēd cyning   Lēofan men   Fæder ūre
> *boy youthful*   *Alfred king*   *dear men*   *father our*

When a noun had two modifiers, sometimes one preceded the noun and one followed. If the modifiers were connected by *and*, both frequently followed the noun:

> mīne þegnas twēgen   ān fæt fyðer-scyte and brād
> *my servants two*   *a vessel four-cornered and broad*

As in PDE, adjectival modifiers consisting of an entire phrase or clause normally followed the words they modified.

> hlāford ofer alle hlāforden
> *lord over all lords*

> Ēadmund clypode ǣnne bisceop þe him þa gehendost wæs
> *Edmund summoned a bishop who (to) him then most convenient was*

However, a number of basic characteristics of adjectival modification in PDE were totally lacking in OE. Noun adjuncts, the use of one or more nouns to modify another without any change in the form (*bicycle chain, ink bottle, wallpaper hanger*), did not appear because a modifying noun was always inflected. Possessives (genitives) were also always inflected; there was no possessive with *of*. The group possessive (*the house on the corner's roof*) was not to appear for several hundred years. Comparative and superlative adjectives were always inflected; *more* and *most* were adjectives, adverbs, or pronouns, but never markers of comparison. Except for the group possessive, all of these features of PDE are those of an analytic language; OE was still highly synthetic.

ADVERBIAL MODIFIERS

Again like PDE, adverbial modifiers in OE were freer in their placement than adjectives. In general, however, they tended to precede the words they modified. The adverb *ne* always came directly before the verb it negated.

> þises godspelles geendung is <u>swīðe</u> ondrædenlic
> *this gospel's ending is very terrifying*

> And hī þā <u>sōna</u> <u>hider</u> sendon māran sciphere
> *And they then immediately here sent (a) bigger navy*

> se cynincg <u>ne</u> sceall arīsan of ðām bedde
> *the king not shall arise from the bed*

In OE, the taboo against double negatives had not yet been invented, and multiple negatives are common.

> <u>Ne</u> ūre <u>nænig</u> his līf <u>ne</u> fadode swā swā he scolde ... and <u>nāðer</u> <u>ne</u>
> *Not of us none his life not arranges as he ought to   and neither not*

> heoldan <u>ne</u> lārc <u>ne</u> lage <u>ne</u> manna swā swā we scoldan
> *(we) observe neither teaching nor law nor of men as we ought to*

PREPOSITIONAL PHRASES

As in PDE, prepositions in OE generally preceded their objects.

> būton hī <u>on</u> iugoðe liornan
> *unless they in youth learn*

> <u>On</u> þissum gēare cōm Harold cyng <u>of</u> Eoferwic <u>to</u> Westmynstre
> *In this year came Harold king from York to Westminster*

However, prepositions also frequently followed their objects, especially if the object was a pronoun. PDE of course has lost this freedom of placement, but the inverted position does survive in a few idioms such as *the world over* and *sleep the clock around*.

> and cwæð þā æt nēxtan cynlice him <u>to</u>, "Ēala þū bisceop ..."
> *and said then finally regally him to, "Oh, you bishop"*

VERB PHRASES

Old English lacked the rich and complex system of verb phrases that characterizes PDE; a phrase like *I should have been traveling* would have been impossible. There was no regular progressive tense, and the perfect tense was only just beginning to appear in its present function. The much wider use of the subjunctive in OE replaced to some extent the verb phrases of today. For example, where PDE has *if I had been*, OE could use *gif ic wǣre* (past subjunctive). In general, though, adverbs and context substituted for the multiword verb phrases of PDE.

Impersonal verbs (those without any expressed nominative subject) are almost totally unfamiliar in PDE, but were common in OE, where they frequently were accompanied by a dative or accusative reflexive pronoun.

> him limpð oft æfter hiora āgnum willan
> *(to) them happens often according to their own desire*

> þinceð him tō lītel þæt hē lange hēold
> *seems (to) him too little which he for long (has) held*

The only survival in PDE of this once-common construction is the archaic *methinks* (literally, "(it) thinks to me"), which most modern speakers probably construe as a quaint and ungrammatical way of saying "I think." To some extent, PDE has substituted the use of *there* and *it* for the OE impersonal verbs ("It seems to me the color has changed"; "There's a unicorn in the garden"). OE never used *there* in this way and used *it* as a dummy subject less frequently than PDE does.

Old English also never used *to* to mark the infinitive; the *-an* ending of the infinitive provided sufficient identification. OE did use *do* as a pro-verb to substitute for an entire verb phrase:

> Harold cyng ... gegædrade swā micelne sciphere and ēac landhere,
> *Harold king   gathered such (a) large navy and also army*

> swā nān cyng hēr on lande ǣr ne dyde
> *as no king here in land before not did*

However, *do* was never used in OE to form the negative or interrogative. A verb was negated simply by putting *ne* before it, and interrogatives were formed by inverting the subject and the verb.

> Hē cwæþ þæt nān man ne būde be norðan him.
> *He said that no man not lived to (the) north (of) him.*

> Hwilce fixas gefēhst þu?
> *Which fishes catch you? (Which fish do you catch?)*

Syntax Within Clauses

If we take the basic elements of a clause as subject (S), verb (V), and object/complement (O), then there are six theoretically possible orders in which these elements may occur: SVO, SOV, VSO, VOS, OSV, and OVS. All of these orders occurred, at least occasionally, in Old English. Nonetheless, order of elements was by no means random; in fact, word order in OE was in many ways similar to that of PDE. In particular, the subject usually preceded the verb. The favorite order in independent declarative clauses was SVO, as it remains in PDE:

and mæsse-prēost āsinge fēower mæssan ofer þān turfon
and (the) mass priest (should) sing four masses over (the) turves

Sēo stōw is gehāten Heofonfeld on Englisc
That place is called Heavenfield in English

Se fērde on his iugoðe fram frēondum and māgum tō Scotlande on sǣ
He went in his youth (away) from friends and relatives to Scotland by sea

However, in dependent clauses, the typical order was SOV. Indeed, the SOV order was common even in independent clauses when the object was a pronoun.

þām þe his willan on worolde gewyrcað
(to) those who his will in (the) world do

for ðan Ælmær hī becyrde
because Elmer them betrayed

ond hē hine sōna to þære abbudissan gelǣdde
and he him at once to the abbess led

This SOV order is virtually impossible in PDE, though it survives marginally in verse and song lyrics ("while I the pipes did play").

The order VSO was the rule in interrogative clauses and imperative clauses with an expressed subject. It was normal, but not universal, in declarative clauses preceded by an adverbial.

Interrogative
Hæfst ðu hafocas? ... Canst ðu temman hafocas? ... Hwæt
Have you hawks? Know how you to tame hawks? What

secge wē be þǣm cōce?
say we about the cook?

Imperative
Ne sleh þū, Abraham, þīn āgen bearn
Not slay you, Abraham, your own son

Preceded by Adverbial
Hēr gefeaht Ecgbryht cyning wiþ xxxv sciphlæsta æt Carrum
Here fought Egbert   king against 35 shiploads at Carhampton

Ðā cwæþ se fæder tō his þēowum ...
Then said the father to his servants

Ond þā se here eft hāmweard wende
And then the army again homeward turned (no inversion of S and V)

Of these three types of constructions, PDE regularly has inversion in interrogatives ("Why do you say that?" "Can he play backgammon?"). The VSO order is obligatory in PDE after a preceding *negative* adverbial ("Never have I seen such a mess"; "Rarely does the class begin on time"), and is a familiar stylistic variant after other adverbials, especially of direction or position ("Here comes the rain"; "On the table was a yellow cat"). In imperatives, PDE normally does not include a subject; but when it does, the order is SVO ("You eat your porridge!"), except in the idiom *mind you*.

The three remaining possible orders of OSV, OVS, and VOS all appear in OE texts, but are relatively rare, especially in prose. They seem to have been stylistic variants used primarily to emphasize the object or complement, though they also offered convenient metrical options to poets.

OVS   Fela spella him sǣdon þā Beormas
Many stories (to) him told the Karelians.

OSV   bēot hē gelǣste
vow he fulfilled

Strained as these examples may appear to the modern ear or eye, both are still used in certain circumstances in PDE. Fronting of an object or complement for emphasis is common in PDE, though perhaps more in speech than in writing ("Time I have, money I don't"). Even the seemingly bizarre order OVS is acceptable in PDE if the object is both negated (which provides the stimulus for inverting S and V) and emphasized ("No evidence have I seen to support that assumption"). In written, though not in spoken PDE, the OVS order is conventional in reporting direct speech ("'I don't care,' said Beulah.").

Syntax of Sentences

For the most part, the structure of entire sentences in OE prose was much looser than we would find elegant today—more like the typical sentence structures of spoken PDE; today's composition teachers would mark OE sentences "rambling" or "run-on." There was much less of the complex subordination that characterizes careful PDE prose; clauses within the sentence tended to be linked simply by the conjunctions *and* and *þā* 'then'. Although OE used such basic subordinating conjunctions as *þā* 'when', *gif* 'if', and *for þan* 'because', it lacked the rich array of subordinating conjunctions that PDE has, and the relative pronoun system was poorly developed.

One of the reasons why OE sentences were generally loose and cumulative in structure was the lack of models for tighter, more hypotactic structures. Although most writers were familiar with Latin, its grammar differed so much from OE grammar that its structures simply could not be transferred wholesale into English. Indeed, even in glosses, where scribes "translated" Latin texts simply by writing an English equivalent over each Latin word, scribes often changed the original word order, apparently feeling that a word-for-word translation in such instances would be too distorted to be comprehensible to a native speaker of English.

The sentence below, from the entry for the year 893 in the Parker version of the *Anglo-Saxon Chronicle*, is a fairly typical example of the loose but generally lucid style of unselfconscious OE prose. The punctuation here is modern.

þā hīe gefēngon micle herehȳð ond þā woldon ferian norþweardes ofer
When they seized great plunder and it wanted to carry northward over

Temese, in on Ēastseaxe ongēan þā scipu, þā forrād sio fierd
Thames, into Essex toward the ships, then intercepted the army

hīe foran ond him wið gefeaht æt Fearnhamme, ond þone here
them in front and them against fought at Farnham, and the (enemy) army

geflīemde ond þā herehȳþa āhreddon; ond hīe flugon ofer Temese
put to flight and the plunder rescued; and they fled over Thames

būton ǣlcum forda, þā ūp be Colne on ānne iggað.
without any fords, then up along Colne (River) onto an islet.

    The works of two writers, Wulfstan and the prolific Ælfric, were exceptions to the general rule of loose, rambling prose. Both men drew much of their conscious artistry from poetic devices, using, in particular, heavy alliteration and parallelism to embellish their styles. The following passage is from Wulfstan's famous bombastic sermon, "Sermo Lupi ad Anglos." Again, the punctuation is modern.

Hēr syndan mannslagan and mǣgslagan and mǣsserbanan and
Here are homicides and kinsmen-slayers and priest-killers and

mynsterhatan, and hēr syndan mānsworan and morþorwyrhtan, and
church-persecutors, and here are perjurers and murderers, and

hēr syndan myltestran and bearnmyrðran and fūle forlegene
here are harlots and infanticides and foul fornicated

hōringas manege, and hēr syndan wiccan and wælcyrian, and her
whores many, and here are witches and sorceresses, and here

syndan rȳperas and rēaferas and woruldstrūderas, and hrǣdest
are robbers and thieves and plunderers, and most hastily

is tō cweþenne, māna and misdǣda ungerīm ealra.
is to say, wickednesses and crimes countless number of all.

Note the heavy alliteration—Wulfstan even manages to use seven consecutive nouns all alliterating on [m] at the beginning of the selection. Later he uses series of doublets linked both by *and* and by alliteration. So carefully has he chosen his words that coordinated nouns are of the same class and hence have the same endings, adding weak rhyme to the alliteration (*mannslagan and mǣgslagan*; *rȳperas and rēaferas*; *māna and misdǣda*). Extensive use of parallelism (*and hēr ... and hēr ... and hēr*) keeps what would otherwise be an overly long and cumbersome passage from getting out of hand. This style is a far cry from "naive" prose. If it seems a bit too ornate and overblown for modern tastes, we still must admire its craftsmanship and power.
    The basic syntax of OE poetry did not differ greatly from that of prose. However, one important option that poets exercised was an extensive use of apposition (technically known as **variation**). Appositive phrases in poetry could move relatively freely to fit the demands of the alliterative line, as this example from *Beowulf* illustrates:

Lēoht ēastan cōm,
Light from east came

beorht bēacen Godes,   brimu swaþredon,
bright beacon God's,   *waves subsided,*

þæt ic sǣnæssas   gesēon mihte,
so that I headlands   *see could,*

windige weallas.
windy walls.

Here, *beorht bēacen Godes* is in apposition to *Lēoht*, and *windige weallas* is in apposition to *sǣnæssas*. Note that the basic S + V order of prose is preserved in the independent clauses (*Lēoht ēastan cōm; brimu swaþredon*) and that the adverb *ēastan* precedes the verb it modifies. In the dependent clause, the expected SOV order appears (*ic sǣnæssas gesēon mihte*).

Idioms and Latin Influence

All natural languages have idioms, constructions that do not fit the normal patterns of the language. Some OE idioms are still used today; for example, what could be called the "correlative comparative" as illustrated by *the bigger, the better* dates back to an OE idiom using the instrumental case. Old English nouns following a numeral, particularly numerals over three, often took the genitive plural: *twēntig gēara* 'twenty years'. Although the *-a* of the genitive plural was lost by the end of Middle English, making the noun identical with the singular, Standard English today still uses an uninflected noun after a numeral when the group is used attributively (*four-day wait, seven-year itch, ten-year-old girl*), rather than adding *-s* to the plural noun.

Many other OE idioms have been lost. For example, when an OE verb preceded its subject, the verb was often singular even if the subject was plural; in the phrase *gefeaht Æþerēd cyning ond Ælfrēd* 'King Æþered and Ælfred fought', the verb is singular. An idiom highly confusing to speakers of PDE can be illustrated by *eahta sum*, literally "of eight some," but meaning "one of eight" or "one and seven others."

As implied earlier, Latin syntax had little permanent influence on Old English syntax, even though most scribes were familiar with Latin. Nonetheless, a few Latinisms do appear, especially in direct translations from Latin. In particular, the occasional use in OE of a dative absolute is borrowed from the Latin ablative absolute. Present participles, rare in original OE writing, are more frequent in translations from Latin. The use of *nelle* (*ne* + *wille*) in negative imperatives is common in translations from Latin, but never appears elsewhere; it is an obvious borrowing of Latin *noli*. For example, OE *nelle þu beon gedreht* 'don't be troubled' translates Latin *noli vexari*.

NAMING THE STONES

The etymologies of some of our most valuable gemstones are not especially interesting. *Diamond* means simply "hard" and *ruby* means "red." More entertaining are the etymologies of some of the semiprecious stones. For example, *onyx* is from Greek *onux* 'claw' because onyx occasionally has a vein of white on a pink background like the half-moon of a fingernail. Greek also is the origin of the word *amethyst*; Greek *amethustos* means "anti-intoxicant" because amethyst was once thought to be a remedy for intoxication. Another supposedly medicinal stone was *jade*, from Spanish *ijada* 'flank, loin', so named because it was considered a cure for colic of the kidneys. The word *pearl* ultimately derives from Latin *perna* 'ham' because of the ham-shaped stalk of the sea-mussel that was the source of pearls.

Old English Lexicon

The Extensive Vocabulary

No matter how physically impoverished a culture may be, there is seemingly no limit to the richness its vocabulary may have. Even if the culture is technologically primitive and preliterate, its language may still express fine nuances of meaning by different words, and it may still have large numbers of synonyms or near-synonyms for the same object or concept. The vocabulary of Old English, although only a fraction of that of PDE, was still rich indeed. Thousands of different lexical items are found in OE texts, despite the fact that the majority of OE texts have not survived. Furthermore, any culture has hundreds of words that are unlikely to be written down in the first place simply because the contexts in which they are normally used are not appropriate subjects for written texts. For example, in a sample of one million words of edited written PDE text,[4] the words *snore*, *tricycle*, and *toadstool* (as well as many other familiar words) do not appear once. Yet these words are known to virtually every native speaker of English. For all these reasons, it is impossible to estimate with any confidence the total size of the OE vocabulary.

One of the explanations for the extraordinary richness of the surviving OE vocabulary is the nature of OE poetry. Because this verse was alliterative, a poet needed a variety of synonyms for the same concept in order to have a word that began with the right sound. In addition, OE poetry made extensive use of variation, or the repetition of the same idea in different words. This practice, too, required many synonyms. For example, to express the meaning of "messenger" alone, OE had at least the following words: *ǣboda*, *ǣrendraca*, *ǣrendsecg*, *ār*, *boda*, *engel*, *fērend*, *foreboda*, *forridel*, *rynel*, *sand*, *spellboda*, *wilboda*, and *yfelberende*. These terms were not complete synonyms—a *wilboda* brought good news, and an *yfelberende* brought bad news, for instance—but, depending on the context, many of them were interchangeable for poetic purposes.

Hundreds of the surviving OE words appear only in poetry. However, this fact does not mean that the "poetic" words were totally unfamiliar in ordinary speech. In some cases, it is simply an accident that a word is recorded only in poetry and not in prose. Second, the great majority of "poetic" words were compounds, both elements of which often were used in prose as well as poetry. For example, *frēomǣg* 'free kinsman' appears only in poetry, but both elements of this compound appear in nonpoetic contexts: *frēo* 'free', *frēolǣta* 'freedman', *frēodōm* 'freedom', and so on; and *mǣg* 'male kinsman', *mǣgburg* 'family, tribe', *mǣgmyrðra* 'parricide', and so on.

Loanwords

The largest proportion by far of the OE lexicon was native in origin and of two types, Indo-European or Germanic. The IE portion comprises those words found not only in Germanic languages but also in other IE languages (and not borrowed from one IE language into another). It includes the most essential vocabulary, such as the names of the numbers from 1 to 10, kinship terms for the nuclear family, and basic terms essential to any language, like the words meaning sun, water, to eat, head, property, tree, high, cold, flat, red, to stand, to have, to run, to laugh. The

---

[4] Henry Kučera and W. Nelson Francis, *Computational Analysis of Present-Day American English* (Providence: Brown Univ. Press, 1967).

Germanic element consists of items either common to all branches of Germanic or to West Germanic alone, but not found in other IE languages. Some of the Common Germanic words in OE are *bæc* 'back', *bān* 'bone', *folc* 'folk', *grund* 'ground', *rotian* 'to rot', *sēoc* 'sick', *swellan* 'to swell', *wērig* 'weary', and *wīf* 'woman'. Common only to West Germanic are OE *brōc* 'brook', *crafian* 'to crave', *īdel* 'idle', *cniht* 'boy, knight', *sōna* 'immediately', and *wēod* 'weed'.

CELTIC INFLUENCE

Despite extensive contacts between Germanic and Celtic speakers on the Continent and both extensive and intensive contacts after the Anglo-Saxons came to England, OE had only a handful of loanwords from Celtic languages. Some of these were originally from Latin (late OE *cros* from Old Irish *cross* from Latin *crux*), and some had been borrowed while the Anglo-Saxons were still on the Continent (OE *rīce* 'kingdom'). Of the half dozen or so words apparently borrowed after the Anglo-Saxons came to England, only *bin* 'storage box, crib' and perhaps *hog* and *dun* 'grayish-brown' have survived in the standard language to the present day. Much more Celtic influence is shown in place names and place-name elements; *Thames, Dover, London, Cornwall, Carlisle*, and *Avon* are the most familiar of many surviving Celtic place names in Britain.

Scholars usually explain the lack of Celtic influence on English vocabulary as resulting from the fact that the Celts were a conquered people whose language would have had little prestige, and hence the English would have had little incentive to borrow vocabulary from them. While this is true, it is not an adequate explanation, particularly in view of the fact that, in other situations, conquerors have borrowed proportionally more vocabulary items from their subject populations, even when the general cultural level of the conquerors was much higher than that of the conquered peoples. For example, the Romans borrowed scores of words from Germanic, and American English has retained well over a hundred words from the various American Indian languages. Even granting that the English colonists found more unfamiliar things to be named in the New World than the Anglo-Saxons found in England, the paucity of Celtic loans in OE is still puzzling.

SCANDINAVIAN INFLUENCE

The extensive—and usually unpleasant—contacts between the English and the Scandinavians began well within the Old English period. However, few certain Scandinavian loans appear in OE texts, partly because Old English and Old Norse were so similar that loans from Old Norse are not always easy to detect, partly because there would have been no prestige attached to the use of Scandinavian words, but primarily because there is always a lag between contact of two different languages and the assimilation of loanwords from one language into the other.

The few Old Norse words that do appear in OE texts chronicle the relationship between the English and the Norse. Although the English themselves were no mean seamen, the Norse were even better, and so we find the Norse loans *hā* 'rowlock' and *cnearr* 'kind of small ship' in OE. *Orrest* 'battle' and *rān* 'rapine' reflect the context in which the English met the Norsemen. The structure of Norse society and social classes differed in many ways from that of the English; hence the loanwords *hofðing* 'chief, leader', *hold* 'chief, notable', and *hūscarl* 'member of the king's bodyguard'. A dozen or so additional Old Norse words are recorded during the OE period, but the extensive influence of ON on English was not to appear until Middle English.

LATIN INFLUENCE

The only major foreign influence on OE vocabulary was Latin, an influence beginning in Common Germanic times, when such words as *belt, cheese, copper, linen,* and *pole* were borrowed. While the ancestors of the English were still on the Continent, West Germanic dialects borrowed several score Latin words, including *beer, butter, cheap, dish, mile, pit, plum, shrive, sickle, stop, street, tile,* and *wine.* (PDE spellings are given; the OE spellings were usually somewhat different.)

Because the language of the Church was Latin, Christianization predictably brought Latin loanwords to English. Among the many Latin loans in OE relating to religious practice or intellectual life are

alter 'altar'	*clūstor* 'cloister'
calic 'chalice'	*fers* 'verse'
candel 'candle'	*lētanīa* 'litany'
cantic 'canticle'	*mæsse* 'mass'
carte 'document'	*traht* 'tract'

The English, however, were also resourceful in adapting existing native words to express Christian concepts. For Latin *sanctus*, native *hālig* 'holy' was used; for Latin *deus*, native *god*; for Latin *dominus*, native *hlāford*. Native *gāst* translated Latin *spiritus*; *synn* served for Latin *peccatum*; and *biddan* 'pray' for Latin *orare*. Some of these ingenious translations may seem humorously irreverent to modern ears; for example, OE translated Epiphany as *bæðdæg* 'bath day' because Epiphany was supposedly the day of Christ's baptism.

The introduction of Christianity brought not just a new religion, but also administrative personnel, monastic life, and various secular concepts and products previously unfamiliar in England. Consequently, OE borrowed many secular Latin terms as well as religious terms. For some reason, there was an especially large number of borrowings for plant life—trees, fruits, vegetables, herbs, and flowers. A few examples are *ceder* 'cedar', *peru* 'pear', *bēte* 'beet', *rædic* 'radish', *pollegie* 'pennyroyal', *lilie* 'lily', and *peonie* 'peony'. Other Latin loans are too miscellaneous to be classified: *lamprede* 'lamprey eel', *fann* 'fan', *cancer* 'cancer', *gīgant* 'giant', *mūl* 'mule', and *ostre* 'oyster'.

From the beginning, the English did not hesitate to hybridize by combining Latin roots with native prefixes or suffixes and by forming compounds consisting of one Latin and one English element. Thus OE *bemūtian* 'to exchange for' has an English prefix on a Latin stem (L. *mutare*). OE *candeltrēow* 'candelabrum' has a Latin first element and an English second element (*trēow* 'tree').

Latin influence on OE vocabulary is also occasionally reflected in **calques**, or loan translations, in which the semantic elements of a foreign word are translated element by element into the borrowing language. For example, Latin *unicornis* 'unicorn' was loan-translated as *ānhorn* 'one horn'. Probably the best-known OE calque is *godspell* 'gospel', literally "good news," from Latin *evangelium*.

The Latin loans from the Continental period had been exclusively oral. The earliest Latin loans from the missionary period were also heavily oral, but as literacy in Latin increased in England, more and more Latin loans came in through writing, especially during the Benedictine reform of the late tenth century. Many of these later loans were of a highly esoteric nature and often were not even anglicized by removal of Latin endings. Not surprisingly, many of these loans that smell of the cloister have not survived into PDE, or were lost and then reintroduced at a later date. A few examples are *carbunculus* 'carbuncle', *corōna* 'crown', *eclypsis* 'eclipse', *fenester* 'window', *paradīs* 'paradise', and *termen* 'term'.

Formation of New Words

Any healthy language must have ways of creating new lexical items without resorting exclusively to borrowing or loan-translation. By the time of written OE, the earlier devices of ablaut and umlaut were no longer productive, and OE relied primarily on compounding and affixing to form new words, both devices inherited from IE and still widely used in PDE.

COMPOUNDING

An occasional compound can be found among all the parts of speech in OE, but the great majority of compounds are nouns or adjectives. The most common type of compound noun consists of two nouns; usually, the first noun is not inflected.

noun + noun = noun	*sunbēam* 'sunbeam'
	luftācen 'love token'
	þēohseax 'thigh sword'
adjective + noun = noun	*hēahsynn* 'high sin, crime'
	yfelweorc 'evil deed'
	wīdsǣ 'open sea'
adverb + noun = noun	*eftbōt* 'again-healing' (recuperation)
	ongēanhwyrf 'backturn' (return)
	innefeoh 'inside property' (household goods)

OE was innovative among Germanic languages in its occasional use of triple compounds: *winterrǣdingbōc* 'lectionary for the winter'; *biterwyrtdrenc* 'drink of bitter herbs'. Some types of compound nouns found in PDE, however, did not occur in OE. For example, OE did not have verb + adverb compounds (*hangover, kickback, go-between*); noun + verb compounds (*carwash, hairdo, sunshine*); or verb + verb compounds (*hearsay, look-see, lend-lease*).

Compound adjectives in OE most often had an adjective as the second element. The first element was usually a noun or an adjective, less often an adverb. One type of compound adjective rare in PDE, the adjective + noun combination, was relatively common in OE.

noun + adjective = adjective	*dōmgeorn* 'glory-eager'
	īsceald 'ice-cold'
	ǣlfscīene 'elf-bright' (beautiful)
adjective + adjective = adjective	*wīshȳdig* 'wise-minded'
	dēadboren 'stillborn'
	hēahstēap 'high-steep' (very high)
adverb + adjective = adjective	*ūplang* 'upright'
	þurhhefig 'extremely heavy'
adjective + noun = adjective	*blōdigtōþ* 'bloody-tooth'
	glædmōd 'happy-heart' (cheerful)
	feorsibb 'distant relative'

Among the infrequent compound adverbs of OE are the adjective +
adjective combination *eallmǽst* 'almost' and the adverb + adverb combination
nǽfre (ne + ǽfre) 'never'.

Old English did have some compound verbs, but they usually were derived
from preexisting nouns or adjectives. Examples are *līchamian* 'to clothe with flesh'
from *līchama* (body + covering), meaning simply "body," and *goldhordian* 'to
hoard treasure', from the compound noun *goldhord*. One common type of OE verb
resembled a compound, but it is probably better treated as a derived verb
consisting of a prefix plus a verbal stem. This type of verb consisted of an adverbial
particle plus a verb. Examples are numerous: *æfterfolgian* 'pursue', *ofercuman*
'overcome', *onfōn* 'take in, receive', and *underetan* 'undermine'. PDE preserves this
type of verb formation, though it is no longer especially productive.

Affixing

Although compounding is more entertaining and seemingly often more ingenious
than affixing, affixing was by far the most common way of forming new words in
OE. Even though it lacked the many borrowed affixes that PDE has from French
and Latin, OE had a rich stock of prefixes and suffixes. As in PDE, prefixes most
often changed the meaning of the word to which they were attached, whereas
suffixes usually changed the part-of-speech category or subcategory.

The most common prefix in OE is *ge-*, so widely used and in so many
different ways that it came to be virtually meaningless and was ultimately lost from
the language. It was a marker of the past participle of verbs, but it was also used
throughout the entire conjugation of many verbs, usually to indicate perfective
aspect (completion of an action). Sometimes it distinguished a special meaning of
the verb. For example, *gān* meant "to go," while *gegān* meant "to conquer." Often
ge- was attached to a verb with no discernible change in meaning at all: both *mǽnan*
and *gemǽnan* meant "to mean." And *ge-* was used with other parts of speech as well.
Attached to nouns, it often signified association; for example, *brōðor* meant
"brother," while *gebrōðor* meant "a member of a community, a monk." But when
attached to a noun or adjective, *ge-* often meant no more than that the word was
derived from a verb; for instance, from the strong verb *nīpan* came the noun *genīp*
'darkness.' However, *ge-* was not even consistently used in this way. The derived noun
from *hlystan* 'to listen, hear' appears as both *hlyst* and *gehlyst*, both meaning "sense
of hearing."

There was such a wide array of affixes in OE that space limitations prevent
an exhaustive listing. Just for forming abstract nouns from concrete nouns or other
parts of speech, OE had the suffixes *-nes, -ung, -dōm, -scipe, -aþ, -hād, -lāc,* and
-rǽden. Note that *-nes* (-ness) and *-scipe* (-ship) are still productive today, and that
-dōm, -aþ, and *-hād* are familiar, though rarely used to form new abstract nouns
(*wisdom, length, childhood*). For forming agent nouns, OE had *-end, -a, -bora, -ere,*
and *-estre*, of which *-ere* is still highly productive (*key-puncher*), and *-estre* is
marginally productive (*gangster*).

The most common adjective suffixes in OE were *-ig* (compare PDE *speedy*),
-lic (PDE *manly*), *-ful* (*bountiful*), *-lēas* (*mindless*), *-ed* (*bow-legged*), *-isc* (*childish*),
-sum (*handsome*), and the now-extinct *-cund, -fæst,* and *-wende*.

Many of the most frequent OE prefixes are still familiar and even pro-
ductive today, including *un-, in-, ofer-* (over-), *æfter-, fore-, mis-, under-, ūp-,* and *ūt-*
(out-). Still familiar but no longer productive are *ā-* (PDE *abide*), *be-* (*become*), *for-*
(*forget*), *forþ-* (*forthcoming*), *tō-* (*today*), *þurh-* (*throughout*), and *wiþ-* (*withhold*).

Among the numerous OE prefixes now lost are *on-*, used to indicate the beginning of an action; *of-*, used to indicate perfective action; and *ymbe-*, meaning "around." As an example of the productivity and ease of affixing in OE, consider *milde*, an adjective meaning "mild, gentle." From this stem, there was the verb *mildian* 'to become mild', the noun *mildnes* 'mildness', and another adjective *mildelic* 'propitious'. *Mildelic* was also an adverb meaning "kindly." Compounding produced still another adjective *mildheort* 'merciful'; adding a suffix to this gave the noun *mildheortnes* 'loving-kindness'. The prefix *un-* produced the adjectives *unmilde* 'harsh' and *unmildheort* 'merciless'. All of these derived forms are recorded in OE; there may well have been others that were not recorded in surviving manuscripts.

Types of Word-Formation Not Used in Old English

Old English, then, had ample resources for forming new vocabulary items. But it is also worth considering some of the ways for creating words that OE did *not* use. Certainly one of the most productive means of word-formation in PDE is **functional shift**, or using one part of speech as another without changing the form of the original by adding affixes. Nouns and verbs in particular participate freely in this process (*run fast*; *take a run*), but other parts of speech may also be involved. For example, PDE *up* may serve as a preposition (*up the wall*), an adverb (*climb up*), a noun (*ups and downs*), a verb (*to up the prices*), or an adjective (*on the up side*). OE could not employ functional shift because it was a synthetic language, and most parts of speech had to have distinctive inflections.

Another fertile way of creating vocabulary in PDE is the formation of nouns from two-part verbs by shifting the stress from the second element to the first (the verb *take óff* and the noun *tákeoff*). This process was not available to OE for two reasons. First, the accent was strongly fixed on the first syllable or at least the root syllable, so a form like *take óff* would have been impossible. Second, OE did not have verbs of this sort; instead of modifying meaning by a following separable particle like *off* or *up*, it prefixed these particles to verb stems. Thus, where PDE has *come up*, OE had *ūpcuman*; where PDE has *bring in*, OE had *ingebringan*.

Of some of the minor sources for new words in PDE, OE lacked acronyms, probably because the extensive use of acronyms presupposes a fairly high level of literacy—speakers must know the alphabet and what letters words begin with. Folk etymology was rare or absent in OE because most folk etymologies arise from unfamiliar borrowed words, and OE had few foreign loanwords. Aside from shortened forms caused by sound changes, we have little evidence in OE for clipping (as with PDE *fence* from *defense* or *lab* from *laboratory*); perhaps there were some clipped forms in the spoken language that never got recorded. Surely OE created a number of words through onomatopoeia because the process is universal. However, onomatopoetic words tend not to appear in writing, especially formal writing, so it is not surprising if they have not survived. (College dictionaries today do not even list such familiar PDE onomatopoetic words as *eek* and *kerplunk*.)

Lost Vocabulary

A large proportion of the rich Old English vocabulary is gone from PDE. Estimates vary; most assume that between 65 percent and 85 percent of the OE lexicon has been lost since OE times. Such figures are misleading, however. First, it is often not easy to decide whether a word has been "lost" or not: should we consider *fīon* 'to hate' lost, even though the OE noun *fīond* derived from this verb survives in the word *fiend*? Furthermore, raw counts are deceptive. Another way of looking at the overlap between OE and PDE vocabulary is to consider the survival rate of the most common, essential words of the language. Here the statistics present a different picture: of the 100 most frequent words in OE poetry, 80 have survived.[5] Of the 100 most frequent words in written PDE, 96 were in OE, and the remaining four (*are, they, them, their*) are from Old Norse, a Germanic language closely related to English in OE times.[6] Further, the overlap between the two lists is very high; in other words, the most common words of OE are also the most common words of PDE.

The fact remains, however, that a heavy proportion of the total OE lexicon has not survived. Given that there seems to be no upper limit to the size of a language's lexicon, why should any words be lost? There are many reasons, and for some words, multiple reasons.

1. In a few cases, words seem to simply "wear out." Sound changes reduce them to the point where there is phonetically so little left that they are replaced by longer, more distinctive forms. This is probably what happened to OE *ēa* 'river, stream' (which does survive, however, in the first syllable of *island*, though the word has been respelled by false analogy with Latin *insula*). OE *ā* 'always' may have suffered the same fate. Indeed, the first-person singular nominative pronoun came close to extinction when OE *ic* [ič] lost its final consonant and was reduced to [i]; lengthening the vowel saved it.

2. Words may be lost when sound changes make two previously distinct words identical. English usually tolerates the resulting homophones if they do not lead to confusion; hence *reed* (OE *hrēod*) and *read* (OE *rǣdan*) both survive in PDE. However, if the two words are members of the same word class and are used in similar contexts, unacceptable ambiguity can arise. As was mentioned earlier, when sound changes made OE *lǣtan* 'let, allow' and OE *lettan* 'hinder, delay' identical in pronunciation (PDE [lɛt]), one had to give way because both were transitive verbs used in similar contexts. The *let* meaning "hinder" does survive marginally in *let ball* (in tennis) and the legal phrase *without let or hindrance*, but it would be impossible in the context of "I won't let you." For a similar reason, English borrowed the ON third-person plural personal pronouns. Sound changes had made the words for "he" and "they" and the words for "her" and "their" identical in most dialects. Although English had lost and was losing many other grammatical distinctions expressed by inflections, the singular-plural distinction continued strong, so some of the original native forms had to be replaced.

3. Thousands of words are lost because of cultural and technological changes; in a sense, it is not so much the words that are lost as it is their referents. Because our social and legal system is entirely different from that of the Anglo-Saxons, we have no need for the OE words *wergild* 'compensation for a man's life', *forþingian* 'to arrange for a man's *wergild*', *mǣgcwalm* 'murder of a relation', or *ofweorpan* 'to stone to death'. Technological changes have eliminated the referents for *ǣwul* 'basket with a narrow neck for catching fish', *sǣdlēap* 'sower's basket', and *tǣnel* 'wicker basket'.

---

[5] Figures derived from John F. Madden and Francis P. Magoun, Jr., *A Grouped Frequency Word-List of Anglo-Saxon Poetry* (Cambridge, Mass.: Harvard Univ. Press, 1967).

[6] Figures derived from Henry Kučera and W. Nelson Francis, *Computational Analysis of Present-Day American English* (Providence: Brown Univ. Press, 1967).

4. Taboos are responsible for the loss of some words. Words for death and dying, for example, are often replaced by euphemisms, which themselves become tainted by their meanings and are in turn replaced by other words or euphemisms. OE had an extremely common verb, *gewītan*, meaning "to go away." By late OE, it had become a common euphemism for "to die." The ultimate loss of *gewītan* from the language is probably the result of its unpleasant associations with death.

5. Semantic changes in one area of vocabulary may set off a chain reaction that ends up with some words being squeezed out in a kind of linguistic musical chairs. OE *weorðan* 'to become, happen; passive auxiliary' was one of the most frequently used words in the language and seemingly would have had an excellent chance of survival. OE also had the verbs *cuman* 'to come, go', *gān* 'to go, come', and *becuman* 'to come, approach, arrive, happen, come to be'. Over the years, the present clear distinction between *come* and *go* arose, and the usefulness of *becuman* in the meaning of "come" declined. In Middle English, a new verb *happen* was created from the Old Norse loan *hap*; *happen* now encroached on another meaning of both *weorðan* and *becuman*. The French loanwords *approach* and *arrive* further invaded what had once been the territory of *becuman*. At the same time, from OE times on, *weorðan* had had a rival in *bēon* 'to be' as the passive auxiliary. By the twelfth century, *become* was being used in close to its present meaning of a change in state, a slight extension of its OE meaning "come to be." Because the use of *weorðan* as a passive auxiliary was simultaneously giving way to *be*, *becuman* and *weorðan* were now in direct competition for the one remaining area of meaning, change of state. By the fourteenth century, it was clear that *become* was winning, and the last citation of *worth* as a verb dates from the fifteenth century. Though we cannot explain why *worth* should be lost and *become* retained, the process whereby one of them became redundant can be traced.[7]

This is not to imply that a language never can have two ways of expressing the same meaning or grammatical distinction. For example, PDE uses both *get* and *be* as passive auxiliaries. However, there is a definite stylistic difference between the two; *I got fired* is both stronger and more casual than *I was fired*. Moreover, the general tendency is to have only one form to express basic grammatical concepts. Certainly it is hard to imagine any way of expressing the progressive in PDE except by *be* + *-ing* or the agent of a passive construction except with *by*.

6. If two dialects of a language use different words to refer to the same concrete object, confusion results when speakers of the two dialects try to communicate. For example, Americans from one part of the country are often puzzled to discover that what they call a *ground squirrel* is called a *gopher* in another part of the country. If the different dialects merge through continuous contact, one of the terms is likely to be abandoned. The existence of two words meaning "whale" in Old English (*hran* and *hwæl*) may have led to the loss of *hran* from the language. The process can be accelerated if a loanword from another language adds to the number of synonyms. In OE, both *hyht* and *hopa* meant "hope"; *hyht* had the additional meanings of "faith in" and "joy." When *trust*

---

[7] Another contributing factor *may* have been avoidance of homophony. *Worth* as verb was identical in sound to the adjective and noun *worth*, whereas *become* was unique.

was borrowed from Old Norse and *joy* from Old French, *hyht* lost its unique territory and became vulnerable to extinction. This vulnerability was only increased when, by Middle English, the word *hyȝt* (OE *hyht*) had become identical in pronunciation to another noun meaning "haste," adding homonymy to dialect confusion.

7. Fashion leads to the loss of many vocabulary items. This may involve the higher prestige of urban over rural forms, of upper-class words over what are perceived as lower-class words, or of foreign words over native words. After the Conquest, the higher prestige of French as the language of the conquering and ruling class led to the loss of many Old English words. Examples include the replacement of OE *þēod* by French *people*, of *sīþ* by *journey*, of *wuldor* by *glory*, of *æðele* by *noble*, and of *feorh* by *spirit*.

Old English Semantics

Semantic Categories

Semantics is the most difficult aspect of language to treat systematically because it is the interface between language and the real world—and the real world is notoriously complex and unpredictable. Experience can not only be categorized in many different ways, but also in several ways simultaneously. As an example, consider two semantic areas that have been widely studied in recent years, primarily because they are more obviously structured than and hence more amenable to analysis than most aspects of meaning. The two areas are kinship terms and color terms. In both these areas, we find differences between Old English and Present-Day English. Obviously, there has been no change in possible biological relationships of human beings or in the rods and cones of the human eye between Old English times and today. Therefore, if we find differences in the semantic systems, they reflect, not differences in the real world, but differences in the way human beings interpret it.

Considering all the distinctions that could be made in kinship relationships, OE and PDE are really very similar. Neither has core terms expressing order of birth (Chinese, for example, has separate terms for a person's older and younger siblings). Both OE and PDE are "ego-oriented"; that is, the same individual may be *sister* to one person, *daughter* to another, *mother* to a third, and *aunt* to a fourth; the term used to describe the relationship varies according to the individual speaker or subject of conversation. OE and PDE also share terms for the members of the nuclear family: OE *mōdor*, *fæder*, *sunu*, *dohtor*, *sweostor*, *brōðor*. Both distinguish sex in most terms (PDE *cousin* is an exception), and both normally distinguish biological from legal relationships: OE *dohtor* versus *snoru* 'daughter-in-law'.

However, OE tended to put less emphasis on generation differences beyond the nuclear family; *mago* was simply a male relative, *nefene* could be either a granddaughter or a niece, and a *nefa* could be a nephew, a second cousin, a stepson, or a grandson. OE also lacked separate terms for the marriage relationship; OE *wīf* meant simply "woman," and OE *hūsbonda* meant "male head of the household." On the other hand, the distinction between maternal and paternal relatives was more specifically made in OE. A maternal uncle was *ēam*, but a paternal uncle was *fædera*; a *geswigra* was a sister's son.

In PDE, when we use the word *color*, we usually are thinking of only one aspect of color—hue, the dimension of color that ranges from red, orange, yellow, green, blue, violet, and back to red. However, the human eye perceives other dimensions of color, including lightness (how "light" or "dark" the color is), saturation (the amount of gray in the color; its vividness), luster (the amount of light seemingly reflected from the surface), and scintillation (sparkling or twinkling). OE had most of the basic hue words of PDE, including, at least, words for red, yellow, green, violet, white, black, and gray. However, for reasons unknown, these terms for hue were used rather infrequently, at least in surviving texts. Texts rarely mention, for example, the hue of a person's hair, complexion, or clothing. This omission is somewhat surprising because other Germanic cultures like Icelandic and neighboring Celtic cultures such as the Welsh and Irish pay particular attention to hue in their surviving texts.

On the other hand, color terms referring to saturation, lightness, luster, and scintillation appear frequently in OE texts. It is not always possible to be sure precisely what some color words meant, so the glosses are only approximate.

Saturation		Lightness
fealu 'dusky'	*dunn* 'dingy'	*scīr* 'bright'
hasu 'ashen'	*grǣg* 'gray'	*beorht* 'bright'
hār 'hoary'	*wann* 'dark'	*torht* 'bright'
healfhwīt 'half-white'		*scīma* 'brightness'
dungrǣg 'dusky'		*hādor* 'brightness'
brūnwann 'dusky'		
æscfealu 'ash-colored'		

Luster	Scintillation
lēoma 'gleam'	*spircan* 'sparkle'
glæd 'shining'	*scimerian* 'shimmer'
blīcan 'glitter'	*blēobrygd* 'scintillation'
lȳman 'shine'	*brigd* 'play of color'
brūn 'having metallic luster'	*bregdan* 'play of color'
	tȳtan 'sparkle'

It might be tempting to suggest that speakers of OE tended to ignore hue because, first, their culture lacked the wide array of chemical dyes that makes us so conscious of hue today. Second, OE speakers had little artificial lighting in a country notorious for cloudy days and long dark winters. The cones of the eye, required for perceiving hue, do not function well in dim light. We might conclude that OE speakers simply did not see hue as often or in as much variety as we do today. However, this theory does not explain why Celtic speakers and other Germanic speakers in equally gloomy lands reveled in terms descriptive of hue.

In sum, it is dangerous to insist on one-to-one correspondences between a language and the culture that speaks this language. For example, if the proverbial man from Mars examined only the etymology of many common PDE expressions, he might conclude that English speakers are highly religious. Our first meal of the day is "breaking a fast." When we part, we ask the blessing of God upon each other ("goodbye" is historically from "God be with you"). Given the slightest emotional disturbance, we invoke a deity (*Good Lord! Good heavens! My God! God only knows!*) or call down a curse (*What the devil! To hell with it! Damn it all!*). The fact is that there is no tidy and reliable relationship between a culture and the semantic systems of its language.

Semantic Change

It is difficult enough to deal with the semantics of PDE, where we at least have our intuitions as native speakers as a guide; but it is much more difficult to recapture the semantics of a much earlier stage of a language for which surviving texts are few. Many Old English words surely had more meanings than we can detect today. Probably many other OE words had *fewer* meanings; that is, they were more limited in their application than we judge them today.

The basic meanings of the OE core vocabulary do seem to have remained relatively stable over the centuries, though the individual items often have developed extended meanings. For example, the OE meaning for such words as *mother, son, tree, sun, good, have,* and *be* seem to be much the same in OE and in PDE. Thus, OE *habban* had the same basic sense of possession as its PDE reflex *have,* even if PDE has added idiomatic meanings as exemplified in *I've been had, I won't have you talking like that, I had some friends in for the weekend, I had my car stolen,* and even if PDE has lost some of the earlier "fringe" meanings of *have,* as in *Do you, sir, have me for a fool?*

In some instances, we can offer post hoc explanations for semantic shifts. For example, two OE words for "horse" were *hors,* the basic term for equines, and *stēda,* which meant "stud-horse, stallion." OE *hors* has survived with its OE meaning virtually unchanged, but *steed* has lost its earlier close association with breeding potential and has become a "poetic" word for a spirited horse, especially a war-horse. In this case, it is reasonable to assume that when the French loan *stallion* was introduced, it competed directly with *stēda* for the meaning of "uncastrated male horse, stud-horse." *Stēda* survived by shifting its basic meaning to another semantic plane where it was distinguished from *stallion* by its romantic connotations.

In other cases, however, there is no detectable motivation for semantic shifts. Four OE words all referring generally to lack of light were *dimm, sweart, deorc,* and *blæc.* All of them survive in more or less recognizable form in PDE as *dim, swarthy, dark,* and *black.* In OE, *dimm, sweart,* and *deorc* also were used metaphorically to refer to evil, but *blæc* apparently was not. In PDE, *dim* and *swarthy* have lost their extended meaning of evil, *dark* has retained it, and *black* has added it. Today we can speak of a *black heart* or *dark thoughts,* but not of a *dim heart* or *swarthy thoughts.*

There are a number of possible ways of classifying types of semantic change, none of them totally satisfactory. For our purposes here, we will identify the following kinds of change: generalization and narrowing, amelioration and pejoration, strengthening and weakening, shift in stylistic level, and shift in denotation.

GENERALIZATION AND NARROWING

Generalization, or extension of meaning, can be represented by OE *gesūnd* 'safe, healthy, uninjured'; PDE has added the more abstract meanings of "thorough" (*a sound scolding*), "unbroken" (*a sound sleep*), "reliable" (*a sound investment*), and "sensible" (*sound advice*). OE *flicorian* seems to have meant only "to move the wings, to flutter," while PDE *flicker* has been extended to include the movement of light (*a flickering candle*) or even of emotion (*flickering interest*).

It is much easier to find examples of narrowed meaning of words between OE and PDE, perhaps because, as English has incorporated thousands of new loanwords, the semantic domain covered by a single item has been correspondingly limited. For example, OE *wǣd* could refer to any garment, whereas PDE *weeds* is used only to refer to mourning clothes (*widow's weeds*). OE *wēod* referred to herbs or grass in general; PDE *weed* refers only to undesirable, unwanted plants. OE *swǣtan* meant to exude liquid, including blood; PDE *sweat* is usually restricted to the exuding of water, especially perspiration.

AMELIORATION AND PEJORATION

Amelioration, or a change to a more favorable meaning, can be exemplified by OE *prættig* 'tricky, sly, wily'; compare PDE *pretty*. Pejoration, much more common than amelioration, is represented by OE *sǣlig* 'happy, prosperous', which has become PDE *silly*. Other examples are OE *crǣftig* 'skillful, strong, learned', PDE *crafty*; OE *lǣwede* 'laic, layman', PDE *lewd*; and OE *ceorl* 'peasant, freeman', PDE *churl*.

STRENGTHENING AND WEAKENING

Strengthening or intensification is a rare type of semantic change. One example is OE *wrecan*, PDE *wreak*, as in *wreak havoc, wreak vengeance*. The OE word could be used in the strong sense of "avenge, punish," but also often had the milder meaning of "push, impel" or simply "pronounce, relate." Because of the universal tendency to exaggerate, weakening of meaning is much more common than strengthening. A few examples are OE *sōna* 'immediately', PDE *soon*; OE *cwellan* 'kill, murder', PDE *quell*; OE *hraðor* 'more quickly, immediately', PDE *rather*.

SHIFT IN STYLISTIC LEVEL

Shifts in stylistic level are related to amelioration and pejoration, but still constitute a separate category of semantic change. For example, in the lofty and dignified OE heroic poem *Beowulf*, after Beowulf and the dragon have killed each other, Beowulf's people prepare a solemn and majestic funeral for him. During the preparations, they must dispose of the dragon's corpse. The poet describes their actions as *dracan ēc scufun, wyrm ofer weallclif* 'moreover, they shoved the dragon, the serpent over the cliff'. *Scufun* is from the verb *scūfan* 'thrust, push'. The PDE verb *shove* still means to push, but the verb is no longer used in such dignified contexts; we would scarcely say that after Adam and Eve had been banished from Eden, the angel *shoved* the gates shut. Incidentally, another word in this same line has undergone a dramatic shift, involving both narrowing of meaning and, to a lesser extent, a shift in stylistic level. *Wyrm*, glossed here as "serpent," is the ancestor of PDE *worm*. Its PDE meanings, including its use as a contemptuous term for people, date back to earliest OE, but in OE it could also mean "dragon, serpent, snake," even in the most elevated contexts.

SHIFT IN DENOTATION

Occasionally, words undergo such an extreme shift in denotation that it is not easy to trace the path of the change. OE *dwellan* meant "to lead into error, deceive, wander, err," a very different meaning from its PDE descendant *dwell*. The PDE meaning was probably influenced by a similar-sounding Old Norse verb *dvelja* 'delay, stay, remain'. Less explicable is the change in OE *clūd* 'rock, hill', PDE *cloud*.

All of these semantic shifts are relatively simple; they represent one step and one type of shift. Many semantic changes, however, are much more complex. Consider the history of the word *fair*. OE *fæger* meant "beautiful, attractive." By the end of the twelfth century, the word still meant "beautiful," but it was also being used to mean "free of fraud or injustice, legal," a reasonable extension of the basic meaning; this meaning survives in the PDE *fair trial, fair play, fair game*. By the thirteenth century, another specialized meaning had been added, that of "unblemished." *Fair* was used widely in this meaning during ME, but the "unblemished" meaning was later lost again in most contexts, surviving today primarily with respect to weather phenomena (*a fair day, fair-weather friends*). During the sixteenth century, *fair*, still preserving its basic meaning of "beautiful," also came to mean "blond" (a change that suggests something about English speakers' concepts of beauty). This meaning has of course also survived to the present day; it combines with the original meaning of "beautiful" in the expression *fair-haired boy*, meaning a favorite or pet. Then, during the eighteenth century, weakening of the basic meaning took place as *fair* and its corresponding adverb *fairly* came to mean "so-so, adequate." This weakened meaning eventually supplanted the original meaning of "beautiful," which survives today only in highly restricted contexts and in such expressions as *fair maidens* and *Only the brave deserve the fair*. The original basic meaning of "beautiful" has been lost. For most native speakers of PDE, *fair* probably has the two seemingly unrelated core meanings of "so-so" and "free of injustice," and the two additional meanings of "blond" and "uncloudy," used only in the specialized contexts of complexion and hair-color, and weather, respectively.

Because so many semantic changes, subtle and unsubtle, have occurred since OE times, translating OE words with PDE cognates is full of pitfalls. The danger can be exemplified by Ezra Pound's translation of the OE poem "The Seafarer." The translation is a *tour de force* in its preservation of the OE alliterating sounds and its high proportion of native words, but sometimes it is almost disastrous semantically. In the first line, *May I for my own self song's truth reckon*, the word *reckon* strikes a jarring note because, although the OE word *gerecenian* did mean "to relate, to recount," its PDE descendant has undergone a narrowing of meaning to "to compute, calculate," or a degeneration to a colloquialism meaning "to think, assume." An even greater semantic infelicity appears in the line *Narrow nightwatch nigh the ship's head*. OE *nearu* meant "narrow" in the physical sense, but also meant "oppressive, dangerous"; PDE has lost the latter meaning. In the same line, Pound apparently did not know that *head* is PDE sailor's jargon for "toilet." Many other such semantic misfits appear in the translation, but these examples suffice to illustrate the problem of relying too heavily on etymology and earlier meanings. Like all other aspects of language, semantic change is inevitable.

Old English Dialects

Most of our previous discussion of Old English has assumed a homogeneous dialect over both time and place. This was certainly not the case. Great changes occurred in the language between A.D. 450 and A.D. 1100—so great that the Saxon invaders of the fifth century surely would not have been able to understand the speech of the warriors fighting beside Harold Godwineson at Stamford Bridge. The single most important change over these 650 years was the reduction of all unstressed vowels to [ə] and the consequent loss of distinctions between inflectional endings; this change is shown more clearly in Chapter 6.

Even at any given point in time, the language spoken in England varied from place to place. Some of this variation probably arrived with the first settlers, and further differences arose after settlement, although what evidence there is suggests that mutual intelligibility among contemporary dialects was the rule throughout the entire OE period.

From the few remaining texts written outside the West Saxon area and from developments that appear in Middle English, it seems that there were two broad dialectal areas in Anglo-Saxon England: Anglian in the North and Southern in the South. Traditionally, four dialectal areas are recognized—Northumbrian and Mercian in the northern part of the island, and West Saxon and Kentish in the southern part. It should be kept in mind, however, that dialect boundaries are rarely sharp. In the absence of major geographical obstacles such as mountain ranges or unnavigable and unfordable rivers that prevent communication between settlements, the boundaries between dialects are not discrete but rather form a continuum.

For the most part, the differences among OE dialects—as is the case among PDE dialects—lay primarily in phonology, vowels in particular. Unfortunately, we cannot know exactly how any OE vowel was pronounced. In addition, the prestige of the West Saxon dialect in writing may have influenced the spelling (but not necessarily the pronunciation) of vowels in other dialectal areas. Naturally, there were also vocabulary differences, differences that became more striking after the permanent Norse settlements in England. Syntactic differences were of little significance. The morphology was similar in all areas, although the North lost inflectional distinctions earlier than the South did.

A detailed description of OE dialectal differences is beyond our scope here. To the superficial glance, the most striking characteristics include the heavier use of diphthongs (as opposed to pure vowels) and the extensive palatalization of velar consonants in the West Saxon areas, and the corresponding lack of both in the Northern dialects. In Kent, both earlier [y̆] and [æ̆] became [ĕ]; the heavy preponderance of ⟨e⟩ over other vowel symbols is almost enough to identify a manuscript as Kentish in origin.

The problem of defining Old English dialects is exacerbated, of course, by the paucity of surviving texts. Even given texts and that ideal situation of the same text copied at about the same time into two different dialects, one must still take into account the possible eccentricities of the individual scribes. Moreover, because writing is at best an incomplete and imperfect representation of speech, there is always the possibility that what appear to be phonological differences are simply different spelling conventions. For example, early Northumbrian texts often use ⟨u⟩ and ⟨d⟩ where Southern texts use a form of the letter ⟨w⟩, and ⟨ð⟩ or ⟨þ⟩, respectively. This difference does not mean that the North did not have the phonemes /w/ and /θ/; it means simply that the scribes did not have separate graphemes for representing them and so made do with approximations. A further problem is that, because most of our manuscripts are copies, we cannot be sure to what extent the original text has been contaminated by the scribe's own dialectal peculiarities and spelling conventions.

To illustrate some of these problems, we reproduce below five lines from a Northumbrian and a West Saxon version of *Cædmon's Hymn*, one of the few OE works that survive in multiple copies. (In the first line, the words *aelda* and *eorðan* are not dialectal variants; they are entirely different words, meaning "of men" and "of earth," respectively.) We do not indicate vowel length here because the manuscripts themselves do not do so.

North.:	He aerist scop	aelda barnum
West S.:	He ærest sceop	eorðan bearnum
	He first shaped	*of men [earth] for the sons*
North.:	heben til hrofe,	haleg scepen;
West S.:	heofon to hrofe,	halig scyppend;
	heaven as a roof,	*holy creator;*
North.:	tha middungeard	moncynnæs uard,
West S.:	þa middangeard	moncynnes weard,
	then earth	*mankind's guardian,*
North.:	eci dryctin,	æfter tiadæ
West S.:	ece drihten,	æfter teode
	eternal lord,	*afterwards brought forth*
North.:	firum foldu,	frea allmechtig.
West S.:	firum foldan,	frea ælmihtig.
	for men region,	*lord almighty.*

Old English Literature

Today we usually distinguish as literature only writing that has intrinsic artistic merit apart from its other purposes or content. Here we shall ignore this esthetic distinction and use the term "literature" to include all writings in prose or verse from the Old English period. Even with such a broadened definition, our corpus is small. Few OE texts have survived. Of those that have, most exist in only one manuscript, rarely the author's holographic copy.

The surprise, however, is that we have as many texts as we do, considering the enemies of preservation—fire, damp, vermin, negligence, the Viking invasions, the Norman Conquest, the dissolution of the monasteries, the zeal of reformers, and political and religious upheavals in general. Furthermore, the chances that a text would be written were small in the first place. During the entire OE period, literacy was confined to the clergy. There was only a small potential audience for books, and their contents were restricted to what the clergy felt was appropriate to preserve. Decisions to copy any text were not lightly made because books were incredibly expensive by modern standards. Paper had not yet reached Europe, so vellum was the chief writing material, and the production of even one modest volume required the skins of scores of sheep or lambs. The printing press was still several hundred years in the future, so every copy of every book had to be laboriously written out by hand.

Finally, given the decision to write a new book or copy an existing manuscript, the odds against its being written in English were high. Most literate Anglo-Saxons were bilingual in Latin and English (and occasionally in Irish or Gaelic). For the most part, Latin was considered the only appropriate language for

A PAGAN CHARM

Paganism did not disappear absolutely and immediately upon the introduction of Christianity to England. Among the surviving pagan customs for which direct evidence remains are a series of charms. Some of them have a veneer of Christianity overlying the basic paganism; others lack even the veneer. The charms are against such diverse evils as infertile land, delayed childbirth, the "water-elf disease," swarming of bees, theft of cattle, a wen, and the following charm (here translated into modern English) against a sudden stitch.

For a sudden stitch, a good remedy is feverfew and red nettle, which grows throughout the place, and plantain. Boil in butter.

Loud they were, oh! loud, when they rode over the hill;
They were fierce when they rode over the land.
Shield yourself so that now you can survive attack!
Out, little spear, if it be here-in!

I stood under a linden, under a light shield,
Where the mighty women prepared their powers
And they sent forth screaming spears.
I will send another back to them,
A flying arrow directly back.
Out, little spear, if it be here-in!

The smith sat, forged a little knife,
Wondrously crafted of iron.
Out, little spear, if it be here-in!

Six smiths sat, made deadly spears.
Out, little spear, not at all within, spear!

If there be here-in any piece of iron
The work of a witch, it must melt.
If you were shot in the skin or were shot in the flesh
    Or were shot in the blood
Or were shot in a limb, may your life never be injured;
If it were shot by gods or it were shot by elves
Or it were shot by a witch, now I will help you.

This is a remedy to you against the shot of gods; this is a remedy to you
    against the shot of elves,
This is a remedy to you against the shot of a witch. I will help you.
Fly there to the mountain-head.
Be healthy! The Lord help you!

Then take the knife; put it in the liquid.

Translated by C. M. Millward from "For a Sudden Stitch" (MS. Harley 585), in Elliott Van Kirk Dobbie, ed., *The Anglo-Saxon Minor Poems* (New York: Columbia Univ. Press, 1968), pp. 122–23.

serious literature, and Latin was the only language for communication beyond the confines of England.

The miracle is that we have as much OE literature as we do. The use of vellum as a medium was one advantage; vellum is much more durable than paper, particularly most of today's paper, which is made from wood pulp rather than cloth and which is treated with chemicals that hasten its deterioration. The Viking invasions, destructive as they were of many manuscripts, also indirectly contributed to the number of surviving texts in Old English: the accompanying severe decline in Latin scholarship in England meant that more texts had to be written in English. Also, under normal circumstances, books in any language would have been treated with more care in Anglo-Saxon times than we treat our books today. After all, even one book was a major investment; and without electronic media, books were the only means of passing on the wisdom of the past, aside from the notoriously fallible human memory.

With a few notable exceptions, Old English texts are anonymous. Authors received no royalties, so there was no economic motive for asserting one's authorship. The cult of individuality had yet to be invented, and the idea of "creativity" and originality would never have occurred to an Old English author. Indeed, it would have been more important to assure readers that the material was all based on the old authorities and that the author was merely serving as preserver and transmitter. One would never be charged with plagiarism, but one might be faulted for invention.

The overwhelming preponderance of OE literature is religious in nature. To some extent, however, the division into religious and secular is an artificial one; religion so permeated all of life during the Middle Ages that almost no text is free of religious references. A more reasonable distinction might be that between religious subject matter and secular subject matter.

Prose

In the history of the literature of a culture, the evolution of a respectable prose style usually lags behind that of verse. English was the first of the medieval European vernaculars to develop a flexible, lively, yet often sophisticated prose. One reason for this early development is probably the fact that the other possible contenders —chiefly French and Italian—were inhibited by their obvious and close relationship to Latin. In the year 950, Latin would have been a far easier language for a French speaker to master than for an English speaker, and the French writer would turn quite naturally to Latin as a prose vehicle. Even though most literate Englishmen, especially prior to the Viking invasions, would have been literate in Latin as well as English, the great differences between Latin and English would have made many of them less at home in Latin than their Continental counterparts were. After the great decline in English scholarship following the Viking invasions, writing in English and translation of Latin works into English was encouraged, not because English was felt to be superior—it was not—but because it was faster to train clerics to read and write their native tongue than to teach them a foreign language. Whatever the reasons, English writers were using vernacular prose confidently well in advance of other Europeans.

A surprising variety of OE prose writing survives, though a heavy proportion consists of translations from Latin. King Alfred translated or had translated into English Bede's *Ecclesiastical History of the English People*, Pope Gregory the Great's *Pastoral Care*, Boethius' *Consolation of Philosophy*, and Orosius' compendious history (to which Alfred had some original additions made). Among the Biblical translations of the OE period are the *Heptateuch* (the first seven books of the Old Testament), portions of the Psalms, and the late *Anglo-Saxon Gospels*. There are even fragments of prose fiction and fantasy, including *Apollonius of Tyre*, *Alexander's Letter to Aristotle*, and *Wonders of the East*.

King Alfred was also responsible for beginning the *Anglo-Saxon Chronicle* (actually a series of chronicles kept at various centers in England), an invaluable source of information not only about Anglo-Saxon history, but also about the Old English language. Begun in the late ninth century, some of the texts of the *Anglo-Saxon Chronicle* were kept, more or less continuously, for almost three hundred years. The latest version goes down to 1154, almost a century after the Norman Conquest. Most of the writing in the *Chronicle* is natural, matter-of-fact, but undistinguished. Some of the later entries, though, show true craftsmanship and can be read with pleasure and even excitement today.

A large amount of religious writing in prose survives from the OE period. Most notable are the works of Abbot Ælfric, the outstanding prose writer of his time, and Bishop Wulfstan. Most of Ælfric's sources were Latin, but in his sermons, homilies, and saints' lives, Ælfric freely adapted his sources to fit English needs. He wrote a sophisticated, vigorous, often elegant prose that, while showing influence of Latin literary devices, also employs native rhythms and alliteration. The result is so "poetic" that earlier scholars printed passages of his works as verse rather than prose.

Bishop Wulfstan is best known for his bombastic *Sermo Lupi ad Anglos* ("Wulfstan's Sermon to the English"; see p. 97), an eloquent and fiery admonition of the English people for their sins, to which he attributed the evils of the Viking invasions and various natural disasters. Other, usually anonymous, homilies survive in the two collections known as the *Blickling Homilies* and the *Vercelli Homilies*.

Among the miscellaneous prose writings of the OE period are genealogies, glossaries to Latin works (important for their information about OE vocabulary and semantics), laws, charters, and a few letters. Scientific writing is represented by leech books and herbariums and by Byrhtferth's *Manual*, which treats of astronomy and mathematics.

Verse

For the modern student, Old English literature usually means Old English poetry, although only about 30,000 lines of poetry survive—roughly the same number that we have from Chaucer alone in Middle English. OE poetry falls into two broad general classifications, epic verse and shorter poems. *Beowulf*, which at 3182 lines comprises about one-tenth of surviving OE verse, is the only complete secular epic; others, such as *Exodus* and *Judith*, are on Biblical topics. Most of the shorter poems are usually somewhat vaguely classified as lyrical or elegiac (OE poetry could never be called lighthearted); they include such well-known poems as "The Seafarer," "The Wanderer," "The Dream of the Rood," and "Deor." In addition, there are a number of poems that can be generally categorized as didactic verse.

The basis of OE verse was the four-stress, unrhymed, alliterative line, a Germanic form that the Anglo-Saxons brought with them from the Continent.[8] Each OE poetic line was divided into two half-lines, and the first stressed word of the second half-line determined the alliteration for the entire line. The second stressed word of the second half-line did not alliterate, but either or both of the stressed words in the first half-line could alliterate. Rhythmically, OE verse was a time-stressed line, with approximately equal time between major stresses. Unlike the syllable-counting verse more familiar in English today, the number of unstressed syllables in a line could vary; in reading OE verse aloud, one simply speeds up for a series of unstressed syllables and slows down for one (or no) unstressed syllable between major stresses. There were also various conventions with respect to which initial sounds alliterated with each other and to the relative positions of stressed and unstressed syllables in the line.

Although the flow of OE verse was frequently interrupted by variations (or apposition), the syntax did not differ in any essential respects from that of OE prose. There does seem to have been a poetic vocabulary of words used chiefly or exclusively in verse. Of course, an extensive lexicon was essential in order for poets to have at their disposal synonyms beginning with various sounds to fit the alliterative demands of any given line. Reproduced below are lines 6–14 of "The Wanderer," an elegiac lyric from the *Exeter Book*, the largest surviving collection of Old English poetry.

Swa cwæð eardstapa,   earfeþa gemyndig,
Thus spoke earth-stepper,   of hardships mindful,

wraþra wælsleahta,   winemæga hryre:
of horrible slaughters,   of dear kinsmen destruction:

"Oft ic sceolde ana   uhtna gehwylce
"Often I have had to alone   dawn each

mine ceare cwiþan.   Nis nu cwicra nan
my care bemoan.   Not is now alive none

þe ic him modsefan   minne durre
to whom I to him soul   my dare

sweotule asecgan.   Ic to soþe wat
clearly express.   I as truth know

þæt biþ in eorle   indryhten þeaw,
that is in brave man   noble custom

þæt he his ferðlocan   fæste binde,
that he his breast   fast bind,

healde his hordcofan,   hycge swa he wille."
hold his thoughts,   think as he will."

---

[8] Alliteration, or front rhyme, is ideally suited to Germanic languages, with their stress on the root syllables of words. For the same reason, throughout its history, English has been a difficult language in which to rhyme. End-rhyme demands that all sounds after the stressed vowel be the same; the closer the stress is to the beginning of the word, the more complicated the rhyme must be and the less likely that a rhyme will exist in the language. (PDE has a number of common words, such as *orange* and *month*, for which there is no rhyme at all.)

Translation

Thus spoke the wanderer, remembering hardships, horrible slaughter, and the fall of dear kinsmen: "Often, at each dawn, I, alone, have had to bemoan my cares. No one is now alive to whom I dare reveal my soul. I know in truth that it is a noble custom in a brave man to bind fast his heart and hold back his thoughts—whatever he may be thinking."

Because a time-stressed rhythm characterized not only OE verse but also ordinary speech, the dividing line between verse and prose in Old English was less sharp than that between the syllable-counting verse and the prose of today. Some OE writers employed "metrical prose," prose that fell roughly into four-stress phrases. These phrases were further unified by alliteration, sometimes heavy alliteration, although the detailed alliterative rules of OE verse were not strictly observed.

With the Norman Conquest, the long and glorious tradition of alliterative verse in English came to a halt. This is movingly documented by a short fragment written about 1100 and preserved in a manuscript in Worcester Cathedral Library. The piece celebrates Anglo-Saxon learning and laments its decline under foreign (French) teachers. It is doubly sad because it exemplifies what it deplores: the little poem is itself very bad alliterative verse.

þeos lærden ure leodan on englisc.
these taught our people in English

næs deorc heore liht. ac hit fæire glod.
not was dark their light but it bright shone

nu is þeo leore forleten. & þet folc is forloren.
now is the teaching neglected & the people are lost

nu beoþ oþre leoden. þeo læreþ ure folc.
now are other languages which learn our people

& feole of þen lorþeines losiæþ. & þet folc forþ mid.
& many of the teachers are being destroyed & the people forth with

Translation

These taught our people in English. Their light was not dark, but shone brightly. Now their teaching is abandoned and the people are lost. Now our people learn other languages, and many of the teachers are perishing and the people with them.

In summary, the most important features of Old English are

1. Phonologically, the consonant system was similar to that of PDE, but included phonemically long consonants and lacked phonemic /ŋ/ and phonemically voiced fricatives. Length was also phonemic for vowels.
2. Morphologically, OE was still a heavily inflected language, including four cases, three genders, two numbers, two tenses, three persons, and three moods.
3. Syntactically, OE word order resembled that of PDE, but was freer and more varied.
4. Lexically, OE had a rich vocabulary and extensive resources for forming new words; loanwords comprised an insignificant part of the lexicon.

Suggested Further Reading

Anglo-Saxon England, 1972– .
Barney, Stephen A. *Word-Hoard: An Introduction to Old English Vocabulary.*
Blair, Peter Hunter. *An Introduction to Anglo-Saxon England.*
Campbell, A. *Old English Grammar.*
Cassidy, Frederic G., and Richard N. Ringler, eds. *Bright's Old English Grammar & Reader.*
Clark Hall, John R., and Herbert D. Meritt. *A Concise Anglo-Saxon Dictionary.*
Collingwood, R. G., and J. N. L. Myres. *Roman Britain and the English Settlements.*
Lapidge, Michael, and Helmut Gneuss, eds. *Learning and Literature in Anglo-Saxon England.*
Mitchell, Bruce. *Old English Syntax.*
Quirk, Randolph, and C. L. Wrenn. *An Old English Grammar.*
Stenton, Frank M. *Anglo-Saxon England.*
Toller, T. Northcote, ed. *An Anglo-Saxon Dictionary Based on the Manuscript Collections of the Late Joseph Bosworth.*
Traugott, Elizabeth Closs. *The History of English Syntax.*
Whitelock, Dorothy. *The Beginnings of English Society.*

CHAPTER 6

Middle English

*So now they have made our English tongue a
gallimaufry or hodgepodge of all other speeches.*
—Edmund Spenser

OUTER HISTORY

Linguistically, the English language between the mid-eleventh and the sixteenth centuries is sufficiently homogeneous to justify the single label of Middle English. On the other hand, the political and social status of both the language and its speakers changed greatly during this period, and three distinct subperiods can be identified.

1066–1204: English in Decline

The Norman invasion is arguably the single most cataclysmic event in English history. It was the last—but the most thoroughgoing—invasion of England by foreigners. It unified England for the first time in its history. And it was the most important event ever to occur in the outer history of the English language. Politically and linguistically, it was a French conquest of England. Ethnically, it represented the last of the great Germanic invasions of England.

William I (William the Conqueror, Duke of Normandy) was a descendant of Rollo the Dane, the Viking who had terrorized northern France until, in A.D. 911, the harassed French king, Charles the Simple, was forced to conclude an arrangement with him similar to that King Alfred had made with the Danes in England a few years earlier. Rollo and his followers took control of the area of northern France that became known as Normandy (Norman = "north man"). The Normans soon gave up their own language in favor of French, but it was a

French heavily influenced by their original Germanic dialect, a fact that was much later to be of significance in the ultimate resurgence of English in England.

Following his defeat of Harold Godwineson at Hastings, William rapidly subjugated the rest of southeast England. Rebellions in the north and west of England delayed his securing of these areas, but within about ten years after the Conquest, all of England was firmly under William's control. Most of the Anglo-Saxon nobility was killed, either at Hastings or in the subsequent abortive rebellions. The remaining English speakers accepted William's kingship with resignation if not enthusiasm. One of the reasons for this relatively easy acceptance was that William brought the land more unity, peace, and stability than it had experienced for generations. During his reign, the Viking attacks ceased. The numerous internal squabbles came to an end. William established a ring of castles on the Welsh borders and thereby kept the Welsh under control. William himself was a stern and ruthless ruler, but he was not genocidal; his subjugation of England was a business matter, not a holy war. Where existing English laws and customs did not conflict with his own regulations, he allowed English practices to remain.

William replaced Englishmen with Frenchmen in all the high offices of both state and Church, partly to reward his French followers for their support, partly because he, justifiably, felt that he could not trust the English. Even the scriptoria of the monasteries were taken over by French speakers (although at Peterborough the *Anglo-Saxon Chronicle* continued to be written in English until 1154).

Along with his French officials, William also imported the principle of the feudal system, the notion of the state as a hierarchy in which every member was directly responsible to the person above him in the hierarchy. Vassalage was hereditary from the dukes directly under the king at the top to the peasants at the bottom. Although these peasants were not slaves, they were bound to the land. Hence the English speakers of one area had few opportunities to communicate with those of other areas, and dialectal differences among the regions increased. There were few towns of any size in which speakers from various areas could congregate, thereby reconciling the most outstanding dialectal differences. Without literacy and a standard written language—or any written language at all—to act as a brake on change, dialectal differences in English proliferated.

During most of the Middle English period, the kings took French wives and spent most of their reigns in their extensive possessions in France. They did not speak English at all, though some of the later kings apparently understood it. The English court was a French-speaking court. Indeed, some of the finest French literature of the period was written in England for French-speaking English patrons.

The linguistic situation in Britain after the Conquest was complex. French was the native language of a minority of a few thousand speakers, but a minority with influence out of all proportion to their numbers because they controlled the political, ecclesiastical, economic, and cultural life of the nation. The overwhelming majority of the population of England spoke English, but English had no prestige whatsoever. Latin was the written language of the Church and of many secular documents; it was also spoken in the newly emerging universities and in the Church. Scandinavian was still spoken (but not written) in the Danelaw and other areas of heavy Scandinavian settlement, though it was soon to be assimilated to English, its influence being restricted primarily to loanwords in English and to dialectal peculiarities of the area. Beyond the borders of England proper, Celtic languages still prevailed in Wales and Scotland (where a new standard Scots English was eventually to develop, based on the English of Edinburgh).

Within a short time after the Conquest, there was probably a fair amount of bilingualism in England. Even if the kings had no English, most of the nobility would have had to learn at least a number of English words in order to communicate with their Anglo-Saxon underlings. Estate officials and household supervisors must have used English to give orders and to receive reports. Even though the kings usually did not take English wives, many of the nobility soon did; the result would have been bilingual children. Even if both the lord and his lady spoke only French, they probably had English-speaking nurses for their offspring, and the children learned English from these nurses and the other servants. Conversely, many Anglo-Saxons would have attempted to learn French as a means of improving their social and economic status. From the beginning, English speakers would have become familiar with such French words as *tax*, *estate*, *trouble*, *duty*, and *pay*. English household servants would have learned French words like *table*, *boil*, *serve*, *roast*, and *dine*. From French-speaking clergy, the English would have learned such words as *religion*, *savior*, *pray*, and *trinity*. Most of these words do not appear in written English until after 1204, but only because little written English has survived from the period 1066–1204. When such words do appear in writing, they are used with the confidence of familiar, universally known words.

1204–1348: English in the Ascendant

In what must have seemed a bitter fulfillment of the prophecy of his earlier nickname (John Lackland), King John of England lost, in 1204, all of Normandy except the Channel Islands. Thereafter, landowners who held possessions in both France and England were forced to choose between the two and give up their lands in one of the two countries. Although vast parts of southern France remained under nominal English control, they had always been too far away to support the easy and continuous intercommunication that had previously characterized England and Normandy.

With the loss of Normandy came a predictable decline of interest in France and French among those Anglo-Norman landholders who had opted to stay in England. This lack of interest—even hostility—to French was only exacerbated by the fact that the French that they spoke, by now a recognizably different dialect called Anglo-French, was ridiculed by speakers of the rising standard French based on the Parisian dialect. There could have been a reversal to the decline in the influence of French in the mid-thirteenth century when King Henry III of England brought in hundreds of French acquaintances and gave them official positions in England. However, these newcomers were speakers of Central French and were heartily loathed by even the Anglo-French speakers, so Henry III's francophilia had little permanent effect on the erosion of French in England.

Even as the loss of English possessions in France was making French a less important language in England, other conditions were contributing to the rise in use and prestige of English. Among them was increased communication among English speakers of the various regions. This intercourse led to a smoothing out of the most striking dialectal differences and to the beginnings of a new standard English, based on the London dialect but including features from all dialectal areas.

From the time of the First Crusade (1095) on, English speakers from all over the nation congregated periodically in coastal towns to take ship for the Holy Land. The rise in popularity of pilgrimages also brought speakers of many different dialects together; Canterbury became a popular goal of pilgrims shortly after Thomas à Becket's assassination there in 1170, and there were many other shrines popular with the English, both in England itself and on the Continent.

By the thirteenth and fourteenth centuries, the children of the English nobility no longer learned French as their native language and had to be taught it, either by imported teachers or by being sent overseas. For about three hundred years after the Conquest, French was the language in which Latin was taught in the schools, but by the late fourteenth century, English was the normal medium of instruction. The rapid decline in knowledge and use of French during this period is evidenced by rules requiring the use of French and by the appearance of books designed to teach people French.

1348–1509: English Triumphant

Although French remained the official language of England until well into the second half of the fourteenth century, two events of that century scaled its fate and guaranteed the resurgence of English. The first of these events was the Black Death (probably bubonic and/or pneumonic plague). The first cases appeared in England in 1348, and successive outbursts followed every few years for the next three hundred years. Because this epidemic was the first of its kind to strike Europe since the sixth century A.D., the population was extremely susceptible. Precise statistics are impossible, but probably about two-thirds of Europe's population was attacked, and perhaps half the victims died. In other words, roughly one-third of the people in England died of the Black Death between 1348 and 1351. The resulting social turmoil is easy to imagine.

Because of the high mortality rate of the Black Death, labor shortages became chronic, and surviving workers demanded higher pay for their labor. Despite laws designed to keep peasants on the farms, many used the accompanying upheavals and social disorganization to escape to the freedom of towns and cities where they could earn more. Wages increased in spite of legislation fixing them. Like it or not, the ruling classes were forced to respect the lower classes because they needed them so badly. This respect surely increased the prestige of English, which was the only language of the lower classes.

The second event that assured the resurgence of English in England was the Hundred Years War (1337–1453). In this intermittent conflict between England and France, England had several notable successes, such as the famous victories at Crécy (1346), Poitiers (1356), and Agincourt (1415). But the French, galvanized into action by Joan of Arc, eventually defeated the English, and England lost all her Continental holdings except the port of Calais. Once England was without French possessions, the English no longer had important practical reasons for learning and using French.

Well before the end of the Hundred Years War, however, French had already become an artificially maintained second language in England, even among the nobility. By the mid-fourteenth century, English was widely used as the language of instruction in schools. In 1362, English became the official language of legal proceedings. The kings of England had spoken English for some time. The number of manuscripts written in English increased enormously in this same century. By the fifteenth century, English was more common in legal documents than either French or Latin.

Unpopular as France and the French were in England during the Hundred Years War, the substitution of English for French as the official language was not a policy decision based on animosity toward France. Rather, it was the recognition of a *fait accompli*; by the end of the fourteenth century, everyone in England spoke English, and even those who spoke French were bilingual in English. Further, English had supplanted not only French, but also the Norse spoken in the Danelaw. Much more slowly, but just as inexorably, it was also supplanting the Celtic languages spoken in Wales, Cornwall, and Scotland.

Throughout the period, great dialectal differences persisted in the English spoken (and written) in the various parts of the country. At the same time, however, a standard spoken and written English based on the London dialect was emerging. This new standard was not to replace the dialects; instead, it was superimposed upon them. And this London dialect is the basis of all the national standards of today, not just Received Pronunciation in Britain, but also the standard versions of American, Canadian, Australian, New Zealand, South African, and Indian English today.

London English was a logical and obvious basis for a standard language. London speech was essentially an East Midlands dialect, but the city attracted people from all over the country and its speech was to some extent influenced by all these other dialects. It was, therefore, a natural compromise dialect. As the largest city, the major seaport, and the biggest commercial center of the nation, London automatically had a prestige that carried over to its speech. London was near the court at Westminster, and the court lent its glamour to London. When, toward the end of the fifteenth century, printing came to England, the printers set up their establishments in London and printed their books in the London dialect. As these books spread throughout the rest of the country, they brought the written version of London English with them. The greatly increased literacy of the fifteenth century meant that more and more people were exposed to this rising standard dialect.

The ascendancy of Henry VIII to the throne in 1509 coincides with the end of the Middle English period. The revival of English as the national language of England was assured, and a national standard English based on London speech was being disseminated throughout the country by means of the printed word.

INNER HISTORY

Middle English Phonology

Historians of the English language are fortunate in having fairly extensive written records from Old English. They are less fortunate with respect to the early stages of Middle English. Because the Norman Conquest made French the official language of England for about three hundred years, English was written down relatively infrequently, especially during the period 1100–1200. Yet the English language was changing rapidly, and dialectal differences were becoming, if anything, even greater than during Anglo-Saxon times. By the time English was once again written down regularly, many changes had occurred in all aspects of the language. The match between the sound system and the spelling was much worse than in Old English.

French scribes, most of them probably not even fluent in English, let alone being native speakers, had introduced a fair amount of confusion into the spelling system of English.

To make matters worse for the historian of the language, the new standard English that arose in the fourteenth century was not a direct descendant of West Saxon, the dialect in which most of our Old English texts survive. Instead, the new standard in Middle English was based on London speech, essentially an East Midlands dialect, although with some unique characteristics and some features of other dialects. Our discussion of Middle English is necessarily based on this London dialect (roughly, the dialect of Chaucer's writings) and not on the Southern dialect that was a direct descendant of West Saxon.

Consonants

As we saw in the preceding chapter, the inventory of consonants in Old English did not differ dramatically from that of Present-Day English. The Middle English inventory, not surprisingly, looks even more like that of Present-Day English; indeed, it lacks only phonemic /ŋ/ and /ž/ to be identical.

VOICING OF FRICATIVES

Figure 6.1 shows the Middle English consonants. Comparing Figure 6.1 with Figure 5.1 (p. 70), we see that the only system-wide change between the consonants of Old English and those of Middle English is the addition of phonemic voiced fricatives. (Voiced fricatives did occur in Old English, but only as allophones of voiceless fricatives.) None of the Old English consonant phonemes were lost between Old English and Middle English.

Why, when English had gotten along nicely for half a millennium without a voiced/voiceless contrast in its fricatives, should it develop one during the Middle English period? A number of factors contributed to the change. Probably no single one of them would have been sufficient to bring about the change, but the combination of all of them tipped the balance. One pressure came from the great influx of loanwords. French already had a phonemic distinction between /f/ and /v/, so, in English, the only difference between such loans as *vine* and *fine*, or between

Figure 6.1 Middle English Consonants

Manner of Articulation		Point of Articulation					
		Bilabial	*Labiodental*	*Interdental*	*Alveolar*	*Alveopalatal*	*Velar*
Stops	voiceless	p			t		k
	voiced	b			d		g
Affricates	voiceless					č	
	voiced					ǰ	
Fricatives	voiceless		f	θ	s	š	h
	voiced		v	ð	z		
Nasals		m			n		
Lateral					l		
Retroflex					r		
Semivowels		w				j	

the French loans *vetch*, *view*, and *vile* and English *fetch*, *few*, and *file*, respectively, would have been the voiced [v]. However, French did not have [z] in initial position, and it did not have the sounds [θ] and [ð] at all. Nor were the loanwords with contrasting [f] and [v] numerous. Besides, languages can easily tolerate a few homophones. Therefore, the French influence alone would scarcely have been adequate to effect a structural change in the English phonological system.

Another impetus to the development of voiced fricative phonemes was dialect mixture. Even in Old English, some Southern dialects were apparently voicing all fricatives in initial position (*synn* 'sin' was [zyn:], not [syn:]), although this pronunciation was usually not reflected in the standardized spelling of Old English. With the increased communication between regions during the course of Middle English, speakers from various areas would have become accustomed to hearing both voiced and voiceless fricatives at the beginning of words.[1]

A third source of contrastive voiced fricatives was the loss of final vowels. In Old English, fricatives were voiced only when surrounded by voiced sounds. For example, in most forms of the verb *hūsian* 'to house', the *s* was pronounced [z] because it was preceded and followed by (voiced) vowels. After the loss of the final [n] and then the preceding vowel or vowels, the *s* stood in final position in many forms. Nevertheless, it retained its [z] pronunciation, thus contrasting directly with the singular noun *hous* (OE *hūs*), which had always been pronounced with a final [s].[2]

A fourth development producing voiced fricatives in previously unvoiced positions was the voicing of fricatives in very lightly stressed words, especially function words like *is*, *was*, *of*, *his*, *the*, *then*, *that*, and *they*. The usual explanation is that voiced consonants require less energy to produce than do unvoiced consonants; we can still observe the process in the PDE variant pronunciations of *with* as either /wɪθ/ or /wɪð/.

The voiced fricatives became phonemic in English hundreds of years ago, ample time, we might think, for the newcomers to become completely naturalized. Yet /v/, /ð/, and /z/ are still more limited in their distribution than most other English consonants. Almost all words beginning with /v/ or /z/ are loanwords, and only function words like the definite article, the demonstrative pronouns, the third-person plural pronouns, and adverbs like *then*, *thus*, and *there* have initial /ð/. (Try it; how would you pronounce a new word spelled *thale* or *thorvine*?)

Even though /f/, /θ/, and /s/ developed corresponding voiced phonemes during Middle English, /š/ did not. Voiced [ž] was not to become phonemic until the Early Modern English period and then under highly limited conditions. Also, [ŋ] was not yet phonemic in Middle English. The consonant /h/ still could appear after vowels or consonants in the form of the allophones [ç] (ME *niht* [nɪçt] 'night') and [x] (ME *thurh* 'through' [θurx]).

---

[1] Although the Midlands and Northern forms usually prevailed, PDE still retains the Southern *vixen* beside Midlands *fox*. The Southern form *vat* ousted the Midlands *fat* in most dialects only after the eighteenth century; colonial New England records still have the spelling *fat*.

[2] This distinction in *house* as noun and *house* as verb is retained in PDE, despite the identity in spelling. Parallel distinctions remain in such pairs of related forms as *cleave/cleft*, *lose/lost*, and *bathe/bath*. In Old English, a number of nouns had a vowel in plural endings that did not appear in the nominative singular (nom. sg. *cnīf* 'knife'/nom. pl. *cnīfas*). Here also, the alternation in the voicing of the final consonant of the stem remains to this day in such words as *knife/knives*, *path/paths*, *half/halves*, and, of course, the noun *house/houses*.

CHANGES IN DISTRIBUTION OF CONSONANTS

Although the only system-wide change in the English consonant inventory between Old and Middle English was the addition of phonemically voiced fricatives, numerous adjustments within the system affected the distribution of individual consonants. Some of these changes were systemic; that is, they occurred wherever the conditioning factors appeared. Other changes were sporadic, occurring under given conditions in some words but not in others. Among the systemic changes were loss of long consonants, loss of initial /h/ before certain consonants, loss of [γ] as an allophone of /g/, and loss of /j/ in the prefix *ge-*.

1. As was noted in Chapter 5, Old English had had phonemically long consonants; that is, words could be distinguished on the basis of the time spent in producing the consonant. This distinction was probably being lost at the end of words by late Old English, and was lost in all positions by the end of Middle English. Hence the difference between such Old English words as *man* 'indefinite pronoun, one' and *mann* 'man, mankind' disappeared.
2. The consonant /h/ was regularly lost in the clusters /hl/, /hn/, and /hr/. In some dialects /h/ was also lost before /w/, but other dialects have of course retained /hw/ to the present day (as in *what, whale, whimper*). Examples include the change from Old English *hlǣfdige* 'lady', *hnecca* 'neck', and *hræfn* 'raven' to late Middle English *ladi, necke,* and *raven*.
3. The Old English allophone [γ] of the phoneme /g/ regularly vocalized or became the semivowel /w/ after [1] and [r]. Thus Old English *swelgan* 'to swallow' and *fēolaga* 'partner' became Middle English *swolwen* and *felawe*; Old English *morgen* 'morning' and *sorg* became Middle English *morwen* and *sorow*.
4. The very common Old English prefix *ge-* (pronounced /jɛ/ or /jɪ/) lost its initial consonant and was reduced to /ɪ/, spelled *y* or *i*. Thus, for example, Old English *genōg* 'enough', ME *inough*; and OE *genumen* 'taken', ME *inome(n)*.

Among the sporadic changes in consonants during Middle English are the voicing of fricatives under certain conditions, the loss of unstressed final consonants, the simplification of consonant clusters, and the appearance of intrusive consonants.

1. Initial and final fricatives of words that normally received very light stress tended to become voiced in Middle English (see p. 126). However, voicing did not occur (or at least did not remain) in similar words like *for* or *so*. In addition, the final *-s* of plurals and third-person singular present indicative verbs became voiced after voiced sounds, but remained voiceless after voiceless sounds.
2. Unstressed final consonants following a vowel tended to be lost in Middle English. Thus OE *ic* 'I' became ME *i* and the OE adjective ending *-lic* became ME *-ly*. In OE, a final *-n* had characterized various parts of verbal paradigms, including the infinitive, the plural subjunctive, and the plural preterite indicative. During the course of ME, final *-n* was lost in all these positions; it has remained, however, in the past participle of many strong verbs to the present day (*seen, gone, taken*). Final *-n* was also lost in the possessive adjectives *my* and *thy* before words beginning with a consonant sound and in the indefinite article *an*, but remained in the possessive pronouns *mine* and *thine*.
3. Certain consonants tended to be lost when they appeared in clusters with other consonants.
   a. The semivowel /w/ dropped after /s/ or /t/, though it is sometimes still retained in spelling: *sword, sister* (OE *sweostor*), *such* (OE *swilc*), *sough,* and

two. It was retained after /s/ or /t/ in such words as *swallow*, *swim*, *swelter*, *twin*, and *twain*.

b. The consonant /l/ was lost in the vicinity of /č/ in the adjectival pronouns *each*, *such*, *which*, and *much* (OE *ǣlc*, *swilc*, *hwilc*, and *micel*). However, in some other words, /l/ remained in this environment (*filch*, *milch*).

c. The fricative /v/ tended to drop out before a consonant or vowel plus consonant. Compare OE *hlāford* 'lord', *hlǣfdige* 'lady', *hēafod* 'head', and *hæfde* 'had' with ME *lord*, *ladi*, *hed*, *hadde*. The /v/ was not lost in such words as OE *heofon* 'heaven', *hræfn* 'raven', or *dreflian* 'to drivel'.

d. By the end of ME, at least, a final /b/ after /m/ was being lost in pronunciation, though not in spelling (*lamb*, *comb*, *climb*), but the cluster /mb/ remained in medial position (*timber*, *amble*).

4. Intrusive consonants appeared, especially before the resonants /l/, /r/, and /n/, in many words in Middle English.

a. Intrusive /b/ after /m/ and before a consonant was common: OE *brēmel* 'bramble', *nǣmel* 'nimble', *ǣmerge* 'ember' became *bremble*, *nimble*, and *ember* in ME. However, this development was not universal: OE *hamor* 'hammer' and *camel* 'camel' developed no such intrusive /b/. In a few words, an intrusive /b/ appeared after final /m/ in ME, though it was later lost in pronunciation. Thus OE *þūma* 'thumb', ME *thombe*; compare the PDE pronunciation of *thumb* with its derivative *thimble* (OE *þȳmel*).

b. Parallel to intrusive /b/ after /m/ was intrusive /d/ after /n/ in final position or before a resonant: OE *dwīnan*, ME *dwindle*; OE *þunor*, ME *thunder*; late ME *sound* from Old French *son* 'noise'. Again, this was not consistent; OE *fenol* 'fennel' and *canne* 'metal container' developed no intrusive /d/.

c. In a number of words, ME developed an intrusive /t/ after /s/ in the same positions in which intrusive /b/ and /d/ appeared. Thus we find, for example, ME *listnen* 'listen' (OE *hlysnan*), ME *hustle* (from Middle Dutch *husselen*), and ME *beheste* (OE *behǣs*). But no intrusive /t/ appears in similar words such as ME *vessel* (from Old French *vessel*), *lessen* (from the adjective *less*), or *cros* 'cross' (OE *cros*).

Despite the many adjustments in the distribution of consonants during the Middle English period, several combinations remained that have since simplified. The initial stops of the clusters *gn-* and *kn-* were still pronounced in ME: OE *gnæt* and *gnagan*, ME *gnat* and *gnawe(n)*; OE *cnāwan* and *cnafa*, ME *knowe(n)* and *knave*. Also, the fricative /h/ could still appear in positions other than at the beginning of a syllable; *þought* 'thought' was pronounced [θoxt] and *high* was [hiç]. On the other hand, /h/ was often lost in unstressed positions: OE *hit*, ME *it*.

Vowels

The vowels of English have always been less stable than its consonants. The problem of ascertaining exactly what the vowel phonemes were at a given period is exacerbated by the fact that, throughout its history, the English writing system has suffered from a paucity of graphemes (letters) to represent its rich inventory of vowel phonemes. For example, a typical PDE American dialect has fourteen vowels and diphthongs, but only seven graphemes to spell them—including ⟨w⟩ and ⟨y⟩, both of which double as consonants and are restricted in their use as vowel symbols. Because we must rely heavily on written evidence in reconstructing the phonology of earlier stages of the language, our conclusions about vowel phonemes are necessarily much more tentative than our statements about consonants. There is, if anything, less agreement among scholars about both the phonetics and the phonemics of Middle English vowels than there is about Old English vowels. The system presented here for London English during the Middle English period will thus not agree in all details with that postulated by some other scholars.

QUALITATIVE CHANGES

Figure 6.2 presents the regular development of the vowels that Middle English inherited from Old English.

As the chart shows, the majority of OE vowels remained unchanged in ME, at least with respect to their regular development. Changes did occur, however, in eight of the eighteen OE vowels and diphthongs.

1. OE /y/ and /ȳ/ had unrounded to /ɪ/ and /ī/ in some dialects during the OE period. In the West Midlands, they remained as rounded vowels, spelled *u*, until late in the ME period. In the South, they had unrounded to /ɛ/ and /ē/, respectively, during OE, and remained thus during ME. By the end of ME, all dialects had /ɪ/ and /ī/.
2. OE /æ/ apparently had lowered to /ɑ/ in all dialects by the end of ME. However, its development is somewhat obscured by the fact that the graphic symbol ⟨æ⟩ was abandoned early in ME; to what extent the grapheme ⟨a⟩ represented both /æ/ and /ɑ/ is uncertain. In the South, OE /æ/ apparently was /ɛ/, not /ɑ/, during the ME period.
3. In Figure 5.3 (p. 74), we showed only one symbol for /æ/ in West Saxon Old English. However, other OE dialects had had two different phonemes here, reflecting two different origins. One of them, /ǣ/[1], came from West Germanic *ā and had become /ē/ in OE dialects other than West Saxon; this /ē/ remained in ME. The second, /ǣ/[2], arose from the *i*-umlaut (mutation) of OE /ā/. This /ǣ/[2] had become /ɛ̄/ in most of England by ME times.
4. OE /ā/ became ME /ɔ̄/ during the course of ME in all areas except the North, where it remained /ā/ throughout the ME period.
5. All the OE diphthongs smoothed (became pure vowels) in Middle English.

Figure 6.2   Middle English Development of Old English Vowels

Short Vowels		Long Vowels		Diphthongs	
OE	ME*	OE	ME	OE	ME
i	ɪ	ī	ī	eə	ɛ
y	ɪ	ȳ	ī	æə	ɑ
e	ɛ	ē	ē	ēə	ē
æ	ɑ	ǣ	ɛ̄, ē	ǣə	ɛ̄
ɑ	ɑ	ā	ɔ̄		
⟨⟩	ɔ	ō	ō		
ʊ	ʊ	ū	ū		

* We assume, though without direct evidence, that the short vowels had a lax pronunciation, similar to that of PDE, by the end of ME. The difference in the pronunciation of the short vowels in OE and ME would not have been as great as the change in symbols here might suggest.

If only the regular developments just outlined had occurred, the Middle English vowel system would have been rather simple, simpler in fact than that of Old English, with only five short and six long vowels: /ɪ, ɛ, ɑ, ɔ, ʊ/ and /ī, ē, ɛ̄, ɔ̄, ō, ū/. But the total picture is more complex because various phonological developments added the short vowel /ə/ and the long vowel /ā/ to the ME inventory. Other sound changes and French loanwords added as many as seven new diphthongs to the language. Figure 6.3 presents the vowels of ME, their sources, their most common spellings, and illustrative words containing the vowels. On the chart we use slash marks, indicating phonemic status for all the ME vowels and diphthongs. However, the phonemic status of some of the diphthongs is dubious.

As Figure 6.3 shows, the ME short vowel system differs from that of OE in the loss of /y/ and /æ/ and in the addition of /ə/. In addition to the OE sources for the ME short vowels were loanwords from Old Norse and Old French. For example, the Old Norse loans *skin* and *egg* had /ɪ/ and /ɛ/, respectively. The Old French loans *test* and *part* had /ɛ/ and /ɑ/, respectively.

The ME midcentral short vowel /ə/ appeared only in unstressed syllables. Beginning in OE and continuing in ME, the short vowels /ɑ/, /ɛ/, /ɔ/, and /ʊ/ all reduced to /ə/ (most often spelled *e*) in unstressed syllables. Under the same circumstances, the short vowel /ɪ/ tended to remain, as it does to the present day. This reduction of all unstressed vowels to /ə/ or /ɪ/ was one factor in the ultimate loss of most English inflections.

A minor source of ME /ə/ was the development of a "parasitic" vowel (also called an **epenthetic** vowel) between two consonants. This parasitic vowel was spelled various ways, most commonly *e*.

OE	*ME*
þurh	*thorow* 'thorough'
setl	*setel* 'seat'
ǣfre	*ever*
swefn	*sweven* 'dream'

As we saw earlier, the ME long vowel system differed from that of OE in its loss of /ȳ/ and /ǣ/ and its addition of /ɛ̄/ and /ɔ̄/. Note also that the OE combinations of [ʊɣ] and [ūɣ] had completely vocalized by ME, giving ME /ū/. Loanwords also contributed to the ME long vowels; for instance, the ON loans *root* with /ō/ and *thrive* with /ī/, and the OF loan *beste* 'beast' with /ɛ̄/.

Although all the OE diphthongs smoothed to pure vowels in Middle English, an assortment of new diphthongs arose, most of them as the result of vocalization of OE [w], [y], and [v] between two vowels. In addition, French loanwords provided two other diphthongs, /ʊi/ and /ɔi/. They later fell together as /ɔi/ in most dialects of English, but some dialects of English distinguish them to this day. That is, those dialects that have [pɑizən] for *poison* and [bɑil] for *boil* have only the standard [nɔiz] for *noise* and [ǰɔi] for *joy*; the distinction dates from Middle English. The first two diphthongs listed in Figure 6.3, /iu/ and /ɛu/, were rare even in Middle English; they later fell together and appear in PDE as either /u/ or /ju/.

QUANTITATIVE CHANGES

For the later history of English, the quantitative changes in vowels during ME were of greater importance than the qualitative. Phonemic vowel length was retained

Figure 6.3 Middle English Vowels

Vowels	Primary Sources	Common Spelling	Sample Words
Short			
/i/	OE /i/ /y/	i, y	OE *dimm*, ME *dim*; OE *cyssan*, ME *kisse(n)*
/ɛ/	OE /e/ /ea/	e	OE *bedd*, ME *bed*; OE *heorte*, ME *herte* 'heart'
/ə/	unstressed vowels	e	ME *tale, moder* 'mother', *bunden* 'bound'
/a/	OE /a/ /æ/ /æə/	a	OE *þæt*, ME *that*; OE *earm*, ME *arm*; OE *ealu*, ME *ale*
/ʊ/	OE /u/	u, o	OE *full*, ME *full*; OE *sunu*, ME *son*
/ɔ/	OE /o/	o	OE *hoppian*, ME *hoppe(n)* 'hop'
Long			
/ī/	OE /ī/ /ȳ/	i, y	OE *rīpe*, ME *ripe*; OE *fȳr*, ME *fir(e)*
/ē/	OE /ē/, /ǣ/ /ēa/	e, ee	OE *fēlan*, ME *fele(n)* 'feel'; OE *strǣt*, ME *strete* 'street'; OE *dēop*, ME *deep*
/ɛ̄/	OE /ǣ/ /ēa/ /ē/	e, ee	OE *tǣcan*, ME *teche* 'teach'; OE *drēam*, ME *dreem* 'dream',
/ā/	OE /a/ /æ/	a	OE *baþian*, ME *bathe*; OE *blæse*, ME *blase* 'blaze'; OF *save*, ME *save*
/ū/	OE /ū/ [uɣ]	ou, ow	OE *hūs*, ME *hous*; OE *fugel*, ME *fowle*
/ō/	OE /ō/	o, oo	OE *sōna*, ME *sone* 'soon'; OE *pōl*, ME *pool*
/ɔ̄/	OE /o/	o, oo	OE *hām*, ME *home*
Diphthongs			
/iu/	OE [īw] [ēəw]	ew, ue	OE *spīwan*, ME *spewe(n)* 'spew'; OE *trēowe*, ME *trewe* 'true'
/ɛu/	OE [ǣw] [ēəw]	ew	OE *fēawe*, ME *fewe* 'few'; OF *neveu*, ME *neveu* 'nephew'
/u/	OE [aɣj] [aw] [ax]	au, aw	OE *clawu*, ME *clawe* 'claw'; OE *āwiht*, ME *aught*, OF *cause*, ME *cause*
/ɔu/	OE [āw] [āɣj] [āx] [ōw] [ɔɣj] [ɔx]	ou, ow	OE *boga*, ME *bowe* 'bow'; OE *blōwan*, ME *blowe*; OE *dohtor*, ME *doughter* 'daughter'
/æi/	OE [æj] [ɛj] [ej] [æəx]	ai, ei, ay, ey	OE *dæg*, ME *dai* 'day'; OE *weg*, ME *wey* 'way'; ON *steik*, ME *steyke* 'steak'
/ʊi/	Old French	oi, oy	OF *bouillir*, ME *boille(n)* 'boil'; OF *point*, ME *point*
/ɔi/	Old French	oi,oy	OF *noyse*, ME *noise*; OF *choisir*, ME *chois* 'choice'

throughout ME, but, as it became more and more predictable and redundant, its overall importance was greatly reduced. These quantitative changes were to pave the way for the ultimate loss of quantitative distinctions between vowels in Early Modern English.

Lengthening of Short Vowels. As early as Old English, short vowels had lengthened before certain consonant clusters (liquids or nasals followed by a homorganic voiced stop, or /r/ followed by /s/, /ð/, or /l/). Examples are early OE *climban*, ME *clīmbe*; OE *feld*, ME *fēld* 'field'. This lengthening did not take place in words that rarely received full stress in a syllable (for example, *and* or *under*). Nor did it occur if a third consonant followed the cluster (OE *cild*, ME *chīld*; but plural OE *cildru*, ME *childrene*).

With some variation among dialects, these OE lengthenings shortened again during the fourteenth century, *except* for the following combinations:

i, o + mb	early OE *climban*; ME *clīmbe(n)*
	(but OE *dumb*, ME *dumb* where *u* precedes *mb*)
i, u + nd	early OE *grindan*; ME *grīnde(n)*
	(but OE *scrincan*, ME *scrince(n)* 'shrink'
	where *nk* follows the vowel)
any vowel + ld	early OE *hold*; ME *hōld*
	early OE *milde*; ME *mīlde*
	early OE *weald*; ME *wēld* 'forest'
	(The ME form shows the regular development
	of the OE long diphthong *ēa*.)

During the thirteenth century, the short vowels [ɑ], [ɛ], and [ɔ] lengthened in open syllables. (An open syllable is one ending in a vowel.) Thus

OE *ga-tu*	ME *gā-te* 'gate'
OE *ste-lan*	ME *stē-le(n)* 'steal'
OE *ho-pa*	ME *hō-pe* 'hope'

Later in the thirteenth century, /ɪ/ and /ʊ/ sometimes also lengthened in open syllables, but with a simultaneous lowering of the vowel. Hence /ɪ/ became /ē/ and /ʊ/ became /ō/. This lengthening, however, was only sporadic and fails to appear in many words.

OE *pise*, ME *pēse* 'peas' (but not in OE *ficol*, ME *fikel* 'fickle')
OE *wudu*, ME *wōde* 'wood' (but not in OE *hulu*, ME *hule* 'hull')

Shortening of Long Vowels. Beginning as early as the tenth century, there was a parallel shortening of long vowels in stressed closed syllables. (A closed syllable is one ending in one or more consonants.)

OE *sōf-te*	ME *sof-te* 'soft'
OE *gōd-sibb*	ME *god-sib* 'gossip'
OE *scēap-hirde*	ME *scep-herde* 'shepherd'

Shortening did not always occur before *-st*. Thus, beside the predicted ME *last* 'track, last' from OE *lāst*, we also find ME *gōst* 'ghost' from OE *gāst*. Beside the expected shortening of OE *rūst* 'rust' to ME *rust*, there is ME *Chrīst* from OE *crīst*.

If two or more unstressed syllables followed the stressed syllable, the vowel of the stressed syllable always shortened. This rule explains the different vowels still used today in *Christ/Christmas* (ME *Chrīst/Christesmesse*) and *break/breakfast* (ME *brēke/brekefast*).

This process of conditioned lengthening and shortening of vowels depending on whether the syllable was open or closed led to different vowels in different parts of the paradigm of the same word or root. In many instances, regularization across the paradigm later took place. However, some irregularities or apparent irregularities remain to the present day. Examples include the vowels of *five/fifteen*, of *wise/wisdom*, and of the singular *staff*/alternative plural *staves*. In a number of weak verbs, the addition of a /t/ or /d/ closed the preceding syllable, leading to such irregularities as

PDE	ME
hide : hid	*hī-de(n)* : *hid-de*
keep : kept	*kē-pe(n)* : *kep-te*
sleep : slept	*slē-pe(n)* : *slep-te*
hear : heard	*hē-re(n)* : *her-de*

Loss of Unstressed Vowels. During the course of Middle English, unstressed final *-e* (pronounced /ə/) was dropped, although, to judge from the scansion of poetry, its pronunciation remained optional throughout the period. For example:

OE	Early ME	Late ME
heorte 'heart'	*herte* /hɛrtə/	/hɛrt/
milde 'mild'	*milde* /mīldə/	/mīld/
sōna 'immediately'	*sone* /sōnə/	/sōn/
strengþu 'strength'	*strengthe* /strɛnkθə/	/strɛnkθ/

By the end of Middle English, the unstressed *-e* of inflectional endings was also being lost, even when it was followed by a consonant. Thus, although the *e* was still usually written in the plural ending *-es*, the third-person singular present endings *-es* and *-eth*, and the past tense and past participle ending *-ed*, it was no longer pronounced (except in the positions where it is still pronounced today, such as in *wishes, judges, wanted, raided*).

In addition to its drastic consequences for the inflectional system of English (see the next section), this reduction and then loss of unstressed final vowels also eliminated the phonological distinction between many adjectives and adverbs. For a number of common words, the only distinction in Old English between adverb and the nominative form of the adjective had been a final *-e* on the adverb (OE *dēop* 'deep'/*dēope* 'deeply'; OE *heard* [adj.]/*hearde* 'hard' [adv.]). The loss of the *-e* of the adverb in ME made adjective and adverb identical and is the origin of the so-called plain adverbs such as *hard* and *fast* today—although many adverbs have since acquired an *-ly* that distinguishes them from their corresponding adjectives. (Think of the PDE uncertainty between such phrases as *Drive slow* and *Drive slowly*.)

The final *-e* of most French loanwords was not lost in this general decay of final *-e*. These vowels remained because, during ME, most such loans still retained the French stress on the final syllable, even though the stress was to move forward toward the beginning of the word over the coming centuries. Thus the reflexes of ME *cite* 'city' and *purete* 'purity' still have final vowels in PDE.

Prosody

Despite the many changes in the phonology, morphology, syntax, and vocabulary between Old English and Middle English, the stress patterns of native English words changed little; indeed, they remain much the same to the present day. Major stress was on root syllables, while subsequent syllables received minimal stress. Compound words usually had a major stress on the first element and a secondary stress on the second element.

However, the ratio of stressed to unstressed syllables in the sentence as a whole was affected by several factors during Middle English. The loss of many inflectional endings led to a reduction in the number of unstressed syllables. This loss was counterbalanced by an increased use of unstressed particles. Among these were the emerging obligatory definite and indefinite articles, a wider array of prepositions (some of which consisted of two or even more syllables), an increased number of subordinating conjunctions and relative pronouns, the analytic possessive (genitive) with *of*, the marked infinitive with a preceding unstressed *to*, *for to*, or *at*, and compound verb phrases of which only the main verb received full stress.

In addition, among the great influx of French loanwords were many with two, three, or more syllables, of which only one syllable in each word received major stress. Newly borrowed loans of this sort normally were stressed on the final syllable in accordance with French patterns (though there was a general tendency over the years for the stress to migrate toward the front of the word).

The net result of all these changes was a shift in the perceived rhythm of the language. Old English had had what might be termed a generally trochaic rhythm. Words and phrases tended to begin with a stressed syllable and end with unstressed syllables (inflectional endings): *óprĕ sípĕ* 'on another occasion'; *félă míssĕră* 'for many half-years'; *fólcĕ to frófrĕ* 'as a consolation to the people'; *hǽlĕþ wáfĕdŏn* 'the men marveled'. By late Middle English, the rhythm had shifted to a more iambic pattern of unstressed syllables followed by stressed syllables. French loans contributed to this shift, of course, but the wider use of particles was just as important because so many of them formed a unit with a following stressed word: *ŏf mý gráce, fŏr tŏ fýnde, tŏ thĕ péplĕs, shŏlde hăn lóst hĭs héed, whăn thĕ sónne wăs tŏ réste.*

Middle English Graphics

During the Middle English period, spelling and handwriting styles varied greatly over time, in different areas of the country, and even within the work of a single scribe. Even the total inventory of graphemes (letters) occasionally differed; for example, Scots English often used the symbol *β* where other areas had a final *-s* or *-ss*. To some extent, these differences reflect dialectal differences, but in many cases they are simply the predictable inconsistencies of a written language that is not the official language of the nation and hence not standardized. As English gradually replaced French as the official language, as the London dialect became accepted as a national standard, and especially with the advent of printing at the end of the ME period, graphic consistency began to appear, though it was not to become absolute until well into the Early Modern English period. Because of this great disorder, we can make only generalizations, focusing primarily on the most common features and those that have been retained in PDE.

Figure 6.4   The Middle English Alphabet

a	f	k	p	þ
b	g	l	q	u/v
c	ȝ	m	r	w
d	h	n	s	x
e	i/j	o	t	y
				z

During most of the Middle English period and in most areas, there were usually 26 letters in the alphabet. However, as Figure 6.4 illustrates, this alphabet was not identical to that of either Old English or Present-Day English. The OE symbols æ and ð dropped out of use early in Middle English, but two other symbols, þ and ȝ, were retained from the OE alphabet. Further, although *j* and *v* had been introduced by the French, in writing English they were still simply allographs (variants) of *i* and *u*, respectively. That is, both *i* and *j* were used to represent both the vowels /ɪ/ and /i/ and the consonant /ǰ/. *Time* might be spelled *tiim* or *tijm*, and *judge* could be spelled either *iuge* or *juge*. Likewise, both *u* and *v* represented both /ʊ/ and /u/ and the consonant /v/. Thus *up* might be spelled *vp* or *up*, and *even* might be *even* or *euen*. Later in the ME period and continuing into EMnE, there was a strong tendency to reserve *v* for initial position (*vp*, *valeie* 'valley') and *u* for other positions (*euen*, *pur* 'pure').

The letter form ⟨g⟩ was introduced from the Continent to represent /g/. The symbol ⟨ȝ⟩ (derived from the OE form for /g/ and /j/), had a number of different values in ME, the most common of which were [x], as in *poȝt* 'thought' and /j/ as in *ȝung* 'young'. Sometimes ⟨ȝ⟩ represented /ǰ/, as in *bridȝe* 'bridge'. Probably because scribes tended to confuse *ȝ* and *z*, *ȝ* also sometimes was used for /z/, especially in inflectional endings such as in *daiȝ* 'days'.

In OE, the letter *y* had represented the front rounded vowel /y/. As early as late OE, however, this vowel had unrounded in many dialects, becoming identical in sound with /ɪ/ or /i/. Thereafter, and continuing throughout ME, *y* and *i* were used interchangeably to represent both /ɪ/ and /i/. (In the dialects that retained rounded high front vowels in ME, *u*—not *y*—was used to represent /y/ and /ȳ/.) Note that, although *y* is still used in PDE to represent /ɪ/ or /i/, it is no longer in free variation with *i*; today *y* normally represents /ɪ/, /i/, or /ai/ only (a) at the end of a word (*by*, *pay*, *joy*, *party*); (b) in many loanwords ultimately of Greek origin (*system*, *lyre*, *dysentery*); and (c) in a few monosyllabic words (*dye*, *rye*, *lye*).

The letters *q* and *z* had been known in OE, but were rarely used. Under French influence, their use was extended in ME. In particular, the combination *qu* was used for /kw/, replacing the OE *cw* even in native words (OE *cwic* 'alive', ME *quicke*; OE *cwen* 'queen', ME *quene*).

During the course of ME, there was a general tendency to replace þ with the digraph *th* in representing /θ/ or /ð/. The process was gradual, and þ was still being used as late as EMnE, especially in the spelling of function words like *that*, *thou*, and *then*. However, beginning in ME, scribes often formed þ like *y*, so that *ye*, for example, could represent either the second-person plural subject pronoun *ye* or the definite article *the*. This is the origin of the pseudo-archaism *ye olde coffee shoppe*; the *ye* here would properly be pronounced like *the*.

AN EARLY SPELLING REFORMER

Widespread interest in spelling reform for English was not to develop until the sixteenth century. However, one English writer devised his own spelling system at the beginning of the thirteenth century, even though his chief purpose may have been to aid reading aloud rather than to reform the spelling.

Orm—the name is Scandinavian, meaning "serpent"—was an Augustinian canon from the East Midlands who set for himself the task of instructing ordinary people in Church doctrine through a collection of homilies. Each homily consisted of a translation of a passage from the Gospels, followed by an explanation and application of this passage.

If Orm had completed his work, it would have been 150,000 lines long; as it is, 20,000 short verses survive. Orm used a monotonously regular fifteen-syllable line unadorned by either alliteration or rhyme. As literature, the result is worthless, for Orm was unbelievably prolix and repetitive. However, because he did attempt to represent pronunciation in his spelling, the *Ormulum*, as his work is called, is a valuable source of information about the Middle English language. The most noticeable feature of Orm's spelling system is the doubling of consonants to indicate that the preceding vowel is short, although he is not absolutely consistent in this practice. Orm somewhat sporadically employs breve marks (˘) and macrons (¯) to indicate vowel length.

The *Ormulum* survives in a single manuscript today, probably Orm's autographic copy. As the facsimile of the opening lines below shows, it is not an easy text to read.

Facsimile of Orm's Dedication Page

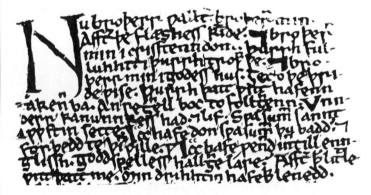

Transliteration

Nu broþerr wallt<u>er</u>. broþerr min.
affter þe flæshess kinde. broþerr
min i crisstenndom. þurrh ful-
uhht & þurrh trowwþe. & broþerr min i godess hus ȝet o þe þri-
de wise. þurrh þatt witt hafenn
täkenn ba. an reȝhell boc to follȝhenn. Vnn-
derr kanunnkess had. & lif. Swasumm sannt

awwstin sette. Icc hafe don swasumm þu badd &
for þedd te þin wille. Iċc hafe wennd innttill enn-
glissh. goddspelless hallʒhe lare. Affter þatt little
wit. þatt me. min drihhtin hafeþþ lenedd.

Translation

Now, Brother Walter—my brother by nature of flesh, and my brother in Christendom through baptism and through faith and my brother in God's house [and] still in the third way—that we two have taken one rule book to follow under canonhood and life, as St. Augustine established [it]. I have done as you asked and performed your will. I have turned into English [the] gospel's holy teaching according to the little wit that my Lord has lent me.

From *The Ormulum*: with the Notes and Glossary of Dr. R. M. White, edited by Rev. Robert Holt, M.A., Vol. I (Oxford: At the Clarendon Press, 1878), dedication page facsimile.

Spelling and Punctuation

Old English spelling had been relatively consistent, though it by no means achieved a perfect match between phonemes and graphemes. The many sound changes between OE and ME discussed in the preceding section meant that the match between sound and symbol became even poorer. In addition, French loanwords introduced new spelling conventions to English, and French scribes, often not fluent in English, extended these conventions to native English words. The different dialectal areas frequently developed different spelling conventions of their own, even for the same sounds, and these conventions had to be reconciled somehow when a standardized spelling finally did arise. Here we will concentrate on the most important spelling changes between OE and ME: single-letter substitutions and the increasing use of **digraphs** (pairs of letters used to represent a single phoneme, as in *th* to represent /θ/).

SINGLE-LETTER CHANGES

We have already mentioned a number of spelling changes brought about by the loss of earlier graphemes or the introduction of new ones during ME. In addition, a number of substitutions were made within the existing inventory of letters, some of them introduced by French scribes, others apparently by English scribes.

1. *o* for /ʊ/. OE had usually spelled short /ʊ/ with *u*. In ME, a number of words containing this sound came to be spelled with *o*, and many of them are still spelled this way. In most such words (such as *come*, *love*, *son*, *won*, *tongue*, *some*), the earlier *u* had preceded another grapheme also formed with minims (a minim is a single vertical stroke). In the handwriting of the time, letters formed with minims were often ambiguous because scribes were not careful, for instance, about leaving *u* open at the top and *n* open at the bottom, or about spacing between letters. Thus the word *minim* itself might appear as 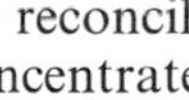 (the letter *i* was not yet "dotted"). By replacing *u* with *o*, some of this ambiguity could be avoided; the word *come*, for example, would appear as 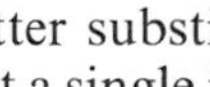 rather than 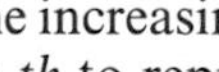.
2. *c* for /s/. In OE, the letter *c* represented either /k/, as in *cuman* 'to come' or /č/, as in *cild* 'child'. The combination *sc* represented /š/, as in *scearp* 'sharp'; and *cg* stood for /ǰ/, as in *hrycg* 'ridge'. French loanwords like *cellar* and *place*

introduced still another value for *c*, that of /s/, which spread to some native English words like *lice* and *mice*. (Note that the singular forms of these words are still spelled with *s*.)

3. *k* for /k/. OE had known the grapheme *k* but used it sparingly; the phoneme /k/ was normally spelled *c*. However, as just noted, *c* was already overburdened in OE and took on the additional value of *s* in ME. During the ME period, the convention arose of using *k* to represent /k/ before the vowel symbols *i* and *e* and before *n*; hence the PDE spellings *keen*, *kiss*, and *knee* (OE *cene*, *cyssan*, and *cneow*) versus *cat*, *cool*, *cut*, *clean*, and *creep*. For some words, this spelling convention meant that different forms of the same word were spelled with different initial letters, which, with increasing literacy, led to the loss of the association in the minds of speakers between the related forms. Few PDE speakers think of *kine* as a plural of *cow* or of *(un)kempt* as a variant past participle of *comb*.

DIGRAPHS

We have already mentioned the increasing use of the digraph *th* to represent /ð/ and /θ/ during ME. Several other digraphs became conventional during the period, most of them under French influence.

1. *ou* and *ow* for /ū/. French scribes introduced the spelling *ou* or *ow* for /ū/ in such loanwords as *hour* and *round*. The convention spread to native words like *how*, *thou*, *house*, *loud*, and *brown* (OE *hu*, *þu*, *hus*, *hlud*, *brun*).
2. Doubling of vowels. The OE writing system did not indicate vowel length; /god/ 'God' and /gōd/ 'good' were both spelled *god*. During ME, vowels were often doubled to indicate length. In the influential London area, which ultimately set standards for the rest of the country, only *o* and *e* were doubled, and only these doublings are permissible in English words today (*beet*, *boot*). In the North, Scots English used a following *i* to indicate length: *guid* 'good', *maid* 'made', and *rois* 'rose'.
3. *sh* for /š/. OE spelled /š/ with the digraph *sc*. Under French influence, *sc* was replaced by *sh* in ME: for example, OE *scamu*, ME *shame*. Depending on the area and the scribe, /š/ was also spelled *ssh*, *sch*, and *ss*, though of course *sh* ultimately became the regular spelling.
4. *ch* for /č/. As noted above, OE spelled /č/ as *c*. Again under French influence, /č/ became spelled *ch* in ME (OE *ceap*, *cinn*; ME *cheap*, *chin*). This spelling was a useful innovation that reduced some of the ambiguity of the letter *c*.
5. *dg(e)* for /ǰ/. OE spelled /ǰ/ as *cg*. In earlier ME, this spelling was replaced by *gg* and later by *dg(e)*: thus OE *bricg*, early ME *brigge*, later ME *bridge*. In OE, /ǰ/ had not occurred initially at all. Norman French loanwords introduced the sound in initial position, and here it was spelled *i* or *j* according to French conventions (ME *just* or *iust*).
6. *gh* for [x]. In OE, the [x] allophone of /h/ was spelled *h*. The use of *gh* to represent this sound began in ME (OE *þoht*, *riht*; ME *thought*, *right*). In the North and particularly in Scotland, *ch* tended to be used instead of *gh*, a practice that is still reflected in the variant spellings of proper names like *McCullough*/ *McCulloch*.
7. *wh* for [ʍ]. OE had used the digraph *hw* to spell the [ʍ] sound (phonetically a voiceless aspirated bilabial fricative): OE *hwæt* 'what' and *hwil* 'while'. In ME, the order of the letters was reversed to *wh*, probably by analogy with other

digraphs that had *h* as the second element. In the South, where the aspiration of such words as *what* and *while* was lost at an early date, spellings like *wat* and *wile* were typical. In the North, where the aspiration remained heavy, the spelling was often *quh* or *qu* (*quhat*, *quile*).

8. *gu* for /g/. The spelling *gu* for /g/ was introduced in a number of French loanwords, such as *guard*, *guile*, and *guide*. This convention spread to some words not of French origin, such as ON *guest* and *guild*, and even to native English words like *guilt* (OE *gylt*).

By modern standards, punctuation in ME manuscripts is sparse and limited in variety. The point (or period or stop) is the most common mark, but its use did not correspond to modern practice. More often than not, it indicated a syntactic break of some kind, but not necessarily the end of a complete sentence. The point was also used to surround Roman numerals and sometimes to follow abbreviations (as it is today).

The comma was not to appear regularly until the sixteenth century, but to some extent its function was served by the *punctus elevatus*, a kind of upside-down and backwards semicolon—though many scribes did not employ the *punctus elevatus* at all. In later ME especially, a virgule (slanted line) indicated syntactic breaks, partially corresponding to the PDE use of the comma.

In many manuscripts, no special mark was used to designate a question; in others, a point with a curved arch over it served as a question mark. To indicate the breaking of a word at the end of a line, two forms of hyphen were used. One was a long, thin oblique stroke; the other, two short parallel strokes like a tilted equals sign. Often no equivalent to the hyphen appeared at all, and the word was simply completed on the following line.

Paragraphs or subheadings were often introduced by a square bracket or a modified form of capital *C* (the ancestor of our paragraph symbol today).

Figure 6.5   Some ME Marks of Punctuation

Punctus elevatus	
Virgule	/
Hyphens	
Paragraph markers	

Handwriting

After the Conquest, the distinctive, elegant, and highly legible Insular hand of Old English, introduced by Irish monks in the sixth century, was gradually replaced by the Carolingian minuscule. This originally rather angular hand later developed a more rounded cursive style (with connected letters) that was less legible but that could be written more rapidly. A more ornate "gothic" hand was often used for formal writing; sometimes the two are mixed in the same manuscript, with the gothic being used for Latin and the cursive script for English.

Figure 6.6 Samples of ME Handwriting

Cursive Hand

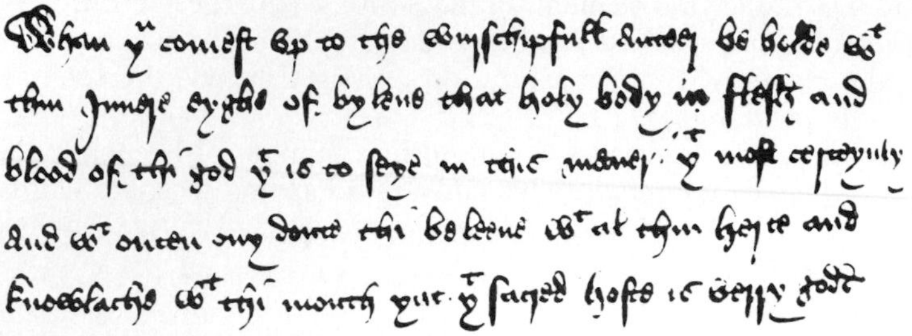

[handwritten cursive text]

Transliteration and Translation

Whan y^u comest vp to the wurschipfull auteer be holde w^t
When thou comest up to the worshipful altar behold with

thin jnnere eyghe of byleue that holy body in flesh and
thine inner eye of belief that holy body in flesh and

blood of thin god y^t is to seye in this maner y^t most certeynly
blood of thy god that is to say in this manner: that most certainly

and w^t outen ony doute thin beleeue w^t al thin herte and
and without any doubt thy belief with all thy heart and

knowlache w^t thin mouth yat y^t sacred hoste is verry goddes
knowledge with thy mouth that that sacred host is very (= true) God's

More Formal Hand

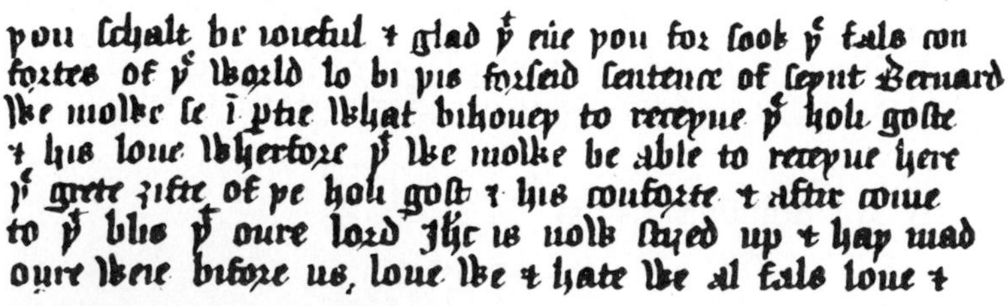

[handwritten formal text]

Transliteration and Translation

þou schalt be ioieful & glad þ^t euer þou for sook þ^e fals con
thou shalt be joyful & glad that ever thou forsook the false com-

fortes of þ^e world lo bi þis forseid sentence of seynt Bernard
forts of the world: Lo by this foresaid sentence of St. Bernard

we mowe se in partie what bihoueþ to receyue þ^e holi goste
we can see in part what is necessary to receive the Holy Ghost

& his loue wherfore þ^t we mowe be able to receyue here
& his love wherefore that we can be able to receive here

þ^e grete ȝifte of þe holi gost & his conforte & aftir come
the great gift of the Holy Ghost & his comfort & afterward come

to þ^t blis þ^t oure lord Jhc is now stiȝed up & haþ mad
to that bliss that our Lord Jesus Christ has now arisen up and has made

oure weie bifore us. loue we & hate we al fals loue &
our way before us. Let us love, & let us hate all false love &

140

Middle English Morphology

Loss of Inflectional Endings

The few major and numerous minor changes in phonology between Old English and Middle English are relatively unimportant compared to the cataclysmic changes in inflectional morphology. By the end of the ME period, English had only a handful of leftover inflections. Along with the loss of inflection came the loss of grammatical gender and its replacement by natural (or biological) gender. Nouns were reduced to two cases (possessive and nonpossessive), and adjectives had lost all inflections as well as the earlier distinction between weak and strong adjectives. Personal endings of verbs were reduced, and mood distinctions blurred. Personal pronouns remained relatively intact, but the distinction between dual and plural number had vanished.

There is no single, simple answer to the question why English should have renounced its Indo-European heritage and changed from a synthetic, inflecting language to an analytic language dependent on word order and particles for indicating the relationships among the words in a sentence. One of the standard explanations is that, exposed to and confused by the varying inflectional systems of three different languages (English, French, and Scandinavian), English speakers abandoned inflections entirely. This explanation is not sufficient. First, the process was well under way in English before the Conquest. French would, however, have tended to support—though not necessarily cause—inflectional loss in English because Old French itself preserved only a distinction between singular and plural. What is more, the plural ended in -*s*, the same ending that was to become universal for the plural in English. Second, Scandinavian influence was heavy only in certain areas of the country; besides, the inflectional systems of Old Norse and Old English were quite similar for many classes of nouns and adjectives (verbal inflections differed more, but English lost fewer verbal inflections than noun and adjective inflections). For example, the declension of the word for "judgment," a strong masculine noun in both languages, was as follows:

	Singular			*Plural*	
	OE	*ON*		*OE*	*ON*
N	dōm	dōmr	N	dōmas	dōmar
A	dōm	dōm	A	dōmas	dōma
G	dōmes	dōms	G	dōma	dōma
D	dōme	dōmi	D	dōmum	dōmum

In particular, Old Norse influences should have, if anything, reinforced the genitive plural -*a* and the dative plural -*um* in English, because almost all nouns of all classes and genders in both languages had these endings.

Certainly one important contributing factor to the loss of inflections in English was the phonological development described earlier in this chapter: the reduction of all unstressed final vowels to /ə/ meant that the distinctions previously signaled by -*e*, -*o*-, -*a*, and -*u* (OE /e o ɑ u/) were all lost as all became /ə/, usually spelled -*e*. Nonetheless, a parallel heavy stress on root syllables and reduced stress on inflectional endings has not led to the loss of all inflections in German, even to the present day, so the English result was not inevitable.

As was mentioned in the preceding chapter, Old English already had a more rigid word order than many other Indo-European languages. While this alone would not *cause* loss of inflections, it would tend to substitute for them. That is, the information formerly carried by inflections could be shifted to word order. Similarly, the increasing use of prepositions and other particles helped carry some of the syntactical information formerly conveyed through inflections.

In sum, while no one factor can be singled out as the sole reason for inflectional loss in Middle English, the combination of various factors provides at least a reasonable post hoc explanation.

As a rule, the North of England, conservative with respect to phonological changes, was far more innovative with respect to morphological changes. Almost without exception, reduction of inflections began in the North, spread to the Midlands, and only slowly reached the South; in some instances, the South preserved features that had been lost centuries before in the North.

Nouns

By late Old English, the *-um* of dative endings had become *-un*. At about the same time, all the vowels of inflectional endings were reduced to /ə/, spelled *e*. Thus *-um*, *-an*, *-on*, and *-en* all became /ən/, usually spelled *-en*. Later, this final *-n* was also lost in most, though not all, noun endings. Finally, by late Middle English, final inflectional *-e* had dropped (though it often continued to be spelled). The result was only three[3] different forms for nearly all nouns—essentially the state we have in English today.

The result of all these sound changes was that case distinctions in nouns were reduced to two: possessive versus nonpossessive. Grammatical gender was lost—though this loss was due as much to changes in the demonstrative and the adjective as to changes in the noun itself, because the form of a noun even in Old English had been a poor indicator of its gender. For the most part, the OE distinctions among the several noun classes vanished, and over time, almost all nouns were generalized to the older strong masculine declension. French loanwords were also adapted to this declension; this was a simple step because French at this time already had lost most of its nominal inflectional endings but preserved a plural in *-s*. The Old English weak noun declension with oblique singular forms and nominative-accusative plurals in *-n* survived into early ME, even spreading to some formerly strong nouns in the South, but eventually coalesced with the regular strong declension. Although PDE preserves only *children*, *brethren*, and *oxen*, *-n* plurals were also common in ME for *eye*, *ear*, *shoe*, *foe*, and *hand*.

As exceptions to the general pattern of noun declensions presented in Figure 6.7, ME retained a few s-less genitives, especially of formerly feminine nouns (*his lady grace*), and of kinship terms (*thi brother wif*; *hir doghter name*). Nouns ending in sibilant sounds like /s z š č/ often appear without a genitive *-s* well beyond the ME period (*for peace sake* occurs as late as the eighteenth century). Some Old English strong neuter nouns had had no ending in the nominative-accusative plural, and this pattern was retained for a number of them into the ME period, including such words as *year*, *thing*, *winter*, and *word*.

---

[3]Four, if we count the possessive plural as separate from the other cases. It was and is different for mutated plurals, such as *man:man's/men:men's*.

Figure 6.7   OE and ME Noun Declensions

Strong Masculine: *hund* 'hound'			Weak Masculine: *nama* 'name'		
Case	*OE*	*ME*	*Case*	*OE*	*ME*
Sg. N	hund	hund	Sg. N	nama	name
A	hund	hund	A	naman	name
G	hundes	hundes	G	naman	names
D	hunde	hund	D	naman	name
Pl. NA	hundas	hundes	Pl. NA	naman	names
G	hunda	hundes	G	namena	names
D	hundum	hundes	D	namum	names

Among the unchanged neuter plurals of OE had been a few names of animals, such as *deor* 'wild animal', *sceap* 'sheep', *swin* 'swine', and *neat* 'animal'. During and beyond ME, this pattern of unmarked plurals for animal names spread by analogy to other words that formerly had belonged to different declensions (*fish, elk*). Ultimately, the subgroup was to become so well-defined that it even attracted to itself loanwords from outside English, including the Portuguese *buffalo* and the Algonquian *moose*.

In ME and even later, measure words like *mile, pound, fathom, pair, score, thousand*, and *stone* frequently appeared without a pluralizing -s, especially after numerals. This practice may have resulted from analogy with the *s*-less plurals of *year* and *winter* in OE. Or such unchanged plurals could be a reflex of former genitive plurals in -*a*; OE used the genitive plural after numerals. Whatever the origin, the practice was common in ME, and it survives dialectally down to the present day. In attributive position as adjectives, such combinations are part of the standard language in PDE (*I took a two-hour walk* versus *I walked for two hours*).

Finally, the OE class of mutated plurals (words that signaled plural number by a vowel change rather than by an ending) was preserved fairly well in Middle English; again, most of them survive to the present day. Examples include *geese, teeth, lice*, and *kine* (the older plural of *cow*).

Adjectives

Of all the parts of speech, the adjective suffered the greatest inflectional losses in Middle English. Although it was the most highly inflected part of speech in Old English, it became totally uninflected by the end of the ME period. Because its case and gender depended on that of the noun it modified, it quite predictably lost case and gender distinctions when the noun lost them, failing to preserve even the possessive endings that the noun retained.

The distinction between strong (indefinite) and weak (definite) adjectives was often blurred even in Old English usage. By Middle English, it had vanished entirely except for monosyllabic adjectives ending in a consonant. Here a final -*e* distinguished the strong singular form from the weak singular and from the plural:

	Strong	**Weak**
Sg.	blind	blinde
Pl.	blinde	blinde

Even this vestigial distinction was frequently not observed: forms without a final -*e* appear where a weak ending would be expected, and, conversely, -*e* appears where a strong ending would be expected.

The reduction and eventual loss of unstressed endings was the chief cause of the loss of the strong-weak distinction. Another contributing factor was surely the rising use of definite and indefinite articles, which conveyed much of the information formerly carried by the adjective endings.

The distinction between singular and plural adjectives generally lasted until unstressed final -*e* was dropped in pronunciation, though it was retained in spelling long after it had been lost in speech.

One might reasonably expect French influence to have helped preserve the singular-plural distinction in ME adjectives. However, the French plural ending was -*s*, and no OE plural adjectives had ended in -*s*, so the French forms would not have reinforced the original English forms. Adjectives borrowed from French frequently do appear with an -*s* in the plural, but normally only when the adjective follows the noun. Thus the -*s* is more a marker of an un-English word order than of plurality. For example, in Chaucer's *Treatise on the Astrolabe*, we find phrases like *houres inequales* and *plages principalis* ('principal regions'); the plural adjective may even modify a native English noun, as in *sterres fixes* ('fixed stars') and *dayes naturales*. But when the adjective precedes the noun, it has no -*s*: *dyverse langages, celestialle bodies, principale divisiouns*. For the last example, note that *principale* appears without an -*s* even though it has an -*s* when it follows the noun in *plages principalis*.

The comparative and superlative forms of adjectives (and adverbs) developed predictably and undramatically in ME. The OE comparative suffix -*ra* became ME -*re* and later, by metathesis, -*er*. The OE superlative endings -*ost* and -*est* became -*est*. Several common adjectives in OE had had *i*-mutation in their comparative and superlative forms. Analogy was eventually to level all of these (except the variant *elder* from *old*) under the base form, but a number still survived in ME, often beside the "regular" analogical comparatives. For instance, ME texts show both *longer* and *lenger* from *long* and both *strongest* and *strengest* from *strong*.

The PDE system of periphrastic comparison (separate words instead of inflectional endings) had its beginnings in ME, but the complexities of the present system were not to be settled until the modern period. After the fourteenth century, *ma* ('more'), *more*, and *most* often appear either along with the -*er* and -*est* inflections or as a substitute for them. Hence we find *swetter* 'sweeter', *more swete*, and even *more swetter*. Double comparison of the type *more swetter* and *moste clennest* is so common that *more* and *most* are perhaps better regarded here as intensifiers (analogous to PDE *awfully nice, real tired*) than as comparative markers. Again, although French influence cannot be called the sole cause of the development of the periphrastic comparative in ME, it was probably a contributing factor—French by this time was using only periphrastic comparatives.

Old English adjectives were frequently used as nouns. This practice continued in ME, probably supported by the parallel practice in French. However, the use of the pronoun *one* to "support" the adjective also began during this period. Thus we find such phrases as *hwon þe sunfule is iturnd* 'when the sinful (one) has turned' and *this olde greye, Humble in his speche* 'this old gray-haired (person), humble in his speech', but also, as time goes on, phrases like *I have the mooste stedefast wyf, And eek the mekeste oon that bereth lyf* 'I have the most steadfast wife, and also the meekest one alive'. Even long after the development of the prop-word *one*, the use of an adjective alone as a noun continued down to almost the modern period.

Pronouns

PERSONAL PRONOUNS

If the Old English personal pronouns had developed regularly in Middle English, much of the differentiation between gender and number would have been lost. In particular, the forms for "he" and "she" would have become identical, resulting in *he* (/he/ in ME and /hi/ in PDE). The explanation for the preservation of gender is not clear; after all, even OE had had no gender distinction in the plural personal pronouns, and gender was lost for nouns, adjectives, and other pronouns during ME. Nor can one argue that gender distinctions in the third-person singular are essential to any language—Chinese, for example, makes no gender distinction in speech and has developed a distinction in writing only in the twentieth century and only as a result of Western influence. Nevertheless, for whatever reason, English has retained gender in the third-person singular pronouns, though at the expense of a great deal of confusion and variation during the entire ME period and of some unexplained sound changes.

Throughout the ME period and, for that matter, up to the present day, English personal pronouns have preserved all their original inflectional categories of number, gender, case, and person. During ME, one case was lost through the coalescence of dative and accusative into a single object case. In addition, the dual number, weak even in OE, disappeared. All other OE inflectional distinctions were preserved in one way or another.

All this is not to say that the phonological changes within the pronominal system were only minor. First, although gender survived, it became natural (or biological) gender instead of grammatical gender. That is, the pronoun selected to substitute for a noun depended on the sex of the referent itself and not on the arbitrary and inherent gender of the noun used to indicate the referent. Some use of natural gender had appeared as early as OE; conversely, the conservative Southern dialects preserved some grammatical gender until well into the fourteenth century.

Further, the number distinction between singular and plural in the second-person pronouns, based solely on actual number in OE, shifted gradually to a more sociologically based number in ME. When addressing more than one person, the speaker always used the plural form. But from the thirteenth century on, plural forms were also increasingly used as polite or respectful forms in addressing only one person. This use of the plural as a singular originated under French influence and probably was more common in writing than in speech, and more carefully observed among the upper classes than the lower. Nonetheless, it remained a feature of English until the singular forms were completely replaced by the plural in the eighteenth century.

Figure 6.8 presents a summary of the ME personal pronoun system, including some of the most frequent variant forms.

1. First-person singular. In accordance with the general rule that unstressed final /ě/ was lost in ME (see p. 127), the subject pronoun became simply /ɪ/; it was later restressed and lengthened to /ī/. ME *me* is the regular development of OE dative *me*; like all other accusative forms except the neuter pronoun, the OE

Figure 6.8 Middle English Personal Pronouns

Case	First-Person Singular	First-Person Plural
Subject	ich, I	we
Object	me	us
Possessive	min(e), mi	ure, our

Case	Second-Person Singular	Second-Person Plural
Subject	þu, thou, etc.	ȝe, ye
Object	þe, thee, etc.	ȝou, eu, you, ȝiu, etc.
Possessive	þin(e), þi, thin(e), etc.	ȝur(e), your(e), etc.

Case	3d Sg. Masc.	3d Sg. Fem.	3d Sg. Neut.	3d Plural
Subject	he	heo, sche, ho, he, ȝho, etc.	hit, it	he, hi, þei, ho, hie, þai, etc.
Object	him	hire, hure, her, heore, etc.	hit, it, him	hem, þem, ham, heom, þaim, þam, etc.
Possessive	his	hir(e), heore, her(e), etc.	his	here, þair, heore, hore, þar, etc.

accusative gave way to the dative, resulting in a single object case. ME *mīn(e)* is also the expected development of OE *mīn*. During the course of ME, the form *mi* began to be used before words beginning with a consonant, while *min* appeared before words beginning with a vowel. (Compare the use of *a* and *an* in PDE.)

2. First-person plural. Both *we* and *us* are regular developments from OE *we* and *us*, with *us* absorbing the functions of both the earlier accusative and dative cases. Absolute pronominal forms (*ours* and also *hers*, *yours*, and *theirs*) began in the North during the ME period and gradually spread south.

3. Second-person singular. Despite some variation in spelling during ME, second-person singular pronouns developed regularly and undramatically in ME. The /θ/ of the subject form often became /t/ when the pronoun followed a verb: thus *wiltou* 'wilt thou' instead of *wilt þou*, or *seiste* 'sayest thou' for *seist þou*.

4. Second-person plural. The ME object form reflects a shift in the stress of the diphthong in OE dative *eow*. The subject and object forms are still distinct (unlike PDE *you*), but *ye* sometimes appears as the spelling for the unstressed object *you*, probably pronounced /jə/.

5. Third-person singular masculine. All of the OE forms developed predictably and regularly in ME.

6. Third-person singular feminine. The object and possessive forms of ME are predictable. However, the subject form varied widely from area to area and over time during the course of ME. The East Midlands and the North acquired forms beginning with /š/; their origins are obscure and the subject of much controversy. Suffice it to say that the /š/ form allowed the feminine pronoun to be distinguished from the masculine and, of course, this form was to prevail in the standard language. Nevertheless, *h*-forms remained in the South throughout the ME period.

7. Third-person singular neuter. The initial /h/ of OE *hit* was lost in some areas as early as the twelfth century, and *it* was regular by the end of the ME period, although *hit* survived in dialects much longer. For most of the period, the OE

dative *him* survived for indirect objects, while *it* (or *hit*) was used for direct objects or objects of prepositions. In accordance with the rule that accusative forms gave way to dative forms, one would expect the object form of the neuter pronoun eventually to have become *him*. However, if this had occurred, the object forms of the masculine and the neuter would have been identical; with the choice of the accusative form of the neuter, the two genders were kept distinct.

8. Third-person plural. If the third-person plural personal pronoun had developed regularly in ME, all of its forms would have been subject to confusion with other, singular pronoun forms—the subject and possessive forms with the feminine forms, and the object form with the masculine object form. By the end of the ME period, this ambiguity had been resolved by an unusual means, borrowing the pronouns from another language, Old Norse (Scandinavian). Unlike Old English, Old Norse distinguished gender in the plural; ME borrowed the masculine forms of the Norse plural pronoun. The Old Norse subject form was *þeir*, the dative form *þeim*, and the possessive form *þeira*. All of these forms were easily adaptable to English. For the subject form, English simply dropped the final *-r*, a process that was familiar from the many Norse loanwords in English whose nominative singular and plural endings had also been in *-r* (for example, English *flat* and *leg* from ON *flatr* and *leggr*). With *þeim*, the diphthong was ultimately smoothed to a pure vowel, and with *þeira* the unstressed final *-a* was predictably dropped.

All of the new forms in [θ] first appeared in the Northeast Midlands and North and gradually spread to the West and South. The nominative *þei* was the first to appear everywhere; for example, Chaucer has *they*, but *here* and *hem* in the oblique cases, and *them* did not appear in London English until the fifteenth century. The Southern areas preserved all the native forms in *h-* until the fifteenth century.

DEMONSTRATIVE PRONOUNS

The two OE demonstrative pronouns had been highly inflected (two numbers, three genders, and five cases), but by the end of the ME period, only one singular and one plural form remained for each. At the same time, morphological fission took place as a separate, indeclinable definite article (*the*) developed, splitting off from the true demonstratives.

For both demonstratives, the new singular was based on the OE neuter nominative-accusative singular (*þæt* and *þis*), but the plural forms of both developed somewhat irregularly. At first, the plural of *that* was *tho*, the expected development of OE *þa*. Late in the ME period, an *-s* was added by analogy with the other plurals in *-s*; however, the plural *tho* survived alongside *thos(e)* until the EMnE period. If it had developed regularly, the OE plural of *this* would have become identical to the plural of *that*. Instead, a new plural, *þise*, originally with the vowel of the singular, arose.

Indeclinable *þe* (*the*) was at first only a substitute for OE *se* and *seo*, the masculine and feminine nominative singular forms of *that*. (*Se* and *seo* were the only OE demonstrative forms that did not begin with /θ/, so were vulnerable to such analogical change.) The more conservative areas of the West and South preserved inflected forms well into the ME period, but the East and North were using *þe* as an indeclinable definite article separate from the demonstrative as early as the twelfth century.

In sum, by the end of the ME period, the modern system of two demonstratives inflected only for number (*this*/*these* and *that*/*those*) and a single indeclinable definite article (*the*) was firmly established for English.

INTERROGATIVE PRONOUNS

Even in Old English, there was no distinction between masculine and feminine gender in the interrogative pronouns, nor was there a singular-plural distinction. In Middle English, the accusative predictably fell together with the dative. The OE instrumental *hwy* was separated from the pronoun declension to become the interrogative adverb *why*. All of the forms except *what* show some irregularities in their phonological development in ME, the most striking being the loss of the /w/ in *who* (and *whom* and *whose*) when it was assimilated to the following back vowel.

Figure 6.9 ME Interrogative Pronouns

Case	Masculine-Feminine	Neuter
Subject	who	what
Object	whom	what (acc.); whom (dat.)
Possessive	whos	whos

That bugbear of modern prescriptive grammarians, the distinction between *who* and *whom*, was confusing English speakers and writers as early as late ME. For example, in the Paston letters (1449), we find *that thai wost ho I ment* 'that they knew who I meant'.

As in OE and in PDE, ME *which* was also used as an interrogative pronoun. *Whether*, used only as a conjunction in PDE, could still be used as an interrogative pronoun meaning "which of two" in ME: *Mid hweþer wult tu þolien?* 'With which of the two will you suffer?'

OTHER PRONOUNS

Old English had used the particle *þe*, either alone or in combination with demonstrative pronouns, as a relative pronoun; less often, *þæt* 'that' was used as a relative. During Middle English, indeclinable *þat* completely supplanted *þe* and became the most common all-purpose relative pronoun, used for all numbers, cases, and genders. (In the North and in Scots English, *at*, a borrowing from Old Norse, appeared alongside *þat* as a relative.) By the fourteenth century, however, the interrogative pronouns were beginning to be used as relatives, possibly under the influence of French and Latin usage. *Which* was the most frequent interrogative used relatively, and it was employed with both human and nonhuman referents. *Which* also appeared in such compound relatives as *which that, which as, the which*, and *the which that*. Although *who* was occasionally also used as a relative, it was rare throughout the ME period.

Omission of the relative pronoun (as in *the tree she climbed*) did not occur in Old English. By the fourteenth century, however, nonexpression of the relative pronoun was fairly common, especially when the relative would have been the subject of the subordinate clause. For example, Chaucer has *he sente after a cherle was in the town* 'he sent for a fellow (who) was in the town'. Nonexpression of a relative that would have been an object is less frequent in ME, but does occur: *the sorowe I suffred* 'the sorrow I suffered'. Note that this is a reversal of PDE usage, where nonexpression of an object relative is common, but nonexpression of a subject relative is considered substandard.

Old English had no reflexive pronouns as such, simply using the dative or accusative forms of the personal pronouns as reflexives. OE *sylf* 'self' was not a true reflexive, but an emphatic pronoun or pronominal adjective. The regular personal pronouns continued to be used as reflexives throughout ME (and beyond), but reflexives with *-self* also began to appear. Apparently because *self* was often regarded as a noun, the personal pronouns that appeared with it often—but not always—were in the possessive case. This confusion over the role of *self* is the origin of the inconsistency in form of the reflexive pronouns today; *myself* and *yourself* have the possessive form of the pronoun, but *himself* and *themselves* have the object form.

Old English had regularly used *man* as an indefinite pronoun (roughly equivalent to *one* in PDE). This use continued into ME but gradually declined, though no completely satisfactory substitute for it has ever been found. The second-person plural *you* (or *ye*) appeared as an indefinite by early ME; *one* and *they* as indefinite pronouns first appeared toward the end of ME.

Verbs

Compared with other branches of Indo-European, Germanic had had few verbal inflections; and compared with other Germanic languages, Old English verbal morphology had been greatly simplified. Therefore, one might expect that this process of reduction of verbal inflections and inflectional categories would have continued until the present day. Perhaps surprisingly, it has not. Despite many changes within the verbal system between OE and ME, ME retained, at least to some extent, all the earlier categories of tense, mood, number, and person. It also preserved the three basic types of verbs (strong, weak, and other), and actually added what might be considered a new type of verb, the two-part or separable verb (*pick up*, *take over*). Finally, ME saw the real beginning of the complex system of periphrastic verb phrases that characterizes PDE.

STRONG VERBS

The biggest casualties, proportionally, occurred among the strong verbs in ME. Strong verbs were particularly vulnerable because, although they included the most frequently used verbs in the language, there were many more weak verbs than strong verbs, even in Old English. Second, the strong verbs were fragmented into seven different classes, with numerous irregularities within most of these classes. Third, sound changes had blurred or eliminated some of the distinctions within and between classes. Fourth, many OE verbs had appeared in pairs consisting of a strong verb and a parallel weak verb derived from it and similar to it in form and meaning (for example, OE *cwelan* 'to die' and *cwellan* 'to kill'; *hweorfan* and *hwierfan* 'to turn'; *fēran* 'to travel' and *ferian* 'to transport'). In ME, these separate but related verbs tended to fall together as a single weak verb. Finally, the many new verbs from French almost always entered English as weak verbs, thus strengthening the class of weak verbs at the expense of the strong verbs. The loss of a strong verb was not, however, sudden; often the strong and weak versions coexisted for centuries; one might compare the PDE situation with *show*, which has the strong past participle *shown* beside the equally acceptable weak participle *showed*.

Despite heavy attrition, the seven classes of strong verbs remained throughout ME, even though every class suffered some casualties, either through outright loss or through change to a weak verb. Class I, still relatively healthy in PDE, preserved its identity well, but among the losses were OE *blīcan* 'shine' and *līpan* 'sail'. *Slītan* 'slit' and *tēon* 'censure' were replaced by or absorbed by weak versions. Class II suffered greater damage, partly because sound changes had destroyed some of the earlier vowel distinctions. *Nēotan* 'use' and *tēon* 'draw' were lost, while *flēon* 'flee' and *cēowan* 'chew' became weak. Class III, a large class in OE, also had heavy losses in ME, though the subclass of verbs with a nasal (*n* or *m*) plus another consonant remains strong to the present day. Totally lost in ME were *limpan* 'become' and *beorgan* 'protect'. *Climban* 'climb' and *meltan* 'melt' became weak verbs.

Class IV had few members even in OE, but they were mostly verbs used very frequently, verbs that resisted loss and weakening remarkably well. *þweran* 'stir' and *hwelan* 'roar' dropped out of the language, but none of the common strong verbs of this class weakened during ME. Class V had numerous anomalies in OE and suffered many losses in ME. Among the total losses were *gefēon* 'rejoice' and *screpan* 'scrape.' (PDE *scrape* is not a descendant of OE *screpan*, but a loan from Old Norse *skrapa*, a weak verb in ON.) Two of the Class V verbs that became weak by the end of ME are *metan* 'measure' and *plegan* 'play.' Class VI fared better, although it lost *alan* 'nourish' and *spanan* 'seduce,' while *bacan* 'bake' and *faran* 'go' became weak. The great variety of infinitive and past participle vowels in Class VII tended to obscure the identity of the class as a whole, and its position was shaky in ME. Among the numerous losses were *blōtan* 'sacrifice' and *lācan* 'leap'; *fealdan* 'fold' and *weaxan* 'grow' became weak verbs.

Though the overwhelming tendency during ME was for strong verbs to give way to weak, there were occasional reversals such as *wear*, *dig*, and *hide*. The French loan *strive* entered as a Class I strong verb instead of a weak verb. The parallels between Old Norse and Old English strong verbs were so close that strong Old Norse verbs usually entered English as members of the corresponding English strong verb class. Examples include *take*, *get*, *give*, *sling*, and *thrive* (but *die* and *leak* came in as weak verbs).

Figure 6.10 ME Strong Verb Classes

Ablaut Series	Infinitive	3d sg. pres.	3d sg. pret.	Pl. pret.	Past part.
Class 1 /ī-ō-ɪ-ɪ/	*rise(n)* 'rise'	riseþ	ros	risen	(y)risen
Class 2 /ē-ɛ-ʊ-ō/	*crepe(n)* 'creep'	crepeþ	crep	crupen	(y)cropen
Class 3 /ɪ-a-ʊ-ʊ/	*singe(n)* 'sing'	singeþ	sang	sungen	(y)sungen
Class 4 /ɛ-a-ē-ō/	*bere(n)* 'bear'	bereþ	bar	beren	(y)boren
Class 5 /ɛ-a-ē-ɛ/	*speke(n)* 'speak'	spekeþ	spak	speken	(y)speken
Class 6 /ā-ō-ō-ā/	*wake(n)* 'wake'	wakeþ	wok	woken	(y)waken
Class 7 /V₁-ē-ē-V₁/	*falle(n)* 'fall'	falleþ	fel	fellen	(y)fallen

Figure 6.10 summarizes the strong verb classes in ME; the forms are listed in typical ME spellings. It presents, however, a highly idealized picture; there was great variation even among the forms for a single verb. In general, the tendency was for the vowels of the singular and plural preterite to become alike and to become identical with the vowel of the past participle. By EMnE, the distinction between singular and plural preterite was lost, but some distinctions between the preterite and the past participle vowels remain, of course, to the present day.

A comparison of the ablaut series of ME listed in Figure 6.10 with those for Old English (Figure 5.10) shows that the vowels of the principal parts of most classes of strong verbs underwent both qualitative and quantitative changes during ME. Regular sound changes affected the quality of the vowels of Classes 2, 4, and 5, in particular. The lengthening of vowels in open syllables affected the vowel of the infinitive in Classes 4, 5, and 6, and that of the past participle in Classes 2, 4, 5, and 6. All of these changes tended to weaken the cohesiveness of the category of strong verbs as a whole and of individual classes of strong verbs. It is no accident that the best-preserved class of strong verbs in PDE, Class 3, has undergone the least change in its vowels over the centuries.

WEAK VERBS

In terms of sheer numbers, far more weak verbs than strong verbs were lost between OE and ME; a handful of examples are *bāsnian* 'await'; *clynnan* 'resound'; *drohtian* 'behave'; *efenlǣcan* 'to be like'; *forcwȳsan* 'to shake violently'; and *hwemman* 'to bend'. However, there were far more weak verbs to begin with, and most of the many new verbs coming into ME from Scandinavian and French came in as weak verbs. Just a few examples of the hundreds of new verbs from French are *cover, join, languish, move, notice, plead, please, save, spend, store,* and *waste.* Among the scores of weak verbs from Norse are *blather, call, cast, clip, crawl, droop, gape, glitter, lift, raise, stagger,* and *want.*

In general, two classes of weak verbs could be identified, those with a preterite in *-ed(e)* and those with a preterite in *-de* or *-te* (without a preceding *e* before the dental ending). However, this distinction was to be lost by the end of ME as the vowel preceding the dental consonant gradually dropped out.

OTHER VERBS

Of the anomalous verbs *be, do, will,* and *go, do* and *will* developed more or less regularly in ME. By the end of the ME period, the two separate present tenses that *to be* had had in OE (see p. 89) had collapsed to one, though the particular forms used varied over the period and from area to area. In the singular present indicative, the older forms from *wesan* (*am, art, is*) eventually prevailed, but the infinitive *wesan* itself gave way to *be(n)*. In the plural present indicative, the older *sind(on)* was lost entirely. *Beoþ* and *be(n)* were both widely used, and a new form *are(n)*, probably influenced by the parallel ON plural forms (*erum, eruþ, eru*) also arose. *Are* was ultimately to prevail in the standard language, but *they be* continued to be acceptable until well into the EMnE period and survives dialectally to the present day. The OE past tense of the verb *to go* (*eode, eodon*) survived into ME, but during ME, the past tense from the verb *wendan* (also meaning "to go") began to replace the older form; *went* of course eventually supplanted *eode* completely, though Chaucer still regularly used *yede* and *yeden* as past tenses of *go*.

Most of the OE preterite-present verbs survived into ME and usually retained their OE functions and meanings. Examples include ME *wot* 'know'; *can* 'know how to'; *þarf* 'need'; *owe* 'possess'; *dar* 'dare'; *mot* 'can, must'; *may* 'be able to'; *shal* 'must, have to'. Most of the preterite-present verbs had had nonfinite forms such as an infinitive and a past participle in OE, but these were lost in ME, and this group of verbs became defective, like the modal auxiliaries of PDE, which lack nonfinite forms.

Figure 6.11 presents the complete conjugation of two ME verbs, the strong verb "to find" and the weak verb "to look." Because there were so many differences in the endings characteristic of the major dialectal regions, separate forms are listed for the North, the Midlands, and the South. Even so, not all variants are listed. However, the actual picture was by no means as neat as Figure 6.11 implies; there was a great deal of fluctuation and mingling of types, and the same ME author frequently used two or more variants within the same text.

A comparison of Figure 6.11 with Figure 5.11 will reveal that the major distinctions of OE were well preserved in most areas during ME. The OE distinction between classes of weak verbs disappeared in ME, so only one weak verb is presented in Figure 6.11.

One other feature of ME verb morphology is worth noting here because it represents still another example of the tendency of English to move from a synthetic to an analytic language. Old English had had an extensive series of verbal prefixes (*ā-, be-, ed-, on-, oþ-, or-, ofer-*) that modified the meaning or function of the verbs to which they were attached. For example, *giefan* meant "give," whereas *āgiefan* meant "give up"; *tēon* meant "draw, tug," but *ontēon* meant "draw to oneself"; *brecan* meant "break," and *forbrecan* meant "break into pieces, destroy." During ME, this process became much less productive (though it still survives, to a limited extent, even in PDE). Gradually replacing these prefixes was the use of separate adverbial particles that altered the meaning in various, often subtle ways. The process was probably at least reinforced by Old Norse influence because such verb + adverb combinations were very common in ON well before they were widely used in English. By the fourteenth century, such two-part verbs occurred frequently, and we find instances like *He put his hand in* and *blowe out þe light*. In the General Prologue to the *Canterbury Tales*, Chaucer says of the Pardoner's hood *For it was trussed up in his walet*.

Uninflected Word Classes

PREPOSITIONS

In Old English, inflections had been a major way of expressing syntactic relationships in the sentence. In Middle English, other means had to fill the gap left by the loss of inflections. One of these means was increased use of prepositions and the adoption of new prepositions to express more delicate relationships. Most of the OE prepositions survived into the ME period, though *mid* 'along with' gave way to *with* by the fifteenth century, and *umbe* 'around, about' was also lost during ME.

New prepositions were formed by compounding two or more existing prepositions, by converting other parts of speech, and by borrowing from Norse, French, and even Latin. Among the new compounds of ME were *above, out of*, and *unto*. Some of the conversions included *along* (from an OE adjective), *among* (from the OE prepositional phrase *on gemong* 'in a crowd'), and *behind* and *beneath* from OE adverbs. French elements provided *according to, around*, and *during*, among others. *Till* came from Old Norse and *except* from Latin.

Figure 6.11 ME Verb Conjugations

		Strong			Weak		
		North	*Midlands*	*South*	*North*	*Midlands*	*South*
Infinitive		find	finde(n)	finde(n)	lok(e)	loke(n)	loke(n)
Present Tense							
Indicative	Sg. 1	find(e)	finde	finde	lok(e)	loke	loke
	2	findes	findest	findest	lokes	lokest	lokest
	3	findes	findeþ, (-es)	findeþ	lokes	lokeþ, (-es)	lokeþ
	Pl.	find(es)	finde(n), (-es)	findeþ	loke(s)	loke(n), (-es)	lokeþ
Subjunctive	Sg.	find(e)	finde	finde	lok(e)	loke	loke
	Pl.	find(en)	finde(n)	finde(n)	lok(en)	loke(n)	loke(n)
Imperative	Sg. 2	find	find	find	lok	lok	lok
	Pl. 2	findes	findeþ	findeþ	lokes	lokeþ	lokeþ
Pres. Participle		findand(e), finding(e)	findende, finding(e)	findinde, finding(e)	lokand(e), loking(e)	lokend(e), loking(e)	lokinde, loking(e)
Preterite Tense							
Indicative	Sg. 1, 3	fand	fond	fond	loked	loked(e)	loked(e)
	2	fand	founde	founde	loked	lokedest	lokedest
	Pl.	fand	founde(n)	founde(n)	loked	loked(en)	loked(en)
Subjunctive	Sg.	fand	founde	founde	loked	loked(e)	loked(e)
	Pl.	fand	founde(n)	founde(n)	loked	loked(en)	loked(en)
Past Participle		funden	(y)founden	(y)founden	loked	(y)loked	(y)loked

153

Indeed, so many new prepositions entered the language during Middle English that a number of them proved superfluous and were later lost. Examples include *forewith* 'in front of', *evenlong* 'along', and *onunder* 'beneath'. French borrowings that eventually fell into disuse include *sans* 'without', *countre* 'against', and *maugre* 'in spite of'.

CONJUNCTIONS

Most of the OE simple coordinating conjunctions survived in ME, including *and*, *ac* 'but, and', and *or* (a contraction of OE *oþþe*, with the final /r/ added by analogy with other conjunctions like *whether* and *either*).

By far the most frequent, all-purpose subordinating conjunction of ME was *þat* 'that', although the OE *þe* survived until the thirteenth century or so. Other subordinating conjunctions inherited from OE included *gif* 'if', *þeah* 'though', and *ere* 'before'. As the language increasingly used subordination where it had earlier made do with coordination and simple parataxis, new subordinators were needed. These developed primarily from other parts of speech, more often than not supported by *þat*. From the interrogative adverbs and pronouns came *how þat*, *which þat*, and *when þat*. Other parts of speech contributed *after þat*, *because þat*, *also soone as þat* 'as soon as', *þe while þat*, and *til þat*. Among the other compound subordinating conjunctions were *þer as*, *for why*, and *right as*.

However, even as new conjunctions were proliferating, an older type was being lost. These were the correlative conjunctions consisting of the same word used before two (or more) clauses (OE *ge ... ge*, *þonne ... þonne*, and so on; see p. 91). Although *þa ... þa* 'when ... then', *so ... so*, and *þat ... þat* were still used in ME, the type was eventually to disappear from English, except for PDE *the ... the*.

ADVERBS

The chief means of forming adverbs in OE had been the addition of *-e* to the base form of the adjective. This process continued to some extent in ME, but, as final *-e* was lost in pronunciation, the distinction between adjective and adverb was lost. Seemingly, the distinction is an important one in the language, for a new way of distinguishing adjective and adverb developed even as the older one was fading. In OE, *-lic* /lič/ had been an adjective-making suffix; a final *-e* could be added to this suffix to form an adverb. During ME, the final consonant was lost, but the suffix *-ly* itself came to be treated as an adverbial marker. Even though many existing adjectives also ended in *-ly* (for example, *earthly*, *manly*, and *homely*), the suffix was no longer productive as a source of new adjectives and came to serve as an adverb marker only.

The comparative and superlative forms of adverbs developed parallel to those of adjectives in ME (see p. 144). During the entire ME period, *ne* 'not' was the normal negating adverb, though *noht* from the OE noun *nāht* 'nothing' began to appear. The word *nothing* was also used adverbially. *Never* was the ME reflex of OE *næfre*.

One of the striking characteristics of ME was its wide assortment of intensifying adverbs, including *all*, *clean*, *downright*, *enough*, *fair*, *fele*, *full*, *passing*, *pure*, *quite*, *right*, *sore*, *swiþe*, and *well*. All of these can, without too much inaccuracy, be translated simply as "very"; *very* itself, however, remained an adjective meaning "true" until after the fifteenth century. Among the numerous adverbs that served to weaken, rather than intensify, the adjectives they preceded were *little*, *nigh* 'nearly', *scarce*, and *somedeal* 'somewhat'.

INTERJECTIONS

By ME times, many texts attempted to reproduce actual speech, so we know more about the interjections used than we do for Old English. Among the various onomatopoetic interjections were *a* for surprise, *ho* for triumph, *ha-ha* for laughter, *fie* for disgust, and *hay* for excitement. *Lo, now,* and *what* were all attention-getting words, and *alas, wo,* and *wei-la-wei* could be used to express grief.

Salutation formulas of the ME period included *hail* and *welcome*. Chaucer uses both *good morrow* and *good night*, abbreviated forms of "have a good morrow (morning)" and "have a good night"—demonstrating that the ubiquitous *have a nice day* of PDE has a long history. *Farewell* first appeared in late ME.

Other social formulas included *gramercy* 'thank you', borrowed from the Old French *grant merci* 'great favor' and originally meaning "may God grant you

---

A MIDDLE ENGLISH RECIPE

By the fourteenth century, collections of recipes—in effect, cookbooks—began to appear in English. The recipe below is for *halekaye,* a parti-colored confection of almond milk and sweet ingredients. The name is probably derived from Arabic *halwā* (marzipan) or *halāwāl* 'sweet dish'. Note the lack of precise measurements and the somewhat disorganized order in which the instructions are given.

Middle English Text

To maken a mete þat is icleped halekaye. Nim alemauns & make heom qwyte, & soþþen braye heom in an morter, and make god mylke ase god ase þou miht. & soþþen boille hit & do þrin a lute vynegre; & qwen hit is iboilled do hit in an cloþ þat hit beo drue. & soþþen do hit in an veyr morter, & do þerto penydes, & a dole of amidon, & of sucre; & qwen hit is ybrayed, do out half vor to tempren wyþ gingebred, & þilke halue dole schal beon icolored wyþ saffroun, & þe oþer halue dele schal beo qwyt. And qwen þus þinges beoþ ysoden, do þe on & þe oþur in an dyhs, & on þe qwyte do þe greyns of poume gernet oþur reysins yfassed, & soþþen ȝef vorþ.

Translation

To make a food that is called "halekaye." Take almonds and make them white [blanch them], and then pound them in a mortar, and make as good milk as you can. And then boil it and put therein a little wine vinegar; and when it is boiled put it in a cloth so that it will be dry. And then put it in a good mortar, and put *penydes* [a kind of candy] in it, and a portion of wheat starch, and of sugar; and when it is pounded, take out half to mix with taffy, and that half shall be colored with saffron, and the other part shall be white. And when these things are boiled, put the one and the other in a dish, and on the white put seeds of pomegranate or seeded raisins, and then serve.

Translated by C. M. Millward from Constance B. Hieatt and Sharon Butler, eds., *Curye on Inglysch: English Culinary Manuscripts of the Fourteenth Century* (Early English Text Society S.S.8; London: Oxford University Press, 1985), p. 56.

great favor (for your kindness)." The modern *thank you* first appeared in late ME. One of the most versatile interjections of the period was *benedicite* 'bless', common as a greeting, as a verbal charm against evil, and simply as an expression of surprise.

Profanity seems to have been as common as it is today; people swore by *God, Deus, Christ, Mary, Peter*, and a wide assortment of favorite saints. Tauno Mustanoja has noted that *Goddamn* was so widely used by English troops in France during the Hundred Years War that the term itself became a synonym for "Englishman" among the French. Some authorities assert that *bigot* has a parallel source (from *by God*) as a derogatory name applied by the French to the Normans, but this etymology is dubious.

Middle English Syntax

The word order of Middle English, predictably, falls between that of Old English and that of Present-Day English, less free than OE but often with more options than PDE allows. Further, the tendency toward rigidity of syntax increases throughout the ME period as inflections are lost. By late ME, we find sentence after sentence with word orders that would be completely acceptable in PDE. For example, if the spelling in the following passage from a 1432 description of a reception in London were modernized, it would read like a slightly rambling but nonetheless contemporary piece of English.

> And when they sawe the kyng come, the maire with the aldermen rode to the kyng, and welcomed hym with all reuerence, honour, and obeysaunce. And the kyng thanked hem [them] and he come ridyng thurgh all the peple; and they obeyed and seid: "Welcom, oure liege and kyng, welcom!"

Syntax Within Phrases

Noun Phrases
As in both OE and PDE, single-word adjectivals usually preceded their nouns.

> an erþely servaunt
> *an earthly servant*
>
> gret heuy rente
> *great heavy rent*
>
> a gentyl and noble esquyer
> *a gentle and noble esquire*

These examples also show the development of articles in ME. The indefinite article originated as an unstressed variant of the numeral *one*; the uninflected definite article represents a split from the demonstrative pronoun. The following example illustrates the definite article in its two major contemporary functions of marking uniqueness (*þe son, þe mone*) and of indicating something that has previously been identified (*þe kandel*). As in PDE, the articles always immediately preceded the noun or the attributive adjective modifying the noun.

> þou sees þe son bryghtar þan a kandele, þe kandel bryghtar þan þe mone
> *you see the sun brighter than a candle, the candle brighter than the moon*

As in Old English, but less frequently, the adjective + noun order was occasionally reversed, especially in poetry or in phrases translated from French or Latin. However, by ME, titles used with a proper name usually preceded the name; titles of foreign personages often were preceded by a definite article.

shoures soote an heven indivisible
showers sweet *a heaven indivisible*

kyng Richarde þe kyng Alexandre
King Richard *the king Alexander*

Again like OE, when a noun had multiple single-word modifiers, one sometimes preceded the noun and the rest followed it.

a gode wyt and a retentyff
a good wit and a retentive

meny cites and tounes, faire, noble, and ryche
many cities and towns, fair, noble, and rich

Phrasal modifiers predictably followed the words they modified.

þe zennes þet comeþ of glotounye and of lecherie
the sins that come from gluttony and from lechery

the cercles abouten here hedes
the circlets around their heads

As in PDE, possessive nouns usually preceded the words they modified. Occasionally, the possessive marker was written as an independent possessive adjective, though this practice was not to become highly frequent until the EMnE period. Note that no apostrophe was used with possessive nouns.

oþer mens prosperite
other men's prosperity

go to þe raven is neste
go to the raven's nest

An innovation in ME was the use of the *of* possessive, a usage at least supported by the parallel French possessive with *de*.

aftyr þe lawes of oure londe
according to the laws of our land

deopnesse of sunne
deepness of sin

The group possessive, so characteristic of PDE (as in *the man in the moon's face*), was only just beginning to appear in ME, and the typical order of such phrases was possessive + noun + noun modifiers:

the Dukes place of Lancastre
the Duke's place of Lancaster ("*the Duke of Lancaster's place*")

Criste, þe keyng sonn of heven
Christ, the king's son of heaven ("*Christ, the king of heaven's son*")

The double possessive (with both an *of* phrase and a possessive noun or pronoun) also made its first appearance during ME:

> the capteyn ... toke awey .j. <u>obligacion of myn</u> þat was due
> *the captain ... took away one obligation of mine that was due*

Noun adjuncts, the use of one noun to modify another without a change in the form of the modifying noun, first appeared in ME, but they too were not to become common until later.

> Take perselly rotes, fenell rotes, perytory and isope.
> *Take parsley roots, fennel roots, pellitory and hyssop.*

ADVERBIAL MODIFIERS

Adverbial modifiers in ME tended to precede the words they modified more frequently than is typical in PDE. Nonetheless, placement after the verbs or other modified words was also common.

> Ye shul <u>first in alle youre werkes mekely</u> biseken <u>to the heighe God</u>
> *You must first in all your works meekly beseech to the high God*

> And <u>ʒet</u> sche wyst <u>ful wel</u> þat ...
> *And yet she knew very well that ...*

The negative *ne* always preceded the verb, and other negatives preceded the verb or verb phrase more often than in PDE. *Ne* often contracted with following common verbs and auxiliaries. However, the PDE placement of the negative after the auxiliary verb also appears in ME, as the second example below shows.

> I <u>nolde</u> fange a ferthynge for seynt Thomas shryne
> *I not would take a farthing for St. Thomas' shrine*

> he shal <u>nat</u> been ashamed to lerne hem
> *he should not be ashamed to learn them*

Double negatives were freely used and indeed could pile up heavily, as in Chaucer's famous description of the Knight in his General Prologue to the *Canterbury Tales* (the second example below).

> <u>ne</u> tolde heo þen engle <u>non</u> tale
> *not told she the angel no tale*

> He <u>nevere</u> yet <u>no</u> vileynye <u>ne</u> sayde / In al his lyf unto <u>no</u> maner wight
> *He never yet no villainy not said / In all his life to no kind (of) creature*

PREPOSITIONAL PHRASES

As has always been true in English, prepositions normally preceded their objects in ME, but, as in OE, prepositions occasionally followed their objects, especially if the object was a pronoun.

> Excuse me <u>of</u> negligence <u>Towardes</u> love <u>in</u> alle wise
> *Excuse me for negligence toward love in all ways*

> rycht <u>till</u> the bra syd he ʒeid / And stert <u>be-hynd</u> hym <u>on</u> his sted
> *straight to the hillside he went / And jumped behind him on his horse*

> he seyde him <u>to</u>
> *he said him to*

Another bugbear of modern prescriptive grammar, the placement of the preposition after its object when its object is a relative pronoun or when the verb is passive, first appeared in ME. In general, the preposition in such constructions came toward the end or at the end of the phrase.

Relative   the place that I of speke
the place that I of speak

Relative   preciouse stanes þat he myght by a kingdom with
precious stones that he could buy a kingdom with

Passive   þes oþir wordis of þis bischop ouȝte to be taken hede to
these other words of this bishop ought to be taken heed to

Verb Phrases

The rich system of compound verb phrases that characterizes PDE was not fully developed, even by the end of ME, but it had its genesis during the ME period. The perfect tense in particular, rare in OE, became common in ME. Both *be* and *have* were used as auxiliaries, but, even as *be* became the only auxiliary for the passive voice, it lost ground as an auxiliary for the perfect. By the end of ME, *be* was limited as a perfect auxiliary to intransitive verbs of motion.

þou hauest don oure kunne wo
You have done our family woe

I am com to myne ende
I have come to my end

summe of the Iewes han gon vp the mountaynes
some of the Jews have gone up the mountains

The perfect infinitive first appeared during the fourteenth century, possibly under French and Latin influence.

tʊ have holden hem under
to have held them under

Although the progressive "tense" came into being during ME, its precise origins are uncertain. Most likely, it represents a fusion (and confusion) of (1) verb + present participle as adjective and (2) verb + *on* + gerund. By late ME, both the present participle and the gerund ended in -*ing*, so confusion between the two forms is understandable. The progressive system was not to be fully developed until late in the EMnE period, but examples of its incipient use are easy to find during the entire ME period. The combination of the progressive and the perfect, however, did not appear until the latter part of the fourteenth century and was never common in ME.

Participle   For now is gode Gawayn goande ryȝt here
For now is good Gawain going right here

Gerund   I am yn beldyng of a pore hous
I am (in) building of a poor house

Perfect Prog.   We han ben waitynge al this fourtenyght
We have been waiting all this fortnight

Old English had used both the verb *wesen* 'to be' and *weorþan* 'to become' to form passive constructions. During the course of ME, the latter verb was lost completely, and only 'to be' was used as the passive auxiliary.

> Hir clothes weren makid of right delye thredes
> *Her clothes were made of very delicate threads*

It was also during the course of ME that *by* became the normal preposition for indicating the agent of a passive verb.

> [men] That wol nat be governed by hir wyves
> *[men] that will not be governed by their wives*

English has never had a separate inflected future tense, and OE normally used the present tense to express the future, allowing context and adverbs of time to make the future meaning clear. By ME, the modal auxiliaries *shall* and *will* appeared more and more frequently as indicators of future time, though some degree of obligation (*shall*) or volition (*will*) usually accompanied the future meaning.

> Quan al mankinde...Sal ben fro dede to live broȝt
> *When all mankind ... shall be from dead to living brought*

> and swiche wolle have the kyngdom of helle, and not of hevene
> *and such will have the kingdom of hell, and not of heaven*

In line with the generally analytic trend of the language, Middle English began increasingly to use modal auxiliaries like *may* and *might* and quasi-modals like *be going to* and *be about to* in place of the inflected subjunctive. Nonetheless, the inflected subjunctive was still used far more frequently in ME than it is in PDE, especially to express an optative meaning and in hypothetical subordinate clauses.

Modal	þat y mowe riche be *that I may rich be*
Modal	the gretteste and strongeste garrysoun that a riche man may *the greatest and strongest garrison that a rich man may*
Subjunctive	have...is that he be biloved *have ... is that he be beloved*
Quasi-modal	Satan is ȝeorne abuten uorto ridlen þe ut of mine corne *Satan is eagerly about to sift you out of my grain*
Quasi-modal	Thys onhappy sowle...was goyng to be broughte into helle *This unhappy soul ... was going to be brought into hell*
Subjunctive	how lawful so it were *however lawful it might be*
Subjunctive	why nere I deed! *why am I not dead!*

The one auxiliary that underwent an almost explosive growth during ME was *do*. Though its use varied dialectally and over time, four main functions of *do* as auxiliary verb can be recognized during the period. First, its earlier use as a pro-verb substituting for an already mentioned verb continued.

they [camels] may forbere drynk ii. dayes or iii. and so may not the hors do.
they   can forgo drinking two days or three and thus can not the horse do

Second, in some parts of England, *do* was used as a causative, more or less equivalent to the PDE use of *make* or *have*. As a causative, it was in competition with *make*, *let*, and (in the North) *ger*.

and al hys halles I wol do peynte with pure gold
and all his halls I will have painted with pure gold

Jesu Crist þat makede to go þe halte
Jesus Christ, who caused the lame to walk

þe princes ... gert nakers strike and trumpes blaw
the princes   had drums struck and trumpets blown

Third, *do* was used periphrastically, seemingly as an alternative to the simple tenses. To the modern reader, this use often looks like that of the PDE "emphatic" *do*, but it frequently occurred in contexts where no emphasis or contradiction is apparent. This use of *do* was to increase greatly in EMnE, only to be lost again in PDE.

unto the mayde that hir doth serve
to the maid that her does serve

Fourth, the PDE use of *do* in negative and interrogative clauses was just beginning during the ME period, though it was never as common as the simple verb in such constructions.

my maister dyd not graunt it
my master did not grant it

'Fader, why do ye wepe?'
'Father, why do you weep?'

Old English had had a number of impersonal verbs, that is, verbs without an expressed subject but often with an accompanying pronoun in the accusative or dative case. The number of such verbs increased during ME, partly under French influence. At the same time, they gradually evolved into personal verbs with expressed subjects in the nominative (subject) case, or with a "dummy" subject *it* (as in the third example below).

Me thristed sare, drinc yee me broght
I was very thirsty, drink you me brought

Me dremyd ... þat I was ledd to durham
I dreamed ... that I was led to Durham

Hit þe likede wel þat þu us adun læidest
It pleased you well that you us down laid

In Old English, the ending *-an* had been sufficient to mark the infinitive. After the loss of final unstressed syllables in ME, a preposition preceding the verb substituted for the inflectional ending. *For to* originally expressed purpose, later became a simple infinitive marker, and finally died out. *Till* and *at* sometimes appeared as infinitive markers in Northern texts; both reflect Scandinavian usage.[4] However, *to* was always the most common, and by the end of the ME period, it had prevailed over the alternative markers.

Syntax Within Clauses

As we saw in the preceding chapter, if we take subject (S), verb (V), and object/complement (O) as the basic elements of a clause, then OE allowed every possible order of elements (SVO, SOV, VSO, VOS, OSV, and OVS). We also saw that OE already had favorite orders, most of them still familiar in PDE. In ME, we find continuations of some OE patterns different from those of PDE, but the trend was toward modern word order, and by the end of ME, PDE patterns were firmly established.

For straight affirmative independent clauses, the SVO order was, as it has always been in English, the most common. Unlike OE, however, the SVO order was also frequent after adverbials and in dependent clauses, including indirect questions.

Independent clause	Thyn Astrolabie hath a ring to putten on the thombe *Your astrolabe has a ring to put on the thumb*

After adverbial	In the contre of Ethyop they slen here childeryn byforn
	In the country of Ethiopia they slay their children in front of
	   here goddys
	   their gods

Dependent clause	þe taverne ys þe scole of þe dyevle huere his deciples studieþ *the tavern is the school of the devil where his disciples study*
Indirect question	men askede hire how scho myghte swa lyffe *people asked her how she could thus live*

The order SOV, almost totally alien to PDE, can at least occasionally be found throughout the entire ME period, especially (a) when the object is a pronoun, (b) in dependent clauses, or (c) with compound tenses, where the object usually comes between the two parts of the verb.

Pronoun object	If a man will þe harme *If a man wants (to) you harm*
Compound tense	wo haueþ þe in þe putte ibroute? *who has you in the well put?*

---

[4] One well-hidden survival of the use of *at* to mark the infinitive is the word *ado*, originally *at do*. We have reinvented this compound with the English preposition *to* in the word *to-do*.

As in OE, the order VS(O) was regular in direct questions and in imperatives with an expressed subject. It was common, but not universal, after introductory adverbials.

Direct question	Gaf ye the chyld any thyng? *Gave you the child any thing?*
Direct question	What seye we eek of hem that deliten hem in sweryng *What say we also of them that delight (themselves) in swearing*
Imperative	And wete ye wel that thour this desert may non hors passe *And know you well that through this desert can no horse pass*
After adverbial	Nowe haue ye herde þe vertues & þe significacouns *Now have you heard the virtues and the meanings*

The order OSV was a fairly common means (as it still is today in speech) of emphasizing the direct object or complement.

This bok I haue mad and wretyn
This book I have made and written

Merchaunt he was in his ȝonghede
Merchant he was in his youth

Another common variant was the order (O)VS.

Clothis have they none but of the skynnys of bestis.
Clothes have they none except of the skins of beasts.

Now more of the deth of kynge Arthur coude I never fynde
Now more about the death of King Arthur could I never find

Old English had frequently had subjectless sentences when the context or the inflections of verbs made the meaning of the sentence clear. During ME, the feeling seems to have arisen that a sentence must have a subject, regardless of whether or not the context requires it. By the end of ME, the "dummy" subjects *there* and *it* were being used regularly to fill the subject slot when no other logical subject was available. Note that the *there* in the first clause below is really a kind of pronoun and not an adverb of place.

Another remedie <u>there</u> is ayenst slouth
Another remedy there is against sloth

And whan the passhion nyghed <u>it</u> is certayne that the tre floterid above
And when the Passion drew near it is certain that the tree floated above

Syntax of Sentences

Like OE, ME favored the cumulative or "run-on" sentence over the periodic sentence. Coordination, rather than heavy subordination, was the general rule for connecting clauses. The result is sentences that are normally easy to understand but that seem somewhat loose and inelegant by modern standards. To illustrate this we use two brief passages, one from relatively early in the ME period and one from the end of the ME period. The first sample is from the *Ancrene Wisse*, or "Behavior of Anchoresses." (An anchoress was a female religious recluse; this book was a manual of rules for such recluses.) The original text was written about the year 1200 by an unknown cleric at the request of three noble sisters who intended to retire to a contemplative life. The text below is from a manuscript copied in the first half of the thirteenth century.

> ʒe mine leoue sustren bute ʒef neod ow driue & ower meistre hit reade. ne
> *You, my dear sisters, unless need you compels & your master it advises, not*

> schulen habbe na beast bute cat ane. Ancre þe haueð ahte. þuncheð bet
> *should have no beast except cat only. Anchoress who has cattle seems more*

> husewif ase Marthe wes. ne lihtlice ne mei ha nawt beo Marie marthe suster
> *housewife than Martha was; not easily not can she not be Mary, Martha's sister,*
> suster
> *sister,*

> wið griðfullnesse of heorte. for þenne mot ha þenchen of þe kues foddre.
> *with serenity of heart. For then must she think of the cow's fodder,*

> of heordemonne hure. Olhnin þe heiward. wearien hwen he punt hire. &
> *of herdsman's hire, flatter the hayward, beware when he impounds it, and*

> ʒelden þah þe hearmes. ladlich þing is hit wat crist hwen me
> *pay, moreover, the damages. Loathly thing is it, Christ knows, when people*

> makeð i tune man of ancre ahte.
> *make in town complaint of anchoress' cattle.*

The second sample is from Thomas Malory's *Morte Darthur*, written about 1460–70. Punctuation and capitalization in this passage have been modernized.

> Than sir Launcelot had a condicion that he used of custom to clatir in
> *Then Sir Launcelot had a condition so that he was accustomed to chatter in*

> his slepe and to speke oftyn of hys lady, quene Gwenyver. So sir Launcelot
> *his sleep and to speak often of his lady, Queen Guinevere. So Sir Launcelot*

> had awayked as longe as hit had pleased hym, and so by course of kynde he
> *had been awake as long as it had pleased him, and so by course of nature he*

> slepte and dame Elayne bothe. And in his slepe he talked and claterde as a
> *slept and Dame Elaine both. And in his sleep he talked and chattered like a*

> jay of the love that had bene betwyxte quene Gwenyver and hym, and so as
> *jay of the love that had been between Queen Guinevere and him, and because*

> he talked so lowde the quene harde hym thereas she lay in her chambir.
> *he talked so loud the queen heard him where she lay in her chamber.*

> And whan she harde hym so clattir she was wrothe oute of mesure, and for
> *And when she heard him thus chatter she was angry beyond limit, and for*

> anger and payne wist not what to do, and than she cowghed so lowde that
> *anger and distress knew not what to do, and then she coughed so loud that*

> sir Launcelot awaked.
> *Sir Launcelot awaked.*

Middle English prose translations often attempted to replicate in English the convoluted and heavily subordinated syntax of their Latin originals. These attempts were usually not especially successful stylistically; not until the EMnE period were English writers to achieve a sophisticated English prose style that incorporated Latinate subordinating devices smoothly into the natural syntax and rhythms of English. The brief passage below from Chaucer's translation of Boethius' *Consolation of Philosophy* is fairly typical of what happened when ME prose writers tried to imitate Latin exemplars.

"This world," quod I, "of so manye and diverse and contraryous parties,
"This world," said I, "of so many and diverse and adverse parts,

ne myghte nevere han ben assembled in o forme, but yif ther ne were oon that
not could never have been united in one form, unless there not were one that
that
that

conjoyned so manye diverse thinges; and the same diversite of here natures,
composed so many diverse things; and the very diversity of their natures,

that so discorden the ton fro that other, most departen and unjoynen the
that so disagree the one from the other, must separate and disjoin the

thinges that ben conjoynid, yif ther ne were oon that contenyde that he
things that are composed, if there not were one that held together what he

hath conjoynid and ybounden. Ne the certein ordre of nature schulde not
has composed and bound. Nor the certain order of nature should not

brynge forth so ordene moevynges by places, by tymes, by doynges, by spaces,
bring forth such regulated movings by places, by times, by actions, by spaces,
spaces,
spaces,

by qualites, yif ther ne were on, that were ay stedfast duellynge, that
by qualities, if there not were one that was always steadfast remaining, that

ordeynide and disponyde thise diversites of moevynges. And thilke thing,
ordained and regulated these diversities of movings. And that same thing,

whatsoevere it be, by which that alle thinges ben ymaked and ilad, y clepe
whatever it be, by which all things are made and conducted, I call

hym 'God', that is a word that is used to alle folk."
him 'God', which is a word that is familiar to all people."

Syntax of Poetry

The syntax of ME verse was essentially the same as that of the prose. However, to meet the exigencies of rhyme or proper stress placement, the poets were likely to employ inversions much more frequently than was typical of prose. Complexity of sentence structure varied widely, from the simple syntax of lyrics and ballads, to slightly more complex structures in many verse romances, to the extraordinarily complex syntax of such carefully wrought poetry as the opening lines of *Sir Gawain and the Green Knight*.

The following lyric, "Mirie It Is While Sumer Ilast," is dated about 1225. The sentence structure is basically simple. There is, however, inversion of the predicate adjective *mirie* in the first line, of subject and verb in the third line, and of adjective and noun in the fourth line—all of these inversions made in order to get rhyming words into the proper position at the end of the line.

Mirie it is while sumer ilast,
Merry it is while summer lasts,

Wið fugheles song.
With birds' song.

Oc nu necheð windes blast
But now draws near wind's blast,

And weder strong.
And weather fierce.

Ej! ej! what þis nicht is long!
Ah! ah! How this night is long!

And ich wið wel michel wrong
And I with very great grief

Soregh and murne and fast.
Sorrow and mourn and fast.

Showing somewhat less inversion but slightly more complicated sentence structure is the following passage from *Sir Orfeo*, a Breton lai (a short romance with supernatural elements) dated about 1325.

Orfeo was a king,
Orfeo was a king,

In Inglond an heiʒe lording,
In England a high lord,

A stalworþ man and hardi bo,
A stalwart man and hardy both,

Large and curteis he was also.
Generous and courteous he was also.

His fader was comen of King Pluto
His father was come from King Pluto

And his moder of King Iuno,
And his mother from King Juno,

þat sumtime were as godes yhold
That once were as gods held

For auentours þat þai dede and told.
For adventures that they did and told.

With this syntactic simplicity may be contrasted the opening lines of Chaucer's General Prologue to the *Canterbury Tales*. Inversion is only moderate, but the syntax is ambitious indeed: the eighteen lines reproduced here comprise a single sentence of eleven clauses, and no independent clause appears until line 12.

Whan that Aprill with his shoures soote
When April with its showers sweet

The droghte of March hath perced to the roote,
The drought of March has pierced to the root,

And bathed every veyne in swich licour
And bathed every vein in such moisture

Of which vertu engendred is the flour;
Of which virtue engendered is the flower;

5   Whan Zephirus eek with his sweete breeth
When Zephirus also with his sweet breath

Inspired hath in every holt and heeth
Breathed on has in every field and heath

The tendre croppes, and the yonge sonne
The tender crops, and the young sun

Hath in the Ram his halve cours yronne,
Has in the Ram its half course run,

And smale foweles maken melodye,
And small birds make melody,

10 That slepen al the nyght with open ye
That sleep all the night with open eye

(So priketh hem nature in hir corages);
(So spurs them nature in their hearts);

Thanne longen folk to goon on pilgrimages,
Then desire people to go on pilgrimages,

And palmeres for to seken straunge strondes,
And palmers to seek strange shores,

To ferne halwes, kowthe in sondry londes;
To remote shrines, familiar in various lands;

15 And specially from every shires ende
And especially from every shire's end

Of Engelond to Caunterbury they wende,
Of England to Canterbury they go,

The hooly blisful martir for to seke,
The holy blessed martyr to seek,

That hem hath holpen whan that they were seeke.
That them has helped when they were sick.

Middle English Lexicon

Perhaps the two most salient characteristics of Present-Day English are its highly analytic grammar and its immense lexicon. Both of these features originated during the ME period. But although English lost all but a handful of its inflections during ME and has undergone little inflectional change since, ME marks only the onset of the burgeoning of the English vocabulary to its current unparalleled size among the languages of the world. Ever since ME, the language has been more than hospitable to loanwords from other languages, and all subsequent periods have seen comparable influxes of loans and increases in vocabulary.

The thousands of loanwords that poured into English after the Norman Conquest had an effect beyond that of merely adding new terms and synonyms to the language. They also provided the raw material for an intricate system of *levels* of vocabulary ranging from the colloquial through the formal, from the everyday to the highly technical, from the general to the highly specialized. Through the thousands of Latin-based roots, they also mark the beginning of the highly cosmopolitan nature of English today.

By the ME period, the English language was well suited linguistically to borrow easily and freely from other languages. Its inflectional simplicity meant that English speakers could adopt words without having to worry about what

LEGAL ENGLISH

Those who have some familiarity with legal English of both the past and the present may think that the language of the law is an exception to the principle that all language changes over time. Indeed, legal English is perhaps more conservative than any other variety of the language. As an illustration, compare the language of the following two selections from indentures. The first was written in 1458, the second in 1972. (The first selection has a few minor changes in spelling to make it easier to read.)

1458

Thys indenture made the xxviij day of august the yere of the reigne of kyng henre the sext after the conquest xxxvi wittenessith that thaghe john sone of william Coldecotes sometyme of wolueton in the countie of lance be boundon to Thomas Norreis of spreke in the saide countie esquier in xl $ of gode & leille money of Englond to be payet to the said Thomas his attorney or executoures at the feft of seynt mighelle archangell next suying the date of thes presesentes ... that if the forsaid john in tyme comyng make none aliencaon morgage nor eschaungegysse nor selle nor none encombraunce make of or in alle those meses londes & tenements rentes & seruices with thaire appurtenaunce or of any parcelle of the same....

1972

This indenture of lease entered into on the day of August 23, A.D. 1972, by and between [R.M.] and [C.M.], hereinafter called the lessors, and [Y. K.], hereinafter called the lessee. Witnesseth: That the said Lessors hereby demise and lease unto said Lessee that certain parcel of land with buildings and improvements thereon situated at [53 F.S., Providence, R.I.]. To have and to hold the same with the appurtenances for and during the term of twelve (12) months ... yielding and paying therefor the total sum of twenty-five hundred and twenty Dollars ... It is further agreed that wherein this lease the words "Lessors" or "Lessee" are used the same both as to rights and as to duties and liabilities shall import and extend to the heirs, executors, administrators and assigns of the Lessors or the Lessee except where the context clearly excludes such meaning.

---

inflectional classes they belonged to—whether they were weak or strong; masculine, feminine, or neuter; whether they should be *i*-stems, *ā*-stems, or special stems reserved for nonnative words. This point may seem trivial, but heavily inflected languages often have difficulty in assimilating loanwords and treat words that are borrowed so specially that their foreignness is not easily lost. In Russian, for example, loanwords often are clearly marked as aliens by (a) violating Russian spelling conventions, (b) having natural rather than grammatical gender, and (c) being indeclinable. The loanword *madam*, for example, is indeclinable even though most Russian nouns are declined for six cases, and feminine even though it would be masculine if it were a native word (because native Russian words ending in a consonant are masculine). Even Japanese, whose proclivity for borrowing English words is sometimes a source of amusement to English speakers, marks loanwords as "different" by writing them in a special syllabary. English, on the other hand, has borrowed so many words from so many sources over the centuries since ME that almost nothing looks or sounds extremely exotic. If it does, that does not matter either, because there are so many other "un-English" words already in the language: *wok* was accepted more readily as an English word because it was preceded by *amok* and *batik* and *kayak*.

To a lesser extent, the wide variety of phonemes and the complex allowable syllable structure of English also facilitates adoption of loanwords in recognizable form. For example, English could borrow the Chinese word *shantung* as the name for a kind of silk fabric manufactured in Shantung, China, because both *shan* and *tung* fit English syllable-structure rules. Chinese, with its highly restricted syllable structure, would have had much more difficulty trying to fit English *polyester* into Chinese; hence, it settled for a kind of loan-translation (or *calque*) and calls the product *ju-zhi* ('assemble' + 'ester').

Loanwords

The greatest inundation of loanwords into ME came from French, but English borrowings from other languages also appeared at this time. In particular, there were numerous Scandinavian (Norse) and Latin contributions to the English lexicon, along with a handful of words from other languages, European and non-European.

SCANDINAVIAN INFLUENCE

Chronologically, the first significant new source of loanwords in ME was Scandinavian. (At this time, the differences among Danish, Swedish, and Norwegian were so slight that it is unnecessary to try to distinguish them; hence we use the more general terms Norse or Scandinavian.) Many of the Scandinavian words that first appear in writing during ME were actually borrowed earlier, but, particularly in a society with a low literacy rate, there is a lag between use in speech and first appearance in writing. When they were written down, it was usually first in the North and the East Midlands, those regions with heaviest Norse settlements. Only later did they spread to other areas of England. The largest number of loanwords came into writing during the period 1150–1250, a few score more appeared 1250–1350, and the influx diminished to a trickle in the period 1350–1500. The listing below is representative but not exhaustive.

c. 1150–1250

> anger, bag, band, bloom, both, bound (going to), bull, cake, call, carp (complain), cast, clip (cut), club, die, egg, fellow, flit, gad, gape, gear, get, hit, husband, ill, kid, kindle, loan, loft, loose, low, meek, muck, raise, ransack, rid, root, rotten, sale, same, scab, scale, scare, scathe, score (20), seat, seem, skill, skin, sky, sly, snare, swain, take, thrall, thrive, thrust, thwart, ugly, wand, wassail, window, wing

c. 1250–1350

> awe, bait, ball, bark (of tree), bat (the animal), birth, blend, bole, bracken, brad, brunt, crawl, dirt, dregs, droop, flat, flaw, geld, gift, girth, glitter, leg, lift, likely, midden, mire, mistake, race, rag, rive, skate (the fish), sleight, slight, snub, stack, stagger, stem, teem, weak, whirl

c. 1350–1500

> awkward, bask, bawl, bulk, down (feathers), eddy, firth, flag, freckle, froth, gap, gasp, keel, leak, link, raft, reef (sail), reindeer, scant, scrap, steak, tatter, tether, tyke

A quick perusal of these lists reveals that almost all these words are so common in English today, so native in appearance, that it is hard to believe that they are loans from another language. Part of their familiarity is explainable by the fact that they have been in the language for so long that they have had plenty of time to become fully assimilated. Further, Scandinavian is so closely related to English that these loans "feel" like English.

Some of the Norse loans (such as *both*, *call*, and *take*) express such basic concepts that we feel that they must be native words, that Old English could not have done without them. Old English did have its own terms for the concepts, but, unlike the majority of ME loans from French or Latin, Norse loans often supplanted rather than supplemented native vocabulary. Thus Norse *call* replaced OE *hātan*, *both* replaced OE *bā*, and *take* replaced OE *niman* and *fōn*. In other instances, the Norse loan took over only part of the domain of the native English word, while the English word survived in a narrowed usage. For example, ON *sky* replaced OE *heofon* as the general term for the upper atmosphere, but *heaven* survives, especially in the sense of "dwelling-place of God." Occasionally, both the native word and the Norse loan survive as almost complete synonyms; few people could specify any distinct difference in meaning between Norse *crawl* and native English *creep*.

A number of the Norse loans are cognates of existing English words. Usually such doublets as have survived have undergone a differentiation in meaning—each has carved out a specialized semantic territory for itself. Examples include Norse *raise*, *skin*, and *skirt*, cognates of native *rear*, *shin*, and *shirt*. In a few instances, blends have occurred. For example, *reindeer* is a blend of ON *hrein* 'reindeer' and English *deer* (from OE *dēor* 'wild animal').

Most of these early Norse loans represent basic homely concepts and lack the apparent intellectual sophistication of so many French and Latin loans. Nonetheless, a number of them have come to express remarkably subtle distinctions of meaning. *Awkward* has a domain of its own, separate from its many near-synonyms such as *clumsy*, *ungainly*, *ungraceful*, *gauche*, *gawky*, *maladroit*, or *unskillful*. Similarly, none of the words like *mild*, *submissive*, *humble*, *patient*, *stoical*, *gentle*, *forbearing*, *long-suffering*, *unresisting*, or *unassuming* quite captures the precise meaning of *meek*.

In addition to its contributions to the general vocabulary, Norse introduced a number of new place-name elements into English, especially into the areas heavily settled by Scandinavians. Chief among these were *-beck* 'brook', *-by* 'town', *-dale* 'valley', *-thorp* 'village', *-thwaite* 'piece of land', and *-toft* 'piece of ground'. Within a relatively small area of Cumberland and Westmorland, for instance, are settlements named Grizebeck, Troutbeck, Thursby, Glassonby, Knarsdale, Uldale, Braithwaite, and Seathwaite. In the old Danelaw area in the east, *-beck* and *-thwaite* names are scarcer, but the map is dotted with such places as Easttoft, Langtoft, Ugthorpe, and Fridaythorpe. English settlers were later to import these names to all parts of the globe—from Yelvertoft, Australia, to Uniondale, South Africa, to Oglethorpe, Georgia, to Moresby Island, British Columbia.

Finally, Norse influence was heavy at about the time the English began to use surnames, so Norse was able to give English the common surname suffix *-son*. This suffix proved so popular that it was attached not only to first names of Norse origin (*Nelson, Anderson*), but also to native English names (*Edwardson, Edmundson*) and even to French names (*Jackson, Henryson*). English did not, however, adopt the Scandinavian practice of using *-datter* 'daughter' as a surname suffix for females.

FRENCH INFLUENCE

Important as the Norse influence has been to English, it looks small beside that of French. By 1400, the entire nature of the English lexicon had been transformed by the flood of loanwords from French. For the first hundred years after the Conquest, the rate at which the French loans entered English seems to have been relatively slow. The usual explanation for this slow start is that it took several generations of bilingualism for English speakers to be comfortable with French words. Another factor, however, is the paucity of texts in English prior to 1200; if we have no texts, we have no way of telling how many French words were being used by English speakers. Probably the borrowing varied greatly from area to area and from individual to individual. The *Ormulum* and Layamon's *Brut*, both written in English about the year 1200, have few French loans—this is particularly surprising in the case of the *Brut* because it is a translation from a French original. On the other hand, *The Owl and the Nightingale*, written at approximately the same time, has dozens of different French loanwords within its 1794 lines. These range from legal or quasi-legal terms like *accord, plead, rent,* and *spouse,* to humbler words like *carter, flower, pie* (magpie), and *stubble,* to adjectives such as *gent* ('noble-born'), *jealous,* and *poor.* There are even hybrids with French roots and English affixes, such as *disputing* and *overquatie* ('glut').

Such a wide variety of types of words suggests that French loans had already thoroughly permeated the English vocabulary, and that they were not limited to specific semantic fields. By way of contrast, consider the status of Italian loanwords in PDE. In certain fields, such as music, architecture, and painting, the Italian influence is extraordinarily heavy (for example, *piano, cello, sonata, forte, poco, prima donna, vibrato, bel canto*). However, beyond these areas, the Italian influence on English is slight. Even though Italian cooking is very popular in the United States and Italian restaurants probably outnumber French ones by ten to one, most of the Italian cookery terms in English are restricted to the names of specific Italian foods or dishes (*lasagne, spaghetti, pizza, ricotta, tortoni*). When we prepare these Italian foods, we use English or French words to describe the process (*bake, sauté, serve, plate, casserole, fork, stir, mince, roast, fry*). Nor have the Italian loans expanded beyond their restricted semantic domains: *poco* 'little' remains a musical term only. On the other hand, the French word *petit,* also meaning "little," appears as part of the general English vocabulary in two different forms, *petty* and *petite,* not to mention its specialized use in terms like *petit larceny, petit point,* and *petit mal.*

The number of French loans making their first appearance in English texts increased steadily during the thirteenth century, crested during the fourteenth century, and then began to decline toward the end of the fourteenth century. Almost every aspect of civilization was represented in these French loans. Space prevents more than a fractional sampling of the thousands of French words still used today that entered the language during ME, so we have simply selected a dozen broad semantic areas and listed a score or so of French loans representing each.

Relationships and Ranks
parentage, ancestor, aunt, uncle, cousin, gentle(man), noble, peer, peasant, servant, villein, page, courtier, squire, madam, sir, princess, duke, count, marquis, baron

The House and Its Furnishings
porch, cellar, pantry, closet, parlor, chimney, arch, (window)pane, wardrobe, chair, table, lamp, couch, cushion, mirror, curtain, quilt, counterpane, towel, blanket

Food and Eating
dinner, supper, taste, broil, fry, plate, goblet, serve, beverage, sauce, salad, gravy, fruit, grape, beef, pork, mutton, salmon, sugar, onion, cloves, mustard

Fashion
fashion, dress, garment, coat, cloak, pantaloons, bonnet, boots, serge, cotton, satin, fur, button, ribbon, baste, embroider, pleat, gusset, jewel, pearl, bracelet

Sports and Entertainment
joust, tournament, kennel, scent, terrier, falcon, stallion, park, dance, chess, checkers, minstrel, fool, prize, tennis, racket, disport, audience, entertain, amusement, recreation

Arts, Music, Literature
art, painting, sculpture, portrait, color, music, melody, lute, tabor, hautboy, carol, poet, story, rime, chapter, title, romance, lay, tragedy, rondel, ballad

Education
study, science, reason, university, college, dean, form, train, grammar, noun, subject, test, indite, pupil, copy, pen, pencil, paper, page, chapter, tome, lectern, dais

Medicine
medicine, surgeon, pain, disease, remedy, cure, contagious, plague, humor, pulse, fracture, ague, gout, distemper, drug, balm, herb, powder, sulfur, bandage, ointment, poison

Government
government, state, country, city, village, office, rule, reign, public, crown, court, police, tyranny, subsidy, tax, counselor, treasurer, exchequer, register, mayor, citizen

Law
judge, jury, appeal, evidence, inquest, accuse, proof, convict, pardon, attorney, heir, statute, broker, fine, punish, prison, crime, felony, arson, innocent, just

The Church
chapel, choir, cloister, crucifix, religion, clergy, chaplain, parson, sermon, matins, confession, penance, pray, anoint, absolve, trinity, faith, miracle, temptation, heresy, divine, salvation

The Military
enemy, battle, defense, peace, force, advance, capture, siege, attack, retreat, army, navy, soldier, guard, sergeant, captain, spy, moat, order, march, trophy

In addition to its contribution to the vocabulary of specialized areas, French has given English hundreds of "little" words, words so familiar and so widely used that they seem completely native today. Again, we can give only a small sample:

age, blame, catch, chance, change, close, cry, dally, enter, face, fail, fine, flower, fresh, grease, grouch, hello, hurt, join, kerchief, large, letter, line, mischief, move, offer, part, pay, people, piece, place, please, poor, pure, rock, roll, save, search, sign, square, stuff, strange, sure, touch, try, turn, use

With this pervasive influence of French in so many semantic areas, it is surprising (and even consoling) to discover that some aspects of English life remained relatively untouched by French loanwords. One of these areas was shipping and seafaring, though, as we shall see, this area had many loans from Low German and Dutch. Another area was farming and agriculture in general. The word *farm* itself is from French, and *agriculture* is a loan from Latin. However, the Norman masters themselves apparently left their English servants to work the fields by themselves, for most basic farming terminology remains native English to this day. All of the following words come down directly from Old English:

acre, field, hedge, furrow, sow, till, reap, harvest, plough, sickle, scythe, spade, rake, seed, wheat, barley, oats, grass, hay, fodder, ox, horse, cow, swine, sheep, hen, goose, duck, sty, pen, barn, fold

Finally, because the French came to England as administrators and did not make entirely new settlements consisting only of French-speaking inhabitants, the French, unlike the Norse, contributed no place-name elements to England.

Almost all the thousands of French loans that came into the language during ME were nouns, verbs, or adjectives. Unlike Norse, French contributed little to the basic grammar of English. We have no pronouns from French. Though a few of our prepositions and conjunctions (*in spite of*, *because*, *during*, *regarding*, *in case*) are ultimately French, they came into English as nouns or verbs and were converted to function words only after they had been thoroughly naturalized. The noun *cause*, for instance, is first recorded in English during the early thirteenth century, but the phrase *by cause of* does not appear until the mid-fourteenth century, and the conjunction *because* only in the late fourteenth century.

As our earlier examples from *The Owl and the Nightingale* illustrated, French roots were combined freely with English affixes from the beginning. Further, English was soon borrowing French affixes. Sometimes French suffixes were applied to English roots (for example, *starvation*), but most of them were usually reserved for use with French (or Latin) roots. French prefixes were borrowed even more freely and were used on both native and borrowed roots. So extensive was this practice that some native prefixes were totally replaced by their French equivalents. French *counter-* supplanted the native English *with-* 'against'; although *with-* survives in a few words like *withhold*, *withstand*, and *withdraw*, we can no longer use it to make new words. Even with native roots, we must say *countersink* and *counterblow*, not **withsink* and **withblow*.

Most of the earliest French loanwords into Middle English came from Norman French, but by the fourteenth century, the majority of loans were from Central, or Parisian, French, which had become the prestigious dialect in France. In many instances, it is impossible to identify the original French dialect, but in other cases phonological differences distinguish the forms. In words originally borrowed from Germanic, Germanic /gw/ became /w/ in Norman and /g/ in Central French. Thus, beside Norman *wile, warrant, war,* and *wage,* English also has the Central French forms *guile, guaranty, garrison,* and *gauge.* In Norman French, Latin /k/ before /a/ remained, while in Central French it became /č/. Hence we have such doublets in English as Norman *canal, cattle, catch,* and *car* versus Central French *channel, chattels, chase,* and *chariot.*

A surprisingly large number of the French words borrowed into English during ME were words that French itself had originally borrowed from Germanic. Often doublets of these words still exist, though changed in form and meaning. For example, the French loan *equip* is from the same Germanic root as English *ship.* French *soup* is a doublet of native English *sop,* and *grape* is a doublet of native *grapple.*

LATIN INFLUENCE

By the late fourteenth century, no one could have written an English text of any length without using any loanwords from French, but it still would have been possible to write on many topics without using Latin loanwords. Of course, most French loans were ultimately from Latin, but direct loans from Latin into ME tended to be learned words borrowed through the written translation of Latin texts. Because Latin was the official language of the Church, a number of religious terms came directly into English from Latin, such as *apocalypse, dirge, limbo, purgatory,* and *remit.* Latin was also frequently used in legal documents, so English borrowed such words as *testament* and *confederate.* A few of the other miscellaneous learned words directly from Latin are *admit, divide, comprehend, lunatic, lapidary,* and *temporal.* All in all, although a great many Latin loans came into ME, the real deluge was not to take place until the Early Modern English period.

CELTIC INFLUENCE

Loanwords from Celtic into English have always been few. Still, several are recorded for the first time during ME, including *bard, clan, crag, glen,* and *loch.* Possibly—but not certainly—from Celtic are *bald, bray, bug, gull, hog,* and *loop.* French had a large number of words of Celtic origin, and some of them (*car, change, garter, mutton, socket, vassal*) came into English via French, but these were of course only indirect loans.

DUTCH AND LOW GERMAN INFLUENCE

During the latter part of the ME period, commerce between England and the Low Countries increased greatly, particularly as a result of the wool trade, and several dozen loans from Dutch and/or Low German entered English as a result of this contact. Reflecting the seafaring interests of the Dutch are words like *halibut, pump, shore, skipper,* and *whiting.* The containers in which merchandise was shipped brought words like *bundle, bung, cork, dowel, firkin,* and *tub.* Trade in general gave English words like *trade* and *huckster;* the wool trade in particular provided *nap* (of cloth) and *selvage.* There were also miscellaneous words, such as *clock, damp, grime, luck, scour, speckle, splinter, tallow,* and *wriggle.*

INFLUENCE FROM OTHER LANGUAGES

There was little Greek scholarship in England during the ME period and therefore almost no direct borrowing from Greek. Indirectly through French, English acquired a few items like *squirrel*, *diaper*, and *cinnamon*. More learned Greek words entered through Latin; a few examples are *philosophy*, *paradigm*, *phlegm*, *synod*, and *physic*.

As Europe increased its knowledge of the Levant through the Crusades and the spread of Islam, many Arabic and Persian words were borrowed into European languages. English, however, almost always acquired these secondhand through French or Medieval Latin. Among the indirect borrowings from Arabic during ME are the words *azimuth*, *ream*, *saffron*, *cipher*, and *alkali*. Ultimately from Persian, though sometimes filtered through several other languages on the way to English, are *borax*, *mummy*, *musk*, *spinach*, *taffeta*, and *lemon*. From Hebrew via French or Latin are *jubilee*, *leviathan*, and *cider*. Middle English received Slavic *sable* and Hungarian *coach* via French.

At all periods of its history, English has received words whose origins simply cannot be traced to any source. Among the items of unknown origin that are first recorded in ME are such familiar words as *bicker*, *big*, *boy*, *clasp*, *junk*, *kidney*, *lass*, *noose*, *puzzle*, *roam*, *slender*, *throb*, and *wallet*.

Formation of New Words

Despite the thousands of loanwords from French and other sources that poured into English during ME, the language did not stop creating new words by the older processes of compounding and affixing. Indeed, the loanwords provided new raw material for both processes, and new processes of formation developed during the period.

COMPOUNDING

The loss of inflections made compounding even easier, although, because of this loss and because of functional shift, it is often hard to decide whether an element in a compound is, say, a noun or a verb. Thus the compound *windfall* could be interpreted as noun + noun (a fall caused by the wind) or as noun + verb (the wind makes it fall). As in OE, the majority of the many new compounds in ME were nouns or adjectives. Foreign elements entered freely into the new compounds (for instance, *gentleman* consists of French *gentle* + native *man*).

The most productive types of OE compound nouns continued in ME. New noun + noun compounds included such words as *cheesecake*, *toadstool*, *bagpipe*, *nightmare*, and *wheelbarrow*. Adjective + noun compounds can be illustrated by *sweetheart*, *wildfire*, *quicksand*, and *commonwealth*. Among the adverb + noun compounds were *insight*, *afternoon*, and *upland*. Just coming into use during ME were noun + verb compounds like *sunshine* and *nosebleed*. We also begin to find verb + noun combinations such as *hangman*, *pastime*, and *whirlwind*. ME also saw the beginning of a type that was eventually to become highly productive in English, the verb + adverb compound; two examples from ME are *runabout* and *lean-to*. Another new type was adverb + verb, including words like *outcome*, *outcast*, and *upset*. English also borrowed—or loan-translated—a number of French and Latin phrases with the order noun + adjective (*knight-errant*, *heir-apparent*, *sum total*). However, this type violated the basic English principle that an attributive adjective precedes its noun, and the type has never become productive in English.

Among the compound adjectives, the OE type noun + adjective continued to be productive; ME examples include *threadbare*, *bloodred*, and *headstrong*. Much less common was the adjective + noun type (*everyday*).

As in OE, compound verbs in ME were usually formed from preexisting compound nouns or adjectives. The OE type of adverb (or particle) + verb continued to be employed: *outline, uphold, overturn, underwrite* all appeared for the first time in ME. Just coming into English was a new type consisting of noun + verb, as in *manhandle*; most of these compounds, however, were the products of back-formation from nouns (compare modern *babysit* from *babysitter*), and the type would not become common until Early Modern English.

Some of the compounds that first appear in ME have since lost their transparency as compounds because of sound changes or because one or both of the constituents have become obsolete as independent words. Few native speakers today would recognize *cockney* as consisting of *cock + egg*, or *gossamer* as *goose + summer*. *Wanton* does not look like a compound because both *wan* 'deficient' and *towen* 'to bring up, educate' have been lost from the language; the original compound meant "poorly brought up."

A number of the loanwords borrowed from French or Latin during ME were compounds or phrases in origin, but were treated as single units in English. For example, Latin *dies mali* 'evil days' has become *dismal*; French *porc espin* 'spiny pig' has been anglicized as *porcupine*.

Affixing

Despite the extensive borrowing of words from French, the continued productiveness of compounding, and the loss of a number of native prefixes and suffixes, affixing continued to be one of the chief ways of creating new words in Middle English.

A few OE affixes were totally lost, not even surviving in already-formed words (or not being recognized as affixes if they did). Among these were *ed-* 'again' (replaced by French/Latin *re-*); *el-* 'foreign'; *ymb-* 'around'; *to-* 'motion toward'; and *-end*, which was used in OE to form agentive nouns. Other native affixes survived in preexisting words, but lost most or all of their productiveness. Examples include *with-* as in *withstand*; *for-* as in *forsake, forswear*; and *-hood* as in *motherhood, childhood*.

Among the new prefixes borrowed from French during ME are *counter-*, *de-, in-* 'not', *inter-, mal-*, and *re-*. Suffixes from French include *-able, -age, -al, -ery*, *-ess, -ify, -ist, -ity*, and *-ment*. Some of them, such as *re-*, were freely attached to native words and loanwords alike. Others have always retained their association with French or Latin; for example, despite the hundreds of words in English ending in *-ment*, we would hesitate to form an abstract noun by attaching *-ment* to a native root. In other words, although we are thoroughly comfortable with *discernment*, which received its *-ment* after entering English, we find *understandment* or *knowment* decidedly unacceptable and prefer to use the native gerund suffix *-ing* instead (*understanding, knowing*).

Minor Sources of New Words

As was mentioned in the preceding chapter, PDE has a number of minor sources of new vocabulary items, sources for which we have no evidence in surviving OE texts. However, in the more extensive and more diversified texts from ME, a number of these processes make their first appearance.

Clipping, the process whereby one or more syllables are subtracted from a word, became common in ME with words of French origin. This is not surprising. Native English words usually have their major stress on the first syllable; hence the native speaker hearing a French word would tend to interpret it as beginning with the onset of the major stress.[5] Often both the clipped and the full forms have survived in English, usually with a differentiation in meaning. A few of the many possible examples from ME are *fray* (< *affray*), *squire* (< *esquire*), *stress* (< *distress*), *peal* (< *appeal*), and *mend* (< *amend*).

Somewhat similar to clipping in result, though not in principle, is the **back formation**, a new word formed by mistakenly interpreting an existing word as having been derived from it. Thus English speakers interpreted the final -*s* of French *orfreis* as a plural suffix and created the new word *orphrey*. Similarly, *asp* is a back formation of the (singular) Latin *aspis*, *fog* a back formation from the Scandinavian loan *foggy*, and *dawn* from earlier English *dawning*.

Blends, also called **portmanteau** words, are combinations of two existing words to form a new word. In PDE, the process is often deliberate (*sexational* from *sex + sensational*; *smog* from *smoke + fog*), but it was probably still an unconscious process in Middle English. Particularly for earlier periods, it is not always easy to be sure precisely what the original components of a blend were, or even whether a particular item should be considered a blend or an echoic word. However, among the numerous probable blends from ME are *scroll* from *escrow + roll*; *scrawl* from *sprout + crawl*; and *quaver* from *quake + waver*.

Common nouns that originated as proper nouns also begin to appear in Middle English. These could be from a person's name, like *jay* from Latin *Gaius* and *jacket* from French *Jacques*; or they could be from place names, like *magnet* from *Magnesia*, *scallion* from *Ascalo*, and *damson* (plum) from *Damascus*.

Among the fairly numerous onomatopoetic (echoic) words first recorded in ME are *blubber*, *buzz*, and the now archaic or dialectal word *dush* 'to crash'. One of the more famous echoic words from the period is *tehee*, representing the sound of a giggle, first recorded in Chaucer.

Old English does not provide us with clear-cut examples of folk etymology, primarily because folk etymologies normally originate as attempts to make semantic sense of unfamiliar words or parts of words. By ME, many OE words had become obsolete; when these appeared in compounds still in use, the compounds were often restructured with more familiar elements. One example is *earwig* from OE *earwicga*, originally a compound of *ēar* 'ear' and *wicga* 'insect'. After *wicga* fell into disuse as an independent word, the earlier compound was altered to *earwig*. Similarly, OE *hlēapwince* (from *hlēapan* 'jump' and *wince* 'wink'), the name of a plover-like bird, was altered in ME to *lapwing*.

Lost Vocabulary

Much of the extensive vocabulary of Old English was lost during the ME period. In the preceding chapter, we outlined some of the major reasons for vocabulary loss in a language; cultural and technological change is responsible for the vast majority of losses from the native vocabulary during ME. The imposition of a foreign culture upon a nation is bound to have drastic effects upon its language. The miracle, perhaps, is that English survived as intact as it did.

---

[5] This tendency is still strong in English. Young children often pass through a stage during which they clip all syllables prior to the major stress of words. Such children will say *brella* for *umbrella*, *cide* for *decide*, etc.

A YOUNG WIFE'S LETTER

By the late Middle English period, literacy in England was sufficiently widespread for personal letter-writing to be common. The family letters of several English families have survived; the best known are those of the Pastons, a Norfolk family. Their correspondence provides us with vivid first-hand accounts of life in fifteenth-century England and, incidentally, with fine examples of the Norfolk dialect of the time. The following excerpt is from a letter of Margaret Paston, then a young bride pregnant with her first son John Paston II, to her husband John Paston I.

Ryth reverent and worscheful husbond, I recomau[n]de me to yow, desyryng hertyly to here of yowre wylfare, thankyng yow for the tokyn that ye sent me be Edmunde Perys, preyng yow to wete that my modyr sent to my fadyr to London for a goune cloth of mustyrddevyllers to make of a goune for me; and he tolde my modyr and me, wanne he was comme hom, that he cargeyt yow to bey it aftyr that he were come oute of London. I pre yow, yf it be not bowt, that ye wyl wechesaf to by it and send yt hom as sone as ye may; for I have no goune to werre this wyntyr but my blak and my grene a lyere, and that ys so comerus that I ham wery to wer yt.

As for the gyrdyl that my fadyr behestyt me, I spake to hym therof a lytyl before he yede to London last, and he seyde to me that the faute was in yow, that ye wolde not thynke ther uppe on to do mak yt; but I sopose that ys not so—he seyd yt but for a skeusacion. I pre yow, yf ye dor tak yt uppe on yow, that ye wyl wechesafe to do mak yt ayens ye come hom; for I hadde never more nede therof than I have now, for I ham waxse so fetys that I may not be gyrte in no barre of no gyrdyl that I have but of on. . . .

I pre yow that ye wyl were the reyng wyth the emage of Seynt Margrete that I sent yow for a rememrau[n]se tyl ye come hom. Ye have lefte me sweche a rememrau[n]se that makyth me to thynke uppe on yow bothe day and nyth wanne I wold sclepe.

Yowre ys, M. P.

To state exactly how many OE words were lost by the end of the ME period is impossible. Of the recorded OE words, we often do not know how widely used and generally familiar many were during Old English itself.

The vocabulary loss seems particularly heavy among compounds. However, here we cannot always be sure how many of the OE compounds recorded only once or twice were nonce formations, not part of the permanent vocabulary. Contemporary speakers of English constantly make up new compound words according to the same principles used by OE speakers. For example, if I have a special implement that I use to dust my books, I may call it my *bookmop*. I pronounce this combination with heavy stress on the first syllable; it is an inseparable compound in my speech; I write it as one word. Yet I would hesitate to call it an English "word," and I certainly would not expect to find it listed in a contemporary dictionary. In any case, though hundreds of recorded OE compounds are no longer in use, both components of many of them are still in the language. For instance, *cwenfugol* 'hen' is gone, but both *queen* and *fowl* survive. We have lost the compound adjective *limsēoc*, but retain both *limb* and *sick*.

Conversely, the language sometimes preserves what once were independent words only as parts of compounds (though they may not always be recognized as compounds today). *Gār* 'spear' is gone, but *garlic* 'spear' + 'leek' remains. *Hrif* 'belly' is no longer used, but survives marginally in *midriff*.

Close Translation

Right reverend and worshipful husband, I recommend myself to you, desiring heartily to hear of your welfare, thanking you for the token that you sent me by Edmund Perys, praying you to know that my mother sent to my father to London for a gown cloth of Mouster de Villers [a gray woolen cloth] to make a gown for me; and he told my mother and me, when he came home, that he charged you to buy it after he had left London. I pray you, if it has not been bought, that you will vouchsafe to buy it and send it home as soon as you can; for I have no gown to wear this winter except my black and my ivy-green, and that is so cumbrous that I am reluctant to wear it.

As for the belt that my father promised me, I spoke to him hereof a little before he went to London last time, and he said to me that the fault was yours, that you would not think thereupon to have it made; but I imagine that is not so – he said it just for an excuse. I pray you, if you dare take it upon you, that you will vouchsafe to have it made before you come home; for I never had more need thereof than I have now, for I have grown so dainty that I cannot be girt in any band of any belt that I have except one. . . .

I pray you that you will wear the ring with the image of Saint Margaret that I sent you for a remembrance until you come home. You have left me such a remembrance that [it] makes me think about you both day and night when I would like to sleep.

Yours, M.P.

From Norman Davis, ed., *Paston Letters* (Oxford: Clarendon Press, 1958), pp. 4, 5. Reprinted by permission. Translated by C. M. Millward.

Sometimes OE words have been preserved only in specialized vocabularies. The average speaker of English today will not recognize the OE word *ribbe* 'ribwort', but the plant fancier or botanist will see in it the ancestor of PDE *ribgrass* and *ribwort*. Similarly, a particular kind of bird known in OE as a *cūscote* is normally called a *ringdove* today, but in Scotland and other dialectal areas, it is still a *cushat*.

Nevertheless, the fact remains that the bulk of the OE vocabulary is no longer in use today, and the majority of this loss occurred during ME. Most of the commonest words have survived, but most of the rest are gone. Replacement by French words accounts for the preponderance of the loss, including even a number of frequently used words. For example, OE *earm* 'poor' has been replaced by French *poor*; OE *griþ* by French *peace*; OE *herian* by French *praise*; OE *þēod* by French *people*. As mentioned earlier, Scandinavian words also replaced a number of common OE words; for example, OE *giefu* was lost to Norse *gift* and OE *þēon* to Norse *thrive*.

Not all the losses are to loanwords from other languages, however. Sometimes one English word has replaced another. Thus English *spider* has supplanted English *ātor-coppe* (except dialectally), *body* has replaced *līchama*, *mad* has replaced *wōd*, *neck* has replaced *heals*, and *often* has replaced *gelōme*.

In still other instances, cultural and technological changes have simply rendered the referent obsolete. Only a few of the many possible examples are OE *folgoþ* 'body of retainers', *gytfeorm* 'ploughing feast', *hōcīsern* 'small sickle', *hoppāda* 'upper garment'. As any birdwatcher or wild-plant enthusiast knows, the popular names of birds and plants are highly varied and unstable, so it is not surprising if such names for birds as *hice* and *hulfestre*, or such names for plants as *hratele* and *lustmoce*, have been lost.

It is not only native words that have disappeared. Many of the loans from Norse and French were really unnecessary to begin with, so scores of recorded Norse loans and hundreds of recorded French loans have disappeared. Norse *cayre* 'to ride' and *grayþ* 'grief, hurt' did not survive the ME period. Nor did French *alose* 'praise', *manse* 'curse', *rehayte* 'encourage', or *talentif* 'desirous'.

Middle English Semantics

As we noted in Chapter 5, semantic change is difficult to treat systematically because it is so intimately connected to the highly unsystematic real world. The causes of semantic change are multiple and usually undetectable from a distance of several centuries. For many OE words we do not even know the denotative meanings because they occur so infrequently in surviving texts and because there were no English-to-English dictionaries compiled in OE times to record meanings of words. Without knowing the denotation of a word, we cannot know its connotations.

The possibility of dialectal differences in meaning at a given time is another complication. We may think we have discovered a semantic shift over time because the meaning of a given word in a text from year X + 200 is clearly different from its meaning in a text from year X. But it may be that we simply lack texts from another dialectal area for year X, an area in which the word had the same meaning in year X as in year X + 200. A contemporary example would be the word *jumper*. To most American speakers, a *jumper* is a sleeveless dress, but to most British speakers, it is a sweater of the type Americans call a *pullover*. (For that matter, if we asked an American electrician what a *jumper* was, the response would probably be "a wire used to bypass a circuit," illustrating an occupational dialect.)

In Chapter 5, we also discussed various types of semantic change, including generalization and narrowing, amelioration and pejoration, strengthening and weakening, shifts in stylistic level, and extreme shifts in denotation. These classifications are valid enough, but, alas, many semantic changes do not fit comfortably into cut-and-dried categories and may partake of several of them at the same time. Furthermore, semantic change is rarely all-or-none; overlapping in meaning can continue for generations, even centuries. The same word, with essentially the same denotation, may even have different connotations in different contexts. Again, a modern example may make the point clearer. In my dialect at least, the word *tricky* has negative, neutral, and positive connotations, depending on the context. Applied to a person, it is strongly negative (*Tricky Dick*). Applied to a process, it is neutral (*Hanging wallpaper is tricky*). Applied to the solution of a problem, it is often positive (*What a tricky way of doing it!*).

However, as the old proverb says, what can't be cured must be endured. Failing a tidy world with tidy meanings, we must do what we can with a chaotic one. We will continue to use the categories of semantic change introduced in Chapter 5, but with the caveat that they are less than perfect descriptions of the actual semantic changes that occurred between OE and ME.

Generalization and Narrowing

The type of semantic change easiest to find between OE and ME (and during ME) is narrowing of meaning. Upon reflection, we should not find this too surprising: because the language acquired far more new words than it lost old ones, the result had to be either many complete synonyms or a general tendency to narrow meanings. For whatever reason, absolute synonyms are rare in language; hence many OE words acquired narrower, more specific meanings in ME as a direct result of loans from other languages. For example, the OE word *gōma* meant "jaw, palate, inside of the mouth." With the Latin loan *palate* and the new word *jaw* from an unknown source, ME *gome* 'gum' came to refer only to the firm connective tissue that surrounds the teeth. OE *sand* had meant either "sand" or "shore." When Low German *shore* was borrowed to refer to the land itself along a body of water, *sand* narrowed to mean only the granular particles of disintegrated rock that covered this land. OE *feðer* had meant "feather" or, in the plural, "wings"; when ME borrowed *wing* from Scandinavian, *feather* narrowed to refer only to the plumage of birds. OE *frēo* had meant either "free" or "noble." When *noble* was borrowed from French to refer to hereditary rank, *free* gradually lost this aspect of its original meaning. Occasionally, narrowing resulted when one native word replaced another in part of its original meaning. OE *bēam* could mean either "tree" or the product of a tree (beam, timber, cross, and so on). OE *trēow* replaced *bēam* in its meaning of the plant in its living state, and at the same time *trēow* lost its own earlier applications to trees that had been cut up.

Generalization was less common than narrowing in ME, but there are still numerous examples. For instance, OE *bridd* had meant "young bird"; the general term for a bird was *fugel* 'fowl'. During ME, *bird* generalized to include fowl of any age (and *fowl* simultaneously began to narrow in application to refer to larger, edible birds). The OE adjective *rūh* 'rough' meant "coarse (of cloth), hairy, shaggy." In ME, this meaning was extended metaphorically to refer to seas, weather, actions, language, and sounds.

Amelioration and Pejoration

Examples of amelioration and pejoration are harder to pinpoint, partly because we cannot always be sure how pejorative or nonpejorative a word was, partly because much of the vocabulary of a language is not especially susceptible to the process. It is hard to see how some of the words just discussed, words like *sand*, *tree*, or *feather*, could acquire meanings that were either elevated or base. When we do detect pejoration, it is usually through context. For instance, we can be sure that OE *ceorl* 'peasant, freeman, layman' has degenerated in its meaning when we read a ME phrase like *the foule cherl, the swyn* ('the foul churl, the swine'). Similarly, when we read in Chaucer about someone who is *so crafty and so sly*, we can be sure that *crafty* has degenerated from its OE meaning of "strong, skillful, clever." A possible example of amelioration during ME might be—depending on one's viewpoint—the word *dizzy*. In OE it meant "foolish," a meaning that still survives marginally in such expressions as *a dizzy blonde*; but by ME its primary meaning was "suffering from vertigo."

Strengthening and Weakening

Like amelioration and pejoration, the processes of strengthening and weakening are limited to the kinds of words amenable to such change. In general, strengthening is rarer in language than weakening—evidence that people are more prone to exaggeration (which tends to weaken meanings) than to understatement (which tends to strengthen meanings). One example of weakening during ME is that of the word *awe*. Its etymons, OE *ege* and ON *agi*, had meant "terror, dread" in general. In ME, it came to refer especially to attitudes toward God, or "reverential fear and respect." The weakened meaning suggests that fears of unworldly or future things are not as strong as immediate, worldly fears.

Shift in Stylistic Level

Shifts of stylistic level are hard to pinpoint for earlier stages of English because the overwhelming majority of English words are appropriate for any stylistic level and because we are not justified in arguing that, just because a word does *not* appear in, say, a highly formal text, it was therefore inappropriate stylistically. Normally, the only time we can detect a change in stylistic level is when we spot a word in an earlier text that would be totally out of place in a similar text today. The example of the word *shove* was mentioned in Chapter 5. Another is the verb *smear*. OE *smierwan* meant "anoint, salve, smear." With the advent of the French loan *anoint*, *smear* came to have connotations of crudeness and even contempt. Certainly today we could not speak seriously of a bishop's *smearing* someone's head with oil.

Shift in Denotation

Shifts in denotation tend to occur when what was once a subsidiary or extended meaning of a word becomes the central meaning. Examples from ME are numerous. The basic meaning of OE *tīd* had been "time" (as in *Christmastide*). OE also had the words *hwīl* 'time' and *tīma*, which referred primarily to an extent or a period of time. The tides are of course related to time by being periodic. Because of this relationship and because the language already had other words that could take over the "time" meanings of *tide*, the core meaning of *tide* itself could shift. Similarly, when ME acquired the word *boy*, the word *knight* (OE *cniht*) could shift from its earlier meaning of "boy, male youth" to the narrower meaning of "youthful gentleman-soldier."

Analogous shifts in denotation include that of *warp* from "throw" to "twist out of shape," of *quick* from "alive" to "rapid," of *swing* from "strike, whip, rush" to "oscillate," and of *spell* from "discourse, tale" to "incantational formula." Note that all these changes in referent also involve a narrowing of meaning. The shift in denotation of *wan* is slightly different in principle. In OE, *wann* had meant "dark, dusky," but during ME, it came to mean "pale," seemingly a complete reversal of meaning. However, the common thread of the two meanings is *lack* of color (hue).

Many semantic changes are hard to classify because several kinds of changes have occurred simultaneously. The fate of the word *grin* provides a good illustration. OE *grennian* meant "to grimace (either in pain or anger or in pleasure), to gnash the teeth, to draw back the lips and display the teeth"—close to what we mean by "make a face" today, but the involvement of the teeth seems to have been important. By late ME, *grin* had added the meaning of "to smile in a forced, unnatural manner" without losing completely the earlier meanings. By PDE, the core meaning has shifted still further to mean a broad smile. Since OE times, then, the meaning has narrowed to eliminate the meaning of "snarl" and "grimace in pain or anger." It has also broadened to include the idea of smiling. There has been a shift in basic denotative focus from the teeth to the lips. (I can grin without showing my teeth, but not without curling my lips upward.) And there certainly has been a deterioration in stylistic level—we would not say "My hostess grinned politely as I complimented her on the dinner."

In most of our examples illustrating semantic change, we have used native English words. Loanwords undergo the same kinds of changes. The French loan *garret* shifted in denotative meaning during ME from its earlier meaning of "turret on the top of a tower" to "watchtower." By the end of ME, it was shifting again toward its PDE meaning of "room on the top floor." When first introduced into English, the French loan *fairy* meant "fairyland," "fairy people collectively," or "magic." In late ME, the meaning of "an individual supernatural being" was added, and all the other previous meanings were declining (though they were not to be totally lost until EMnE). A dramatic example of semantic amelioration is that of the French loan *nice*. In its earliest uses in English, it meant "foolish, stupid, wanton." During the fifteenth century, it began to improve its status by acquiring the additional meanings of "flamboyant, elegant, rare, modest," but also acquired the pejorative meanings of "slothful, unmanly." We must, however, wait until later periods for its present vague meaning of "pleasant" to develop.

Middle English Dialects

Our discussion of Middle English so far has concentrated primarily on features that were to prevail in the standard language (though "standard language" is itself a somewhat artificial concept). Middle English, however, was characterized by great dialectal diversity, seemingly a greater diversity than existed in Old English. It is possible that dialectal differences did increase during ME: the limited mobility of the English-speaking population in the years following the Conquest may well have led to linguistic isolation and consequent proliferation of dialectal differences. Still, the increase in differences and in the number of identifiable dialects in ME can easily be exaggerated—or, more accurately, the relative homogeneity of Old English is probably only apparent. First, we have a far greater number of surviving texts and texts from a wider geographical area for ME than for OE. Second, OE had a strong scribal tradition that tended to conceal existing dialectal differences under a standardized spelling. A parallel can be drawn with PDE. If we were to use spelling as our only guide, we would conclude that American and British speakers pronounced the words *schedule* and *lieutenant* alike (though they do not). Conversely, the spelling differences between American *realize* and *check* versus British *realise* and *cheque* would suggest that the two groups pronounced the words differently (though they do not). In sum, although there certainly was great dialectal diversity during the ME period, it did not make its first appearance then. Rather, the wider array of surviving texts and the loss of the OE scribal tradition made preexisting dialectal differences much more obvious.

For many years, historians of the language spoke confidently of five major dialect areas for ME: Northern, East Midlands, West Midlands, Southern, and Kentish. Lists of dialectal features for each area were compiled and dialect maps showing quite precise dialect boundaries (or **isoglosses**) were drawn up. However, during the past thirty years or so, Angus McIntosh and his colleagues on the Middle English Dialect Survey have shown that this neat picture is a gross oversimplification. Instead of basing their conclusions on a handful of items and instead of examining texts from the entire ME period, McIntosh and his co-workers use a checklist of about 270 items and restrict their data base to the years

1350–1450—a period for which large numbers of texts are available but also a period prior to the restandardization of spelling in English. Their procedures and their findings are too complex to describe in detail here, but they have shown that sharp dialect boundaries simply did not exist in ME, that virtually every item on their checklist has its own distinctive isoglosses.

McIntosh and his colleagues identify the area in which a text was written, not so much by unique features as by unique *configurations* of features. The procedure can be illustrated by a highly simplified, abstract example. Assume you have four texts, all of which differ in four items. No single text differs from all the others in any one item, but each text has its own pattern or configuration of items, as the diagram below illustrates:

Figure 6.12   Schema of Possible Dialectal Patterns

Text	Item 1	Item 2	Item 3	Item 4
A	sche	are	enough	gif
B	sche	are	enow	if
C	she	ben	enough	if
D	she	ben	enow	gif

In actual practice, many more items are used as test words, and a single text is rarely absolutely consistent, even for a single item; the same text may use both *are* and *ben*, for example. Nonetheless, the principle is the same.

By beginning with "anchor" texts that can be precisely dated in time and located in geographical space, and by extrapolating the information gathered from these anchor texts, McIntosh and his associates have been able to identify the date and place of previously uncertain texts with a high degree of confidence.

McIntosh's work is also innovative in its extensive use of purely graphic features. Without necessarily trying to posit exactly what phonological entity a letter form represented in a given word, he uses the spelling itself or even the particular way of forming certain letters as indicative of dialects. (This is analogous to our previous example of *check* versus *cheque*; we recognize *cheque* as a British form because of its spelling alone—the pronunciation is irrelevant.)

As an example of the kinds of differences typically found in copies of the same text made in different parts of England, we reproduce below twelve six-line excerpts from *The Prick of Conscience*, a fourteenth-century moral poem of 9624 lines designed to encourage righteousness. Despite its lack of interest for most modern readers, this poem must have been extraordinarily popular in its day, for it survives in over a hundred manuscripts, more than any other ME poem, including even the works of Chaucer. (In the sentences below, underlining indicates abbreviations that have been spelled out to facilitate reading.)

1 (Devonshire)

And make the folk hym to honour
As thovgh he were here sauyour
He schal saye thanne ryȝt to cristene man
Was neuer non be-fore hs tyme be-gan
Bote falsly crist he wol hym calle
And saye þᵗ hy be-levyth wrong alle

2 (Northeast Shropshire)

And make þe folk him to honoure
And sey he is oure sauyoure
He schal sey þᵗ riȝt cristene man
Was ner before his tyme bygan
Bᵗ false anᵗ cristus hem he schal calle
And sey þei haue lyued þorȝ wronge at alle

3 (Southeast Surrey)

To make þe folk hym honour
& say he ys here sauyour
He schal seye þat no crysten man
By-fore hys tyme neuer by gan
Bote false anticristys he schal hym calle
And sey þᵗ þy leued in false trowþe alle

5 (Suffolk)

And make þe folk him to honour
And seyn þat he is her saueour
He schal seyn þᵗ ryht cristen man
Was neuere or his tyme be-gan
But false antecrystes he schal hem calle
And seyn þey liuid wrongliche alle

7 (South Lincolnshire)

And so make þe folk hym to honoure
And shal seie þat he is here saueoure
He shal seie þat no cristene man
Was bifore þat his tyme began
And falce cristene he shal hem calle
And seyn þat þei lyuen in falce trouþe alle

9 (Northern)

And mak ye folk him to honoure
And sall say yᵗ he es yair saueoure
He sall say yat na ryght cristen man
Was neuer bi-for his tyme bi-gan
Bot fals anticristes he sall yam call
And say yai lyfed in fals trowth all

11 (South Warwickshire)

And make þe folk hym to honoure
And say þat he is heore sauyore
He schal sey þat no riȝt cristene man
Neuere byfore hys tyme bygan
Bote fals antecristes he schal hem calle
And sey þat þey lyue in a fals truþe alle

4 (Yorkshire/Nottinghamshire border)

& make þo folke hym to honour
& say he es þair soucoure
He schall say þat right cristen man
Was neuer befor his tyme be-gane
Bot fals ancristes he schall hem call
& say þai lifed in wronge trouth all

6 (Northern)

And make ye folke him to honour
And say yat he is yaire saueour
He sall say yat na right cristen man
Was neuer be-fore yis tyme began
Bot fals anticristes he sall yaim call
Yat hase bene fra ye werldes begynnyng

8 (Northeast Lancashire or possibly extreme western Yorkshire)

And make ye folke hym to honour
And say yat he is yair sauyour
He sall say yat right cristen man
Was neuere be-fore or he began
Bot fals ancristes he sall yaim calle
And say yat yai lyued in wronge trouthe
alle

10 (Wiltshire)

And make þe folke hym to honoure
And seiþ þat ys here sauioure
He schal seiþ þᵗ no cristen man
Neuere by fore hys tyme by-ganne
Bote false antecristes he schal hym kalle
And seiþ þᵗ þey lyue in false trowþe all

12 (Monmouthshire, western Gloucestershire, or possibly South Wales)

And make þe folk hym to honoure
And say he ys here sauyoure
He schal say þat ryȝt crystene man
Was neuere or hys tyme be-gan
But fals antecrystes he schal hem calle
And say þey leue in wrong þoru ouȝt alle

Six lines of text is, of course, far too small a sample on which to base a dialect analysis. Nonetheless, even these few lines illustrate some of the more distinctive characteristics of certain areas. For example, note that the Northern texts use the Norse form (with *þ*) for all cases of the third-person plural pronoun, while the other texts have *h-* in the object case and usually in the possessive case, but, except for the southernmost text (1), have *þ-* in the subject case. The Northern texts all have *sall* (instead of *schal*), *na* (instead of *no*), and do not distinguish *y* and *þ* graphically. The southwesternmost texts use the grapheme *ȝ* where other regions

Figure 6.13 Origins of *Prick of Conscience* Manuscripts

have *gh* or *h*. Three different present indicative plural verb endings are illustrated here—*be-levyth* (1), *lyuen* (7), and *lyue* or *leue* (10, 11, 12). In contrast to these relatively neat observations, the wide variety of different spellings and even words for "before" defies easy generalization, at least on the basis of this tiny sample.

Middle English Literature

English was only one of three major literary languages in England during the ME period—and it ran a poor third at that. Latin was the only respectable language for serious literature and the only language for an international audience, and would remain so for several centuries to come. All vernaculars, not just English, were universally regarded as inferior to Latin. Another incentive for writing in Latin was the awareness that English had changed and was continuing to change; if authors wanted their works to be accessible to posterity, they felt obliged to write in Latin. French was the language of the upper classes, and this Anglo-French dialect was, in fact, the vehicle of some of the best writing done in French anywhere during the period. But polylingualism was not restricted to Latin, French, and English. The Celts in Ireland, Scotland, Wales, and Cornwall continued to speak and write in Irish, Scots Gaelic, Welsh, and Cornish.

For most of the ME period, those authors who did write in English used their own dialects, and recognizable though only vaguely defined "schools" of literature arose in various regions. The West Midlands were earlier associated with the so-called Katherine Group of religious prose and later with alliterative poetry such as *Piers Plowman* and the work of the *Pearl* poet. Richard Rolle's mystical works are in a Yorkshire dialect, and Barbour's *Bruce* in a Northern dialect. Toward the end of the period, however, when it became clear that the London dialect would be a standard, authors began to use it even when it was not their native dialect in order to reach a national audience. Chaucer's family was from London, so he could be expected to write London English, but John Gower (from Kent) and John Lydgate (from Suffolk) also wrote in the London dialect.

Compared with what we have from the Old English period, the quantity of surviving ME literature is large, especially after 1250. Obviously the later something was written, the better its chances for preservation, and the advent of printing at the end of the ME period saved much that would otherwise have been lost. Nevertheless, for a small population with a low literacy rate, the ME output is still surprisingly high. To be sure, much of this writing in English consists of translations, primarily from French and Latin, but sometimes from other European vernaculars. For example, the very late ME morality play *Everyman* is now generally agreed to be a translation of a Dutch original.

To modern tastes, the quantity of ME literature is not paralleled by a correspondingly high quality. Part of the explanation is different tastes: most modern readers simply do not care for the religious and didactic works that comprise the overwhelming bulk of ME literature. In addition, much if not most of ME writing was done for oral presentation—relatively few people could read, and even those who could were just as accustomed to being read to as to reading to themselves. A listening audience has different expectations and different requirements from those of individual, silent readers. For example, in oral presentation, a fair amount of repetition is not only acceptable but essential because the audience cannot go back to reread something it missed the first time around. Still another reason for the spotty quality of so much ME literature is the fact that the English writers were still experimenting with new forms and genres borrowed from French and had not yet adapted them to suit English.

As is true of OE literature, the great bulk of ME literature is anonymous. There was no cult of creativity or originality and little or no material incentive for authors to claim works as their own. Copyright had yet to be invented—and would have been virtually meaningless if it had existed because, without printing, books were hand-copied one at a time and no one could ever make a fortune or even a decent profit by reproducing the works of others.

Another characteristic of ME literature alien to modern readers is the heavy proportion of verse to prose. Aside from legal documents, almost any kind of subject matter or genre could be and often was versified: historical works, Biblical translations, religious instruction, fictional tales, even recipes and how-to materials. Furthermore, with a few outstanding exceptions, the prose that was produced was of poor quality. One reason for the preponderance of verse is that verse is easier to memorize than prose, an important consideration for a society in which a book was a major investment and literacy was low. Second, though Old English had had a strong tradition of good prose writing, this was almost totally destroyed by the Conquest. When literature once again began to be produced in English, it was at first primarily in verse; in any culture, good prose develops later than verse.

When writing in English began again after the disruption of the Conquest, English writers adopted French genres and forms wholesale. In most of the country and for most purposes, the native alliterative verse was abandoned for syllable-counting, rhymed verse. The older tradition of heroic poetry gave way to new genres—the romance in particular, but also other, shorter verse forms. Toward the end of the ME period, drama appeared for the first time in English. Shorter poems that fit comfortably into our modern (rather hazy) notions of a lyric appear. In other words, many of the literary types of today are recognizably the descendants of ME forebears. Nonetheless, we still do not find such contemporary types as the novel, the short story, the biography, or the autobiography.

Secular Prose

Secular prose in Middle English includes legal works such as codes of laws, charters, wills, writs, and deeds—little of literary interest but much that is valuable as a source of linguistic and historical information. Also usually, but not always, written in prose were handbooks on such topics as astronomy, mathematics, political theory, medicine, husbandry, and etiquette. Personal letters of the period include some that rise to a level that might well be called literary. The letters of three families in particular, the Stonors, the Celys, and the Pastons, survive in large quantities (see pp. 178–179).

Most medieval chronicles were either written in Latin or French, or were in verse, or both. However, the *Anglo-Saxon Chronicle* (see p. 116) was continued in English prose for nearly a century after the Conquest. Late in the ME period, John Capgrave wrote his *Chronicle of England* (from the Creation to 1417) in prose. Romances also were normally in verse, but a few were in prose. Thomas Malory's late fifteenth-century romance *Morte Darthur* is one of the best prose works of the entire period and one of the few prose works that can still be read today with genuine pleasure. Still another prose work is Thomas Usk's *Testament of Love*; despite its title, it is actually a political allegory.

Defying easy classification is *Travels of Sir John Mandeville*, purportedly the record of Mandeville's journeys to the limits of the then-known world, but actually a fiction based on sheer invention and brazen plagiarism of earlier writings.

Religious Prose

Middle English religious prose is even harder to classify neatly than secular prose because there is so much of it and the types tend to overlap more. We will restrict ourselves to mentioning some of the most important titles and known authors. The early (c. 1200) *Ancrene Riwle* (or, as some versions are called, *Ancrene Wisse*; see p. 163) is one of the few religious works likely to appeal to the contemporary reader. Written by a cleric at the request of three noblewomen, it is dedicated but compassionate, idealistic but realistic, down-to-earth but warm and often humorous. The quality of the writing is high, perhaps higher than that of any other English prose work prior to Malory.

Saints' lives (hagiography) must have been extremely popular with ME audiences because so many of them have survived. Most of them bear about as much resemblance to reality as does the modern political campaign "biography." The same miracles and tortures are repeated for one saint after another. The so-called Katherine Group, written in heavily alliterative prose from the West Midlands, includes the lives of three virgin saints, along with two other religious treatises. Another vast collection, *The Golden Legend*, contains numerous saints' lives in addition to much other ecclesiastical material. Still another very mixed collection is the *South English Legendary*, comprising saints' lives, other narratives, material appropriate for the church calender, and other religious writings.

Collections of sermons and homilies from the period are too numerous even to list exhaustively. Among the better-known such collections are the *Lambeth Homilies* (c. 1180), the *Northern Homily Cycle* (c. 1300), the *Northern Passion* (c. 1325), and the late *Jacob's Well* (c. 1425). John Wycliffe (late fourteenth century) is best known today for the Biblical translations under his name (though he probably did little if any of the actual translating). However, he was also the author of a large number of surviving sermons that provide lively reading to this day. Many ME sermons and homilies include exempla, or short tales with a moral. Often the exemplum has been added more for its entertainment value than for its didactic relevance, and the application of the moral may be far-fetched. The *Gesta Romanorum* (late thirteenth century) is the most famous collection of such exempla.

The writings of the English mystics, or religious visionaries, form a subcategory of their own. The best-known of these mystics were Richard Rolle, Walter Hilton, and the author of *The Cloud of Unknowing*, all from the fourteenth century. Mystical writings by women include Dame Julian of Norwich's *Revelations of Divine Love* (late fourteenth century) and the rather hysterical but lively and colloquial *Book of Margery Kempe* (c. 1430).

Of no literary interest whatsoever is Dan Michel's *Ayenbite of Inwit* (c. 1340), a bad translation into bad English prose of a French book on vices and virtues. However, the work is of linguistic interest as a relatively rare example of the Kentish dialect.

Secular Verse

In secular literature, the ME period is the age of the romance. To most people today, the term *romance* suggests a love story in prose. In medieval literature, however, it refers to a story of knightly adventure in which love is only a subordinate element. Most ME romances are in verse, though a few later ones are in prose. About fifty ME romances survive, varying in length from a few hundred to several thousand lines. Their quality varies from sheer drivel to some of the finest poetry ever written in English (*Sir Gawain and the Green Knight*). The most common meter of the romances is rhymed iambic tetrameter, but a fair number (including *Sir Gawain*) are in the older alliterative meter, with or without accompanying rhyme. Conventionally, romances are classified according to subject matter: (1) Matter of Britain— tales of King Arthur and his knights; (2) Matter of England—tales of English or Germanic heroes; (3) Matter of Greece and Rome— tales of Alexander the Great or of the Trojan War; and (4) Matter of France—tales of Charlemagne and his knights. In addition, a score or so of ME romances are on various topics that fit none of these categories, for example, tales of the long-suffering wife, Oriental stories, and quasi-historical stories.

Another important ME literary type is the debate, of which *The Owl and the Nightingale* (c. 1200) is the earliest and the finest example in English. Topics range widely: body versus soul, rose versus lily, clerical lover versus knightly lover, summer versus winter. Often the author provides no "winner," but overtly tells the readers or listeners to decide for themselves.

The lyric makes its first appearance in English during the ME period, and hundreds of ME lyrics have survived, a number of them with accompanying music, suggesting that the type originated as songs. Celebrations of springtime and the tribulations of lovers are the most popular topics. (There are also many religious lyrics; the Passion and the Virgin Mary are especially prevalent themes.) Many individuals who have never heard of ME are familiar with one of the earliest ME lyrics, "Sumer Is Icumen In":

> Sumer is icumen in,
> Lhude sing, cuccu!
> Groweth sed and bloweth med
> And springth the wude nu.
> Sing, cuccu!

Particularly in the fifteenth century, there was a fair amount of satire written in English. Greed, corruption, the clergy, and unsatisfactory social and political conditions were the favorite topics. Perhaps the most delightful example to the contemporary reader is the late thirteenth-century *Land of Cokaygne*, which describes the life of Cistercian monks in a make-believe land of luxury and sexual permissiveness. Less well represented in ME outside of Chaucer are the *fabliau*, a short, humorous, bawdy tale, and the *beast tale*, a story in which the faults of human beings are indirectly attacked by putting men in the guise of animals.

All of these genres of secular verse were borrowed directly or indirectly from French. The ME romances in particular are often free—or even close—translations of French originals.

Religious and Didactic Verse

The amount of religious and didactic verse in Middle English is so vast that we can do little more here than enumerate some of the most outstanding types and examples. The range of this literature includes scriptural paraphrase and commentary, exempla in verse, saints' legends and lives, homilies, allegories, proverbs, and various combinations of these.

As we employ the term, scriptural paraphrase includes retelling of Biblical material that does not even necessarily follow the sequence of the original and that may include a great deal of homiletic material in addition to the Biblical narrative. One of the earlier and longer of such works is *Cursor Mundi* 'The Way of the World' (c. 1325), an encyclopedic poem of almost 30,000 lines originating in the north of England. It begins with the Creation and ends with Doomsday, making many stops along the way. More limited in range are such pieces as *Genesis and Exodus* and *Harrowing of Hell* (both c. 1250).

Though we earlier mentioned exempla under prose, there were also collections of exempla in verse. The best known of these is John Gower's *Confessio*

Amantis (c. 1390); Gower often seems more interested in the tales themselves than in their moral applications.

Saints' legends, although primarily a prose type, also were sometimes written in verse. Among the more interesting are narratives of visits to Hell, including the highly imaginative *St. Patrick's Purgatory* (c. 1325), *The Vision of St. Paul* (c. 1375), and *The Vision of Tundale* (c. 1400), all translations of Latin originals. Perhaps reflecting the rigors of the northern climate in which they originated, the Hell depicted in these poems includes not only fire and brimstone, but also snow, ice, hail, and bitter winds.

Of the abundant surviving homiletic material in verse, we have already mentioned the *Ormulum* (p. 136). The earliest of the long homiletic works is *Poema Morale* (c. 1170), whose chief claim to fame today is that it is the first surviving poem in English to use the "fourteener"—a fourteen-syllable rhyming iambic line. More interesting, despite its unpromising title, is Robert Mannyng of Brunne's *Handlyng Synne* (c. 1300), a translation of a French original. Other works too numerous to cite deal with such dismal themes as repentance, worldly transitoriness, death, the Last Judgment, and Hell.

We have focused here on works that are primarily or exclusively religio-didactic in nature. It should be noted, however, that many other ME works, though read today for other reasons, contain much didactic and religious material. Examples include *Piers Plowman*, *Pearl*, and even most of Chaucer's works.

Drama

Drama as a literary type and social phenomenon virtually disappeared in Europe from late antiquity until the late Middle Ages. When it did reappear, it was at first in the form of religious drama and indeed probably arose out of dramatization of parts of church services. The earliest English dramas were *mystery plays*, based on Biblical stories and written for the most part in verse. These plays were performed by craftsmen's guilds outdoors on Corpus Christi Day (late May or early June). Several collections, or cycles, of mystery plays survive, of which the best is the Wakefield cycle (or Towneley plays), consisting of thirty-two plays dating from about 1400.

Morality plays, in which the principal characters are personified abstractions such as Vice, Good Deeds, and Friendship, appeared later than mystery plays. Some of these are extremely long with huge casts of characters. The finest of the morality plays, *Everyman*, dates from about 1500, at the very end of the ME period. Its message of the terror and loneliness of impending death has such universal appeal that the play is regularly revived and performed to this day.

In sum, the Middle English period saw not so much a rebirth of English literature as the birth of a new English literature based on Continental models rather than the earlier Germanic traditions. Although Latin remained the language of "serious" literature, English steadily gained respectability as a language for more popular literature. Chaucer could have written in French had he wished to, but he chose English. The fact that his work was not only popular in England but was actually praised in France demonstrates how far the prestige of English had risen since the years immediately following the Conquest.

In summary, the most important features of Middle English are

1. Phonologically, voiced fricatives became phonemic. By the end of ME, phonemic length in consonants had been lost, but length remained phonemic for vowels. Vowels of unstressed syllables became [ə] or [ɪ] or were lost entirely.
2. Morphologically, there was a steady loss of inflections. By the end of ME, the inflectional system was that of PDE except for the preservation of separate second-person singular and second-person plural pronouns and verbs.
3. Syntactically, word order became more like that of PDE, but differences remained; for example, pronoun objects frequently preceded verbs. Indefinite and definite articles began to be used. The complex system of verb phrases that characterizes PDE was developing.
4. Lexically, ME saw an explosion of loanwords. Early in ME, many Norse loans appeared in texts for the first time. Later, vast numbers of French loans entered ME, along with numerous Latin loans. ME continued to form new words from native resources and from both native and borrowed elements.

Suggested Further Reading

Björkman, Erik. *Scandinavian Loan-Words in Middle English.*
Brunner, Karl. *An Outline of Middle English Grammar.*
Clanchy, M. T. *From Memory to Written Record: England 1066–1307.*
Jacob, Ernest Fraser. *The Fifteenth Century, 1399–1485.*
Kurath, Hans, and Sherman M. Kuhn, eds. *Middle English Dictionary.*
McIntosh, Angus, M. L. Samuels, Michael Benskin, et al. *A Linguistic Atlas of Late Mediaeval English.*
McKisack, May. *The Fourteenth Century, 1307–1399.*
Mossé, Fernand. *A Handbook of Middle English.*
Mustanoja, Tauno F. *A Middle English Syntax.*
Myers, A. R. *England in the Late Middle Ages (1307–1536).*
Powicke, F. M. *The Thirteenth Century, 1216–1307.*
Shelly, Percy Dyke. *English and French in England, 1066–1100.*
Stenton, Doris Mary. *English Society in the Early Middle Ages (1066–1307).*
Stratmann, Francis Henry. *A Middle-English Dictionary.*

C H A P T E R 7

Early Modern English

O, good my lord, no Latin!
I am not such a truant since my coming
As not to know the language I have liv'd in.
A strange tongue makes my cause more strange,
*   suspicious;*
Pray, speak in English.

—William Shakespeare

OUTER HISTORY

The Early Modern English (EMnE) period is the first during which English speakers stand back and take a serious look at their language. Often they don't like what they see and attempt to do something about what they perceive as the sorry state of their native tongue. Although it is a golden age of English literature, it is one in which most of the greatest writers are highly self-conscious about their language.

Cultural, Political, and Technological Influences

Of the many events of this highly eventful period, those with the greatest direct effects on the language are (1) the introduction and dissemination of printing, (2) the Renaissance, (3) the Protestant Reformation, (4) the enclosures, (5) the Industrial Revolution, (6) exploration and colonization, and (7) the American Revolution.

Printing

If we were to hold strictly to our dates of 1500–1800 for EMnE, the introduction of printing to England would belong to the ME period because William Caxton imported and set up England's first printing press in 1476. However, the major impact of printing on the language was to be felt in the following centuries; indeed, printing contributes largely toward distinguishing Early Modern English from Middle English.

The effects of printing were manifold. First, it was heavily responsible for freezing English spelling. Unfortunately, this was at a stage just before a major sound change was completed; hence in the twentieth century we are still spelling a language that has not been spoken since the fifteenth century. Second, because printing made books available at a relatively low price, it led to an increased demand for books and literacy, especially among the middle and lower classes. But these middle classes did not have the opportunity or the leisure to obtain a classical education, so they wanted books in English rather than Latin or French. To make the Greek and Latin classics available to those who knew only English, they were translated into English—and these translations led to the introduction of thousands of loanwords from Latin and Greek into English. Still another consequence of printing was that, for the first time, aspiring authors had at least the opportunity (though rarely the actuality) of making a living by writing without the financial support of a rich patron. It is not an exaggeration to say that contemporary Western civilization is the child of the printing press.

The Renaissance

Another important influence on EMnE was the Renaissance. The revival of interest in classical learning resulted in translations of such authors as Caesar, Plutarch, Plato, Virgil, Ovid, and Homer, authors accessible only in Latin (or Greek) prior to the sixteenth century. Even the works of those so important in the religious controversies of the time—figures like Erasmus, Calvin, and Martin Luther—were originally written in Latin and translated only in the sixteenth century. All these translations brought classical loanwords into English. They also gave English authors practice in developing a sophisticated English style that incorporated the features of classical rhetoric compatible with English. The very fact that the works of the great classical authors existed in English translation added to the status of the English language. At the same time, familiarity with classical models forced English writers to compare English to Latin. Not surprisingly, English almost always suffered from the comparison, at least in the eyes of those making it. This in turn prompted attempts to improve the English language.

The Protestant Reformation

One consequence of Henry VIII's disputes with the Pope was the Reformation and the separation of Protestants from the Roman Catholic Church. The Protestant belief that people should read the Bible for themselves led to numerous translations of the Bible, culminating in the Authorized Version (the King James Bible) of 1611, whose language has had a powerful effect on English stylistics ever since its appearance.

The Reformation also tended to break the centuries-old monopoly of the Church on education. Because Latin had always been the official language of the Church, and because most educators had been clergymen, Latin quite understandably had been viewed as the primary language of education. However, the new schools set up by merchants and gentry after the Reformation were staffed by laymen, not clergy (or, if by clergy, by Protestant clergy), a fact that was to lead to increased emphasis on English at the expense of Latin and ultimately to the almost complete transfer of the responsibility for education from the church to the state. In the religious disputes following the Reformation, both Protestants and Catholics looked to the medieval church for historical evidence to support their arguments. This in turn led to an interest in medieval English, to the rediscovery of Old English, and, in general, to an awareness of the ancestry of English.

The Enclosures
Beginning in the late fifteenth century and continuing into the early seventeenth century, English landowners combined small holdings for more efficient management and converted estates into sheep pastures to increase the wool production so important to England's economy. In the process, thousands of former tenants were evicted. The affected peasants frequently revolted, but the process continued, and the dispossessed people gradually drifted to the cities, leading to greater urbanization of the nation as a whole. Cities became melting-pots of dialects from rural areas all over England, and thus the dialectal picture of England was altered.

Urbanization also fostered the rise of a middle class whose members wanted to improve their social and economic standing. Insecure in their status yet eager to move upward still further, the middle classes are typically concerned about correct behavior, including linguistic behavior. In response to these concerns, handbooks of correct usage were written to teach the middle classes how to sound like those they considered their betters. These books were authoritarian in approach, which was precisely what the market demanded: the insecure do not want theory, speculation, abstraction, or exceptions; they want hard and fast practical rules that are easy to understand and memorize.

The Industrial Revolution
Toward the end of the Early Modern English period, the Scots engineer and inventor James Watt made improvements on existing designs that allowed the modern steam engine to become practicable. Though many, many other factors and conditions were involved, Watt's achievement is usually cited as the beginning of the Industrial Revolution. The Industrial Revolution led to even more intensive urbanization because workers had to be clustered in one area to man the factory machines. The Industrial Revolution also eventually led to the massive technical vocabulary based on Latin and Greek roots that is so characteristic of Present-Day English. Initially, however, industrialization of England may have temporarily decreased the percentage of literacy in the nation because so many children were put into the factories instead of being sent to school.

Exploration and Colonization
Compared with the Dutch, Spanish, and Portuguese, the English were dilatory in entering the age of global exploration and colonization. At the beginning of the EMnE period, England had only one overseas possession, the town of Calais, and she lost that in 1558. However, thirty years later, England defeated the Spanish Armada and suddenly found herself a major sea power in Europe. Within the next hundred years, the English were to acquire such far-flung colonies as Bermuda, Jamaica, the Bahamas, British Honduras, the Leeward Islands, Barbados, the Mosquito Coast, Canada, the American colonies, India, St. Helena, Gambia, and

the Gold Coast. By 1800 they had Gibraltar, the Windward Islands, Sierra Leone, Pitcairn Island, Penang, Beukulen (in the Dutch East Indies), Australia, New Zealand, and Pakistan—not to mention a number of colonies which they held for only a few years. The exotic products and processes of these colonies were directly responsible for the introduction of thousands of new loanwords into English from—for the first time—non-Indo-European languages. Conversely, colonization led to the spread of English around the globe and ultimately to the present position of English as the most widely used language in the world.

The American Revolution

At the end of the EMnE period, the American colonies revolted and became an independent nation. At the time, this did not represent a great geographical loss to England; after all, she still held Canada, and the thirteen colonies, strung out in a thin strip along the eastern shores of a large continent, comprised only a few hundred thousand square miles out of an empire of many millions of square miles. These American colonies contained no gold or silver, the furs were already depleted, and the land was not even especially fertile. However, U.S. independence did represent the first political separation of English speakers from their parent country and the beginning of what would become multiple national Englishes.

A LETTER FROM PRISON

The spontaneous writings of colonial Americans are not always easy to read. Even after one has deciphered the handwriting, the spelling and syntax provide additional hurdles. The selection below is perhaps especially bad, but not uniquely so.

> my tender and lvfin wif derlo thou hast thou pay for mee with wipin jes and sarofvl harts wich god abof do know wee thare war forst to part at that dolsvm plas abof riton bvt it my prayers for the and my sweet bab vpon my benddid nies and to the Lord mosthi I shall eaver pray and my sweet bab also the Lord prasarf yov both Crist kip yov all so pray for me swet lvf for my protexon and saf arifel kip well my lvf in stor and til sich times it shall plas god to bringe us to gather again jf plas god as that j hap he is I do in tend as sven as j Cum at that land and dissposed of I do in tend to send for thee....

The passage is touching, but, in fairness to the modern reader, it should be noted that the author wrote it from prison in Boston. His disregard for the law made him a problem for authorities in both Massachusetts and Rhode Island. This was not the first time his name had become a matter of public record.

Thomas Waters, letter "from the prison in boston may 27 1687" to his wife Anne in Providence. *Early Records of the Town of Providence*, Vol. 17 (Providence, R.I.: 1892–1915), pp. 88–89.

The Self-Conscious Language

The victory of English as the spoken language of the English people had been decided by the thirteenth century. English was accepted as a respectable language for "creative" literature by the end of the fourteenth century. Nonetheless, its suitability as a scholarly language was still in doubt in the seventeenth century. Over two hundred years after Chaucer, well after Shakespeare's death, in the same century that Milton wrote *Paradise Lost*, Francis Bacon's *Novum Organum* (1620) and Sir Isaac Newton's *Philosophiae Naturalis Principia Mathematica* (1687) appeared in Latin. Nor were Bacon and Newton fusty old fogies out of touch with their times. Quite the contrary: the basic principles laid down in their works remain the underpinnings of science in the twentieth century. Bacon and Newton wrote in Latin because Latin was still the international language of scholarship. Latin was not even totally extinct as a literary language in England; Milton himself wrote Latin as well as English poetry for most of his creative life.

At the beginning of the Early Modern English period, English had even less of a monopoly on literary and scholarly works. French was still the most prestigious of the European vernaculars, and Latin was almost universally employed for "serious" works. Those who advocated the continued use of Latin had some good arguments. True, a certain amount of vested interest was often involved: They themselves had spent years mastering Latin and it was disconcerting to think that all those years had been wasted. On the other hand, they were right in asserting that English was not understood beyond the shores of England, that English was changing constantly and their English writings would not be easily accessible to future generations, and that English lacked the vocabulary necessary for the learning ushered in by the Renaissance. But history was against them. The burgeoning middle class—the class from whom the majority of scholars were to come in the future—had neither the leisure for nor the interest in devoting years of their education to the study of Latin. Vocabulary deficiencies could and would be remedied by borrowing from Latin and by coining new English words or extending the meanings of existing ones. English would continue to change, yes, but the rate of change in the written language was to decrease; works written in the seventeenth century are more comprehensible to a twentieth-century reader than works written in the fourteenth century were to a seventeenth-century reader.

The problem that English was not understood in the rest of Europe remained, ameliorated to some extent by the fact that when English did increase its vocabulary to accommodate the new learning, it did so by borrowing Latin roots that were familiar to speakers of other European languages. Moreover, the English did not find themselves intellectual outcasts when they gave up Latin because Latin was being replaced by the vernacular all over Europe. For example, the Dutch inventor of the microscope, Leeuwenhoek, wrote only in Dutch, and the secretary of the (British) Royal Society reported in 1665 that even the Italians "love every whit as well to read books in Italian as the English doe to read them in English." Ultimately, though not until the twentieth century, English itself would replace Latin as the international language of scholarship. Many would lament (and continue to lament today) the loss of knowledge of classical languages, but, by the eighteenth century, English had no rival as the language of scholars in England.

The Debate over Vocabulary

The universal acceptance of English as a scholarly language did not mean that English was complacently regarded as a perfect vehicle or taken for granted without second thoughts. Indeed, one might call the entire Early Modern English period the Age of Linguistic Anxiety. Once the inevitability of its universal use had been at least tacitly recognized, disputes immediately arose about its deficiencies and its purity. The earliest perceived glaring inadequacy was in lexicon. Both the translators of the Latin and Greek classics and the practitioners of the new learning spawned by the Renaissance discovered that the existing word stock of English was insufficient to express economically and elegantly the ideas they wanted to convey.

Borrowing was the easiest and most obvious way to fill the gaps in English vocabulary, and Latin was the easiest and most obvious language from which to borrow. English had borrowed before, of course, but the loanwords in EMnE differed from those of earlier periods in several ways. First, the great majority of loans were from Latin and not from some other vernacular. The second difference lay in the sheer number of loanwords: Impressive as the French loans of Middle English had been, they were greatly outnumbered by the Latin loans of the Renaissance. Third, for the first time in the history of English, the borrowing was conscious and was done by specific individuals who were deliberately attempting to improve the language. Fourth, the bulk of the loanwords were, at least initially, learned in nature, though thousands of them were eventually to become part of the general vocabulary of the language.

Many of the conscious borrowers were responsible scholars, borrowing only when they felt a real need and carefully defining the Latinisms they used. Best known of such conscientious borrowers is Sir Thomas Elyot, who took great pains to define his neologisms, in some instances with only a word or two, in other instances with a lengthy explanation of several sentences. For example, in his *The Boke Named the Gouernour*, we find

consultation	This thinge that is called Consultation is the generall denomination of the acte wherin men do deuise to gether & reason what is to be done.
fury	a fury or infernall monstre
majesty	whiche is the holle proporcion and figure of noble astate and is proprelie a beautie or comelynesse in his countenance / langage / & gesture apt to his dignite / and accommodate to time / place / & company: whiche like as the sonne doth his beames / so doth it caste on the beholders and berers a pleasaunt & terrible reuerence.

Most borrowers, however, were less responsible than Elyot, and even Elyot often introduced loans without explaining them. Many writers used unfamiliar Latin terms simply to show off their learning and probably were more pleased than otherwise that the average reader found their work virtually incomprehensible.

Predictably, there were many who objected strenuously to the flood of new words pouring into English. Perhaps the majority of these protesters accepted borrowing in principle, realizing that English was insufficient in some ways, but objected to the foolish excesses, to the use of strange and obscure Latin words when adequate English equivalents already existed. They called such excessive neologisms **inkhorn terms** and mocked their pretentious users in such diatribes as the following statement by Thomas Wilson:

> Some seeke so far for outlandish English, that they forget altogether their mothers tongue. And I dare sweare this, if some of their mothers were aliue, thei were not able to tell what they say:... The vnlearned or foolish phantasticall, that smelles but of learning (such fellowes as haue seen learned men in their daies) wil so Latin their tongues, that the simple can not but

wonder at their talke, and thinke surely they speake by some reuelation. I know them that thinke *Rhetorique* to stande wholie vpon darke wordes, and hee that can catche an ynke horne terme by the taile, him they coumpt to be a fine Englishman, and a good *Rhetorician*.

Wilson, and other writers like Roger Ascham and Sir John Chéke, recognized the need for some borrowing and objected primarily to its overuse and misuse. Still others were concerned about the purity of the English vocabulary and resented borrowing because it contaminated this purity. Most members of this faction did perceive inadequacies in English. But rather than filling all these gaps with Latinate loans, they encouraged reviving older English words that had been lost, coining new words from the basic English stock, and adapting dialectal forms into the standard language.

The poet Edmund Spenser, who greatly admired Chaucer, was one of the most enthusiastic of the archaizers; he used such archaic or dialectal words as *gar* 'make' (a causative verb), *make* 'write verse', *forswatt* 'sweaty from work', and *spill* 'perish' in his works. Though Spenser employed many such terms correctly, few of them were accepted into the general, standard language. Ironically, Spenser's best-known contributions to the English lexicon are probably *braggadocio* and *derring-do*: the first, despite its Middle English base of *brag*, looks like an Italian loan, and the second is only a pseudo-archaism resulting from Spenser's misunderstanding of a Chaucerian term meaning "daring to do." For the most part, attempts to substitute archaic English words for Latin neologisms were unsuccessful.

Among those who tried to augment the language by coining new words from existing English forms was Sir John Cheke, who went so far as to try to translate the New Testament using only English terms. His primary approach was to extend the denotations of existing words or to use functional shift to make one part of speech from another. For example, Cheke substituted *moond* for the Latinate *lunatic*, *crossed* for *crucified*, and *biword* for *parable*. Again, his attempts were fruitless; *byword* does survive today, but only in the meaning "proverb," a meaning which the word has had since Old English times. Similarly, *cross* (which was in fact originally a Latin loan via Old Irish into Old English) is still a verb in PDE, but not with the meaning "crucify."

Another advocate of using English resources was Arthur Golding, who was especially fond of compounding. Many of his compounds are almost self-explanatory and often rather appealing, such as *fleshstrings* (muscles), *grosswitted*, and *heart-biting*, but few of them survived. One that did was *base-minded*—but it was probably already in the language because Queen Elizabeth I used it in a letter the year before Golding's book was published (1587). Another one, *primetime*, looks startlingly modern; Golding, however, used it to mean "an early age of the world," an extension of a contemporary meaning of "springtime." What is more, the word *prime* was an earlier loan from French.

A number of EMnE writers attempted to "English" the technical vocabularies of various subjects. For instance, in mathematics, Robert Recorde used *threlike* for "equilateral (triangle)" and *likejamme* for "parallelogram." In logic, Ralph Lever invented *endsay* for "conclusion" and *saywhat* for "definition." In rhetoric, George Puttenham used *over-reacher* to mean "hyperbole" and *dry mock* to mean "irony." None of these invented terms were adopted, at least partly because the people who were likely to need them were already familiar with the Latin terms.

Despite the protests and despite the efforts to substitute native formations for the inkhorn terms, the Latin loanwords continued to pour into English. Many of them were accepted without comment or objection because the consensus was that the language needed new words, even if there was disagreement about the appropriate source. Familiarity bred acceptance for many others; in fact, it was their very strangeness that had made them deplorable in the first place. Today we find it amusing that people could object to such words as *discretion, exaggerate, expect, industrial,* and *scheme*—all of which were inkhorn terms when they appeared in print for the first time in English between 1530 and 1600. We take these words for granted today because they are so familiar. Our reaction to *contund, effodicate, exinanite, synchysis,* and *transumptive* is quite different because they look so strange and we do not know what they mean. Yet these were also inkhorn terms that entered English during the same period. The only difference between the two sets of words is that the first survived and the second did not. Hundreds of the newly borrowed words from Latin and Greek during the EMnE period were destined to be lost again, some almost immediately and others within a century or so. Still, enough remained in the language to alter permanently the entire texture of the lexicon.

Although Latin (and, to a lesser extent, Greek) was the major source of both neologisms and the debate over them during EMnE, loanwords from other European languages also produced some controversy. French loans continued to come in, as they had ever since the twelfth century. However, by now, English already had thousands of French loans, English spelling had been modified under French influence, and there were standardized ways of adapting French words to English. Thus, new French loans attracted relatively little attention. But when English travelers on the Continent brought back Italian and Spanish words, the travelers were ridiculed for their pretentious "oversea" language. One of the reasons for the attention was that the un-English endings in *-o* and *-a* prevented these words from slipping unnoticed into the general vocabulary. Indeed, some of the Spanish and Italian loans from this period still look exotic today. To most English speakers, such EMnE loans from Italian as *cameo, cupola, piazza,* and *portico* and such words from Spanish as *armada, bravado, desperado,* and *peccadillo* seem much more "foreign" than such French loans from the same period as *comrade, duel, ticket,* and *volunteer.*

The Spelling Reformers

Beginning a little later than the inkhorn controversy and continuing throughout the sixteenth century was a flurry of activity over another aspect of English words: their spelling. Even Old English spelling had been less than perfect. Then French scribes spelled or respelled additional confusion into the system during Middle English. By the sixteenth century, the effects of the Great Vowel Shift were making the English correspondence between vowel and vowel symbol very different from that of such Continental languages as French and Italian. Why a great interest in spelling reform should have occurred at this particular time is not certain. Probably it was partly a by-product of the Renaissance; people noticed the seeming consistency and standardization of Latin spelling and became unhappy with the chaotic conditions in English. An ongoing concern over the pronunciation of Greek perhaps also led to increased awareness of the inadequacies of English spelling. The contemporary French attempts to reform French orthography may have introduced a "keep up with the Joneses" element to the situation. One might even view the movement as an early harbinger of the conservatism and tidying-up impulses of the eighteenth century.

Whatever the reasons, the mid-sixteenth century saw many suggestions for reforming English spelling. Ideally and at its most extreme, reform would result in a simplified, consistent, "phonetic," standardized spelling system for English. In its weakest version, reform would clean up a few of the most glaring deficiencies and provide fixed spellings for all English words, without attempting to remove internal inconsistencies or to change the existing inventory of alphabetic symbols.

Some of the leading figures in the movement for spelling reform were men who also participated in the inkhorn dispute. Among these was Sir John Cheke, whose suggestions for reform were relatively mild compared with those of some of his successors. Cheke (1569) proposed removing all silent letters; where these unsounded letters had indicated vowel length, Cheke would instead have doubled the vowel.

Much more sweeping were the reforms proposed by Sir Thomas Smith (1568), who understandably but wrong-mindedly wanted letter forms to be "pictures" of speech sounds, that is, to have an iconic relationship to the sounds. Smith would also have thrown out redundant letters like c and q, reintroduced the OE thorn ⟨þ⟩ for [θ], and used Greek theta ⟨θ⟩ for [ð]. He wanted to modify the forms of some other letters and to indicate vowel length by various diacritical marks such as the circumflex, the macron, and the umlaut. Smith's suggestions were simply too drastic to be accepted—and the fact that he wrote his treatise on English spelling in Latin did not increase his chances for success.

John Hart's proposals for spelling reform were first published in 1569 and 1570, although they had been written nearly two decades earlier. Like Smith, he proposed several new characters and wanted to discard such letters as y, w, and c. He would have indicated vowel length by a dot under the vowel. Recognizing that capital letters had no counterpart in speech (that is, capital and lowercase letters are pronounced identically), he recommended eliminating them entirely—but then would have put a virgule (slant line) in front of words that would otherwise have been capitalized.

William Bullokar (1580) did not suggest eliminating existing letters from the English alphabet, but did propose using various diacritical marks to distinguish, for example, [ǰ] and [g]. He also wanted new symbols for [š], [θ], [ð], and [hw]. Bullokar's understanding of phonology was extremely fuzzy, but he was more far-sighted than some of the other reformers in that he wanted a dictionary to record and preserve the new spellings and also a grammar to stabilize and set standards for English. Figure 7.1 illustrates Bullokar's reformed spelling.

The latter half of the sixteenth century saw still more spelling reformers, but their suggestions were essentially along the same lines as those already mentioned. Richard Mulcaster, however, took a somewhat different approach. He was more conservative than his fellow reformers in that he was willing to leave the existing alphabet as it was, neither adding nor eliminating characters. On the other hand, he was ahead of his time in recognizing the inevitability of sound changes, in preferring to rely chiefly on current usage, and in realizing that the relationship between speech sound and written symbol is arbitrary. Rather than attempting a perfect match between sound and symbol, he would have been content with eliminating letters that were completely redundant (double consonants in many words, for instance), with adding letters where existing spelling had too few, and

Figure 7.1 William Bullokar's Reformed Spelling*

William Byllokar

þowht, woul∂ æƷ, þat my painƷ.

The ∂esolate
neuer ∂esti-
tute wholie
nor è contra.

I must confes, som fren∂Ʒ I foyn∂,
þat gau me som relef,
with comfortabl' spe∂h, byt yet,
þey æƷ∂ not, al' my gref.

Scorning is a
scourging.

No grefiƷ græter, to þe mýn∂,
þan when, þe scorning train
∂oth gest, an∂ gyb, at vertuƷ gift?,
an∂ such aƷ ∂oo tak pain :

Vn-grate-
fulnes is
greeuous.

Ye, for þeir goo∂, þat ∂eƷeru not,
to hau, so goo∂ a þing :
them-selu' not abl', to ∂oo lýk,
þeir mýn∂?, not so ben∂ing.

If tærƷ shoul∂ fal'-∂own, from mýn yƷ,
it' wær not, of þyl∂ish myn∂,
sith, nærer step?, of þre scor yerƷ,
þan fifty, my yet fýn∂ :

Nor yet, for faintnes, of coƷag',
sith, wiling mýn∂ me læ∂∂,
twýc, intoo foren foƷ contry,
yn∂er þe ensýn spre∂∂,

Soldior vn-
der Sir Rich.
Wingfeeld
in Queene
Maries time.
Vnder Sir
Ad. Poinings
at new Ha-
ven.

Seruing two knihtƷ, riht-worƷhip-fyl,
bóth sol∂yorƷ of renown,
riht-skil-fyl in, warly affairƷ,
to seru in fel∂, or town :

With whoom I vƷ∂ such ∂iligenc',
þat þey pytt tryst in me,

moƷ

with altering spelling when the same spelling represented two different pronunciations (for example, *use* as noun and *use* as verb). Mulcaster would even have accepted highly irregular spellings if they were already widely used and familiar. In essence, he was willing to patch up where possible and did not propose sweeping reforms. His more modest goal was a fixed, uniform spelling for each word.

It is hard to say how much influence the spelling reformers of the sixteenth century had. Certainly "public" spelling was completely standardized within the next two centuries. By 1750, Lord Chesterfield could write to his son:

> Orthography is so absolutely necessary for a man of letters, or a gentleman, that one false spelling may fix a ridicule upon him for the rest of his life; and I know a man of quality who never recovered the ridicule of having spelled *wholesome* without the *w*.

However, the scribes of the Chancery (the royal secretariat) and the printers probably had more to do with this stabilization than the reformers did. Chesterfield's warning notwithstanding, "personal" spelling—that of individuals in their private writing—remained unfixed long after the spelling of printed material had become standardized. None of the reformers' suggested new characters were adopted. English today does not even use any diacritics except in words still regarded as foreign—a pity, perhaps, because judicious use of diacritics could go a long way toward solving the problem of too few vowel symbols in English. Other European languages like French, Spanish, Danish, and Swedish do not find diacritics too cumbersome, but, for whatever reason, English has never adopted them.

The sixteenth century was perhaps the last time a thoroughgoing reform of English spelling was possible. Soon thereafter, the spread of printed books was to make the vested interest in older customs too great to be overthrown, except perhaps by government fiat, a path that England and other English-speaking nations have chosen not to take. The present system, unsatisfactory as it is in so many ways, does have certain advantages. Although English pronunciation both within and across national boundaries differs so greatly as to make some versions almost mutually unintelligible, all native speakers of English write the same language. Our fossilized spelling system unites the English-speaking world.

Furthermore, with the exception of a few, mostly very common, words, English spelling is more systematic and predictable than most people believe. The fact that most of us spell most words correctly is evidence of this. Moreover, again with a few outstanding exceptions, the conversion of spelling to sound is highly predictable. Most of us know how to pronounce most of the new words we encounter in reading. For example, when I asked a group of thirty native speakers to say the nonwords *lape, morantishly, permaction,* and *phorin,* there was virtual unanimity in their pronunciation, including even the placement of the major stress. Complex though it is, there is a systematic relationship between English spelling and English pronunciation. George Bernard Shaw was simply being silly (as he

---

*From William Bullokar, *Booke at Large* (1580) and *Bref Grammar for English* (1586) (Delmar, N.Y.: Scholars' Facsimiles & Reprints, 1977), n.p. Translated into traditional modern spelling, the first two full paragraphs on this page are as follows: "I must confess, some friends I found, / that gave me some relief, / with comfortable speech, but yet, / they eased not, all my grief. / No grief is greater, to the mind, / than when, the scorning train / doth jest, and gibe, at virtue's gifts, / and such as do take pain:"

probably knew) if he actually said that English *fish* could be spelled *ghoti* (*gh* as in *rough*; *o* as in *women*; *ti* as in *lotion*): *gh* is never pronounced [f] at the beginning of a word, *ti* never spells [š] at the end of a word, and *o* spells [ɪ] only in *women*. If perchance there were a literate English speaker who had never seen the word [fɪš], he or she would still spell it *fish*. And most literate speakers would pronounce *ghoti* as [goti], even though *gh* is rare at the beginning of English words and *i* is relatively rare at the end of words.

The Dictionary Makers

On first thought, it may seem surprising that the earliest English-to-English dictionary dates only from the first part of the seventeenth century. "But how did people get along without dictionaries?" is our likely response. On second thought, it should not be surprising: There were no English-to-English dictionaries because there was no real need for them. After all, what do we use a dictionary for? Most people today consult a dictionary primarily to check the spelling of words they want to write. When most people never wrote at all because they did not know how, and when spelling was not fixed anyway, a spelling "error" was not a social embarrassment, so there was no need to check spelling. Further, until the widespread dissemination of printing, people used their memories more than they do today and were less prone to forget what they had previously seen or read. Prior to the introduction of inkhorn terms and the explosion of knowledge brought in by the Renaissance, most literate speakers of English would have known the meaning of most English words that they were likely to encounter. Even today, dictionaries are not consulted especially frequently to determine correct pronunciation, and pronunciation was even less of a problem before the introduction of large numbers of Latin and Greek words into the lexicon. Probably still fewer people today consult a dictionary for usage, part-of-speech category, or etymology. Some people use a dictionary as a convenient source for finding out the capital of a country, the population of a state, the dates of a prominent author, and the like—but this sort of information is actually the domain of an encyclopedia or an almanac, and its inclusion in modern dictionaries is only for convenience. In sum, there were no English-to-English dictionaries prior to the seventeenth century because there was no particular need for them.

All of this changed with the expansion of literacy and the Renaissance. Another incentive to the production of English-to-English dictionaries at this time was the increasing desire, already noted with respect to the inkhorn controversy and spelling reform, to refine, standardize, and fix the language, a desire that was only to intensify throughout the seventeenth and eighteenth centuries.

The first English-to-English dictionaries did, however, have antecedents. As far back as Anglo-Saxon times, manuscripts written in Latin often had interlinear translations in Old English. Indeed, a modern reader may be shocked to see a magnificent manuscript page defaced by hastily scribbled Old English words inserted above the elegantly executed Latin text—in exactly the same way that contemporary students of a foreign language write English equivalents over the unfamiliar words in their reading. Figure 7.2 shows Old English glosses in the famous Book of Lindisfarne. For example, in the upper left corner, over the Latin words *incipit euangelium* are the Old English words *onginneð godspell* 'begins gospel'.

Besides these interlinear translations or **glosses**, there were separate word lists, or **glossaries,** for the "hard" words of particular texts. Several of these lists

Figure 7.2   Old English Glosses in the Book of Lindisfarne

survive from the OE period; Ælfric (see p. 116) prepared a Latin-Old English list. Such bilingual word lists continued to be prepared throughout the Middle English period; for example, Alexander Neckham compiled the trilingual Latin-French-English *De nominibus utensilium* around 1200. These early bilingual or trilingual lists were usually organized by subject matter and not alphabetized (even though the principle of alphabetization was known). The first alphabetical bilingual dictionaries did not appear until the mid-sixteenth century.

In addition to glossaries of unusual or hard words, bilingual vocabularies, the predecessors of our modern Berlitz phrase books, were prepared for travelers on the Continent. Caxton printed such a 52-page French-English vocabulary in 1480. Nor were all these word lists restricted to the familiar European languages and Hebrew. In America, Roger Williams wrote his *Key into the Languages of America* (1643) partly as a grammar, but primarily as a series of word lists arranged by subject matter.

Approaching the principle of the monolingual dictionary from another direction, Richard Mulcaster compiled a list of about 8000 English words in the first part of his treatise on education, *The Elementarie* (1582). However, he included no definitions.

Finally, in 1604, the schoolmaster Robert Cawdrey (with the help of his son Thomas, also a schoolmaster) published *A Table Alphabeticall*, the first true alphabetically arranged English-to-English dictionary. It contained about 2500 rare and borrowed words with definitions in English. The complete title of Cawdrey's little dictionary was *A Table Alphabeticall, conteyning and teaching the true writing, and understanding of hard usuall English wordes, borrowed from the Hebrew, Greeke, Latine, or French, &c. With the interpretation thereof by plaine English words, gathered for the benefit & helpe of Ladies, Gentlewomen, or any other unskilfull persons. Whereby they may the more easilie and better understand many hard English wordes, which they shall heare or read in Scriptures, Sermons, or elswhere, and also be made able to use the same aptly themselues.*

This cumbersome title reveals a great deal about the times in which it appeared. First, it is addressed to a new audience created by the Renaissance— literate women who did not know Latin or French. Second, it reflects the effects of the Reformation in its assumption that such women would be reading the Bible for themselves. Third, it shows the rising concern for correctness in its statement "and also be made able to use the same aptly themselves." Incidentally, the variant spellings *wordes* and *words* show that spelling was not yet absolutely fixed. Apparently there were a lot of ladies, gentlewomen, and other "unskilfull persons" eager to improve themselves, for Cawdrey's little dictionary went into four editions.

After Cawdrey, the number of English-to-English dictionaries proliferated, each of them more complete and complex than its predecessors. Each compiler borrowed heavily from previously published dictionaries (as dictionary makers to this day still do); Cawdrey himself had taken about half his entries from Thomas Thomas' 1588 Latin-English dictionary.

John Bullokar's *An English Expositor* (1616) included about 60 percent more entries than Cawdrey's dictionary. His definitions were in general more complete than Cawdrey's, and he marked archaic words (Cawdrey had marked French and Greek loans, but not Latin loans). Henry Cockeram's popular *English Dictionarie* (1623 and many later editions) contained three parts: an alphabetical list of "refined" words, another list of "vulgar" words, and, anticipating some of the encyclopedic information of modern dictionaries, a short dictionary of mythology.

Though Thomas Blount's *Glossographia* (1656) was based heavily on preceding dictionaries, it was larger (11,000 entries) and was innovative in being the first English dictionary to cite sources and to give etymologies, imperfect as many of them were. In 1658, John Milton's nephew, Edward Philipps, published *The New World of English Words*, so heavily plagiarized from Blount that Blount wrote an attack on it entitled *A World of Errors*. However, Philipps' 1678 revision, *New World of Words or a General English Dictionary*, added to the usual hard

Figure 7.3 Sample Page from Cawdrey's *A Table Alphabeticall*

40 An Alphabeticall table

D

DAmnable, not to be allowed.
deacon, (g) prouider for the poore
demonaicke, (g) possessed with a deuill.
deambulation, a walking abroade
§ debate, strife, contention
debar, let:
debilitie, weakenes, faintnes.
§ debonnayre, gentle, curteous, affable,
decalogue, (g) the ten commaundements:
decacordon, (g) an instrument with tenne strings
decent, comlie, or beséeming
decease, a departing, or giuing place too.
decide, to determine, or make an end of.
decipher, describe, or open the meaning, or to count.
decision, cutting away.
declamation, an oration of a matter feyned.
decline, fall away, or swarue from,
decoction, liquor, wherein things are sod for phisicke.
decorum, comlines
decrepite, very old
dedicate, to giue for euer.

deduct,

words a large number of ordinary words, thereby doubling the number of entries to over 20,000. Elisha Coles' *English Dictionary* of 1676 was based on Philipps' *New World of English Words*, but was expanded to include dialect and cant words. It had about 25,000 entries, but was still essentially a hard-words dictionary. The first English dictionary to include everyday words was John Kersey's *A New English Dictionary* (1702, with later revisions).

Nathaniel Bailey can perhaps be called the earliest truly modern lexicographer. He was the author of *An Universal Etymological English Dictionary* (1721 and later supplements) and a coauthor of the 950-page 1730 edition of *Dictionarium Britannicum* with its 48,000 entries. In addition to his regular inclusion of ordinary words, etymologies, and cognate forms, Bailey's dictionary was the first to indicate the stress placement of words. Bailey's conscientious and complete scholarship made him the standard reference until the publication of Johnson's dictionary.

When Samuel Johnson announced his plan for a dictionary in 1747, he stated that his purpose was to refine and fix the language. In the course of his seven years of compiling *A Dictionary of the English Language* (two volumes, 1755), he gradually recognized the impossibility of achieving this goal, realizing that no living language could ever be fixed and that language change was inevitable. Yet, ironically, Johnson probably did more to "fix" at least some aspects of the language than any other person before or since—almost all the spellings we use today are those he recommended. Although Johnson's 40,000 entries were 8000 fewer than those of Bailey, his dictionary was two and a half times as large and much more complete and accurate. Johnson's use of illustrative quotations was a first in English dictionary-making and helped to establish his dictionary's immediate influence and popularity. It remained *the* authoritative dictionary of English until the publication of Noah Webster's American dictionary in the following century. Johnson's use of quotations to establish the meanings of words in context was to be adopted by the editors of the most magnificent feat of dictionary-making ever accomplished in any language, the *Oxford English Dictionary*.

At about the same time that the first English-to-English general dictionaries were being published, specialized dictionaries began to appear in response to the expansion of knowledge and education brought about by the Renaissance. There were dictionaries (or glossaries) of cant words, of legal terms, of specialized technical fields like mathematics and science. Thomas Wilson compiled *A Christian Dictionarie* (1612) for words of the Bible, and Sir Henry Manwayring wrote *The Sea-Mans Dictionary* (1644) of maritime terms. Polyglot dictionaries continued to appear; one of the most inclusive was John Minsheu's *Guide into the Tongues* (1617), which included words from Latin, Greek, Hebrew, English, French, Dutch, German, Italian, Spanish, Portuguese, and British. Late in the EMnE period, pronouncing dictionaries such as John Walker's *Critical Pronouncing Dictionary and Expositor of the English Language* (1791) appeared.

The great flurry of dictionary-making during the EMnE period had several important effects on the subsequent history of English. The general availability of dictionaries encouraged standardized spelling. The heavy emphasis on learned, Latinate words, especially in the earlier hard-word dictionaries, hastened the adoption of these new words into the general vocabulary. Finally, the high quality of Bailey's and especially Johnson's dictionaries established the almost unquestioned authority of The Dictionary, an authority to which most people still bow unquestioningly.

The Movement for an English Academy

To the modern speaker and writer of English, the idea of a national academy that would legislate standards of English, settle disputes about usage and spelling, eradicate unfortunate solecisms that have sneaked into the language, and in general serve as a watchdog over the English tongue probably seems either ridiculous or outrageous. We tend to smile condescendingly at the current futile attempts of the French Academy to halt the flow of Anglicisms and Americanisms into contemporary French. However, during the latter part of the seventeenth and the early part of the eighteenth centuries, there was a strong movement in favor of just such an academy for English. This demand for an official sentinel over the language was of a piece with the earlier inkhorn controversy, the attempts at spelling reform, and the dictionary-making: All reflected a desire to tidy up and regulate after the linguistic exuberance of the Renaissance. In particular, the formation of the Italian Accademia della Crusca (1582) and the Académie Française (1635) served, to some at least, as models of what could be done to make the English language more respectable.

One of the earliest to call for an academy was Robert Hooke, the scientist and philosopher, in his continuation (1660) of Francis Bacon's unfinished *New Atlantis*. As curator of experiments of the Royal Society, Hooke may well have been influential in that group's appointment of a subcommittee consisting of both scientists and men of letters to look into the formation of an academy under royal patronage (1664). This subcommittee apparently did little beyond meeting several times and eventually simply disbanded. Still, others continued to press for a national academy, including Daniel Defoe in his *Essay Upon Projects* (1697) and Joseph Addison in *Spectator* 135 (1711). In an open letter to the Earl of Oxford (who was the Lord Treasurer of England) in 1712, Jonathan Swift proposed that the Earl establish an academy to purify and regulate the language. Queen Anne supported the idea, and for a brief time it looked as if an English academy would actually be founded. But when Anne died in 1714, her successor, George I of Hannover, was a German who paid relatively little attention to affairs in Great Britain and did not even speak English. Without royal support, the movement languished.

Even during the height of agitation for a national academy, it had had its opponents. Some of the opposition was on other than linguistic grounds—the Whigs saw the movement as a power play by the Tories and opposed it for political reasons. Others felt that its authoritarian nature ran contrary to English notions of liberty. Still others sensed that the models, the French and Italian academies, had not been especially successful after all and suspected or realized that efforts to control and purify a living language would be futile.

After the publication of Samuel Johnson's dictionary in 1755, the movement for an English academy died out completely. To some extent, the authority that Johnson's dictionary achieved immediately after its publication made it a substitute for an academy. In addition, in the course of his work, Johnson himself came to recognize the inevitability of language change and the futility and undesirability of trying to legislate it. This attitude on his part at least temporarily squelched whatever impetus for a national academy may have remained.

Within a few years, the establishment of a national academy to legislate for all of English became permanently unfeasible. The English-speaking citizens of the newly independent United States were both too feisty and too insecure to accept docilely the linguistic authority of a body created and staffed by their recent enemy. Nor did John Adams' proposal for a home-grown American Academy meet with any widespread enthusiasm. Today, when the number of independent nations using English as their national language has multiplied, the infeasibility has become impossibility.

The Discovery of Grammar

In the earlier part of the Early Modern English period, concern about the English language focused primarily on the most obvious and intuitive unit of language, the word—its origin, its spelling, and its codification in dictionaries. Later in the period, language-watchers extended their attention to grammar, and especially to "proper" and "improper" usage. This is not to say that no one had previously noticed that different people and groups used different constructions or that grammatical usage was not one of many shibboleths distinguishing classes. However, such variation had been pretty much taken for granted, and few scholars had stood back, looked at the grammar of the language as a whole, and found it sadly wanting. Nor had there been a great demand for putting rules of grammar into print and making them accessible to all. A number of factors, most of them arising outside the world of letters, converged after the mid-eighteenth century to make this an era of anguishing over usage and of attempting to improve it.

One of these factors was the aspirations of the rising middle class. Aware that linguistic usage was one of the things that marked them as different from those they regarded as their betters, they sought guidance in the form of "how-to" books that would help them acquire appropriate linguistic behavior. Another important factor was the spirit of the times. The eighteenth century is often called the Age of Reason. Although generalities are always dangerous, it is certainly true that this period was one of great faith in logic, reason, and organization. Isaac Newton (1642–1727) had seemingly demonstrated that the universe itself was one of order and harmony ruled by a system of ascertainable and immutable divine laws. More recently, Carolus Linnaeus (1707–1778) had devised a taxonomic classification system for all living creatures, plant and animal. If the contents of the universe could be categorized logically and if its behavior could be reduced to laws, then surely the grammar of a language could be defined and regulated.

Still a third factor that encouraged attempts to codify, clean up, and improve English grammar was the prevailing notion that language was of divine origin and that there existed a "universal" grammar from which contemporary languages had deteriorated. Greek and Latin were (wrongly) assumed to have deviated less from this original purity than had the various European vernaculars, and thus they (especially Latin) were regarded as models upon which an improved English grammar should be based.

Misguided as this notion is, it is understandable in the context of the times. Little was known about human languages outside the Indo-European languages of Europe and, to some extent, the Semitic languages (chiefly Hebrew). Even William Jones' demonstration of the unity of the Indo-European languages was not to appear until the end of the eighteenth century. All of these known languages were inflecting languages, and the older the stages of the languages, the more highly inflecting they were. Hence grammar was equated with inflection. Hence the fewer the inflections of a language, the more it must have fallen away from its original purity. Because English had almost no inflections, it was assumed to have little or no grammar and to be extremely corrupt. Obviously, then, if English was to regain any degree of its original purity, it must be provided with rules, cleansed of its corruption, and then prevented from decaying further. These were precisely the goals that most eighteenth-century grammarians set for themselves: to *ascertain* (or to establish rules), to *refine* (or to purify), and, once these two goals had been accomplished, to *fix* (or to stabilize and prevent future change) by publishing the rules of the language.

Although the eighteenth century was the heyday of the prescriptive grammar, books indirectly or directly concerned with English grammar had been appearing since the sixteenth century. The Renaissance concern over eloquence and elegance is reflected in such books as Thomas Wilson's *The Arte of Rhetorique* (1553), a rather lengthy and detailed work based primarily on classical models. Henry Peacham's *The Garden of Eloquence* (1577) is essentially a dictionary of rhetorical tropes (for example, metaphor, synecdoche, allegory, irony, and hyperbole) and schemes (for example, zeugma, tautology, and hysteron proteron), but Peacham uses as illustrations either actual English examples or English translations of classical and Biblical quotations.

Beginning in the late sixteenth century, numerous "grammars" of English began to appear, though few of them were to have widespread influence, partly because many of them were not designed for the general public or for schoolchildren. The earliest known such grammar is that by William Bullokar (the spelling reformer; see p. 201). Heavily dependent on Latin terminology, Bullokar's *Bref Grammar* (1586) is printed in his own proposed reformed spelling—which surely did not add to its popularity. Alexander Gil's *Logonomia Anglica* (1621) is quite detailed, but even more slavishly tied to Latin. Indeed, the book itself is written in Latin, and English examples are in Gil's phonetic transcription, making it even less accessible to the general public than Bullokar's grammar. John Wallis' *Grammatica Linguae Anglicanae* (1653) was also in Latin.

By this time, however, some writers were beginning to break out of the Latin mold. Jeremiah Wharton, for instance, in his *The English Grammar* (1654) recognized the lack of inflection in English without deploring the fact:

> Genders of Nouns in Latine bee seven; but the consideration of them in English is useless; but onely to observ, that som words do signifie Males; som females; and som neither; and that of the first wee must say *hee*; of the second *shee*; of the third *it*:

More clearly pedagogical in intent was Joseph Aickin's *The English Grammar* (1693), whose preface was addressed "To the School-masters of the English Tongue and other Candid Readers" and whose first chapter begins

> My Child: your Parents have desired me, to teach you the English-Tongue. For though you can speak English already; yet you are not an English Scholar, till you can read, write, and speak English truly.

It was the eighteenth-century school grammars, however, that were to have the greatest audience and influence, an influence continuing down to the present day. Of these, Robert Lowth's *A Short Introduction to English Grammar* (1762 and many subsequent editions) was the most prominent. Lowth was bishop of London, privy councillor, professor of poetry at Oxford, and a scholar of Latin, Greek, Hebrew, and several modern languages—clearly a man with impressive credentials. Lowth had no doubts about what was correct and no hesitations about condemning roundly what was incorrect. His little book abounds in such phrases as "This abuse has been long growing upon us," "Adjectives of this sort are sometimes very improperly used," and "Mistakes in the use of them [conjunctions] are very common." Many of his decisions about English usage have come down to us virtually unchanged; few modern readers will fail to recognize such quotations from Lowth as

> Two negatives in English destroy one another, or are equivalent to an affirmative.

> Thus it is commonly said, "I *only* spake three words": when the intention of the speaker manifestly requires, "I spake *only* three words."

Joseph Priestley's *The Rudiments of English Grammar* (1761) is often contrasted (favorably from the modern point of view) with Lowth's grammar. Although probably best known as the discoverer of oxygen, Priestley was also a chemist, inventor, philosopher, traveler, nonconformist minister, and the founder of the Unitarian Church in America. Born and bred in England, he was made an honorary citizen of France, and eventually settled and later died in Pennsylvania. If Lowth stands for the conservative establishment of the time, Priestley may well be considered the liberal opposition. To some extent, this political difference is reflected in their approaches to grammar; certainly, Priestley more willingly accepted prevailing custom than did Lowth. However, the differences between their two works lie more in their attitudes than in the substance of what they say. Where Lowth is horrified by what he sees as error and says so emphatically, Priestley is gentler in his disapproval and tries to use reason rather than condemnation to persuade readers to change their ways. The following quotations concerning the use of *was* with *you* illustrate this difference:

> *You was*, the second person plural of the pronoun placed in agreement with the first or third person singular of the verb, is an enormous solecism, and yet authors of the first rank have inadvertently fallen into it. [Lowth]

> Many writers of no small reputation say *you was*, when speaking of a single person: but as the word *you* is confessedly *plural*, ought not the *verb*, agreeable to the analogy of all languages, to be plural too? moreover, we always say *you are*. [Priestley]

Both authors define grammar the same way:

> Grammar is the art of rightly expressing our thoughts by words. [Lowth]

> Grammar is the art of using words properly. [Priestley]

That is, to both Lowth and Priestley, grammar is an art (rather than a science) and is chiefly concerned with propriety. Both are concerned with the importance of analogy. Lowth was less willing to accept contemporary usage as a guide to correctness, perhaps partly because he had such a strong background in the classical languages and even knew Old English well enough to allow him to compare earlier stages of the language with contemporary usage. Indeed, in his grammar, he frequently includes the Old English forms of words.

For most of the EMnE period, American schools used British grammars. But after the Revolution, many Americans were eager to assert their linguistic independence from the mother country. In 1784, Noah Webster published his *Plain and Comprehensive Grammar* to compete with the grammars of Lowth and other British authors. The emancipation from British models is, however, more apparent in intent than in content. Webster said that he would base his rules on existing usage, but he himself was dismayed by the usage of English-speaking immigrants (especially Irish and Scots), and his grammar ended up almost as prescriptive as the contemporary British grammars. His definition of grammar is virtually identical to those of Lowth and Priestley (though some might say that his addition of *dispatch* reflects an early American emphasis on speed and efficiency):

> Grammar is the art of communicating thoughts by words with propriety and dispatch.

Still, on the whole, Webster was less dogmatic in his pronouncements and more willing to accept the inevitability of language change, as the following two quotations illustrate:

> It is very common to hear these phrases, *it is me, it was him.* These appear not strictly grammatical, but have such a prevalence in English, and in other modern languages derived from the same source, it inclines me to think, that there may be reasons for them, which are not now understood.

> *Enough* was once used in the singular only; *enow* in the plural is still used by some writers, particularly the Scotch; but *enough* is now generally used in both numbers.

The specific rules of usage established—sometimes manufactured—by the eighteenth-century grammarians have a mixed record of survival in the late twentieth century. Most educated users of English take for granted and automatically observe the strictures against double negatives and double comparatives and superlatives. Repeated but not observed (or observed in writing only) are the rule against split infinitives and the distinction between *between* and *among*. Few native users, even in writing, employ *shall* for the first-person future or bother to avoid ending a sentence with a preposition.

The deeper, more pervasive, and more pernicious influence of the eighteenth-century prescriptive grammarians lies in their having made "correct" usage a moral rather than simply a practical matter. If we want to be respected and admired, we must conform to the linguistic practices of the groups by whom we wish to be accepted. However, using *ain't* is not sinful; it is simply against our self-interest. The blurring of this distinction has led to widespread feelings of guilt about one's own usage; it is the direct inheritance of the school grammarians of the eighteenth century.

The eighteenth-century grammarians can be forgiven their optimism that linguistic behavior could be controlled like traffic in a tunnel—after all, this was the age of codification and classification, a time with a place for everything and everything in its place. Less forgivable was their approach to the anomalies of linguistic reality. For all his beautifully logical taxonomy, Linnaeus had to make do, to make ad hoc adjustments to his system when he encountered, say, a duck-billed platypus. He could not and did not ignore the data of the real world. But when the grammarians encountered such embarrassments, their approach was to try to get rid of them entirely, to legislate them out of the language. We can justifiably criticize them for attempting to exterminate rather than accommodate inconvenient facts.

Nonetheless, we should not overmalign the school grammarians. They were not deliberate linguistic tyrants, nor did they promote class warfare. They responded to a real demand on the part of people who wanted simple, clear-cut

PURPLE PROSE

Shakespeare is the best-known practitioner of Renaissance verbal exuberance, but some of his contemporaries were as flamboyant, if not as successful, in their linguistic experimentation. Among them was John Lyly, whose prose romance *Euphues, The Anatomy of Wit* (1578) has given its name to an affected, overblown elegance of style characterized by elaborate similes, antitheses, and alliteration. Prolixity is inherent in euphuism, so a lengthy quotation is necessary to convey the flavor of Lyly's prose:

> The freshest colors soonest fade, the teenest razor soonest turneth his edge, the finest cloth is soonest eaten with moths, and the cambric sooner stained than the coarse canvas; which appeared well in this Euphues, whose wit being like wax apt to receive any impression, and having the bridle in his own hands either to use the rein or the spur, disdaining counsel, leaving his country, loathing his old acquaintance, thought either by wit to obtain some conquest or by shame to abide some conflict, and leaving the rule of reason, rashly ran unto destruction, who, preferring fancy before friends and his present humor before honor to come, laid reason in water, being too salt for his taste, and followed unbridled affection, most pleasant for his tooth. When parents have more care how to leave their children wealthy than wise, and are more desirous to have them maintain the name than the nature of a gentleman; when they put gold into the hands of youth where they should put a rod under their girdle; when instead of awe they make them past grace, and leave them rich executors of goods and poor executors of godliness; then it is no marvel that the son, being left rich by his father's will, become retchless by his own will.*

Over two centuries later, Walter Scott parodied euphuism in the character of Sir Piercie Shafton in his novel *The Monastery* (1820):

> "Ah, that I had with me my *Anatomy of Wit*—that all-to-be-unparalleled volume —that quintessence of human wit—that treasury of quaint invention—that exquis- itely-pleasant-to-read, and inevitably-necessary-to-be-remembered manual of all that is worthy to be known—which indoctrines the rude in civility, the dull in intellectuality, the heavy in jocosity, the blunt in gentility, the vulgar in nobility, and all of them in that unutterable perfection of human utterance, that eloquence which no other eloquence is sufficient to praise, that art which, when we call it by its own name of Euphuism, we bestow on it its richest panegyric....
>
> "Even thus," said he, "do hogs contemn the splendor of Oriental pearls; even thus are the delicacies of a choice repast in vain offered to the long-eared grazer of the common, who turneth from them to devour a thistle. Surely as idle is it to pour forth the treasures of oratory before the eyes of the ignorant, and to spread the dainties of the intellectual banquet before those who are, morally and metaphysically speaking, no better than asses."†

* Reprinted from *The Golden Hind, An Anthology of Elizabethan Prose and Poetry*, Revised Edition, Selected and Edited by Roy Lamson and Hallett Smith. By permission of W. W. Norton & Company, Inc. Copyright 1942, © 1956 by W. W. Norton & Company, Inc.

† From Sir Walter Scott, Bart., *The Monastery* (Boston: Dana Estes & Company, Publishers, n.d.), pp. 122–23.

answers to usage questions, people who asked for concrete instruction and not abstract theory. We can fault the grammarians for the false information they gave, but not for the fact that they gave information. Today's linguists assume that grammars have orderly rules and that their task is to discover and describe them; the eighteenth-century grammarians saw their task as one of imposing rules where they assumed that none had previously existed. It is unfair to condemn Lowth and his contemporaries for not knowing what has been learned in the two centuries since he wrote his *Short Introduction*. If anything, we should criticize the present age for having improved so little upon his example.

INNER HISTORY
Early Modern English Phonology

The Early Modern English period is the first in the history of English from which ample texts are available to illustrate the use of the language. A larger population, greater literacy, proliferation of texts through printing, and the increased chances of survival of materials because of the relative nearness in time to the present all have contributed to the vast numbers of texts dating from 1500–1800. On the other hand, the standardization and fossilization of spelling during this period have meant that most printed texts are of little help in reconstructing the phonological changes that occurred. In this respect, the poorly educated writer is of more assistance than the well-educated one because the former is more likely to spell "phonetically." Some of our most valuable sources of information are personal letters, diaries, and governmental records kept by ill-educated clerks (particularly in colonial America). In addition, we have for the first time written statements about the language and its sounds. These, however, must be used with caution because the writers usually were not trained phoneticians and they apparently often indulged more in wishful thinking than in objective reporting.

As was true of Middle English, there were many local dialects, and, indeed, it seems that there were more acceptable variants *within* the standard language than is the case today. By the end of the EMnE period, new dialects were rising in the American colonies. Unfortunately, much of this dialectal variation is poorly understood today; in any case, its detail is beyond the scope of this book. Our discussion will be based primarily on the standard language in England.

Consonants
The present-day inventory of English consonants was established during the Early Modern English period. By 1800, the system was identical to that of today, so we can simply refer to Figure 2.2 (p. 23). A comparison of Figure 2.2 with Figure 6.1 (p. 125) reveals that the only system-wide difference between Middle English and Early Modern English is the addition of phonemic /ŋ/ and /ž/ to the EMnE inventory.

The specific origins of /ŋ/ and /ž/ will be discussed below; we will note here only that both could be accommodated easily because both filled gaps in the system. The addition of /ŋ/ gave three nasals parallel to the three sets of stops. That is, for the stops /p/ and /b/, there was the homorganic nasal /m/; for /t/ and /d/ the homorganic nasal /n/; and now, for /k/ and /g/, the homorganic nasal /ŋ/. Prior to the addition of /ž/, there had been the pairs of voiceless and voiced fricatives /f/ ~ /v/; /θ/ ~ /ð/; and /s/ ~ /z/. Only /š/ had been without a corresponding voiced phoneme. The addition of /ž/ filled this gap.[1]

CHANGES IN DISTRIBUTION OF CONSONANTS

Although the only system-wide change in consonants between Middle English and Early Modern English was the addition of /ŋ/ and /ž/, numerous changes in the distribution of individual consonant phonemes occurred, some systemic, some only sporadic. Most of the systemic changes involved loss of consonants in particular environments, or, occasionally, the substitution of one consonant for another. The sporadic changes involved either substitution or spelling pronunciations (or both).

1. The postvocalic allophones of /h/, [ç] and [x], disappeared in most dialects during the course of EMnE, though [x] has survived in Scots until PDE. With some variation due to dialect mixture, [ç] and [x] usually disappeared completely before /t/ (*sight, straight, caught,* for example). In final position, they were either lost completely (*sigh, although,* for example) or became /f/ (*tough, laugh, cough*). In either position, the total loss of [x] or [ç] lengthened a preceding short vowel; hence ME [sɪçt] 'sight', EMnE [sit] (and ultimately PDE [saɪt] because of the Great Vowel Shift).

2. The consonant /l/ was lost after low back vowels and before labial or velar consonants (*half, palm, folk, talk*), but not after other vowels (*film, silk, hulk*) or before dental or palatal consonants (*salt, bolt, Walsh*).

3. The consonant /t/ and, to a lesser extent, /d/ tended to drop in consonant clusters involving /s/. Hence the normal PDE pronunciation of such words as *castle, hasten, wrestle* (without /t/) and *handsome* and *landscape* (without /d/). Sometimes these losses were of a /t/ that had itself been an unetymological intrusive /t/ in ME (*listen, hustle*). The loss of /t/ and /d/ was also, at least in some dialects, widespread in final position after another consonant. Colonial American records, for example, are full of such forms as *par, wes,* and *adjormen* (for *part, west,* and *adjournment*), and *lan, Arnol,* and *pown* (for *land, Arnold,* and *pound*).

4. Probably in the late seventeenth century, /g/ and /k/ were lost in initial position before /n/, as in *gnaw, gnome, know,* and *knight.* During the eighteenth century, /w/ was lost before /r/ in initial position (*wrong, wrinkle, wrist*).

5. During OE and ME, the combination *ng* had been pronounced [ŋg], with the [ŋ] being merely the allophone of /n/ that appeared before /k/ or /g/. During EMnE, the /g/ was lost when the combination appeared in final position. This loss made [ŋ] phonemic, because it now contrasted with /n/ in final position, as in *sin* versus *sing.* In some dialects at least, however, a final unstressed /ŋ/ tended to become /n/, a phenomenon commonly though erroneously called "*g*-dropping." In many dialects, the /ŋ/ has been replaced today under the influence of spelling, but the /n/ pronunciation during EMnE is attested by the high frequency of such semiliterate spellings as *tacklin, stockens,* and *shilin* (for *tackling, stockings,* and *shilling*) and even of reverse spellings like *garding, muzling,* and *ruinge* for *garden, muslin,* and *ruin.*

---

[1] The phoneme /h/ is also a fricative and does not have a phonemic voiced counterpart. However, /h/ is anomalous in so many ways that it really is not a proper member of the set of fricatives in English.

The combination of the tendency for final unstressed /ŋ/ to become /n/ and the tendency for /t/ and /d/ to be lost after /n/ explains such otherwise inexplicable EMnE misspellings as *behing* and *bearind* for *behind* and *bearing*. These words were pronounced [bihain] and [bɛrɪn]. The writers, however, knew that many such words were properly spelled with an additional consonant at the end. In these cases, the writers simply guessed wrong and used *g* instead of *d* in *behind* and *d* instead of *g* in *bearing*.

6. The loss of /r/ before /s/ had begun as early as ME. By EMnE, its loss had extended to other positions, at least in some dialects. By the late seventeenth and early eighteenth centuries, semiliterate spellings like *quater*, *Mach*, and *brothe* (for *quarter*, *March*, and *brother*) and reverse spellings like *curtlass* and *Marthere* (for *cutlass* and *Martha*) reveal that it was regularly dropped in unstressed positions and even in stressed positions after back vowels. During the eighteenth century, the loss of /r/ before a consonant or finally became general in the standard language in England (though not in all dialects, most notably Scots). In America, *r*-lessness prevailed along the Atlantic seaboard areas with close ties to England, but not in the more inland settlements, a pattern that survives to the present day.

7. As was noted in Chapter 6, unstressed vowels were reduced to /ɪ/ or /ə/ during ME. This process continued during most of the EMnE period; contemporary spellings like *tenner*, *venter*, and *pecular* (for *tenure*, *venture*, *peculiar*) suggest how far it had progressed. But also during EMnE, a tendency arose to develop the palatal semivowel /j/ before an unstressed vowel in medial position *after* the major stress. Thereafter, words like *tenure* and *peculiar*, formerly pronounced /ténər/ and /pəkjúlər/, became /ténjər/ and /pəkjúljər/.[2] However, if the preceding consonant was /s/, /z/, /t/, or /d/, a further change took place whereby the consonant fused with the following /j/ to produce a palatal fricative or affricate.

/sj/	> /š/	as in *nation, pressure, ocean*
/zj/	> /ž/	as in *seizure, pleasure, usual, vision*
/tj/	> /č/	as in *creature, ancient, lecture, fortune*
/dj/	> /ǰ/	as in *soldier, gradual, residual, grandeur*

This **assibilation** is the origin of the phoneme /ž/ in English. Once /ž/ had become phonemic, it could be extended to other positions, in particular, to newly introduced loanwords from French like *garage* and *beige* (though many speakers still use /ǰ/ and not /ž/ in such words).

Assibilation was not without exception, and dialectal differences remain to this day. For example, the noun *graduate* is frequently heard as /grǽdjuət/, especially in British English. Conversely, *immediately* is often pronounced with assibilation as /ɪmiǰətli/ in Britain, much less often so in American English. Further, the pronunciations of a number of words that once had assibilated consonants have reverted to their earlier forms, at least in standard English. Examples include *idiot*, *tedious*, and *Indian* (compare the old dialect spelling *Injun*).

8. In a relatively minor change, earlier English /d/ changed to /ð/ when it followed the major stress and preceded /r/. For example, OE *fæder*, *mōdor*, *slidrian*,

---

[2] The prepalatalization stage has left traces in such colloquial pronunciations as /fɪgər/ for *figure* and /partɪkələr/ for *particular*, or in the dialectal *critter* for *creature*.

gadrian, ME *widderen* became *father, mother, slither, gather*, and *wither*. This change did not occur in French loanwords (*modern, consider*), in the comparative suffix *-er* (*wider*), or in the agentive suffix (*reader*). In a kind of reverse change, earlier /ð/ often became /d/ after /r/ or before /l/: thus OE *morðor, byrðen, fiðele* and PDE *murder, burden, fiddle*. This latter change did not always occur, so we still have /ð/ in *farthing* and *further* (but the spelling *furder* for *further* is so frequent in the seventeenth century that some dialects must have undergone the change here too).

SPELLING PRONUNCIATIONS

In the course of EMnE, literacy became sufficiently widespread to cause a number of spelling pronunciations. For instance, a number of loanwords from French and Latin used *th* to spell /t/. Because *th* was the normal English spelling for /θ/, English speakers altered their pronunciations in such words to /θ/. Examples include *anthem, throne, author*, and *orthography*. The process extended even to native words in which *t* and *h* had come together as the result of compounding; hence *Gotham, Wrentham*, and *Waltham*, all originally compounds with the second element *-ham* (as if today we were to pronounce *courthouse* as /kɔrθaus/). The change was even more common in America than in Britain: The British still pronounce the name *Anthony* with a /t/, but speakers of American English have /θ/. As we noted earlier, the *Thames* River in England is /tɛmz/, but in Connecticut it is the /θemz/.

Middle English had borrowed many words from French or Latin that were spelled with an unpronounced initial *h*. By spelling pronunciation almost all of these loans came to be pronounced with /h/ during EMnE (for example, *habit, hectic, history, horror, human*). *Hour, honor*, and *heir* escaped this almost universal trend (but *heritage*, from the same ultimate root as *heir*, acquired /h/). In British English *herb* also has /h/, but in American English it does not.

Knowledge of Latin roots caused the unhistorical introduction of *l* into the spelling of loans that had entered English in a French form without the *l*. Again, the influence of spelling led to the pronunciation of the *l*. Examples include *fault, assault, falcon, vault* (ME and Old French *faute, assaut, faucon, vaute*; Vulgar Latin *fallita, assaltus, falcō, volūtum*). Among the numerous other words respelled under Latin influence and then repronounced during EMnE are *adventure, admiral, perfect*, and *baptism* (ME *aventure, amiral, perfit, bapteme*).

Spelling pronunciations did not, however, always prevail. For instance, despite the respelling of the French loans *receite, dette*, and *doute* as *receipt, debt*, and *doubt* under the influence of Latin *receptus, dēbitus*, and *dubitāre*, English speakers have thus far resisted pronouncing the unhistorical *p* and *b* in these words.

Vowels

The changes in English consonants during EMnE were relatively minor. The two new phonemes (/ŋ/ and /ž/) both filled preexisting gaps, so they actually helped to stabilize the system. Otherwise, there were only slight readjustments in the distribution of some consonants. However, the vocalic system of English underwent a greater change than at any other time in the history of the language. The short vowels experienced a number of adjustments, but the major activity concerned the ME long vowels. The ultimate result of the sweeping sound change known as the Great Vowel Shift (GVS) was the loss of length as a distinctive feature of English vowels and hence a restructuring of the entire system, a

Figure 7.4   EMnE Development of ME Vowels

Short Vowels		Long Vowels (GVS)		Diphthongs	
ME	*EMnE*	*ME*	*EMnE*	*ME*	*EMnE*
ɪ	ɪ	ī	ɑi	iu	u, ju
ɛ	ɛ	ē	i	ɛu	u, ju
ə	ə	ɛ̄ → ē →	i, e	ɑu	ɔ
ɑ	æ, ɑ	ā → ɛ̄ →	e	ɔu	o
ʊ	ə, ʊ	ū	ɑu	æi	e
ɔ	ɔ, ɑ, æ	ō	u	ui	ɔi
		ɔ̄	o	ɔi	ɔi

phonological change as far-reaching in its effects as the prehistoric consonant change described by Grimm's and Verner's Laws.

Although the vowel changes of EMnE are fairly well understood, dating them precisely is difficult because the standardization of English spelling early in EMnE meant that future changes were usually not reflected in spelling. In addition, English has always had fewer vowel graphemes than phonemes (and it lost one of these graphemes, ⟨æ⟩, early in ME). Even when misspellings make us suspect that a change has taken place, we normally cannot be sure exactly what the misspelling represents.

Before launching into the details of the Great Vowel Shift, let us summarize the major changes between Middle English and Early Modern English. Figure 7.4 presents the vowel picture for the standard language at the end of Middle English. It does not include minor conditioned or sporadic changes, nor does it reflect the varying developments of different dialects.

A comparison of the EMnE columns of Figure 7.4 with Figures 2.3 and 2.4 (pp. 25 and 26) reveals that the PDE vowel inventory was achieved by the end of the EMnE period, although there have been some allophonic and distributional changes since 1800, and although a number of dialects have developed somewhat differently.

THE GREAT VOWEL SHIFT

Under the sound change known as the Great Vowel Shift (GVS), all the ME long vowels came to be pronounced in a higher position. Those that were already in the highest position "fell off the top" and became diphthongs. Short vowels were not affected. Figure 7.5 illustrates the ME long vowels, the changes involved in the GVS, and the resulting configuration.

Precise dating of the GVS is impossible and, in any case, varied from dialect to dialect. In general, the process began in late ME and was pretty much over by the end of the sixteenth century, although the change of ME /ɛ̄/ to /i/ was not complete in standard English until the eighteenth century (and is not uniformly complete in all dialects to this day).

Scholars do not agree on all the details, but it is likely that at least some of the changes took several generations to reach their final stage. For example, by Shakespeare's day, ME [ī] and [ū] were probably pronounced [əi] and [əu], respectively. The earliest changes must have been with the ME high vowels [ī] and

Figure 7.5   The Great Vowel Shift

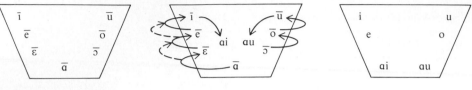

ME Long Vowels   The Great Vowel Shift   Result of the Great Vowel Shift

[ū]; after they had undergone a clearly perceptible shift, the next highest vowels, [ē] and [ō], were free to move into the positions formerly held by ME [ī] and [ū]. In other words, if ME [ē] had changed *before* ME [ī], it would have coalesced with ME [ī], and ME words with [ī] and with [ē] would both be pronounced with [ai] today. This merger did not occur: ME *bite* 'bite' and *bete* 'beet' are still distinct in PDE.

Note that we have not indicated vowel length by a macron in the right-hand diagram in Figure 7.5. This omission is intentional. After the GVS, vowel length was no longer phonemic in English, and only qualitative differences distinguished most English vowels in most dialects. The long/short distinction had been eroding since ME, when length became tied to syllable structure in many words and hence was often redundant (see pp. 130–33). But the "pairing" of long and short vowels was still relatively easy in ME because they were qualitatively similar. However, the GVS destroyed this match (even though it was often retained in spelling). That is, for the ME speakers, the vowels of *bit* [bɪt] and *bite* [bīt] were still clearly similar, if not identical, except for length. After the GVS, these words were [bɪt] and [bait]; the phonological relationship between the two vowels had been destroyed. Of course, PDE vowels do vary in their actual phonetic length—the vowel of *bee* is much longer than the vowel of *beet*—but the distinction today is no longer phonemic. It is allophonic only, conditioned by the environment of the vowel.

Because of dialectal variation followed by dialect mixture, there are a few apparent exceptions to the GVS, most of them concerning ME [ɛ̄] and [ō]. ME [ɛ̄] normally became [i], but in some words it apparently shortened prior to the GVS; hence such words as *threat, head, death*, and *deaf* still have [ɛ] today. (*Cheat, plead, wreath, leaf*, and so on show the regular development of ME [ɛ̄].) In a few other words, ME [ɛ̄] stopped at [ē] and did not become [i]; examples include *break, yea, steak, great*. The situation was still undergoing change in late EMnE, as the following couplet from Alexander Pope's *Rape of the Lock* illustrates; Pope would have pronounced *tea* as [te].

> Soft yielding minds to water glide away,
> And sip, with Nymphs, their elemental tea. (ll. 61–62)

There is even greater fluctuation among words with ME [ō]. Many predictably became [u], for example, *boot, loose, mood, pool, soon*. Others then shortened from [u] to [ʊ]; they include *foot, good, hook*, and *wood*. In a few cases, this [ʊ] further unrounded to [ə], as in *flood* and *blood*. Pope's rhyming of *good* and *blood* in these lines from "Elegy to the Memory of an Unfortunate Lady" (1717) shows that the vowel of *blood* had not yet unrounded to [ə].

> But thou, false guardian of a charge too good,
> Thou, mean deserter of thy brother's blood! (ll. 29–30)

This indecisive state of affairs has persisted into PDE for a number of words whose pronunciation varies between [u] and [ʊ], even within the same dialectal area. Examples include *root, hoop, soot, roof, room.*

DEVELOPMENT OF SHORT VOWELS
EMnE saw no sweeping, systemic changes in ME short vowels parallel to the GVS of ME long vowels. Nonetheless, all the ME short vowels were involved in changes of one kind or another, some more limited or temporary than others.

1. All remaining final unstressed -*e*'s (=[ə]) from ME were lost during EMnE, including those of noun plurals and third-person present indicative singular past-tense endings, except in the environments where they remain to this day as [ə] or [ɪ] (as in the final vowels of *judges, passes, wanted*).
2. In general, ME /ɑ/, if indeed it had been /ɑ/ and not /æ/, became /æ/ in EMnE. However, in the seventeenth century, this /æ/ reverted to /ɑ/ before /r/, as in *harm, scarf, hard, park.* During the eighteenth century, /æ/ became /ɑ/ before voiceless fricatives in the standard English of southern England and in the New England dialects of areas most closely tied to the mother country. In these dialects, /ɑ/ remains to this day in this environment (*staff, class, path, fast, half*). The change, however, never occurred in the first place if the fricative was followed by another vowel (*classical, passage*).
   Before /l/, /ɑ/ became /ɔ/ instead of /æ/ (*all, fall, walk, salt, chalk, halt*). In many dialects, ME /ɑ/ also became /ɔ/ after /w/ (*want, wash, reward, swan, quart*). This change did not occur if the vowel preceded a velar consonant (*wax, quack, wag, wangle, swagger, twang*).
3. ME /u/ centered and unrounded to /ə/ in most environments (*run, mud, gull, cut, hum, cup*). The unrounding did not occur if /u/ was "protected" by a preceding labial consonant and followed by /l/, /š/, or /č/ (*full, pull, bull, push, bush, butcher*). There were some exceptions, and dialectal variation remains to this day in the pronunciation of such words as *bulky, bulge,* and *shrub.*
4. Over the long course, English /ɪ/ and /ɛ/ have remained remarkably stable. Nevertheless, the two sounds seem to have been confused in many dialects during EMnE, a confusion revealed in hundreds of semiliterate spellings such as *rever, skellet, wedth, tell,* and *derect* (for *river, skillet, width, till,* and *direct*). Conversely, we find spellings like *niver, Nigro, dwilling, divell,* and *chist* (for *never, Negro, dwelling, devil,* and *chest*). Most of these vowels have since reverted to their original values, but the colloquial pronunciations *pritty, git,* and *nigger* still reflect the EMnE situation.
   Also during EMnE, /ɛ/ followed by a nasal regularly and permanently changed to /ɪ/ in many words. Examples include *wing, single, hinge, fringe, mingle,* and *nimble* (ME *wenge, sengle, heng, frenge, mengle(n), nem(b)yl*). This tendency of a following nasal to raise /ɛ/ to /ɪ/ dates to prehistoric times in Germanic languages, and continues to the present day. In many contemporary American dialects, especially in the southern areas of the country, words like *pen, sense,* and *them* are pronounced with /ɪ/.
5. Before /l/, ME /ɔ/ generally became /o/ (*bolt, cold, old, bowl, hold*). In other environments, ME /ɔ/ was retained in standard British English and some American dialects. However, a dialectal variant in Britain that was to become extensively used in the United States was /ɑ/ for ME /ɔ/. Examples are numerous including *hot, rock, pocket, yonder, top,* and *shot.* Dialect mixture in

the United States is so widespread that the same speaker may have, say, /ɑ/ in *frog* and /ɔ/ in *log*.

THE INFLUENCE OF A FOLLOWING /r/

In general, a following /r/ tends to lower vowels. During late ME and continuing throughout EMnE, there was a widespread lowering of /ɛr/ to /ar/. In some instances, the lowering was permanent, and the words involved were eventually respelled to reflect the change. For example, modern *far, star, dark, farm,* and *barn* were *fer, sterre, derk, ferme,* and *bern* in Middle English. In most cases, however, the pronunciation later reverted to /ɛr/ (which then became /ər/); it did so, for example, in the words often spelled *sarvant, sarmon, sartain, vardict,* and *starling* in EMnE (PDE *servant, sermon, certain, verdict, sterling*). Occasionally, doublets have survived: *clerk/Clark; vermin/varmint; person/parson;* and *university/varsity*. In the case of *sergeant,* the spelling has not changed to reflect the /ar/ pronunciation.

Later than the lowering of /ɛr/ to /ar/, /ɪ/, /ɛ/, and /ʊ/ all lowered and centered to /ə/ before a following /r/; hence the present-day pronunciations of such words as *girl, dirty, her, fern, early, hurt,* and *curse*. This change is so recent that the various dialects of English do not reflect it in the same way. In particular, most Scots dialects still retain the original vowels in this position.

In many other words, a following /r/ blocked the GVS's raising or diphthongization of ME /ɛ̄/, /ō/, and /ū/ to /i/, /u/, and /aʊ/, respectively. Thus we find apparent exceptions to the GVS in such words as *wear, bear, floor, sword, course,* and *court*. Again there is still a fair amount of dialectal variation in words like *poor, tour,* and *moor*.

DEVELOPMENT OF DIPHTHONGS

At all periods in the history of English, the tendency has existed for diphthongs to "smooth," that is, to become simple vowels, and for new diphthongs to arise. The GVS provided EMnE with a number of new diphthongs, but at the same time almost all the ME diphthongs smoothed. As Figure 7.4 shows, ME probably had seven diphthongs: /iu/, /ɛu/, /aʊ/, /ɔu/, /æi/, /ʊi/, and /ɔi/. All but /ʊi/ and /ɔi/ became simple vowels, and these two coalesced into the single diphthong /ɔi/.

1. ME /iu/ and /ɛu/. By late ME, /iu/ and /ɛu/ had fallen together as /iu/. Then, perhaps in the sixteenth centrury, this /iu/ became /ju/ and has remained /ju/ in scores of words to the present day. Examples include *pure, mute, hew, cute, beauty, accuse,* and *pewter*. After a labial consonant, /ju/ almost always remains, but after other consonants, many dialects have simplified /ju/ to /u/. Among the words that show dialectal variation in PDE are *new, fruit, glue, shrew, rude, duty,* and *lute*.
2. ME /aʊ/. ME /aʊ/ became /ɔ/ in EMnE. A few examples are *cause, hawk, claw, autumn,* and *aught*. Before /l/ plus a labial consonant, however, ME /aʊ/ became /ɑ/ or /æ/, as in *half, calf, calm, palm,* and /l/ was lost.
3. ME /ɔu/. ME /ɔu/ became EMnE /o/, as in *know, blow, soul,* and *grow*. Note that this /o/ is actually diphthongized in most dialects of English today.
4. ME /æi/. ME /æi/ smoothed to EMnE /e/; examples include *day, pay, raise, stake,* and *eight*. Like /o/, /e/ is usually somewhat diphthongized in PDE.
5. ME /ʊi/ and /ɔi/. ME had acquired the two diphthongs /ʊi/ and /ɔi/ in French loanwords. These diphthongs coalesced as /ɔi/ in most dialects by EMnE, but remained as /əi/ (from earlier /ɔi/) and /ɔi/ (from earlier /ʊi/) in some dialects

into the PDE period. In the following lines from the Earl of Rochester's "A Satire Against Mankind" (1675), the vowel of both *design* and *join* was probably [əi].

> Look to the bottom of his vast design
> Wherein Man's wisdom, power, and glory join; (ll. 153–54)

Examples of earlier /ui/ are *toil*, *boil*, *poison*, *soil*, and *destroy*; from earlier /ɔi/ are *joy*, *avoid*, *royal*, *boy*, and *choice*.

Prosody

So far as we can tell, the clause and sentence rhythms of English have remained essentially the same from Old English times on. Questions to which an answer of "yes" or "no" is expected have risen in pitch at the end, statements have ended with a falling pitch, and so forth. Furthermore, the general tendency to stress the first syllable of words has always characterized English. We have no reason to believe that Early Modern English differed significantly from Present-Day English in these respects.

Nonetheless, the evidence of poetry and of occasional statements by contemporary speakers indicates that there were a number of minor differences between the prosody of EMnE and that of PDE. The most obvious is variation in the placement of the major stress of polysyllabic words, especially loanwords from French or Latin. For example, an initial stress (as in PDE) on *sinister* in the following line from Shakespeare's *Henry V* results in a rough scansion, but stressing the second syllable makes it a smooth line.

> 'Tis nó siníster nór no áwkward cláim

Similarly, Shakespeare seems to have had the major stress on the second syllable of words such as *opportune*, *welcome*, and *contract* (as noun). On the other hand, Shakespeare sometimes has the major stress on the first syllable of words that today usually have it on the second syllable; examples include *cement*, *concealed*, *humane*, and *mature*. The evidence of poetry also suggests that secondary stresses often occurred on syllables that today have reduced stress. In this respect, EMnE perhaps was more like American English today than like contemporary British English; compare British *sécretary* with American *sécretàry*, or, conversely, the Scots and Irish pronunciation *Lóndondèrry* (Northern Ireland) with American *Lóndonderry* (New Hampshire).

The Elizabethans seemingly accepted variant pronunciations of many more words than do English speakers today; for example, Shakespeare sometimes stressed *commendable* and *triumphing* on the first syllable, sometimes on the second. Such variation is explainable by the fact that it was during this period that English was in the process of developing the complex but automatic rules for stress placement of Latinate words and their derivatives that characterize the language today.

Some contractions appear in texts written prior to the EMnE period (such as OE *nelle* for *ne wille* 'not want'). However, it was not until EMnE that extensive patterns of contractions of pronouns, auxiliary verbs, and prepositions appear in writing. The rules for contracting in EMnE were not, however, those of PDE. In general, EMnE contracted forms tended to be **proclitic** (contracting the first word, as in *'tis*), whereas PDE contractions are **enclitic** (contracting the second word, as in *it's*). Therefore we find in Shakespeare such forms as *'twill* and *h'were* for *it will* and *he were*. Also unlike PDE was the contraction of prepositions with a following pronoun, as in *in's* 'in his' and *w'us* 'with us', and even three-part contractions like *i'th'eye* 'in the eye'. EMnE did have some enclitic contractions, such as *did't* and *don't* (for *did it* and *done it*), but this particular enclitic pattern has not survived into PDE. Conspicuously absent from Shakespearean English is the contraction of auxiliary verbs and a following *not* (as in PDE *isn't*, *can't*); this was not to appear until the seventeenth century, and was infrequent until the eighteenth century.

Early Modern English Graphics

Paradoxical though it may seem, the spelling patterns of PDE were established at the beginning of EMnE, but the graphemes (letters) themselves were not established in their current forms until well into the EMnE period. Figure 6.4 (p. 135) shows the English alphabet at the end of Middle English. Early in EMnE, the *yogh* (ȝ) was abandoned, being replaced by *gh*, *y*, or *s*. The thorn (*þ*) lasted somewhat longer. By the seventeenth century, however, it had become identical in shape to *y* and was used to represent /ð/ or /θ/ only in function words like *thou* and *that*, as illustrated in Figure 7.6, reproductions of printed lines from the First Folio of Shakespeare; the first passage is from *Henry IV, Part* 2 and the second is from *The Merry Wives of Windsor*.

As Figure 7.6 shows, *þ* was not universal even in words like *thou*; in line 5, *thou* is spelled with *th*. Actually, in the First Folio, *þ* is used primarily in abbreviations, to save space in the line. It appears chiefly in prose passages where the line extends to the right margin.

Figure 7.6 also reveals that the present-day practice of using *i* and *u* only as vowel symbols and *j* and *v* only as consonants was not yet established—this change

Figure 7.6 EMnE Graphic Forms

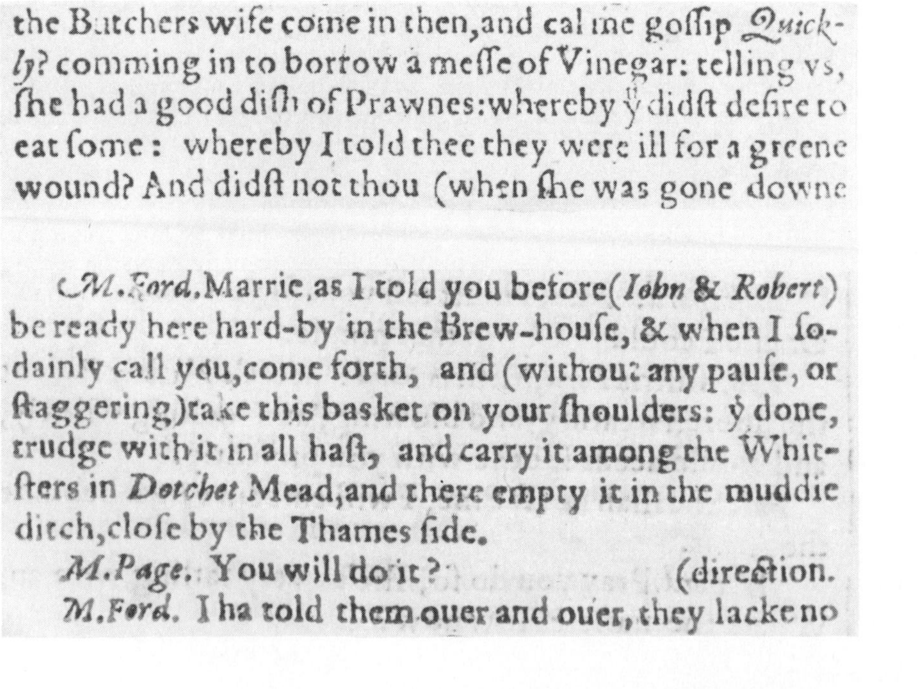
the Butchers wife come in then, and cal me goſſip *Quickly*? comming in to borrow a meſſe of Vinegar: telling vs, ſhe had a good diſh of Prawnes: whereby yͧ didſt deſire to eat ſome: whereby I told thee they were ill for a greene wound? And didſt not thou (when ſhe was gone downe

M.Ford. Marrie, as I told you before (*Iohn* & *Robert*) be ready here hard-by in the Brew-houſe, & when I ſodainly call you, come forth, and (without any pauſe, or ſtaggering) take this basket on your ſhoulders: yͭ done, trudge with it in all haſt, and carry it among the Whitſters in *Dotchet* Mead, and there empty it in the muddie ditch, cloſe by the Thames ſide.
M.Page. You will do it? (direction.
M.Ford. I ha told them ouer and ouer, they lacke no

occurred later in the seventeenth century. Prior to then, *j* was rarely used at all, and *i* represented both the vowel and the consonant /j/. Line 6 illustrates *i* in its consonant function (*Iohn*). During the same period, *v* stood for both vowel and consonant at the beginning of a word (*vs* and *Vinegar*, l. 2), and *u* for both vowel and consonant elsewhere (*muddie*, l. 11; *ouer*, l. 14).

Until the eighteenth century, "long *s*" (*messe*, l. 2, *desire*, l. 3, *close* and *side*, l. 12) was normally used everywhere except at the end of words (*vs*, l. 2, *was*, l. 5). However, even in the First Folio, "long *s*" can be seen giving way to the form used everywhere today; in the word *basket* (l. 9), the short *s* is used where long *s* would be expected.

Spelling and Punctuation

As we described earlier in this chapter, modern spelling patterns had been formulated in their essential details during late ME and early EMnE. (See pp. 200–204.) By the end of the seventeenth century, the principle of a fixed spelling for every word was firmly established for printed works, and, over the course of the following century, "personal" spelling followed suit.

As was mentioned earlier, during the sixteenth and early seventeenth centuries, knowledge of Latin roots was responsible for changing the spelling (though not the pronunciation) of a number of French loans into English. For example, ME *vitaille*, *rime*, and *endite(n)* were respelled as *victual(s)*, *rhyme*, and *indict*, respectively, under the influence of Latin *victualia*, *rhythmus*, and *indictus*. Sometimes the etymologies were false: even though it was a native English word, OE *īegland*, ME *ilond* was mistakenly assumed to have come from Latin *insula* or Old French *isle*, so it was respelled *island*. Compounding the confusion, ME *eile* was associated somehow with *isle* and respelled *aisle*, despite its actual origin in Latin *āla* 'wing'. By analogy with native words like *bright* and *light*, ME *delite* was respelled *delight* (etymologically, it goes back to Latin *delectare*).

During most of the EMnE period, capitalization remained, if not exactly random, at least haphazard. The first words of sentences were capitalized, as were proper nouns. However, common nouns were also often capitalized for no reason apparent to the modern eye. For instance, in Figure 7.6, the common nouns *Butchers*, *Vinegar*, *Prawnes*, and *Brew-house* are all capitalized, though the nouns *gossip*, *messe*, *dish*, *wound*, *pause*, and *basket* are not.

Punctuation during the EMnE period usually followed the models of Continental printers. During the sixteenth century, the comma replaced the virgule as the primary mark of internal punctuation in the sentence. The apostrophe was used for contractions (and more contractions appeared in print than is conventional today), but often not consistently. For example, Shakespeare's First Folio has both *Ile* and *I'le* for *I'll*; *ith* and *i'th* for *in the*. Past tense and past participle endings appear in the First Folio in both contracted and uncontracted spellings, frequently for no apparent metrical reason; *banished*, for instance, is spelled *banisht*, *banished*, and *banish'd*. The apostrophe was not used to mark possessives until late in EMnE; see *the Butchers wife* in line 1 of Figure 7.6. Nevertheless, by the end of EMnE, modern patterns of punctuation had been established, although eighteenth-century punctuation was usually much "heavier" than that of PDE, with the colon in particular being used much more often.

Handwriting

After the introduction of the printing press to England at the end of the ME period, books (and later, periodicals) were printed rather than handwritten. Nonetheless, the typewriter—not to mention the word processor—is very much a product of the PDE era, and many things that are normally typewritten today still were written in longhand during the EMnE period. These texts include legal documents, records of all kinds, authors' manuscripts of books, and business and personal letters. Clerks and amanuenses (secretaries) were expected to have a legible hand, even though nonprofessional handwriting was often as illegible and inelegant as it is today.

Figure 7.7 presents samples of English handwriting from three different dates during EMnE. (A) is a letter written by Thomas Cranmer on 2 November

Figure 7.7 Samples of EMnE Handwriting

(A)

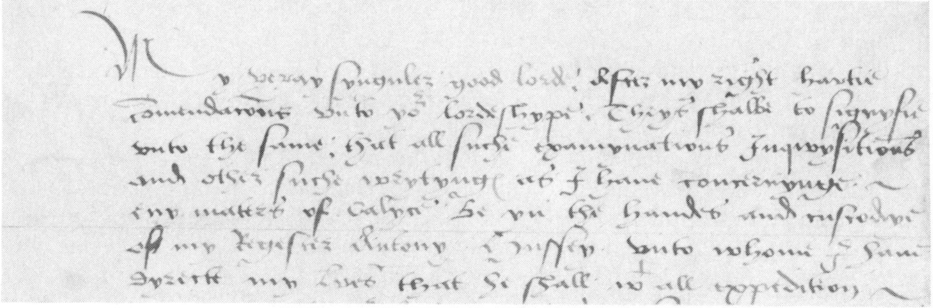

My veray synguler good lorde, After my right hartie Comendaçons unto yor lordeshype, Thiys shalbe to sygnyfie unto the same, that all suche examyna-tions Inquysitions and other suche wrytyngs as I haue concernynge any maters of Calyse be yn the hands and custodye of my Regester Antony Hussey unto whome I haue dyrecte by Lres that he shall w^t all expedition

(B)

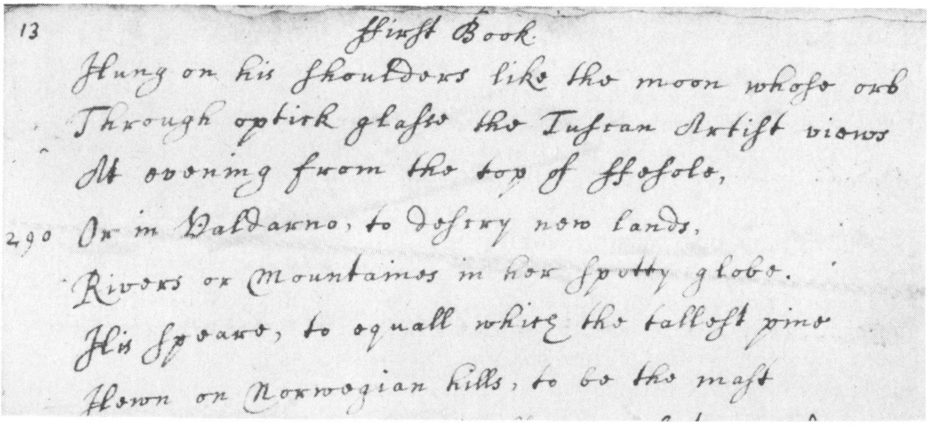

Hung on his shoulders like the moon whose orb
Through optick glasse the Tuscan Artist views
At evening from the top of Fesole,
Or in Valdarno, to descry new lands,
Rivers or Mountaines in her spotty globe.
His speare, to equall which the tallest pine
Hewn on Norwegian hills, to be the mast

(C)

We had yesterday a very crouded Club. St Asaph, Fox, Bourke, Althrop, and about sixteen more. And the talk was of Mrs Siddons. Can you talk skilfully of Mrs Siddons? I had nothing to say. There was talk of Cecilia,—and I did better.

1539. (B) is a page from the manuscript of John Milton's *Paradise Lost*, about 1665, probably written by an amanuensis because Milton himself was totally blind by this time. (C) is a personal letter written by Samuel Johnson and dated 11 December 1782. The steady progress toward a handwriting that is modern in overall appearance is obvious, but note that even Johnson still uses the long *s*.

Early Modern English Morphology

After the radical inflectional losses that characterized Middle English, so few inflections were left that, from about 1500 on, most of the "grammar" of English was carried by syntax rather than morphology. Indeed, by EMnE, it is hard to draw a sharp line between morphology and syntax. Of the inflections that remained at the end of ME, only two were lost during EMnE—the second-person singular pronoun and the corresponding second-person singular indicative endings of verbs. There were, however, a number of distributional changes within the inflectional categories.

Nouns

In all essentials, noun morphology in EMnE was the same as that of PDE. The distinction between singular and plural remained, but cases were reduced to two—common case and possessive (genitive) case. All traces of grammatical gender were gone, and biological gender prevailed.

EMnE observed the same mutated plurals that we have today (*mice, feet, teeth, men,* and so on). Particularly in the early part of the period, a few -*n* plurals remained, often side by side with -s plurals. For example, Shakespeare used *shoes* as the plural of *shoe* in one act of *Hamlet* but *shoon* in the next act. (The form *shoon*, however, appears in a song and is necessary for the rhyme.)

> two Provinciall Roses on my rac'd *Shooes* (3.2.277)

> How should I your true love know from another one?
> By his Cockle hat and staffe, and his Sandal *shoone* (4.5.25–26)

Other -*n* plurals to be found occasionally in EMnE texts include *housen, hosen, eyen,* and the still marginally familiar *kine* as a plural of *cow*.

Measure words after numbers often—but not invariably—had unmarked plurals throughout the EMnE period. To use Shakespearean examples again:

> but this our purpose now is twelve *month* old (1 H4 1.1.28)
> so hard that it seems the length of seven *year* (AYL 3.2.317)
> a man of fourscore *pound* a year (MM 2.1.123)
> digt himself four *yard* under the countermines (H5 3.2.62)

The neuter noun *kind* had had an unmarked plural in OE, and it frequently remained unmarked in EMnE (as it still often does today in speech):

> all the *kind* of the launces have this very fault (TGV 2.3.2)

Usage varied with the names of many animals; sometimes they took an -s plural, and sometimes an unmarked plural:

> but a team of *horse* shall not pluck that from me (TGV 3.1.267)
> presents me with a brace of *horses* (TNK 3.1.20)

> fowls have no feathers, and *fish* have no fin (ERR 3.1.79)
> canst thou catch any *fishes* then? (PER 2.1.66)

By EMnE, the -'s possessive for both singular and plural nouns was almost universal, although traces of OE uninflected genitives remained for some kinship terms and formerly feminine nouns. By the end of the EMnE period, these traces were restricted primarily to fixed expressions where the genitive relationship was no longer clearly perceived—*mother tongue, fatherland, ladyfinger, lady slipper*. In addition, the -'s possessive was often omitted in expressions where the genitive noun ended in a sibilant or the following noun began with one, such as *for posteritie sake, for peace sake*. Here, however, the difference between EMnE and PDE is only in the written language; speakers today do not lengthen the sibilant or add an extra [s] when they say such phrases, even though they do use the -'s in writing.

In one respect, the use of the possessive differed startlingly in EMnE from its use in PDE. Apparently people interpreted the final [s] (or [z] or [ɪz]) of the possessive nouns as a contraction of the possessive adjective *his* rather than what it historically is, an inflectional ending. Then, in writing, they would spell out the full possessive adjective. This misinterpretation appears earliest and most frequently with *his*, but spread to the other possessive adjectives by analogy. For example, the town records of colonial Rhode Island have such examples as

> John Browne *his* meaddow
> the said Daniell Williams *my* heirs
> Wallings & Abbott *there* up land
> Ann Harris *her* lot

Sometimes the same text, written by the same clerk, contains both the historically correct form and the form with the possessive adjective:

> his Mothers decease
> his deceased mother *her* will

The group genitive, that is, the addition of the possessive inflection to the end of the entire noun phrase instead of to the noun to which it logically belongs, is frequent in PDE, especially in speech (*a day or two's time, the Duke of Edinburgh's arrival*). The construction occurred in EMnE, but less often than today. Combined with the *his* possessive, it can be confusing to the modern reader, as in the following examples.

> his Brother Thomas Barnes who is deceased his son
> her said deceased husband who belonged & was an Jnhabitant of
>   Mashantatuck in Providence his Estate

Occasionally, the same phrase contains both the inflected genitive and the *his* genitive, or both the "logical" inflected genitive and the group genitive.

> after mine & my wifes her decease
> the Governors of Boston his letter

Adjectives

English adjectives had lost all their inflections except the comparative -*er* and the superlative -*est* by the end of ME, so there was little adjective morphology left to be changed by EMnE times. The rules for the use of the comparative and superlative, however, had not yet achieved their modern form. *More* and *most* were historically not comparative markers, but intensifiers (as they still can be in such expressions as *a most enjoyable evening*). In EMnE, this intensifying function was felt much more strongly; hence writers did not find it ungrammatical or pleonastic to use both a comparative adverb and -*er* or -*est* with the same adjective. Examples from Shakespeare include *in the calmest and most stillest night* and *against the envy of less happier lands*. Further, the rules for when to use the periphrastic comparative had not yet reached their PDE rigidity. Therefore Shakespeare could say *violentest* and *certainer* and also *more bold* and *the most brave*.

Pronouns

Though personal pronouns remain to this day the most heavily inflected of English word classes, there were still a number of changes in the pronominal system between the end of ME and the end of EMnE, both in the personal pronouns and in other types of pronouns.

PERSONAL PRONOUNS

One system-wide change in the personal pronouns during EMnE was the development of separate forms for possessive adjectives and possessive pronouns. In OE, the form *mīn*, for example, had been used both adjectivally and pronominally. In ME, *my* (or *mi*) began to appear as the adjective form used before a word beginning with a consonant, while *min* was used before words beginning with a vowel and as the absolute (or pronominal) form. In EMnE, *my* generalized as the adjective form in all environments, and *mine* became reserved for pronominal functions, the present distribution of the two. The use of *thy* and *thine* paralleled that of *my* and *mine* until the second-person singular pronoun itself dropped out of the language. By analogy with possessive nouns, the absolute forms *hers, ours, theirs,* and *yours* had appeared as early as ME. *His,* already ending in a sibilant, did not develop a separate pronominal form.

This left only *it* to be settled. In OE, ME, and the first part of EMnE, the possessive form of *it* had been *his,* identical to the masculine singular. By the late sixteenth century, however, the subject/object form *it* was also often used as a possessive, as in the 1611 King James Bible's *That which groweth of it owne accord ... thou shalt not reape.* At about the same time, the possessive *its* appeared. Though Shakespeare normally used *his* or *it* (as in *Rebellion in this land shall lose his sway*), he has several examples of *its* (but spelled with an apostrophe): *The Cradle-babe, Dying with mothers dugge betweene it's lips.* By the mid-seventeenth century, *its,* without an apostrophe, was the regular form. Note, however, that the absolute use of *its* is, although grammatical, still uncomfortable and relatively rare in PDE.

As was pointed out in Chapter 6, the originally plural forms *ye* and *you* were already being used as polite singular forms during Middle English. During the seventeenth century, the singular *thou/thee* forms dropped out completely. Thus, by the beginning of the eighteenth century, English had lost the singular-plural distinction in the second person; it survives today only in the forms *yourself/ yourselves.*

The earlier subject form *ye* gave way to *you* during the sixteenth century. Although *ye* continued to be spelled in texts for several decades afterwards, it appears as both subject and object pronoun and probably represents simply the reduced pronunciation of *you* [jə] still familiar in speech today.

DEMONSTRATIVE AND INTERROGATIVE PRONOUNS

The PDE system of demonstrative and interrogative pronouns was established in all its essentials during ME. However, EMnE still had a few minor differences from PDE. For example, although the plural form *those* appeared as early as late ME, the earlier plural *tho* remained in use until the mid-sixteenth century or so. *Whether* is today only a conjunction, but historically it is an interrogative pronoun meaning "which of two." It could still be used this way throughout the EMnE period, in both direct and indirect questions:

> *Whether* of them, think you, is the plainer pledge of ... Providence?
> It is indifferent to me ... *whether* of the two sit in Parliament.

RELATIVE PRONOUNS

English has been a long time in developing a stable system of relative pronouns —indeed, considering current disputes about the use of *which* to introduce restrictive clauses, some might argue that the system is still not stable. By the eighteenth century, the PDE pattern was established in all its essentials, but practice varied during the EMnE period itself.

As has always been true in English, *that* was the all-purpose and most widely used relative pronoun. During EMnE, it could have a human or a nonhuman referent, and it often was used to introduce nonrestrictive as well as restrictive clauses ("Another error, *that* hath also some affinity with the former, is a conceit ..." [Bacon, 1625]). Frequently, *that* was combined with *which* to form a compound relative in constructions where we would use only one or the other today ("God's ordinary mercy, *that which* he exhibits to all" [Donne, 1624]).

Which first appeared as a relative pronoun during Middle English and was used both by itself and in compounds during EMnE. In addition to *that which*, the compound *the which* was also common. *Which* could have animate as well as inanimate referents (for example, the King James Bible's "Our Father *which* art in heaven").

Although *who* appeared as a relative occasionally in late ME, it did not become frequent until the EMnE period, and even then it was rare before restrictive clauses. On the other hand, in constructions in which the relative clause was embedded within the main clause, simple *who* could serve as the subject of both clauses ("*Who* steals my purse steals trash"). Today we use a personal pronoun followed by *who* in such constructions ("*He who* steals my purse steals trash").

In addition to *who, that,* and *which, as* was fairly common as a relative in EMnE. A typical example is "all the goods *as* was brought to our view." Though *as* is still sometimes used as a relative pronoun today, it is of course considered substandard.

Complete omission of the relative pronoun, even when it would have been subject of the relative clause, was still acceptable. For example, Shakespeare could write "I have a brother is condemn'd to die."

A final difference between EMnE and PDE worth noting is the frequent redundant use of a subject pronoun after a relative clause. This usage was especially common if the relative clause was lengthy, as in the following example from George Puttenham (1589):

> Others *who* more delighted to write songs or ballads of pleasure to be sung with the voice and to the harp, lute, or citheron, and such other musical instruments, *they* were called melodious poets....

REFLEXIVE PRONOUNS

Forming reflexive pronouns by combining *-self* with the personal pronouns had begun in ME. The construction became more frequent in EMnE, but the older practice of using the simple object form of the pronoun as a reflexive also continued throughout most of the period. The following examples from Shakespeare are typical.

> Get *thee* a good husband (AWW 1.1)
> thou does *thyself* a pleasure (OTH 1.3.369)
> I will shelter *me* heere (Wives 5.5)
> if I drown *myself* wittingly (HAM 5.1.18)

Although the compound reflexive has replaced the simple pronoun in standard PDE, the simple form still survives dialectally, especially as an indirect object. That the form is still recognized is illustrated by the fact that a twentieth-century popular song could contain the line "I'm gonna buy *me* a paper doll to call my own."

Even as *-self* forms were being fixed as the normal reflexives, however, the use of reflexive pronouns in general was decreasing in the language. Verbs that had formerly been unvaryingly transitive, taking a reflexive pronoun when the direct object was the same as the subject, came to be used both transitively and intransitively. Among such verbs that Shakespeare often used reflexively were *complain, repent, fear, repose,* and *advise.* However, as the third of the following quotations illustrates, the reflexive object was not obligatory (and eventually would never be used).

> to all the host of heaven I complain *me* (LUC 598)
> where then, alas, may I complain *myself*? (R2 1.2.42)
> to whom should I complain? (MM 2.4.171)

Self was originally an independent pronoun in English and could be used as subject as well as object. This usage was still acceptable in EMnE. (In the second example below, note also that *him* is used as a reflexive pronoun.)

> because *myself* do want my servants' fortune (TGV 3.1.147)
> he commends him to your noble *self* (R3 3.2.8)

INDEFINITE PRONOUNS

The indefinite pronouns of EMnE are for the most part those still familiar to us today. One difference is that, whereas in PDE *every* is used only as a pronominal adjective meaning "all" or "each," in EMnE it could also be used as an independent pronoun meaning either "all" or "each of two":

> If *every* of your wishes had a womb (A&C, 1.2.38)
> There be two sortes of Blites . . . and *every* of them is diuided
>   againe into two kindes.

Other without a pluralizing *-s* could be used in EMnE as both singular and plural pronoun ("The best ground work whereon to build both the *other*"). In PDE, the pronominal adjective *some* can modify singular, plural, or uncountable nouns, but as an indefinite pronoun, it cannot refer to a singular, countable noun; in EMnE this was still possible: "*Some* will blushe that readeth this, if *he* be bitten."

In PDE, the compound *somewhat* is only an adverb; *something* is the corresponding pronoun. In EMnE, both *somewhat* and *something* were used both as adverbs and as pronouns:

Pronoun	this gentleman told *somewhat* of my tale (MM 5.1.84)
	I'll give you *something* else (TRO 5.2.86)
Adverb	he's *somewhat* bigger than the knight he spoke of (TNK 4.2.94)
	he's *something* stained with grief (TEM 1.2.415)

In general, then, the use of indefinite pronouns in EMnE was less rigid than it is in PDE.

Verbs

The most significant changes in verbs between ME and the end of EMnE involved the development of verb phrases and hence are really more a question of syntax than of morphology. Nonetheless, EMnE saw the continuation of a number of processes that had been going on since OE times, processes such as the change of strong verbs to weak, the further reduction of verbal inflections, and the gradual decline in the use of the subjunctive.

STRONG VERBS

By the end of the EMnE period, the division of English verbs into strong and weak categories was no longer a viable one. The majority of OE strong verbs had disappeared, become weak, or lost separate past and past participle forms. Further, sound changes in weak verbs during ME had created irregularities in many weak verbs (for example, *keep/kept*). From EMnE on, it is really more reasonable to speak of regular and irregular verbs than of strong and weak verbs.

As can be seen by the present-day fluctuation between, say, *throve* and *thrived* as the past tense of *thrive*, strong verbs do not become weak all at once. Instead, alternate strong and weak forms are used together for decades or even centuries. EMnE seems to have been a time when alternate forms for many verbs were acceptable. For instance, seventeenth- and eighteenth-century documents show such variants in past participle forms as *gave/given*, *hald/holden*, *wrott/ wratten/written*, *shewed/shewn*, *drank/drunk*, and *chose/chosen*.

Another general tendency of the period was the collapse of the distinction between the past tense and the past participle, with one vowel characterizing both forms, as in *cling/clung/clung* or *shine/shone/shone*. Perhaps one factor encouraging this coalescence was the existence of a rather large number of (weak) irregular verbs with vowel changes but a single form for preterite and past participle, verbs like *hear/heard/heard* and *sleep/slept/slept*.

Despite fluctuation and indecision, a score or more of earlier strong verbs became unambiguously weak during EMnE. Among these are *brew*, *writhe*, *creep*, *seethe*, *yield*, *carve*, *reap*, *wash*, *laugh*, *flow*, *starve*, and *knead*. In some instances, earlier strong past participles have survived as adjectives, *molten* and *sodden*, for example.

WEAK VERBS

By the end of ME, weak verbs had become the "regular" verbs of English, and almost any new verb entering the language would follow this paradigm. Nonetheless, at least three formerly weak verbs did become strong during the period: *dig*, *spit*, and *stick*. On the other hand, some weak verbs that had had irregularities in their paradigm due to earlier sound changes were regularized by analogy. Examples include *work*, whose earlier preterite and past participle survive today only as an adjective (*wrought iron*). Earlier *kemb* gave way to *comb*, formed from the noun; again, the former participle survives adjectivally in *unkempt*.

A general tendency during the period was for Latinate loans ending in [t] (for example, *situate*, *convict*, *degenerate*, *contract*) to take no ending at all in the past participle. This tendency was probably partly the result of analogy with Latin past participles, but it also had a parallel in native verbs like *hit* and *set*.[3]

Middle English had seen a great attrition in the number of verb inflections and, at the same time, a wide variety of dialectal variants in the surviving inflections. By the end of EMnE, the total number of inflections had been reduced to its PDE state, and the few remaining ones had become standardized across the language. During EMnE, the last vestiges of the *-n* ending on infinitives disappeared, as did the present indicative plural endings *-n* or *-th*. The present participle suffix *-ing* became universal in all dialects. The second-person singular present indicative ending *-(e)st* (or sometimes *-s*) survived intact until the category itself was lost—that is, until *you* supplanted *thou*.

The printed editions of Shakespeare's works show both *-s* and *-th* as the third-person singular present indicative; sometimes the two appear in a single line,

---

[3] The process of reducing past and past participle endings of verbs ending in [t] is still going on in English. Most speakers accept either *knit* or *knitted*, for example. In my own speech, I distinguish between past *fit* 'conformed in size or shape, was suitable' and *fitted* 'altered to make conform'.

as in *Macbeth* 1.3.79: "The Earth *hath* bubbles, as the Water *ha's.*" Nevertheless, although *-th* was still being written as the third-person singular ending as late as the eighteenth century, the *-s* ending was universal in speech from the seventeenth century on. A number of writers of the period comment on this written archaism.

OTHER VERBS

The anomalous verbs *be*, *do*, and *go* had essentially taken on their modern forms by the end of ME, and there has been little change in them since. During EMnE, *went* completely supplanted *yede* as the past tense of *go*, and *gone* replaced *yeden* as the past participle. For the verb *to be*, *are* became the standard present plural indicative form, though the alternate *be* was possible throughout the period (and survives dialectally to the present day).

The preterite-present verbs (or modal auxiliaries, as they can be called now) have historically been unstable, as is attested by their origin as verbs whose past tenses came to be used as present tenses (see p. 89). EMnE was a period of particularly great changes in their form, function, and meaning. First, the membership of the class of modal auxiliaries continued to decline. OE *unnan* 'to grant' and *(ge)munan* 'to remember' had been lost in ME. During EMnE, OE *þurfan* 'to need' and *dugan* 'to avail' were totally lost, and *witan* 'to know' survived only dialectally and in such archaic expressions as "God wot." Of the surviving modals, *couthe*, the earlier past tense of *can*, gave way to *could*. The present *mote* was lost entirely, and the earlier past tense *must* came to be used with present (or future) meaning. For *dare*, a regular weak past, *dared*, began to compete with the earlier past *durst*. By the end of EMnE, *might* had supplanted earlier *mought* as the past form of *may* in the standard language, though *mought* is found as late as the eighteenth century ("authority that they had or mought have" [1720]).

Even in OE, some of the preterite-present verbs had been defective, lacking some of the nonfinite forms (infinitive, past participle, and present participle). The attrition continued during ME, and, by the end of EMnE, most of these verbs lacked all nonfinite forms. At the same time, *will* moved into the category of modal auxiliaries. *Dare* began to acquire characteristics of a regular weak verb; it developed an infinitive form *to dare* and could be followed by a marked infinitive ("what we dared to say"). An originally regular weak verb, *need*, also acquired some of the characteristics of a modal, such as that of not being followed by a marked infinitive ("we need not say").

In PDE, the modal auxiliaries are always followed by an unmarked infinitive, which serves as the lexical verb. In EMnE, the modals were still sufficiently independent verbs to appear without a following infinitive when a verb of motion was implied and was clear from the context. Examples from Shakespeare include

> I *must* away this night toward Padua (MV 4.1.403)
> it *will* out at the casement (AYL 4.1.162)
> thou *shalt* to prison (LLL 1.2.158)

Most of the present-day meanings of the modal auxiliaries existed during EMnE, but older meanings also often survived. For example, *can* could still mean "know," but it was not used in its contemporary sense of "receive permission." *Shall* retained a sense of obligation throughout the period (as in the King James Bible's "Thou *shalt* not kill"), as it still does to some extent in legal language today.

Will implied prediction and was regularly used as a marker of the future, but also retained a strong sense of desire; *would* was still the regular past tense of *will* in this meaning.

As was noted in the preceding chapter, verb + adverb combinations (or two-part verbs, as they are often called) appeared at least occasionally in ME. By EMnE, they were extremely common, perhaps as common as they are in PDE. The following are but a tiny sample of the numerous instances to be found in Shakespeare.

> *shorten up* their sinews with aged cramps (TEM 4.1.269)
> have *worn* your eyes almost *out* in the service (MM 1.2.110)
> when she had writ it, and was *reading* it *over* (ADO 2.3.137)
> I were best to *cut* my left hand *off* (MV 5.1.177)

Uninflected Word Classes

PREPOSITIONS

As any foreign learner of the language can attest, the meanings and usages of English prepositions are highly specific and idiomatic. There are to this day numerous dialectal differences with respect to prepositional usage. For example, in one English-speaking area, people say "stand *in* line" and in another area "stand *on* line." One person is "sick *to* his stomach"; another is "sick *at* his stomach." Since the situation today is so fluid and unstable, it is no surprise that prepositional usage changed between ME and EMnE or that EMnE usage differs in many ways from that of PDE.

With the loss of most inflections that indicated grammatical relationships, ME developed or borrowed a large number of new prepositions. By the end of EMnE, a number of these had been lost again, including the French loans *maugre* and *sans*, but also the native or Old Norse *betwixt*, *forth*, *next*, *fro*, and *sith* (as in "*next* the bank" and "the matter depending *betwixt* them"). On the other hand, a number of new prepositions entered the language during the same period. For the most part, these were not entirely new words, but compounds consisting of existing prepositions plus nouns. Some examples of these new phrasal prepositions are *by means of*, *in spite of*, *because of*, *with regard to*, and *in accordance with*.

Modern readers of EMnE texts are not likely to be confused by the lack of such prepositions as *in connection with*. They are more likely to misinterpret sentences in which a familiar preposition is used in an unfamiliar way. There are many such differences between EMnE and PDE. Space limitations forbid even a summary of all these changes; a handful are illustrated below.

> I have no power *upon* [= over] you. (A&C 1.3.23)
> We were dead *of* [= from] sleep. (TEM 5.1.221)
> *without* [= outside] the seven mile line (1711)
> the highway *against* [= beside] John Whipples house (17th c.)
> What think you *on't* [= of] (HAM 1.1.55)

CONJUNCTIONS

The most common coordinating and subordinating conjunctions of ME continued to be used in EMnE, including *and*, *or*, *though*, *if*, and *that*. Earlier *ac* gave way completely to *but*, however. Many of the compound subordinating conjunctions with *that* which had arisen in ME (see p. 154) remained in EMnE: for example, *while that*, *after that*, *when that*, and *for that*. Though these were to be lost by PDE, other new compound subordinating conjunctions developed during EMnE, including *provided that*, *insofar as*, and the correlative *just as ... so*.

Even when conjunctions themselves have survived through the centuries, their meanings and usage have often shifted. For example, in EMnE, *and* and *and if* were often used where we would use *if* today. *But* appears where PDE would have *unless*, and *since* where PDE has *when*.

they may tell it *and* [= if] they please (Shelton, 1612)

A sheepe doth very often stray, / *And if* [= if] the Shepheard
be awhile away (2 GV 1.1.75)

He is of an yll inclinacion, *but* [= unless] he be forced (Lord Berners, 1534)

He can remember *since* [= when] we had not above three merchants ships of 300 tons. (Child, 1690)

In general, membership in the class of subordinating conjunctions and the meanings of these conjunctions have tended to be unstable throughout the history of English. Older ones are lost and new ones arise, even to the present day. For example, PDE British English has *immediately* (*that*) and *directly* (*that*) as subordinating conjunctions, while American English does not.

ADVERBS

As in PDE, the chief means of forming new adverbs from existing adjectives in EMnE was by adding the suffix *-ly*. However, plain adverbs, those without any suffix distinguishing them from adjectives, were still widely used and apparently completely acceptable, as is shown by such examples as *exceeding much worn*, *to be absolute dead*, *cannot possible come*, *this day grows wondrous hot*.

The wide assortment of intensifying adverbs used in ME was also characteristic of EMnE, though some of the earlier ones such as *fele* and *swithe* were lost. *Very* became more common as the period progressed, and *pretty* arose as an intensifier during the seventeenth century (*pretty near square*). Colloquial PDE uses as intensifiers many Latinate words originally referring to fear or great size. This practice began in EMnE, but was not as extensive as it is today. For example, Shakespeare says "I will be *horribly* in love with her" (ADO 2.3.235), and *wondrous* is common as an intensifier in his works. *Exceedingly* and *extraordinarily* also occur, though infrequently. *Terribly* still retains its etymological sense, as in "it strook mine ear most *terribly*." Shakespeare does not use *tremendously*, *enormously*, *frightfully*, *fearfully*, or *awfully* at all.

INTERJECTIONS

Most of the ME interjections mentioned in Chapter 6 continued to be used in EMnE. *Excuse me* as a general formula for apology arose during EMnE. *Please* was used, but still not in its reduced contemporary form; it appeared in phrases like *if it please you*, *please you*, or *please* followed by an infinitive as in *please to taste this*. The cry *hollo* was used to attract attention or to express exultation (somewhat similar to PDE *hey*!)—modern *hello* did not become a standard greeting formula until the PDE period.

Expressions of surprise included *what*! *O*!, *lo*!, and *hay*! The contemporary American English *wow*! first appeared in print in the sixteenth century, but was primarily Scottish during the EMnE period.

The most striking feature of EMnE interjections was the large number of euphemistic distortions of the name of the deity that appeared in the late sixteenth and especially the seventeenth century, when Puritan influence was strong in England. These exclamations include *sblood* (God's blood), *zounds* (God's wounds), *egad* (Ah, God), and a wide variety of compounds beginning with *od* (short for *God*): *odsbones, odslife, odstruth, od's pithkins* (God's pity), and even nonsensical formations like *od's haricots* (God's French beans) and *od's kilderkins* (God's little barrels).

Early Modern English Syntax

In most of the larger patterns, the syntax of Early Modern English is like that of Present-Day English. Indeed, it is so similar that the real differences may escape attention because they are minor and the context makes the meaning clear. Further, because EMnE texts are still widely read and familiar, their differing constructions are at least passively familiar to the modern reader. Quotations from Shakespeare and the King James Bible are so much part of our cultural heritage that we normally do not think of an expression like "They toil not, neither do they spin" as being ungrammatical in PDE. When contemporary writers or speakers use such earlier constructions for stylistic effect, we recognize them as "elevated" or "oratorical," but nonetheless completely intelligible and acceptable. Hence John F. Kennedy could say "Ask not what your country can do for you" without fear of being misinterpreted.

More elusive are the differences that are merely statistical, such as the greater use of the inflected subjunctive in EMnE. We still use the subjunctive today and under many of the same circumstances that it was used in EMnE, but we do not use it as often. Finally, a number of the ways in which EMnE syntax differs from that of PDE are negative ones, and we are much less likely to observe that something is *not* present than we are to notice that a strange construction *is* present in a text. For instance, few modern readers will be struck by the fact that EMnE texts do not contain extensive noun-adjunct constructions of the type *market data analysis sheets*.

Syntax Within Phrases

NOUN PHRASES

As was noted in Chapter 6, most of the word-order patterns of PDE noun phrases were firmly established in ME and have changed little since then. EMnE use of the definite and indefinite articles differed in a few minor ways from that of PDE, but these are really matters of idioms rather than basic structural differences. For example, John Donne could write *a child that is embalmed to make mummy*, where PDE would have an indefinite article before *mummy*. Conversely, the names of scholarly disciplines and of diseases often were preceded by the definite article, where we would use no article at all today. Thus Francis Bacon wrote *let him study the mathematics* and *bowling is good for the stone* [kidney stones]. (Compare PDE *the measles, the mumps, the flu*.)

Early Modern English also sometimes modified a noun with both a demonstrative adjective and a possessive adjective, where PDE would use a demonstrative and *of* + possessive pronoun. Where Bacon wrote *atheists will ever be talking of that their opinion*, we would write *of that opinion of theirs*. Possessive adjectives also occasionally followed attributive adjectives in a noun phrase, as in Shakespeare's *ah! poor our sex*.

The ME legacy of allowing single adjective modifiers (especially Latinate adjectives) to follow rather than precede their noun head continued in EMnE, though the frequency of such constructions decreased throughout the period. Some sixteenth-century examples include *faith invincible, God's promises infallible, a means convenient*, and *the line royal*.

The use of noun adjuncts, which had just begun in ME, increased greatly during the EMnE period; a few random eighteenth-century examples are *hackney coach, neighborhood broker, sugar almonds, merchant goods*. Nonetheless, the frequency of such constructions was lower than in PDE, and the appearance of more than one adjunct per noun head was still rare.

ADVERBIAL MODIFIERS

The syntax of adverbial modifiers in EMnE was in general similar to that of PDE, though a tendency remained throughout the period to place the adverbial before rather than after the words being modified. Especially common was the insertion of an adverbial modifier between an auxiliary verb and a past participle. The following examples are from the late seventeenth and early eighteenth centuries.

> is *again* come together
> the Councill have *to them* Granted Administration
> which he *behind him* left
> and was *by them* Examined

Double negatives, common in ME, became less common in EMnE, but still appeared and apparently were considered acceptable until at least the eighteenth century; the following two examples are from the late seventeenth century.

> they are *not* bound to stand to *no* determination
> *nor* that she *never* was married

VERB PHRASES

As was noted in Chapter 6, the modern system of compound verb phrases began, but was by no means fully developed, in Middle English. During EMnE, the system developed much further, although it still had not quite reached its PDE stage by the end of EMnE. The period had a full-fledged perfect tense, used in essentially the same way that the perfect is used today, although, particularly in the early part of EMnE, the auxiliary for intransitive verbs of motion was still *be* rather than *have*. By the sixteenth century, *have* was encroaching on the territory of *be*. Shakespeare used both *be* and *have* as the perfect auxiliary for verbs of motion; *have* is especially frequent in phrases with a modal auxiliary.

> this gentleman *is* happily arriv'd (SHR 1.2.212)
> I *have* since arriv'd but hither (TN 2.2.4)

> did he not say my brother *was* fled? (ADO 5.1.205)
> love's golden arrow at him should *have* fled (VEN 947)

In speech, *have* as auxiliary was reduced to [ə] (as it normally is today), as the following late-seventeenth-century examples illustrate: *should a return'd*; *should ahad notice.*

The perfect infinitive came later than the perfect tense, but it too was being used by the seventeenth century:

> I had hopes *to haue got* away (1652)
> we did not intend *to have baffelled* you in our pay (1696)

The progressive tense originated in ME, increased greatly during EMnE, and was fully developed by the end of the sixteenth century. Nonetheless, it was used less frequently than it is in PDE; often we find the simple present or simple past where the progressive would be obligatory today. For example, in *Henry VI, Part III*, Warwick asks the already dead Clifford, "Speak, Clifford, dost thou know who *speaks* to thee?" In PDE, we would have to say *who is speaking.*

Although both the perfect and the progressive tenses were used extensively during EMnE, the combination of the two in a single verb phrase ("I have been watching you") was rare. The progressive-passive combination ("you are being watched") did not develop until the late eighteenth century. The three-way combination of progressive, passive, and perfect ("you have been being watched") was not to appear at all until PDE. In fact, passive constructions in general were less common in EMnE than they are in PDE.

As was noted in Chapter 6, *do* in ME could serve as a causative auxiliary, as a periphrastic alternative to the simple present or past, and was just beginning to be used in forming negatives and interrogatives. By EMnE, causative *do* had disappeared. Unemphatic periphrastic *do* continued into EMnE, and Shakespeare has numerous examples:

> thou shin'st in every tear that I *do* weep (LLL 4.3.32)
> so sorrow's heaviness *doth* heavier grow (MD 3.2.84)
> unnatural deeds *do* breed unnatural troubles (MAC 5.1.72)
> the cry *did* knock against my very heart (TEM 1.2.8)

The use of *do* as a "dummy" auxiliary for forming interrogatives and negatives was fully developed by EMnE, but was not obligatory. That is, one could either use the auxiliary *do* or employ simple inversion. Shakespeare employs both constructions freely:

> I doubt it not (ROM 3.5.52)
> I do not doubt you (2 H4 4.2.77)

> Why do you look on me? (AYL 3.5.41)
> Why look you so upon me? (AYL 3.5.69)

PDE has an extensive and complex system of quasi-modals, or verb phrases that behave like modals by modifying the aspect of the lexical verb. The beginnings of this system go back to ME, and it continued to develop during EMnE. *Be going to* as a future auxiliary, *have to* 'be obliged', and *be about to* 'be on the point of' all became common during EMnE. The phrase *used to* was employed in its PDE sense, but, unlike in PDE, could also be employed with present reference, as in *the meadow he useth to mow* (1710), meaning "the meadow he is accustomed to mow." Still, the extraordinarily rich variety of quasi-modal constructions that characterizes modern English was not yet fully developed. We cannot find in an EMnE text a verb phrase like *I don't like to have to keep on nagging you*, with its three quasi-modals in succession.

Impersonal verbs were common in Old English, decreased in use in late OE, then were temporarily reinforced under French influence during ME. However, such constructions are seemingly alien to English, for they began to decline again by late ME and were almost totally lost by the end of the sixteenth century. The verbs themselves remained in the language but came to be used personally, that is, with a nominative subject. Of the common impersonal verbs of ME, Shakespeare never uses *meet*, *repent*, *chance*, *hunger*, *thirst*, or *happen* impersonally. He uses *yearn* and *dislike* impersonally once each, *fear* twice, and *like* several times, all with an expressed subject. However, he also uses all of these verbs personally.

> *it yearns me* not if men my garments wear (H5 4.3.26)
> I'll do't, but *it dislikes me* (OTH 2.3.47)
>
> only *this fears me*, the law will have ... (TNK 3.6.129)
> his *countenance likes me* not (LR 2.2.90)

The only impersonal construction that is common in Shakespeare is *methinks* (and *methought*). However, *himthought, *usthinks, *youthinks, and so on, never appear, and Shakespeare regularly uses *think* as a personal verb, so even *methinks* is better regarded as a fossilized idiom in EMnE than as a true impersonal verb.

Syntax Within Clauses

As was noted in Chapter 6, most of the PDE patterns of subject (S), verb (V), and object/complement (O) were established by the end of ME. Still, EMnE, and especially the sixteenth and seventeenth centuries, had more flexibility than we do today.

By the seventeenth century, the SVO order was regular in both independent and dependent declarative clauses. It was also typical after adverbials, and, unlike PDE, could be used even after negative adverbials:

> I confess nothing, *nor* I deny nothing (ADO 4.1.272)
> *never* faith could hold, if not to beauty (LLL 4.2.106)

The SOV order was still an available option during most of the EMnE period for pronoun objects and for emphasis, particularly in dependent clauses:

> as the law should *them* direct (1708)
> By Richard that *dead* is (1 H4 1.3.146)

As in PDE, the order VSO was regular in direct questions and in conditional statements *not* preceded by a subordinator:

> How *hast thou* offended? (Shrew 5.1.107)
> *is not this* my Cambio (Shrew 5.1.114)
>
> *Were he* my kinsman ... it should be thus with him. (MM 2.2.86)

Unlike PDE, imperatives in EMnE frequently had an expressed subject. When they did, the subject followed the finite verb (VSO order):

> go, go, my servant, *take thou* Troilus' horse (TRO 5.5.1)
> *Do thou* but *call* my resolution wise (ROM 4.1.53)

The VSO order was also often—but by no means invariably—used after introductory adverbials, including nonnegative as well as negative adverbials.

> therefore *was thou* deservedly confin'd (TEM 1.2.360)
> So haply *are they* friends to Antony (A&C 3.13.48)
> Still *have I* borne it with a patient shrug (MV 1.3.109)

> nor *can imagination* form a shape (TEM 3.1.56)
> never till this day *saw I* him touched (TEM 4.1.144)

To emphasize an object or complement, the order OSV or OVS was occasionally employed:

OSV   A bursten-belly inkhorn orator called Vander hulke they pick'd out to present him with an oration (Thos. Nashe, *Unfortunate Traveler*, 1594)

OVS   These conjectures did they cast in their heads (Lodge, *Rosalynde*, 1590)

OVS   But answer made it none (HAM 1.2.216)

Syntax of Sentences

Because Latin had always been the language of education, it had had a certain amount of influence on the syntax of written English from the earliest days on. With the revival of Classical learning that accompanied the Renaissance, however, this influence increased greatly. "Elegant" English came to be characterized by long, heavily subordinated, periodic sentences and by such devices as parallelism, couplets, balanced clauses, and use of absolute participles. At the same time, the older, native tradition of cumulative, paratactic sentences was never completely lost. Indeed, it always characterized the spoken language and much of religious writing, such as homilies and Biblical translation. A nice contrast between the two stylistic conventions can be found in the King James Bible (1611). The translation itself is in the older tradition of loosely constructed cumulative sentences and clauses, connected primarily by the coordinators *and*, *but*, and *for*. The Dedication is composed in the then-fashionable Latinate style. Note the different flavor of the two passages below, despite their similarity of subject matter. Note also that the difference between the two is not simply a question of lexicon—the passage from Mark has such Latinate loans as *deliver*, *councils*, *testimony*, and *premeditate*, and the passage from the Dedication has such homely native expressions as *run their own ways* and *hammered on their anvil*.

> But take heed to yourselves: for they shall deliver you up to councils; and in the synagogues ye shall be beaten: and ye shall be brought before rulers and kings for my sake, for a testimony against them. And the gospel must first be published among all nations. But when they shall lead you, and deliver you up, take no thought beforehand what ye shall speak, neither do ye premeditate: but whatsoever shall be given you in that hour, that speak ye: for it is not ye that speak, but the Holy Ghost.
> —Mark 13.9–11

So that if, on the one side, we shall be traduced by Popish persons at home or abroad, who therefore will malign us, because we are poor instruments to make God's holy truth to be yet more and more known unto the people, whom they desire still to keep in ignorance and darkness; or if, on the other side, we shall be maligned by self-conceited brethren, who run their own ways, and give liking unto nothing but what is framed by themselves, and hammered on their anvil, we may rest secure, supported within by the truth and innocency of a good conscience, having walked the ways of simplicity and integrity, as before the Lord, and sustained without by the powerful protection of Your Majesty's grace and favour, which will ever give countenance to honest and Christian endeavours against bitter censures and uncharitable imputations.

—Dedication of the King James Bible

These two stylistic traditions were to remain distinct throughout the EMnE period. Over 150 years after the King James Bible, Benjamin Franklin's *Autobiography* illustrates the native paratactic tradition, while Edward Gibbon's *Decline and Fall of the Roman Empire* is a fine example of the Latinate, hypotactic tradition.

John was bred a dyer, I believe of woolens. Benjamin was bred a silk dyer, serving an apprenticeship at London. He was an ingenious man. I remember him well, for when I was a boy he came over to my father in Boston, and lived in the house with us some years. He lived to a great age. His grandson, Samuel Franklin, now lives in Boston. He left behind him two quarto volumes, MS., of his own poetry, consisting of little occasional pieces addressed to his friends and relations, of which the following, sent to me, is a specimen. He had formed a short-hand of his own, which he taught me, but, never practising it, I have now forgot it. I was named after this uncle, there being a particular affection between him and my father. He was very pious, a great attender of sermons of the best preachers, which he took down in his short-hand, and had with him many volumes of them. He was also much of a politician; too much, perhaps, for his station.

—Benjamin Franklin, *Autobiography* (1771)

The superstition of the people was not embittered by any mixture of theological rancour; nor was it confined by the chains of any speculative system. The devout polytheist, though fondly attached to his national rites, admitted with implicit faith the different religions of the earth. Fear, gratitude, and curiosity, a dream or an omen, a singular disorder, or a distant journey, perpetually disposed him to multiply the articles of his belief, and to enlarge the list of his protectors. The thin texture of the Pagan mythology was interwoven with various but not discordant materials. As soon as it was allowed that sages and heroes, who had lived, or who had died for the benefit of their country, were exalted to a state of power and immortality, it was universally confessed that they deserved, if not the adoration, at least the reverence of all mankind. The deities of a thousand groves and a thousand streams possessed, in peace, their local and respective influence; nor could the Roman who deprecated the wrath of the Tiber, deride the Egyptian who presented his offering to the beneficent genius of the Nile. The visible powers of Nature, the planets, and the elements, were the same throughout the universe.

—Edward Gibbon, *Decline and Fall of the Roman Empire*, Vol. I (1776)

HIDDEN ANIMALS

Like those pictures in which we are told to find concealed faces in unlikely spots, some English words contain the hidden names of animals. For example, *chenille,* the tufted fabric from which bedspreads and rugs are made, is the French word for "caterpillar." The French word itself is from Latin *canīcula,* a diminutive of *canis* 'dog'—caterpillars were so called because of their furry bodies. Another doggy word is *cynosure,* from Greek *kunosoura* 'dog's tail'; *kunosoura* is the Greek name for the Little Dipper.

   The word *pedigree* is from Old French *pie de grue* 'crane's foot', named thus from the claw-shaped marks used to show lines of succession. Also from Old French is *dauphin* 'dolphin'. The term goes back to the coat of arms of the lords of Viennois, France, which had three dolphins on it. The word *muscle* is ultimately from Latin *mūsculus* 'little mouse', presumably from the appearance of muscles rippling beneath the skin. *Easel* comes from Dutch *ezel* 'ass' and got its name because of its shape, just as *sawhorse* did.

Early Modern English Lexicon

Earlier in this chapter we discussed the great increase in the English vocabulary during the EMnE period and the attendant debate over inkhorn terms, borrowing, and "oversea language." Most of this increase came from borrowing, and most of the borrowing was from Latin. Still, other languages also contributed to the English lexicon during these centuries, and, for the first time, words from non-Indo-European languages entered English in fairly large numbers.

Loanwords

CLASSICAL LOANS

It is impossible to give even a reasonable estimate of the total number of words from the Classical languages that entered English during the EMnE period. For one thing, we often cannot determine whether a word came directly from a Classical language or entered via one of the Romance languages, especially French. Furthermore, from the Renaissance on, English borrowed roots and affixes to form new words that had not existed in the Classical languages themselves. Should the word *cortical* be counted as a loan separate from *cortex* even though *cortical* was formed in English and was never a Latin word? How do we treat a word like *fibroma*, manufactured in English from the Latin root *fibr-* and the Greek suffix *-oma*? In sum, it is more reasonable simply to note that borrowings from the Classical languages were extraordinarily heavy and that they provided English not only with thousands of direct borrowings but also with the raw materials for manufacturing thousands more.

This fact should not be surprising because it was scholars who introduced them, and the language of scholarship and education was Latin. Space limitations prevent an extensive listing of loans from the period, but perhaps an A–Z sample will convey the general flavor of the borrowings.

ambiguous	identical	quotation
biceps	joke	ratio
census	lichen	scintillate
decorate	mandible	tangent
emotion	navigate	ultimate
fanatic	opponent	vacuum
gladiator	perfidious	zone
harmonica		

Many of the Latin loans of EMnE were **doublets** (two words from the same source that enter a language by different routes) of words previously borrowed from French or Latin during Middle English. These recycled words could be introduced and retained because they were different in form and meaning from the earlier borrowings. For example, Latin *invidiōsus* gave English *envious* (via French) in Middle English and *invidious* (directly from Latin) in Early Modern English. For the most part, the EMnE borrowings are closer to the original Latin in form. A few other such doublets are

ME	*EMnE*	*ME*	*EMnE*
armor	armature	pale	pallid
challenge	calumny	palsy	paralysis
chamber	camera	porch	portico
choir	chorus	prove	probe
crimson	carmine	spice	species
frail	fragile	strait	strict
gender	genus	strange	extraneous
jealous	zealous	treasure	thesaurus
mould	module	voyage	viaticum

Most of the EMnE Latin loans came into English as nouns, verbs, or adjectives. However, the part-of-speech category sometimes underwent a shift in English. For instance, the English noun *affidavit* derives from the perfect tense of the Latin verb *affidare*; *affidavit* meant "he has stated on oath" in Medieval Latin. Other Latin verb forms that ended up as nouns in English include *caret, deficit, fiat, tenet,* and *veto. Facsimile* is from Latin *fac simile*, an imperative phrase meaning "make similar." English *propaganda* originated as a gerund from the phrase *Sacra Congregatio de Propaganda Fide* 'Sacred Congregation for Propagating the Faith'.

English has thousands of words that are Greek in origin, but the majority of these have come into English by way of Latin, or sometimes French. To consider only a sampling of items beginning with *a*, Early Modern English borrowed directly from Greek such words as *anarchy, aorist, aphrodisiac, apothegm, autarchy,* and *autochthon*. By way of Latin or French, it acquired Greek words like *analysis, anathema, angina, anonymous, antidote, archetype, autograph,* and *azalea*. As these examples suggest, most borrowings from Greek are highly specialized, scholarly words.

LOANS FROM OTHER EUROPEAN LANGUAGES

Although Latin was the most fertile and most obvious source of loanwords into English during EMnE, other European languages also contributed hundreds, even thousands, of new vocabulary items.

French.   French influence on the English lexicon was heaviest during ME, but the flow of loans continued throughout EMnE and into Present-Day English. In EMnE, French loans outnumbered those from any other contemporary language. By this time, however, the majority of French loans were fairly specialized words. Typical examples are *admire, barbarian, compute, density, effigy, formidable, gratitude, hospitable, identity, javelin, liaison, manipulation, notoriety, optic, parade, ramify,* and *sociable.*

Italian.   Contacts between England and Italy increased after the sixteenth century and, not surprisingly, were accompanied by many English loans from Italian. Borrowings were especially heavy in trade, architecture, and the arts, with musical terms being particularly prominent (*adagio, alto, andante, aria, operetta, oratorio, solo, sonata*). A wide variety of other semantic fields was also represented in the Italian loans, as is evidenced by words like *balcony, bandit, ghetto, motto, regatta, vermicelli, carnival, ditto, malaria, zany, antic, archipelago, arsenal, artichoke, tariff,* and *belladonna.*

Spanish and Portuguese.   Spanish and Portuguese can be treated together because the two languages are much alike and the nature of their loans to EMnE is similar; indeed, for many loans (for instance, *hurricane, jaguar, rusk*), it is impossible to tell whether the immediate source was Spanish or Portuguese. Both the Spanish and the Portuguese had a long head start on the English in the exploration, establishment of commercial relations, and colonization of the non-European world. Hence many of our terms for the exotic products and life-forms found in the Far East and the New World come directly from one of these two languages, though indirectly from some non-Indo-European language. Portuguese examples include *mango, albacore, betel, pagoda, tank, yam, tapioca,* and *cashew.* A few of the many Spanish examples are *cigar, papaya, potato, puma, alpaca, avocado, cannibal, canoe, chili, maize, tomato, coyote, llama, iguana,* and *hammock.* Among the native Portuguese words borrowed by EMnE are *auto-da-fé, palaver, molasses, albino,* and *dodo.* EMnE borrowings of native Spanish words include *anchovy, breeze, castanet, cockroach, sombrero,* and *tortilla.*

Dutch.   Geographic proximity and extensive political and commercial relations between England and the Low Countries facilitated the borrowing of scores of Dutch words into English during EMnE. Dutch prominence in seafaring gave such nautical words as *avast, boom, commodore, cruise, deck, reef, scow, sloop, smack, smuggle, splice, stoke,* and *yacht.* Their famous school of painting provided words like *easel, etch, landscape, sketch,* and *stipple.* Miscellaneous loans include *blunderbuss, brandy, clapboard, drill, foist, gruff, muff, ravel, sleigh, snuff, sputter,* and *uproar.* These examples show that Dutch loans tended to be less scholarly and abstract than the typical French and Latin loans of the period; even when the words are specialized (like *stipple* or *smack*), they are practical and concrete.

German. Partly because Germany was so late in achieving political unification, hence in developing a standard language, German loans into English have never been especially heavy. German preeminence in geology and mining provided the eighteenth-century loans *bismuth, cobalt, gneiss, meerschaum, quartz,* and *zinc.* Miscellaneous loans of the period include *carouse, fife, halt, knapsack, noodle, plunder, swindle, veneer,* and *waltz.*

Celtic Languages. A respectable number of Celtic loans entered English during EMnE—proportionally more than in previous periods. From one Celtic language or another came *banshee, brogue, caber, cairn, galore, hubbub, leprechaun, plaid, ptarmigan, shamrock, shillelagh, slogan, trousers,* and *whiskey.*

Other European Languages. Borrowing from European languages other than those already mentioned was minimal. The few loans that did come into English were chiefly the names of specialized products or topographical features not indigenous to England. From Russian came *beluga, kvass, mammoth,* and *steppe.* Norwegian contributed *auk, fjord, lemming,* and *troll. Eider* and *geyser* are from Icelandic, and *tungsten* from Swedish. Hungarian gave *hussar.*

LOANS FROM NON-INDO-EUROPEAN LANGUAGES

During the Renaissance, Europe greatly increased its contact with the world beyond its own confines and discovered a New World hitherto unknown to Europeans. This new traffic led to the introduction of many loanwords into European languages, including English.

Amerindian Languages. We have already noted that EMnE received a number of loans from New World languages via Spanish, Portuguese, and even French. In addition, several dozen words were borrowed from American Indian languages directly into English as a result of the English settlements in North America. These settlements were on the Eastern seaboard, where the dominant Indian linguistic family was Algonquian, so most of the loans are from Algonquian languages. The semantic areas represented by the loans reflect the nature of the contact between the English and the Indians; because the English actually settled among the Indians, we find a number of cultural terms in addition to the predictable names of unfamiliar plants, animals, and artifacts. On the other hand, because the topography of eastern North America is not strikingly different from that of England and the Continent, we do not find new names for topographical features.

Animals:	menhaden, moose, muskrat, opossum, raccoon, skunk, terrapin, woodchuck
Plants and Food Products:	hickory, hominy, pecan, persimmon, poke(weed), pone, squash, succotash, tamarack
Artifacts:	moccasin, tomahawk, totem, wampum, wigwam
Cultural Relations:	caucus, manitou, papoose, powwow, sachem, sagamore, squaw

Asian Languages. During the seventeenth and eighteenth centuries, the British successfully vied with the Portuguese, French, and Dutch for control of the Indian subcontinent. As a result of their conquest, the English language acquired many new loanwords. The most important contributor was Hindi, which gave such words as *bandanna, bangle, bungalow, cheetah, cowrie, cummerbund, dungaree, gunny, guru, jungle, myna, nabob, pundit, sari, seersucker, shampoo, toddy,* and *veranda.* Tamil provided *catamaran, cheroot, corundum, curry,* and *pariah.* From Bengali are *dinghy* and *jute,* and from Urdu is *coolie.*

Malay-speaking areas of the southeastern Asian islands were the source of loanwords like *amuck, caddy, cassowary, kapok, orangutan, rattan, sago,* and *teak.*

Considering their high levels of civilization and even technology, we might expect China and Japan to have contributed many loans to EMnE. But both these nations had closed their borders to foreign intrusion, so their influence on the English lexicon was relatively light. From Chinese, EMnE borrowed, for instance, *ginseng, ketchup, kumquat, litchi, nankeen, pekoe, pongee, sampan, tea,* and *typhoon.* Japanese provided a few terms like *mikado, sake, shogun,* and *soy.* Remote and inaccessible as Tibet was, English still borrowed Tibetan *lama* and *yak* during EMnE.

Near and Middle Eastern Languages. From the time of the Crusades onwards, loanwords from the Near and Middle East had been trickling into European languages. This flow continued during the EMnE period. Turkish was the largest direct source, although many of the Turkish loans were themselves borrowed from Persian or Arabic. From Turkish, English acquired *dervish, divan, jackal, pasha, pilaf, sherbet, turban, vizier,* and *yogurt.* Probably directly from Persian were *attar, bazaar, percale,* and *shawl.* Arabic is the source of *ghoul, harem, hashish, henna, hookah,* and *sheik.*

African Languages. Sub-Saharan Africa was not to be opened to significant European influence until the nineteenth century. Consequently, few loanwords entered EMnE from languages spoken in this area. Probably African in origin are *chigger, marimba,* and *okra.*

Formation of New Words

Although borrowing greatly increased the size of the English vocabulary during the EMnE period, English speakers did not stop forming new words from existing elements. The familiar processes of compounding and affixation continued. Functional shift (also called **zero derivation**) became common. Minor processes of forming words, such as clipping and blending, continued to be employed. In fact, it is only to be expected that new formation should be a more productive source of new words than borrowing: borrowing is necessarily restricted to those with some familiarity with a foreign language, but every native speaker is a potential creator of new words from the existing lexicon.

COMPOUNDING

As has always been true in English, the majority of new compounds in EMnE were nouns and adjectives, with verbs and adverbs being less frequent and other parts of speech only occasional.

As in ME, the most productive type of EMnE compound noun was noun + noun. Hundreds of them appeared, the majority being concrete nouns naming new or newly discovered products or processes. A few examples are *air pump, buttercup, copyright, daybed, figurehead, gunboat, jellyfish, nutcracker, punch bowl, saucepan, skinflint,* and *windowsill.*[4] A variant of the noun + noun combination was gerund + noun, as in *laughingstock, spelling book, stumbling block,* and *walking stick.* Another minor variant was possessive noun + noun; in many of these compounds, the apostrophe is not used in PDE. A few examples are *cat's-paw, death's-head, foolscap, helmsman, saleswoman, townspeople.* Verb + noun compounds were also frequent: for example, *blowpipe, catchword, daredevil, leapfrog, pickpocket, ramrod, scatterbrain, snapdragon,* and *turncoat.* Among the many new compound nouns consisting of adjective + noun were *broadside, commonplace, dry dock, easy chair, hotbed, lazybones, poorhouse, shortcake, sweetbread,* and *wet nurse.*

The compound noun consisting of adverb + noun seemingly decreased in productivity between ME and EMnE, but a few examples are still to be found: *afterbirth, by-blow, inroad, upcountry.* Increasing in frequency, but still much less common than in PDE, was the verb + adverb combination, as in *castaway, drawback, lookout, pinafore, say-so,* and *turnout.*

One of the most frequent types of compound adjectives in EMnE was the noun + adjective combination, for instance, *bloodthirsty, duty-free, heartsick, knee-deep, lifelong, noteworthy,* and *top-heavy.* Also common was the compound adjective consisting of an adjective and a noun with an *-ed* "inflection." A few of the many examples from EMnE are *cold-blooded, double-barreled, eagle-eyed, good-natured, mealy-mouthed, public-spirited, red-haired, stouthearted,* and *thick-skinned.*

A third relatively common type of compound adjective had a noun or adjective as the first element and a present or past participle as the second. Instances with a noun as the first element are *painstaking, earthborn,* and *henpecked*; with an adjective as the first element, *easygoing, good-looking, heavy-handed, old-fashioned.*

Throughout the history of English, compound verbs have tended to be formed from preexisting compound nouns or adjectives. This practice continued in EMnE. For example, *breakfast* is first recorded as a noun in 1463 but as a verb only in 1679. The noun *horsewhip* had appeared in print by 1694, but the verb did not appear until 1768. Nonetheless, for a few compounds, the verbal function is recorded well before the nominal function, suggesting that the word was initially created as a verb. Most of these compounds are made up of a noun plus a verb: *handcuff, hoodwink, rib roast, spoon-feed, whitewash.* Another fairly productive type of compound verb during the period was the adverb + verb combination, as in *backslide, cross-examine, inlay,* and *roughhew.* For the enormous increase in two-part verbs of the type *pick up,* see p. 235.

AFFIXING

English had lost most of its inflectional affixes by the end of the ME period, but it has increased the number of productive derivational affixes over the centuries;

---

[4] In deciding whether to spell the compounds discussed in this section as one word, two words, or a hyphenated word, I have followed one contemporary dictionary, *Webster's Third New International Dictionary* (1981). Other dictionaries and even other editions of the same dictionary vary somewhat in their practice. The treatment of compounds is perhaps the last frontier of even marginal creativity allowed in English spelling today.

affixing has always been the single largest source of new vocabulary items in English. By EMnE, the language had not only its native affixes and those borrowed from French during ME, but also an array of new derivational affixes from Latin and Greek. For every compound in English, the OED lists at least a score of new words formed by affixing. We might take the treatment of the Latin noun *numerus* 'number' in English as an example of the tremendous productivity of the affixing process. The noun *numeral*, borrowed directly from Latin, is first recorded in English in 1530. To this stem, English had added *-ity* (*numerality*) and *-ly* (*numerally*) by 1646, and *-ant* (*numerant*) by 1660. The Latin adjective form *numerous* is first recorded in English in 1586. By 1611, English had formed *numerosity* and *numerously*, and by 1631 *numerousness*. From Medieval Latin *numericus*, English formed *numerical* (1628), *numerically* (1628), *numerist* (1646), and *numerication* (1694). These examples are only some of the words formed from *numerus* by derivative suffixes; we have not even considered additional words formed by prefixes such as *in-*, *de-*, and *re-*. Note also that native suffixes like *-ly* and *-ness* are used freely alongside borrowed suffixes like *-ity* and *-ant*.

FUNCTIONAL SHIFT

With the loss of most inflections in Middle English, functional shift became one of the important ways of forming new words in the language. This process accelerated during EMnE, and, aside from borrowing, was perhaps the third most common way of expanding the vocabulary (after affixing and compounding). Of the various parts of speech, nouns and verbs participated most freely in the process. For the EMnE period, Hans Marchand[5] records such noun-to-verb conversions as *badger*, *capture*, *guarantee*, *pioneer*, and *segment*. Among his examples of verb-to-noun shifts are *cheat*, *contest*, *slur*, *split*, and *whimper*. Other parts of speech can also be involved. For instance, the adjectives *lower*, *muddy*, *numb*, and *tense* all underwent functional shift to verbs during EMnE. The OED records many, many more instances that have not survived to the present day.

MINOR SOURCES OF NEW WORDS

All of the minor processes for forming new words mentioned in Chapter 6 continued to provide at least a few new items in EMnE. In addition, some more modern sources made their first tentative appearances in EMnE.

1. *Clipping.* Clipping, whereby initial or final syllables are dropped from an existing word, provided such new words as *rear* (<*arrear*), *hack* (<*hackney*), *spinet* (<*espinette*), and *van* (<*vanguard*). Several not especially complimentary terms for people have their origin in clipping. From *rakehell* there was *rake*, and from *chapman* there was *chap*. French *cadet* had already provided the word *cuddie*, which was then clipped to *cad*. Similar to clipping is the formation of new words by internal contraction of old ones. Thus from *fantasy* comes *fancy*. *Fourteen-night* is reduced to *fortnight*, *godfather* to *gaffer*, and *triumph* to *trump*.
2. *Back-formation.* Back-formation of the existing adjectives *disheveled, foggy*, and *greedy* gave the verb *dishevel* and the nouns *fog* and *greed*. Misinterpretation of the archaic adverb suffix *-ling* as a present participle ending provided the verbs *sidle* and *grovel* from *sideling* and *groveling*. From nouns ending in *-y* came such back-formations as *difficult* (<*difficulty*) and *unit* (<*unity*). Interpreting a

---

[5] Hans Marchand, *The Categories and Types of Present-Day English Word-Formation* (Birmingham: University of Alabama Press, 1966), pp. 293–306.

French loanword whose singular form ended in -s as an English plural (a common source of back-formations) resulted in, for example, *tabby* from *tabis* and *marquee* from *marquise*. Somewhat more complex is the origin of English *gendarme*; its source is the French phrase *gens d'armes* 'men of arms', which was taken as a single plural word *gendarmes* and then made singular by dropping the final -s.

3. *Blends.* Blends were not to proliferate until PDE, but a number of new ones did appear in EMnE. Among them were *dumfound* (from *dumb + confound*), *apathetic* (from *apathy + pathetic*), and *splutter* (probably from *splash + sputter*).

4. *Proper names.* Scores of common nouns or other parts of speech were made from proper nouns during EMnE. From the names of places came, for instance, the words *calico, clink, coach, cognac, delft, duffel, finnan* (haddie), *frieze, jersey, landau, mocha, sardonic,* and *tangerine.*[6] Inventors or people associated with a process, event, or type of behavior gave their names to such words as *batiste, derrick, doily, dunce, galvanic, grog, mansard, martinet, pompadour,* and *praline.* Classical literature and mythology provided scores of vocabulary items; a few of these are *bacchanal, fauna, flora, gorgon, hector, hermetic, panic,* and *stentorian.* Even nicknames could give common nouns; *Richard* is the ultimate source of *dickey* and *hick; John* of *jackanapes;* and *Dorothy* of *doll.*

Botanical discoveries in the New World or the Far East, the pressure for classification and labeling brought about by Linnaean taxonomy, and a general interest in horticulture all led to the need for naming scores of newly identified or newly developed plants. During the EMnE period, the convention arose of naming new plants after their discoverer or developer; today, we can be fairly confident that any plant whose name ends in -*ia* has as its base a proper name. Some of the flower names thus given during EMnE include *begonia, camellia, fuchsia, gardenia, gloxinia,* and *magnolia.*

5. *Echoic words.* By EMnE, words that were echoic in origin were being recorded in fairly large numbers. To list only some items beginning with *b*-, the following echoic (or probably echoic) words first appeared in writing during the EMnE period: *baa, bah, bash, blob, blurt, bobolink, booby, boohoo, boom, bowwow, bump, bungle.*

6. *Folk etymology.* EMnE produced a number of words formed or altered by folk etymology. Among the native words or phrases thus created was *stark naked* from earlier *start naked* 'naked to the tail'. *Start* here was the same word that appears in the bird name *redstart;* OE *steort* meant simply "tail." The bird name *wheatear* was also altered by folk etymology, probably from earlier *hwit* 'white' + *ers* 'ass'.

The large number of foreign loans in EMnE was a rich source of misinterpretation and consequent folk etymologizing. For example, French *musseroun, puliol real, curtal,* and *chartreuse* became *mushroom, pennyroyal, curtail,* and *charterhouse,* respectively. Portuguese *mangue* ended up as *mangrove;* Dutch *oproer* ('up' + 'motion') as *uproar.* German *ribbesper* (from *ribbe* 'rib' + *sper* 'spit') not only was folk-etymologized, but also underwent metathesis of its two constituent elements when it became English *spareribs.*

7. *Verb + adverb.* A rich source of both verbs and nouns in PDE is the verb + adverb combination, as in *take out, pickup,* and *run-in.* As we have noted

---

[6] The original place or personal names that gave rise to the common nouns mentioned here can be found in any good college dictionary.

elsewhere, the process of forming new verbs in this fashion began in ME and became highly productive in EMnE. Nonetheless, the conversion of such verbs to nouns by shifting the major stress to the first syllable is a PDE phenomenon. Only a handful of such compound nouns are recorded prior to the nineteenth century; two examples are *comeoff* (1634) and *breakup* (1795).

8. *Reduplication.* In many languages, **reduplication**, or the formation of new words by doubling the initial syllable or all of an existing word, is a highly productive source of new lexical items. English seemingly has never been amenable to extensive reduplication. (We exclude here the use of reduplicating letters as an attempt to represent in writing nonspeech sounds, as in *ha-ha* for laughter; this type of reduplication dates back to Old English.) Reduplicated words do not appear at all until the EMnE period. When they do appear, they are usually direct borrowings from some other language, such as Portuguese *dodo* (1628), Spanish *grugru* (1796) and *motmot* (1651), French *haha* 'ditch' (1712), and Maori *kaka* (1774). Even the nursery words *mama* and *papa* were borrowed from French in the seventeenth century. *So-so* is probably the sole native formation from the EMnE period; it is first recorded in 1530.

9. *Unknown origin.* As is the case for all periods of English, a large number of words whose origin is unknown first appear in EMnE. A few of the many examples from EMnE are *aroint, baffle, chubby, dapple, filch, gale, huddle, jaunt, lazy, mope, noggin, pet, qualm, rickets, sleazy, taunt, wraith,* and *yaw.*

Lost Vocabulary

In one sense, the only truly lost words are those that have not survived in writing and perhaps were never written down in the first place. As we saw in Chapter 5 (p. 99), PDE speakers regularly use many words that do not appear in even hundreds of thousands of lines of printed text. Therefore it is likely that many words familiar to most speakers of ME are irretrievably lost because they were never recorded in writing and dropped out of the spoken language. Obviously, we can say nothing at all about these words.

More generally, the term "lost" is applied to words not used in the standard language today. Here, however, there is the problem that specialists still use words that have become obsolete in the general vocabulary. For example, large dictionaries still list such words as *tuille* and *vambrace* without any label that they are archaic or obsolete; yet these names of pieces of armor are "lost" to most speakers of PDE because armor is no longer worn.

Still another problem that arises in defining "lost" vocabulary is that words often survive in regional dialects long after having been lost in the standard language. For instance, most speakers of modern English are not familiar with the word *orts* unless they are language specialists or crossword enthusiasts. Yet I was recently told of an old woman in rural New Hampshire who still uses the term naturally and unselfconsciously. Should *orts* be considered part of the lost vocabulary of English or not?

The problem of defining "lost" notwithstanding, we cannot read any lengthy ME text without encountering a number of words that are not found in EMnE or PDE texts. Clearly, these words have been lost in some sense. An examination of the first few hundred lines or so of Chaucer's "Melibee" is instructive in this respect. Because the tale is in prose and aimed at a general audience, we avoid the possible contamination of the vocabulary by special poetic terms or by the esoteric words of a highly specialized treatise. Excluding simple variant spellings, at least a score of words appearing in these lines were no longer in use by the end of EMnE or, in some instances, by the end of ME. Of these, one loan from French, *warisshen* 'to cure, recover' has disappeared completely. Several native English words have totally dropped out: *forthy* 'therefore', *cleped* 'called', *noot* 'not know', *algates* 'nevertheless', and *bihight* 'promised'. What were originally dialectal forms (*give, their*) have replaced two forms once standard (*yeve, hire*). However, the majority of the now obsolete words are variant forms of still surviving French loans, or French loans later influenced by Latin:

semblaunt 'semblance'	*avoutrie* 'adultery'
ententif 'attentive'	*noyous* 'annoying'
agreggen 'aggravate'	*secree* 'secret'
garnisoun 'garrison'	*perfourne* 'perform'
espace 'space (of time)'	

It would be foolish to take these few lines from a single text as representative of the entire vocabulary of "standard" Middle English. Nonetheless, the heavy proportion of lost words that are merely alternative forms of other, surviving words does suggest that a great deal of the lexical loss between ME and EMnE consisted of the sloughing off of unnecessary variants of French loanwords.

THE UBIQUITOUS JOHN

Over the centuries, no masculine given name has been more popular than *John,* a name that has never gone out of fashion. Its popularity is reflected in the scores of common nouns or other words that have been made from *John* or a variant of *John.* Thus we have *John Bull* as a personification of England, *John Barleycorn* as a personification of liquor, *John Doe* as a fictitious legal person, and *John Dory* as the name of two different kinds of fish. When a woman wants to tell a man that she prefers someone else, she writes him a *Dear John;* and of course, in the United States people answer the call of nature in an uncapitalized *john.*

A *Johnny-jump-up* is a plant, a *Johnny-on-the-spot* is a person in the right place at the right time, a *Johnny Reb* is a Confederate soldier, a *Johnny-come-lately* is a recent arrival, and a *stagedoor Johnny* seeks the company of actresses. Cornbread is also known as *johnnycake,* and people who have medical examinations may be asked to put on a *johnny,* a kind of robe open in the back.

The diminutive *Jack* has spawned as many common nouns as its original form *John. Jack Frost* is the personification of cold weather, while a *Jack-tar* is a sailor. Then there are *jack-o'-lantern, jack-in-the-box, jack-in-the-pulpit* (a plant), *jack-of-all-trades, every man jack,* and *jackanapes*—not to mention *jack pine, jackdaw, jackknife, jacksnipe* (a bird), *jackpot, jackstraws, jackrabbit,* and *jackass.* Finally, there are *jacks,* which include playing cards, devices to lift cars, braces, six-pointed metal objects used in a children's game also called *jacks,* and flags. *Jack* is also common as the second part of compounds: *applejack, blackjack, bootjack, crackerjack, flapjack, hijack, lumberjack,* and *steeplejack.*

The Scots version of *Jack* is *Jock,* from which we have *jocks* and *jockeys.* The noun *jacket* is, however, probably from the name *Jacques,* which is the French form of *James,* not of *John.*

Early Modern English Semantics

In some respects, semantic change is much easier to study for the EMnE period than for preceding periods because the number of surviving texts is so much greater. We have multiple examples of most words in context, so subtle differences in meaning are easier to detect. On the other hand, the very abundance of textual material can be intimidating. Furthermore, the great increase in the total English lexicon caused by the extensive Latinate borrowing makes the task of determining and analyzing the complex semantic interrelationships of individual words extremely difficult.

One of the reasons why semantic change is so frustrating to investigate is that it is so inextricably related to other kinds of linguistic change. We have already seen that semantic change is highly correlated with lexical loss and gain. It is also intimately related to morphological and syntactical change. For example, in EMnE, the verb *have* first came to be used as a kind of modal auxiliary in constructions of the form *have* + *to* + infinitive (*we have to leave now*). This represents a morphological and syntactic change in that a new modal construction has entered the language. It also represents a semantic change in the word *have* itself. (For that matter, there is also a phonological change in *have* and *has* because the final fricatives in both have become unvoiced in this modal construction.)

Generalization and Narrowing

The most obvious type of semantic change both from ME to EMnE and during EMnE is narrowing of meaning. As we noted in Chapter 6, this is to be expected: If the language is to retain the vast numbers of new loanwords, the meanings of already existing words must be narrowed to accommodate them. Indeed, as we examine the changes in meaning that appear in EMnE, there are scores of examples of narrowed meaning for each example of generalized meaning. The following list is but a tiny sample of the words that underwent semantic narrowing.

Word	Meaning Prior to EMnE	Meaning After EMnE
acorn	fruits	fruit of oak tree
adventure	chance, luck, fortune, accident, danger, circumstance	unusual and exciting experience
battle	armed fight, battalion, troop, line of troops	armed fight
courage	heart, mind, disposition, nature, bravery, valor	bravery, valor
deer	animal	mammals of the family Cervidae
error	mistake, wandering, doubt, perplexity, chagrin, vexation	mistake, deviance from the right
girl	young person of either sex	young female
harlot	rascal, thief (of either sex)	unchaste woman
read	think, suppose, estimate, teach, speak, mention, comprehend written matter, interpret	comprehend written matter, interpret, perceive, study
sermon	speech, account, religious discourse	religious discourse

A few examples of generalization can also be found. For example, prior to the seventeenth century, the noun *twist* referred to a twig, tendril, or branch, whereas today it can refer to almost anything that has been twisted or entwined, such as yarn, tobacco, slices of lemon, ankles, or the action of twisting itself. Until the eighteenth century, the word *crop* was restricted to sprouts or new shoots, and the word *plant* to shrubs, saplings, or seedlings. The verb *trend* formerly meant "to revolve, roll, or go in a circular motion," whereas since the seventeenth century, it has generalized to mean "movement in a specified direction; tendency."

Amelioration and Pejoration

Pejoration during EMnE can be illustrated by such words as *lust*, which formerly meant simply "pleasure, delight" without necessarily implying sexual desire. *Carp* once meant "speech, talk" and not constant complaining. *Coy* meant "quiet, shy, modest" until the seventeenth and eighteenth centuries, without the connotations of pretense or deviousness that it has since acquired. A *knave* was simply a boy until the end of the ME period, then referred to a page or other servant until the seventeenth century, when its present meaning of an unprincipled, crafty man took over.

There are also numerous examples of amelioration, though it is often the result of narrowing. That is, amelioration has occurred, not because the entire meaning of the word has changed, but rather because earlier pejorative meanings or connotations have been lost. Thus *scant* no longer implies "sparing, niggardly"; *jolly* does not mean "arrogant, wanton, lustful"; and *bare* is not "useless, worthless." Even as *lust* was degenerating to mean "excessive sexual craving," *luxury* was losing its earlier meanings of "lust, licentiousness." Similarly, though *knave* underwent great degeneration, *boy* came up in the world by losing earlier meanings of "rascal, servant, slave." *Fond* no longer means "idiotic, mad." *Prowl* retains connotations of stealth, but at least does not mean "plunder, rob, pilfer, get by cheating." *Await* has ameliorated by shaking off the meanings "contrive, plot, lie in wait for."

Certain semantic categories seem particularly prone to semantic shift for psychological or sociological rather than strictly linguistic reasons. For instance, it may be a universal of human behavior to mistrust people who are more gifted than average. Therefore, adjectives referring to cleverness tend to degenerate in their connotations. *Calculating* and *scheming* have always been pejorative in English— even though the nouns *calculation* and *scheme* do not necessarily have bad connotations. The words *sly* and *designing* once could be used in a favorable sense, even though their unfavorable senses have also been with them from the beginning. The adjectives *artful*, *crafty*, and *cunning* were all once exclusively favorable; *crafty* became pejorative in Middle English, and *artful* and *cunning* in Early Modern English. Although *clever* is typically favorable today, signs of its ultimate degeneration appear in such expressions as "too clever by half" and "too clever for one's own good." Nonetheless, even this strong tendency is not without its exceptions: *shrewd* was once strictly unfavorable and became more neutral in EMnE (though it should be noted that the earliest meaning of *shrewd* was "malicious, bad, evil"; it did not begin life as a word having to do with cleverness). *Subtle* had bad as well as neutral connotations in ME and EMnE, but has lost most of its bad associations in PDE.

Strengthening and Weakening

As was noted in Chapter 6, intensification of meaning is much less common than weakening. A few examples of intensification can, however, be identified from the EMnE period. The meaning of *jeopardy* intensified from "uncertainty" to "danger, peril." *Appalled* intensified from "pale, weakened" to "filled with consternation or dismay."

The much more common process of semantic weakening can be illustrated by such words as *quell*, which once meant "put to death"; *spill*, which formerly meant "destroy, kill, lay waste"; and *dissolve*, which meant "cause the death of." Prior to the seventeenth century, *dreary* meant "gory, bloody, cruel, dire," and *spite* could mean "evil deed, outrage." *Fret* has weakened from its earlier meaning of "eat, devour, consume."

Shift in Stylistic Level

As we have noted before, stylistic shifts of meaning are often not easy to document. One unambiguous example of a lowering of stylistic status from EMnE is the verb *stuff*, once used in serious writing to mean "supply with defenders, munitions, provisions." Another example of a decline in stylistic level is that of the noun *heap*, which is normally informal today, especially if used to refer to human beings. That it was not always so informal is shown by the following quotation from *Richard II*:

> Among this princely *heap*, if any here,
> By false intelligence, or wrong surmise,
> Hold me a foe ... I desire
> To reconcile me to his friendly peace.

Shift in Denotation

Shifts in denotation are also common for the EMnE period. To cite merely a few examples, *blush* once meant "look, gaze"; *discover* meant "uncover, reveal"; and *yelp* meant "boast." *Error* could mean "chagrin, vexation," and *harmless* meant "innocent" (a meaning still retained today in some legal documents).

The dictionary definitions of *astrology* as "the foretelling influence of planets and stars on human affairs" or of *element* as "one of the simple substances out of which all material bodies are compounded" applied as well in EMnE as they do today, yet because our beliefs about the nature of the universe have changed so much since then, we cannot say that *astrology* and *element* have the "same" meaning today as they did in 1600. Although *grace* is still "favor and good-will," the widespread loss of religious faith has deeply altered what *grace* now means to us. Similarly, *courtesy* can still be defined as "politeness and considerateness toward others," but it no longer has the connotations it would have had for those Middle English speakers to whom the word stood for an entire way of life. Ultimately, semantic change involves, not just the history of the word itself, but all the outer history of the speakers of the language.

Early Modern English Dialects

Contrary to what one might expect, a great deal more is known about Middle English dialects than about Early Modern English dialects. The standardization of the written language at the beginning of EMnE has concealed most dialectal differences, phonological differences in particular. However, in combination with widespread education, a standardized writing system can even conceal dialectal differences in morphology and syntax. For instance, though I regularly use the dialectal construction "The cat wants in" (without an infinitive) in speech, I do not use it in writing—except when referring to it.

Although we have no extensive descriptions of nonstandard dialects for the EMnE period, people were certainly aware of their existence. A few writers comment on them, and some dramatists attempt to represent dialect. One famous example is Edgar's use of Somerset dialect in *King Lear*:

> Chill not let go, zir, without vurther 'casion. ("I will not let go, sir, without further occasion.")

Here, '*Chill* represents a contraction of *ich will*, and *zir* and *vurther* reflect the voicing of initial fricatives. In the same scene, Edgar uses the word *ballow* to mean "cudgel, stick"; because this word appears only in the Folios of Shakespeare, we assume it was his attempt to represent a dialectal variation in vocabulary.

However, even the scant evidence that the dramatists provide is not trustworthy because certain nonconventional spellings were conventionally used to represent rustic speech from any dialectal area whatsoever. Even if a writer tried to be faithful to the dialect, ambiguities and inaccuracies were inevitable because the English alphabet is not suited for representing subtle distinctions in pronunciation. Further, writers who were not native speakers of the dialect were likely to err in representing it (just as British writers today often make mistakes in their assumptions about the use of American English forms such as *got* versus *gotten* and the phrase *I guess*).

A fair amount of information about regional dialects could be garnered from personal letters, diaries, documents, and town records written by persons too poorly educated to have mastered standard spelling. For example, in the town records of colonial New England the high frequency of spellings like *Edwad*, *capetts*, *octobe*, and *fofeitures* (for *Edward*, *carpets*, *October*, and *forfeitures*) are so common that we must assume a general loss of preconsonantal and final [r]. Similarly, the high frequency of spellings like *par*, *nex*, *warran*, *bine*, *Collwell*, and *lan* (for *part*, *next*, *warrant*, *bind*, *Caldwell*, and *land*) reveal a general loss of [t] and [d] after another consonant. Much painstaking research remains to be done before we have a clear picture of the EMnE dialectal situation, either in Great Britain or in colonial America.

In summary, the most important features of Early Modern English are

1. Phonologically, the Great Vowel Shift affected all ME long vowels and resulted in the loss of phonemically long vowels in English. The consonants /ž/ and /ŋ/ were added to the inventory of phonemes.
2. Morphologically, EMnE was much like late ME, with only minor changes, such as the continued weakening of originally strong verbs.
3. Syntactically, EMnE was similar to PDE, although the complex PDE system of verb phrases was not yet fully developed, and the use of noun adjuncts was still not as common as in PDE.

4. Lexically, English continued to borrow heavily, especially from the Classical languages. Many loanwords came into English from non-Indo-European languages. Functional shift, clipping, and folk etymology became significant sources of new words for the first time.
5. Culturally, English became an important language of the world, and English speakers began their attempts to improve it or at least to prevent what they regarded as further deterioration.

Suggested Further Reading

Abbott, E. A. *A Shakespearian Grammar.*
Barber, Charles. *Early Modern English.*
Blake, N. F. *Caxton and His World.*
Bolton, W. F. *The English Language*: *Essays by English & American Men of Letters, 1490–1839.*
Brook, G. L. *The Language of Shakespeare.*
Craigie, William Alexander. *The Critique of Pure English from Caxton to Smollett.*
Dobson, E. J. *English Pronunciation, 1500–1700.*
Ekwall, Eilert. *A History of Modern English Sounds and Morphology.*
Jones, Richard Foster. *The Triumph of the English Language.*
Kökeritz, Helge. *Shakespeare's Pronunciation.*
Leonard, Sterling Andrus. *The Doctrine of Correctness in English Usage, 1700–1800.*
Lounsbury, Thomas R. *English Spelling and Spelling Reform.*
Michael, Ian. *English Grammatical Categories and the Tradition to 1800.*
Padley, G. A. *Grammatical Theory in Western Europe, 1500–1700: The Latin Tradition.*
Partridge, A. C. *Tudor to Augustan English*: *A Study in Syntax and Style from Caxton to Johnson.*
Starnes, DeWitt Talmage, and Gertrude E. Noyes. *The English Dictionary from Cawdrey to Johnson, 1604–1755.*
Vorlat, Emma. *The Development of English Grammatical Theory, 1586-1737.*

CHAPTER 8

Present-Day English

Life may be lengthened by care, though death cannot be ultimately defeated: tongues, like governments, have a natural tendency to degeneration; we have long preserved our constitution, let us make some struggles for our language.

—Samuel Johnson

OUTER HISTORY

The Language Comes of Age

At the beginning of the nineteenth century, the position of English as the national language of Great Britain, the United States, and Canada was secure. Its fitness as a language of scholarship and literature was no longer questioned. This is not to say, however, that it was universally regarded as perfect and safe from present or future deterioration. The intensity of the EMnE debate over vocabulary was not to be repeated, but various attempts at spelling reform have continued to the present day. Even if there has been no popular support for an academy to serve as a watchdog over the language, there have always been those who see English in grave danger of contamination and degradation from its enemies within and without.

The Question of Vocabulary
By the beginning of the PDE period, the controversy over the English vocabulary and over loanwords in particular had died down. In the United States, during the

258

colonial period and the early days of the republic, some Americans were urging that borrowing, especially borrowing from French, should be avoided. Noah Webster, for example, resented what he considered a "servile imitation of the manners, the language, and the vices of foreigners." But others, most notably Thomas Jefferson, supported at least "judicious neology" as a means of gaining the words needed to express new ideas. The average American probably did not care one way or the other.

Later in the nineteenth century, British writers such as William Morris often consciously strove to use "Saxon" terms and to avoid Latinate words. Morris's reasons, however, were more stylistic than puristic; he simply felt that the native words were better suited for his translations from Old Norse literature. Certainly, there was no mass movement of the sort that took place in Germany to "purify" the language by purging it of foreign loans.

In sum, most English speakers today are not xenophobic regarding foreign loans or the Latinate loans and hybrids being manufactured by English speakers themselves. If some feel a mild regret over the virtually unlimited hospitality of English to foreign imports, others take pride in the cosmopolitan nature of the vocabulary of English.

The Question of Spelling Reform[1]

Since the latter part of the EMnE period, interest in English spelling has focused more on consistent spelling than on reform of the entire spelling system. From the nineteenth century on, great emphasis has been placed on correct spelling. Spelling is now taught as a separate subject in elementary schools. Correct spelling is not regarded as an infallible sign of the well-educated person, but incorrect spelling is usually treated as a hallmark of illiteracy.

Although the pervasive concern has been to promote traditional spelling, the PDE period has also seen a number of attempts to reform the spelling system, some extreme, some involving only minor adjustments.

In Great Britain, interest in spelling reform died down after the sixteenth century but revived during the mid-nineteenth century, especially as a means to make learning to read easier and to help foreigners master English. Isaac Pitman, the inventor of the phonologically sophisticated shorthand system widely used to this day, proposed a completely new regular alphabet in 1842. In collaboration with A. J. Ellis, Pitman later made extensive revisions to this earlier alphabet, ending up with the 38-character Phonotype alphabet of 1870. The 1870 version consisted primarily of familiar Latin characters and of modifications of these characters to represent sounds that had no unique representations in the standard Latin alphabet. For example, s represented /s/, but ʃ was used for /š/. Similarly, ð, ɛ, ŋ, and ɰ represented /ð/, /e/, /ŋ/, and /u/, respectively. Though Phonotype was not, of course, universally adopted, a number of books and pamphlets were published using it. Figure 8.1 is a reproduction of the first few verses of the Gospel of St. John printed in Pitman's Phonotype.

In the second half of the nineteenth century, spelling reform received the support of various organizations. For instance, in 1876, the National Union of Elementary Teachers urged the formation of a commission to study spelling

---

[1]Much of the material in this section has been adapted from D. G. Scragg, *A History of English Spelling* (New York: Barnes & Noble Books, 1974).

Figure 8.1   Illustration of Pitman's Phonotype*

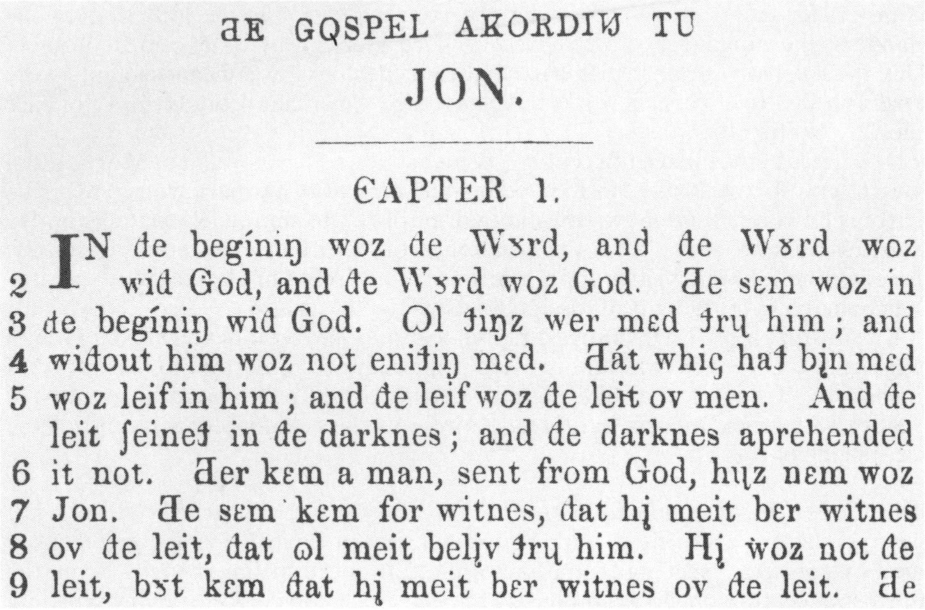

ðE GQSPEL AKORDIꞶ TU
JON.

ꞔAPTER 1.

IN ðe begíniŋ woz ðe Wꞧrd, and ðe Wꞧrd woz
2   wið God, and ðe Wꞧrd woz God.   ꝺe sɛm woz in
3 ðe begíniŋ wið God.   Ọl ꝼiŋz wer mɛd ꝼrụ him ; and
4 wiðout him woz not eniꝼiŋ mɛd.   ꝺát whiꞔ haꝼ bịn mɛd
5 woz leif in him ; and ðe leifwoz ðe leɨt ov men.   And ðe
   leit ſeineꝼ in ðe darknes ; and ðe darknes aprehended
6 it not.   ꝺer kɛm a man, sent from God, hụz nɛm woz
7 Jon.   ꝺe sɛm kɛm for witnes, ðat hị meit bɛr witnes
8 ov ðe leit, ðat ọl meit beljv ꝼrụ him.   Hị woz not ðe
9 leit, bꞧt kɛm ðat hị meit bɛr witnes ov ðe leit.   ꝺe

*David Abercrombie, *Isaac Pitman—A Centenary of Phonography, 1837–1937* (Sir Isaac Pitman & Sons Ltd, 1937). Reproduced by permission of Pitman Publishing, London.

reform. In 1871, A. J. Ellis produced still another revised alphabet (called Glossic) for the British Philological Society. The British Spelling Reform Association was organized in 1879 and proposed several modifications of the traditional system. Despite the efforts of these groups, however, the public as a whole never supported extensive spelling reform, and once again reform attempts died down for several decades.

During the twentieth century, there have been a number of new proposals for spelling reform. R. E. Zachrisson's Anglic was modified to become the New Spelling of 1941. Like Axel Wijk's Regularized Inglish, it deviated only minimally from traditional English spelling. George Bernard Shaw is the best-known modern proponent of spelling reform; his will left money to promote a new 40-character alphabet for the language. As late as the 1960s, Shaw's own *Androcles and the Lion* was published in his revised alphabet—but the fact that few people have even heard of the Shavian spelling reform shows how futile the effort has been.

In colonial America, the pedagogical interest in spelling reform was reinforced by rising nationalism and the desire to see an American English distinct from Anglo-English. As early as 1768, Benjamin Franklin had proposed a reformed alphabet. Like the traditional alphabet, it had 26 characters, but it omitted such redundant letters as *c, j, q,* and *x* and used modified versions of existing letters to represent phonemes like /θ/, /ð/, /ŋ/, and /š/. The underrepresentation of vowels was partly solved by doubling "long" vowels.

The best-known and ultimately the most effective American spelling reformer was Noah Webster. His earliest book, *A Grammatical Institute of the English Language* (1783), retained the spellings of Johnson's dictionary, but his

Dissertations on the English Language (1789) included some fairly drastic reforms of spelling (though not of the alphabet itself). For instance, he spelled *is* as *iz*, *tongue* as *tung*, and *prove* as *proov*. Webster later modified these extreme revisions, and his *An American Dictionary of the English Language* (1828) for the most part included only those revisions that distinguish British spelling from American spelling today, spellings like *favor* (instead of *favour*), *meter* (instead of *metre*), *check* (instead of *cheque*), and *defense* (instead of *defence*). His omission of final *-k* on words like *music* and *logic* was later adopted in England.

As in Great Britain, interest in spelling reform reappeared in the latter half of the nineteenth century, and for the same practical reasons of facilitating the teaching of literacy. In 1876, a group of reformers headed by Francis Marsh formed the American Spelling Reform Association; its revised alphabet of 32 letters met with little success. By the beginning of the twentieth century, concern over spelling reform had spread beyond the ranks of philologists and educators. Supported by a big grant from the industrialist-philanthropist Andrew Carnegie, the Simplified Spelling Board was established in 1906. In the same year, President Theodore Roosevelt ordered that government publications adopt the revised spellings recommended by the Simplified Spelling Board. Roosevelt's order and the proposed revisions were simply ignored. For fifty years, the Chicago *Tribune* attempted to get at least minor reforms accepted by using simplified spellings like *thru*, *tho*, and *synagog* in its own publications—but it finally admitted defeat of even its most modest aims and returned to traditional spellings.

At present, the chances for spelling reform extending beyond occasional individual items appear very dim. Americans are seemingly even more attached to traditional spellings than the British. Indeed, in many instances of mismatch between spelling and pronunciation, Americans have opted to alter their pronunciations rather than their spelling; hence, unlike their English cousins, they now regularly pronounce /h/ in *forehead* and /l/ in *Ralph*.

Dictionary-Making

Dominating the history of dictionary-making in the Present-Day English period has been the publication of the *Oxford English Dictionary*, a work for which even descriptive terms like "monumental" and "unparalleled" seem inadequate. The project began in 1857, when the Dean of Westminster suggested that the Philological Society make plans for a new dictionary of English to be based on historical principles and to include every word that had appeared in English since the year A.D. 1000. (This date was later moved forward to 1150.) As work got under way, thousands of volunteers in both Great Britain and the United States were recruited to read texts and make up slips listing words and the contexts in which they appeared. Over five million excerpts were made, of which 1.8 million were eventually printed. The first section was issued in 1884 and the final one in 1928, followed by a supplement in 1933.

During the three-quarters of a century required for its production, the *OED*, as it is usually called today, had six different editors: Herbert Coleridge, Frederick J. Furnivall, James A. H. Murray, Henry Bradley, William A. Craigie, and Charles T. Onions. Murray made the greatest contribution; he essentially dedicated his life to the dictionary, serving as editor from 1879 until his death in 1915. Of the total of 15,487 pages, Murray edited nearly half.

The 1933 Supplement to the *OED* appeared over fifty years ago, but in a sense, the work is still not complete and will never be complete as long as English remains a living language. In 1971, a two-volume microprint edition appeared. Its relatively low price and its widespread distribution through book clubs have made the *OED* available to thousands of people who otherwise would probably have never even heard of it, and who certainly could not have afforded the full-size edition. During the 1970s and 1980s, a new four-volume supplement updated the original thirteen volumes. At present, a project is getting under way to put the entire *OED* on computer disk. Once this is completed, users will be able to ask for such information as all the words recorded before the year 1250, all words ending in -*th*, all words listed as being of Finnish origin, and so on.

Dictionary-making in the United States began not long after the nation became independent. In 1806, the educator and lexicographer Noah Webster published a small dictionary of 28,000 words, *A Compendious Dictionary of the English Language*. In 1828, his most important work, the two-volume *American Dictionary of the English Language*, appeared. With 70,000 entries, it was the largest dictionary to date in English. It was not, however, without its problems: The pronunciations listed were biased heavily toward those of New England, and the etymologies were not up to the standards previously established by Johnson's dictionary.

When Noah Webster died in 1843, George and Charles Merriam bought the publishing rights to the 1828 dictionary, and in 1847 they published the first Merriam-Webster unabridged dictionary. Later editions followed in 1864, 1890, 1909, 1934, and 1961. The current edition, the 1961 *Webster's Third New International Dictionary*, has approximately 450,000 entries; this figure represents 150,000 fewer entries than the 1934 edition, but still includes 100,000 new entries.

Although the line of dictionaries established by Noah Webster still dominates American lexicography, at least in the popular mind, many other good dictionaries have been produced in the United States. For example, beginning in 1830, Joseph E. Worcester, a former assistant to Noah Webster, began publishing a series of dictionaries. More conservative and more favorable to British usage than Webster's dictionaries, Worcester's dictionaries outsold Webster's for a number of years. In 1889–91, the six-volume *Century Dictionary* appeared. Dictionary buyers today can choose from a number of fine "college" or "desk" dictionaries, each with tens of thousands of entries. These include Houghton Mifflin's *American Heritage Dictionary*, the World Publishing Company's *New World Dictionary*, and the college dictionaries published by Random House, Funk & Wagnalls, and the G. & C. Merriam Company.

In addition to all the general dictionaries of the language, many specialized dictionaries are now available. By the beginning of the nineteenth century, lexical differences between British and American English had become obvious. An early attempt to list some of these Americanisms was John Pickering's *A Vocabulary, or Collection of Words and Phrases Which Have Been Supposed to be Peculiar to the United States of America*. More complete and more systematic was John Russell Bartlett's *Dictionary of Americanisms* (1848, 1859). As a kind of extension to the *OED*, William Craigie and James Hulbert edited the four-volume *Dictionary of American English* (1938–44). More recent is Mitford M. Mathews' two-volume *Dictionary of Americanisms* (1951). The *Dictionary of American Regional English* (1985–) will provide a record of thousands of dialectal forms. There are also dictionaries of several other national varieties of English, such as Scots, Canadian, Australian, Indian, and South African English.

Exhaustive dictionaries of both Old English and Middle English have recently appeared or are soon to appear. Numerous specialized fields like medicine, archeology, and literary criticism have their own dictionaries. The emergence of English as a world language has resulted in vast amounts of material to aid in teaching English as a second language. Among these materials are dictionaries of various types, ranging from the earlier Kenyon and Knott's *Pronouncing Dictionary of American English* (1949) to Rosemary Courtney's *Longman Dictionary of Phrasal Verbs* (1983).

The Question of a National Academy

By the nineteenth century, even the zealous purists had for the most part abandoned attempts to establish a governmentally sponsored and supported national academy to serve as a watchdog over the English language. Plans for a national academy were either dropped altogether or were replaced by private groups. In general, the goals of such private organizations were modest; rather than attempt to reform, regulate, and fix the language, they proposed simply to guide, advise, and support good usage.

The most important of these groups in Great Britain has been the Society for Pure English, formed in 1913. In the first tract published by the Society, its head, the poet Robert Bridges, describes its aim as that of "informing popular taste on sound principles, . . . guiding educational authorities, and . . . introducing into practice certain modifications and advantageous changes."[2] Since its foundation, the SPE has published numerous tracts on such varied topics as the split infinitive, English handwriting, American pronunciation, and Arabic words in English.

In the newly independent United States, sentiments for an academy were inextricably mingled with nationalism and the desire to be linguistically as well as politically independent of England. In what was perhaps the last serious attempt to establish a governmentally backed language academy, the poet Joel Barlow proposed (1806) an organization that would serve both as academy and as national university. However, even though President James Madison approved of the idea, both the House and the Senate defeated the bill.

Somewhat more successful, at least with respect to the amount of publicity it received, was the American Academy of Language and Belles Lettres founded in 1820 by the grammarian and author William S. Cardell. Cardell's goals were both ambitious and diverse; he proposed that the Academy should be a guiding influence for correct usage, promote uniformity of language throughout the United States, make recommendations in cases of disputed usage, and encourage linguistic independence from Great Britain. What is more, it would encourage the production of American textbooks, support American literature, and even undertake the study of native (Amerindian) languages. Despite the support of a number of prominent people, including John Adams, the Academy was opposed by such influential figures as Thomas Jefferson, who believed that such an organization would inevitably try to fix and to legislate rather than to guide and to develop. Other opponents included the statesman and teacher Edward Everett, who attacked the vagueness of the Academy's goals and urged a stronger position in favor of an independent American English.

Later attempts to organize a private but national language academy were the National Institute of Letters, Arts, and Sciences (1868) and the American

---

[2] *Society for Pure English, Tract No. 1* (Oxford: The Clarendon Press, 1919), p. 6.

Academy of Arts and Letters, founded at the turn of the twentieth century. The latter was a conservative group, leaning more to British than to American English. It printed a few lectures and then quietly dropped out of sight.

In summary, no attempt to establish a national academy, either publicly or privately supported, for overseeing the language has been truly successful, either in Great Britain or in other parts of the English-speaking world. To a large extent, the authoritative dictionaries, beginning with Johnson's dictionary and continuing with the *Oxford English Dictionary* in Britain and Webster's dictionaries in the United States, have served as a substitute for a national academy. This explains the furor that followed the publication of *Webster's Third New International Dictionary* in 1961. Its editors had emphasized descriptiveness and used prescriptive labels like "slang" and "nonstandard" very sparingly. Reviewers from the world of letters and journalism (who were not qualified linguists) denounced what they perceived as the excessive "permissiveness" of the new dictionary and accused structural linguists of contributing to the decay of the English language. A number of institutions announced that they would continue to regard the Second edition of 1934 as their authority rather than bow to the populism and lawlessness of the Third. In direct response to their horror over Merriam-Webster's having disavowed its responsibility as guardian of the English language, the editors of the American Heritage Publishing Company announced their own "deep sense of responsibility as custodians of the American tradition in language" and prepared a new dictionary that "would add the essential dimension of guidance," including the opinions on usage of a 100-member panel of writers and other prominent public figures.

The excitement has since abated, and American institutions have quietly accepted Webster's Third as their ultimate lexicographical authority. The new *American Heritage Dictionary*, while more prescriptive and conservative than Webster's Third, is still probably much more "permissive" than its editors had anticipated. Nevertheless, the basic problem has not disappeared: people still long for a single authority that will define linguistic morality in unambiguous terms and that will halt misuse and change in the language. The fact that the dream is an impossible one makes it no less real.

Approaches to Grammar

As we saw in Chapter 7, to the extent that there was concern with English grammar at all during the EMnE period, it was overwhelmingly a concern with correctness. Books on grammar focused almost exclusively on what was viewed as correct and incorrect usage. The PDE period, especially the twentieth century, has seen a split into three distinct approaches to grammar: (1) continuation of prescriptive grammar, (2) "traditional" grammar, and (3) "scientific" grammar.

Dominating the prescriptive or school approach during the nineteenth century was Lindley Murray's *English Grammar*, a continuation of the type of normative grammar established by Robert Lowth (see p. 211). First published in 1795, Murray's grammar went through scores of editions, expansions, and abridgments, and sold millions of copies in Britain and the United States. In general, Murray is predictably indignant about what he considers improper English (such as the double negative), but he does accept a number of widespread usages such as *none* with a plural verb. Other popular school grammars of the nineteenth century include Samuel Kirkham's *English Grammar in Familiar Lectures* (1825) and Goold Brown's *Grammar of English Grammars* (1851). The tradition is continued to this day in the plethora of grammar handbooks used in elementary, secondary, and university English classes.

As a group, the prescriptive grammars take a moral approach to language usage, concentrating on right and wrong—especially on wrong. Most are grossly incomplete, ignoring vast areas of grammar if native speakers rarely make mistakes in them. For example, although most school grammars will remind students to use *an* before words beginning with a vowel sound, they will contain little or no discussion of when to use the definite versus the indefinite article. Further, most such grammars make few attempts to explain *why* one usage is preferable to another apart from unhelpful statements that certain forms are "inappropriate" or "illiterate" or "illogical."

Traditional grammars are descriptive rather than prescriptive, focusing on what actually occurs or has occurred and passing few if any moral judgments. The framework of such grammars is usually the Greco-Roman model, but, more concerned with completeness and accuracy than with internal consistency, they are eclectic and pragmatic rather than being confined to any one theoretical bent. Their heavy use of citations from the written language tends to make them data-oriented, historically oriented, and writing-oriented. The traditional grammars are, to date at least, the most complete grammars of English available, running to thousands of pages and several volumes. Interestingly, except for *A Grammar of Contemporary English* (1972) by Randolph Quirk, Sidney Greenbaum, Geoffrey Leech, and Jan Svartvik, the most important traditional grammars of English have been written by scholars who are native speakers not of English but of closely related Germanic languages. Etsko Kruisinga, author of the three-volume *Handbook of Present-Day English*, was Dutch, as was Henrik Poutsma, author of the five-volume *Grammar of Late Modern English*. The linguist Otto Jespersen, author of the seven-volume *A Modern English Grammar on Historical Principles*, was a Dane. Even one of the coauthors of *A Grammar of Contemporary English*, Jan Svartvik, was born in Sweden.

A discussion of the so-called scientific grammars might seem to belong more to a work on the mainstream of contemporary linguistics than to a history of the English language. However, a brief note on a few of the major theoretical schools is justified because many of their findings have influenced the writings of traditional grammarians and histories of the language (including this one).[3] Further, a large, even disproportionate, amount of their work has been based on English. Disparate as the approaches of the various schools are, they share an emphasis on internally consistent theory; we might loosely characterize scientific grammars as deductive in focus, whereas traditional grammar is inductive.

The earliest of the groups was the Prague School, dating from the 1920s and 1930s and centered in Prague. The Prague group's most important contribution was their distinction between phonetics and phonology. Their concepts of distinctive features and of the binary principle are influential to this day.

American Structuralism arose in the 1920s under the leadership of Leonard Bloomfield. Heavily influenced by behaviorism in psychology, the school stressed objectivity and antimentalism. Most of its contributions were in phonology and

---

[3] The following summary owes much to Dwight Bolinger, *Aspects of Language*, 2d ed. (New York: Harcourt Brace Jovanovich, 1975), pp. 514–50.

morphology; it did little with syntax and would scarcely admit that there was such a thing as meaning.

Meanwhile, in Britain, the Firthian school (named for the linguist J. R. Firth) was developing. The Firthians shared with the American structuralists a strong behaviorist and antimentalist bias. Unlike the structuralists, they were oriented heavily toward the total context of language—linguistic and nonlinguistic—an approach somewhat similar to that of sociolinguistics today. An offshoot of the Firthian school is M. A. K. Halliday's systemic grammar, which views language as a complex network of systems.

Of all the twentieth-century schools of grammar, the one best known to (though not necessarily understood by) nonspecialists is transformational (or generative-transformational) grammar, the approach headed by Noam Chomsky of M.I.T. Chomsky rejects the antimentalism of the structuralists and emphasizes the notion of grammar as a dynamic process (hence the term "generative"). The tenets of the school have changed greatly since its inception during the 1950s, but it continues to make a distinction between deep structure and surface structure, and of phrase-structure rules and transformations that translate the deep structure to surface structure. A more recent offshoot of generative-transformational grammar has been generative semantics, which would eliminate the level of deep structure and generate sentences directly from meaning. Still another offshoot is case grammar, which posits underlying cases seemingly rather like those of Latin or Greek; the approach in general owes much to the predicate calculus of formal logic.

Whether or not generative-transformational grammar (or one of its derivatives) turns out to be the approach of the future, it has had an enormous impact on modern grammatical thought. Unfortunately, none of the so-called scientific approaches outlined here has produced a sufficiently complete grammar of English to allow us to evaluate its acceptability and accuracy.

A FUTURE DIALECT

Most dialect writers are content to represent the spoken language of the past or present. But in *Riddley Walker*, Russell Hoban writes in what he imagines the English of a distant future to be.

> That wer when I clappt my han over his mouf it wer giving me the creaps how he wer going on. He wer stomping in the mud he wer dantsing and shouting and his face all wite with no eyes in the litening flashes. He begun to groan then like some terbel thing wer taking him and got inside him. He startit to fall and I easit him down I knowit he wer having a fit I seen that kynd of thing befor. I stuck the clof part of the hump back figger be twean his teef so he wunt bite his tung. I wer on my knees in the mud and holding him wylst he twissit and groant and that hook nose head all black and smyling nodding in the litening flashes. The dogs all gethert roun and them close to him grovvelt with ther ears laid back.

Russell Hoban, *Riddley Walker* (New York: Washington Square Press, 1980), p. 95.

INNER HISTORY
Present-Day English Phonology

If we had to rely on written records alone, we would be forced to conclude that the phonology of English has remained unchanged since before the beginning of the Present-Day English (PDE) period. Our fixed spelling system hides both changes in the language over time and dialectal differences among speakers at any given point in time. Luckily for the historian of English, linguistics as a discipline came into being in the late eighteenth and early nineteenth centuries. With linguistics —and its subdisciplines of historical linguistics and dialectology—came a heightened awareness of language change and tools for describing and recording the sounds of the language. The various kinds of phonetic alphabets developed in the nineteenth century preserve sounds for the eye, and the phonograph records and tape recordings of the twentieth century preserve them for the ear as well.

Despite the regret and even resentment of many, the language continues to change; change is inevitable. Ongoing changes today are seen as dialectal differences in different geographical areas or as differences among the various groups within one geographical area. Substandard or dialectal deviations from the standard language may represent the continuation of older patterns after the standard language has changed. Such is the case, for example, with the preservation of [hw] (aspirated voiceless [w]) by some speakers in words like *what*, *whistle*, and *whip*. Other deviations may represent genuinely new patterns resulting from tendencies within the language or pressures from outside the language. An example would be the voicing of intervocalic, post-stress /t/ in most American English dialects in words like *bitter* or *hottest*.

The large amount of variation in the phonology of English today was true of earlier periods of the language as well; the variation of the past merely seems less obvious because we do not have living speakers all around us to remind us of it. Still, despite the myriad of allophonic differences that have arisen since EMnE in the various dialects of PDE, the basic phonemic system of most dialects of English today was established by the beginning of the PDE period. Most of the changes since EMnE and across contemporary dialects are allophonic rather than phonemic. For instance, a glottal stop [ʔ] is characteristic of many dialects of contemporary English. The sound itself, or at least the pervasiveness of it, is apparently a recent phenomenon in English. Yet in no dialect is [ʔ] a phoneme; in most dialects, it is simply an allophone of /t/.[4] The system itself has neither added nor lost a phoneme.

Because such a large proportion of the native speakers of English today are literate, spelling pronunciations have had a greater influence on PDE phonology than they ever did in the past. Most of these involve the reinsertion of previously lost sounds in isolated words. For example, we frequently hear /h/ in *forehead*, /p/ in *clapboard*, and /t/ in *often* (but in *silhouette*, *cupboard*, and *soften*, the *h*, *p*, and *t* are not pronounced). In other instances, the spelling pronunciation clearly results from the pressures of more common sound-spelling correspondences. American *schedule* with /sk/ arose because the *sch-* combination in such words as *scheme*, *school*, *schooner*, and *scherzo* is pronounced /sk/, whereas the /š/ pronunciation of

---

[4] In some dialects, it is also an allophone of other stops, particularly in final position.

sch- is for the most part confined to rarer or obviously foreign words like *schuss*, *schmaltz*, *Schumann*, and *schist*. Similarly, *sumac* is /sumæk/ rather than the traditional /šumæk/ for many speakers today because most words beginning with *s* plus a vowel are pronounced with /s/, not /š/; the two major exceptions, *sugar* and *sure*, retain their /š/ pronunciations because children learn them before they learn to read. The traditional pronunciation /hjustən/ for the Texas city is retained in the United States where speakers hear the name constantly; in Britain, it is often pronounced /hustən/ or even /haustən/.

Occasionally, spelling pronunciations take over entire patterns. Many younger speakers in the United States regularly have /l/ in *calm*, *palm*, *psalm*, *balm*, and *alms*. This spelling pronunciation has not yet spread to *talk* and *chalk* or *folk* and *yolk*, but could do so in the future; many speakers already have /l/ in *polka*.

Consonants

The PDE inventory of consonants was established in EMnE; they are listed and described in Chapter 2 (pp. 22–24). The most recent additions to the system, /ŋ/ and /ž/, continue to have a low functional load. Indeed, for many native speakers, /ŋ/ is still not phonemic, but simply an allophone of /n/ that appears before /k/ or /g/.

The distribution of individual consonant phonemes has also remained fairly stable since the beginning of the nineteenth century. Perhaps the greatest amount of activity has centered around the voiceless stop /t/. American English now normally voices this sound when it occurs intervocalically and after the major stress of a word. For most younger speakers, such pairs as *betting/bedding*, *citing/siding*, *title/tidal*, and *matter/madder* are total homophones. There is evidence that voicing in this position will spread to the other voiceless stops as well. Confusion of the graphemes *g* and *q* may explain spelling errors like *conseguently*, but cannot explain the even more frequent misspelling *signifigant*. Such pronunciations as /hɪstɔrɪgəl/ for *historical* are frequent. Certainly, intervocalic /k/ seems to be moving toward /g/ when under minimal stress, though the eventual coalescence of such pairs as *picky/piggy* or *locker/lager* is not yet obvious.

Especially in urban dialects, the most common allophones of /θ/ and /ð/ are frequently retracted to such an extent that, to the speaker of standard English, they may sound like /t/ and /d/, respectively. Closer inspection, however, will usually reveal that, for native speakers, the fricatives and stops have *not* coalesced here; instead, /θ/ and /ð/ are being pronounced as dental, not interdental, fricatives.

We mentioned earlier that one striking modern development in PDE phonology is the use of [ʔ] as an allophone of /t/ in many positions. In American English, this glottal stop is virtually universal before /n/ and after the major stress (in words like *satin, rotten, mitten*).[5] If /n/ also precedes the /t/, the /n/ is lost and the preceding vowel is nasalized (*fountain, mountain, wanton*). Note that, for many speakers, this glottalization is strictly limited to post-stress position—it does not occur in *maintain* or *Brentano*, for example. Furthermore, glottalization occurs only before /n/ and not before other nasals; *atom* and *sitting*, for instance, have the predictable "voiced /t/." However, if "*g*-dropping" occurs—if /n/ replaces /ŋ/ at the end of *sitting*—then the /t/ *is* glottalized: [sɪʔɪn].

---

[5] Glottalization of /t/ takes precedence over the voicing of /t/. That is, in a word like *satin*, one would expect [sædɪn] because the /t/ is intervocalic and post-stress, but the following /n/ conditions a [ʔ] instead of a [d].

In many dialects, even educated dialects, of American English, the glottal allophone of /t/ is also common in final position after both vowels and consonants (as in *put, fight, felt, want*). Other dialects of English have [ʔ] for /t/ in more extensive environments. Its appearance before /l/ is a shibboleth of some New York City speech (as in *bottle, title, shuttle*). Glottal /t/ is also common in urban dialects in England and Scotland, and researchers have reported that in some dialects of Black English it appears for word-final /b/, /d/, and /g/—that is, for final *voiced* stops. Clearly, [ʔ] is spreading rapidly throughout English.

Preconsonantal /r/ was generally lost in the eighteenth century in both Received Pronunciation in Britain and on the Eastern seaboard and the South in the United States. One striking innovation of mid-twentieth-century American English has been the reintroduction of /r/ in this position in many areas, including such former strongholds as coastal New England and the Deep South.

Vowels

The diagram of Present-Day English vowel phonemes presented in Chapter 2 (p. 25) will fit the phonemic patterns of many American English speakers well, will fit others with slight modifications, and will be a poor fit for some speakers. Along with prosodic variations, differences in vowel allophones—and even phonemes—constitute the chief distinctions among dialects. Unfortunately, the picture is so complex that we cannot go into details here and must content ourselves with noting that, by the PDE period, unstressed vowels have almost universally been reduced to either /ə/ or /ɪ/. For the stressed vowels, the Great Vowel Shift was completed in most dialects by the beginning of the PDE period. This is not, however, to say that the stressed vowels of English are absolutely stable today. For example, both diphthongization of simple vowels and smoothing of former diphthongs are characteristic of a number of American dialects of the South. The most familiar examples are the tendency to diphthongize the (phonetically long) simple vowel /æ/ to [æə] and to smooth the diphthong /aɪ/ to [ɑ].

Prosody

The PDE period has seen the rise of the differences in sentence rhythms and pitch variations that characterize the prosodic distinctions between, roughly, American and Canadian English on the one hand and most other dialects of English on the other hand. It is difficult to state exactly when these differences arose because of the vague terminology used by early commentators on the American language. The major characteristics of American speech that eighteenth- and nineteenth-century observers noted were nasality and drawling. A drawl is hard to define; it may be that the term included the smaller variation in pitch that typifies American English as compared to Received Pronunciation today.

Many dialects of British English use fewer secondary stresses in poly-syllabic words than do most American dialects; compare British *sécretary* and *mílitary* with American *sécretàry* and *mílitàry*. In such words, British English may even elide the same vowel to which American English gives secondary stress; thus *secretary* is often pronounced [sékrətrɪ] in Britain, but [sékrətèrɪ] in the United States.

PDE has seen the continued tendency to move the stress of words back to the first syllable, a tendency that has characterized English since prehistoric times. We can see the process in operation in the pronunciation of such words as *pólice, défense,* and *Détroit.* Various dialects, however, select different words; hence British *labóratory* and *coróllary* versus American *láboratory* and *córollary*, but British *gárage* and *chágrin* versus American *garáge* and *chagrín.*

Present-Day English Graphics

The graphemes (letters) of the English alphabet have not changed since the end of the EMnE period. Nor have the essentials of the punctuation system. Punctuation tends to be lighter today than at the end of EMnE; on the whole, there are fewer marks of punctuation per sentence. This lighter punctuation is, however, at least partly due to the stylistic trend toward shorter, less complicated sentences that require less punctuation to block off the major syntactic units. Capitalization has been restricted to the first words of sentences, the word *I*, and proper names (though the definition of a proper noun remains fuzzy, so there is more variation in capitalization than many people realize).

The major spelling patterns of English were settled by the end of ME, were refined and adjusted for many individual words during EMnE, and have become rigid during PDE. In many ways, English spelling today is more morphographemic than phonemic. That is, the tendency is for a single morpheme to have a single spelling, regardless of the differences in pronunciation among different forms. Hence we write *autumn* and *autumnal*, despite the fact that *autumn* is pronounced /ɔtəm/ and *autumnal* is pronounced /ɔtəmnəl/. The past tense of regular verbs has three different pronunciations ([d] [t] [əd]), but they can all be spelled *-ed*. Another tendency is to preserve etymology despite sound changes. Thus we spell many silent letters, as in *wrong, through, sword,* and *comb*—and do not add new letters when new phonemes appear, as in *one, Europe,* or *music.*

American English has accepted some of the patterned spelling changes proposed by Noah Webster that British English has not. This explains the national differences exemplified by such words as British *honour, centre, realise, judgement,* and *connexion* versus American *honor, center, realize, judgment,* and *connection.* Even here, the distinction is in practice blurred. Because they had read so many American books, the students I taught in a British university regularly used American spellings. Conversely, my American students so universally spell *judgement* (with two *e*s) that I have given up trying to persuade them otherwise. Even the diligent may be foiled: A British-trained graduate student now studying in the United States decided to do as the Romans do and always use American spellings where they differ from British ones. However, not quite grasping the essence of the *-ise/-ize* difference, he twice wrote *surprize* in a paper (not realizing that the American *z* spelling was used only for the verb-making suffix).

Proper spelling has become so culturally important that "Thou shalt not spell incorrectly" has almost the status of an eleventh commandment. At the same time, an attractive and legible handwriting carries no prestige whatsoever; in fact, many people actually pride themselves on having a handwriting so bad that no one, not even they themselves, can read it. Part of this disdain for handwriting results from the widespread accessibility of typewriters and printing; as a rule, only one's personal correspondents and teachers are forced to decipher one's illegible scrawls. Even these people may be lucky enough to receive typewritten copy.

Present-Day English Morphology

As we saw in Chapter 7, most of the inflections that characterized Old English and the early part of Middle English had been lost by Early Modern English. The inflectional categories that did survive into Early Modern English (plural, possessive, past, past participle, present participle, third-person singular indicative, and comparative and superlative) have remained in Present-Day English, though not without some attrition and a few distributional changes.

Nouns

The categories of PDE noun morphology are identical to those of EMnE. Nouns are inflectionally distinguished only for singular versus plural and for possessive versus nonpossessive.

Seven native words retain mutated plurals (*feet, teeth, geese, lice, mice, men, women*), and three *-n* plurals remain (*brethren, children, oxen*). As in EMnE, a few words have unmarked plurals (for example, *sheep, deer, salmon*), and several more have either an *-s* plural or an unmarked plural (for example, *fish/fishes*; *elk/elks*). Otherwise, the *-s* plural has become universal for native and naturalized words. Foreign plurals are restricted primarily to learned words of Latin and Greek origin and, occasionally, Italian (*librettos* or *libretti*), French (*trousseaus* or *trousseaux*), and Hebrew (*seraphs* or *seraphim*). In general, when such loanwords become more familiar or are used in nontechnical senses, they take an analogical English *-s* plural; examples include *indexes* (versus *indices*), *stadiums* (versus *stadia*), and *antennas* (versus *antennae*).

The group genitive (see p. 229) has become widely used in PDE speech, though its more extreme manifestations are usually edited out of the written language. Thus, although we might say *that plant he was describing's flowers*, we would normally write *the flowers of that plant he was describing*.

The inflected (or *-'s*) genitive remains very much alive in English. Nonetheless, the periphrastic (or *of*) possessive has been encroaching upon it ever since ME times. As a general rule of thumb, the *-'s* possessive is used for the higher animals, including human beings, but lower animals and inanimates take the *of* possessive. Of course, many idiomatic expressions like *a day's work*, *your money's worth*, and *a stone's throw* still take only the *-'s* possessive.

Adjectives

Like EMnE adjectives, PDE adjectives can be inflected only for comparative (*-er*) and superlative (*-est*), and this remaining inflection alternates with the periphrastic forms *more* and *most*. In PDE, however, *more* and *most* have almost completely lost their intensifying function and have become purely grammatical markers of comparison. "Double" comparatives like Shakespeare's *most stillest* are no longer acceptable in the standard language. Further, the rules for the use of the inflected versus the periphrastic comparative have become more rigid, and the domain of the inflections *-er* and *-est* has been eroded. In general, monosyllabic adjectives take only inflected forms (*big, bigger*, but **more big*). Many common disyllabic adjectives can take either form (*healthy, healthier, more healthy*). Adjectives of more than two syllables can take only the periphrastic form (*wonderful, more wonderful*,

but *wonderfuller). Probably the inflected comparative and superlative will continue to lose ground to the periphrastic forms; even today, many younger speakers
express discomfort with inflected disyllabic adjectives like *handsomer* or *hollowest*.

Pronouns

The personal pronouns are the only class of words in PDE that preserve two
numbers and three distinct cases (subject, object, possessive). Demonstrative
pronouns retain separate singular and plural forms. Other types of pronouns, such
as relative and indefinite pronouns, had lost all inflections by EMnE, but their
distribution and use has since changed somewhat.

PERSONAL PRONOUNS

The only major change in the personal pronouns since the end of EMnE has been
the total replacement of the earlier second-person singular forms *thou, thee,* and
thine by the originally plural forms *you* and *yours*. Because the first- and third-
person pronouns continue to distinguish number (*I/we; she/they*), and because
nouns also distinguish number, it is not surprising that a new singular/plural
distinction in the second person has developed in some dialects of English. One
substandard version has singular *you* versus plural *youse*. Another version,
widespread in the southern United States, has singular *you* versus plural *y'all*. It is
at least possible that a separate second-person plural pronoun will be adopted in
the standard language at some time in the future. This addition would restore
balance to a system in which the singular-plural distinction is universally observed
for nouns and for the other personal pronouns.

DEMONSTRATIVE AND INTERROGATIVE PRONOUNS

The demonstrative pronouns *this* and *that* have not undergone significant change
since EMnE. Likewise, the interrogative pronouns have remained stable. However,
as was mentioned in Chapter 7, the dual pronoun *whether*, formerly used to mean
"which of two," has been lost and its earlier functions have been absorbed by *which*.
This change is not surprising because, although English does retain some vestiges
of a dual number (*both, neither*), the category is neither widespread nor strong in
the language.

RELATIVE PRONOUNS

No new relative pronouns entered the language between EMnE and PDE, but a
number of changes have occurred in the use of existing relatives. *Which* can no
longer be used with a human antecedent. In the standard language, only *who* or
which can introduce a nonrestrictive clause; *that* is now used only before restrictive
clauses. The use of *as* as a relative pronoun, at least marginally acceptable in
EMnE, is unquestionably substandard today. Finally, the standard language today
does not permit the omission of the relative pronoun when it is the subject of the
relative clause, although omission is optional when the relative has another
function. That is, in the first sentence below, we have the option of including or
omitting the relative pronoun *that*, but in the second sentence it cannot be omitted
in standard English.

This is the camera (that) I was reading about in the photography column.
This is the camera that was written up in the photography column.

REFLEXIVE PRONOUNS

Although the simple object forms of the personal pronouns could still be used as reflexives in EMnE, this usage has been almost completely replaced by compound forms of -self in PDE. Inconsistent though it may be, the use of the possessive forms of the personal pronoun in *myself, ourselves,* and *yourself* (-ves), but the object forms in *himself, itself,* and *themselves,* is probably here to stay. The distribution is not totally random; the first and second persons use the possessive forms, while the third person uses the object forms. As was noted in Chapter 7, the simple object form of pronouns is still used reflexively in some dialects (*I got me a new shotgun*).

INDEFINITE PRONOUNS

The changes in indefinite pronouns since EMnE have been minor, consisting primarily of small adjustments that usually have simply curtailed previous options. In other words, most changes have tended to make the system more rigid and less flexible.

Every has been lost as a pronoun and remains only as an indefinite adjective. As a pronoun, *somewhat* has given way totally to *something.* The pronoun *some* can no longer stand in for a singular countable noun, but only for a mass noun or a plural noun. *Other,* formerly used unchanged with either singular or plural reference, has acquired an analogous plural *others.*

Verbs

With the loss of the second-person singular pronoun by the end of the EMnE period, English also lost the corresponding verbal inflection -st (as in *thou hast, thou didst*). Only four verbal inflections remain in PDE: (1) the third-person singular present indicative in -s, (2) the past tense -ed (or irregular, as with *brought, gave,* and *hid*), (3) the past participle -ed (or irregular, as with *bound, chosen,* and *rung*), and (4) the present participle -ing. An inflectional subjunctive maintains a precarious existence but has no distinctive forms; the present subjunctive is always identical to the infinitive (*that he be*), and the past subjunctive is the same as the past plural (*if he were*). The inflected subjunctive will eventually probably be lost altogether except for fixed phrases like *God bless you* and *far be it from me.*

STRONG AND IRREGULAR VERBS

The steady change of strong verbs to weak, along with numerous sound changes, has so blurred the distinctions among the original classes of strong verbs and between strong verbs and irregular weak verbs that, in some ways, it is not meaningful to speak of a separate category of strong verbs in PDE. Originally strong verbs are today merely one component of a larger class of irregular verbs.

Of the hundred or so verbs in PDE that are still conjugated strong, many are well on their way to becoming regular (weak) verbs. By the end of EMnE, such verbs as *climb, delve,* and *help* were always weak in the standard language. Probably most speakers of English today normally conjugate *crow, grave, heave,* and *lade* as weak verbs. Other promising candidates for fully weak status include *abide, chide, hew, mow, prove, saw, shave, shear, sow, strew, strive, swell,* and *thrive.*

One minor tendency with respect to originally strong verbs is to preserve the strong forms in the core, intransitive meanings of the verb, but to use weak forms for derived, transitive meanings. For instance, we say *the sun shone* and *the bell rang,* but *I shined my shoes* and *I ringed the birch tree.*

WEAK VERBS

The "regular" verbs of PDE are of course weak verbs, but not all weak verbs are regular verbs. Weak verbs often underwent vowel changes in the past tense and past participle during ME as a result of the shortening of vowels in closed syllables. Some of these variations were later regularized, but many remain to the present day (*leave/left/left*). The remaining irregular weak verbs are subject to the same pressures for regularization that strong verbs are. For example, the past forms of *bereave, clothe,* and *plead* frequently appear as *bereaved, clothed,* and *pleaded,* rather than the traditional *bereft, clad,* and *pled.* One subcategory of weak verbs, those with a past tense in *-t* (sometimes with an accompanying vowel change), are commonly regularized in American English, less commonly in British English. Examples include *burn, dream, dwell, kneel, lean, leap, learn, spell, spill, spoil.*

OTHER VERBS

There have been no changes in the standard forms of the modal auxiliaries since the end of the EMnE period, but modals can no longer be used without a following infinitive, even when the meaning is clear without it (see p. 234). Further, the prehistorical English process whereby original past forms came to have present meaning and new past forms had to be developed is being repeated in PDE. The modals *might, could, should, would* are regularly used today with present or future meaning; younger speakers say, for example, "It *might* rain," where older, more conservative speakers say, "It *may* rain." Only *could* and *would* can indicate past time by themselves (*I could tell he was unhappy*; *He would play for hours at a stretch*). The remaining original past forms always have to be "supported" by the perfect tense to convey past meaning (*You should have gone,* not *You should go*; or *They might have slept,* not *They might sleep*).

Verb + adverb combinations (or two-part verbs or phrasal verbs), which first appeared in ME and proliferated in EMnE, have flourished in PDE. The process has even extended, at least in colloquial language, to combinations in which the first element is a noun rather than a verb (*louse up, freak out*). In addition, PDE has developed a numerous category of three-part verbs consisting of verb + adverb + preposition; typical examples are *come down with* (the flu), *get away with* (murder), *look forward to* (a vacation), and *watch out for* (wet paint). Note that these combinations must be treated as units because their meanings are not predictable from their component parts.

Uninflected Word Classes

PREPOSITIONS

The number of prepositions in English has steadily increased over the centuries, and their meanings and usage tend to be unstable. In PDE, new prepositions have developed primarily from participial forms of verbs (*pending, granted*) and from noun phrases that include older prepositions (*in return for, on the basis of*). Shifting usage is especially noticeable after specific verbs, adjectives, or phrases. Composition teachers who protest student constructions like *convince about, married with, take charge over,* and *in search for* (as opposed to the traditional *convince of, married to, take charge of,* and *in search of*) are probably fighting a hopeless battle; usage of specific prepositions will undoubtedly continue to shift from generation to generation and from one dialectal area to another.

CONJUNCTIONS

Throughout the history of English, the language has had far fewer coordinating than subordinating conjunctions. What is more, the small class of coordinating conjunctions has remained remarkably stable from OE times to the present. The three regular coordinating conjunctions of today—*and*, *but*, and *or*—all go back to Old English (although their usage and meanings have changed somewhat over the years). *For* and *yet*, both of which have a marginal status as coordinating conjunctions today, also date back to OE. No new coordinating conjunctions have appeared over the centuries.

The picture is quite different for subordinating conjunctions. In general, the tendency has been for the total number to increase over the centuries. Still, even as new ones are being added, some of the older ones are lost. Since EMnE, the subordinating conjunctions *albeit*, *lest*, *whence*, *whereas*, and *whither* have become much less frequently used in speech and are generally restricted to formal levels of writing. All have an archaic flavor today. As is true of prepositions, new subordinating conjunctions tend to be phrasal. For example, the multiword phrases *assuming that*, *on the ground(s) that*, and *in view of the fact that* have all become subordinating conjunctions during PDE.

ADVERBS

Perhaps the most striking change in the morphology of adverbs between EMnE and PDE has been the development of the feeling that all adverbs derived from adjectives should be overtly marked as adverbs by the suffix *-ly*. In EMnE, plain adverbs (those identical in form to adjectives) were widely used, even by careful writers. The list of acceptable plain adverbs today has shrunk to a few frequent ones, which often seem to have survived only because the corresponding form in *-ly* has a different meaning. We say "I worked *hard* until very *late*" because *hardly* and *lately* do not mean the same thing as *hard* and *late*. Except for a handful of common time words like *early*, *daily*, *weekly*, and *hourly*, even adjectives that already end in *-ly* are at best uncomfortable when used adverbially. For example, although contemporary dictionaries still list *friendly* as an adverb, most of us would hesitate to write it as such, preferring a paraphrase like *in a friendly manner* or even the phonological monstrosity *friendlily* (also recognized by some dictionaries).

Some of the common closed-list adverbs (those not derived from adjectives) of EMnE have since become obsolete or at least archaic. Examples include *afore* 'before', *ere long*, *without* 'outside, out of doors', *hither*, and *thither*. The adverbial use of *something* in EMnE was mentioned earlier.

Present-Day English Syntax

The larger syntactic patterns of Present-Day English were established by the Early Modern English period, and most of the changes since that time have either been minor or more quantitative than qualitative in nature.

Syntax Within Phrases

NOUN PHRASES

There was little change in the rules for the formation of noun phrases between EMnE and PDE. Under "Morphology" (p. 271) we discussed the extension of the *of* genitive at the expense of the inflected genitive and also the greater use of the group genitive in PDE. The most striking difference between the two periods is the great increase in the use of noun adjunct phrases during PDE. This process of modifying one noun with another, uninflected noun originated in ME and became common in EMnE. However, its extensive use and the use of several noun adjuncts to modify a single head is a PDE phenomenon. We cannot so much as glance at a contemporary periodical without encountering such phrases as *death penalty*, *lifetime ambition, group hysteria*, and *factory smokestacks*. A slightly more careful perusal, especially of technical or governmental writing, will produce three-part examples like *university press publications, interagency task force, deep-sea marine sequence*, and *pro-choice women activists*. Indeed, an extraordinarily heavy density of noun adjuncts is one of the things that makes reading bureaucratese so difficult and annoying.

VERB PHRASES

Most of the syntactic differences between EMnE and PDE involve verb phrases; yet few of these changes concern new structures. Rather, most of them involve either an extension of patterns established at an earlier stage of the language, or a loss of previous options.

From OE times on, verb phrases in English have been increasing in complexity. OE had a phrasal passive formed with either *weorþan* 'become' or *beon* 'be' plus the past participle. The progressive tense began in ME and became common in EMnE. The combination of the two—the progressive passive as in *we are being watched*—first appeared at the end of EMnE, and its regular use is only a PDE phenomenon. Finally, the perfect progressive passive (*I have been being annoyed*) is a PDE development and, in fact, is still relatively rare in English.

Passives formed in the traditional way with *be* + past participle tend to have a static sense and are often indistinguishable from *be* + adjectival (for instance, *I was interested*; *the walls were painted*). Perhaps because of a felt need to convey more forcefully the sense of the action of the verb, a new passive with *get* as the auxiliary arose in the nineteenth century and is common today, although it is still restricted primarily to colloquial style. Some have said jokingly that we use the *get* passive when we really mean it. There is a certain amount of truth in this remark: Compare the much stronger *they got beaten* with the weaker *they were beaten*.

All of the preceding changes have involved either new syntactical structures or extensions of older ones. PDE has also lost some options that existed as late as EMnE. First, *have* is now the only auxiliary that we can use to form the perfect tense; *be* is no longer possible, even for verbs of motion. Second, as late as the seventeenth century, ongoing action limited in duration could be expressed by either the simple present or by the progressive tense. In PDE, the progressive tense is obligatory for such ongoing action, and the simple present has become a "timeless" tense. (Compare the difference in meaning between *she reads German* and *she is reading German*.)

Still another loss in PDE is that of the unemphatic periphrastic *do* of EMnE (see p. 239). Even as English has lost this option, however, the use of *do* as an "empty" auxiliary when no other auxiliary is present has become obligatory in negative and interrogative sentences, in tag questions, and in emphatic constructions that often imply a contradiction of a previously expressed idea:

Negative	She *didn't* eat her lunch.
Interrogative	*Did* she eat her lunch?
Tag question	She ate her lunch, *didn't* she?
Emphatic	Despite what you say, she *did* eat her lunch.

The use of *do* as a substitute for a full verb when no other auxiliary is available goes back to OE and is, of course, standard in PDE ("She brought an umbrella, but I *didn't*"). In British English, this usage is sometimes extended to constructions in which another auxiliary is present in the original clause:

> "Will you be coming tonight?" "I may *do*."
> "It's hard to believe that anyone could have come so far, but Janie might have *done*."

Syntax Within Clauses

Throughout the history of English, the SVO word order has always been the favorite for declarative statements in independent clauses, and many of the changes that have taken place over the centuries have involved extensions of this pattern to other contexts or loss of other options. Since EMnE, the language has lost the option of VSO order after a nonnegative adverbial. We can no longer say, as Shakespeare could, "therefore *was I created* with a stubborn outside" (H5 5.2.226). Also gone is the option of SOV order when the object is a pronoun. On the other hand, PDE cannot use SVO in a clause that begins with a negative adverbial; inversion to VSO is now obligatory. That is, where Shakespeare says "seldom he smiles" (JC 1.2.205), we would have to say "seldom does he smile."

Since OE times, when both a direct and an indirect object are present in a clause, English has preferred the order IO + DO. However, when the verb has the general meaning of giving and when both the direct and the indirect objects are pronouns, the alternative order of DO + IO has been possible. To use another Shakespearian example, "'twas men I lack'd, and you will give *them me*" (2 H6 3.1.345). This option is still available in British English, but has been lost in American English, where *give me it* is acceptable, but *give it me* is not.

Syntax of Sentences

The basic grammar of the sentence as a whole has changed little since Middle English times; indeed, the syntax of many Old English prose sentences would be acceptable in PDE. What has changed and continues to change is the fashionable stylistics of written sentences. Much of the surviving OE prose consists chiefly of highly paratactic, cumulative sentences that probably were fairly close to speech patterns. Middle English saw a continuation of this style but also early attempts to model English prose on ornate Latin patterns. This Latin influence increased during EMnE, and by the end of the period, the best writers had succeeded in creating a highly formal hypotactic Latinate style in English. But the older traditions persisted too, as the examples in Chapter 7 illustrate.

PDE has experienced a reaction against the intricate, balanced, periodic high style of EMnE. To some extent, there has been a blending of the Latinate hypotactic and the native paratactic. That is, much contemporary prose looks paratactic, but closer examination reveals a deeper hypotaxis whose superficial simplicity is achieved by heavy use of participles and deletion of subordinating conjunctions. To illustrate this, we can examine a brief passage from Ernest

Hemingway, an author whose name has become a byword for stripped-down, simple prose.

> (1) It was bright sunlight in the room when I woke. (2) I thought I was back at the front and stretched out in bed. (3) My legs hurt me and I looked down at them still in the dirty bandages, and seeing them knew where I was. (4) I reached up for the bell-cord and pushed the button. (5) I heard it buzz down the hall and then some one coming on rubber soles along the hall. (6) It was Miss Gage and she looked a little older in the bright sunlight and not so pretty.
>
> —Ernest Hemingway, *A Farewell to Arms* (1929)

The first sentence of this paragraph has overt subordination with the clause *when I woke*. In sentence 2, Hemingway has drawn the reader's attention away from the subordination by deleting the subordinator *that* after *I thought*. Sentence 3 has another example of overt subordination with the brief clause *where I was* at the end. It also has "hidden" subordination; by using the participle *seeing*, Hemingway can avoid a subordinate clause something like *when I saw them*, and he also can delete the subject *I* of the verb *knew*. In sentence 5, *I heard it buzz* is a compression of *I heard it as it buzzed* or some such construction. Furthermore, the participial *coming* is an abridged form of *someone who was coming*. Sentences 4 and 6 are both straightforward, sentence 4 being merely a simple sentence with a compound verb, and sentence 6 a compound sentence with the two independent clauses connected by *and*.[6]

Of course, other features make this paragraph very different stylistically from, say, the Gibbon passage on p. 242. In particular, it lacks the heavy parallelism and balance of the Gibbon passage, and Hemingway's sentences are primarily cumulative, whereas Gibbon's are heavily periodic. Indeed, Hemingway seems almost deliberately to avoid periodic structure by placing adverbial modifiers at the end rather than at the beginning of sentences (see *when I woke* above).

It is not necessary to use such an extreme example to illustrate the change in stylistics between EMnE and PDE: after all, Gibbon's prose was highly mannered even for his own day, and Hemingway is famous for his stark style. A fairer comparison would be between the formal prose of Gibbon and a serious contemporary historian. The passage below was published in 1983.

> (1) It is worth pausing a moment to consider this temporal discipline of Christianity, especially of Western Christianity, which distinguishes it sharply from the other monotheistic religions and has not been adequately examined in the literature on time measurement. (2) In Judaism the worshiper is obliged to pray three times a day, but at no set times: in the morning (after daybreak), afternoon (before sunset), and evening (after dark). (3) A pious Jew will recite his prayers as soon as possible after the permissible time; but if circumstances require, he has substantial leeway in which to perform his obligation. (4) Today some of the starting times of worship are given on calendars to the minute, thanks to astronomical calculations. (5) In ancient and medieval times, however, nature gave the

---

[6] Hemingway's paragraph is more artful than it initially appears in other ways, too. Notice the "envelope" structure achieved by repeating *bright sunlight* in the first and last sentences and by beginning the first and last sentences with *It* and the others with *I* or *My*.

signals. (6) The animals woke the Jew to prayer, and the first of the morning blessings thanks God for giving the rooster the wit to distinguish between day and night. (7) The evening prayer could be recited as soon as three stars were visible; if the sky was cloudy, one waited until one could no longer distinguish between blue and black. (8) No timepiece or alarm was needed.

—David S. Landes, *Revolution in Time* (1983)

Without going into great detail, we can note that Landes' shortest and longest sentences are both shorter than Gibbon's shortest and longest, respectively. Landes' sentences lack the almost compulsive balance of Gibbon's sentences, and Landes uses slightly less overt subordination than Gibbon (though the latter's paragraph is not especially heavily subordinated, either). One of the ways by which Gibbon achieves such a strong sense of balance is through the use of parallel "couplets" like *was not embittered by . . . nor was it confined by*; *to multiply . . . and to enlarge*; *who had lived, or who had died*; *power and immortality*; *a thousand groves and a thousand streams*; and so on. Not only is the Landes passage missing this parallelism, it sometimes lacks parallelism even where the structure would seem to demand it. For instance, the subordinate clause in the first sentence has compound verbs, one of which is active (*which distinguishes it*) and the other of which is passive (*and has not been adequately examined*).

IN THE VERNACULAR

Of all those who have attempted to capture in writing the flavor of the spoken American vernacular, no one has been more successful than Ring Lardner (1885–1933), sportswriter, novelist, essayist, and short-story writer. The following passage is from his nonfiction book *First and Last*.

But while I was raised in a kennel, you might say, and some of my most intimate childhood friends was of the canine gender, still in all I believe dogs is better in some climates than others, the same as oysters, and I don't think it should ought to be held against a man if he don't feel the same towards N.Y. dogs as he felt towards Michigan dogs, and I am free to confess that the 4 dogs who I have grew to know personly here on Long Island has failed to arouse tender yearnings anyways near similar to those inspired by the flea bearers of my youth. . . .

[No. 4] is our present incumbrance which we didn't ask for him and nobody give him to us but here he is and he has got the insomonia and he has picked a spot outside my window to enjoy it but not only that but he has learnt that if you jump at a screen often enough it will finely give way and the result is that they ain't a door or window on the first floor that you couldn't drive a rhinoceros through it and all the bugs that didn't already live in the house is moveing in and bringing their family.

That is a true record of the dogs who I have met since takeing up my abode in Nassau county so when people ask me do I like dogs I say I'm crazy about them and I think they are all right in their place but it ain't Long Island.

Ring Lardner, *First and Last* (New York: Charles Scribner's Sons, 1938), pp. 262, 264–65.

Present-Day English Lexicon

The previous two chapters emphasized the great increases in the English lexicon during Middle English and Early Modern English. We might think that, after the remarkable expansions of these centuries, Present-Day English would be a fallow period, a time for the language to settle down and absorb its gains. Such is not the case; the vocabulary has increased and continues to increase at an incredible rate during PDE. Measuring this growth precisely is impossible, but in sheer numbers of words, the vocabulary of English has acquired more items during PDE than in all its preceding history.

There are, however, differences between the new vocabulary of PDE and that of earlier periods. The bulk of acquisitions during ME were borrowings from French that ranged across the entire spectrum of semantic areas and stylistic levels. In EMnE, the new items were also chiefly borrowings, but this time from Latin, and they tended to be more learned words, concentrated at the formal end of the stylistic range. The PDE growth has been overwhelmingly in Greco-Latin scientific and technical terms.

Loanwords

CLASSICAL INFLUENCE

Borrowing from the classical languages has characterized every period of English and has continued at a high rate in PDE. However, the nature of this borrowing and its effects on the total lexicon of the language differ somewhat in PDE from earlier periods. To be sure, many of the PDE borrowings have become part of the general vocabulary: *petunia, creosote, latex, television, antibiotic, transistor, electron,* and *psychoanalyze* are familiar to most native speakers. Once-erudite words may even be treated with the breezy irreverence accorded homely native terms. For instance, the bacteriological term *streptococcus* first appeared in print only in 1877. It has since undergone clipping to *strep*, as in *strep infection* or *I've got a strep* (with a blithe disregard for the fact that the etymologically "correct" clipped form would be *strepto*).

The bulk of the recent borrowings are, however, so technical and esoteric that only highly educated specialists understand and use them. A quick glance through the pages of *Science*—considered a journal of general interest to scientists, not restricted to specialized fields—reveals such terms as *polypeptide, atracurium besylate, immunogenicity, pentraxin, electrophoresis, hypomethylation,* and *interferometry*, several of which are not even listed in so-called unabridged dictionaries. So inaccessible is much of the technical terminology today that *Science* itself has begun summarizing several of its articles each week in simpler language so that scientists working outside the narrow area of the articles can get at least a general notion of what is being reported. The problem of inkhorn terms is still with us.

Another way in which PDE borrowings from the classical languages differ from those of earlier periods is that the term "borrowed" itself is, in a sense, inaccurate. Some of the newer words are indeed simply borrowed directly from Greek or Latin. For example, *hormone*, first recorded in 1905, is from the Greek verb *horman* 'to urge on'. *Clone*, first recorded two years earlier, is from Greek *klōn* 'twig'. Nevertheless, the majority of PDE "loanwords" from the classical languages never existed in the classical languages. Instead, they have been manufactured in

English out of previously borrowed classical elements. For instance, the word *retrovirus* is so new (or so specialized) that it does not appear in *Webster's Third New International*. It is composed of *retro-*, from Latin *rētro* 'backward', used as a prefix in English since the sixteenth century, and *virus*, from Latin *vīrus* 'poison', also first appearing in English in the sixteenth century and used in its present meaning since the eighteenth century. The word *retrovirus* itself was never used when Latin was a spoken language.

The classical vocabulary of English today is larger than the *total* known vocabularies of classical Greek and Latin because English has composed so many "new" Greek and Latin words. This composition may be similar to regular compounding in English; in the case of, say, *phylloclade*, from Greek *phullon* 'leaf' plus Greek *klados* 'branch', two nouns are used to make a compound noun. Even more common is the use of affixes. PDE has borrowed many prefixes and a few suffixes from Greek and Latin, and uses them extensively to form new classical "loanwords." Among the prefixes either first borrowed or first used productively in PDE are *auto-*, *epi-*, *ex-*, *hypo-*, *intra-*, *meta-*, *micro-*, *mini-*, *multi-*, *neo-*, *para-*, and *ultra-*. Much less productive are the new suffixes like *-athon*, *-itis*, *-mania*, and *-orium*.

One other way in which the Greco-Latin technical vocabulary of PDE differs from that of earlier periods is that it is shared to a large extent by other European languages. For example, beside English *antitoxin* are French *antitoxine*, Italian *antitossina*, Swedish *antitoxin*, Russian *antitoksin*. Even German *Gegengift*, literally "against poison," is a loan-translation of the same term. Nor has English always been the initiator. English borrowed *oxygen* and *hydrogen* from French late in the EMnE period, and the immediate source of the terms *allele* and *gene* was German. Scholars often speak of an "international scientific vocabulary," on the whole an apt description.

OTHER EUROPEAN INFLUENCES

For all its undisputed dominance among the world's languages today, English has continued to borrow freely from other living languages, both Indo-European and non-Indo-European.

French.   French continues to influence the English lexicon more heavily than any other living language, and it has contributed hundreds of loanwords to PDE. France's preeminence in fashion explains such words as *beige, beret, blouse, crepe, lingerie, negligee, suede,* and *trousseau*. Among the many terms borrowed from France's famous cuisine are *au gratin, chef, éclair, gourmet, margarine, menu, restaurant,* and *sauté*. Miscellaneous items include *au pair, camouflage, chauffeur, coupon, elite, garage, genre,* and *semantics*. American French has given a few new words to PDE, including *bayou, shanty,* and *toboggan*.

Italian.   Italian influence on the English vocabulary has not been as heavy in PDE as it was in EMnE. The popularity of Italian cooking is responsible for a number of food-related words, such as *lasagna, pasta, salami, scaloppine,* and *zucchini*. Miscellaneous words include *fiasco, inferno, mafia, ocarina,* and *piccolo*.

Spanish.   Spanish continues to be a source of English loanwords, though the rate of borrowing has decreased during the twentieth century. Among nineteenth-century loans are *adobe, alfalfa, bonanza, chaparral, mescal, quinine, silo,* and *vamoose.* American Spanish has probably been more influential than Continental Spanish; a few of its PDE contributions are *abalone, bronco, gaucho, gringo, mesquite, mustang, peyote, ranch, serape, taco,* and *tamale.* We might expect the recent heavy influx of Spanish-speaking immigrants into the United States to have been accompanied by many new Spanish loanwords, but it has not.

Dutch and Afrikaans. Dutch loanwords into English have always tended to be concrete, down-to-earth words, and their PDE contributions are no exception, as is evidenced by loans like *boss, bushwhack, coleslaw, cruller, poppycock, snoop, spook,* and *waffle.* More exotic are the loans from Afrikaans, the Dutch dialect of South Africa: *aardvark, apartheid, spoor, trek, veldt,* and *wildebeest.*

German. A number of factors led to an increase in German loanwords in PDE. Among these were Germany's unification and emergence as a major international power, her early supremacy in graduate education, and the heavy German immigration into the United States during the nineteenth century. Among the educational or intellectual borrowings are *seminar, semester, kindergarten, gestalt,* and *leitmotif.* Terms for food and beverages include *lager, schnapps, pretzel, strudel,* and *zwieback.* Contributions to the vocabulary of popular music include *accordion,*

A TOUGH ROUGH TO HOUGH

English spelling is—not always deservedly—the despair of foreign learners, the perennial target of reformers, and the butt of general ridicule. But some observers find it a source of fun, as the following piece of whimsy by the contemporary American poet George Starbuck illustrates.

The Barraclough Foofarough

We Barracloughs are tough.
We Barracloughs are thorough.
We've shaken every bough.
We've beaten every borough.
Directories we plough
Methodically through
Are each a very trough
Of Goughs and Houghs—a slough
Of Cloughs and Bloughs. What though
We come down with the cough?
What though we squander dough
And time? It is enough
To *know* there is no -ough
That rhymes with Barraclough.

glockenspiel, yodel, and *zither.* Some miscellaneous loans are *dachshund, poodle, ersatz, kaput, strafe, paraffin, stalag, hinterland,* and *klutz.*

Yiddish.   The heavy immigration of Yiddish-speaking Jews into the United States has brought with it a number of Yiddish words. Unlike most of the other recent loans discussed so far, however, many of them—though by no means all—are familiar primarily in areas with a dense Jewish population. Such is true, for example, of *halvah, knish, kvetch, schlep, schlock,* and *tsuris.* More generally familiar are words like *bagel, kibitzer, kosher, lox, matzo,* and *pastrami.*

Celtic Languages.   As has been true in the past, Celtic loans in PDE have been relatively few; Irish has contributed most of them. These include *blarney, brogan, colleen, dolmen, drumlin, keen* 'to lament', and *slew.*

Other European Languages.   Other European languages have been the source of few loanwords in PDE. Norwegian has provided *ski* and *vole,* Danish *flense,* and Swedish *rutabaga.* Czech has given *polka* and *robot,* and Polish *mazurka. Paprika* and *goulash* come from Hungarian. Russian has been a somewhat more productive source: *babushka, balalaika, borscht, borzoi, intelligentsia, pogrom, samovar, troika, tundra,* and *vodka* all date from the PDE period.

NON-EUROPEAN INFLUENCES

The continued involvement of English-speaking peoples with the rest of the world has meant a continued influx of loanwords from exotic languages.

Amerindian Languages.   The majority of Amerindian loanwords entered English during the EMnE period. Among the few nineteenth-century loans are Algonquian *mugwump, muskeg, pemmican, quahog,* and *wickiup.* Navaho has given *hogan* and Siouan *tepee.* Relatively recent Eskimo loans are *anorak, husky,* and *igloo.*

Asian Languages.   Of the Asian languages, Japanese, predictably, has been the largest contributor to the English vocabulary in the PDE period. Too miscellaneous to categorize, some of these recent loans are *banzai, bonsai, geisha, ginkgo, hara-kiri, hibachi, jinrikisha, judo, jujitsu, kamikaze, karate, kimono, obi, origami, samurai, sukiyaki, tempura, tsunami,* and *tycoon.* More isolated than Japan from the European world until very recently, China has provided fewer loanwords to English; among these few are *fan-tan, gung-ho, kowtow, mahjong, oolong, shanghai, shangtung,* and *yen,* 'yearning'.

   The majority of the English borrowings from Hindi came prior to the PDE period, but the nineteenth century saw a few new loans, including *chutney, loot, pajamas, puttee,* and *thug.* Urdu provided *khaki.* The words *sutra* and *mantra,* both from Sanskrit, were borrowed as scholarly terms around the turn of the nineteenth century, but only in the past two or three decades have they become popular as a result of the recent interest in Oriental religions.

   From the Pacific Island languages, PDE has received Hawaiian *aloha, hula, lei, poi,* and *ukulele,* as well as native Australian words like *boomerang, koala,* and *wallaby.* From Malay is *raffia,* and *boondocks* is from Tagalog.

African Languages. African languages have continued to be only a minor source of loanwords into English. Among the few terms that have been borrowed during PDE are *bongo, dashiki, goober, gumbo, hoodoo, impala,* and *safari.*

Formation of New Words

Although an occasional voice bemoans the lost ability of English to form new words and its too-extensive use of foreign borrowings, such complaints are unjustified. The language has continued to create new words at a high rate during the PDE period. As in the past, affixing and compounding are the major sources. Moreover, most of the minor processes of forming new words are still productive, and the language has even adopted a new process, that of making acronyms.

COMPOUNDING

Compounding continues to be a highly productive source of new vocabulary items. Most of the earlier kinds of compounds are still being formed today, though not necessarily at a high rate. The most common type by far is the noun created by compounding two preexisting nouns. We can find multiple examples simply by glancing at any contemporary newspaper or magazine. A handful of recent examples are *acid rock, birdbrain, body stocking, cable TV, ghetto blaster, granny glasses, group therapy, power station,* and *row house.*

AFFIXING

As has always been true in English, affixing is the single largest source of new lexical items. The prefixes borrowed from the classical languages have added to the pool of raw material for affixing. A few examples that involve these recently borrowed prefixes are *autosuggestion, epicenter, hypodermic, intraorbital, microwave, miniskirt, multimedia, neo-Nazi, paraplegic,* and *ultrasonic.*

FUNCTIONAL SHIFT

From EMnE times on, functional shift, or creating one part of speech from another without altering its form, has been a highly productive source of new vocabulary in English. All parts of speech can participate, at least to a limited extent, but the major types involve nouns to verbs, verbs to nouns, and adjectives to either nouns or verbs. Noun-to-verb conversion has given PDE *to blackmail, to eyeball,* and *to trash,* for instance. Verb-to-noun shift is exemplified by *a commute, a flare, an interrupt. To savage* and *to total* are adjective-to-verb shifts, and *a crazy* and *a gay* are adjective-to-noun conversions.

MINOR SOURCES OF NEW WORDS

None of the minor sources of new words mentioned in Chapter 7 has fallen into total disuse, some of them have increased in productivity, and at least one new source has been added to the language.

1. *Clipping.* Whenever a long word or phrase has to be used repeatedly, some sort of abbreviation is almost inevitable. Clipping, or the dropping off of initial or final syllables, is one way of shortening awkward words or phrases. Many

clipped forms are idiosyncratic or at least confined to a limited dialectal or occupational area, but among some of the more generally familiar PDE clipped forms are *cello*, *coon*, and *mall* from *violincello*, *raccoon*, and *pall-mall*, respectively. These words all underwent clipping of their initial parts. More common is clipping of the final portions of a word or phrase, as in *chimp*, *decal*, *tarp*, *deli*, *porn*, and *razz*, from *chimpanzee*, *decalcomania*, *tarpaulin*, *delicatessen*, *pornography*, and *razzberry*, respectively.

2. *Back Formation.* Back formation is like functional shift in that one part of speech is derived from another, and most back formations involve nouns, verbs, or adjectives. Unlike functional shift, it entails the sloughing off of what appears to be a derivative affix before the shift takes place. For example, since the beginning of the PDE period, the nouns *diplomat*, *peeve*, and *paramedic* have been formed from the adjectives *diplomatic*, *peevish*, and *paramedical*. From the nouns *editor*, *jelly*, *manipulation*, *television*, and *self-destruction* have come the verbs *edit*, *jell*, *manipulate*, *televise*, and *self-destruct*.

3. *Blends.* The umbrella label of "blend" covers a number of different kinds of word formation, but we will note here only two gross subdivisions. The first, older type can be represented by *squawk*, seemingly a blend of *squall* and *squeak*. Such blends probably were first made unconsciously, and the original elements are often uncertain. The type shares features of echoic, reduplicative, and synesthetic word formation; in fact, dictionaries frequently disagree not only on the formative elements, but even on whether a given word is a blend, an echoic form, a dialectal variant of another word, or even a loanword from another language. For example, three contemporary college dictionaries treat *frazzle* as a blend of *fray* + *fazzle*; one considers it a variant of a dialectal word *fazzle*, and one says it is from Low German *vrāsen*. For the word *wangle*, two dictionaries suggest it may be a blend of *waggle* + *wankle*, one dictionary suggests that it is a blend of *wag* + *dangle*, another says it is perhaps an altered form of *waggle*, and still another thinks it a slang formation based on *angle*. The lack of a clear-cut pedigree has not prevented many such words from entering the language during PDE. A few of the possible or probable blends from the PDE period are

Blend	Possible Source
brash	break + rash
crunch	craunch + crush
hassle	haggle + tussle
muss	mess + fuss
prissy	prim + sissy
slosh	slop + slush
squiggle	squirm + wriggle

The second type of blend, a more recent variety, can be represented by *transistor*, a blend of *transfer* and *resistor*. Though the exact rules for forming such blends vary, they are usually consciously made, and the original elements are clear. Some formations, such as the computer term *bit* from *binary* + *digit*, resemble acronyms, except that the end of the second word is incorporated into the new form rather than the beginning. Other formations resemble affixing, clipping, or even compounding in some ways. A representative sample of the numerous such formations in PDE is the following:

Blend	*Source*
apathetic	apathy + pathetic
boron	borax + carbon
medieval	medium + aevum
neutron	neutral + -on
permafrost	permanent + frost
pulsar	pulse + quasar

4. *Proper Names.* PDE has acquired hundreds of new words, most of them nouns, from the names of places, people, and literary characters. Details about the sources of the words in the following list can be found in any good college dictionary.

atropine	jodhpurs	ritzy
badminton	karakul	shrapnel
cardigan	limousine	tuxedo
derringer	mackinaw	volt
euphuism	negus	welch
forsythia	ohm	ytterbium
gorilla	poinsettia	zeppelin
hollandaise	quonset	

5. *Echoic Words.* Echoic words, which sound like their referents, have continued to be a minor source of new vocabulary items in PDE. Among the words first recorded after 1800 are *chug, clop, honk, shush, wham,* and *zap.* Bird names form an entertaining subdivision of echoic words; PDE additions include *bobwhite, chickadee, phoebe,* and *veery,* all names of native American birds (British birds all had already been named before the PDE period).

Words formed through phonetic symbolism constitute a kind of second-generation echoic category. That is, if a number of words more or less accidentally share both a common sound or cluster of sounds and a certain amount of common meaning, then new words to express a similar meaning may be created incorporating this common sound. The process is older than PDE, but by PDE, a sufficient number of examples have accumulated to demonstrate that the process is indeed a real one. For example, over the centuries, the cluster /gr/ has come to be associated with the meaning "menacing noise, grumbling."[7] *Grunt* and *grim* date back to OE, *growl* appeared in ME, *grumble* and *gruff* in EMnE, and *grouse* in PDE. The cluster /sw/ often conveys the idea of swaying or swinging motion, so over the centuries *sweep, swing, sway, swirl, swagger,* and *swash* have appeared; to this list *swoosh* has been added in PDE. The symbolic sound need not be in initial position; the final cluster /ɪdəl/ seems to convey the sense of "trifle" in such words as *fiddle, twiddle, piddle,* and the PDE *diddle.*

---

[7] These examples have been adapted from Hans Marchand, *The Categories and Types of Present-Day English Word-Formation* (University, Ala.: Univ. of Alabama Press, 1966), pp. 313 ff.

6. *Folk Etymology.* Folk etymology does not seem to be an especially productive source of new words in PDE; perhaps universal literacy has made the original forms of most words too familiar. Among the few new terms are (beef) *jerky* from Spanish *charqui* and ultimately Quechua *ch'arki*; *hackamore*, again from Spanish but ultimately from Arabic *shakīmah*; and *sockeye* (salmon) from Salish *suk-kegh.*

7. *Verb + Adverb.* Verb + adverb combinations continue to be highly productive in PDE, as they were in EMnE. A new development in PDE is the easy conversion of the resulting verb to a noun by shifting the stress from the second element to the first. First recorded as nouns only in PDE are, to mention only a few of the many, many examples, *breakdown, breakoff, comeback, comedown, makeup, payoff, pickup, playback, rundown, runoff, sendoff, takeoff, takeover,* and *takeup.*

8. *Reduplication.* As we noted in Chapter 7, English has never made much use of reduplication to form new words, and most of the reduplicated words that we do have today are loans from other languages. A few new ones have been created in PDE, chiefly of the baby-talk or slang variety: *boo-boo, buddy-buddy, choo-choo, goody-goody, hush-hush, no-no, putt-putt, rah-rah, yum-yum.*

   Straight reduplication may be varied by changing the vowel of one of the elements, a process sometimes called ablaut reduplication. This process was perhaps more productive in EMnE, which saw such new terms as *chiff-chaff, dilly-dally, fiddle-faddle, knickknack, tittle-tattle,* and *zigzag.* PDE has produced *clip-clop, criss-cross, hee-haw, ping-pong, ric-rac,* and *tick-tock.*

   Still another variant of straight reduplication is reduplicating rhyme, that is, changing the initial consonant of one of the elements. A few examples of reduplicated rhymes appear as early as EMnE (*boohoo, helterskelter, hodgepodge, hurdygurdy,* and *roly-poly*). The process has apparently become more popular in PDE, which has produced such terms as *boogie-woogie, fuddy-duddy, hanky-panky,* and *yoo-hoo.* A recent trend has been to form reduplicating rhymes in which each element is meaningful, such as *brain drain, chop shop, culture vulture, gang bang,* and *walkie-talkie.*

9. *Calques.* A very minor source of new vocabulary is calques, or loan-translations. Under this process (which could also be treated as a form of borrowing), a word is translated element by element from another language. Most of the few calques that PDE has are from closely related languages, primarily German—perhaps because the grammar of compounds in English is similar to that of German.

Original Language	*English Calque*
French *vers libre*	free verse
German *Lehnwort*	loanword
German *Abdruck*	offprint
German *Oberton*	overtone
Dutch *zaagbok*	sawbuck
German *Stosstruppen*	shock troops
German *Übermensch*	superman

10. *Trade Names.* As a source of new vocabulary, trade names are restricted to the PDE period. Indeed, they have to be because the economic system of capitalistic manufacturing and advertising that has produced the trade names

is itself a product of the modern age. A few familiar terms that originated as trade names are *freon, frisbee, heroin, hovercraft, jello, klaxon, mimeograph, pogo*(stick), *saran, spackle, yo-yo,* and *zipper.* Some of these still are legally protected by copyright, but neither the law nor the copyright holders themselves can control popular usage. Both General Foods, which owns the copyright to the name *Jell-O,* and Nabisco, which manufactures a competing product, would probably prefer consumers to use the term *gelatin dessert* as a generic term. The British call the same product *jelly,* but in the United States *jelly* already refers to preserves without pieces of whole fruit, so the term *jello* fills a need. In some instances, brand names have become common nouns for a time, only to be replaced by other terms later. Such is the case with *kodak* and *victrola,* for instance, and may eventually be true for such contemporary borderline words as *kleenex, walkman, bandaid,* and *xerox.*

11. *Acronyms.* Acronyms, or words formed from the initial letters of preexisting words, are another modern phenomenon, virtually unheard-of in English prior to the PDE period and having mushroomed only in the twentieth century. They are particularly useful for compacting the extremely long names so dear to governmental agencies and chemists; hence such acronyms as UNESCO from *United Nations Educational, Scientific,* and *Cultural Organization* and *amphetamine* from *alpha methyl phenyl ethyl amine.* Both of these examples are pronounced as words, but many such formations are pronounced as a sequence of letters, such as *VCR, MSG, IUD,* and *BLT.* Some prefer to call the latter type *initialisms,* but the distinction is scarcely worth making, especially since some formations are pronounced both ways; *ROTC,* for instance, may be either [ɑr-o-ti-si] or [rɔt-si].

      Once the process of forming acronyms was well under way, it was inevitable that coiners would attempt to insure that the resulting acronym itself formed a meaningful word. Relatively early examples of such tinkering are *Basic* (English) from *British American Scientific International Commercial,* and *WAVES* from *Women Accepted for Volunteer Emergency Service.* More recently, we have seen such names as *NOW* (*National Organization for Women*), a multitude of computer-connected acronyms like *Prolog* (for *Programming Logic*), and *MADD* (for *Mothers Against Drunk Drivers*)—the latter having spawned an imaginary counterorganization *DAMM* (or *Drunks Against Mad Mothers*).

12. *Root Creations.* On first thought, nothing seems simpler than to coin a brand-new word that is not derived from or related to any existing word. In actuality, root creation of this sort is extremely rare; most words purported to be root creations bear a strong resemblance to an existing word or root. For example, *gobbledygook* is obviously related to *gobble,* the meaningless noise made by turkeys. *Golliwog,* supposedly coined as the name for a grotesque doll, immediately reminds one of *polliwog.* More acceptable as lacking an etymology are *kodak, heebie-jeebies, googol,* and *quark*—though the last as a name for a subatomic particle originated in James Joyce's *Finnegans Wake.* Although they are not normally included in the category of root creations, some of the nineteenth-century American English mock-Latinate words like *conniption* 'tantrum' and *absquatulate* 'leave hastily' are perhaps better candidates for true root creation. They have Latinate-looking affixes like *-tion* and *ab-,* but their roots do not appear in Latin, nor can they reasonably be connected with existing English words.

13. *Unknown Origin.* As we have noted before, all periods of the history of English have produced a number of words whose origin is simply unknown—though tentative etymologies may suggest ablaut variation, dialect forms, echoic terms, or root creation. PDE is no exception, and we have scores of pedigreeless words like *bogus, cavort, dander, fad, gadget, hike, jalopy, kilter, lurch* 'stagger', *malarkey, nifty, pandowdy, raunchy, skimp, tatting* 'lace-making', and *yank* 'pull'. Several of these words and many others besides (for example, *floozy, grungy, mosey, rowdy, shoddy, snazzy, spiffy*) end in the affective diminutive *-y*. The majority of them are highly informal and some are strictly colloquial.

LOOKING BACKWARD

Ever since the Renaissance, Englishmen have been interested in the language of their forebears. The attraction of the Middle Ages was especially strong during the nineteenth century, and the English author, artist, craftsman, and utopian socialist William Morris was among those most fascinated by medieval life. In his fantasy *A Dream of John Ball*, Morris attempts to write in fourteenth-century English, albeit with contemporary spelling. The following passage is from the dialogue that Morris, the dreamer, has with John Ball, the leader of the Peasants' Revolt of 1381. Ball is speaking.

> Yea, the road is long, but the end cometh at last. Friend, many a day have I been dying; for my sister, with whom I have played and been merry in the autumn tide about the edges of the stubble fields; and we gathered the nuts and bramble-berries there, and started thence the missel-thrush, and wondered at his voice and thought him big; and the sparrow-hawk wheeled and turned over the hedges and the weasel ran across the path, and the sound of the sheep-bells came to us from the downs as we sat happy on the grass; and she is dead and gone from the earth, for she pined from famine after the years of the great sickness; and my brother was slain in the French wars, and none thanked him for dying save he that stripped him of his gear; and my unwedded wife with whom I dwelt in love after I had taken the tonsure, and all men said she was good and fair, and true she was and lovely; she also is dead and gone from the earth; and why should I abide save for the deeds of the flesh which must be done? Truly, friend, this is but an old tale that men must die; and I will tell thee another, to wit, that they live: and I live now and shall live. Tell me then what shall befall?

Morris had a good ear for Middle English, and the passage "sounds" authentic. Still, it is difficult to avoid anachronism when attempting to reproduce the language of the past. For example, the *Oxford English Dictionary*'s first citation for *stubble-field* is 1614, and for *missel-thrush* is 1774. In the fourteenth century, English speakers would probably have said that one pined or died *for famine* rather than *from famine*. The use of such complex tense forms as *have I been dying* and *after I had taken*, although not impossible in the late fourteenth century, is much more characteristic of the English of later periods.

Three Works by William Morris (New York: International Publishers, 1968), p. 93.

Lost Vocabulary

In previous chapters, we have discussed the problem of identifying—even of defining—"lost" vocabulary. It is relatively easy to determine when a new word enters the language, much harder to say when a word has left. This is particularly true for the PDE period, when not only the standard language but also dialectal forms and specialized vocabularies of all sorts have been preserved in dictionaries.

One reason why identifying lost vocabulary is so difficult is that the loss or gain of lexical elements normally has little effect on the language as a whole. By contrast, if English were to lose a phoneme, even one with a low functional load like /ŋ/, the language would suddenly acquire a number of new homophones and, at a deeper level, the balance of the phonological system as a whole would shift. At the morphological level, if the third-person singular present indicative -*s* were to drop out entirely, the loss would be immediately obvious even if the total morphological system were not violently disturbed. The lexical system of any natural language, however, is relatively so amorphous that individual additions and losses are usually not apparent. If technological change produces the loss, then it will probably remain unnoticed because there is no need for the word. For example, few people under 50 years of age have ever heard of *waterglass*, and fewer would recognize it as a process for preserving eggs over a long period of time. No one bemoans the lack of the word because the process itself has been replaced by refrigeration. Even if the referent of a lost word does still exist, the language usually has enough synonyms or near-synonyms to fill the gap. For example, the two verbs *cleave* 'to split' and *cleave* 'to adhere' are rarely used as active verbs today because, though they are antonyms in meaning, sound changes over the centuries have made them homophones and thus potentially the source of serious misunderstanding. Nonetheless, the obsolescence of these verbs creates no difficulty because their meanings are easily expressed by words like *split* and *stick*.

Present-Day English Semantics

Identifying and explaining recent semantic changes is for the most part as difficult as explaining those of the more distant past. True, there are a few exceptions, instances in which the newer meaning is so emotionally loaded that we are aware that we can no longer use the word in an older meaning; an obvious example would be the word *gay*. In other cases, the new meaning may be used so widely that earlier meanings are forgotten and we are momentarily bewildered if we do encounter the word in its previous meaning. An example would be the word *condominium*, which today is so extensively used as a concrete noun meaning "apartment in a jointly owned building" that, if we see it in its original meaning of "joint rule or sovereignty," we are at once struck by the semantic change.

Nonetheless, most changes are more subtle. The shift in meaning is slight and hard to pinpoint. Older meanings are retained and overlap with newer ones, at least for a number of years, and identifying the precise point at which the real change took place is impossible. When we read a 400-year-old Shakespeare play, we often realize (though probably not as often as we should) that there have been semantic changes between his day and ours. We are less often aware of how much change has occurred between the eighteenth and the twentieth centuries because the drifts in meaning have been smaller; we usually understand everything—or think we do—and merely find the text "quaint" or "old-fashioned." The following paragraph from Daniel Defoe's *Journal of the Plague Year* illustrates a number of such slight alterations in meaning. (In earlier paragraphs, Defoe has explained how townspeople have begun to be charitable to a group of refugees from the plague who have camped outside the town.)

> Encouraged by this good usage, their carpenter in a few days built them a large shed or house with rafters, and a roof in form, and an upper floor, in which they lodged warm, for the weather began to be damp and cold in the beginning of September. But this house, being very well thatched, and the sides and roof made very thick, kept out the cold well enough. He made, also, an earthen wall at one end with a chimney in it, and another of the company, with a vast deal of trouble and pains, made a funnel to the chimney to carry out the smoak.

Leaving aside a change in spelling (*smoak*) and several syntactic constructions that would seem unidiomatic today (*their carpenter in a few days built*), the passage contains at least eight words whose meaning has shifted in one way or another since Defoe's time.

1. *Encouraged.* Defoe means "inspired with courage sufficient for an undertaking; made confident," not today's more common meaning of "stimulate by assistance; reward; foster."[8]
2. *Usage.* We would probably say *use* or *treatment*, not *usage*, because *usage* has tended to become restricted to the meaning of habitual, established behavior.
3. *A roof in form.* Defoe apparently means the framework of a roof (before thatching), and *framework* would probably be used today.
4. *Another (of the company).* PDE usage rarely has *another* as an independent pronoun without a supporting *one*. We would say *another person* or *someone else*.
5. *Company.* PDE prefers in general to reserve *company* for formally organized groups. We would use *group* or perhaps *band* in this context.
6. *Vast.* Today's usage allows *a great deal* or *a good deal* but not *a vast deal*; the range of usage of *vast* has narrowed.
7. *Pains.* We can *take great pains* or *be at great pains* to do something, but we would not say *a vast deal of pains*. Like *vast*, *pains* has narrowed its range of application.
8. *Funnel.* PDE would use *flue* instead of *funnel*. Apparently the word *flue* was just beginning to replace *funnel* in this meaning at the time Defoe wrote this paragraph. The OED gives a 1715 citation "Builders have ... carried the Flue or

---

[8] Because of this shift in the meaning of English *encourage*, Voltaire's famous aphorism is probably misunderstood by many contemporary English speakers. Voltaire wrote "Dans ce pays-ci il est bon de tuer de temps en temps un amiral pour encourager les autres." In the French, *encourager* means "to make courageous." However, the usual English translation, "In this country [England], it's a good idea to kill an admiral now and then to encourage the others," will be interpreted according to the second meaning above.

Funnel bending." The fact that the writer has to define a flue as a "funnel" indicates that the word *flue* was not yet universally familiar.

In our discussions of semantics in these chapters, we have been unable to give changes in meaning the tightly structured kind of analysis that characterizes descriptions of phonological or even syntactic change. Semantics is simply too close to the messiness of the world out there to be amenable to neat, rigorous analysis. Also, until recently, semantics in general has been ignored as a topic for scientific study, and semantic change remains almost virgin territory. An enormous amount of work must be done—tedious, tiresome work that cannot, alas, be relegated to a computer. Still, the drudgery will pay handsome dividends to our understanding of human language and language change.

One possible approach to the study of semantic change is to trace the entire history of groups of synonyms or near-synonyms in an effort to identify patterns of change. For example, an examination of the history of fourteen nouns referring to smell reveals that at least five of them (*odor, aroma, smell, scent, savor*) have developed an extended, metaphorical meaning of "distinctive quality, aura." Is this kind of semantic change characteristic of other sensory nouns? If so, what does this imply? If not, why is smell unique?

To take another example, out of thirteen adjectives all meaning "laughable" in one way or another (*amusing, comic, comical, droll, facetious, funny, hilarious, humorous, laughable, ludicrous, mirthful, ridiculous, witty*), not one had the basic meaning of "funny" prior to the mid-sixteenth century, and most did not acquire it until long after that. This would suggest that the very concept of humor in its present-day meaning is modern. Yet we need go back no further than Chaucer to see that he wrote many lines obviously intended to be funny, in the modern sense of the word *funny* (as opposed, say, to producing derisive laughter, or joyful laughter, or delight at ingenuity). Then why have we no earlier word to describe it? An organized investigation might reveal whole categories of meaning that have been gained or lost over time.

In summary, the most important features of Present-Day English are

1. Phonologically, the system has, to date, remained stable, with no additions or losses among the phonemes. Minor changes in the distribution of existing phonemes continue to occur.
2. Morphologically, no systemic changes have taken place, although certain categories, such as the inflected genitive and the inflected comparative, have been losing ground.
3. Syntactically, the major patterns remain those of EMnE, but verb phrases have continued to become more complex and the use of quasi-modals has increased. The use of noun adjuncts has mushroomed.
4. Lexically, the English vocabulary has undergone a vast expansion, especially in scientific and technical words created from Greco-Latin roots.
5. Culturally, English is now as close to a world language as any language has ever been throughout history.

Suggested Further Reading

Aarsleff, H. *The Study of Language in England, 1780–1860.*
Barber, Charles. *Linguistic Change in Present-Day English.*
Baron, Dennis E. *Grammar and Good Taste: Reforming the American Language.*
Bauer, Laurie. *English Word Formation.*
Bolton, W. F., and D. Crystal. *The English Language: Essays by Linguists and Men of Letters, 1858–1964.*
Craigie, William A., and James R. Hulbert, eds. *A Dictionary of American English on Historical Principles.*
Dohan, Mary Helen. *Our Own Words.*
Gordan, Ian A. *The Movement of English Prose.*
Greenough, James Bradstreet, and George Lyman Kittredge. *Words and Their Ways in English Speech.*
Lewis, C. S. *Studies in Words.*
Marchand, Hans. *The Categories and Types of Present-Day English Word-Formation.*
Murray, K. M. Elisabeth. *Caught in the Web of Words: James Murray and the Oxford English Dictionary.*
The Oxford English Dictionary.
Quirk, Randolph, et al. *A Grammar of Contemporary English.*
Serjeantson, Mary S. *A History of Foreign Words in English.*
Sheard, J. A. *The Words of English.*
Sledd, James H., and Wilma R. Ebbitt, eds. *Dictionaries and THAT Dictionary: A Casebook on the Aims of Lexicographers and the Targets of Reviewers.*

CHAPTER 9

English Around the World

One common language I'm afraid we'll never get:
Oh, why can't the English learn to set
A good example to people whose English is
*   painful to your ears:*
The Scotch and the Irish leave you close to
*   tears.*
There even are places where English completely
*   disappears—*
In America they haven't used it for years.
                                    —Alan Jay Lerner

In the highly developed nations of the world today, native speakers of English are unique in their widespread—some would say virtually universal—lack of proficiency in other languages. In most English-speaking countries, students do not begin the study of foreign languages until their high-school years, if then. Even at the university level, many colleges do not require a foreign language at all; those that do demand only a minimum ability, certainly not a level high enough to permit the person to function satisfactorily in an environment where only that language is used. Most universities still require master's and doctoral candidates to "demonstrate proficiency" in one or two foreign languages, but, again, the acceptable level is so low that few Ph.D.'s can translate a technical article written in the foreign language in which they are supposedly proficient. Even when students do achieve some fluency through their schooling, most of them rapidly lose this skill after their formal training stops because they rarely use the foreign language after leaving the classroom.

There is a kind of arrogance in the monolingualism of native speakers of English: They can't be bothered learning foreign languages. This arrogance is not necessarily accompanied by contempt, by a feeling that other languages are inferior or barbaric. Quite the opposite—most English speakers feel that English is simple and that other languages are, by comparison, impenetrably complex and hard to learn. Nor, of course, is there any genetic reason why native speakers of English are so incompetent in other languages. Rather, English speakers do not learn other languages because they realize, implicitly or explicitly, that it is not a matter of burning self-interest for them to do so. Most native speakers live in countries where English is both the overwhelmingly dominant language and the only prestigious language. When they go beyond their own borders, they see that, not only is English widely used, but everyone there wants to learn and use English. Why go to the trouble of learning and using other people's language when they are eager to learn and use yours?

An International Language

Insofar as there has ever been such a thing as a world language, English is one today. Certainly English is the worldwide language of technology and communication. The majority of the world's mail is addressed in English, English is the language of international air controllers, and English is the medium of 80 percent of the information stored in computers around the world.[1] Scholars from every nation publish in English in order to reach the widest possible audience, and scholars from some countries publish almost exclusively in English. Particularly in the sciences, English is so much the language of scholarship that, for example, a Swedish scientist once told me that, when he is working in his own specialty, he even thinks in English and often automatically and unconsciously switches to English when discussing scientific questions with his Swedish colleagues.

The pervasiveness of English can be seen in other, less global ways. When bad weather forced me to wait for six hours in the airport in Reykjavík, Iceland, I was apparently one of only a handful of Americans or British there, yet all the conversation around me was in English, albeit often halting English—like that of the Japanese tourist who asked for "a piece of Coca-Cola." (Indeed, I had to return to Kennedy Airport in New York to encounter people who did not understand me when I addressed them in English.) Matches manufactured in the Soviet Union for export to Eastern European countries are labeled "Made in the U.S.S.R." I own a fountain pen, a perfect replica of the famous Parker pen. It was manufactured in the People's Republic of China, exclusively for sale to Chinese within China. It does have the Chinese characters for "everlasting" on it, but it also says, in the Latin alphabet and in English, "Made in China." All over the world, from France to Thailand, young people wear shirts and jackets with English words printed on them, even though the English words often make no sense. These anecdotal examples show that English today is a *koine* for those who do not speak the same language and also that its prestige and popularity outstrip even its actual use.

---

[1] This figure and some of the following statistics were taken from "English Out to Conquer the World," *U.S. News and World Report*, Feb. 18, 1985, pp. 49–52; and from "The New English Empire," *The Economist*, Dec. 20, 1986, pp. 129–33.

There are, of course, a great many native speakers of English. Since 1800, the beginning of the PDE period, the number of people whose first language is English has increased by 2000 percent, and today there are approximately 350 million native speakers. Another 400 million or so use English as a second language. Nonetheless, the number of speakers of Mandarin Chinese, approximately three-quarters of a billion, outstrips even the combined number of native and nonnative English speakers. But Mandarin Chinese is confined primarily to the northern half of the People's Republic of China, while English is spoken as a first language on every continent except South America, and even there it is widely used as a second language.

English is the first language of at least a significant portion of the population in the United States, the British Isles (including Ireland), Canada, Australia, New Zealand, South Africa, Jamaica, Trinidad, Guyana, Barbados, the Leewards, and the Bahamas. India has a small population of native English speakers, but millions use it as a second language; a similar situation applies in Sri Lanka, Pakistan, Bangladesh, and Nepal. Though the number of native speakers is small, English is the official state language of Liberia, Nigeria, Ghana, Sierra Leone, Gambia, Malawi, Zambia, Zimbabwe, Botswana, Swaziland, Lesotho, and Namibia. English is widely used and was once an official language in Kenya, Uganda, and Tanzania. English shares official or semiofficial status with other languages in Singapore and the Philippines.

The widespread use of English and its current position as *the* world language is not accidental, nor is it attributable to any intrinsic linguistic superiority of English as a language. It began with the establishment of the British Empire in the eighteenth and nineteenth centuries. Wherever the British acquired colonies, they brought English with them as the language of administration. Britain lost most of its Empire after World War II, but even as the sun was setting on the Empire, the United States was simultaneously rising as a political, economic, and military superpower. Thus the spread of English has continued without a break.

Nevertheless, English could not have achieved the dominant position it has today without its almost worldwide uniformity. Were it split up into numerous mutually unintelligible dialects, it would not even be a candidate for a world language. This homogeneity of English is due to several factors. First, the diffusion of English throughout the world is a recent phenomenon, and widely disparate dialects simply have not had time to develop. Second, nearly universal literacy in most English-speaking countries has retarded change, especially in the written language. Third, modern developments in communications—telephone, radio, motion picture, tape recordings, satellite television—have united English speakers, retarding dialectal differences, familiarizing all speakers with the sound of other Englishes, and superimposing a kind of world standard over regional varieties.

All this is not to deny the existence of differences among the Englishes used around the world. There is great disparity in phonology, especially of vowels and of intonation patterns. There are also differences in vocabulary and even in the semantics of common vocabulary. Variation in morphology and syntax is less extensive, except for creoles such as Krio. In the larger countries in which English is the first language (the United States, Canada, Australia), national varieties of English with their own standards, standards different from those of Great Britain, have arisen.

Nor has English itself been unaffected by its diffusion throughout the world. Most of the phonological differences among the regional varieties are attributable to the influence of other languages spoken or formerly spoken in the regions. Lexical items from indigenous languages have entered not only the English spoken in a particular region but also the common vocabulary of all varieties of English. Examples include such words as Hindi *dungaree* and *jungle* or Turkish *shawl*. Conversely, the pervasive influence of English-speaking cultures has led to the introduction of English loanwords into virtually every other language of the world.

Linguistic Variation

This chapter will outline some of the most salient features of the major varieties of English around the world. To make the discussion easier to follow, a few definitions of terms relating to linguistic variation are in order.

The most frequently used—and most fuzzily defined—term referring to linguistic variation is *dialect*. A **dialect** is a variety of a language distinguished from other varieties in such aspects as pronunciation, grammar, lexicon, and semantics. Without further modification, the term usually refers to regional (geographical) variety. Nonetheless, regional variation is only one of many possible types of differences among speakers of the same language. For example, there are occupational dialects (the word *bugs* means something quite different to a computer programmer and an exterminator), sexual dialects (women are far more likely than men to call a new house *adorable*), and educational dialects (the more education people have, the less likely they are to use double negatives). There are dialects of age (teenagers have their own in-group slang, and even the phonology of older speakers is likely to differ from that of young speakers in the same geographical region) and dialects of social context (we do not talk the same way to our intimate friends as we do to new acquaintances, or to the paperboy and to our employer). Certain subject matters comprise almost separate dialects in and of themselves; to the uninitiated, legal language or the language of medical technology is almost incomprehensible. In the following discussion, the word *dialect* will, unless specifically stated otherwise, refer to regional variation, but it should be remembered that regional dialects are only one of many types of linguistic variation.

In contrast to *dialect*, which can be applied to linguistic variation of any type, the term **accent** refers to phonological characteristics only, and especially to a nonnative speaker's pronunciation of English, which is influenced by his or her native language (a German accent, a Korean accent).

A **standard language** is a variety of a language that is socially and culturally predominant and is generally accepted as the most proper form of that language. Written Standard English is, with minor differences, primarily in spelling, the same the world over. However, with reference to the spoken language, the term Standard English must be further qualified. The Standard English of New Zealand is by no means identical to the Standard English of Ireland. Indeed, even within a given country, what is considered standard may vary from area to area. For instance, in much of the southern United States, *y'all* is the standard second-person plural pronoun in speech; but *y'all* is not used in other parts of the country.

In the following pages we will, of necessity, speak in generalities. But language is a human activity, subject to as much inconstancy as other kinds of human behavior, so dialects can be described only statistically, only as tendencies and not as absolutes. Dialectal variation is a messy continuum, not a series of discrete points along a scale. For example, one catalog of "Americanisms" lists *faucet* as American English in contrast to British English *tap*. Now, in my dialect (and, I suspect, that of many of my compatriots), the mechanical device itself is indeed a *faucet*; I would speak of a *broken faucet* and not a *broken tap*. I probably (though I am not absolutely sure) would say *leaky faucet* rather than *leaky tap*. On the other hand, I always say *tap water* and *beer on tap* and never *faucet water* and *beer on faucet*. Another discussion of American/British dialectal differences categorically states that American English has /ɑ/ in such words as *frog*, *pocket*, and *bother*. This would be disconcerting news to millions of Americans who have /ɔ/ in these words, and puzzling to many others who do not even have a phonemic distinction between [ɑ] and [ɔ]. To cite a syntactic example, British English supposedly differs from American English in inverting the transitive verb *have* in questions while American English uses the auxiliary *do*. That is, the British speaker is likely to say *Have you another alarm clock?* whereas the American would say *Do you have another alarm clock?* In general, this is true, but if the object of *have* is an abstract noun and especially the word *idea*, many Americans do not use the auxiliary *do*: *Have you any idea who that is?*

Our survey of English around the world will be divided into two major categories—English as a native language and as a nonnative language. Variations among native dialects of English are primarily historical in origin, and phonological differences are, with some exceptions, allophonic and not phonemic. On the other hand, variations among nonnative dialects are usually the results of interference from the speakers' first languages.

ENGLISH AS A NATIVE LANGUAGE

Even though the fact of dialectal diversity is not mentioned in surviving Old English texts, there have been dialects in English from the beginnings of English itself. By Middle English times, awareness of geographical variation in English speech was high enough for Chaucer to use it to add local color to the *Reeve's Tale*: Chaucer tells us that his two students John and Aleyn were from a town "Fer in the north, I kan nat telle where." He then puts Northern forms in their dialogue, as in John's statement

> I have herd seyd, 'man sal taa of twa thynges
> Slyk as he fyndes, or taa slyk as he brynges'.

in which *sal* (for more Southern *shal*), *twa* (*two*), *taa* (*taken*), *slyk* (*swich* 'such'), and the use of *-es* instead of *-(e)th* as the third-person singular present indicative ending are all Northernisms.

Some years later, in the *Second Shepherds' Play*, the Wakefield Master, writing in Northern English, has the scoundrel Mak pretend to be from southern England:

> What! ich be a yoman ... Goyth hence

in which *ich* (instead of Northern *I*), *be* (*am*), and *goyth* (*go*) are all Southernisms. Lest the point be missed, the playwright has one of Mak's companions say

> Now take outt that sothren tothe [tooth]
> And sett in a torde!

At the end of the fifteenth century, the printer William Caxton relates his famous anecdote about a misunderstanding that arises because of dialectal differences in the word for "egg," to which Caxton adds his own comment, "certaynly it is harde to playse euery man / by cause of dyuersite & chaunge of langage."

By the sixteenth century, many English authors, especially the writers of handbooks of rhetoric and usage, are commenting, usually unfavorably, on the dialectal diversity of England. In his *Arte of English Poesie* (1589), George Puttenham says that the speech of the London area is best and condemns Northern speech as old-fashioned and inelegant. Edmund Coote (1597) cites dialectal pronunciations as a source of spelling errors. Alexander Gil (1619) censures western dialects for being the most "barbarous" of all.

By the eighteenth century, pronunciation based on educated London speech was securely established as a standard. At the same time, a somewhat more objective interest in local dialects led to the compilation of glossaries of local vocabulary items. Systematic study of dialects in England did not, however, begin until after the mid-nineteenth century. The English Dialect Society was formed in 1873 and, during its two decades of operation, put out numerous bibliographies, glossaries, and miscellaneous publications. The fifth volume of A. J. Ellis' *Early English Pronunciation* (1889) was a study of modern English dialects. In 1898–1905, Joseph Wright's monumental six-volume *English Dialect Dictionary* appeared, its findings based on a postal questionnaire sent to 12,000 people as well as on previously published glossaries, county histories, and miscellaneous sources.

The twentieth century has seen comprehensive dialect studies of all of England, Scotland, and Wales. Begun in 1946, the Leeds Survey, directed by Harold Orton, culminated in the publication of the *Survey of English Dialects* (1962–71) and the *Word Geography of England* (1974). The Linguistic Survey of Scotland, directed by Angus McIntosh, Kenneth Jackson, and David Abercrombie, was begun in 1949; in 1975–77, the two-volume *Linguistic Atlas of Scotland*, Scots section, was published. The *Scottish National Dictionary* (edited by David Murison), a project independent of the Linguistic Survey of Scotland, was completed in 1976. Alan Thomas edited the *Linguistic Geography of Wales: A Contribution to Welsh Dialectology* (1973).

England

Diversity among the regional dialects of England, particularly in pronunciation, is greater than in any other part of the world where English is spoken as a native language. England is also the only English-speaking nation with an official or quasi-official standard dialect, which we can call Standard British English (SBE). This dialect is a social and educational, rather than a regional, dialect. It is superimposed upon regional dialects; in effect, many of its users are bidialectal to some extent, able to speak both SBE and a regional dialect. SBE is the English taught in the public (that is, private) schools of England and Wales. Until a few years ago, it was the English demanded of all BBC announcers. Though its prestige has declined somewhat in recent years, especially among younger people, it remains a powerful social phenomenon and is still a marker of the upper-middle and upper classes. In the following pages, we will first briefly sketch the most salient characteristics of SBE and then outline ways in which regional dialects of England differ in pronunciation from SBE.

Standard British English

PHONOLOGY

It is traditional to refer to the pronunciation of Standard British English as Received Pronunciation, or, more economically, simply RP. Rather than attempting a complete description of the sound system of RP, the following discussion will concentrate on the most important ways in which RP differs from General American (GA) pronunciation.

Consonants. The inventory of RP consonants is identical to that of GA, the only differences between the two dialects lying in the distribution of the phonemes and in their allophonic realizations.

RP is nonrhotic (*r*-less); that is, historical /r/ is not pronounced when it appears before a consonant or at the end of a word. If the following word begins with a vowel, /r/ is retained (for instance, *near them* [nɪə ðɛm]; *near it* [nɪr ɪt]). Though it is stigmatized, intrusive [r], an unhistorical [r] inserted between a word ending in a vowel and another word beginning with a vowel (for instance, *idea of* [ɑɪdíərəv]), is not uncommon. In some RP speech, intervocalic /r/ is a flap rather than a retroflex and may sound like /d/ to American ears; that is, *very* may be perceived as "veddy." This pronunciation, however, is old-fashioned and dying out.

Intervocalic /t/ is not voiced in RP as it is in GA, and the use of the glottal stop [ʔ] as an allophone of /t/ is normally limited to the end of syllables before another consonant. RP does not distinguish /hw/ from /w/; *which* and *witch* are homophones. After alveolars, the semivowel /j/ appears before /u/ in many words (for example, *new, tune, assume, due*).

Vowels. Comparison of the vowels of RP and GA is complicated by the fact that British and American linguists have traditionally used dissimilar methods to analyze the two systems, making the differences between the two appear greater than they are. Here we will simply "translate" the British terminology into the transcription used elsewhere in this book as far as possible.

To Americans, the most familiar difference between RP and GA vowel phonology is probably the RP use of /ɑ/ (as opposed to GA /æ/) before some fricatives and nasals, as in *bath, dance,* and *pass.* In words like *hot* and *frog,* where American English has /ɑ/ or /ɔ/, RP has a slightly rounded back vowel, transcribed as /ɒ/. Stressed schwa /ə/ in RP tends to be pronounced lower and farther back than in GA—phonetically [ʌ], as in *some* [sʌm].[2] The back diphthongs /o/ and /u/ normally have a more central on-glide in RP than in GA: RP *toad* [təʊd] and *loop* [lɨup]. ([ɨ] is an unrounded high central vowel.)

RP pronunciation of a number of individual words differs phonemically from GA pronunciation; perhaps the most familiar are RP *lieutenant* [lɛ́ftɛnənt], *schedule* [šɛ́djul], *clerk* [klɑːk], and *herb* [hɜːb]. Others include *garage* [gǽrɪǰ], *renaissance* [rɪnésəns], *premier* [prɛ́mjə], *charade* [šərɑ́ːd], and *dynasty* [dínəstɪ]. In still other instances, the RP pronunciation also occurs in the United States, but only as a regional or even substandard variant; a few examples are RP *ate* [ɛt], *figure* [fɪ́gə(r)], *neither* [nɑ́ɪðə(r)], *leisure* [lɛ́žə(r)], *tomato* [təmɑ́to], and *nephew*

---

[2] British analyses, for reasons that we need not go into here, usually treat RP [ə] as a separate phoneme from [ʌ].

[névju]. All of these are isolated unpatterned variants; systematic differences between RP and GA in the pronunciation of individual words are rare. One of the few patterned differences that do exist involves words ending in the suffix *-ile*. In RP this is usually pronounced [aɪl], but in GA it is normally [əl]. For example, RP *missile* (mɪsaɪl) is GA [mɪsəl], and the suffixes of *fertile, fragile, tactile, volatile,* and *sterile* are pronounced similarly. Even here there are exceptions: *reptile, servile,* and *juvenile* are often pronounced with [aɪl] in the United States, and *mobile* can be [əl], [aɪl], or even [il] in the United States.

Prosody. For all the allophonic differences betwen RP and GA in the pronunciation of consonants and vowels, by far the most important distinguishing characteristic of RP to American ears is its prosodic patterns. Unfortunately, little is known about the details of these differences and their perception. As a general rule, the pitch range—the range from the lowest pitch to the highest pitch within a given phrase or utterance—is greater in RP than in GA. Because they associate a wider pitch range with female speech and especially with excited female speech, Americans may initially perceive a male RP speaker as effeminate and impatient or annoyed when he is actually using a "neutral" intonation pattern. Conversely, the RP speaker may hear GA speech as a drawled monotone.

Both RP and GA, of course, have a stress-timed rhythm, and both have at least three levels of stress for syllables: primary, secondary, and minimal stress. In polysyllabic words, however, RP tends to use minimal stress on many syllables that have secondary stress in GA. In particular, words ending in *-ary, -ery,* or *-ory* usually have a penultimate secondary stress in GA but not in RP. For example, the word *secondary* itself is stressed *sécŏndàrў* in GA; but in RP the secondary stress is lowered to minimal, or is even so reduced that the syllable is dropped entirely: /sékǝndrĭ/. Other examples are *auditory, territory, cemetery, monastery, legendary,* and *dictionary.*

Morphology and Syntax

In morphology and syntax, Standard British English (SBE) and General American (GA) differ in numerous minor details, none of which is likely to cause more than momentary confusion to speakers of either variety.

SBE frequently uses a plural verb with such collective nouns as *government, team,* or *hotel* that normally take a singular verb in GA: "Labour *seem* likely to win" or "The hotel *make* a point of insulting their guests." SBE uses no article in the phrases *be in hospital* and *go to university* (compare GA *go to college*), but does require an article with the word *class,* where GA normally omits it in such contexts as "He's *in class* right now." Both SBE and GA use a definite article with river names, but SBE puts the word *River* before the specific name whereas GA puts it after (SBE *the River Trent* versus GA *the Illinois River*).

Pronominal usage in SBE differs chiefly in the wider use of *one* as an indefinite pronoun. That is, SBE not only does not substitute *he* (*him, his*) after the first mention, it also uses *one* in less formal contexts than is usual in GA: "*One* can't pick *one*'s own parents out ahead of time, can *one*?"

There are a number of general differences in prepositional usage between SBE and GA, though probably no more than can be found between or among different dialects of American English. In SBE, *in* (as opposed to GA *on*) is used in the expressions *to live in X Street, be in a team,* and *to be in a sale* (compare New York City *to stand on line* with upstate New York *to stand in line*). Conversely, in speaking of students following a particular academic program, SBE has *on the course* where GA has *in the course* (or *in the program*). SBE uses the word *round* as a preposition where GA has *around*; Americans are familiar with the British usage from such phrases as in "Here we go *round* the mulberry bush" and "*round* Robin Hood's barn." Students in the United States may agonize over whether to write *different from* or *different than*, but rarely would write *different to*, both common and acceptable in SBE.

In verbal morphology, the only patterned difference between SBE and GA is the British tendency to retain the historical but irregular past tense and past participle in *-t* of a number of weak verbs, especially those that do not have a vowel change in the past forms (*burn/burnt/burnt*; similarly for *dwell, rend, smell, spell, spill, spoil*).[3] Note that GA normally retains the past forms in *-t* if the verb ends in *-nd* (*bend, send, spend*) or if there is a vowel change, as in *creep, sweep, sell, deal,* and *feel*. For the verb *get*, GA has two past participles: *got*, meaning "have possession of," and *gotten*, meaning "obtain or receive" (compare "Have you *got* a pen?" with "Have you *gotten* a pen?"). SBE lacks the participle *gotten* and employs *got* in both meanings. SBE also uses *shall* as a future auxiliary to express somewhat tentative intention far more frequently than GA does. Simple inversion of *have* (rather than the use of the *do* auxiliary) as a full verb meaning "possess" is much more common in SBE than in GA:

SBE	Have you a room of your own?
	Hasn't he a dependable car?
GA	Do you have (*or* Have you got) a room of your own?
	(also used in SBE)
	Doesn't he have (*or* Hasn't he got) a dependable car?

The inflected subjunctive is far less common in SBE than in GA. For instance, where GA would have "The judge ordered that *he be held*," SBE would more likely have "The judge ordered that *he should be held*" or "The judge ordered *him to be held*." SBE allows the pro-verb *do* after an auxiliary, a construction impossible in GA: "Have you read the papers yet?" "No, but I shall *do*." In clauses with both a direct object and an indirect object, SBE allows the direct object to precede the indirect object when both objects are pronouns ("Give it me"), also impossible in GA.

SBE uses *directly* and *immediately* as subordinating conjunctions, as in "I'll come immediately my class is over." Finally, SBE can use a gerund after the preposition *like* in constructions such as "It looks like raining all day," where GA would require a full clause such as "It looks like (as if) it's going to rain all day."

LEXICON AND SEMANTICS

After I had been living in Britain for two or three months, an acquaintance approached me at a rather noisy party and said in a low voice, "Have you seen the john?" I replied, "John who?" She looked baffled for a moment, then laughed and said, "Do you know where the loo is?" She, knowing that I was from the United

---

[3] GA often retains the earlier past participle forms as adjectives, for example, *burnt toast* or *spilt milk*.

States, had used the colloquial American English term for a toilet to be sure she would be understood. I, having lived long enough in Britain to have acquired a British "set," was not expecting to hear the American term. In the noisy surroundings, I did not hear the definite article *the*, so I assumed she was using *john* as a proper name. This anecdote illustrates that, although there are hundreds of vocabulary items that differ in SBE and GA, speakers of SBE are often familiar with the GA term, and vice versa.

Many of the terms regularly used by speakers of one variety of English are at least passively familiar to speakers of the other. What is more, for many lexical items, the supposedly SBE term may actually be the normal term in some GA dialects, while the purported GA term is never used. For example, in a list that I saw recently, *couch*, *davenport*, and *chesterfield* were cited as American terms corresponding to the British term *sofa*. In my dialect, *sofa* is the normal, neutral term, though I also use *couch*. I have known people who call the piece of furniture a *davenport*, but I have never actually heard anyone speak of a *chesterfield*. The situation may be even more complex: Trudgill and Hannah, for example, state that *quite* (as in *quite good*) has a negative or neutral connotation in English English but a positive connotation in American English.[4] Most Americans of my acquaintance use *quite* in both meanings; if I put emphatic stress on the word *quite* ("It was *quite* good"), I mean "somewhat, rather," but I am expressing reservations and certainly do not mean "very, extremely." On the other hand, if I stress the adjective ("It was quite *good*"), my intended meaning is more positive. Finally, if I use *quite* as an adverb modifying a verb or an entire sentence ("That is *quite* a different matter"), I do mean "completely, altogether."

Three broad semantic areas in which British-American lexical differences are especially noticeable are food, clothing, and transportation. Historically, this is because new foods and new ways of processing and cooking foods have arisen since the separation of the two nations. The vagaries of fashion have caused divergence in the vocabulary of clothing. The many differences in the terminology of transportation result from the fact that the railroad (British *railway*) and motor-car industries developed after the separation of the United States and Great Britain. The inventory below is intended to be suggestive rather than exhaustive. The SBE forms are listed, with the corresponding American English terms in parentheses.

Food

aubergine (eggplant)
biscuit (cookie or cracker)
bloaters (smoked fish)
boiled sweets (hard candy)
chips (french fries)
chocolate beans (M & Ms)
cooker (kitchen stove)
courgette (zucchini)
crisps (potato chips)
gigot (leg of lamb or pork)

to grill (to broil)
jelly (jello)
joint (a roast)
marrow (squash)
mince (hamburger)
monkey nuts (peanuts)
porridge (oatmeal)
scone (biscuit or muffin)
treacle (molasses)

---

[4] Peter Trudgill and Jean Hannah, *International English: A Guide to Varieties of Standard English* (London: Edward Arnold, 1982), p. 76.

Clothing

basketball boots (high sneakers)
jumper (pullover sweater)
knickers (women's underpants)
nappy (diaper)
overall (smock)

pants (underpants)
turn-ups (cuffs)
vest (undershirt)
waistcoat (vest)

Transportation

bonnet (hood)
boot (trunk of a car)
caravan (trailer)
diversion (detour)
dual carriageway (divided highway)
high street (main street)
lay-by (roughly, turnout or rest area)
lollipop man (school crossing guard)
loose chippings (roughly, soft
    shoulder)
lorry (truck)

motorway (turnpike)
return ticket (round-trip ticket)
roundabout (traffic circle)
season-ticket holder (commuter)
semi-articulated lorry (tractor-trailer)
superelevated (banked curve)
no tipping (no dumping)
verge (shoulder of a road)
wing (fender)
zebra [zɛbrə] (striped pedestrian
    crossing)

Miscellaneous

camp bed (cot)
cot (crib)
cupboard (closet)
dummy (pacifier)
dustbin (trash can)
fringe (bangs)

fruit machine (slot machine)
garden (yard)
off-license store (liquor store)
portfolio (briefcase)
slot machine (vending machine)
sticking plaster (band-aid)

Occasionally, the unwary American traveler in Britain may use a term that is perfectly innocent in its connotations in the United States but that is considered vulgar or even taboo in England. For example, both *knickers* and *pants* refer to outer garments in American English; in British English they are slightly vulgar terms for undergarments. *Fanny* is a polite euphemism for the buttocks in American English, but a taboo term for the female genitalia in England. *Bug* is an all-purpose colloquial term for "insect" in American English, but can have the narrowed meaning of "bedbug" in British English.

Conversely, terms that are vulgar or taboo in the United States may be completely acceptable in Britain. The advertising slogan for a vacuum cleaner, "Nothing sucks like Electrolux," could never be used, even humorously, in the United States. If Britishers say that they will *knock you up* later, they mean that they will drop by your residence to see you; if they are *all knocked up*, they are exhausted. A *rubber* is an eraser. Where Americans say *rooster*, the British are much less hesitant to say *cock*. One can approach a salesclerk in London and ask if he has a *prick* without provoking an international incident; a *prick* is an *egg prick*, used to make a tiny hole in an egg to prevent its shell from breaking when it is boiled.

A SCOTS SONNET

Of all written English dialects, the only one to achieve and retain the status of a literary language has been Scots, whose success is attributable in part to Scotland's long independence from England. As the following sonnet by Robert Garioch, a twentieth-century poet, illustrates, Scots is still a distinctive and lively medium for literary expression.

Elegy

They are lang deid, folk that I used to ken,
their firm-set lips aa mowdert and agley,
sherp-tempert een rusty amang the cley:
they are baith deid, thae wycelike, bienlie men,

heidmaisters, that had been in pouer for ten
or twenty year afore fate's taiglie wey
brocht me, a young, weill-harnit, blate and fey
new-cleckit dominie, intill their den.

Ane tellt me it was time I learnt to write—
round-haund, he meant—and saw about my hair:
I mind of him, beld-heidit, wi a kyte.

Ane sneerit quarterly—I cudna square
my savings-bank—and sniftert in his spite.
Weill, gin they arena deid, it's time they were.

Translation

They are long dead, people that I used to know,
their firm-set lips all decayed and awry,
sharp-tempered eyes rusty in the clay:
they are both dead, those prudent, good-willed men,

headmasters, that had been in power for ten
or twenty years before fate's snaring way
brought me, a young, brainy, shy and other-worldly
new-hatched schoolmaster, into their den.

One told me it was time I learned to write—
round-hand, he meant—and looked after my hair:
I remember him, bald-headed, with a paunch.

One sneered every quarter—I couldn't balance
my savings-bank—and snorted in his spite.
Well, if they aren't dead, it's time they were.

Reprinted by permission from Robin Fulton, ed., *Robert Garioch: Complete Poetical Works* (Edinburgh: Macdonald Publishers, 1983), p. 87. Translation by C. M. Millward.

Regional Variation in England

As we noted earlier, dialectal variation in the British Isles, and particularly in England, is greater than in any other part of the English-speaking world. So complex is the dialectal picture that we can here only sketch in broadest outline some of the more salient characteristics of the dialectal areas, remembering as we do so that RP is universally understood and taught and that dialect boundaries are never sharp but rather comprise a continuum. Further, we shall discuss only phonological traits and not morphological, syntactic, or lexical characteristics.

As is true of American dialects, the broadest dialectal division in England is between North and South, with the London area comprising a separate division within the South. According to Wells' classification,[5] the South includes (1) the home counties of Middlesex, Essex, Kent, Surrey, Hertfordshire, and Sussex, for which London speech is the dominant influence; (2) East Anglia, including Norfolk, Suffolk, and nearby parts of Cambridgeshire; and (3) the West Country in the southwestern part of England, including Gloucestershire, Avon, Somerset, Devon, and the Wessex area of Dorsetshire, Hampshire, and Wiltshire. The North as a dialectal area is roughly defined by a line running southwest to northeast from the mouth of the River Severn to the Wash. Within this larger area, further subdivisions include (1) the East Midlands, centered around Leicester and Nottingham; (2) the West Midlands, centered around Birmingham; (3) the middle North, including the industrial cities of Manchester, Leeds, and Sheffield; and (4) the far North, extending roughly from the mouth of the River Tee up to the Scottish border and including the distinctive subregions of Tees-side, County Durham, and Tyneside.

THE LONDON AREA (COCKNEY)

The term *Cockney* in its strictest usage refers to a native of the East End of London and more specifically to someone born within hearing of the bells of St. Mary-le-Bow, but we shall employ the term more loosely to refer to the working-class dialect of all of London and the immediately surrounding area.

Because no American dialects "drop" /h/ in stressed syllables, the widespread *h*-dropping of Cockney is one of its most striking characteristics to American ears. Another common feature is the vocalization of syllable-final /l/ to [o] or [u]; for example, *pill* may be realized as [p'io]. Word-final /t/ regularly becomes the glottal stop ['] (as, indeed, is common in many dialects of English). Glottalization is not, however, limited to /t/ or to word-final position. All three voiceless stops /p t k/ may be either accompanied by glottal closure ([p'] [t'] [k']) or totally replaced by a glottal stop both intervocalically and finally. Thus *fatter* becomes [fæ'ə], and I have heard the word *people* pronounced [pi'o], with a glottal stop for the second /p/ and vocalization of the final /l/.

The interdental fricatives /θ ð/ are sometimes realized as the bilabial fricatives [f v], but the phonemic distinction between the two sets of fricatives is still preserved. Assibilation of an alveolar stop and a following /j/ is common; hence, the initial sounds of *tune* and *duke*, for instance, are often [č] and [ǰ], respectively. Voicing of intervocalic, post-stress /t/ is not characteristic of Cockney; where American English typically has [wɔdər] for *water*, Cockney has [wɔ'ə]. As

---

[5] J. C. Wells, *Accents of English*, 3 vols. (Cambridge: Cambridge Univ. Press, 1982). Much of the following discussion is indebted to Wells.

the preceding transcription indicates, Cockney is nonrhotic (it drops preconsonantal /r/).

The vowel system of Cockney is isomorphic with that of RP; that is, it has the same set of vowel phonemes. The typical phonetic realizations of these vowels are, however, noticeably different. In particular, the vowels /i e u o/ have a strongly centralized onset, so that the word *James*, for example, appears as [ǰʌɪmz]. On the other hand, the diphthongs /aɪ/ and /aʊ/ tend to be smoothed to pure vowels; *mine* may be [mɔ:n] and *gown* [gæ:n]. Nasalization of vowels is common, so much so that a following nasal consonant may be completely replaced by heavy nasalization of the preceding vowel; for example, *pen* may be [pɛ̃].

The intonation patterns of Cockney are similar to those of RP.

THE SOUTH

East Anglia.   Among the most salient features of the speech of East Anglia is the extensive loss of /j/ before /u/, not only after alveolar consonants, as in *tune* and *new*, but even after labials, as in *pew*, *music*, and *feud*. Before orthographical *r*, the vowels /ɪ/ and /ɛ/ often merge, making homophones of words like *peer* and *pare*, *here* and *hair*, *dear* and *dare*, all of which may be pronounced with [ɛ:] or [ɛə]. Wells reports that the speech of East Anglia is noted for its special rhythm created by lengthening stressed long vowels and reducing or omitting unstressed vowels.

The West Country.   In a few ways, the speech of the West Country of England resembles American English more than other dialects of England do. For one thing, graphic *r* tends to be preserved, even in educated speech. Further, the vowel of words like *hot* often is [a], as in much of the United States, rather than [ɒ] as in RP. On the other hand, the voicing of the initial voiceless fricatives /f θ s š/ (for example, *furrow* with initial [v], *see* with [z], *shame* with [ž] is totally alien to American dialects. This voicing is now disappearing, but it dates back to early Middle English at least.

In many dialects of English, there is a tendency to vocalize /l/ after a vowel. The speech of the city of Bristol is famous for the reverse tendency—intrusive [l] after [ə]. In fact, the very name of the city illustrates this tendency: *Bristol* was formerly *Bristow*. Wells reports jokes about this trait of Bristol speech, such as the one about the man who had "three daughters, Idle, Evil, and Normal."

THE NORTH

Traditional dialect is better preserved in the North than in other parts of England, and the Great Vowel Shift of Early Modern English has been arrested throughout much of the area, though details vary from locality to locality. In particular, the merger of ME [ɛ̄] and [ē] is not complete; words like *meet* and *meat* are not always homophones and may have various pronunciations. In some places, words that had had [ɪ] before a velar fricative in ME (for example, *fight*, ME [fɪçt]) show loss of the fricative and lengthening, but no diphthongization of the vowel: *right* is [rit] rather than [raɪt] or [rʌɪt]. (In such words, the fricative was not lost until after the GVS was effective; hence the vowel remained short during the time when the GVS was diphthongizing ME [ī].)

In the far North, ME [ū] also escaped the effects of the GVS and remains [u] in regional speech to this day: *about* is pronounced [əbut]. Another characteristically Northern feature is the use of [æ] instead of RP [a] in words like *glass*, *path*, and *France*. ME [ʊ] did not undergo phonemic split in this area, so there is no phonemic distinction today between [ə] and [ʊ], and such words as *shuck* and *shook* or *cud* and *could* are homophones.

The preservation of preconsonantal /r/ varies throughout the North. In general, the urban industrial areas of the west (Liverpool-Manchester area) resemble RP in being nonrhotic, but rhoticity increases as one goes north, with the far north being fully rhotic. The Northumbrian burr, a uvular fricative [ʁ] realization of /r/, can still be heard in the far north, although it is gradually dying out.

Within the extensive area comprising the North are pockets of distinctive dialects associated with specific urban areas. One of these is the Liverpool accent, popularly called *Scouse*, whose uniqueness is at least partly due to the influence of heavy Irish immigration during the nineteenth century. Some working-class speakers use dental or alveolar stops for /θ/ and /ð/; this feature is not, however, typical of all Scouse speech. More widespread is the replacement of syllable-final stops by fricatives; /p t k/ are realized as [ɸ ţ x] in this position, thus a word like *take* becomes [teɪx]. Liverpudlian speech is famous for its merger of /ə/ and /ɛ/ before orthographic *r*, a merger that leads to such homophones as *purr* and *pear* or *her* and *hare*.

Another dialectal pocket is Tyneside, the urban area of the far north centered on Newcastle-on-Tyne. The accent, popularly called *Geordie*, is perhaps best known for its extensive glottalization of voiceless stops, as in *couple* [kʊpˀəl] or *city* [sɪtˀi]. In the broadest Geordie accents, /ə/ and /ɔ/ merge before orthographic *r*, producing such homophones as *shirt* and *short* [šɔ:t]. Many words that have /ɔ/ or /o/ in RP have [æ:] or [a:] in Geordie, including *talk* [ta:k] and *know* [na:]. Unlike other urban dialects, Geordie does not have *h*-dropping. Geordie also has a highly distinctive intonation pattern, although it has not been well described.

Scotland

Scotland has shared much of the history of England throughout the Christian era, although it has been politically joined to England only for the past three and a half centuries. The Romans, who successfully subjugated southern Scotland, called it Caledonia during their period of control from the first through the fourth centuries. With the Germanic invasions, the Anglo-Saxons moved as far north as Edinburgh, and most of Scotland was converted to Christianity through the missionary efforts of St. Columba in the sixth century. Still, for most of the first millennium after the Anglo-Saxon incursions into the area, Scotland was an independent nation. England first took at least nominal control in 1174 through a treaty obtained by Henry II, but Scotland's independence was decisively asserted again in 1314 when Robert Bruce defeated Edward II (of England) at Bannockburn. In 1513 the Scots were badly defeated by the English at Flodden Field. The two thrones of England and Scotland were finally united in 1603 when the Scots king James VI, son of Mary Queen of Scots, succeeded to the English throne as James I of England. In 1707, the two parliaments were united, and since then Scotland has been part of Great Britain, although Scotland to this day retains a certain degree of independence in its legal and educational systems, and its banks even issue their own currency.

Although the Celtic dialect called Scots Gaelic can still be heard in parts of Highland Scotland, English has been spoken in southeastern Scotland almost as long as it has in England. First known as Inglis and then as Scots, this Scottish dialect is a descendant of the Northumbrian dialect of Old English, heavily influenced by Norse and, later, French. It is the only dialect of English (apart, of course, from the East Midlands dialect, which is the ancestor of both SBE and all other standard varieties of English today) to have developed an independent literary tradition that has persisted, at least to some extent, to the present day. Initiated as a literary language in the fourteenth century by such figures as John Barbour (c. 1320–c. 1395), it flourished in the fifteenth century under major writers like Robert Henryson, William Dunbar, Gawin Douglas, and David Lindsay, and experienced an eighteenth-century revival with Allan Ramsay, Robert Fergusson, and Robert Burns—who named this dialect *Lallans* (Lowlands). Although it is not particularly in favor today, the tradition was continued into the twentieth century by poets, most notably Hugh MacDiarmid (1892–1978). Educated spoken Scots, however, has been so heavily influenced by SBE that today it is nearly identical to it except for pronunciation and a few vocabulary items and idioms.

Phonology
Scots English is distinctive among varieties of English for its extremely conservative phonology, both in consonants and in vowels.

CONSONANTS
Among the conservative features of Scots English consonants are the preservation of the phonemic distinction between /hw/ and /w/ (*while* differs from *wile*), the lack of *h*-dropping, and the retention of /r/ in all positions in the word. Even more conservative is the use of /θ/, rather than /ð/, in *though*, *with*, and *without*; these words did not undergo the voicing of voiceless fricatives that took place during EMnE in other dialects. Other dialects also lost [x] during EMnE, but Scots still retains this sound in specifically Scottish words like *loch* or proper names like *MacColloch*. In the Highlands and the Hebrides, direct influence from Gaelic is revealed in the extremely heavy aspiration of the voiceless stops and a parallel tendency to make the normally voiced stops /b d g/ voiceless.

VOWELS
Scots pronunciation of vowels is unique in a number of ways. First, it is the only native dialect of English in which most of the vowels remain phonemically distinct before /r/; for example, *sir* and *fur*, *early* and *surly*, and *horn* and *mourn* do not rhyme. On the other hand, Scots lacks a phonemic distinction between /ʊ/ and /u/, so that *full* and *fool* are both /ful/. Similarly, RP /ɒ/ and /ɔ:/ have coalesced as /ɔ/ (*tot* and *taught* are both /tɔt/, and RP /æ/ and /ɑ:/ appear as /a/ (*cam* and *calm* are /kam/). The vowels /i e o/ are usually phonetically monophthongs in Scots, rather than diphthongs as in RP. In unstressed styllables, /ɪ/ tends to be used, even in words for which RP or GA favors /ə/, such as *better* /bɛtɪr/. Although highly educated speakers avoid it, popular speech often has /u/ instead of /ɑʊ/ in such words as *mouse* and *out*.

Grammar and Lexicon
The grammar of written and educated spoken Scots differs little from that of SBE, though there are a number of minor differences at the informal, colloquial level.

Some of these will not be apparent to American speakers because they share them: for example, the use of *will* to the near exclusion of *shall* or the use of *yet* in sentences without a perfect tense ("Did you tell her yet?" instead of "Have you told her yet?"). Even *need* followed by a past participle ("That house needs painted") and *need* and *want* followed by a directional adverb ("The cat needs out"; "The baby wants up") also occur in some American dialects. Less familiar is the pervasive use of tag questions, including contexts that would seem not to require them at all ("Well, I haven't done anything about that, have I?").

A morphological habit striking to non-Scots ears is the highly frequent use of the suffix *-ie* /i/ as a kind of hypocoristic, a habit well exemplified in the Scots prayer "From ghoulies and ghosties and long-leggety beasties / And things that go bump in the night, / Good Lord deliver us!"

At the informal spoken level in particular, Scots has scores of unique idioms and vocabulary items. Some of these simply represent extensive use of words known but rarely used in other dialects. Examples are *wee* (small), *aye* (yes), and *dram* (a small drink of liquor). In other cases, the word has an entirely different meaning in Scots; for example, (*lord*) *provost* means "mayor" and *sober* means "poor, miserable, humble." In still other instances, the word is not used at all in SBE or GA. Examples are *fash* 'to trouble, annoy', *haar* 'sea mist', and *dreich* 'dreary, tiresome'. Uniquely Scots idioms include *back of four o'clock* 'soon after four' and *miss yourself* 'miss something good by being absent', as in "You really missed yourself at the concert yesterday."

Wales

Much of North America has been English-speaking longer than most of Wales, despite the proximity of Wales to England. Wales has not fully shared in the history of England until relatively recently. During their occupation of the British Isles, the Romans tended to ignore Wales. The Anglo-Saxons pushed the Celts back into what are today Wales and Cornwall, but made no serious attempts to take over these areas. Complete conquest did not come until 1282, under the English king Edward I. Even so, Owen Glendower was able to lead a successful (though short-lived) rebellion in the fifteenth century. Total political assimilation into England was finally achieved with the Act of Union (1536), whereby English law was established in Wales and English was made the official language. Even after the Act of Union, however, English remained a foreign language for most of the Welsh until the last century, and even now bilingualism is widespread. According to one estimate, for about 20 percent of today's population, English is a second language. Because Welsh is still extensively spoken in Wales, it is, understandably, the dominant influence on Welsh English, although not every unique characteristic of Welsh English has its origin or parallel in Welsh.

Phonology
The inventory of phonemes in Welsh English is, for most speakers, iso-morphic with that of RP, and highly educated Welsh English is similar to RP. It is the allophonic variants of less well-educated speakers that make Welsh English so distinctive.

CONSONANTS

Like RP, educated Welsh is nonrhotic and has both linking and intrusive /r/ (though the latter is frowned upon). In the positions where /r/ does occur, its realization can be retroflex, rolled, or even uvular. The dark allophone ([ɫ]) of /l/ is not used in Welsh English; /l/ is clear in all positions. Some speakers of northern Welsh have no voiced alveolar fricatives, and [s] and [š] appear for /z/ and /ž/. Welsh English lacks the glottalized allophones of stops typical of many varieties of English, but the voiceless stops are heavily aspirated in all positions except after /s/. The consonants /t d n/ are often dental rather than alveolar. One of the most striking characteristics of Welsh English is the tendency to lengthen intervocalic consonants before an unstressed syllable: *funny* is [fən:i] and *nothing* is [nəθ:ɪŋ]. Like many other speakers of British English, the Welsh tend to drop /h/, even in stressed syllables. In words like *white* and *when*, /w/ rather than /hw/ is the norm.

VOWELS

While RP tends to diphthongize the vowels /i e u o/ even more obviously than American English, Welsh English typically makes all of these monophthongs, giving the vocalic system a more Continental flavor than most native dialects of English. Further, Welsh English tends to use full vowels rather than /ə/ in unstressed syllables; thus, it often has /ɛ/ in the final syllable of *shortest*, /æ/ in the second syllable of *sofa*, and /ɒ/ in the first syllable of *convey*.

In words like *few*, *tune*, and *music*, where RP has /j/ after the initial consonant, Welsh English has the vowel /ɪ/ instead; *tune* is [tɪʊn], not [tjun]. There is a tendency to use /æ/ and not /ɑ/ before fricatives and nasal + fricative in such words as *last* and *France*, but practice varies here.

PROSODY

Even if Welsh English were to use exactly the same allophones of consonants and vowels as RP, it would still be easily identifiable because of its unique intonation patterns, which produce what is usually described as a "sing-song" impression. Exactly what constitutes this effect is not well understood, although part of it may result from the Welsh English tendency to avoid secondary stresses in words and to use only primary and reduced stress.

Grammar and Lexicon

Written Welsh English is indistinguishable from other varieties, but the spoken language has a number of characteristic traits, usually the result of influence from Welsh (Celtic). One of the most conspicuous traits is the tendency to invert the normal English order of sentence elements for emphasis (a characteristic also of Irish English and some Scots usage), as in "Staying away too long you are." *Isn't it* is sometimes employed as a universal (unvarying) tag question: "They've told you already, isn't it?" The adverb *too* (instead of *either*) may be used in negative as well as affirmative statements, as in "She wasn't listening, too."

As is typical of the relationship between Celtic languages and English throughout their history of contiguity in the British Isles, Welsh has had little influence on the vocabulary of Welsh English. Trudgill and Hannah report *del* as a term of endearment and *llymru* as the name of a porridge dish, in addition to the more widely familiar term *eisteddfod* for a competitive congress of Welsh artists, musicians, and dramatists.

Ireland

Although Ireland shared much of the early history of England, the English language was late in coming to Ireland. Celtic tribes settled there during the last few centuries before the birth of Christ, but the Romans did not attempt to conquer it when they made England part of their empire. In the fifth century A.D., St. Patrick converted the Irish to Christianity, and, beginning in the eighth century, the Vikings invaded Ireland and even founded the city of Dublin. The Norse remained a major influence in Ireland until their defeat by the Irish king Brian Boru in 1014.

The centuries-old antagonism between England and Ireland began in the twelfth century with Henry II's conquest of Ireland. In the seventeenth century, England settled large numbers of Scottish and English Protestants in northern Ireland, initiating the religious and political conflicts that have continued to the present day. In 1921, England offered dominion status to Ireland, though northern Ireland remained part of the United Kingdom. Ireland withdrew from the Commonwealth in 1948, six northern counties, however, remaining under the control of the British Parliament.

English has been spoken in Ireland since the twelfth century, and, in fact, there was a recognizable Anglo-Irish dialect during Middle English. Nevertheless, the number of native speakers of English was inconsiderable until the plantations of the seventeenth century introduced Scots English to northern Ireland and the dialects of western England to the rest of Ireland. Since that time, English has steadily expanded at the expense of Irish. In the early nineteenth century, perhaps half the population spoke Irish, but today only a handful use it as their everyday language, and even these people are bilingual in English as well. Irish today survives only through the life-sustaining apparatus of being the *de jure* official language and of being a required (though often detested) subject in schools. In a curious reversal of the pattern in many African and Asian countries, English is the native language of the Irish but is *not* the official language of Eire.

Because the major influence on the English of northern Ireland was Scots, while that on the English of the south was the English of western England, there are numerous differences between the dialects of the two areas, and the two are treated separately here.

Northern Ireland

PHONOLOGY
Like that of Scots, the phonology of Northern Irish English tends to be conservative, preserving a number of features that have been lost or altered in RP.

Consonants.   Northern Irish English (NIE) is rhotic, with the /r/ typically being a retroflex semivowel much like that of American English. Also like American English is the tendency to voice intervocalic post-stress /t/. The liquid /l/ is normally clear in all positions. Another conservative feature is the retention of /hw/, though this is being replaced by /w/ in some urban areas. Like some American English dialects, NIE frequently palatalizes syllable-initial /k/ and /g/ in such words as *cab* and *car*. Unlike Southern Irish English, NIE preserves the distinction between /θ ð/ and /t d/.

Vowels. Although there are a number of differences between NIE and RP in the pronunciation of consonants, the two dialects vary most strikingly in their vocalic systems. The details are highly complex, so we can summarize here only some of the more obvious differences. In NIE, the vowels /æ/ and /ɑ/ have merged: *wrap, path,* and *palm* all have [a], a vowel midway between [æ] and [ɑ] in articulation. Another merger is that of /ɒ/ and /ɔ/, resulting in the same vowel in *tot, taught,* and *cloth.* Unlike Scots, NIE does not have merger of /ʊ/ and /u/.

Like Scots, NIE tends to preserve some distinctions before /r/ that have been lost in other dialects. Among these is that between /ɛr/ and /ʌr/; for example, in rural areas, *swerve* may have /ɛr/, while *curve* has /ʌr/. Similarly, *morning* may have /ɔr/, while *mourning* has /or/. Characteristically Irish is the incomplete merger of ME [ɛ̄] and [e]. Though it is now recessive, some speakers still have [i] in *beet,* but [e] in *beat.* Unlike any other native dialect of English, NIE permits /ɛ/ in open syllables (such as at the end of words) and excludes /e/ from this position. Accordingly, a word such as *pay* is pronounced [pɛː], not [pe]. As in many American and Canadian dialects, the onset of the diphthong /aʊ/ is often heavily fronted; for instance, *mouse* may be [mæʉs] or even [mɛʉs].

Prosody. One of the most easily noted differences between NIE and Southern Irish English (SIE) is in intonation patterns. Unlike SIE and RP, NIE uses a neutral instead of a falling pitch for statements and imperatives; the falling tone is reserved for tag questions and exclamations.

GRAMMAR AND LEXICON

For the most part, the grammar of NIE is the same as that of SBE. The differences that do occur are usually either conservative usages lost in SBE or the results of influence from Gaelic and hence also shared by Scots and SIE. Examples of the former are the use of *doubt* to mean "to think, fear" rather than "to think not," as in *I doubt she won't come* (compare Shakespeare's "I doubt some danger does approach you nearly" [*Macbeth* 4.2.67]), and the phrase *to go (do) the messages,* meaning "do errands, go shopping" (Shakespeare's "Henceforward do your messages yourself" [*Romeo & Juliet* 2.5.64]). An example of the latter is the use of gerunds where SBE would have another construction such as an infinitive (for example, *He couldn't get sleeping,* meaning "he couldn't manage to go to sleep" or "he wasn't allowed to go to sleep"). Trudgill and Hannah report a uniquely NIE use of *whenever* to refer to a single occasion, as in *Whenever I got married, I left home.*

As is true of grammar, lexical differences between NIE and SBE are usually shared by Scots and/or SIE. Among the terms common to NIE and Scots are *aye, wee, burn* 'brook', *to skite* 'to splash', and *throughother* 'mixed-up, confused, untidy'. Terms shared with SIE include *bold* 'naughty' (also in Filipino English), *to cog* 'to cheat', and *to mitch* 'to play hooky, to be a truant from school'.

Southern Ireland

PHONOLOGY

Consonants. Unlike RP, Southern Irish English (SIE) is rhotic, using a retroflex /r/ similar to that of General American. It usually preserves the /hw/ ~ /w/ distinction (as in *where* versus *wear*), and *h*-dropping is not typical. The liquid /l/ is clear in all positions. The voicing of intervocalic /t/ characteristic of American and

Canadian English can be heard in urban areas, especially Dublin.[6] Distinctively SIE is the aspiration of the final voiceless stops /p t k/. Unlike RP and NIE, the phonemic distinction between /t d/ and /θ ð/ is blurred for some speakers, with dental stops [t d] being used for both sets of consonants. For other speakers, /t d/ may be alveolar stops, and /θ ð/ dental stops.

Vowels.   The vocalic system of SIE differs so much and in such complex ways from that of RP that we can only sketch some of its characteristics here. In general, there is a tendency to front the low back vowels. For instance, where RP has [ɔ:], as in *talk* or *law*, SIE has [ɑ:], and where RP has [ɑ:], as in *bath* or *calm*, SIE has [a:]. In some areas, the onset of the diphthong /ɔɪ/ is fronted to such an extent that it overlaps with the diphthong /aɪ/; for example, *oil* is [aɪl]. As in NIE, the /ɒ/ ~ /ɔ/ distinction may be lost, so *cot* and *caught* have the same vowel, though the vowel may be different in NIE and SIE. As in Scots, the RP three-way distinction /ʌ/ ~ /ʊ/ ~ /u/ is often blurred; hence *cook* and *book* may have /u/.

SIE also often has pure vowels rather than diphthongs for RP /e/ and /o/; *may* is [me:] and *goat* is [go:t]. In parts of western Ireland, as in much of the southern United States, the /ɪ/ ~ /ɛ/ distinction is neutralized before a nasal, so that both *since* and *sense* appear as [sɪns]. Although the realization of ME [ɛ̄] as [e] (as in *tea* [te]) is popularly thought of as a typical Irishism, this is now recessive and restricted for the most part to uneducated speech. Unique to SIE English is the pronunciation of *many* and *any* with [a] rather than [ɛ]. As in Australian English, /ɪ/ and /ə/ tend to merge in unstressed syllables, making such words as *habit* and *abbot* perfect rhymes.

Prosody.   The intonation or sentence rhythm of SIE is similar to that of RP. The most striking prosodic feature of SIE is its untypical or flexible placement of word stresses. For example, distinctively SIE are the penultimate stress in words like *architécture*, or the final stress of *concentráte* and *recogníze*. Examples of variable stress are SIE *áffluence* as well as *afflúence*, or *órchestra* as well as *orchéstra*.

GRAMMAR AND LEXICON
For all practical purposes, the grammar and lexicon of educated SIE are identical to that of SBE. At the colloquial and uneducated level, however, there are a number of obvious differences. Like American and Scots English, SIE tends to use *will* to the exclusion of *shall* and to employ a simple past tense where SBE would have a perfect ("Did you see that film yet?"). Reminiscent of U.S. Black English is the use of *do* to indicate habitual or timeless states or actions ("Dublin does be a dirty city"). The use of -*een* as a hypocoristic suffix is endemic; it can be added to virtually any noun ("It's only a small *houseen*, but I love it").

Direct or indirect influence from the Irish language is responsible for many "Irishisms." Irish has no separate words for *yes* and *no*; hence Irish English frequently has a phrase where other dialects would use simply *yes* or *no*. Examples are "Do you know her?" "I do not" or "Are you ready?" "I am indeed." Probably the extensive use of participial forms in Irish is responsible for the wider use of the

---

[6] In the 1960s, South Dublin Catholic children had a song they sang to (or at) Protestant children: "Proddy, Proddy, sitting on the wall, / Sure, we're going to hit you, / And sure, you're going to fall."

progressive in Irish English than in other dialects. Thus, where SBE would have "He looks like his father," SIE might have "He is looking like his father." A direct loan translation from Irish gives *after* + progressive where SBE uses *just* and a perfect tense, as in "I'm just after speaking to her" (SBE "I have just spoken to her"). All varieties of English use cleft sentences (those in which a single sentence is divided into two sections, each with its own subject and verb) to provide emphasis, as in "It was his sneer that annoyed me" rather than "His sneer annoyed me." Irish English uses clefting much more frequently than other dialects, often where no emphasis is intended, as in "It was too late that you came" or "Is it for the night you'll be stopping?" Again, the widespread use of clefting in Irish English is a carry-over from Irish constructions.

The lexicon of educated Irish English is virtually identical to that of SBE, though it shares some items with NIE or Scots English (*wee, cog*). Trudgill and Hannah report as distinctively Irish the directional terms *back* (in the West), *below* (in the North), *over* (in the East), and *up above* (in the South). Among the more colloquial vocabulary items is *messing*, meaning "joking, pulling one's leg," as in "Ah, sure, he's only messing." A victim who is not fooled by a joke may reply, "Pull the other one; it's got bells on it."

Australia

During the first half of the seventeenth century, the Dutch became the first Europeans to explore the coast of Australia, but the Englishman James Cook's exploration of the east coast followed not long afterwards (1770). Because America was no longer available for the purpose, England began settling convicts in Sydney Cove, N.S.W., in 1788, and New South Wales remained a convict settlement until 1840. For all their infamy, most of these convicts were not what we would classify today as violent hardened criminals (such criminals were hanged), but rather political offenders, embezzlers, union organizers, petty thieves, and general trouble-makers. When their sentences expired, they became free. Many returned to England, but many stayed in Australia. These convicts and the civil and military officers assigned to oversee them were primarily from southern England, but heavy immigration from Scotland also took place for a decade or so around the turn of the nineteenth century. Western Australia was founded in 1829 as a free settlement, although the colony took in convicts for labor during the mid-nineteenth century. The remaining Australian states never were convict settlements.

The overwhelming majority of the population of Australia—about 90 percent—is of British origin, and most Australians today were born in Australia. Only about 1 percent of the population speak Aboriginal languages, which have provided the only significant foreign influence on the English vocabulary there.

Phonology

The Australian accent is often said to be like Cockney. Historically, this makes sense, for the two dialects share the geographical origin of urban southern England. Nonetheless, the resemblance is only superficial, lying chiefly in the tendency of both to have more open and centralized diphthongs than is typical of, say, Received Pronunciation or General American. Otherwise, Australian differs from Cockney in its slower delivery, its less frequent use of the glottal stop, and its lack of affricatization of stops.

The most striking characteristic of Australian pronunciation is its remarkable homogeneity; there is virtually no geographically based variation over the nearly three million square miles of the Australian continent, an area nearly as large as that of the continental United States. Where variation does exist, it is a matter primarily of educational, social, and stylistic differences among speakers. Three main types of pronunciation are recognized—Cultivated, General, and Broad—differing chiefly in the pronunciation of vowels. Cultivated Australian is close to RP, Broad is the most different from other accents of English, and General falls between the two. Even Broad Australian, however, differs from RP only phonetically, not phonologically. That is, the systemic repertoire of phonemes is that of RP, but the allophonic realizations of these phonemes are different.

CONSONANTS

Like RP, Australian English is nonrhotic (r-less); it has both linking /r/ and intrusive /r/. Unlike RP, intervocalic post-stress /t/ may be voiced, although this voicing is by no means as universal as it is in American English. As mentioned above, there is little substitution of the glottal stop [ʔ] for /t/, and no glottalization of other stop consonants. Occasional h-dropping may be heard, but again, it is not widespread. Some authorities report the lack of a clear distinction between dark [ɫ] and clear [l], with /l/ tending to be rather dark in all positions. The claim that the distinction between /w/ and /hw/ is regularly maintained is dubious; still, probably at least some older speakers do distinguish *where* and *wear*.

VOWELS

The unmistakable Australian accent resides primarily in the pronunciation of vowels. In general, two systematic differences from General American are obvious. First, front and low lax "pure" vowels are all raised and tensed. To the American ear, this raising is most conspicuous for /æ/ and /ɛ/; the words *bat* and *bet* may even be heard as *bet* and *bait*, respectively. In Sydney and surrounding areas, /ɪ/ may be raised and tensed to the extent that the two vowels of *Sydney* sound the same: [sidni]. Second, diphthongs are more "open" and have a more centralized onset than in General American. An open diphthong is one in which the tongue and mouth undergo extensive changes of position during its production. For example, /ɑɪ/ is an open diphthong in GA, whereas /u/ is a close diphthong. In GA, /i e o u/ are close diphthongs (and often are actually monophthongs phonetically) and /ɑɪ ɑu ɔɪ/ are open diphthongs. In Australian English, on the other hand, *all* diphthongs are open, with /i e o u/ having a much more centralized onset point than in GA. The jocular name *Strine* for Australian English reflects this shifting of /e/ from [e] or [eɪ] to [ʌɪ].

Apart from these overall allophonic differences, Australian English is distinguished by some distributional differences from many other dialects. In particular, there is a tendency to use /ə/ in all unstressed syllables, rather than both /ɪ/ and /ə/. That is, where many English and American dialects would have /ə/ in the unstressed syllable of *famous* but /ɪ/ in the same position in *village*, Australian has /ə/ in both words. Australian most often has /ɑ/ before a voiceless fricative in such words as *class*, *bath*, and *laugh*, but usage varies before a nasal (words like *France, sample*); many speakers have /æ/ here, while others have /æ/ in some words and /ɑ/ in others.

PROSODY

To Americans, Australian intonation patterns may sound "English," but to British ears, the intonation is flatter than that of RP, with less variation between the highest and lowest pitches used in neutral statements. British speakers also sometimes say that Australians tend to use the rising intonation typical of yes-no questions in simple statements, though this is perhaps less obvious to Americans.

Morphology and Syntax

As is true of native varieties of English the world over, Australian English has no significant differences from other standard varieties in morphology and syntax. Like American English, it normally uses singular verbs with collective nouns such as *government* and *team*, and it tends to use *will/would* where British English typically has *shall/should*. The pro-verb *do* is also less frequently used after an auxiliary than in British English; Australians tend *not* to say "I may do" in reply to the question "Will you see her this afternoon?" The once uniquely Australian use of *but* at the end of a sentence as an adverb meaning "however" is now spreading to New Zealand.

At the colloquial level, Australian English is well known for its use of an *-o* suffix: *beauto* as a term of approval, *spello* for "a rest," or *prego* for "pregnant." Another colloquialism is the widespread use of *she* to refer to inanimate nouns or in impersonal constructions. For example, Trudgill and Hannah report the use of *She'll be right* in the meaning "Everything will be all right."

Lexicon and Semantics

The song "Waltzing Mathilda" has probably familiarized more people with more Australian vocabulary items than any other single source; the first fifteen words alone include three specifically Australian terms: *swagman*, *billabong*, and *coolibah*. As this song exemplifies, Australian English is best known for its vigorous slang and its borrowings from Aboriginal languages. Australian is also distinctive in its specialized terms created from English roots and in the semantic shifts that have occurred in existing English words.

Predictably, the majority of the borrowings from native Australian languages are terms for natural phenomena that the English settlers had not previously encountered; zoos have made some of the animal and bird names familiar to the rest of the English-speaking world. Among the names for animals are *kangaroo*, *dingo*, *koala*, *wallaby*, *wombat*, and *jumbuck* (sheep). Bird names include *budgerigar*, *bulla bulla*, and *kookaburra* (also known by the English term *laughing jackass*). *Coolibah*, *yertchuk*, and *mugga* are tree names. Miscellaneous borrowings include *boomerang*, *billabong* (a waterhole or pond), and *gunyah* (a roughly built shelter).

The peculiar circumstances of life in Australia have led its inhabitants to create numerous new words from existing elements. The noun *outback* 'back country, hinterland' has spread beyond Australia to be widely used in the United States. Less familiar are such terms as *billy* 'tin used for cooking', *swagman* 'itinerant worker', and *dog tucker* 'old sheep kept as food for dogs'. Although most Americans associate the expression *to stonewall* with the Watergate scandal of the 1970s, it originated a century earlier in Australia as a term for parliamentary obstruction.

Because most slang is, almost by definition, ephemeral, any attempt at an extensive listing of contemporary Australian slang would be obsolete before the book was in print. We will mention here only a few of the seemingly more enduring Australian colloquial expressions that may survive. *Bonzer* means "fine, enjoyable," *scratchy* means "not much good," and *crook* means "bad, angry." A *wowser* is an obnoxiously puritanical person. Any living language is sure to have slang terms for inebriation and mental instability. Two such Australian expressions are *shikkered* 'drunk' and *a shingle short* 'a loose screw; not playing with a full deck'. Patrick White, the 1973 winner of the Nobel Prize for Literature, uses the colloquialism *whinge* 'complain' in his novel *The Eye of the Storm*; the term is also common in New Zealand.

The terrain and wildlife of Australia are so unlike those of England that it is not surprising if a number of English topographical terms have undergone semantic shifts in Australian usage. Best known among such changes, perhaps, is the use of *bush* to mean "country" as opposed to "town," a usage that has spread to the United States. The term has spawned many derivatives, such as *bush telegraph* 'rumor, grapevine' and *bushranger* 'outlaw who lives in the bush'. In Australian, *scrub* can refer to large forests containing tall trees as well as to areas with stunted trees and shrubs. The term *gully* refers to what the rest of the English-speaking world would call a valley. A *mob* is a group of a single kind of animals or birds; the term is not restricted to human beings. A *muster* is a round-up of cattle, especially sheep. Although they are familiar with them from books, Australians as a rule do not use the topographical terms *field*, *meadow*, *brook*, or *stream*, finding them quaint or romantic (as Americans respond to the English words *copse*, *spinney*, *moor*, and *heath*).

New Zealand

New Zealand's first European explorer was the Dutch captain Abel Tasman (1642). Tasman was, however, prevented from landing by hostile natives. In 1769 the Englishman James Cook circumnavigated both the main islands and took possession for the British crown. Organized British settlement began after 1840, when the islands became part of New South Wales (Australia); they were made a separate crown colony in 1841. Unlike New South Wales, New Zealand never was a convict settlement. Further, while Australia experienced virtually no organized native opposition to European exploration and settlement, the aboriginal inhabitants of New Zealand, the Maori, put up a fierce resistance to the Europeans. Europeans' respect, if not their affection, for the Maori was only increased by their reputation for cannibalism. From 1852 to 1907 New Zealand was a self-governing colony, in 1907 it was declared a Dominion, and today it is an independent member of the Commonwealth.

Though natives of both Christchurch and Brisbane would probably emphatically deny it, New Zealand English is, at least to speakers of other English dialects, very similar to Australian English. In particular, New Zealand English shares the Australian raising and tensing of front vowels and the opening and centralizing of diphthongs. Because the two varieties of English are so alike, in the discussion below we will concentrate on the few differences between the two;

aspects of New Zealand English that are not mentioned can be assumed to be similar to Australian English.

Phonology

CONSONANTS

New Zealand English is generally nonrhotic (*r*-less), though preconsonantal /r/ does survive to some extent in areas with heavy Scottish settlement, primarily the far south. As in Australian, /l/ tends to be dark [ɫ] in all environments. The distinction between /w/ and /hw/ as in *wet* and *whet* is apparently better preserved than in Australia. Some investigators have reported the tendency for New Zealanders to simplify the sequence [kwɔ:], as in *quart*, *quarrel*, to [kɔ:].

VOWELS

As was noted above, New Zealand English has undergone the same shifting of diphthongs and of front vowels that Australian English has. In fact, the front vowels /æ/ and /ɛ/ tend to be even closer than in Australian, so *pat* may be [pɛt]. However, the vowel /ɪ/, rather than being raised to /i/, tends to be centralized to [ə] or [ɨ], so that, for example, *bit* may be pronounced [bət]. Indeed, for many New Zealanders, there seems to be no phonemic contrast between /ɪ/ and /ə/.

A number of vocalic contrasts are neutralized before /l/ in New Zealand English, at least in the broader accents. The contrasts /o/ ~ /ɒ/ ~ /ʌ/ may all be lost, making *dole*, *doll*, and *dull* identical. Similarly, before /l/ the distinction /ɛ/ ~ /æ/ may disappear, so *mallow* is pronounced the same as *mellow*.

Another characteristically New Zealand feature is the coalescence of /ɪ/ and /ɛ/ before orthographic *r*. That is, where RP would have /stɪə/ for *steer* and /stɛə/ for *stare*, New Zealand English tends to merge the two into something that is, impressionistically at least, closer to [stɪə].

Unlike Australian English, New Zealand English tends to have "broad *a*" ([ɑ]), not only before voiceless fricatives in words like *path* and *ask*, but also before nasals in words like *example* and *dance*. The diphthong /aɪ/ tends to have a back onset; for instance, the pronoun *I* sounds like "oy" to American ears. Conversely, the diphthong [aʊ] is fronted to [æʊ], as in *now* [næʊ].

Lexicon and Semantics

Considering the significant presence of Maori culture in New Zealand life, it is surprising that there are relatively few loanwords from Maori in New Zealand English, and even fewer that have spread beyond the Australasian area. Predictably, the loanwords from Maori that do appear tend to be names for natural phenomena. They include such tree names as *totara*, *rata*, and *nikau*, and fish and shellfish names like *pipi*, *hapuka*, and *terakihi*. More familiar to Americans are the names of the flightless birds *kiwi* and the now-extinct *moa*. *Kiwi* has in turn given its name to the fuzzy Asian fruit now frequently sold in American markets. Despite the paucity of Maori common nouns as loans into New Zealand English, there are more Maori place-names in New Zealand than there are aboriginal place-names in Australia, names such as Kekerengu, Takapuna, Wanganui, Lake Wanaka, the Waikato River, Urewera National Park, and Mt. Tatawera.

As a rule, New Zealand shares its specialized derived terms and even colloquialisms and slang with Australia. Trudgill and Hannah mention as unique to New Zealand a few words such as *gutzer* 'a fall'; *school* 'a group of drinkers'; *puckerooed* 'broken down' (from Maori); and *hooray!* as a leave-taking formula equivalent to *goodbye*.

Most of the semantic shifts mentioned in the discussion of Australian English also apply to New Zealand. *Bush*, however, does not have as extended a meaning in New Zealand English as it does in Australian; in New Zealand, *bush* refers to the extensive indigenous forest or native "bush," but not to country as opposed to town. Also, in New Zealand English, the term *forest* normally refers to large plantations of nonindigenous trees, such as pines to be harvested for the paper industry.

South Africa

The Portuguese navigator Bartholomeu Dias was probably the first European to see the Cape of Good Hope (1488). The earliest significant European influence, however, came nearly two centuries later, in the seventeenth century, when the Dutch East India Company began organized settlement. At the turn of the nineteenth century, Great Britain seized the Cape area. Rather than live under British rule, many of the Dutch settlers trekked north and founded two republics, the Transvaal and the Orange Free State, both of which were later annexed by the British. Antagonism between Dutch settlers (Boers) and British colonials eventually led to the Boer War, 1899–1902. The British won the war and, in 1910, created the Union of South Africa, incorporating the Cape Colony, Natal, Transvaal, and the Orange Free State. After a referendum in 1961, the Union became the Republic of South Africa and withdrew from the Commonwealth.

South Africa today has two official languages, Afrikaans (a descendant of seventeenth-century Dutch) and English, neither of which is the native language of the majority of the population. Of the population of 31 million (1983 estimate), roughly 10 percent have English as their first language, perhaps 16 percent have Afrikaans, and most of the rest have one Bantu language or another. There are also fairly large communities of speakers of other languages, especially Indians.

Most of the native speakers of English are of English background, though the Indian populations are progressively abandoning their native languages for English. English is the native tongue of a few blacks, also. Many "coloureds" (people of mixed racial background) and speakers of Afrikaans also have English as a second language.

English in South Africa is the first language of a minority of the white population, which itself is a minority of the total population. But the influence of English is far greater than the number of its native speakers might suggest. Its white native speakers include many people of wealth and power. English is the principal language of commerce and industry and also the language of education. As someone has pointed out, for the victims of apartheid, English is both the language of the oppressor *and* of the voices for freedom.

Phonology
The model for the pronunciation of English in South Africa is RP, and the accent of many well-educated native speakers is virtually identical to RP. Broad South African English is phonemically much the same as RP, but allophonically closer to

New Zealand English. Further, there is some influence from Afrikaans, even in those who do not speak Afrikaans.

Consonants

South African English is normally nonrhotic (historical *r* is lost before consonants and finally), but neither intrusive *r* nor linking *r* is characteristic. In the environments in which *r* is retained, it is often realized as a fricative or a tap. The liquid /l/ is usually clear. A distinction between /hw/ and /w/ (as in *while* versus *wile*) is rare. Intervocalic /t/ tends, though not as strongly as in American English, to be voiced. In the broader accents, Afrikaans influence appears in the tendency for /p t k č/ to be unaspirated and for voiced consonants to be devoiced in final position; for example, *led* and *let* both may be pronounced [let].

Vowels

Like Australian and New Zealand English, broad South African is characterized by a raising and tensing of lax vowels, most noticeably /ɛ/ and /æ/. The midfront /ɛ/ is often raised all the way to [e], and /æ/ may be as high as [ɛ]. Hence, to American speakers, *fed* may sound like *fade*, and *fad* may sound like *fed*.

Also as in Australian and New Zealand English, /ə/ is the normal vowel in unstressed syllables, even in environments where other varieties have /ɪ/, as in the final syllables of *wretched* and *postage*. Like New Zealand English, the phonemic distinction between /ɪ/ and /ə/ is somewhat blurred. In stressed syllables, a raised allophone of /ɪ/—almost [i]—is used next to a velar consonant, initially, and after /h/. Otherwise, a [ə]-like allophone of /ɪ/ appears. Hence such pairs as *kiss* and *miss* may not rhyme, the former being [kis] and the latter [məs]. South African English has a general tendency to monophthongize diphthongs, particularly /e/ and /o/. The vowel of words like *bath* and *dance* is a very back, only slightly rounded /ɑ/.

Morphology and Syntax

The morphology and syntax of educated South African English is essentially that of educated British English. Trudgill and Hannah report that broader varieties may delete noun phrases after transitive verbs (for instance, "Did he take?" "Have you put?"), and an invariable tag question *is it?* is common ("He's working late today." "Oh, is it?"). *With* may be used without an object, as in "Have you bought anything for them to take with?"

Lexicon and Semantics

The most striking feature of the South African English lexicon is its large number of borrowings from Afrikaans and from African languages (primarily Bantu). Among the many loans from Afrikaans are *aandblom* 'evening flower', *grysbok* 'a small antelope', *vry* 'to caress', *ouma* 'granny', *dikkop* 'blockhead', and *melktert* 'a kind of custard pie'. Predictably, the loans from African languages involve primarily natural phenomena for which English had no existing terms, or cultural phenomena with no parallel in European societies. A few examples are *mabela* 'ground kaffir corn', *mopani* 'turpentine tree', *nyala* 'a large antelope', *daba* (grass) 'coarse grass for thatching huts', and *lobola* 'means of acquiring a wife by an exchange for cattle'.

YANKEE TALK

James Russell Lowell's *The Biglow Papers* appeared in two series, published in 1848 and 1868. Though they were originally intended as political satire concerning the Mexican War and the U.S. Civil War, respectively, their interest today lies primarily in Lowell's representation of New England dialect of the time. The bulk of *The Biglow Papers* is in verse, but we have selected a prose passage here in order to ensure that the exigencies of meter and rhyme had not influenced the language. The selection is a mine of interesting dialectal characteristics; note the following ones in particular.

1. Simplification of final consonant clusters ending in [d] or [t]: *las'* (2), *wine* (6), *expec'* (4), *tole* (16). Conversely, intrusive final [t] appears in *onct* (14).
2. Final unstressed [ŋ] becomes [n]: *noticin'* (1), *sunthin'* (4). The reverse change appears as a hypercorrection in *huming* 'human' (9).
3. Loss of [r] before [s]: *Fust* (14). Intrusive [r] appears in *dror out* (6) and *penderlum* (6).
4. Etymological [hw] appears as [w]: *wut* (1), *ware* (22).
5. [ɪ] is lowered to [ɛ]: *deffrence* (2), *Sence* (5), *tell* (7).
6. [æ] is raised to [ɛ]: *ez* (13), *plen* (22).
7. [ɛ] is lowered to [a] before [r]: *whare* (21), *Etarnity* (25).
8. [oi] appears as [ai] in *ile* 'oil' (13).
9. The spelling *nater* 'nature' (9) suggests that no [j] had developed before the final unstressed syllable in this word; hence assibilation had not taken place.
10. The original [juzd] of *used* in the quasi-modal phrase *used to* has assimilated to the following [t] of *to*; probably the spelling *ust to* (19) represents the pronunciation [justə].
11. The still-familiar pronunciation [kɛč] for *catch* appears in this dialect (17).
12. The plural of *house* is *housen* (21).

The United States

Because not only the language but also the dominant cultural patterns of the United States today are based on English models, we tend to forget that the English were not the first Europeans to make permanent settlements in North America. The Spanish were in Texas almost a century before the Jamestown settlement. Both the Spanish and the French had colonies in South Carolina in the sixteenth century. Before the Pilgrims landed at Plymouth Rock, the Spanish had founded the city of Santa Fe (New Mexico) and the Dutch were settling New York. At about the same time that English colonists were coming into Maryland, Swedes were establishing settlements in neighboring Delaware. Of course, by the eighteenth century, English speakers were dominant in the only part of the North American continent with a relatively dense European population, and when these colonies achieved their independence later in the century, the linguistic fate of the nation was assured—though this was not apparent at the time.

Satisfying as it would be to be able to pinpoint the English regional origins of the speech of particular areas in the United States, it is impossible to do so. From the time of the earliest English settlements, immigrants came from different parts of Great Britain, so the speech of any given area in America was a dialectal potpourri

> ### Mr. Hosea Biglow's Speech in March Meeting.
>
> To the Editor of the Atlantic Monthly.
>
> Jaalam, April 5, 1866.
>
> My dear Sir,—
>
> (an' noticin' by your kiver thet you're some dearer than wut you wuz, I enclose the deffrence) I dunno ez I know jest how to interdooce this las' perduction of my mews, ez Parson Wilbur allus called 'em, which is goin' to *be* the last an' *stay* the last onless sunthin' pertikler sh'd interfear which I don't expec' ner I wun't yield tu ef it
> 5 wuz ez pressin' ez a deppity Shiriff. Sence Mr. Wilbur's disease I hev n't hed no one thet could dror out my talons. He ust to kind o' wine me up an' set the penderlum agoin', an' then somehow I seemed to go on tick as it wear tell I run down, but the noo minister ain't of the same brewin' nor I can't seem to git ahold of no kine of huming nater in him but sort of slide rite off as you du on the eedge of a mow.
> 10 Minnysteeril natur is wal enough an' a site better 'n most other kines I know on, but the other sort sech as Welbor hed wuz of the Lord's makin' an' naterally more wonderfle an' sweet tastin' leastways to me so fur as heerd from. He used to interdooce 'em smooth ez ile athout sayin' nothin' in pertickler an' I misdoubt he did n't set so much by the sec'nd Ceres as wut he done by the Fust, fact, he let on onct
> 15 thet his mine misgive him of a sort of fallin' off in spots. He wuz as outspoken as a norwester *he* wuz, but I tole him I hoped the fall wuz from so high up thet a feller could ketch a good many times fust afore comin' bunt onto the ground as I see Jethro C. Swett from the meetin' house steeple up to th' old perrish, an' took up for dead but he's alive now an' spry as wut you be. Turnin' of it over I recclected how they ust to
> 20 put wut they called Argymunce onto the frunts of poymns, like poorches afore housen whare you could rest ye a spell whilst you wuz concludin' whether you'd go in or nut espeshully ware tha wuz darters, though I most allus found it the best plen to go in fust an' think afterwards an' the gals likes it best tu. I dno as speechis ever hez any argimunts to 'em, I never see none thet hed an' I guess they never du but tha
> 25 must allus be a B'ginnin' to everythin' athout it is Eternity so I'll begin rite away an' anybody may put it afore any of his speeches ef it soots an' welcome. I don't claim no paytent.
>
> James Russell Lowell, *The Biglow Papers* (Boston: Houghton Mifflin Company, 1894), pp. 487–89.

of Early Modern English. To be sure, we can make the broad generalization that the earliest settlers came mostly from southern and eastern areas of England, while immigrants to western New England and Pennsylvania were often from north of London. Unfortunately, only rarely do we have extensive documentation about the origins of settlers. Contemporary written records are of only marginal usefulness because English spelling had become so standardized by the seventeenth century that it concealed dialectal variations in pronunciation. In vocabulary, the one aspect of language where one might hope to find indisputable regional evidence, the evidence can be perversely contradictory. For example, in early Rhode Island records, the few unequivocally regional words that appear are primarily from northern England, yet supposedly northern England supplied few immigrants to this part of the country. Little research is being done at present to try to identify specific English origins for early American speech, partly because the few studies that have been made have produced such inconclusive and frustrating results. It is quite likely that dialectal differences in American English were less apparent in the seventeenth and eighteenth centuries than they were to become later.

The spread of English speakers to the interior of North America was slow at first, being limited by hostile Indians and lack of good transportation routes. In the early eighteenth century, immigrant Ulster Scots (the so-called Scotch-Irish) gravitated toward the frontier areas, moving first into Pennsylvania, then into West Virginia, western Virginia, and southern Ohio. Another group went south into the western part of the Carolinas and down into northern Georgia. With the exception of these Ulster Scots, however, movement inland tended to follow an east-west direction and to take the form of secondary settlement from existing colonies.

Eastern New England contributed relatively little to the eighteenth-century movement westward, but pioneers from western New England and eastern New York moved across New York and northern Pennsylvania, the northern Midwest, and ultimately all the way to the Great Plains. The speech of these settlers was the basis for what would become the North Central dialect area (see below).

To the south, settlers from western Pennsylvania moved across central Ohio, Indiana, and Illinois, eventually tapering off at the Mississippi River. Still farther south, a third band of settlers moved west and southwest from the Appalachians, reaching all the way to eastern Texas.

By the time settlers reached the Midwest, however, the lines of migration had begun to cross and even recross, and, especially from the Rocky Mountains west, the three relatively neat bands of westward movement are no longer obvious.

In the nineteenth century, the dialectal streams were further muddied by large numbers of immigrants coming directly from Europe, all of these except some of the Irish being non-English-speaking at the time of their arrival. The Great Potato Famine of 1845–49 brought hundreds of thousands of Irish immigrants, the majority of whom settled in eastern cities. Midwestern cities were inundated by Germans fleeing the chaos resulting from the 1848 revolutions. Scandinavians were especially attracted to the upper Midwest. In the late nineteenth and early twentieth centuries, millions of immigrants from eastern and southern Europe entered the United States—Italians, Hungarians, Poles, Serbo-Croatians, Greeks, and Czechs. The West Coast received Chinese, Japanese, and Filipino immigrants. Still more recently, political and economic problems in their homelands have led to large numbers of immigrants from Central and South America, the Caribbean, and Southeast Asia. With few exceptions, all these immigrants have adopted English almost immediately, and their children born in this country have been native speakers of English. Nonetheless, they have left their mark on American English, even if this influence is only imperfectly understood.

Scientific investigation of regional dialects in the United States began at about the same time as it did in Great Britain, in the closing decades of the nineteenth century. The American Dialect Society was founded in 1889 and, within a few years, was carrying out various dialectal studies. The journal *American Speech* (among whose founders was H. L. Mencken) published its first issue in 1925. In the late 1920s and early 1930s, the American Linguistic Atlas Project got under way, headed by Hans Kurath and Bernard Bloch. The first unit of a planned linguistic atlas that would eventually cover the entire United States and Canada was published in 1939–43. This was the massive three-volume *Linguistic Atlas of New England*, edited by Hans Kurath and his colleagues. Harold Allen's three-volume *Linguistic Atlas of the Upper Midwest* appeared in 1973–76. In 1980, publication began of the *Linguistic Atlas of the Middle and South Atlantic States*. A linguistic atlas of the Gulf States is currently being prepared under the editorship of

Lee Pederson, and beginnings have been made for regional studies of such areas as the Rocky Mountain states, Louisiana, and the Pacific Coast.

In addition to these linguistic atlases, more specialized dialect studies have appeared, including E. B. Atwood's *Survey of Verb Forms in the Eastern United States* (1953) and his *Regional Vocabulary of Texas* (1962). Probably the most comprehensive vocabulary study ever undertaken is Frederic Cassidy's *Dictionary of American Regional English*, the first volume of which was published in 1985.

Unlike most English dialect surveys, the American studies have, from the beginning, investigated social and educational as well as regional variation. The New England Atlas Project deliberately divided its informants into three types: (1) older, poorly educated speakers; (2) younger, better educated speakers with at least two years of high school; and (3) well-educated speakers, usually with a college degree. This concern for social and educational variation has only intensified over the years; a landmark publication was William Labov's *Social Stratification of English in New York City* (1966).

General American

Unlike Great Britain or, for that matter, most Western nations, the United States has no single metropolitan center whose speech serves as the basis for an accepted standard language. The size, age, prestige, and cultural and economic influence of New York City make it an obvious candidate, yet New York City speech is almost universally ridiculed, even by those for whom it is a native dialect. Nor have such other centers as Boston, Chicago, or Los Angeles filled the gap. Nonetheless, there is a recognizable form of English that can be termed General American. In a sense, it is a "negative" dialect, defined as much by the lack of striking features that characterize some of the regional dialects as by the presence of specific identifying features. It also allows a considerable amount of allophonic or even phonemic variation, primarily in the pronunciation of vowels.

Among the characteristics of General American (GA) are

1. Rhoticism, that is, the preservation of preconsonantal /r/ and (usually) lack of intrusive /r/.
2. Voicing of post-stress intervocalic /t/.
3. A "darker" (more velar) /l/ than is typical of British RP.
4. The use of /æ/ in words like *bath*, *dance*, and *class*.
5. Phonemically different vowels in *tot* and *taught* (but with great variation in the distribution of /ɔ/ and /ɑ/).
6. Clearly diphthongized pronunciation of /aɪ/ and /ɔɪ/.
7. The use of /i/ as the final unstressed vowel in words like *cloudy* or *shiny*.
8. Retention of the vowel in unstressed syllables and wider use of secondary stress than is the case in RP.
9. Lack of the three-way phonemic distinction /ɑ/ ∼ /ɒ/ ∼ /ɔ/ of RP.
10. A narrowed range of pitch variation in "neutral" speech as compared to RP.

Failure to meet any of these criteria will normally mark the speech of an individual as "dialectal" in some way. On the other hand, careful attention to the speech of different persons all of whom are considered speakers of General American will reveal that GA allows some rather extensive differences in pronunciation. For example, most speakers of American English, at least, do not notice whether another American speaker has: (1) /æ/ or /ɛ/ in words like *carry* and *various*; (2) /ɔ/

or /ɑ/ in words like *forest*, *doll*, and *log*; (3) [ʌ] or [ɜ] in *hurry* and *fur*; (4) [hw] or [w] in *where* and *whimper*; or (5) /j/ in words like *tune* and *new*. ([ɜ] is a slightly raised mid-central allophone of [ə] that occurs before /r/ in stressed syllables.)

Regional Variation in the United States

Strictly speaking, virtually every individual's speech comprises a separate dialect of the language. On the other hand, everyone knows that valid generalizations about the speech of most people in different regions of the country can be made; we quite rightly recognize a "Southern" or a "Boston" accent as different from a Chicago accent. The problem lies, first, in deciding exactly how many different dialectal areas it is reasonable to posit, and, second, in drawing the boundary lines between these areas. Given the present state of dialect studies in the United States, many scholars agree on ten major areas, varying in geographical size from a few score square miles to over a million square miles. These ten areas are (A) Eastern New England, (B) New York City, (C) Middle Atlantic, (D) Western Pennsylvania, (E) Southern Mountain, (F) Southern, (G) North Central, (H) Central Midlands, (I) Northwest, and (J) Southwest. As more regional studies are completed, it may become necessary to increase the number of dialectal areas and to redefine the boundaries of the areas.

One aspect of regional dialects that has been relatively neglected is prosody, despite the fact that prosodic differences are among the features that we respond to most quickly and easily in recognizing dialects. To the extent that prosodic features are identified, the descriptions tend to be vague and impressionistic: the Southern "drawl," the "staccato" delivery of large urban centers, the "breathless" and "soft" speech of many people from the Pacific Northwest. Much more work needs to be done on regional differences in prosody.

A. Eastern New England (ENE)

The dialectal area of Eastern New England includes the urban centers of Boston, Providence, and Portland. It extends to the Atlantic Ocean on the east, westward to the Connecticut River, north to the Canadian border, and south into northeastern Connecticut.

The best-known features of ENE speech are its traditional nonrhoticity (its loss of /r/ before a consonant) and its use of [a], an allophone of /ɑ/, before a fricative or a nasal plus fricative in certain words such as *class*, *bath*, and *dance*. Both of these features now are recessive, especially among the middle classes in the cities.

Depending on the specific place within the region, ENE speech may or may not have a phonemic distinction between the vowels of *tot* and *taught*; if the distinction is made, *tot* is phonemically /tɑt/ and *taught* is /tɔt/. The characteristic vowel in words like *forest*, *foreign*, *orange*, and *horrid* is [ɑ]. Words like *hurry*, *furry*, *worry*, and *courage* usually have [ʌ], while words like *carry*, *marry*, *narrow*, and *barren* normally have [æ]. Words such as *fog*, *on*, *crop*, and *pocket* are phonemically /ɔ/, allophonically [ɔ] or [ɒ].

In general, ENE speech does not distinguish /hw/ and /w/; hence *whale* and *wail* are homophones. Insertion of /j/ after the initial alveolar consonant and before /u/ in words like *new*, *tune*, *due*, and *stew* occurs sporadically, but it is not characteristic of the area as a whole.

B. New York City (NYC)

The New York City dialectal area includes the five boroughs of the city itself, Long Island, the Hudson River Valley up into Westchester County, the region to the south down into northern New Jersey, and southwestern Connecticut.

Many of the features that have traditionally uniquely identified NYC speech are stigmatized, even by the speakers themselves; consequently, most of them are recessive today, confined to older or lower-class speakers. NYC is still usually classified as a nonrhotic area, with both linking and intrusive [r]. But the middle classes are becoming increasingly rhotic, particularly in their more formal speech styles. Highly recessive is the fronting of the onset of the diphthong /ɔɪ/ to [ɜɪ] (*choice* and *boil* as [čɜɪs] and [bɜɪl]). Many NYC speakers use the glottal stop [ʔ] as an allophone of /t/ in a wider range of environments than do speakers of other dialects, especially before /l/, as in *shuttle* and *battle*. Also typical of the NYC dialect is a lack of phonemic distinction between [ŋ] and [ŋg]; [ŋg] tends to appear in such words as *wrong* and *singer*. This feature, however, appears in a number of other dialects, and especially in urban areas.

Some attribute the tendency in NYC speech to a dental (rather than alveolar) articulation of /t d n l/ to the influence of foreign speakers. Similarly, the use of a dental stop or affricate (rather than an interdental fricative) in /θ ð/ is also often considered a foreignism. Although it is true that both of these pronunciations are characteristic of many nonnative speakers, it should be pointed out that both occur in a number of other dialects of English around the world for which foreign influence does not seem to be a factor.

Palatalization (/j/) of words in the *tune, new, due* class is common. No distinction is made between the initial sounds of *where* and *wear*; [hw] is not phonemic or even regularly allophonic.

NYC shares with Eastern New England the use of [ɑ] in words like *forest* and *foreign*, [ʌ] in words like *hurry* and *courage*, and [æ] in *carry* and *narrow*. The vowels of *cot* and *caught* are usually phonemically different.

C. Middle Atlantic (MA)

The Middle Atlantic dialectal area is centered in southeastern Pennsylvania and radiates northward to include all of New Jersey not within the NYC belt of influence. It extends south to the District of Columbia, covering Delaware and parts of Maryland.

One of the most conspicuous characteristics of the MA area is a negative one; unlike NE and NYC to the north and the Southern dialectal area to the south, it is historically rhotic ("r-ful"), the only dialect region on the Atlantic for which this is true. Another salient feature of MA is its fronted allophones of /u/ and /o/. For example, *coop* may be [küp] or [küʊp], and *fold* is often [föld] or [foʊld]. Some speakers have /j/ in words of the *new* and *tune* class. Normally, no distinction is made between /hw/ and /w/, with [w] appearing in words like *which* and *whether*. In the parts of the area bordering the Southern dialectal region, the vowels in *for* and *horse* may be phonemically distinct from those in *four* and *hoarse*, with /ɔ/ appearing in the former and /o/ in the latter.

The *tot* and *taught* vowels of MA are usually different; *tot* is /tɑt/ and *taught* is /tɔt/. As in both NYC and ENE, the *hurry* vowel is most commonly [ʌ], the *carry* vowel is usually [æ], and words of the *forest* and *orange* class normally have /ɑ/.

D. Western Pennsylvania (WP)

Pittsburgh is the center of the WP dialect region, which includes not only western Pennsylvania but also bordering areas of eastern Ohio and northern West Virginia. WP is traditional Pennsylvania Dutch country, and the dialect is most famous for its German-influenced syntax and vocabulary. In places where German influence has been especially heavy, it may even be reflected in the phonology of native English speakers; for example, some speakers have devoicing of final voiced stops.

The WP area is firmly rhotic, with little or no intrusive [r]. No distinction is made between the initial consonants of *which* and *witch*; both have /w/. Palatalization of words of the *tune* and *new* class is rare; these words are /tun/ and /nu/, respectively.

The vowels of *tot* and *taught* are not distinguished, and both of them may have [ɒ], [ɔ], or [ɑ]. The usual vowel of *forest* and *horrid* is [ɔ], and words like *hurry* and *courage* have [ʌ]. *Carry* normally has [æ], but similar words, such as *various*, usually have [ɛ].

E. Southern Mountain (SM)

The Southern Mountain region represents a transitional zone between the Central Midlands dialect to the north and the Southern dialect to the south. Geographically, the area is an extension of the Appalachian Mountain chain, including most of West Virginia and Kentucky, eastern Tennessee, and the contiguous parts of western North Carolina and South Carolina, and northern Georgia, Alabama, and Mississippi.

Among the dialectal features that SM shares with the South are the realization of /ɑɪ/ as [a:], especially before [r], as in *wire*, which is usually [war] or [wa:r]; once, when I asked a native of the region what kind of a tool was used to cut stone, I at first misinterpreted his reply as "Warsaw"—he had, of course, said *wire saw*. In most parts of the area, /ɔɪ/ is also monophthongized, appearing as [ɔ:]. Other features common to both SM and the South are /z/ in *greasy* (instead of /s/); [ɪ] as the most frequent vowel in final unstressed syllables of words like *coffee*, *handy*, and *happy*; and a distinction between the vowels of *horse* (with [ɔ]) and *hoarse* (with [o]). Unlike the Southern dialectal area, SM is firmly rhotic, though intrusive [r] does appear occasionally ("pianer," "idear").

Words like *tot* and *taught* are regularly distinguished as /tɑt/ and /tɔt/, respectively. Both [ɑ] and [ɔ] appear in words of the *forest* class. *Hurry* has [ʌ] in most of the area, and [æ] is the normal vowel of words of the *carry* type, though West Virginia in particular may also have [ɛ] in these words. Words like *path*, *ask*, and *dance* usually have [æ], sometimes a diphthongized [æɪ].

The region as a whole tends to retain a distinction between /hw/ and /w/, as in *which* versus *witch*. Words like *tune*, *new*, and *duke* usually have /j/ after the initial alveolar.

F. Southern (SO)

Southern is a catchall term for a variety of regional dialects, some of them, such as those of Florida, New Orleans, and Tidewater Virginia, quite disparate. The area as a whole extends from Maryland south to Florida and west through the eastern two-thirds of Texas. So diverse is the speech of the region that in some places even the shibboleths of *r*-lessness and diphthongization of simple vowels do not hold.

Further research will surely result in recognizing a number of distinct dialects in the region.

In general, the SO dialect has historically been nonrhotic, though intrusive and linking [r] are not common. Recent research has shown, however, that rhoticity is making a strong comeback in the area, especially among the middle classes. Other familiar characteristics are the monophthongization of /aɪ/ and /ɔɪ/ to [a:] and [ɔ:], respectively, as in *mine* [ma:n] and *soil* [sɔ:l]. Conversely, the short simple vowels tend to "break" (diphthongize) to end in a centering glide; hence, such pronunciations as *lid* [lɨəd], *map* [mæəp], *wreck* [rɛək], *fog* [fɔəg], and *should* [šuəd]. One feature that seems to be spreading beyond the boundaries of the SO area is the raising of historical /ɛ/ to /ɪ/ before a nasal; for instance, *them* becomes [ðɪm] or [ðɪəm], and words like *pen* and *pin* are homophones. As noted above, the final unstressed vowel of words like *handy* and *coffee* is often [ɪ], rather than [i] as in more northern dialects.

The SO area tends to preserve more vocalic distinctions before [r] than most other areas; for example, there is usually a three-way distinction among *merry* (with [ɛ]), *Mary* (with [e]), and *marry* (with [æ]). Like Southern Mountain speech, SO tends to distinguish *horse* [hɔ:s] from *hoarse* [hoəs]. The diphthong /au/ tends to be fronted to /æu/, as in *mouth* [mæuθ].

Words of the *hurry* class usually have [ʌ], *carry* has [æ], and *forest* has [ɑ]. *Tot* and *taught* remain distinct as /tat/ and /tɔt/. *Greasy* regularly has /z/, and *tune* normally has /j/ ([tjun] or [tiun]).

G. North Central (NC)

As one moves inland from the Atlantic coast, dialectal differences become less obvious. The areas themselves are larger and their boundaries are less easy to define. This is true of the North Central (NC) area, whose very lack of salient dialectal features makes it a good candidate for a General American dialect. North Central American English extends from western New England west across upstate New York and the northern portions of Pennsylvania, Ohio, and Illinois. It includes all of Michigan and Minnesota, and most of Iowa and the Dakotas.

The region is universally rhotic, without intrusive [r]. Particularly in larger urban areas, /hw/ is often not retained. For the most part, /i e o u/ are more monophthongal—or less diphthongized—than elsewhere in the United States. There is extensive neutralization of vowels before [r]; for instance, *Mary*, *merry*, and *marry* all frequently have [ɛ] (as do other words of the *carry* class). Both *horse* and *hoarse* have /ɔ/. Words like *borrow* and *sorry* vary between /ɔ/ and /ɑ/. *Hurry* words usually have [ɜr] rather than [ʌr]. *Tot* and *taught* have /ɑ/ and /ɔ/, respectively.

Words like *new* and *due* are /nu/ and /du/, without a /j/ between the alveolar consonant and the /u/. *Greasy* regularly has /s/, not /z/.

H. Central Midlands (CM)

The Central Midlands dialect area extends from southern Ohio, Indiana, and Illinois in the east to Utah in the west, and from Wyoming and Nebraska in the north to New Mexico, western Texas, and Oklahoma in the South. Another good candidate for a General American dialect, it shares many features with the North Central region and even with the Southern Mountain, Northwest, and Southwest regions.

Like all of these other dialect areas, Central Midlands (CM) is rhotic, distinguishes /ɑ/ from /ɔ/ in words like *tot* and *taught*, regularly employs [ɛ] in words like *carry* and *marry*, and does not have /j/ in words like *new* and *tune*. *Forest* and *orange* normally have [ɔ]. The word *greasy* tends to have /z/ in the southern part of the CM area, but /s/ is common in the northern part. The diphthong of *out*, *found*, and *town* frequently has a fronted onset; *town*, for instance, appears as [tæʊn]. The vowels /i e o u/ tend to be noticeably diphthongized. Distinction between [o] and [ɔ] before [r] (as in *hoarse* versus *horse*) is more common here than in most other regions.

I. Northwest (NW)

The Northwest dialect region includes the western part of the Dakotas, Montana and Idaho along with northwestern Wyoming, the Pacific coastal states of Washington and Oregon, and the extreme northern tips of California, Nevada, and Utah. The dialect strongly resembles those of both the North Central and the Central Midlands regions.

NW is rhotic. It regularly has [ɜr] in *hurry* and *worry*, [ɔ] in words of the *forest* class, [ɛ] in *narrow* and *various*, and [ɔ] in both *horse* and *hoarse*. The phonemic distinction between *tot* and *taught* is preserved, though there may be variation in other individual words. *Greasy* usually has /s/. Words of the *new* and *due* class normally do not have /j/.

J. Southwest (SW)

The Southwest dialect area consists of Arizona and all but the northern tips of Nevada and California. Because there has been so much recent immigration into the area from other parts of the United States, the speech tends to be mixed. Nonetheless, its general affinities with the North Central dialect area are clearly recognizable.

The SW dialect is rhotic. The usual vowel in words of the *horrid* and *forest* type is /ɔ/. *Hurry* words normally have [ɜ], and *marry* words have [ɛ], with some instances of [æ]. The phonemic distinction between /ɑ/ and /ɔ/ is maintained in words like *tot* and *taught*. Both *horse* and *hoarse* usually have /ɔ/. In keeping with its association with northern dialects, *greasy* usually has /s/, though immigration from more southern regions has brought some instances of /z/. Words of the *new* and *duke* class have no /j/; for example, *do* and *due* are homophones. Diphthongization of /i e o u/ is more obvious than in the North Central dialect area.

Black English

All the dialects of American English discussed thus far have been regional dialects, dialects whose boundaries are geographical. Black English (BE), on the other hand, is an ethnic and socioeconomic variety of the language, defined by the social position and education of its speakers. That is, BE is the nonstandard English used by some blacks in the United States; when blacks use standard English, it has no distinguishing label. When whites use nonstandard English, it is called simply nonstandard English, not White English.

Partly because of the very term Black English, the differences between BE and other dialects of English are often exaggerated—by blacks and whites alike. Most of the phonology, syntax, and lexicon of Black English is isomorphic with that of white speakers and, for that matter, with standard English. Furthermore, as the research of Labov in particular has shown, the features of Black English are probabilistic rather than absolute. No speaker of BE simplifies all final consonant clusters all the time, and even university-educated black professionals simplify them at least sometimes (as, indeed, do most white speakers). Especially among middle-class blacks, specifically BE characteristics vary according to the social situation, appearing more frequently in casual, informal speech than in formal situations.

Another point that should be stressed is that BE is just as grammatical—in the sense that a grammar is a set of rules—as standard English. For example, the BE omission of the copula is far from random sloppiness; in fact, it is dropped only when standard English can contract it, and not otherwise (see below). In some instances, the grammar of BE allows subtle distinctions impossible to make efficiently in SE; an example would be the BE use of *done* as an auxiliary for the recent past versus *been* for the distant past.

The precise origins of BE have long been a subject of controversy. One of the earliest theories was that it resulted when African slaves learned English imperfectly from their masters; because of the social separation of whites and blacks, their errors were passed on to their offspring rather than being corrected. Another theory holds that BE is a creole of West African languages and English. Some investigators have suggested affinities with Irish English brought about by the early contact of black slaves with Irish settlers in the Caribbean and the southern United States. Obviously, the historical separation of whites and blacks has been a contributing factor, permitting BE to develop somewhat independently of SE, in a manner similar to that of geographically separated dialects. Probably all of these facts have contributed to the formation of Black English.

Over the years, BE has contributed a number of lexical items to SE, including direct loans from African languages (such as *goober*, *okra*, and *yam*) as well as idioms and slang expressions that have originated within the black culture in the United States (for example, *nitty-gritty*, *jam* 'to play jazz improvisations', *jazz*, and *rap*). For the most part, however, the lexicon of BE is identical to that of SE. Therefore, we will discuss here only the phonology and grammar of Black English.

PHONOLOGY

Because BE is a continuum, even for a given speaker, ranging from the broadest BE varieties to standard or near-standard English, it would be futile to attempt to present a monolithic phonological system for it. Instead, we will discuss some of the most salient features, always bearing in mind that most of these are probabilistic only and many are shared by other dialects of English.

Consonants. Like many non-black dialects of English, BE is nonrhotic, but intrusive and linking [r] are not typical. In extreme cases, loss of [r] may even extend to positions between vowels. That is, such words as *Harold* and *Hal*, or *carrot* and *cat*, may become homophones. In a development parallel to the loss or vocalization of [r], [l] in preconsonantal position may be vocalized to a high back unrounded vowel [ɯ]. (Note that both [r] and [l] are liquids.) Thus, *help* appears as [hɛɯp] and *silk* as [sɪɯk]. In final position, especially, [l] may be lost entirely; *tall* becomes [tɔ] and goal [go].

Another characteristic of BE is the simplification (reduction) of consonant clusters, primarily at the ends of words. Hence, *missed* may appear as [mɪs], *band* as [bæn], and *talks* as [tɔk]. It has been pointed out that when the two consonants of the cluster differ in voicing, the cluster is more likely to be retained. That is, while *send* may be [sɪn], *rent* will often be [rɪnʔ] (with the glottal stop as an allophone of /t/); or *thumbs* may contrast with *thump* as [θəm] and [θəmp], respectively.

As is true of some other English dialects, the interdental fricatives /θ/ and /ð/ frequently suffer in BE. In general, they tend to become the stops [t] and [d] at the beginning of words, and, in extreme cases, they become the labiodental fricatives [f] and [v] in medial or final position. Thus, *them* is [dɪm], but *something* is [səmfɪn] and *soothe* is [suv]. Like many English dialects, BE normally has [ɪn] rather than [ɪŋ] in the unstressed participial and gerund ending *-ing*.

Vowels. The vowels of BE are much like those of Southern American. In particular, both /aɪ/ and /ɔɪ/ tend to be monophthongized as [ɑ] and [ɔ], respectively; *buy* is [bɑ] and *toy* is [tɔ]. As the transcriptions of *send* and *rent* above indicate, the distinction between /ɪ/ and /ɛ/ is neutralized before nasal consonants.

Prosody. As is true of all dialects of English, the prosodic features of Black English have not been extensively studied. One feature that has been observed has been the tendency to move the major stress of words to the initial syllable, as in *défense*, *Détroit*, and *pólice*. Such front-shifting of stress has been a characteristic of English (and Germanic) throughout the centuries. Impressionistically, BE often seems to utilize a wider pitch range than other varieties of American English, though it is unclear to what extent this is a stylistic as opposed to a systemic feature.

GRAMMAR

Black English perhaps differs more from other varieties of English in its grammar than in its phonology. Still, the differences can easily be overstated: many of them appear in other dialects of English and are not unique to BE. Furthermore, a number of the grammatical features are related to the phonology of BE and thus are not truly independent morphological or syntactic developments. It is in the expression of tense and aspect relationships that BE differs most from other varieties.

Among the features of BE shared by other dialects of nonstandard English is the use of multiple negation, as in "He *don't never* say *nothing*." Note that not only is multiple negation common in all varieties of nonstandard English, but its condemnation is a recent phenomenon in SE; respectable writers still employed it as late as the eighteenth century. A kind of double negation even remains in contemporary SE in the obligatory change of the indefinite pronoun in such clauses as "I have *some*" versus "I *don't* have *any*."

Other grammatical characteristics of BE include: (a) redundant subjects ("My brother, *he* took me"); (b) deviant verb forms ("She *begun* working just yesterday"); (c) deviant prepositional usage ("different *to* mine," "married *with* him"); (d) use of *ain't* rather than *haven't* (*hasn't*) as an auxiliary ("I *ain't* been told," "They *ain't* never come back"); (e) use of *a* instead of *an* before words beginning with a vowel sound ("You want *a* orange?"); (f) inversion after an interrogative adverb that introduces a subordinate clause ("He asked me when did I come"); and (g) omission of the *have* auxiliary in perfect tenses ("We been eating popcorn," "We seen that before"). In the last case, it is sometimes difficult to say whether the *have* auxiliary has been dropped or whether a nonstandard form of the past has been used; should the SE translation of "We seen that before" be "We have seen that before" or "We saw that before"? Again, all of these characteristics appear in other, non-black dialects of English.

Loss of inflections is a well-known feature of BE. In particular, the plural marker -s is often omitted, especially when the meaning is clear without it ("I got three *sister*"). Similarly, the possessive marker may be deleted when the context makes it redundant: "That *Jim* bike" and "This *you* hat?" but *not* *"That hat *you*?" Also frequently absent is the third-person singular present indicative verbal ending (as in "She *make* me breakfast every morning") and past-tense endings ("He *talk* to me last week"). Note, however, that failure to mark these grammatical categories overtly does not mean that the categories are totally absent from the grammar of BE, just as the existence of SE "Today I *cut*" / "Yesterday I *cut*" does not indicate that SE fails to distinguish present from past tense. Often, the same speaker of BE who regularly says "Yesterday I *walk* home" also says "Yesterday I *went* home" (not *"Yesterday I *go* home"). In other words, the SE /t/ of *walked* may be dropped because a phonological rule simplifies final consonant clusters, not because BE has no grammatical category of past tense.

All of the features of BE discussed thus far have parallels in other English dialects. More specifically characteristic of BE is the omission of the copula, as in "He talking now" or "I tired." Even here, as was mentioned earlier, BE merely extends the contraction rule of SE one step further, from contraction to complete deletion. Where SE allows "We're going home," BE has "We going home." Where SE does not permit contraction of the copula, it is retained in BE: "Can you tell me where I *am*?"

Less easily explainable as an extension of SE grammatical rules is the BE use of invariant (noninflected) *be* to indicate continuing or repeated actions or states. For instance, the sentence "She *be* grouchy" means that she is often grouchy or always grouchy, and may contrast with "She grouchy," meaning that she happens to be grouchy at the time of speaking.

A sometimes misinterpreted grammatical feature of BE is the use of *done* as an auxiliary to indicate that the action took place in the recent past. Thus, "That cat *done* bit me" means that the cat just bit me, or "He *done* broke the jar" means that he broke the jar recently. For some BE speakers, the *done* auxiliary can contrast with the *been* auxiliary, which indicates that the action or state took place in the more distant past. "That *been* gone" would, then, mean that it has been gone for a long time. It is reported, however, that the use of the *been* auxiliary is now recessive and probably on its way out.

Canada

The Vikings were probably the first Europeans to reach the eastern coast of Canada, but, despite persistent reports of "rune stones" as far inland as the American Midwest, the Vikings left little evidence, linguistic or otherwise, of their exploration and settlement. Several hundred years later (1497), the Genoese seaman John Cabot, exploring for England, sighted Newfoundland and Cape Breton. His reports of vast schools of codfish brought fishing fleets from England, France, Portugal, and Spain to the area, but no attempts at colonization. Credit for systematic exploration farther inland goes to the Frenchman Jacques Cartier, who discovered the Gulf of St. Lawrence in 1534. In the early seventeenth century, the French made the first European settlements in Canada, and New France was declared a French colony in 1663. For the next century, control of various parts of eastern Canada passed back and forth between France and England. After the French and Indian War (the Seven Years War), however, the Peace of Paris (1763) recognized British sovereignty over the entire territory.

The English-speaking population of Canada increased greatly after 1776 with the immigration of large numbers of Loyalists from the thirteen colonies. Indeed, from the later eighteenth century down to the twentieth, the major source of immigration to Canada was the United States. Still, speakers of other dialects and languages have had an impact too. Thousands of Scots came to Canada at the end of the eighteenth century and the beginning of the nineteenth. With the potato famine of 1846, about 90,000 Irish entered the country. Perhaps 800,000 immigrants from England came in during the first half of the nineteenth century. Free land in western Canada attracted over a million and a half new immigrants in the first decade of the twentieth century. This immigration was divided roughly equally among Britain, the United States, and non-English-speaking nations.

Canada today is officially bilingual. Its population of approximately 25 million is about one-third French-speaking, although a higher proportion of the French speakers than of the English speakers are bilingual. Canadian English is very similar to American English, so similar that British people usually think that Canadians are from the United States, or vice versa; when I lived in Scotland, I was often asked if I were Canadian. This similarity is only to be expected, considering the heavy American component in the Canadian population and the fact that the great majority of Canadians live within 100 miles of the U.S. border.

The pronunciation of Canadian English, with the important exception of Newfoundland, is extraordinarily homogeneous from coast to coast, and even the variation attributable to educational and social differences is slight. Canada, like the United States, has no "official" pronunciation parallel to English Received Pronunciation. In general, the CBC tends to recommend RP when there is a difference between RP and GA pronunciation, but these recommendations are by no means slavishly followed by the Canadians themselves. Because Canadian English is so much like American English, the following discussion will concentrate on the differences between the two varieties, taking the similarities as given.

Phonology

Some dialectologists divide Canada into three major areas: Newfoundland, eastern Canada, and western Canada. However, the differences in pronunciation between the latter two areas are too slight to be of significance. Newfoundland English will be treated separately.

CONSONANTS

The inventory of Canadian English consonants and even their allophonic realizations are nearly identical to those of American English. Canadian English is normally rhotic (r-ful). Voicing of post-stress intervocalic /t/ is usual. The consonant /l/ is said to be rather "dark" in all environments. Some speakers still distinguish /hw/ and /w/ (as in *whale* versus *wail*), but this distinction is highly recessive. Like the majority of American English speakers, most Canadians pronounce such words as *tune*, *due*, and *new* without a /j/ following the initial alveolar consonant. Shibboleth items like *lieutenant* and *schedule* are perhaps most often pronounced as in American English, but older, well-educated speakers in particular may have the British pronunciations /léftənənt/ and /šédjul/.

VOWELS

The single truly distinctive characteristic of Canadian pronunciation is the allophones of the diphthongs /aɪ/ and /aʊ/ that appear before a following voiceless consonant. Instead of starting with a low vowel ([ɑ] or [æ]), they have a mid or mid-back onset ([ə] or [ʌ]). For example, *house*, *out*, and *write* are realized as [həʊs], [əʊt], and [rəɪt]. American ears may even perceive the Canadian [əʊ] as phonemic /u/ instead of /aʊ/. In some instances, these allophones may distinguish words that would otherwise have become homophones. For instance, because of the voicing of intervocalic /t/, most younger American speakers pronounce *writer* and *rider* identically as [raɪdər]; the typical younger Canadian would have [rəɪdər] for *writer* and [raɪdər] for *rider*.

Most Canadians, like many Americans, lack a phonemic distinction between /ɑ/ and /ɔ/, having the same phoneme in, for example, *bought*, *pot*, *calm*, and *part*. Hence such pairs as *taught* and *tot*, and *chalk* and *chock*, are homophones. In words like *half*, *ask*, and *class*, the typical Canadian vowel is /æ/, though some speakers have /ɑ/. Before a nasal, /æ/ (rather than RP /ɑ/), as in *aunt* or *France*, is even more prevalent. The word *been* is perhaps more often /bin/ than /bɪn/, and *either* and *neither* frequently have /aɪ/ rather than the more typically American English /i/.

PROSODY

As noted earlier, the intonation patterns of Canadian English and American English are similar, and these two national varieties of English are the most important members of a natural grouping that some scholars call North American English. Some Canadians follow British practice and put the stress of a few words like *laboratory* and *corollary* on the second syllable, rather than on the first syllable as in American English.

Morphology and Syntax

The morphology and syntax of Canadian English is for all practical purposes identical to that of American English. At least some Canadians follow British practice in not distinguishing between *got* and *gotten*, using *got* everywhere. Trudgill and Hannah report that, unlike American English, Canadian English allows the deletion of *here* or *there* in sentences where *to be* is used to mean "come" or "go," such as "Has the paperboy been yet?"

Lexicon and Semantics

The differences in vocabulary and semantics between Canadian English and American English are few; where they do exist, Canadian English typically uses—or is at least familiar with—British English terms like *fortnight*.

Even with respect to loanwords from aboriginal languages, it is difficult to distinguish Canadian from American English, because the majority of such borrowings are familiar to both varieties of English and are drawn from the same family of Amerindian languages, Algonquian. By the time a loanword has been anglicized, it is almost impossible to tell whether it came from a Canadian Algonquian dialect (such as Cree) or an American Algonquian dialect (such as

Narragansett). Probably Canadians were the first to borrow the words *muskeg*, *pemmican*, *toboggan*, *wapiti*, and *bogan* (a term for a marshy cove).

Specifically Canadian, of course, is the term *Mountie* for a Royal Canadian Mounted Policeman. Canadians are also usually credited with a number of compounds such as *grid road*, *steelhead* (trout), *goldeye* (a fish), *fiddlehead* (a kind of edible fern), *chuck wagon*, and *bush pilot*.

Newfoundland[7]

A glance at a map of Canada will go a long way toward explaining why the English language should have developed so differently in Newfoundland from the way it did in the rest of Canada. The island of Newfoundland, where the bulk of the province's population lives, is separated from the mainland by the Strait of Belle Isle, which is frozen over from November to June. Even during summer months icebergs may enter the strait, sometimes breaking up there. The climate of the mainland portion of Newfoundland (including Labrador) is geographically subpolar and is made even more hostile by the Labrador Current, which passes down along its coast. Between Newfoundland and the major settled areas of Canada lie vast stretches of sparsely populated land. Hence, communication between Newfoundland and the rest of Canada has always been difficult. Newfoundlanders have always regarded themselves as being different from other Canadians. Indeed, Newfoundland at first refused to join the rest of Canada when the Confederation was established; it remained a British colony until 1949.

Another reason for the highly distinctive flavor of Newfoundland English is historical; Newfoundland is one of the earliest overseas British settlements, so dialectal variation has had a long time in which to develop here. The first British settlements were in the early seventeenth century, and the uniqueness of the language was noticed as early as the late eighteenth century, when George Cartwright published a glossary of Newfoundland dialect words. The forebears of today's Newfoundlanders were primarily from southeast Ireland and the West Country of England. Most nineteenth-century comments on the language stressed the Irish element, but a comparison of the most salient features of Irish and Newfoundland English (see pp. 312–15 for Irish English) will reveal that the two varieties really are very different.

PHONOLOGY

In the broadest Newfoundland accents, the interdental fricatives /θ/ and /ð/ have coalesced with the alveolar stops /t/ and /d/, so *thought* is [tɔt] and *then* is [dɛn]. After a vowel, however, standard English /θ/ sometimes appears as [f], as in *path* [pæf]. Most of Newfoundland is rhotic, although there are areas of *r*-lessness, especially the Avalon Peninsula. The distinction between /hw/ and /w/ (as in *where* versus *wear*) is absent everywhere. Broad Newfoundland English also has extensive simplification of final consonant clusters.

On the mainland of Newfoundland, the distinction between /ɪ/ and /ɛ/ has been lost, and the two vowels have merged as [ɪ], except before /r/, where only [ɛ] appears. For example, *fear* and *fair* are homonyms [fɛr]. The diphthong /aɪ/ is generally realized as [əɪ], as in *time* [təɪm] and *like* [ləɪk]. Where the rest of Canada

---

[7] For material on the vocabulary of Newfoundland, I am especially indebted to Christopher S. Wren, "Newfoundland Nurtures Its Outlandish Old Nouns," *New York Times*, January 3, 1986, p. 2.

has /e/, Newfoundland has /ɛ:/, as in *race* [rɛ:s]. In those words that have /ɑ/ in RP and /æ/ in most American English dialects, Newfoundland English has a long [æ:] (*half, bath, glass*).

MORPHOLOGY AND SYNTAX
In morphology and syntax, broad Newfoundland English can differ greatly from other varieties of Canadian English. Perhaps the most striking difference is the use of invariable consuetudinal (referring to habitual actions or states) *bees* in contrast to the normal inflected forms of *to be* for the true present: *I bees tall, she bees tall, they bees tall*, but *I am tired today, you are tired today, they are tired today.* (Compare Black English *be*, p. 333.)

As in many other varieties of English, the use of *-ly* as an adverb marker distinguishing adverbs from adjectives is infrequent. Newfoundlanders employ not only *real* (common everywhere) and *right* (archaic and regional elsewhere), but also *some* as an intensifier. Thus, *that was some exciting* means "that was very exciting."

LEXICON AND SEMANTICS
For all its other differences from standard Canadian, it is in the area of vocabulary that Newfoundland English has attracted the most interest, primarily because so many of these lexical items have not been adopted into other English dialects and hence sound exotic.

In some instances, words or expressions have been confined to Newfoundland itself because the referents are so specialized. This is true, for example, of Indian and Eskimo loanwords like *tabanask* and *komatik*, both terms for types of sled. In other instances, the isolation of Newfoundland has allowed retention of terms that have become obsolete or at least strictly regional and dialectal in other parts of the English-speaking world. Examples include *barm* 'yeast', *glutch* 'to swallow', *pook* 'a mound of hay', and *yaffle* 'armful'. Newfoundland English also contains many expressions coined from native English elements to describe local phenomena. Thus an *outport* is a small coastal settlement, a *come-from-away* is an outsider, and a *stun breeze* is a sea wind of at least 20 knots.

The most entertaining lexical items in Newfoundland English, however, are the colloquial terms, often of unknown origin. *The diddies* is a nightmare; a *bangbelly* is a kind of pudding; a *willigiggin* is something between a whisper and a giggle.

Newfoundland English also has a number of words that are familiar in other varieties of English but have undergone semantic shift in Newfoundland English. For instance, *bread* is hard biscuit, *rind* is the bark of a tree, a *spurt* is a short time, and a *brief* is a disease that rapidly proves fatal.

Western Atlantic English

One area of the world sometimes overlooked in enumerations of English-speaking peoples is the Western Atlantic, despite the fact that the region has as many as five and a half million native speakers (more than New Zealand, for example). In the island group extending from the Straits of Florida to the Venezuelan coast are the Bahamas, Jamaica, the Caymans, Turks and Caicos, Anguilla, the Virgin Islands, St. Kitts and Nevis, Antigua, Montserrat, St. Vincent, Barbados, Grenada, and

Trinidad and Tobago. Farther out in the Atlantic is Bermuda. Guyana (formerly British Guiana) is on the northern coast of South America. Significant pockets of English speakers also live on the Caribbean side of Central America, including the eastern coasts of Belize, Honduras, Nicaragua (the Costa de Mosquitos), Costa Rica, and Panama.

Western Atlantic English (WAE) is unique in several respects. First, this is "Columbus territory"; most of the islands were discovered by Columbus on his various voyages between 1492 and 1503. Consequently, English has often replaced not only earlier Amerindian languages but European colonial languages, often Spanish but also Dutch, French, and even, in the case of the U.S. Virgin Islands, Danish. Second, because of its colonial history, the area's English is based on British rather than American models, despite its proximity to the United States. (The exception is the U.S. Virgin Islands.) Third, this is the only area of the world in which the great majority of the native speakers of English are black. It is the only area where English is a native language yet the English spoken ranges from pidgin to creole to indigenous vernacular to RP. Finally, because almost every island, every coastal strip of the region, has its own history, generalizations about the

---

A STORY IN GULLAH

The only English-based creole on the North American continent is Gullah, spoken by a few blacks living along the coast of the Carolinas and on the offshore Sea Islands. The following passage is from a Gullah story published in 1918. Despite the difficulties of trying to represent the finer details of a dialect or creole in conventional English spelling, the passage does successfully illustrate a number of linguistic features. For example, regular phonological alterations from Standard English include the substitution of [b] for [v] (as in *shabe* and *ebbuh*), extensive clipping (as in *'bout* and *'gen*), and simplification of consonant clusters (as in *'trike* and *groun'*). Morphological simplification can be seen in, for instance, the omission of the plural marker and the reduction of the third-person pronouns to the form *dem*. Gullah also retains a number of lexical items from African languages, though none are apparent in the passage reproduced here.

"Uncle John, mekso oonuh ent shabe dem mule tail?" inquired one of a group that squatted upon the platform.

"Sistuh, you ebbuh yeddy 'bout Johossee muskittuh'?"

"No, suh."

"Ahnhn, uh t'awt so. Gal, you ebbuh see blackbu'd' 'puntop'uh rice rick? You *is* shum, enty? Berry well; dem muskittuh' een Johossee maa'sh stan' same fashi'n. W'en dem light 'puntop'uh mule, dem kibbuhr'um 'tell oonuh cyan' see dem haa'ness! One time, jis' attuh daa'k, uh binnuh dribe comin' een late f'um Adam' Run, en' w'en uh 'trike de causeway, all ub uh sudd'nt uh nebbuh yeddy no mule' foot duh trot 'puntop'uh de groun'! De cyaaridge duh moobe, but uh yent yeddy no soun' f'um de mule' foot. Uh say tuh mese'f, eh, eh, duh warruh dish'yuh? Uh look 'gen, en', uh 'cla' tuh goodness, de muskittuh' *dat* t'ick 'puntop de mule' belly, dem hice'um up off de groun', en' duh flew t'ru de ellyment duh cya'um 'long! Dem wing' duh sing sukkuh bee duh swawm, en' de mule' duh trot wid all fo' dem foot, but 'e nebbuh tetch no groun'! Uh nebbuh do nutt'n' 'tell uh cross de bridge, 'cause de bridge mek out'uh pole, en' dem berry slip'ry duh night time, en'uh glad de mule' ent haffuh pit dem foot 'puntop'um, but attuh uh done cross de bridge, uh tek me lash en' uh cut de mule'

dialectal features of the area are difficult, even if we limit the discussion to, say, middle-class or highly educated speech. For example, even such an obvious feature as rhoticity can vary not only among the islands but among the different levels of English spoken on a given island. The same is true of *h*-dropping. The vocalic picture is so complex as almost to defy analysis. The speech of most of the area has been only scantily described, if at all; Jamaica is a notable exception. For discussion of some of the features of the pidgins and creoles spoken in the Western Atlantic, see pp. 349–51.

ENGLISH AS A NONNATIVE LANGUAGE

We suggested earlier that the differences between nonnative and native varieties of English are not dialectal in the usual sense. That is, they do not come about when an originally homogeneous language diverges in different ways and at different rates in different geographical areas. Rather, they result from interference by the

---

two't'ree time onduhneet' dem belly, en', uh 'cla' tuh my Mastuh, t'ree peck uh muskittuh' drap 'puntop de groun' en' uh yeddy de mule' foot duh trot 'gen een de road! So, attuh dat, uh nebbuh shabe de Gub'nuh' cyaaridge mule' tail no mo', en' now you shum stan' dey, dem kin lick muskittuh', fly en' t'ing' same lukkuh hawss."

Translation

"Uncle John, why haven't you shaved the mules' tails?" inquired one of a group that squatted upon the platform.

"Sister, have you ever heard about Jehossee mosquitoes?"

"No, sir."

"Ah, I thought so. Gal, have you ever seen blackbirds up on top of a rice rick [stack]? You *have* seen them, haven't you? Very well; them mosquitoes in Jehossee marsh look the same way. When they light up on top of a mule, they cover them until you can't see their harness! One time, just after dark, I was driving, coming in late from Adam's Run, and when I struck the causeway, all of a sudden I never heard no mules' feet trotting up on top of the ground! The carriage was moving, but I ain't heard no sound from the mules' feet. I said to myself, eh, eh, what is this here? I looked again, and, I declare to goodness, the mosquitoes were *that* thick on top of the mules' belly, they had hoisted them up off the ground, and flew through the element [air] carrying them along! Their wings were singing just like a bee swarming, and the mules were trotting with all four of their feet, but they never touched no ground! I never did nothing until I crossed the bridge, because the bridge was made out of poles, and they are very slippery at night time, and I was glad the mules didn't have to put their feet up on top of them, but after I had crossed the bridge, I took my lash [whip] and I cut the mules two or three times underneath the belly, and, I declare to my Master, three pecks of mosquitoes dropped up on top of the ground and I heard the mules' feet trotting again in the road! So, after that, I never shaved the Governor's carriage mules' tail no more, and now you saw them standing there, they can lick mosquitoes, flies and things just like a horse."

Ambrose E. Gonzales, "The Wiles That in the Women Are," in *The Black Border: Gullah Stories of the Carolina Coast* (Columbia, S.C.: The State Printing Company, 1964), pp. 128–29. Translation by C. M. Millward.

native language and from imperfect learning of English. Another way in which nonnative English differs from native English lies in where it is used: nonnative English is normally used in education, very often in commerce, government, and the mass media, but rarely in the home. Most nonnative versions take a native version such as British English or American English as a standard, and the discrepancies between the nonnative version and the standard diminish or even disappear with extensive education and practice. Finally, the *kinds* of variation between native and nonnative English are unlike those between different dialects of native English. For instance, no native dialect of English (aside from perhaps creoles, if one treats creoles as dialects of native English) is syllable-timed rather than stress-timed.

Most nonnative varieties of English share a number of characteristic features, regardless of the geographical location and native language of the speakers. That is, the English spoken by Chinese in Singapore and that spoken by Hausa in Nigeria diverge from native English in a number of similar and even predictable ways. Common to many unrelated varieties of nonnative English are at least the following features:

1. A tendency to reduce the number of vowel phonemes, especially by coalescing /ɪ/ and /i/, /ɛ/ and /e/, /ɑ/ and /æ/, and /ʊ/ and /u/.
2. Pronunciation of /θ/ and /ð/ as [t] and [d] or, less often, as [s] and [z].
3. A syllable-timed sentence rhythm.
4. Erratically incorrect stress placement on individual words.
5. Confusion of countable and uncountable nouns, especially in the pluralization of uncountable nouns ("The flood destroyed our furnitures").
6. Mistakes in the use of verb tenses and verb phrases, particularly in the progressive where standard English uses the present ("I am having an earache").
7. Extensive misuse of prepositions.
8. Reversal of the native English use of *yes* and *no* in answering negative questions ("Haven't you finished yet?" "Yes [I haven't finished]" or "No [I have finished]").
9. A tendency to employ a single, invariable tag question, regardless of the antecedents of the pronoun ("We'll be there soon, *is it*?").
10. Heavy input from the vocabulary of the native language.
11. A tendency to lack stylistic differentiation according to context and in particular to use polysyllabic words and flowery expressions (*desire* instead of *want*, *secure* instead of *safe*, and so on).

English in Asia

English is widely studied and spoken in virtually every Asian nation, but we will treat here only three Asian countries. Even though there are probably more Chinese studying English today than there are native American speakers of English, English is not an official language or a lingua franca in China and hence has not developed stable and predictable characteristics there. The same is true of English in Japan. We will confine our discussion here to India, Singapore, and the Philippines because, in all of these nations, English is an official or semi-official language. All three have English as a legacy of colonialism, but different circumstances have molded the particular shape that English has taken in each country. In all these nations, the number of native speakers of English is minuscule, and the control of English ranges from near-native down to pidgin. All three varieties have predictable and even accepted phonological differences from either British or American English that give them a "foreign accent" to native ears.

India

Many of the numerous native languages of India are Indo-European, descendants of the Sanskrit spoken by the Aryan tribes who invaded northern India from the northwest in the second millennium B.C. and merged with the earlier inhabitants. India was subsequently invaded by the Arabs in the eighth century A.D., controlled by Turkish Muslims in the twelfth century, and ruled by Mogul emperors from the sixteenth to the nineteenth centuries. Portugal became the first significant European influence in India when Vasco da Gama established trading posts there at the beginning of the sixteenth century. The Dutch and the French followed, but the English, operating as the East India Company, were successful in getting sole control of most of India during the seventeenth century. In 1947, Britain partitioned India into the dominions of India and Pakistan, and India became a self-governing member of the Commonwealth. In 1950, India became a republic.

Missionaries were the first English teachers in India. Beginning in 1614, mission schools continued to teach English, at least sporadically, until independence. In the mid-nineteenth century, the British promulgated an official policy of training natives in English and established a number of universities. By the early twentieth century, English was the official language of India.

India has scores of native languages, of which the most widely spoken are Hindi, Telugu, Bengali, Marathi, Tamil, Urdu, Gujarati, Kannada, Malayalam, Oriya, Punjabi, and Assamese. Hindi is the official language of the nation and the native language of about a third of the population; English is the "associate official" language. English is taught as a second language all over India; about 20 percent of the newspapers are in English. One estimate has it that about 40 percent of the population use English to some extent.

As in all areas where English is widely used as a second language, English proficiency in India can be classified roughly as high, intermediate, and low, with regional variations superimposed on these levels. British English speakers speak derogatively of Indian English as "Babu English" or of the Anglo-Indian accent as the "chee-chee accent." The Indians themselves are aware of this, but they have been unable to agree whether the standard for Indian English should remain British English or whether a separate Indian Standard should be established that would openly accept widely used Indianisms.

PHONOLOGY

Consonants. As an offshoot of British English, Indian English is usually nonrhotic (*r*-less). The voiceless stops /p t k/ tend to be unaspirated in all positions. Through interference from native languages, the alveolar consonants /t d s z l/ are often replaced by the retroflex consonants [ṭ ḍ ṣ ẓ ḷ]. The pronunciation of /l/ is always clear. At lower levels of mastery of English, and depending on the native language, the distinctions /v/ ~ /w/, /p/ ~ /f/, /t/ ~ /θ/, /d/ ~ /ð/, /s/ ~ /š/, and /z/ ~ /ǰ/ may be lost.

Vowels. Indian English normally lacks the distinctions between /ɑ/ and /ɔ/, and between /ɒ/ and /æ/. The diphthongs /e/ and /o/ are usually pronounced as pure vowels. Full vowels tend to be retained in unstressed syllables instead of being reduced to /ə/ or /ɪ/; for example, *usage* is likely to have [e] or [ɛ] in the second syllable.

Prosody. The most striking difference between RP and Indian English is in sentence intonation and rhythm, Indian English being syllable-timed rather than stress-timed. Further, instead of stress, Indian English usually has a falling or a low-rising pitch on the "stressed" syllable, with a rise in pitch on the following syllable. This produces a sing-song effect so much like South Welsh that Indian English is even sometimes called "Bombay Welsh." Suffixes, weak function words like *to* and *of*, and auxiliary verbs may be stressed, and incorrect word stresses are common, though idiosyncratic (for instance, *necéssary, miníster*).

MORPHOLOGY AND SYNTAX

Indian English shares with other nonnative varieties of English the tendency to make mass nouns into count nouns ("The street is filled with *litters*"), nonnative use of *yes* and *no* in answering negative questions, and an undifferentiated tag question *isn't it* ("You are coming tomorrow, isn't it?"). Also typical of nonnative English are unidiomatic use of prepositions ("I want to get *down from* the bus"; "Please pay attention *on* what I say"), improper inversion after interrogative words ("Why you came so early?" "I wonder who is she"), and unidiomatic verbal constructions ("I am living here since 1984"; "When he will come, he will talk to you"; "She is having many books").

More specifically characteristic of Indian English is the improper placement of the pronoun *there* ("You know good reasons are there"). Indian English also makes extensive use of compounding where native varieties would use an *of* phrase (*bread-loaf, key-bunch*).

LEXICON AND SEMANTICS

Not surprisingly, Indian English has many borrowings from native languages, such as *durzi* 'tailor', *swadeshi* 'native', and *sahib* 'sir'. Hybrid Indianisms, or compounds of which one part is English and the other from a native language, include *police jamadar* (rank corresponding to lieutenant), *kumkum mark* (the Hindu mark on the forehead), and *punkah-boy* (operator of a fan). Among the new words formed by compounding preexisting English words are *betel-bag* and *saucer-lamp*. Semantic change has occurred in, for instance, the use of *hotel* to refer to a restaurant without lodging facilities or of *appreciable* to mean *appreciated*.

Perhaps no nonnative variety of English is better known for its predilection for elegant or pompous words and constructions, for hyperbole, and for mixed or ludicrous metaphors than is Indian English. A friend will be *of tender years* rather than *young*; one feels *melancholy* rather than *sad*. An illustration of Indian English hyperbole is "I am bubbling with zeal and enthusiasm to serve as a research assistant." A typical mixed metaphor is "Land is a well of honeyed ambrosia. In order to get at it we need buckets—the buckets of our intellectual capacity."[8]

---

[8] Examples from Raja Ram Mehrotra, "Indian English: A Sociolinguistic Profile," in John B. Pride, ed., *New Englishes* (Rowley, Mass.: Newbury House Publishers, Inc., 1983), p. 164.

Singapore

Singapore was founded in 1819 by Sir Thomas Stamford Raffles and remained a British colony until 1959, when it became an autonomous nation within the Commonwealth. After an unsuccessful attempt at federation with Malaya, Sarawak, and Sabah in 1963, Singapore once again became a separate nation in 1965. Ethnically, the population of roughly two and a half million is about 76 percent Chinese, 15 percent Malay, 7 percent Indian, and 2 percent other. The five major languages spoken in Singapore are Mandarin Chinese, Hokkien (a dialect of Chinese), Malay, Tamil, and English. All of these except Hokkien are official languages, and Malay has been designated the "national language." Less than 5 percent of the population are native speakers of English, although 30 to 40 percent speak at least some English, the level of proficiency ranging from pidgin English to a variety close to standard British English except for phonology. English in Singapore, however, has an importance far greater than the number of speakers might suggest. English is the dominant working language of government, the legal system, and commerce. It is used for driver's licenses, legal contracts, identity cards, and job interviews. It is frequently the lingua franca among native speakers of other languages.

Of the four official languages of Singapore, only Mandarin and English are gaining in number of speakers. Mandarin is increasing faster than English, but English is more prestigious than Mandarin, being associated with high income. English is also beginning to replace Tamil among the Indian population. About three-quarters of Singapore's schoolchildren attend English-language schools; in 1975, Nanying University switched from Mandarin to English. As one scholar has put it, ethnic identity in Singapore is expressed by Chinese, Malay, and Tamil, but *national* identity is expressed by English.

Phonology

In general, the distinctive characteristics of Singaporean English are due to interference from Chinese, though Indian speakers may have their own patterns, such as failure to distinguish /v/ from /w/.

Consonants.   The consonant system of highly proficient Singaporean speakers is identical to that of RP. Less proficient speakers tend to devoice final stops, affricates, and fricatives; for example, both *leaf* and *leave* are [lif]. The interdental fricatives /θ/ and /ð/ are often replaced by /t/ and /d/, respectively. There is a tendency to reduce final consonant clusters such as /nt nd sk ld/ by dropping the second member; for instance, *coal* and *cold* may be homophones. With less education, speakers may glottalize all final stops and fricatives so that *rip, rib, writ, rid, rick, rig, rich,* and *ridge* are all pronounced identically as [riʔ]. Speakers at the lowest level of proficiency interchange /s/ and /š/, and /r/ and /l/.

Vowels.   Perhaps the most noticeable difference between the vowels of Singaporean English and those of native varieties is the lack of tense-lax distinctions. For example, both /ɪ/ and /i/ are [i]. The diphthongs /e/ and /o/ are regularly monophthongized as long pure vowels [e:] and [o:]. There is no phonemic distinction between /ɑ/ and /ɔ/. Unstressed vowels are not reduced to /ə/ or /ɪ/, but retain the value they would have if stressed, as in *complain* [kɔmplen].

Prosody. As is typical of many nonnative varieties of English, Singaporean English is syllable-timed rather than stress-timed. There is a tendency to stress compounds on the second instead of the first element, as in *door-kéy*. Deviant word stresses like *catalóg* or *charácter* are common, but tend to be sporadic and idiosyncratic instead of generally accepted.

MORPHOLOGY AND SYNTAX

At the less well-educated level, Singaporean English shares most of the morphological and syntactic characteristics of nonnative English described earlier. Such utterances as *I am having a house in the country* and *I want to know what is your name* are typical. *Isn't it* is the universal tag question. Those with extremely poor control of English drop virtually all inflectional and other grammatical markers such as tenses, plurals, and auxiliaries.

One unique characteristic of Singaporean English shared even by highly proficient speakers is the use of the particle *la* at the ends of sentences. *La* may appear after any part of speech and in any sentence type (question, command, statement). Its use is optional and is sociologically instead of grammatically determined: it appears only in settings that are informal, familiar, and friendly. The particle *la* itself is a loan from Chinese, but in Chinese it is obligatory and has specific grammatical functions. Thus its widespread use in Singaporean English is not a straightforward loan, but an adaptation.

LEXICON AND SEMANTICS

Among the many dialect words that have been adopted by Singaporean English from various other languages are *chop* 'stamp', *peon* 'office boy', *towkay* 'proprietor', and *makan* 'food'. Many borrowings are made because there is no existing English word for the referent; for instance, a *kwali* is a special kind of cooking pot (compare the recent adoption of *wok* in American English). An example of semantic shift is *bungalow*, which, in Singaporean English, refers to a two-storied rather than a single-storied building.

The Philippines

The earliest European contact with the Philippines was Magellan's visit in 1521. The Spanish founded Manila in 1571, and the islands were named for King Philip II of Spain. The Philippines remained a Spanish possession until 1898, when, after the Spanish-American War, Spain ceded them to the United States for $20 million. They were occupied by Japan in World War II, and were granted independence on July 4, 1946.

During the long period when the Philippines were a Spanish colony, they of course received extensive influence from the Spanish language. However, after the United States took control, American teachers were sent to the Philippines, and English was made the language of government, education, and business. Today the official languages of the Philippines are *Pilipino* (based on Tagalog) and English. Tagalog is the native language of perhaps half the population; the rest speak a variety of native languages or Spanish-based creoles. The 1960 census reported that about 40 percent of the population could speak English, nearly always as a second language but often with near-native fluency.

Unlike many other countries in which English is extensively used, the

Philippines do have a Standard Filipino English, which accepts specifically Filipino deviations from American English but which is distinguished from creolized "bamboo English" or the mixture of Tagalog and English that the Filipinos call *halo-halo* ('mix-mix').

PHONOLOGY
Filipino English phonology is theoretically identical to that of General American, although allophonic differences are fully acceptable.

Consonants. Because it is American-based, Filipino English is rhotic (*r*-ful). The consonants /t d n l/ tend to have a dental rather than alveolar articulation. In formal styles, the voiceless stops /p t k/ are aspirated, but this aspiration is dropped in informal speech.

Vowels. Phonemically, the Filipino English vowel system is that of American English. Allophonically, /i/ and /u/ are not diphthongized, and the tense-lax distinction is frequently blurred. In formal style, the vowels of unstressed syllables are reduced to /ə/ as in native varieties of English. In casual styles, however, unstressed vowels tend to keep their full value.

Prosody. Like many nonnative varieties of English, Filipino English is syllable-timed rather than stress-timed. Some observers report a tendency to put the major stress of words of three or more syllables on the penultimate syllable (*cemetéry, necessáry*).

MORPHOLOGY AND SYNTAX
The morphology and syntax of Filipino English is essentially the same as that of native varieties of English, but it does accept a number of idioms that would be considered ungrammatical in British or American English. A few examples are

> Close the light. Open the light. (turn off and turn on a light)
> She slept late all this week. (went to bed late)
> We can't come also. (either)
> Did you enjoy? (enjoy yourself)
> Try to cope up with your problems. (cope with your problems)
> He will pass by for me this afternoon. (come by for me)

LEXICON AND SEMANTICS
In addition to the use of native words for objects or concepts with no appropriate existing English term (for example, *ninang* 'godmother'), Filipino English freely creates new English compounds. Examples include the verb *eagle-spread* 'to stretch out one's limbs', *bed-spacer* 'someone who rents a bed, without board, in a dormitory', and *captain ball* 'a team captain in basketball'.

The use of *colgate* to mean toothpaste is an example of the conversion of a brand name into a common noun. Filipino English *career* can mean "college course," an instance of Spanish influence (Sp. *carrera*). Semantic shift can be illustrated by *grandfather* for "great-uncle" and *bold* for naughty films (roughly equivalent to "X-rated").

English in Africa

Because the native peoples of Africa speak such a plethora of mutually unintelligible languages and because European nations colonized most of Africa during the nineteenth and early twentieth centuries, the official languages of the great majority of African nations today are nonindigenous languages. In sub-Saharan Africa in particular, few citizens have their nation's official language as their first language. The cohesive force of Islam has made Arabic official in northern and northeastern Africa—Morocco, Algeria, Libya, Egypt, Sudan, and Somalia (where Somali is also an official language). Portuguese is official in Angola, Mozambique, and Guinea Bissau, and Spanish is official in Equatorial Guinea. Mauritania, Mali, Niger, Chad, Senegal, Ivory Coast, Guinea, Togo, Benin, Gabon, Congo, Central African Republic, Zaire, Rwanda, and Bourkina Fasso (Upper Volta) all have French as their official language.

In most of the remaining nations, English is the official language. In West Africa, this is true of Gambia, Sierra Leone, Liberia, Ghana, Nigeria, and part of Cameroon (where French is also official). In southern Africa, English is the official language of Namibia, Botswana, Lesotho, Swaziland, Zimbabwe, Zambia, and Malawi. In East Africa, English is the official language of Uganda, shares official status with Swahili in Tanzania, and is still an important language in Kenya, though it is no longer official there.

Space limitations and lack of detailed information preclude discussion of all the varieties of English spoken in all the African nations where it is an official language, so we will limit our discussion to a few generalities about West African English, followed by a slightly closer look at English in three West African nations in which the history and status of the English language are all quite different.

West African in General

The following generalities are just that: Although the characteristics discussed are widespread, they are not universal. Individual speakers may have different patterns, depending on the context and nature of interference from their native language and on their education and practice with English. Note that many of the features listed here are also typical of English as a second language in Asia.

PHONOLOGY

Consonants.   West African English is normally nonrhotic (*r*-less), and difficulty in distinguishing /r/ and /l/ is widespread. The fricatives /θ/ and /ð/ are frequently replaced by [t] and [d], occasionally by [s] and [z]. Speakers of Bantu languages in particular have problems in differentiating voiced and voiceless fricatives; many speakers also have trouble distinguishing /v/ from /b/. There is a tendency to devoice final consonants. Less proficient speakers often confuse /š/ with /s/ or /č/, and /ž/ with /z/ or /ǰ/. Perhaps the most common deviation from RP is the reduction of consonant clusters. In final position, the second consonant of the cluster is often simply dropped: *find* becomes [faɪn] and *least* [lis]. In initial position, an epenthetic vowel may break up the cluster (as in *stew* [sutu]). Because so many English words contain consonant clusters, this characteristic can have drastic effects on intelligibility. For example, Wells cites the pronunciation [sukuru direba] for *screw driver* among Hausa speakers.

Many West Africans learn English only in the schoolroom and acquire new vocabulary through reading rather than conversing. Hence even those with good control of English phonology often use spelling pronunciations like *fasten* [fæstɛn] and *limb* [limb].

Vowels. Many African languages have only five vowel phonemes. Therefore, the English system of 12–15 contrastive vowels and diphthongs is a major source of difficulty. The most common result in West African English is the loss of some tense-lax distinctions, leaving a seven-vowel system of /i e ɛ a ɔ o u/ plus the three diphthongs /aɪ aʊ ɔɪ/. Thus, such sets as *leave/live, pull/pool, cot/cut/caught/court*, and *burn/born/bun* all become homophones. Speakers of Bantu languages may pronounce the diphthongs /aɪ aʊ ɔɪ/ disyllabically, as in *tie* [taji]. Vowels followed by /n/ are typically nasalized and the /n/ is dropped: *moon* is [mũ].

Prosody. West African English is normally syllable-timed rather than stress-timed. Many African languages are tone languages, and speakers tend to carry this over into English, substituting high tone for stress in English words. Like other nonnative varieties of English, West African English does not use minimal "stress" on function words like pronouns and prepositions.

MORPHOLOGY AND SYNTAX

Many of the morphological and syntactic differences between West African English and native English are the same as those encountered in other nonnative varieties—confusion of count and mass nouns, a universal tag question *is it*?, and erroneous use of *yes* and *no* in replying to negative questions. Omission of articles is common, and often there is no distinction between reflexive and reciprocal pronouns (*They distrust themselves* for "They distrust each other").

LEXICON AND SEMANTICS

Lexical and semantic deviations from native varieties of English vary widely from area to area and even from speaker to speaker. Predictably, there is widespread use of words from African languages, but the particular words used depend on the native languages and the situation. Often, English words have, not only their usual meanings, but also extended meanings; *serviceable* can have the meaning "willing to serve" and *amount* the meaning of "money." A widely used coinage in West Africa is the noun *a been-to*, a somewhat derogatory term for a person who has been to Europe or America.

Typical of nonnative English learned primarily through literary texts studied in the classroom is the failure to distinguish between formal or literary styles and colloquial styles. Thus ornate diction and long Latinate words are favored even in casual conversation (*converse* for *talk*; *manifest* for *show*).

Nigeria

With a population of over 85 million (1983 estimate), Nigeria is Africa's most populous country and has the largest concentration of blacks in the world. Its first contact with Europeans came with Portuguese and British slavers during the fifteenth and sixteenth centuries. During an anti-slave trade campaign in 1861, the British seized Lagos and gradually extended their control inland. In 1914, they combined the protectorates of northern and southern Nigeria into a single unit. Nigeria became an independent nation in 1960 and a republic in 1963.

Mission schools teaching English were established in southern Nigeria as early as 1842, but the north was a Muslim area and missionaries were not allowed to operate there, so it received schools only later.

Nigeria today has an extraordinarily large number of indigenous languages; estimates vary from 200 to 400. However, there are three major native languages: Ibo in the east, Hausa in the north, and Yoruba in the west. Few Nigerians speak more than one of these three major languages. Mistrust among the regions, most spectacularly evidenced by the unsuccessful secession of the eastern region in 1967 as the short-lived Republic of Biafra, means that it is unlikely that one of the three major languages could be made the official language of the country. Thus English has become the official language by default.

Nigeria has only a handful of native speakers of English, most of them Scots or Americans. Perhaps one-quarter of the people know at least some English. English is the language of government, commerce, the mass media, and education after the first three years. Ten daily newspapers are published in English. Among the better-educated, English is the lingua franca. All important literary works are published in English. Nigeria has yet to establish what could be called Standard Nigerian English; British pronunciation is preferred to American.

Most of the characteristics listed earlier for West African English in general apply to the phonology of English in Nigeria, with variations depending on the amount of education and the native language of the speaker. For example, speakers of Hausa tend to confuse English /p/ and /f/ because Hausa has no phonemic /p/. Predictably, /θ/ and /ð/ cause difficulty and are often realized as [t] and [d], or as [s] and [z]. Most of Nigeria's indigenous languages are tone languages; this affects the treatment of English stress. Like so many other nonnative varieties of English, Nigerian English usually lacks weak forms of function words such as prepositions, pronouns, and auxiliaries.

Morphologically and syntactically, Nigerian English differs from native varieties of English in a number of ways, including the tendency to omit tense markers of verbs, the frequent omission or erroneous use of articles, the pluralizing of uncountable nouns, and the nonnative use of prepositions. Typical idioms include *to be on seat* 'to be in the office' and *to move with* 'to associate with'.

Among the numerous loans into Nigerian English from indigenous languages are *danfo* for very small buses with notoriously reckless drivers, and *buka* for roadside restaurants selling inexpensive food. Nigerian English also has a number of loan translations, especially from Yoruba. For example, the greeting *You're enjoying* is a calque of Yoruba *Eku igbadun* 'I greet you as you enjoy yourself'. Extensions in meaning of existing English words include *fellow* for any person, male or female (compare American colloquial *guys*), *globe* for light bulb, *cup* for a drinking glass, and *drop* for the longest distance a passenger can travel in a taxi for the minimum fare.

Liberia

During the fifteenth century, the Portuguese were the first Europeans to make settlements in Liberia. They were later driven out by traders from England, France, and the Netherlands. No real occupation by non-Africans took place until the nineteenth century. Then, in 1822, freed U.S. black slaves settled at Monrovia (named for U.S. president James Monroe) with the aid of American colonization societies. Today, the 20,000 or so descendants of these freed slaves dominate the government, even though they constitute only about 0.5 percent of the total

Liberian population of over two million. These freed slaves of course spoke American English, and Liberia today is the only African country in which American English is taken as a standard. Liberia is also the only African nation in which English is spoken as a native language by blacks.

Liberian English shares some of the characteristics of English in other West African countries, but it also is similar in many ways to Black English in the United States. It is nonrhotic (r-less), and the distinction between /hw/ and /w/ is maintained. The fricatives /θ/ and /ð/ usually become [t] and [d] in initial position, but [f] and [v] finally (for example, *bathe* is [bev]). Intervocalic post-stress /t/ is voiced as in American English. There is a tendency to omit final /t/, /d/, and fricatives, but this is not an invariable rule.

The relationship of Liberian English to American English is most obvious in the vowel system, where the full range of tense-lax oppositions is preserved. That is, /i/ is distinct from /ɪ/, /u/ from /ʊ/, and so on.

Cameroon

As is true of much of West Africa, the Portuguese were the first Europeans to visit the area that is now Cameroon. Later the European and American slave trade was active in the region. The Germans took control of the area in 1884, and German became the official language. After 1919, Britain and France shared control under League of Nations mandates and later United Nations trusteeships, about four-fifths of the area going to France and one-fifth to Great Britain. In 1960, French Cameroon received its independence; in 1961, part of British Cameroon joined Nigeria and the other part joined Cameroon.

Cameroon has as many as 200 indigenous languages, but the official languages are French and English. However, the most widely used language in the country is Pidgin English (see below), which has heavily influenced Cameroon English. According to one estimate, 70–80 percent of the urban English speakers and up to 60 percent of the urban French speakers also have a working knowledge of Cameroon Pidgin.

The phonology, morphology, and syntax of Cameroon English share most of the features of West African English described earlier. The influence of Pidgin appears in the universal tag question *not so* (Pidgin *no bi so?*).

Among the loans from local languages into Cameroon English are such words as *mbonga* (a type of flat fish), *danshiki* (a local shirt), and *ashu* (a kind of paste). From Cameroon Pidgin come *foot* 'foot, leg, trouser-leg', *hear* 'understand', *skin* 'body', and *sweet* 'tasty'. Unique to Cameroon is the heavy and increasing French influence on the English vocabulary. Examples include "Would you like some *odine*?" (from French *bière ordinaire*) and "We made a nice *sorti*" (from French *sortie* 'trip, excursion').

English-Based Pidgins and Creoles

Many thousands of people in the world regularly use an English-based form of language that is neither a standard native English nor English as a second language in the usual sense of that term. These are the speakers of pidgin English and of English-based creoles.

A **pidgin** is nobody's native language, but rather a contact language used between groups whose native languages are mutually unintelligible. (The word *pidgin* itself comes from the pidgin pronunciation of *business.*) A source language, usually that of the dominant group, is the major component of a pidgin, but the language of the subordinate group also contributes, especially to the vocabulary. Normally, the pidgin form of a regular language is greatly simplified and reduced in phonology, morphology, grammar, and vocabulary. For example, English-based pidgins may have as few as five vowels, may lose all English inflections, and may have vocabularies as small as a thousand words. This is not to say that pidgins have no structure at all: Word order is usually extremely important, and complex aspectual distinctions may be made by the use of particles. In some instances, grammatical distinctions are made that do not even exist in the source language.

When what originated as a pidgin becomes the native language of a group of speakers, a **creole** has developed. Typically, this occurs when pidgin speakers whose native languages are mutually unintelligible intermarry. Their children grow up having the pidgin as their first language. If the linguistic situation stabilizes, the creole increases in vocabulary and grammatical complexity, eventually becoming a full-fledged language in its own right. If regular contact with the source language is lost at a later point, the creole and the source language will become mutually unintelligible; this has occurred with Sranan, the English-based creole that is the official language of Surinam. On the other hand, when access to a prestigious source language continues, the creole usually is steadily modified in the direction of this source language, eventually becoming in effect another dialect of that language. This is taking place today with most of the Caribbean creoles, such as Jamaican.

In theory, it should be simple to distinguish a pidgin from a creole, but in practice the line is not always easy to draw. For example, in parts of Africa, nonnative speakers of the creole called Krio use it as a pidgin for intercommunication. Is the result a creole or a pidgin?

English-based creoles include Sranan, mentioned above as the official language of Surinam (formerly Dutch Guiana, in northern South America). Two other English-based creoles are spoken in the interior of Surinam, both of them mutually unintelligible with each other, with Sranan, and with English. In Africa, Krio, spoken in the general area of Freetown, Sierra Leone, and another West African creole sometimes called Cameroon Creole (or Bush English) seem to be converging into a single West African creole. Both Jamaican Creole and Hawaiian Creole are receding in favor of English, though Jamaican is still widely used. Gullah is the English-African creole spoken by a group of blacks inhabiting the Sea Islands and coastal areas of South Carolina and Georgia. The sample passage below is of Krio, the western African English creole; with the help of the translation, we can see that, strange as Krio may appear to a speaker of standard English, it *is* nonetheless a variety of English.

Krio Narrative[9]

Na wan uman bin dey. So i sen inh pikin foh go was doti-pan na watasai. Wey di pikin go nomoh, na i teyk di ibakoh, na i lef am. So wey i go na ows nau, wey inh mama wanh pul it nomoh, na inh di uman tel am sey, i kol am, i sey, i sey, "Awa! wey mi ibakoh?"

---

[9] Passage and translation from S. Modupe Broderick, "Time and Structure in Narrative: A Study of Internal Relationships in a Krio Oral Narrative," in Ian F. Hancock, ed., *Diversity and Development in English-Related Creoles* (Ann Arbor, Mich.: Karoma Publishers, Inc., 1985), pp. 113, 107. Reproduced by permission.

I sey, "A put am na di pleyt-blai, ma."

I sey, "Yu put am na di pleyt-blai, na inh a noh si am?" I sey, "Pas go luk foh mi ibakoh na di watasai bifo a bit yu jisnoh!"

Na inh di pikin go. I bigin foh krai. I dey krai. Na inh wan grani si am. Na inh i sey, "Titi, weytin yu dey krai foh?"

Na inh i sey, "Na mi ibakoh los, ma."

Na inh i sey, "Kam was mi so fut." I sey, "A go sho yu usai yu mama ibakoh dey."

Na inh di pikin go. I krob di uman inh so fut. I put meresin dey. Na inh di grani sey, "Go bifo." I sey, "Yu go mit oda uman dey dey."

Translation

There was a woman. She sent her child to wash some soiled pots and pans at a stream. The child arrived at the stream. While she was washing the utensils, the *ibakoh* [a flat spoon made from wood and used for serving rice] fell into the water and floated away. The child returned to the house. Her mother wanted to serve the rice she had prepared. She called the child and said, "Hawa, where is my *ibakoh*?"

The child replied, "I placed it in the basket containing the pots and pans that I washed at the stream."

The mother snapped at her. She said, "Do you think that I would not see it if you placed it in the basket containing the pots and pans? You better run off to the stream and find that *ibakoh* before I tan your hide."

The girl left. She went to the stream. She was crying and crying. Then an old woman saw her. The old woman said, "Little girl, why are you crying?"

"I have lost my mother's *ibakoh*," replied the child.

"Little girl, come and clean the sores on my feet," requested the old woman, "then I will show you where to locate your mother's *ibakoh*."

The girl approached the old woman. She scrubbed her sores and applied medicine to them.

The old woman said, "Follow the stream. You will meet another old woman."

Of the English-based pidgins, one of the most important in terms of number of users is Neo-Melanesian (also known as Tok Pisin, from "Talk Pidgin"), spoken in New Guinea. West African Pidgin English, along with the related Liberian Pidgin English and Kru Pidgin English, is the pidgin version of creoles spoken in West Africa. Chinese Pidgin English was once important but was forbidden by the Chinese government, which understandably perceived it as an object of some contempt and as a symbol of China's humiliation by foreign powers.

Suggested Further Reading

Bailey, Richard W., and Jay L. Robinson. *Varieties of Present-Day English.*

Baker, Sidney J. *The Australian Language.*

Brook, G. L. *English Dialects.*

Brook, G. L. *Varieties of English.*

Carr, Elizabeth Ball. *Da Kine Talk: From Pidgin to Standard English in Hawaii.*

Cassidy, Frederic G., ed. *Dictionary of American Regional English.*

Cassidy, Frederic G. *Jamaica Talk: Three Hundred Years of the English Language in Jamaica.*

Chambers, J. K., ed. *Canadian English.*

Crewe, William J., ed. *The English Language in Singapore.*

De Villiers, André, ed. *English-Speaking South Africa Today.*

Dillard, J. L. *Black English: Its History and Usage in the United States.*

Ferguson, Charles A., and Shirley Brice Heath, eds. *Language in the USA.*

Hughes, Arthur, and Peter Trudgill. *English Accents and Dialects: An Introduction to Social and Regional Varieties of British English.*

Labov, William. *Language in the Inner City: Studies in the Black English Vernacular.*

Lanham, L. W. *The Pronunciation of South African English.*

Llamzon, Teodoro A. *Standard Filipino English.*

Marckwardt, Albert H. *American English.*

Masica, C., and P. B. Dave. *The Sound System of Indian English.*

Mencken, H. L. *The American Language.*

Mitchell, A. G. *The Pronunciation of English in Australia.*

Orkin, Mark M. *Speaking Canadian English.*

Orton, Harold, et al., eds. *Survey of English Dialects.*

Pride, John B., ed. *New Englishes.*

Reed, Carroll E. *Dialects of American English.*

Reinecke, John E. *Language and Dialect in Hawaii: A Socio-linguistic History to 1935.*

Scargill, M. H. *Modern Canadian English Usage.*

Shuy, Roger W. *Discovering American Dialects.*

Spencer, J., ed. *The English Language in West Africa.*

Trudgill, Peter, and Jean Hannah. *International English: A Guide to Varieties of Standard English.*

Turner, G. W. *The English Language in Australia and New Zealand.*

Wakelin, Martyn Francis. *English Dialects: An Introduction.*

Wells, J. C. *Accents of English.*

Williamson, Juanita V., and Virginia M. Burke, eds. *A Various Language: Perspectives on American Dialects.*

Wolfram, Walter A., and Ralph W. Fasold. *The Study of Social Dialects in American English.*

A P P E N D I X

Phonetic Symbols

The charts below present an abridged and modified version of the International Phonetic Alphabet (IPA), a set of symbols devised to provide a consistent and uniform system to represent all languages of the world. Sounds rarely or never found in English (for example, clicks or pharyngal consonants) have been omitted. Some IPA symbols have been replaced by symbols more commonly used for representing English sounds. Note that these charts are of phonetic symbols; see the text for tables of English phonemes.

CONSONANTS		*Bilabial*	*Labiodental*	*Interdental*	*Alveolar*	*Alveopalatal*	*Velar*	*Uvular*	*Glottal*
Stops	*Voiceless*	p			t		k		ʔ
	Voiced	b			d		g		
Affricates	*Voiceless*					č			
	Voiced					ǰ			
Fricatives	*Voiceless*	φ	f	θ	s	š ç	x		h
	Voiced	β	v	ð	z	ž	γ	ʁ	ɦ
Nasals		m			n		ŋ		
Laterals					l		ɫ		
Retroflex					r				
Trill								R	
Semivowels		w				j			

VOWELS*

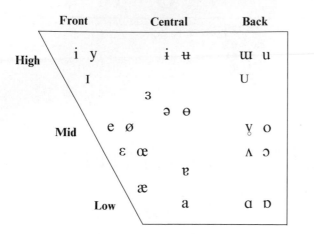

Frequently Used Diacritics

:	Long	[u:] = [ū]
ˇ	Short	[ŭ]
ᶜ	Aspiration	[tᶜ] = [th]
ₒ	Voiceless	[w̥]
ˇ	Voiced	[ṭ]
~	Nasalization	[õ]
ʷ	Velarization	[gʷ]
ˌ	Palatalization	[ɲ]
¨	Rounding of front or mid vowel	[ö] = [ɵ]
ˌ	Syllabic consonant	[ṇ]

---

* When two vowel symbols appear side by side, the symbol to the left represents an unrounded vowel, and the symbol to the right represents the corresponding rounded vowel.

G L O S S A R Y

Abbreviation. A shortened form of a word or phrase, such as *gym* for *gymnasium* or *cm* for *centimeter*.

Ablative. In inflecting languages, a grammatical case indicating separation, direction away from, and sometimes other functions usually expressed in modern English by various prepositions.

Ablaut. A change in a vowel, originally caused by a change in stress or accent. Remnants in PDE include the varying vowels of strong verbs, as in *sing/sang/sung*. Also called *gradation* or *apophony*.

Accusative. In inflecting languages, a grammatical case used for direct objects and the objects of some prepositions.

Acronym. A pronounceable word created from the first letter or first few letters of a group of words, such as *NATO* from *North Atlantic Treaty Organization* or *sonar* from *sound navigation ranging*.

Active voice. The form of the verb indicating that the subject is the doer or cause of the action expressed by the verb. In the sentence *Cows eat hay, eat* is in the active voice. *See also* Passive voice.

Adjectival. A word, phrase, or clause used to modify a noun, pronoun, or other nominal. The italicized words in the following sentence are adjectivals: "*Two charming* policemen *in summer uniform* retrieved the keys *that I had dropped through a grating*."

Adjective. A word that modifies a noun, pronoun, gerund, or other nominal. Types of adjectives include descriptive, proper, demonstrative, indefinite, possessive, numerical, and interrogative adjectives.

Interr.	Num.	Proper		
Which	four	Shakespearian plays will		

	Descriptive		Poss.
the	slave-driving	instructor ask	his

	Indef.	Demon.
	many students to read	this week?

Adverb. A word that modifies a verb, adverb, adjective, or entire clause or sentence. The italicized words in the following sentence are all adverbs: "This coat is *so* small that it will *never* fit me *comfortably*."

Adverbial. Any word, phrase, or clause that functions as an adverb. The italicized words in the following sentence are adverbials: "*In my opinion*, it is *never* appropriate to serve snails *to preschoolers*."

Affirmative. A statement that asserts that something is true; not negative.

Affix. A bound form (not an independent word), such as a prefix or suffix, added to a base, stem, or root. In the word *unlucky*, *un-* and *-y* are affixes.

Affricate. A sound produced by complete stoppage of the flow of air followed by slow constricted release as a fricative. English affricates are /č/ and /ǰ/.

Agglutinative language. A language in which the morphemes undergo little or no change when combined to form words. Swahili and Turkish are examples.

Alliteration. The occurrence in a phrase of two or more words beginning with the same initial sound: "fair, fat, and forty." Also called *front rhyme*.

Allophone. Any of the nondistinctive variants of a phoneme. For instance, aspirated [pʿ] and unaspirated [p] are both allophones of the phoneme /p/.

Alphabet. A writing system consisting of symbols that represent individual sounds (phonemes).

Alveolar. A sound produced by the tip or blade of the tongue touching the alveolar ridge. Among the English alveolar sounds are [t d l n].

Alveolar ridge. The bony ridge above and behind the upper teeth that contains the sockets for the upper teeth.

Alveopalatal. A sound produced by the blade of the tongue touching the back of the alveolar ridge and the front part of the palate. English alveopalatal sounds include /č/ and /ǰ/.

Amelioration. In semantics, a change to a more favorable meaning.

Analogy. Change in existing forms or creation of new forms on the basis of association with other, preexisting forms. For example, many irregular English nouns such as earlier *shoe/shoon* have taken *-s* plurals by analogy with regular plurals like *coat/coats*.

Analytic language. A language that tends to express grammatical relationships by means of separate words rather than inflections. PDE is much more analytic than OE was.

Anomalous verb. A verb that deviates from regular patterns, for example, by sharing features of two or more classes. In OE, the verb *dōn* 'to do' was anomalous because it had characteristics of both strong and weak verbs.

Antonym. A word having the opposite meaning to another word. For instance, *hot* is an antonym of *cold*.

Aorist. A verb tense of Indo-European roughly equivalent to simple past tense in PDE.

Apex. The tip of the tongue.

Apophony. *See* Ablaut.

Article. A member of a subgroup of adjectives used to signal a following noun. In PDE, the *definite article* (*the*) specifies a particular individual, and the *indefinite article* (*a/an*) indicates that the following noun is a member of a class.

Articulator. A movable part of the mouth, such as the lips or the tongue, used in producing speech sounds.

Ash. The conventional name for the OE grapheme (letter) æ [æ].

Aspect. A category of verb inflection denoting the completion, duration, repetition, and so on, of the action expressed by the verb. PDE verbs do not express aspect by inflections, but rather by means of (1) particles, as in *The house burned up* (compare *The house burned*); (2) separate verbs, as in *The stars twinkled*, where

twinkled expresses repetitive action (compare *The stars shone*); and (3) verb phrases, as in *I am speaking English*, where *am* indicates ongoing, limited action (compare *I speak English*).

Aspirate. A sound whose production is accompanied by a puff of air, as in the initial consonants of *pop, top,* and *cop*.

Assibilation. The process by which sounds change to sibilants.

Assimilation. The process by which neighboring sounds become more like each other.

Auxiliary. A verb that accompanies the main verb to indicate the tense, mood, voice, or aspect. The italicized words in the following sentence are auxiliaries: "I *would have* won if I *had*n't *been* disqualified."

Back formation. Making a new word from an existing word, where the existing word is mistakenly assumed to be a derivative of the new word. Usually this involves removing what looks like an affix from the existing word. For example, by analogy with such pairs as *rain/rainy* and *cloud/cloudy*, the back formation of *fog* was created from *foggy*.

Back mutation. Diphthongization of OE vowels caused by a following back vowel.

Back vowel. A vowel formed with the highest part of the tongue arched toward the soft palate at the back of the mouth. English back vowels include [u ʊ o ɔ].

Base. A form to which affixes are added, such as *like* in *likes, liked, liking, unlike,* and *likely*.

Bilabial. A sound made with the two lips as articulators, such as [b p m].

Biological gender. Gender distinction that is based on the actual sex of the referents, as in PDE. Also called *natural gender*.

Blade. The upper surface of the tongue just behind the tip.

Blend. A word formed by combining parts of two different words, such as *smog* from *smoke* and *fog*. Also called a *portmanteau* word.

Borrowed word. A word taken from another language; the source language may or may not be related to the target language. For example, English *paternal* is a borrowed word from Latin. Same as *loanword*.

Bound form. A morpheme that occurs only as part of a larger form, such as the *-s* in *lamps,* the *un-* in *unlike,* or both the *per-* and the *-tain* in *pertain.*

Breaking. The diphthongization of certain vowels under the influence of certain following consonants.

Calque. *See* Loan-translation.

Case. The relationship of nouns, pronouns, or adjectives to other words in the sentence. In inflecting languages, case is indicated by inflectional endings or other changes of form. In PDE, *he* is the nominative case, *him* the object case, and *his* the genitive case of the masculine singular personal pronoun.

Central vowel. A vowel pronounced with the tongue in a "neutral" position. In PDE, [ə] is a central vowel.

Centum languages. IE languages in which IE *[k] appears as [k] (unless later changes have occurred). The *centum* languages are Hellenic, Celtic, Germanic, Anatolian, and Tocharian.

Clause. A group of words containing both a subject and a predicate. The sentence *When I arrived, he was sleeping* has two clauses, *When I arrived* and *he was sleeping.*

Clipping. Forming a word by cutting off the beginning or the end of another word; *lab* and *fridge* are clipped forms of *laboratory* and *refrigerator.*

Closed-list words. Words belonging to categories to which new members are not easily added, such as articles, prepositions, pronouns, and conjunctions.

Closed syllable. A syllable that ends in one or more consonants. *Salt, stop, pass,* and *sink* are all closed syllables.

Cognates. Words in different but related languages that have the same origin in their common parent language. English *father* and French *père* are cognates.

Common Germanic. The features of the ancestor language shared by all the branches of Germanic.

Common Indo-European. The features of the ancestor language shared by all descendants of Indo-European, such as Indo-Iranian, Celtic, Italic, and Germanic.

Comparative reconstruction. The process of establishing hypothetical earlier forms by comparing cognate forms in related descendant languages or dialects. Reconstructed forms are indicated by a preceding asterisk, as in *[trei], the reconstruction of the IE form of which PDE *three,* French *trois,* German *drei,* Russian *tri,* and so on, are descendants.

Comparison. Changing the form of an adjective or adverb to indicate that something possesses the quality to a greater degree or a lesser degree than something else. For example, *more exciting* and *slower* are PDE comparative forms.

Complement. A noun or adjective following a linking verb and referring to the subject. Noun complements are also called *predicate nominatives* or *predicate nouns,* and adjective complements are called *predicate adjectives.* Both are called *subject complements.* An *object complement* is the complement of a direct object; the word *foolish* is an object complement in the sentence "I consider him foolish." Some grammarians also treat direct and indirect objects as complements.

Composition. An alternative term for *compounding.*

Compounding. Combining two or more words to make a single word, such as *bookcase* or *hearsay.*

Conditioned change. Linguistic change caused by the influence of nearby sounds or other linguistic features. An example is the change of the prefix *con-* to *com-, col-,* or *cor-* before roots beginning with [m], [l], or [r], respectively, as in *commit, collect,* and *correct.*

Conjugation. The set of inflections of a particular verb, *or* a set of verbs having the same kind of inflections (such as all the weak verbs).

Conjunction. A word or group of words used to connect words, phrases, or clauses and to indicate the relationship between them. PDE examples include *and, because,* and *when.*

Connotation. The emotional meaning of a word; its implications, suggestions, or associations, as opposed to its explicit literal meaning.

Consonant. A sound produced by restricting or blocking the passage of air from the lungs through the mouth and/or nose. Among the PDE consonants are [p g s v l m].

Consonant cluster. A group of two or more contiguous consonants, such as [str] in the word *strong*.

Construction. A somewhat vague term for a group of words arranged grammatically.

Continuous tense. *See* Progressive tense.

Contraction. The shortening of a word or group of words by omission of one or more sounds or letters; for example, *I've, won't, nor'easter.*

Coordinating conjunction. A conjunction that connects sentence elements that are grammatically parallel. The primary coordinating conjunctions of PDE are *and, but, or,* and *nor.*

Coordination. The joining of two or more elements of the same level of importance, such as two nouns, two adjectives, or two independent clauses. In the sentence *Sticks and stones may break my bones,* the nouns *sticks* and *stones* are coordinated by the conjunction *and.*

Copula. A verb that connects a subject with a subject complement (predicate adjective or predicate noun). The most common copulative verbs of PDE are *be, become, seem, appear, remain,* and the verbs of sensation *see, smell, feel, sound,* and *taste.* Copulas are also called *linking verbs.*

Correlative conjunctions. Conjunctions used in pairs to join grammatically parallel sentence elements. PDE examples include *either ... or* and *both ... and.*

Count noun. *See* Countable noun.

Countable noun. A noun that has both singular and plural forms and that can be modified by numerals. Also called *count noun.* Examples of countable nouns are *table, topic, toy,* and *tax.*

Creole language. A pidgin language that has acquired native speakers.

Cumulative sentence. A sentence in which the amplifying detail follows the statement of the main idea. For example, *She ate the apple that was sitting on the counter in the kitchen* is a cumulative sentence.

Cuneiform. A syllabic writing system consisting of wedge-shaped signs used by various Middle Eastern cultures from the fourth to the first millennium B.C.

Dative. A grammatical case indicating the indirect object or the object of certain prepositions.

Declarative sentence. A sentence which makes a statement of fact or opinion. For example, *The right rear tire is flat* is a declarative sentence.

Declension. The inflections of nouns, pronouns, and adjectives.

Defective verb. A verb that lacks one or more of the normal inflected forms. PDE *shall* is defective because it has no infinitive or participles.

Definite adjective. *See* Weak adjective.

Definite article. An article that specifies a particular member or members of the class that it designates. PDE has one definite article, *the.*

Degeneration. *See* Pejoration.

Demonstrative. A pronoun or adjective that singles out or specifies the nominal that it refers to. In PDE, *this/these* and *that/those* are the demonstrative pronouns or adjectives.

Denotation. The basic, specific, literal meaning of a word or phrase as opposed to its emotional meaning and associations.

Dental. A sound made when the tip of the tongue is touching the upper teeth. Sometimes used synonymously with *alveolar.*

Dental preterite. The past tense ending in [d] or [t] of weak verbs in Germanic languages.

Dependent clause. *See* Subordinate clause.

Derivational affix. An affix used to form a new word by derivation. For example, the adjective *boilable* is formed from the verb *boil* by adding the derivational suffix *-able.*

Diachronic. Referring to the historical changes in languages. *See also* Synchronic.

Diacritic. A mark added to a grapheme (letter) indicating a change in its normal pronunciation. Examples of letters with diacritical marks are *é, â, ø, ü, ç, ñ.*

Dialect. The form of a language spoken in a particular geographic area, *or* the form spoken by a particular group within a given area, such as an occupational, social, or ethnic dialect.

Digraph. A pair of graphemes that represents a single phoneme, such as *th* in *thing* or *ch* in *charge*.

Diphthong. A glide from one vowel position to another within a single syllable. For example, in the word *toy*, the sound represented by *oy* is a diphthong [oi] that glides from [o] to [i].

Direct object. The person or thing receiving the action of the verb in a sentence. *Bumblebees* is the direct object in the sentence *Our cat eats bumblebees*, and *Hannah* is the direct object in the sentence *Melvin secretly adores Hannah*.

Dissimilation. The process whereby two similar or identical sounds become less like or different from each other.

Dorsum. The back of the tongue.

Double possessive. A possessive form that uses both *of* before the noun and *-'s* on the noun, as in the phrase *a friend of my sister's*.

Doublets. Words derived from the same source by different paths. *Major* and *mayor* are doublets in English.

Dual. A grammatical number in addition to singular and plural, used to indicate two of something. OE had dual pronouns for the first and second persons.

Early Modern English. The English language from approximately A.D. 1500 to 1800.

East Germanic. The branch, now extinct, of the Germanic group of Indo-European that included Gothic, Burgundian, and Vandalic.

Echoic. Imitating natural sounds. Words such as *quack* and *bang* are echoic. Also called *onomatopoetic*.

Ellipsis. The omission from a sentence of words or phrases that can be identified by the context. In the sentence *I like pasta better than bread*, there is ellipsis of the words *I like* before the word *bread*.

Emphatic pronoun. A pronoun used to express emphasis. In PDE, the emphatic pronouns are those that end in *-self* or *-selves*.

Enclitic. Referring to a word that has no independent stress of its own but is pronounced as part of a preceding word. In *can't*, the negative (*not*) is enclitic to the verb *can*.

Epenthetic. Referring to the insertion of a nonetymological sound or letter into a word, often to facilitate pronunciation. For example, the pronunciation [æθəlɛt-ɪks] for *athletics* has an epenthetic vowel [ə].

Epiglottis. The cartilage at the base of the tongue which folds over the glottis to prevent food from entering the trachea during swallowing.

Eth. The name of the character (ð) in the Old English alphabet that represented [θ] or [ð]. Also spelled *edh*.

Etymology. The study of the origin, history, or derivation of words.

Euphemism. The substitution of a word with a neutral or pleasant connotation for one with an unpleasant connotation. *Little girl's room* is a euphemism for *women's toilet*.

External history. Nonlinguistic events in the lives of speakers of a language that lead to changes in the language. An invasion by a foreign country would be one such event. Also called *outer history*.

Extralinguistic. Outside or beyond the language itself. The Viking invasions of England were an extralinguistic event, even though they had profound linguistic effects.

Feminine. One of the grammatical genders. *See* Gender.

Finite verb. A verb that is inflected for person, tense, and number and can serve as a complete predicate. In the sentence *You are being watched*, *are* is finite, but *being* and *watched* are nonfinite.

First Consonant Shift. Grimm's Law and Verner's Law taken together.

Fission. The process whereby variants of a single form become independent forms in their own right. For example, phonemic fission occurred when voiced fricatives became phonemic in ME.

Folk etymology. Changing an unfamiliar word or phrase to make it look and/or sound more familiar and meaningful. *Mushroom* is a folk etymology from French *mousseron*.

Fracture. The diphthongization of a vowel under the influence of neighboring sounds.

Fricative.   A consonant produced by forcing air through a constricted passage, creating audible friction. Among the PDE fricatives are [θ v z]. Also called *spirant*.

Front mutation.   *See* Umlaut.

Front rhyme.   *See* Alliteration.

Front vowel.   A vowel formed with the highest part of the tongue arched toward the hard palate at the front of the mouth. PDE front vowels are /i ɪ e ɛ æ/.

Function word.   A word used primarily to indicate the relationships or functions of other words. Many prepositions and conjunctions and some adverbs are function words. In the sentence *If you like to surf, you'll love Hawaii and Newport, if, to,* and *and* are function words.

Functional shift.   Using one part of speech as another part of speech without changing its form. Also called *zero-morpheme derivation*. In the sentence *They will up the price tomorrow, up* is functionally shifted from preposition to verb.

Fusion.   The process whereby formerly distinct forms become "fused." They may become simply nonsignificant variants, as is the case in many PDE dialects for [hw] and [w] in words like *white* and *whale*. Or one of the original forms may change to the other form, as has been the case for English speakers who always use [w] and never use [hw] in words like *white* and *whale*.

Futhorc.   The runic alphabet. The name *futhorc* is formed from the first six symbols of the alphabet, which stand for the sounds [f u θ o r k].

Gender.   A set of categories into which words are divided. One of the most common gender divisions is into masculine, feminine, and neuter. If this division corresponds to the actual gender of the referent (as with English *he, she,* and *it*), it is called *natural* or *biological gender*. If the division is arbitrary, it is called *grammatical gender* (as in French).

Generalization.   Semantic change whereby a word comes to have a wider or more general application. For example, the Germanic ancestor of the English word *thing* once meant an assembly or legal case, but the word has generalized to be applicable to any topic whatsoever.

Genitive.   In inflecting languages, a grammatical case indicating possession and sometimes also source or measurement. Also called *possessive* case.

Germanic.   One of the branches of Indo-European. After leaving the original homeland, Germanic speakers moved to southern Scandinavia and northern Europe. Often subdivided into East Germanic, West Germanic, and North Germanic.

Gerund.   A nominal made from a verb by adding the ending *-ing*. In the sentence *She hates reading, reading* is a gerund.

Glide.   A transitional sound produced between the articulation of one phoneme and the next.

Gloss.   An explanatory note or close translation, usually inserted between the lines of a text.

Glottal stop.   A consonant formed by closing the glottis and then opening it and releasing the air suddenly. Glottal stops are most often only allophones of /t/ in English, but they are phonemic in their own right in some languages.

Glottis.   The opening between the vocal cords.

Gradation.   *See* Ablaut.

Grammar.   The structure of a language and the rules that govern it.

Grammatical gender.   *See* Gender.

Grapheme.   A single unit in a writing system; loosely, a letter of an alphabet.

Graphics.   In linguistics, the study of writing systems.

Great Vowel Shift.   The sound change of the fifteenth through eighteenth centuries under which all the ME long vowels qualitatively changed by moving upward in their articulation.

Grimm's Law.   Rules formulated by Jakob Grimm, detailing the regular changes in the IE stops that occurred in Germanic languages.

Group genitive.   A construction in which the genitive (possessive) marker is attached to the end of an entire noun phrase rather than to the noun to which it logically applies. In *this book I bought's price,* the -'s is attached to *bought* rather than to *book*.

Hard palate. The front part of the roof of the mouth that is supported by bony material.

High vowel. A vowel produced with the tongue raised toward the top of the mouth. In PDE, [i] and [u] are high vowels.

Hiragana. The Japanese syllabary used for most everyday purposes.

Homonyms. Words that are pronounced the same, perhaps spelled the same, but have different meanings. *Bat* (the mammal) and *bat* (the wooden club) are homonyms in English.

Homophones. Words with the same pronunciation but different spellings and meanings. *Eye, aye,* and *I* are homophones in English.

Homorganic. Articulated with the same organs or in the same area. For example, English [n] and [t] are homorganic sounds because both are pronounced with the tongue touching the alveolar ridge.

Hypotaxis. The subordination of one clause to another by means of special subordinating words such as *because* or *if.* Frequently contrasted with *parataxis.*

Ideogram. A graphic symbol that represents an idea or meaning without expressing a specific word. For example, @, ≠ , and ° are ideograms.

Idiom. An expression whose meaning is not predictable from the meaning of its individual words and which may not even fit the normal grammatical patterns of the language. *To give someone a hand* is an idiom.

Imperative. The verbal mood used for expressing commands and requests. In the sentence *Get a horse,* the verb *get* is in the imperative mood.

Imperfect tense. A verbal tense referring to continuous, habitual, or incompleted action.

Impersonal pronoun. *See* Indefinite pronoun.

Impersonal verb. A verb denoting action by an unspecified agent. It is used in the third-person singular and either with no subject or with a "dummy" subject like *it.* PDE has few impersonal verbs; one is *behoove,* as in *It behooves you to watch your language.*

Indefinite adjective. *See* Strong adjective.

Indefinite article. A function word indicating that the following noun is a member of a class rather than a specific individual. *A (an)* is the PDE indefinite article.

Indefinite pronoun. A pronoun that does not refer to a specific person or thing. PDE examples include *some, everybody, whoever,* and *none.* Also called *impersonal pronoun.*

Independent clause. A clause that can form a complete sentence by itself.

Indicative. The verbal mood used for stating facts. In the sentence *She gets tired easily, gets* is in the indicative mood.

Indirect object. A noun or pronoun that specifies who or what is the receiver of the direct object. In the sentence *She gave Tony a black eye, Tony* is the indirect object.

Infinitive. A verb form not inflected for person, number, or tense. PDE infinitives may be *marked* (with *to,* as in "I am able *to stop*") or *unmarked* (as in "I can *stop*").

Infix. An affix inserted within a word, as opposed to being attached to the beginning or end.

Inflection. Variation in the form of a word to indicate a change in meaning or in grammatical relationships with other elements in the sentence. Inflection of nouns and pronouns is called *declension;* inflection of PDE adjectives is called *comparison;* inflection of verbs is called *conjugation.*

Inflectional affix. An affix used to indicate an inflection. For example, the plural *-s* is an inflectional affix in PDE.

Inflectional language. A language that expresses grammatical relationships primarily by means of affixes attached to the roots of words. Classical Greek and Latin were highly inflectional languages.

Injunctive. A verbal mood of Indo-European for expressing unreality.

Inkhorn term. A borrowing from Latin or Greek to which someone objects.

Inner history. *See* Internal history.

Instrumental. In inflecting languages, a grammatical case indicating the means or agent by which something is done.

Intensification. A semantic change strengthening the notion expressed by a word. For example, the word *jeopardy* underwent intensification when its meaning changed from "uncertainty" to "danger, peril."

Interdental. Referring to consonants formed with the tongue between the teeth. Both [θ] as in *think* and [ð] as in *they* are interdental sounds.

Interjection. A word grammatically independent of the rest of its sentence and used to attract attention or express emotion. PDE examples include *ouch! hey!* and *oh!*

Internal history. Changes within a language that cannot be attributed directly to external forces. For example, the raising of [ɛ] to [ɪ] before a nasal in PDE is an internal event. Also called *inner history*.

Interrogative. Referring to words or word order used in asking questions. For example, *why* is an interrogative adverb in PDE.

Intervocalic. Occurring between two vowels.

Isogloss. On dialect maps, a line separating areas in which the language differs with respect to one or more features.

Isolating language. A language in which words are invariable in form, and grammatical relationships are indicated by word order and particles. Modern Chinese and Vietnamese are isolating languages.

Katakana. The Japanese syllabary used primarily for writing documents or foreign words.

Koine. A form of a language, usually a mixture of several dialects or languages, that is used as a trade language.

Labial. A sound formed with the lips. PDE labials include [p b f v].

Labiodental. Referring to sounds made when the upper teeth are on the lower lip. In PDE the labiodental phonemes are /f/ and /v/.

Labiovelar. Referring to sounds with simultaneous labial and velar articulation. PDE [w] is a labiovelar.

Language family. A group of languages all derived from the same parent language.

Larynx. The upper end of the trachea, containing the vocal cords.

Lateral. A consonant pronounced by blocking the front of the mouth but allowing air to escape from one or both sides. In PDE, /l/ is a lateral.

Latinate. Referring to words or constructions either borrowed from Latin or from a derivative of Latin such as French.

Lax vowel. A vowel produced with relatively little muscular tension. In PDE, [ɪ ɛ ʊ ɔ ə] are lax vowels.

Least effort. The theory that language change occurs because speakers are lazy and attempt to simplify their speech to save themselves effort.

Lexicon. The total inventory (including words) of the morphemes of a language.

Ligature. A single written symbol that is a combination of two or more symbols. For example, æ is a ligature of *a* and *e*.

Linking verb. *See* Copula.

Liquid. A consonant produced without friction. The term normally refers to /r/ and /l/ in English.

Loan-translation. A form of borrowing in which the components of a word in one language are translated literally into their equivalents in the borrowing language. For example, English *superman* is a loan-translation of German *Übermensch*; German *über* means "over" or "super" and German *Mensch* means "man." Also called *calque*.

Loanword. A word adopted from another language or dialect. Same as *borrowed word*.

Locative. In inflecting languages, a grammatical case indicating place or place where.

Logogram. A written symbol that stands for an entire word. For example, ¢ is a logogram for *cents*.

Low vowel. A vowel produced with the tongue relatively low in the mouth and the jaws relatively wide open. PDE low vowels are [æ ɑ].

Masculine. One of the grammatical genders. *See* Gender.

Mass noun. A noun that has no plural form and that cannot be modified by *a* or *one*; *furniture, devotion,* and *ink* are mass nouns in PDE. Also called *uncountable noun*.

Medial. Occurring in the middle of a word.

Metathesis. Transposition of sounds within a word, as from OE *wæps* to PDE *wasp*.

Mid vowel. A vowel pronounced with the tongue neither particularly high nor particularly low in the mouth. In PDE [e ɛ ə ɔ] are mid vowels.

Middle English. The English language from about A.D. 1100 to 1500.

Middle voice. A voice of verbs intermediate between active and passive, indicating that the subject is acting upon itself. It is roughly equivalent in meaning to a reflexive.

Modal auxiliary. One of the PDE verbs *can* (*could*), *may* (*might*), *will* (*would*), *shall* (*should*), *dare*, *need*, *ought*, or *must* that occur with other verbs to express mood.

Modifier. A word, phrase, or clause that qualifies or limits another word, phrase, clause, or sentence. Modifiers are most commonly classified as either adjectival or adverbial.

Mood. A variation in verb forms to indicate factuality, probability, or desirability of the action or state expressed by the verb. PDE has three moods: indicative, subjunctive, and imperative.

Morpheme. The smallest meaningful unit of a language. The word *unlikely*, for example, consists of three morphemes: *un-*, *like-*, and *-ly*.

Morphology. The study of the combination of stems and affixes to form words.

Mutation. *See* Umlaut.

Narrowing. A semantic change restricting the meaning of a word to a smaller domain. OE *feðer* meant "wing, feather"; it narrowed when it lost the meaning "wing."

Nasal. Referring to a sound produced while the velum is lowered so that much of the air escapes through the nose. In PDE, /m n ŋ/ are nasal sounds.

Native word. A word that belongs to the original inventory of words of a given language and that cannot be attributed to borrowing from any other language.

Natural gender. *See* Biological gender.

Negative. A word or morpheme denying the truth of the word or phrase to which it is attached or otherwise associated.

Neologism. A newly coined word or phrase.

Neuter. One of the grammatical genders. *See* Gender.

Nominal. A noun or any word or group of words serving the functions of a noun. In the sentence *To play hockey was his only ambition*, the nominals are *To play hockey* and *his only ambition*.

Nominative. In inflecting languages, a grammatical case indicating the subject (or subject complement) of a clause or sentence.

Nonce word. A word made up for a specific occasion.

Normative grammar. *See* Prescriptive grammar.

North Germanic. The subdivision of the Germanic branch of Indo-European languages consisting of Danish, Swedish, Norwegian, Faroese, and Icelandic.

Noun. A word designating a person, place, thing, or concept. In PDE, nouns are inflected for number and for possessive case; they are used as subjects, objects, and complements.

Number. The inflection of words to indicate singular or plural (and, in some languages, dual).

Object. The noun or other nominal that receives or is affected by the action of the verb in a clause or sentence. *See also* Direct object *and* Indirect object.

Oblique case. For inflecting languages, a cover-all term for any case except the nominative (subject) case.

Old English. The English language from about A.D. 450 to 1100.

Onomatopoetic. *See* Echoic.

Open-class words. Words belonging to classes to which new members are relatively easily added, such as nouns, verbs, and derivative adverbs.

Open syllable. A syllable that ends in a vowel sound. The words *sigh*, *go*, *pay*, *me*, and *paw* are all open syllables.

Outer history. *See* External history.

Palate. The roof of the mouth, consisting of the bony hard palate in front and the fleshy soft palate in back.

Paradigm. The complete set of all the inflectional forms of a word. For example, the paradigm for the first-person singular pronoun in PDE is *I/me/mine*.

Parataxis. The coordination or juxtaposition of grammatical units of the same rank, with or without the use of coordinating conjunctions. Frequently contrasted with *hypotaxis*.

Participle. A nonfinite verb form used in PDE as an adjectival and to form verb phrases. The *present participle* ends in *-ing*; the *past participle* (also called *passive participle*) ends in *-ed* (or *-n, -t,* and so on) or has a vowel change (as in *stood, sung*).

Particle. An uninflected word used to indicate grammatical relationships. Typical PDE particles are *of, to, a,* and *as*.

Passive voice. The verbal voice indicating that the subject is the recipient of the action expressed by the verb. In the sentence *Hay is eaten by cows,* the verb *is eaten* is in the passive voice. *See also* Active voice.

Past participle. *See* Participle.

Past perfect tense. *See* Pluperfect tense.

Pejoration. A semantic change for the worse. For example, in OE, *sælig* meant "happy, blessed," but through pejoration its PDE derivative *silly* means "foolish, stupid." Also called *degeneration*.

Perfect tense. In Indo-European, the tense for completed action. In PDE, the verbal "tense" formed by *have* + past participle, signifying current relevance.

Periodic sentence. A sentence in which the completion of the main idea is postponed until after all amplifying material has been stated. For example, "After hitting an iceberg in the north Atlantic, the *Titanic,* supposedly unsinkable, sank."

Periphrastic. Using separate words instead of inflections to express a grammatical relationship. The PDE passive is periphrastic because it consists of the auxiliary *be* plus the past participle of the main verb, instead of a verb base to which a special inflection is added.

Person. A grammatical category that distinguishes the speaker (first person), the person spoken to (second person), and the person or thing spoken about (third person).

Personal pronoun. A pronoun that indicates grammatical person. PDE personal pronouns are inflected for three persons (*I, you, she*), two numbers (*I, we*), and three cases (*I, me, mine*). The third-person singular pronoun is also inflected for three genders (*he, she, it*).

Petroglyph. A carving or drawing on rock.

Pharynx. The back of the mouth between the nasal passages and the larynx. Consonants that have the pharynx as a point of articulation are called *pharyngeal* consonants.

Phone. A vocal sound, whether phonemic or not.

Phoneme. The smallest speech unit that can distinguish one word or group of words from another. For example, /f/ and /v/ are separate phonemes in PDE because they distinguish such words as *fat/vat* and *strife/strive*.

Phonemics. The study of phonemes.

Phonetics. The study of speech sounds, whether phonemic or not.

Phonology. The system of speech sounds of a language, especially at a given period or in a particular area; for instance, we might speak of the phonology of the Northumberland dialect in late Middle English.

Phrase. A group of grammatically related words that does not contain both a subject and a complete predicate. *Over my dead body, slowly sipping a cup of tea,* and *the door being locked* are all phrases.

Pictogram. A written symbol representing a specific object; a picture of that object. Also called *pictograph*.

Pictograph. *See* Pictogram.

Pidgin. A simplified, mixed language used among people who have no common language.

Pitch (accent). Highness or lowness of the voice during speech.

Plosive. *See* Stop.

Pluperfect tense. A tense indicating that the action specified by the verb had occurred before or by the time another action occurred. In the sentence *He had read the book three days earlier, had read* is in the pluperfect tense. Also called *past perfect tense*.

Point of articulation. A nonmovable portion of the speech tract with which an articulator comes in contact or near contact during speech.

Portmanteau word. *See* Blend.

Possessive. *See* Genitive.

Postvocalic. Occurring after a vowel.

Predicate. The part of a clause or sentence that expresses what is said about the subject. It consists of a verb or verb phrase and any objects, complements, or modifiers of the verb. In the sentence *Her brother in Syracuse often calls her late at night*, the predicate is *often calls her late at night*.

Prefix. An affix attached to the beginning of a stem or word. Typical PDE prefixes are *un-*, *dis-*, *re-*, *over-*, and *counter-*.

Preposition. A part of speech used with a noun or other nominal (called its *object*) connecting it with another part of the sentence. The preposition together with its object is called a *prepositional phrase*. Examples of PDE prepositions are *to*, *with*, *from*, and *because of*.

Prescriptive grammar. Grammar regarded as a set of rules that must be obeyed if one is not to be considered ignorant and a substandard speaker. Also called *normative grammar*.

Present participle. *See* Participle.

Present tense. In general, the tense that indicates that the action expressed by the verb is going on at the time of speaking. For PDE, the so-called present tense is actually a "timeless" tense, or, more precisely, a nonpast tense.

Present-day English. The English language from roughly A.D. 1800 to the present.

Preterite. The simple past tense. Also spelled *preterit*.

Preterite-present verb. In Old English, a verb whose present-tense form was originally a past tense, not a present tense.

Prevocalic. Occurring before a vowel.

Proclitic. Referring to a word that has no independent stress of its own but is pronounced as part of the following word. For example, in *'tis*, the pronoun *it* is proclitic to the verb *is*.

Progressive tense. A verbal form indicating that the action is, was, or will be in progress at the time specified or implied. In the sentence *She is studying Sanskrit*, the verb *is studying* is in the progressive tense. Also called *continuous tense*.

Pronoun. A member of a small class of words used to replace nouns or to avoid repetition of nouns. Typical PDE pronouns are *me*, *you*, *them*, *both*, *some*, *anyone*, and *several*.

Prosody. The stress or pitch patterns that give a language its perceived rhythms.

Qualitative. Referring to differences in articulation of vowels, as opposed to quantitative differences, which are of duration only.

Quantitative. Referring to duration of vowels, or the time taken to pronounce them.

Received Pronunciation. Educated British English from the London and southern areas of England.

Reflex. The result of the historical development of an earlier form. PDE *oak* is the reflex of Germanic **aik-*.

Reflexive pronoun. A pronoun that indicates that the object of the verb has the same referent as the subject of the verb. In PDE, the reflexive pronouns end in *-self* or *-selves*.

Relative pronoun. A pronoun that connects a dependent clause to an independent clause and serves as subject or object in the dependent clause. The PDE relative pronouns are *that*, *who*, and *which*.

Resonant. A vague term for a voiced speech sound.

Retroflex. Referring to a sound produced with the tongue tip raised and curled up toward the alveolar ridge. PDE /r/ is retroflex.

Rhotic. Referring to dialects that pronounce *r* in all positions of a word.

Romance language. One of the modern descendants of Latin (such as French, Spanish, Italian, Portuguese, Romanian, and Sardinian).

Root. A word or element from which other words are formed. Also, a base to which affixes can be added. For example, *-tain* is a root from which such words as *contain*, *maintain*, *retain*, *detainment*, and *sustainable* are formed.

Rounded. Articulated with rounded lips. In PDE, /w u o/ are rounded phonemes.

Runic alphabet. An alphabet used by ancient Germanic peoples. Also called *futhorc*. Individual characters in the alphabet are called *runes*.

Satem languages. Those IE languages in which IE *[k] appears as [s] (unless later changes have occurred). The *satem* languages are Indo-Iranian, Armenian, Balto-Slavic, and Albanian.

Schwa. The vowel [ə], as in *alone, harem,* and *color.*

Semantics. The study of meaning in language.

Semivowel. A sound that shares characteristics of both vowels and consonants. The PDE semivowels are /w/ and /j/; some also treat /r/ as a semivowel.

Sentence. A grammatical unit independent of any other grammatical construction. It usually contains a subject and a predicate with a finite verb.

Separable verb. *See* Two-part verb.

Sibilant. A hissing or *s*-like sound. In PDE, the sibilant phonemes are /s z š ž č ǰ/.

Spectrogram. A physical photograph of a speech sound or sounds, recording the energy level over time at various frequencies.

Spelling pronunciation. A change in the traditional pronunciation of a word brought about by its spelling. For example, [ɔftən] for *often* is a spelling pronunciation because the word is not traditionally spoken with a [t].

Spirant. *See* Fricative.

Stammbaumtheorie. The "family-tree" model of language relationships, which likens the connections among related languages to human genealogy.

Standard language. The dialect of a language accepted by most speakers as "good" or "proper."

Stem. The main part of a word to which affixes are added. It may be the same as the root, or it may consist of the root plus a morpheme to which affixes are added.

Stop. A consonant produced by completely closing the air passages and then suddenly opening them. The English stops are /p b t d k g/. Also called *plosive.*

Stress. Variations of loudness between or among syllables; also, special emphasis placed on a sound or syllable.

Strong adjective. In OE, an adjective *not* accompanied by a demonstrative, numeral, or possessive adjective. Also called *indefinite adjective.*

Strong verb. A verb that forms its past tense and past participle by internal vowel changes rather than by the addition of *-ed.* An example is *sing/sang/sung.*

Subject. The noun or nominal in a clause or sentence about which the predicate says or asks something. In an active sentence, the subject is the doer of the action.

Subjunctive mood. In Indo-European, the mood expressing will; in PDE, forms expressing hypothetical, contingent, or suggested action. For example, in the sentence *I wouldn't look down if I were you,* were is in the subjunctive mood.

Subordinate clause. A clause that does not form a complete sentence by itself, but must be attached to an independent clause. In the sentence *If you scratch that bite, it will itch even more,* the subordinate clause is *If you scratch that bite.* Also called *dependent clause.*

Subordinating conjunction. A conjunction that connects two clauses and indicates that one of them is dependent upon the other. Common English subordinating conjunctions include *because, if, although, whenever,* and *after.*

Subordination. The joining of two clauses in such a way that one of them is made grammatically dependent on the other. *See* Subordinate clause.

Substantive. A noun or group of words functioning as a noun. In the sentence *His concern was for the poor,* concern and *poor* are substantives.

Suffix. An affix added to the end of a word. In the word *needlessly, -less* and *-ly* are suffixes.

Superlative. The form of an adjective or adverb that indicates that something possesses a quality to the maximum degree. For example, *the most exciting* and *the slowest* are PDE superlative forms.

Syllabary. The list of characters of a writing system that represents the syllables, as opposed to the individual vowels and consonants, of a language.

Syllable. A unit of speech consisting of a vowel or diphthong, alone or combined with one or more consonants. For example, in spoken English the indefinite article *a* is a single syllable, as is the word *strengths. Spoke* consists of one syllable, but *speaking* consists of two.

Synchronic. Referring to the study of a language at a given point in time, as opposed to the study of its historical development. *See also* Diachronic.

Synonyms. Words that have the same or nearly the same meanings in the same language. In PDE, *little* and *small* are synonyms.

Syntax. The way in which words are arranged to form phrases, clauses, and sentences; the word order or structure of sentences.

Synthetic language. A language in which syntactic relations are expressed primarily by means of inflections. Classical Greek and modern Russian are synthetic languages.

Tense. The forms of a verb that indicate time or duration of the action or state expressed by the verb. English has five tenses: present, progressive, past, perfect, and future. The progressive and perfect tenses may be combined with each other and with the present or past or future to form compound tenses, such as the present perfect progressive (*I have been standing*).

Tense vowel. A vowel produced with relatively great muscular tension of the tongue and its associated muscles. In PDE, [i] and [e] are tense vowels, for example.

Thorn. The name of the character þ in the runic alphabet; it represented the sounds [θ] and [ð] and was incorporated into the Latin alphabet during OE and ME times.

Trachea. The tube going from the back of the mouth to the lungs; the windpipe.

Two-part verb. A verb consisting of a base verb and a separate prepositional adverb. PDE examples include *pick up, take over,* and *run down.* Also sometimes called a *separable verb.*

Umlaut. An internal vowel change, usually caused by a vowel or semivowel in the following syllable. Also called *mutation* or *front mutation.*

Unconditioned change. Linguistic change that cannot be attributed to the influence of nearby sounds or other linguistic features.

Uncountable noun. *See* Mass noun.

Unrounded. Pronounced without rounding the lips. In PDE, [i], [e], and [æ], for example, are unrounded vowels.

Uvula. The triangular piece of soft tissue that hangs down over the throat behind the soft palate.

Uvular trill. An *r*-like sound made by vibrating the uvula.

Velar. Referring to consonants formed by approaching or touching the back of the tongue to the soft palate (velum). In PDE, /k/ and /g/ are both velar sounds.

Velum. The soft palate.

Verb. The part of speech serving as the main element in a predicate. English verbs typically express an action or state of being, are inflected for tense, voice, and mood, and show agreement with their subjects.

Vernacular. The ordinary spoken language of a group or geographical area, as opposed to a literary language.

Verner's Law. The rule formulated by Karl Verner to explain apparent exceptions to Grimm's Law.

Vocal cords. Bands of cartilage in the larynx. When they are tensed and air from the lungs passes through them making them vibrate, sound (voice) results.

Vocative. In inflecting languages, a grammatical case used for words in direct address.

Voice. A verbal category that expresses the relationship between the subject and the object. *See also* Active voice, Passive voice, *and* Middle voice.

Voiced. Referring to sounds pronounced while the vocal cords are vibrating. PDE voiced phonemes include all vowels and consonants like /b d v ǰ l j/.

Voiceless. Referring to sounds produced without simultaneous vibration of the vocal cords. Among the PDE voiceless phonemes are /p t f θ š/.

Vowel. A sound produced by relatively unrestricted passage of air through the mouth, usually accompanied by vibration of the vocal cords.

Weak adjective. In OE, an adjective accompanied by a demonstrative, numeral, or possessive adjective. Also called *definite adjective.*

Weak verb. An English verb whose past tense and past participle are formed by adding a suffix ending in [d] or [t]. *Ask, beg, request,* and *pray* are all weak verbs.

Weakening. A semantic change whereby a word decreases in the force or quality of the meaning it expresses. For example, the word *spill,* which once meant "destroy, kill," has undergone weakening.

Wellentheorie. A theory of language change positing that changes begin in a specific geographic area and spread out concentrically from that point like waves created when a pebble is dropped into a pool. Also called the theory of *waves of innovation.*

Wen. The name of the character *p* in the runic alphabet. It was incorporated into the Latin alphabet to represent [w] during Old English times.

West Germanic. The branch of the Germanic group of Indo-European to which English belongs. Other West Germanic languages include German, Dutch, Flemish, and Frisian.

Yogh. The conventional name for the ME letter *ȝ.*

Zero-morpheme derivation. *See* Functional shift.

GENERAL BIBLIOGRAPHY

Aarsleff, H. *The Study of Language in England, 1780–1860.* Minneapolis: U of Minnesota P, 1983.

Abbott, E. A. *A Shakespearian Grammar.* 1870. New York: Dover, 1966.

Aitchison, Jean. *Language Change: Progress or Decay?* New York: Universe, 1985.

Allen, H. B. *The Linguistic Atlas of the Upper Midwest.* Minneapolis: U of Minnesota P, 1976.

Andrew, S. O. *Syntax and Style in Old English.* Cambridge: Cambridge UP, 1940.

Anglo-Saxon England, 1972– .

Anttila, Raimo. *An Introduction to Historical and Comparative Linguistics.* New York: Macmillan, 1972.

Arlotto, Anthony. *Introduction to Historical Linguistics.* Boston: Houghton Mifflin, 1972.

Bacquet, Paul. *La structure de la phrase verbale à l'époque alfrédienne.* Paris: Société d'Éditions: Les belles lettres, 1962.

Bailey, Richard W., and Jay L. Robinson. *Varieties of Present-Day English.* New York: Macmillan, 1973.

Baker, Sidney J. *The Australian Language.* Sydney: Currawong, 1966.

Baldi, Philip. *An Introduction to the Indo-European Languages.* Carbondale, Ill.: Southern Illinois UP, 1983.

Barber, Charles. *Early Modern English.* London: André Deutsch, 1976.

Barber, Charles. *Linguistic Change in Present-Day English.* University, Ala.: U of Alabama P, 1964.

Barltrop, R., and J. Wolveridge. *The Muvver Tongue.* London: Journeyman P, 1980.

Barney, Stephen A. *Word-Hoard: An Introduction to Old English Vocabulary.* New Haven: Yale UP, 1977.

Baron, Dennis E. *Grammar and Good Taste: Reforming the American Language.* New Haven: Yale UP, 1982.

Bauer, Laurie. *English Word-Formation.* Cambridge: Cambridge UP, 1983.

Baugh, Albert C., and Thomas Cable. *A History of the English Language.* 3d ed. Englewood Cliffs, N.J.: Prentice-Hall, 1978.

Beeton, D. R., and Helen Dorner. *A Dictionary of English Usage in Southern Africa.* Cape Town: Oxford UP, 1975.

Benveniste, Émile. *Le vocabulaire des institutions indo-européennes.* 2 vols. Paris: Éditions de Minuit, 1969.

Birnbaum, Henrik, and Jaan Puhvel, eds. *Ancient Indo-European Dialects.* Berkeley: U of California P, 1966.

Björkman, Erik. *Scandinavian Loan-Words in Middle English.* Halle: Niemeyer, 1900–1902.

Blair, Peter Hunter. *An Introduction to Anglo-Saxon England.* 2d ed. Cambridge: Cambridge UP, 1977.

Blake, N. F. *Caxton and His World.* London: André Deutsch, 1969.

Bolinger, Dwight. *Aspects of Language.* 2d ed. New York: Harcourt, 1975.

Bolton, W. F. *The English Language: Essays by English & American Men of Letters, 1490–1839.* Cambridge: Cambridge UP, 1966.

Bolton, W. F., and D. Crystal. *The English Language: Essays by Linguists and Men of Letters, 1858–1964.* Cambridge: Cambridge UP, 1969.

Bourcier, Georges. *An Introduction to the History of the English Language.* Trans. Cecily Clark. Cheltenham: Stanley Thornes, 1981.

Bronstein, Arthur. *The Pronunciation of American English.* New York: Appleton, 1960.

Brook, G. L. *English Dialects.* New York: Oxford UP, 1963.

Brook, G. L. *A History of the English Language.* New York: Norton, 1964.

Brook, G. L. *The Language of Shakespeare.* London: André Deutsch, 1976.

Brook, G. L. *Varieties of English.* New York: St. Martin's, 1973.

Brunner, Karl. *An Outline of Middle English Grammar.* Trans. G. K. W. Johnston. Oxford: Basil Blackwell, 1970.

Burchfield, Robert, ed. *Studies in Lexicography.* Oxford: Clarendon, 1986.

Bynon, Theodora. *Historical Linguistics.* Cambridge: Cambridge UP, 1983.

Campbell, A. *Old English Grammar.* Oxford: Oxford UP, 1959.

Cardona, George, Henry M. Hoenigswald, and Alfred Senn, eds. *Indo-European and Indo-Europeans.* Philadelphia: U of Pennsylvania P, 1970.

Carr, Elizabeth Ball. *Da Kine Talk: From Pidgin to Standard English in Hawaii.* Honolulu: UP of Hawaii, 1972.

Cassidy, Frederic G., ed. *Dictionary of American Regional English.* 5 vols. Cambridge, Mass.: Harvard UP, 1985–

Cassidy, Frederic G. *Jamaica Talk: Three Hundred Years of the English Language in Jamaica.* London: Macmillan, 1961.

Cassidy, Frederic G., and Richard N. Ringler, eds. *Bright's Old English Grammar & Reader.* 3d ed. New York: Holt, Rinehart and Winston, 1971.

Chadwick, John. *The Decipherment of Linear B.* New York: Random House, 1958.

Chambers, J. K., ed. *Canadian English.* Toronto: Methuen, 1975.

Clanchy, M. T. *From Memory to Written Record: England 1066–1307.* Cambridge: Harvard UP, 1979.

Clark Hall, John R., and Herbert D. Meritt. *A Concise Anglo-Saxon Dictionary.* 4th ed. Cambridge: Cambridge UP, 1969.

Collingwood, R. G., and J. N. L. Myres. *Roman Britain and the English Settlements.* 2d ed. Oxford: Clarendon, 1937.

Craigie, William Alexander. *The Critique of Pure English from Caxton to Smollett.* London: Clarendon, 1946.

Craigie, William A., and James Hulbert, eds. *A Dictionary of American English on Historical Principles.* Chicago: U of Chicago P, 1938–44.

Crewe, William J., ed. *The English Language in Singapore.* Singapore: Eastern Universities P, 1977.

De Villiers, André, ed. *English-Speaking South Africa Today.* Cape Town: Oxford UP, 1976.

Dillard, J. L. *Black English: Its History and Usage in the United States.* New York: Random House, 1972.

Dillard, J. L., ed. *Perspectives on Black English.* The Hague: Mouton, 1975.

Diringer, David. *The Alphabet: A Key to the History of Mankind.* 3d ed. London: Hutchinson, 1968.

Dobson, E. J. *English Pronunciation, 1500–1700.* 2d ed. Oxford: Clarendon, 1968.

Dohan, Mary Helen. *Our Own Words.* New York: Knopf, 1976.

Ekwall, Eilert. *A History of Modern English Sounds and Morphology.* Trans. A. Ward. Totowa, N.J.: Rowman, 1975.

Elliott, Ralph W. V. *Runes: An Introduction.* Manchester: Manchester UP, 1963.

Ferguson, Charles A., and Shirley Brice Heath, eds. *Language in the USA.* Cambridge: Cambridge UP, 1981.

Fisiak, Jacek. *Morphemic Structure of Chaucer's English.* University, Ala.: U of Alabama P, 1965.

Frank, Roberta, and Angus Cameron, eds. *A Plan for the Dictionary of Old English.* Toronto: U of Toronto P, 1973.

Fromkin, Victoria, and Robert Rodman. *An Introduction to Language.* 2d ed. New York: Holt, Rinehart and Winston, 1974.

Garbáty, Thomas J. *Medieval English Literature.* Lexington, Mass.: Heath, 1984.

Gelb, I. J. *A Study of Writing.* Rev. ed. Chicago: U of Chicago P, 1963.

Gordon, Ian A. *The Movement of English Prose.* Bloomington: Indiana UP, 1966.

Gordon, James D. *The English Language: An Historical Introduction.* New York: Crowell, 1972.

Greenough, James Bradstreet, and George Lyman Kittredge. *Words and Their Ways in English Speech.* 1900. Boston: Beacon, 1962.

Harris, Roy. *The Language Makers.* Ithaca: Cornell UP, 1980.

Harris, Roy. *The Origin of Writing.* London, Duckworth, 1986.

Hayakawa, S. I. *Language in Thought and Action.* 3d ed. New York: Harcourt, 1972.

Hoenigswald, Henry M. *Language Change and Linguistic Reconstruction.* Chicago: U of Chicago P, 1960.

Hughes, Arthur, and Peter Trudgill. *English Accents and Dialects: An Introduction to Social and Regional Varieties of British*

English. Baltimore: University Park P, 1979.

Jacob, Ernest Fraser. *The Fifteenth Century, 1399–1485*. Oxford: Clarendon, 1961.

Jeffers, Robert J., and Ilse Lehiste. *Principles and Methods for Historical Linguistics*. Cambridge, Mass.: MIT P, 1979.

Jespersen, Otto. *Growth and Structure of the English Language*. Garden City: Doubleday, 1955.

Jones, Daniel. *The Pronunciation of English*. 4th ed. Cambridge: Cambridge UP, 1956.

Jones, Richard Foster. *The Triumph of the English Language*. Stanford: Stanford UP, 1953.

Kachru, Braj B. *The Indianization of English*. Delhi: Oxford UP, 1983.

Kökeritz, Helge. *Shakespeare's Pronunciation*. New Haven: Yale UP, 1953.

Kurath, Hans. *A Phonology and Prosody of Modern English*. Ann Arbor: U of Michigan P, 1964.

Kurath, Hans, and Sherman M. Kuhn, eds. *Middle English Dictionary*. Ann Arbor: U of Michigan P, 1954–   .

Kurath, Hans, and Raven I. McDavid. *The Pronunciation of English in the Atlantic States*. Ann Arbor: U of Michigan P, 1961.

Labov, William. *Language in the Inner City: Studies in the Black English Vernacular*. Philadelphia: U of Pennsylvania P, 1972.

Lanham, L. W. *The Pronunciation of South African English*. Cape Town: Balkema, 1967.

Lapidge, Michael, and Helmut Gneuss, eds. *Learning and Literature in Anglo-Saxon England*. Cambridge: Cambridge UP, 1985.

Lass, Roger, ed. *Approaches to English Historical Linguistics: An Anthology*. New York: Holt, Rinehart and Winston, 1969.

Leech, Geoffrey. *Semantics*. Harmondsworth: Penguin, 1974.

Leonard, Sterling Andrus. *The Doctrine of Correctness in English Usage, 1700–1800*. Madison: U of Wisconsin P, 1929.

LePage, R. B., and D. DeCamp. *Jamaican Creole*. London: Macmillan, 1960.

Lewis, C. S. *Studies in Words*. Cambridge: Cambridge UP, 1967.

Llamzon, Teodoro A. *Standard Filipino English*. Manila: Ateneo UP, 1969.

Lockwood, W. B. *Indo-European Philology*. London: Hutchinson, 1971.

Lockwood, W. B. *Languages of the British Isles, Past and Present*. André Deutsch, 1975.

Lockwood, W. B. *A Panorama of Indo-European Languages*. London: Hutchinson, 1972.

Lounsbury, Thomas R. *English Spelling and Spelling Reform*. New York: Harper, 1909.

Lyons, John. *Semantics*. Cambridge: Cambridge UP, 1977.

McIntosh, Angus, M. L. Samuels, Michael Benskin, et al. *A Linguistic Atlas of Late Mediaeval English*. Aberdeen, Scotland: Aberdeen UP, 1985–   .

McKisack, May. *The Fourteenth Century, 1307–1399*. Oxford: Clarendon, 1959.

Marchand, Hans. *The Categories and Types of Present-Day English Word-Formation*. University, Ala.: U of Alabama P, [1966].

Marckwardt, Albert H. *American English*. 2d ed. New York: Oxford UP, 1980.

Markman, Alan M., and Erwin R. Steinberg. *English Then and Now*. New York: Random House, 1970.

Masica, C., and P. B. Dave. *The Sound System of Indian English*. Hyderabad: Central Institute of English, 1972.

Mather, J. Y., and H.-H. Speitel, eds. *The Linguistic Atlas of Scotland: Scots Section*. London: Croom Helm, 1975–77.

Meillet, Antoine. *General Characteristics of the Germanic Languages*. Trans. William P. Dismukes. Coral Gables, Fla.: U of Miami P, 1970.

Meillet, Antoine. *Introduction à l'étude comparative des langues indo-européennes*. University, Ala.: U of Alabama P, 1964.

Mencken, H. L. *The American Language*. Annot. and ed. Raven I. McDavid, Jr. New York: Knopf, 1977.

Michael, Ian. *English Grammatical Categories and the Tradition to 1800*. Cambridge: Cambridge UP, 1970.

Michaels, Leonard, and Christopher Ricks, eds. *The State of the Language*. Berkeley: U of California P, 1980.

Millward, Celia M. *Imperative Constructions in Old English*. The Hague: Mouton, 1971.

Mitchell, A. G. *The Pronunciation of English in Australia*. Sydney: Angus & Robertson, 1965.

Mitchell, Bruce. *Old English Syntax*. Oxford: Clarendon, 1985.

Mossé, Fernand. *A Handbook of Middle English*. Trans. James A. Walker. Baltimore: Johns Hopkins, 1952.

Murison, N., ed. *The Guid Scots Tongue*. Edinburgh: Blackwood, 1977.

Murray, K. M. Elisabeth. *Caught in the Web of Words: James Murray and the Oxford English Dictionary*. Oxford: Oxford UP, 1979.

Mustanoja, Tauno F. *A Middle English Syntax. Part I: Parts of Speech*. Helsinki: Société Néophilologique, 1960.

Myers, A. R. *England in the Late Middle Ages (1307–1536)*. Harmondsworth: Penguin, 1963.

Myers, L. M., and Richard L. Hoffman. *The Roots of Modern English*. 2d ed. Boston: Little, Brown, 1979.

Noss, Richard B., ed. *Varieties of English in Southeast Asia*. Singapore: Singapore UP, 1983.

Orkin, Mark M. *Speaking Canadian English*. New York: McKay, 1970.

Orton, Harold, et al., eds. *Survey of English Dialects*. Leeds: Arnold, 1962–71.

Orton, Harold, and Nathalia Wright, eds. *A Word Geography of England*. London: Seminar, 1974.

The Oxford English Dictionary. London: Oxford UP, 1933 + Supplements.

Padley, G. A. *Grammatical Theory in Western Europe, 1500–1700: The Latin Tradition*. Cambridge: Cambridge UP, 1976.

Page, R. I. *An Introduction to English Runes*. London: Methuen, 1973.

Palmer, Leonard R. *Descriptive and Comparative Linguistics: A Critical Introduction*. London: Faber, 1972.

Partridge, A. C. *Tudor to Augustan English: A Study in Syntax and Style from Caxton to Johnson*. London: André Deutsch, 1969.

Pedersen, Holger. *The Discovery of Language: Linguistic Science in the Nineteenth Century*. Trans. John Webster Spargo. Bloomington: Indiana UP, 1962.

Peinovich, Michael P. *Old English Noun Morphology: A Diachronic Study*. Amsterdam: North-Holland, 1979.

Powicke, F. M. *The Thirteenth Century, 1216–1307*. 2d ed. Oxford: Clarendon, 1962.

Pride, John B., ed. *New Englishes*. Rowley, Mass.: Newbury House, 1982.

Prins, Anton Adriaan. *A History of English Phonemes: From Indo-European to Present-Day English*. Leiden: Leiden UP, 1972.

Prokosch, E. *A Comparative Germanic Grammar*. Baltimore: Linguistic Society of America, 1938.

Pyles, Thomas, and John Algeo. *The Origins and Development of the English Language*. 3d ed. New York: Harcourt, 1982.

Quirk, Randolph, et al. *A Grammar of Contemporary English*. London: Longman, 1972.

Quirk, Randolph, and C. L. Wrenn. *An Old English Grammar*. New York: Holt, Rinehart and Winston, 1957.

Reed, Carroll E. *Dialects of American English*. 1967. Amherst: U of Massachusetts P, 1973.

Reinecke, John E. *Language and Dialect in Hawaii: A Socio-linguistic History to 1935*. Ed. Stanley M. Tsuzaki. Honolulu: U of Hawaii P, 1969.

Robins, R. H. *A Short History of Linguistics*. Bloomington: Indiana UP, 1967.

Ruhlen, Merritt. *A Guide to the World's Languages*. Stanford: Stanford UP, 1987.

Samuels, M. L. *Linguistic Evolution: With Special Reference to English*. Cambridge: Cambridge UP, 1972.

Sapir, Edward. *Language: An Introduction to the Study of Speech*. 1949. New York: Harcourt, 1961.

Scargill, M. H. *Modern Canadian English Usage*. Toronto: McClelland, 1974.

Schneider, G. D. *West African Pidgin English*. Athens, Ohio: G. D. Schneider, 1966.

Serjeantson, Mary S. *A History of Foreign Words in English*. 1935. London: Routledge, 1961.

Sey, K. A. *Ghanian English*. London: Macmillan, 1973.

Sheard, J. A. *The Words of English*. New York: Norton, 1966.

Shelly, Percy Dyke. *English and French in England, 1066–1100*. Philadelphia: n.p., 1921.

Shuy, Roger W. *Discovering American Dialects*. Champaign, Ill.: National Council of Teachers of English, 1967.

Sledd, James H., and Wilma R. Ebbitt, eds. *Dictionaries and THAT Dictionary: A*

Casebook on the Aims of Lexicographers and the Targets of Reviewers. Chicago: Scott, 1962.

Spencer, J., ed. *The English Language in West Africa.* London: Longman, 1971.

Starnes, DeWitt Talmage, and Gertrude E. Noyes. *The English Dictionary from Cawdrey to Johnson, 1604–1755.* Chapel Hill: U of North Carolina P, 1946.

Stenton, Doris Mary. *English Society in the Early Middle Ages (1066–1307).* Harmondsworth: Penguin, 1962.

Stenton, Frank M. *Anglo-Saxon England.* 3d ed. Oxford: Clarendon, 1971.

Strang, Barbara M. H. *A History of English.* London: Methuen, 1970.

Stratmann, Francis Henry. *A Middle-English Dictionary.* Rev. Henry Bradley. Oxford: Oxford UP, 1891.

Streadbeck, Arval L. *A Short Introduction to Germanic Linguistics.* Boulder, Colo.: Pruett, 1966.

Sturtevant, E. H. *Linguistic Change: An Introduction to the Historical Study of Language.* 1917. Chicago: U of Chicago P, 1961.

Thomas, Alan R. *The Linguistic Geography of Wales.* Cardiff: U of Wales P, 1973.

Thomas, Charles Kenneth. *An Introduction to the Phonetics of American English.* 2d ed. New York: Ronald, 1958.

Todd, L. *Pidgins and Creoles.* London: Routledge, 1974.

Toller, T. Northcote, ed. *An Anglo-Saxon Dictionary Based on the Manuscript Collections of the Late Joseph Bosworth.* Supp. with rev. and addenda by Alistair Campbell. London: Oxford UP, 1898, 1921, 1972.

Traugott, Elizabeth Closs. *The History of English Syntax.* New York: Holt, Rinehart and Winston, 1972.

Traugott, Elizabeth Closs, and Mary Louise Pratt. *Linguistics for Students of Literature.* New York: Harcourt, 1980.

Trudgill, Peter, and Jean Hannah. *International English: A Guide to Varieties of Standard English.* London: Arnold, 1982.

Turner, G. W. *The English Language in Australia and New Zealand.* London: Longman, 1966.

Ullman, Berthold Louis. *Ancient Writing and Its Influence.* 1932. Cambridge, Mass.: MIT P, 1969.

Visser, F. Th. *An Historical Syntax of the English Language.* Leiden: Brill, 1963–73.

Vorlat, Emma. *The Development of English Grammatical Theory, 1586–1737.* Leuven: University P, 1975.

Wakelin, Martyn Francis. *English Dialects: An Introduction.* London: Athlone, 1972.

Wells, J. C. *Accents of English. Vol. 1: An Introduction; Vol. 2: The British Isles; Vol. 3: Beyond the British Isles.* Cambridge: Cambridge UP, 1982.

Whitelock, Dorothy. *The Beginnings of English Society.* Harmondsworth: Penguin, 1952.

Williamson, Juanita V., and Virginia M. Burke, eds. *A Various Language: Perspectives on American Dialects.* New York: Holt, Rinehart and Winston, 1971.

Wolfram, Walter A., and Ralph W. Fasold. *The Study of Social Dialects in American English.* Englewood Cliffs, N.J.: Prentice-Hall, 1974.

Yule, George. *The Study of Language.* Cambridge: Cambridge UP, 1985.

INDEX

Credits continued from p. iv.